Leaves of Grass

and

Selected Prose

Walt Whitman

Edited by
Lawrence Buell
Oberlin College

The Modern Library
New York
Distributed by McGraw-Hill, Inc.

First Edition

Library of Congress Cataloging in Publication Data

Whitman, Walt, 1819-1892.
  Leaves of grass and selected prose.
  (Modern library college editions)
  Bibliography: p.
  I. Buell, Lawrence. II. Title.
PS3200.F81   818'.309   80-22578
ISBN: 0-07-554263-3

Cover design by Sara Eisenman
Manufactured in the United States of America

Permissions Acknowledgments

Randall Jarrell, "Some Lines from Whitman," *Poetry and the Age,*
  by Randall Jarrell. Copyright 1953 by Randall Jarrell. Reprinted
  by permission of Alfred A. Knopf, Inc.
Odell Shepard, *The Journals of Bronson Alcott.* Copyright 1938 by
  Odell Shepard; Copyright renewed © 1966 by Odell Shepard.
  Reprinted by permission of Little, Brown and Company in asso-
  ciation with the Atlantic Monthly Press.
Walt Whitman, "Old Age Echoes," from *Leaves of Grass.* Copy-
  right, 1924. Reprinted by permission of Doubleday & Company,
  Inc.

CONTENTS

LEAVES OF GRASS

	first publication date	page

SELECTED PROSE

INTRODUCTION

Walt Whitman (1819-92) approached his poetic career with high expectations. He dared to hope that he might become *the* poet of America. For many years the reception was cool enough to shake even Whitman's boundless optimism. But the twentieth century has justified him. We now recognize Whitman not only as a major writer, but as unique among American poets for his innovativeness, for his influence on world literature, and for the fullness with which he expressed American values.

To sum up Whitman's achievement in a way that would have pleased him, he did for poetry what the American Revolution did for political science. In *Leaves of Grass* he declared independence from traditional restrictions of form and subject matter more aggressively than anyone had done before. American poetry before Whitman was written in familiar patterns of rhythm and rhyme, and it relied heavily on stock "poetic" language and effects. Longfellow's lines "On sunny slope and beechen swell, / The shadowed light of evening fell" are all too typical. Whitman went far beyond this timid prettiness. He virtually invented free verse. He was the only major poet of his day to write intimately about sex, to explore the life of the unconscious in depth, to reproduce the stream of consciousness on the printed page, to celebrate the industrial revolution with discernment, and to capture the rhythms of city life.

Above all, Whitman went beyond his predecessors both in the degree to which he dramatized his innermost feelings and in his range of empathy for the commonest, most "unpoetic" objects. Consider, for instance,

The carpenter dresses his plank, the tongue of his foreplane whistles its wild ascending lisp . . .

This is one of many lines in which Whitman glances for an instant at some ordinary action and makes it seem magical even as he pretends to do nothing more than photograph it. He catches the rough-smooth cutting noise of the carpenter's plane and at the same time the motion of arm and tool that makes the plane itself seem a living thing, with a tongue and a whistle and a lisp. Sometimes such attempts fall flat, as in the very next line:

> The married and unmarried children ride home to their
>   Thanksgiving dinner . . .

But Whitman succeeded often enough so that, by the time he stopped writing, he had immeasurably extended the scope of poetry's "legitimate" subject matter.

Perhaps the most striking example is an earlier passage in the same poem, "Song of Myself." It describes a mystical experience in which "my soul" takes possession of the speaker's body and raises him to a plane of awareness in which he feels at one with God and the universe, so that he knows "that the hand of God is the promise of my own." The onset of this experience is described in frankly sexual terms:

> I mind how once we [soul and body] lay such a trans-
>   parent summer morning,
> How you settled your head athwart my hips and
>   gently turn'd over upon me,
> And parted the shirt from my bosom-bone, and
>   plunged your tongue to my bare-stript heart,
> And reach'd till you felt my beard, and reach'd till
>   you held my feet.

At this point the vision starts. The passage is daring not only in its use of a homosexual encounter as a springboard to the experience of equality with God, but also in the way the vision takes the lofty insight "that a kelson of creation is love" and extends it to the minutest, most microscopic corners of that creation—to

> limitless . . . leaves stiff or drooping in the fields,
> And brown ants in the little wells beneath them,
> And mossy scabs of the worm fence, heap'd stones,
>   elder, mullein and poke-weed.

Who but John Donne, snorted the eighteenth-century critic Samuel Johnson, would have compared a good man to a telescope? Unsympathetic nineteenth-century readers asked the same about Whitman's intermixture of sacred and profane, lofty and trivial. Not to mention Whitman's obscene blasphemy, as it would have appeared to such readers, do unpleasant trivia like mossy scabs on worm fences belong in a poetic vision? Is this art? But modern readers, prepared by several generations of American poets who learned from Whitman—Ezra Pound (grudgingly), Hart Crane (enthusiastically), Robinson Jeffers, Theodore Roethke, Allen Ginsberg, A. R. Ammons, and many others—will much more readily admire the great energy and keenness of vision in the above lines. At his best Whitman fully demonstrates the truth of William Blake's aphorism that the unclouded eye can see a world in a grain of sand.

Whitman's antitraditional style and his ability to find poetry in ordinary people and objects show a spirit of egalitarianism, a truly "democratic" conception of art, that American writers and critics had long been calling for but never so well exhibited. Emerson, for instance, expressed this idea when he declared in his "American Scholar" (a speech later dubbed America's "intellectual declaration of literary independence") that "I embrace the common, I explore and sit at the feet of the familiar, the low." But Whitman did so much more naturally than the genteel, Harvard-educated Emerson. The loose-hanging, wide-ranging quality of Whitman's writing, full of tributes to the average person, was really more in keeping than Emerson's intellectualized essays with their fellow citizens' optimistic view of America as a forward-moving, fast-expanding, proud young nation of limitless possibilities. It was more than just coincidence that Whitman had three brothers named after George Washington, Thomas Jefferson, and Andrew Jackson. Whitman fully shared the fierce patriotism that led his parents—and many others of the day—to choose such names, and he might well have used them for his own sons, if he had had any.

Whitman's life and career also followed a distinctively democratic pattern. Sponsored by no rich patrons, aided by no special advantages of birth or education, he was a self-taught writer who had to work his way up from the ranks of third-rate scribblers by a long process of imitation, questioning, and trial-and-error experiment. He was altogether the most unlikely member of the first truly distinguished group of American writers—Ralph Waldo Emerson, Henry David Thoreau, Nathaniel Hawthorne, Herman Melville, Edgar Allan Poe, Emily Dickinson—all born between 1800 and 1835. As literary pioneers, most of them, like Whitman, also took a long time to develop their distinctive styles. But none had to overcome more obstacles than he. Whitman was the only one of genuine working-class background, the second of eight children of a testy, restless, unsuccessful carpenter-builder and sometime farmer, and a mother who was strong, warm, and supportive but neither well educated nor particularly interested in Walt's writing. Several of the Whitman children led tragic or unstable lives. The oldest died of syphilis in an insane asylum; another brother became an alcoholic; Walt's favorite sister fell by an unhappy marriage into a life of chronic poverty and depression; his youngest brother was an invalid imbecile with whom Whitman shared a bed for some years of their adult lives.

Whitman himself always expressed pride in his descent from good American yeoman stock (Yankee on his father's side, New York Dutch on his mother's), and throughout his life always seemed more comfortable in the company of workingmen such as streetcar conductors (his special favorites) than with gentry or his fellow artists. His identification with ordinary people helped to give his work a more sympathetic understanding of the full range of American society than we find in the writings of his great contemporaries. Yet in the short run he was lucky to avoid the fate of some of his siblings, and the fact that he managed to make himself into a major poet is a literary rags-to-riches story more remarkable than Benjamin Franklin's.

Whitman was born on May 31, 1819, on a farm in central Long Island. Four years later the family moved to Brooklyn (then a village of less than 10,000 but growing fast). Until the Civil War he spent most of his life here, though he also lived for periods in Manhattan, rural Long Island, and (briefly)

New Orleans. Country and city scenes attracted him almost equally (see "Give Me the Splendid Silent Sun"), and both figure importantly in his poems. Like many of his generation, Whitman saw no necessary conflict between praising unspoiled nature, traditional rural life, and rapid industrial growth: all seemed "natural" expressions of the American spirit. By today's standards even the biggest urban centers were still little more than dots on the countryside.

After six years of elementary schooling, Whitman was sent to work at the age of eleven. For the next two decades he pursued a checkered career involving a score of jobs, mostly in journalism. He started as a printer's apprentice and worked his way up to the editorships of several newspapers, the most important being the Brooklyn *Daily Eagle* (1846-48), a Democratic paper that dumped him for his support of the Wilmot Proviso—a bill to ban slavery from the territories recently won from Mexico. On this and other occasions Whitman's identification with the reformist wing of the Democratic party got him in trouble with the state's party establishment and may have contributed to his decision, around 1850, to change the major direction of his life and make poetry—a side interest hitherto—his main goal. Apparently with this aim in mind, between 1850 and 1855 Whitman seems to have deliberately chosen underemployment, first in a small-scale printing and bookselling operation, then as a builder—the family trade.

Until this time Whitman had been at least a mildly ambitious man in a conventional way, conscientiously if not passionately filling the roles of professional journalist and associate family breadwinner. He may even have flirted with the idea of a political career. In its own way, his career to this point had somewhat resembled that of his father, whose liberal politics Whitman shared. Father and son probably typified the average blue- and white-collar attempts to make a living from greater New York's almost incredibly rapid growth during the nineteenth century. These attempts involved frequent job changes, intermittent times of unemployment, alternations of hope and disappointment, and a generally marginal standard of living. This was the unpleasant side of the social openness and capacity for individual change that Whitman later celebrated in his poetry.

His father never broke out of the occupational pattern he had set for himself, but Whitman, as he approached mid-life, began to question it. Indeed, there had always been at least two Walt Whitmans. One was, and remained, a gregarious, sociable person, fond of theater going, the New York restaurant scene, and other such entertainments to which newspaper work had introduced him. The other was an introspective, solitude-loving person who liked to muse under a tree or walk alone on the beach declaiming Homer to the waves.

Since his teens Whitman had dabbled in magazine poetry and fiction. Most of these efforts were entirely unoriginal; some were deliberate commercial potboilers—like his syrupy temperance novel, *Franklin Evans; or The Inebriate* (1842), which (to Whitman's disgust) turned out to be the one truly popular work he ever wrote. Such a production was a predictable spinoff for a respectable, reform-minded journalist; it was also an effective means of capitalizing on one of the many reform movements that gained a large following in the antebellum North. New York, along with Boston, become a key public relations center for these movements. In the newspaper field, Whitman for a time became a minor Horace Greeley.

Starting in the late 1840s, however, Whitman began to lose interest in conventional appeals to the mass media and to experiment in a series of notebooks with the long, loosely connected, image-packed free verse that characterizes his mature style. These first experiments are crude, as is to be expected, since they represented a radically new approach to poetry and since Whitman's literary education had been so skimpy to start with. Indeed, throughout his life he was capable of reverting at a moment's notice to the trite, tasteless rhetoric of early verses: "Before the dark brow'd sons of Spain, /A captive Indian maiden stood."

But in another sense, Whitman's very lack of a thorough literary education, such as Emerson and Longfellow enjoyed, made him more of an original. Even the first experimental manuscripts foreshadow some of the distinctive approaches of *Leaves of Grass*: the use of the omniscient yet intimate speaker, who is both "a simple separate person" and also a spokesman and prophet for all humankind; and the slice-of-life catalogues of ordinary but for that very reason uncharted experience. The American boosterism and opinionatedness on all topics, typical of brassy New York journalism, reappears in a new key, with an overlay of mystical enthusiasm about the miraculousness of all creation and the boundless possibilities of human life, American life especially. Altogether, by 1850 Whitman seems to have known pretty much what he wanted to say, though he couldn't yet say it well. Slowly and tentatively he was fusing a personal style from a collage of models: newspaper reportage; political oratory; the poetic prose of Emerson, Carlyle, and other contemporary writers; the speech and gestures he encountered daily on the street and at home; and the rhythms of the Bible.

Just what transformed Whitman's poetry from mediocrity to (at best) greatness is even more mysterious than what caused his change in primary vocation. Various explanations of both have been advanced, in addition to the theory of his disillusionment with the politics of journalism and the instability of editorial tenure. Some have attributed the change to a mystical experience, the original of the one quoted earlier; others to the influence of Emerson (Whitman later said: "I was simmering, simmering, simmering; Emerson brought me to a boil"); others postulate something like a mid-life crisis. Still another contributing factor might have been the imaginative impact of the growing conflict in the Northern states, starting in the late 1840s, between the romantic reformers—particularly the abolitionists—and the compromisers who maintained control of the government through Buchanan's administration. This conflict helped bring about some major changes in the careers of several important Yankee authors. The writings of Emerson, Thoreau, and Harriet Beecher Stowe became more socially conscious and politically radical. Whitman's approach, the obverse of theirs, was to attempt a parallel reorientation in his audience's outlook—not for the most part by direct discussion of political issues as he had once done, but by affirmation of fundamental American values (liberty, equality, hopefulness, brotherhood, pride in the national past, etc.) in a new and radical way.

As we might expect of anyone seeking to carve out a new identity, Whitman deliberately chose to give his first book of poems the air of a mysterious and epochal event. A slim, ninety-five page quarto called *Leaves of Grass* appeared immediately after the symbolic date of July 4, 1855. Instead of putting his name on the title page, the author (who had set part of the type himself) printed an engraving of himself in work clothes and casual pose, in keeping with his claim in the Preface that the American poet should be "one of the mass." His expression was staunch and proud and even a bit defiant, in keeping with his view of how true Americans—and especially true American poets—should behave. The Preface, a manifesto for the new American poetry that was to supersede the "corpse" of tradition, was followed by twelve poems, the first six all called "*Leaves of Grass*," the rest untitled. Here is their order, as retitled, revised, and repositioned in the present text, based on Whitman's final edition almost forty years later:

"Song of Myself" (p. 23)
"A Song for Occupations" (p. 169)
"To Think of Time" (p. 338)
"The Sleepers" (p. 330)
"I Sing the Body Electric" (p. 78)
"Faces" (p. 361)
"Song of the Answerer" (p. 133)
"Europe" (p. 214)
"A Boston Ballad" (p. 212)
"There Was a Child Went Forth" (p. 287)
"Who Learns My Lesson Complete" (p. 309)
"Great Are the Myths" (wisely rejected except for
   the lines that form "Youth, Day, Old Age, and
   Night," p. 181)

The 1855 *Leaves* contained much of Whitman's best work, notably "Song of Myself," which many critics consider the greatest poem in American literature. Here Whitman directly unmasks "himself" in a passage meant to correspond to the portrait:*

> Walt Whitman, an American, one of the roughs, a kosmos,
> Disorderly and fleshy and sensual . . . eating drinking and breeding,
> No sentimentalist . . . no stander above men and women or apart from them . . . no more modest than immodest.

It is interesting to contrast this self-portrait with the picture Whitman chose for the frontispiece of the third edition of *Leaves*. In the latter he looks much more like a "poet," quite dressy in a bohemian fashion, with loose-fitting black coat and floppy tie. Whitman clearly wanted to establish himself both as a serious artist and as the archetypal average American. In both goals he was sincere, but the combination led him into a certain amount of role playing, as even friendly observers noted (Document 4). Perhaps the greatest paradox about Whitman was his mixture of forthright candor and exaggerated posing. Because he was to such an unusual extent a self-made poet, he sometimes behaved like the literary equivalent of a *nouveau riche* (Documents 2, 3c). This was still another way in which he mirrored his countrymen — nineteenth-century Americans were notorious for being brashly proud and culturally insecure by turns.

In his bid for literary recognition, Whitman sent complimentary copies of *Leaves* to many of America's leading authors. Some ignored it or were scandalized by passages of sexual and religious radicalism. But Whitman received one

---

*Though elsewhere I quote from Whitman's final edition, here and at other points where I describe the first appearances of his poems, I quote the texts as originally published. Some were extensively revised later. The reader is invited to compare such quotations with the versions in this text, as samples of Whitman's tinkering, sometimes effective but sometimes not. The next quotation is an especially good example of Whitman's habits of revision; see p. 43 for the later, "official" version.

welcome that made up for any amount of disdain. Emerson, the American writer he most admired, responded with a warm congratulatory letter (Document 1) greeting Whitman "at the beginning of a great career" and praising *Leaves* as "the most extraordinary piece of wit and wisdom America has yet contributed." Whitman was overjoyed. Another admiring reader, quite unknown to him, was Abraham Lincoln, whose law partner somehow managed to get a copy of the book to faraway Illinois.

Altogether, *Leaves* met with as hospitable a reception from reviewers (Documents 3a, 3b) as could be expected of a book so new, so strange, so un-Victorian. But the edition of 795 copies did not sell well. Whitman's biographer Gay Wilson Allen estimates that no more than three dozen were bought. To promote his work, Whitman followed the occasional practice of the day and wrote several laudatory reviews himself. One (Document 3c) begins "An American bard at last!" Another marketing device in questionable taste was Whitman's unauthorized use of Emerson's letter as an advertising gimmick for the second edition (1856), accompanied by a fulsome manifesto-rejoinder (Document 2), in which Whitman presents his "dear Friend and Master" with a much-expanded new volume (thirty-two poems), falsely asserting that the first edition "readily sold" and ventilating his poetic aims in more detail.

The 1856 edition was the first of a series of expansion-revisions of *Leaves*. Other editions followed in 1860, 1867, 1871, 1876, 1881, 1888, and 1891–92. At several points in his life Whitman temporarily considered the book complete and launched out with new volumes, like *Drum-Taps* (1865), a collection of Civil War poems. For an example of a manifesto announcing such a new departure, see the 1872 Preface, p. 525. In the end, however, Whitman pulled all the poetry he thought worth saving back into *Leaves of Grass*. Indeed, by its very nature *Leaves* became a book that could end only with its author's death. Whitman summed up his purpose in his last manifesto, "A Backward Glance O'er Travel'd Roads" (1888), which he requested to be put at the end of all future editions of *Leaves*. The purpose was

to articulate and faithfully express in literary or
poetic form, and uncompromisingly, my own
physical, emotional, moral, intellectual, and aesthet-
ic Personality, in the midst of, and tallying, the
momentous spirit and facts of its immediate days,
and of current America.

In other words, the book was to be an organic expression
both of himself and of the national spirit, a comprehensive
record of a unique yet representative personality both in
itself and in response to the key events of the mid-nineteenth
century. Small wonder, then, that Whitman had difficulty
ending *Leaves*, which includes in addition to its "final"
section ("Songs of Parting") two "annexes" ("Sands at
Seventy" and "Good-Bye My Fancy"). Whitman even
supplied his literary executor with the title for a possible
collection of posthumous pieces, "Old Age Echoes," which
were duly gathered up and published with *Leaves* five years
after his death. Like the speaker of one of his many farewell
poems, Whitman was

> loth, O so loth to depart!
> Garrulous to the very last.

Although at times Whitman liked to think that *Leaves* was
composed as deliberately as a cathedral, he was really well
aware that it grew more or less spontaneously. Several stages
of inspiration can be distinguished. The first two editions
represent Whitman in his most "transcendental," Emersonian
phase. He here tends to emphasize the essential holiness of
human nature ("It is . . . not consistent with the reality
of the soul to admit that there is anything in the known universe more divine than men and women"); to stress the enormous powers of the speaker, who often addresses the reader
as a kind of deity ("I am an acme of things accomplished,
and I an encloser of things to be"). This way of speaking
carries to an extreme the Emersonian doctrine of
"self-reliance," the essential oneness of each individual with
Spirit or God. Whitman's versatile, ever-metamorphosing "I"
can be looked at as a creation of Emersonian logic. "I" can
refer either to myself as a separate person; to different

aspects of myself (the "real" me and the superficial me, for instance), to the collective identity of me with everyone else; or to divinity itself, by reason of my power to be divinely inspired, from which perspective "I" can speak with godlike authority to others not yet illuminated. This deeply serious wordplay accounts for the initially baffling but, on closer inspection, marvelously supple transitions in "Song of Myself." The multiple meanings of the "I," furthermore, amount to a kind of democratic religion—the apotheosis of the average person.

The transcendental Whitman is incorrigibly optimistic about his own gifts and about the possibilities of human and societal transformation. He is even so bold as to deny death. "The smallest sprout" of grass

> shows there is really no death,
> And if ever there was it led forward life, and does
>   not wait at the end to arrest it,
> And ceased the moment life appeared.

But there are some important exceptions to this tone of confidence even in the early poetry, such as "The Sleepers" (a nightmare vision to offset "Song of Myself") and "A Boston Ballad" (a bitter satire against the Fugitive Slave Law). Starting with the third edition (1860), a more pensive, limited, vulnerable speaker becomes distinctly audible. This third edition is especially notable for the first appearance of the complementary sections "Enfans d'Adam" (later "Children of Adam") and "Calamus," the first celebrating the greatness of the body, heterosexual love, and procreation in a rather noisy and programmatic way; the second, more shyly and subtly celebrating the need for (male) companionship. The great lyric "Out of the Cradle Endlessly Rocking," here called "A Word out of the Sea," which stands at the center of the 1860 edition, may also be a sort of Calamus poem, centering as it does on the boy poet's reaction to the bird's loss of its mate.

On the basis of this poem, and hints dropped elsewhere, some readers have speculated that the 1860 edition may reflect a tragic love relationship during the late 1850s. "I loved a certain person ardently and my love was not return'd," says one of the Calamus poems; "Yet out of that I have written these songs." But it is risky to link speaker and author literally, in view of Whitman's capacity for role playing and the additional fact that these lines were added *after* 1860. We have no conclusive evidence of any genuine love affair between Whitman and anyone of either sex, despite occasional veiled allusions in manuscript notebooks and Whitman's old-age reply to a British admirer's suggestion that the Calamus poems condoned homosexuality. To this Whitman responded with a panicky disclaimer and a barefaced lie that he had fathered six illegitimate children. The change in tone between 1856 and 1860 might conceivably have been caused by quite different factors, such as professional disappointment: Whitman quickly found that he would not get the income and recognition from his poems for which he had originally hoped. He had to return to newspaper work, and indeed, despite modest profits from some editions, throughout his life he was forced to eke out his livelihood through short-term jobs or through the bounty of admirers.

At any rate, for whatever reason, we find a new humility of tone in the third edition:

> You, up there, walking or sitting,
> Whoever you are—we too lie in drifts at your feet.

So ends a despondent walk by the seaside. When the boy in "Out of the Cradle" asks the sea for the word that will unlock his destiny, the reply is "Death." This insight, says the poem, awoke "my own songs...from that hour." Here we have another mystical experience, parallel to the one in "Song of Myself," and equally prophetic. Death—the fear of it alternating with the celebration of it—becomes an increasingly important theme in Whitman's poetry.

The Civil War helped both to ensure this and to retard the process somewhat. Quite by accident the war made possible the most exciting, meaningful episode in Whitman's external life, and it inspired his writing more profoundly than that of his major contemporaries. The reflections on the war of Emerson, Thoreau, Hawthorne, Melville, and Dickinson seem stereotyped and tangential by comparison. Whitman's involvement in the war was much more immediate than theirs. Late in 1862 he went south as the family's representative to locate his younger brother George, a Union lieutenant who had been reported wounded. Whitman found George back on active duty, but he was so moved by the plight of the wounded that he remained in and around Washington until after the war's end doing volunteer work as a male nurse. The story is told indirectly in the "Drum-Taps" section of *Leaves*. This section starts with jingoistic pro-Union tub thumping done while Whitman was still in Brooklyn watching military parades ("It's O for a manly life in the camp!"). Later the tone changes markedly. Whitman explains the shift in a passage added to the original version of "The Wound-Dresser":

> Arous'd and angry, I'd thought to beat the alarum,
>   and urge relentless war,
> But soon my fingers fail'd me, my face droop'd and
>   I resign'd myself,
> To sit by the wounded and soothe them, or silently
>   watch the dead.

The war was traumatic for Whitman; he never forgot his first glimpse of a camp hospital: "a heap of amputated feet, legs, arms, hands, &c., a full load for a one-horse cart." Yet the experience was in some ways exhilarating. At last Whitman was able to act out the role of heroic healer envisioned in "Song of Myself." In the process he saw the Calamus ideal demonstrated to his complete satisfaction. He knew that *his* comradeship was crucial for the wounded men he treated. He was affectionate with them, and they with him; he could point to cases where his "tact and magnetic sympathy and unction" had made the difference between life and death. Whitman also took note of comradeship among the soldiers. On a more abstract level, more explicitly than ever before he came to identify the principle of comradeship as the key force that would bond the reunited states together.

The bravery of the soldiers on both sides, especially the enlisted men, confirmed Whitman's faith in the American character. "I never before so realized the majesty and reality of the American people *en masse*," he says in his autobiography. Unsung soldiers such as Sergeant Calvin F. Harlowe of Massachusetts were as noble "as any hero in the books, ancient or modern." For this reason, when Whitman came to write "When Lilacs Last in the Dooryard Bloom'd," the elegy for Abraham Lincoln that is the best of his war poems and indeed one of the greatest elegies ever written, Whitman chose to treat the assassination not as a single tragedy but as a final, representative casualty of the war as a whole:

> Nor for you, for one alone,
> Blossoms and branches green to coffins all I bring...

Eight years later (1873), when Whitman suffered a paralytic stroke from which he never fully recovered, he extended the same idea to himself, explaining the sudden lapse from the perfect health of which he had boasted for twenty years as a result of overstrain during the war. His status as the war's laureate was confirmed by his status as another war casualty.

In "A Backward Glance" Whitman made the astonishing statement that without his war experiences "'Leaves of Grass' would not now be existing." "Although I had made a start before," he says, "only from the strong flare and provocation of that war's sights and scenes the final reasons-for-being of an autochthonic and passionate song definitely came forth." Although this assertion grossly underestimates the value of his prewar poetry, it makes sense when we consider Whitman's long-range goal of making his book the expression of the nation's identity as well as his own. The Civil War was, beyond doubt, *the* great public event of Whitman's lifetime. Furthermore, he must have known that his own spiritual odyssey from jingoism to horrified disillusionment to fresh confidence in the reunited nation was more or less representative of the tide of feeling in the nation as a whole. Probably for such reasons as these the war poetry, in the loose-knit structure of the final edition of

Leaves, comes as the climax of the large batch of poems that deal primarily with social themes. These are concentrated mostly in the central portion of the book, starting with "Salut au Monde!" (p. 109), after the prefatory "Inscriptions" section, two long semiautobiographical poems announcing the poet's aims in detail, and the two sections on the complementary forms of love. Thus Whitman gave his impressions of the war a central position in his final poetic record of the American scene.

Undoubtedly another reason the war seemed so important to Whitman in retrospect was that his later career was anticlimactic by contrast. Always older looking than his chronological age, he was a semi-invalid for most of his final nineteen years. He involved himself in no new causes or enterprises of the significance of his hospital work or his editorships before 1860. He wrote little first-rate poetry after 1865, and almost none after 1873. From that year, shaken by the almost simultaneous blows of illness and his mother's death, he lived a rather quiet life in very modest circumstances, mostly in or near Camden, New Jersey, where he initially moved to be cared for by his brother George. He did a little traveling and lecturing, a good deal of writing and reminiscing. He continued to tinker with the arrangement of *Leaves of Grass*, publishing several new editions. But his later comments on his own work show that he looked at his effective career as over and betray an unprecedented uneasiness about what he had managed to achieve. In 1855 Whitman had insisted, and he always continued to insist, that "the proof of a poet is that his country absorbs him as affectionately as he has absorbed it." He knew that this had not yet happened, although he had begun to gather around him a circle of devoted admirers, like the naturalist John Burroughs (Document 5b), on whom Whitman became more and more dependent emotionally and monetarily.

In his later poems Whitman is increasingly preoccupied with aging, imminent death, and particularly the continuity of life beyond death. Many of the poems of the 1870s and after envision death in what is for him a newly metaphysical, quasi-orthodox manner as the soul's voyage from this world to other worlds unknown. In the most ambitious of these efforts, "Passage to India," the speaker jumps abruptly from a familiar Whitmanesque celebration of new technological advances (the Suez Canal and the Atlantic Cable) that have linked the hemispheres in fulfillment of Columbus's dream to the vision of a spiritual "Passage to more than India" that will whisk the poet away from the globe entirely, into the arms of the "Comrade perfect."

The adventuresome bravado of "Passage," however, alternates in the later poetry with the chastened mood of works like "Prayer of Columbus," perhaps the most powerful of the late poems. In a dramatic monologue the explorer speaks as

> A batter'd, wreck'd old man,
> Thrown on this savage shore, far, far from home,

consoled only by his trust in God and by a flickering vision of future fame: "anthems in new tongues I hear saluting me." The aging Whitman often liked to compare himself to Columbus, the now-famous discoverer unappreciated by his own era. In fact, Whitman's last completed poem was in all probability "A Thought of Columbus."

Whitman's postwar poetry is, overall, less important than his prose. In addition to his most significant later literary criticism and self-criticism, the present text includes his two most important long prose works: *Democratic Vistas*, an essay on the nature, shortcomings, needs, and prospects of American society; and *Specimen Days*, an impressionistic autobiography.

Democratic Vistas is Whitman's most comprehensive and searching piece of social criticism. It expresses in more systematic form many of the social concerns found in his poems and, going back further, in almost two decades of newspaper editorializing about the American scene. As such it provides a link between the prewar era of romantic reform, characterized by such idealistic movements as abolitionism, feminism, utopian socialism, and temperance (all interested Whitman in varying degrees) and late nineteenth-century social protest in the wake of robber baronism, the scandals of the Grant administration, the failure of Reconstruction, and the slow progress of such earlier reform efforts as the women's suffrage movement. *Democratic Vistas* is one of the first important expressions of disillusionment following the temporary euphoria that briefly encouraged Whitman and many other Americans to expect the quick emergence of a heroic new America as a consequence of the heroic struggles and sacrifices of the war.

Democratic Vistas is perhaps especially notable as an early indictment of the materialism and rapacity of America's Gilded Age, a common complaint of the postwar writers but one not usually associated with Whitman, a self-styled booster of material progress and American virtue.* The predominant tone is hopeful, yet in it Whitman pictures America as a gigantic body with an underdeveloped soul that sorely needs to be nurtured by a class of great poet-seers who will give shape and direction to the inherent nobility of the American masses. Here as in the 1855 Preface Whitman teeters uneasily between an elitist and a populist definition of the intellectual's role. The older Whitman is predictably more conservative, and it comes as a bit of a shock to hear him declare that "the present is but the legitimate birth of the past" and that he is writing in response to "the appalling dangers of universal suffrage in the United States," to close the gap "between democracy's convictions, aspirations, and the people's crudeness, vice, caprices." This respect for tradition and fear of democratic excess are new motifs for him. But even stronger, as we read on, is Whitman's familiar egalitarian insistence that the American personality is and should be something quite different from the old "oriental, feudal, ecclesiatical" models. These crosscurrents of opinion make *Democratic Vistas* a notable expression of two classic dilemmas of American intellectual liberalism: how to declare cultural independence without throwing culture out the window, and

---

*Whitman had, however, always been capable of criticizing the American society of his day as harshly as he criticized the reigning conventions in poetry. This is clear as early as "Song of Myself" and, before that, from some of Whitman's newspaper editorials.

how to provide intellectual leadership in a society whose materialistic drift one disapproves without falling into an antidemocratic elitism.

Specimen Days is a prose counterpart to *Leaves of Grass*: Whitman's life story irregularly told in the form of reminiscences of public and personal events, with general philosophizing thrown in. Readers of the two works will enjoy comparing the self-portraits conveyed by each. The contrasts are striking. The most obvious stem from the difference between prose versus poetic form and from the fact that *Specimen Days* is clearly an old man's book whereas *Leaves* is mostly the work of a writer in his prime. But there are also many similarities: egoism, elusiveness, sympathy, descriptive skill, digressiveness, a preference for impressionistic rather than carefully argued discourse. The staccato quality of the reminiscences, many of which are little more than a paragraph or two, reminds us that Whitman was, to an extent not always appreciated, an artist of short pieces. He was a master of both the long poem and the brief imagistic poem, such as "Cavalry Crossing a Ford" and "A Noiseless Patient Spider." He began by favoring the first form, but starting in 1860 he concentrated on the second. In old age Whitman credited Poe with having convinced him that "there can be no such thing as a long poem," that such works tend to break down into short lyric bursts. This is very true of some of Whitman's longer poems. But the shift was more likely a spontaneous process, hastened by the failure of sustained inspiration as he aged.

Whitman's prose is sometimes clogged and turgid, sometimes racy and effective. For a summary—severe yet sensitive—of the old-fashionedness of his great British contemporary Tennyson, against whom Whitman liked to measure his own poetic goals, we need go no further than this sentence:

> The odor of English social life in its highest range—a melancholy, affectionate, very manly, but dainty breed—pervading the pages like an invisible scent; the idleness, the traditions, the mannerisms, the stately *ennui*; the yearning of love, like a spinal

> marrow, inside of all; the costumes, brocade and satin
> the old houses and furniture-solid oak, no mere veneer-
> ing—the moldy secrets everywhere; the verdure, the ivy
> on the walls, the moat, the English landscape outside,
> the buzzing fly in the sun inside the window pane.

It is of course as a poet, not as a prose stylist, that Whitman will always be best known. Today, with a suspension
bridge (between Camden and Philadelphia) and several
schools named after him, with his first and last dwellings
honored as historic shrines, with a scholarly journal devoted
exclusively to articles about him, Whitman is in little more
danger of being forgotten than Columbus. Yet it is not always
easy for the modern reader, even the receptive reader, to
understand Whitman's poetic aims. In fact, he had only a
limited interest in being a poet in the usual sense of an artist
in words. He warns the reader in "A Backward Glance" that
"No one will get at my verses who insists upon viewing them
as a literary performance, or attempt at such performance, or
as aiming mainly toward art or aestheticism." Rather,
Whitman proposed to break through the frontiers of conventional poetry in several directions at once.

First, Whitman regarded poetry as a form of prophecy—as
a means of raising the consciousness of his audience to truths
of the highest importance.

> Know you, solely to drop in the earth the germs of a
>   greater religion,
> The following chants each for its kind I sing.

So he writes in "Starting from Paumanok." Like his
sometime mentor Emerson, only to a greater degree,
Whitman saw himself in rivalry with established creeds and
philosophical systems. He looked to poetry as a means of
imparting a more meaningful, living inspiration to his audiences than they could get from ministerial sermons and tracts.

Hostile critics were not far wrong in likening Whitmanism
to Mormonism as upstart, "disreputable" faiths. What the
critics objected to was mainly sexual impropriety: Mormon
polygamy and Whitman's supposed advocacy of free love.
But beyond this, both reflected the extraordinary religious

ferment in nineteenth-century America, unmatched before
or since—a yearning for spiritual renewal that was at least
in part a response to the dizzying pace of social change that
within Whitman's lifetime turned Brooklyn from a country
village into a part of one of the world's great metropolises.
The combination of rapid territorial expansion, an unprecedented rise in immigration and population growth, mass
migration westward, and the industrial revolution (especially
in Whitman's Northeast) made his age America's first
"modern" generation—the first generation in which perpetual
change seemed to become a primary fact of human life.
Many Americans, as a result, became disenchanted with
traditional forms of belief and began to search restlessly after
new philosophies that would speak more meaningfully to an
age of change. This led simultaneously to the reform of old
churches, to the formation of new ones, and to completely
noninstitutional, free-lance philosophical and artistic
utterances like those of Emerson and Whitman, both of
whom preached a gospel of limitless personal and social
development.

Then too, Whitman sought to break down the barrier
between art and reality. In the 1855 Preface he emphasizes
that "The United States themselves are essentially the
greatest poem." In other words, poetry exists in reality itself,
rather than in the books made about it. The closer
book-poetry comes to the texture of reality the better. "The
true use for the imaginative faculty of modern times is to
give ultimate vivification to facts, to science, and to common
lives, endowing them with the glows and glories and final
illustriousness which belong to every real thing, and to real
things only." Hence Whitman places strong emphasis on the
individual image and on "catalogues" of images, without
attending much to working them into neat packages. "Roots
and leaves themselves alone are these," insists one poem. The
title *Leaves* suggests at the very start that its pages are to be
regarded as living things.

Again, Whitman's highly individual style also expressed
prevalent American values—in this case, the American
distrust of art, or of any other intellectual endeavor, that is
cut off from practical, tangible reality. Whitman's emphasis

on simply presenting the image or scene without poetic
gilding links his work with American painting of the
period—with the genre scenes of William Sidney Mount and
Winslow Homer and with the attentiveness to anatomical and
descriptive detail valued by Whitman's friend Thomas Eakins.

For similar reasons Whitman sought to break down the
barrier that the medium of print imposes between author and
reader. "Camerado," insists one poem,

> this is no book,
> Who touches this touches a man,
> (Is it night? are we here together alone?)
> It is I you hold and who holds you,
> I spring from the pages into your arms...

Whitman's book is meant, then, not simply as an organism
but as a human being: an expression of himself so close to
the real thing that the two are inseparable. If the speaker
elsewhere makes a point of being cagey with his reader ("I
am not what you supposed, but far different") this only
reinforces his humanness by dramatizing his complexity as a
person and the difficulty of full communication even
between intimates. No poet ever took more pains to express
himself, and no poet ever took more pains to co-opt the
reader into his poems. The following passage, for instance,
spells out what many writers must have dreamed of but few
have declared explicitly:

> What thought you have of me now, I had as much of
>   you—I laid in my stores in advance,
> I consider'd long and seriously of you before you
>   were born....
> Who knows but I am enjoying this?
> Who knows, for all the distance, but I am as good
>   as looking at you now, for all you cannot see me?

The reader who approaches Whitman with defenses down gets
an uncanny sense of personal presence from his poems,
notwithstanding their frequent abstractness and argumenta-
tiveness as the speaker periodically assumes the teacher's role.

In all three of these extensions of poetry's usual domain, Whitman was carrying out assumptions of the romantic movement in literature exemplified in England by such writers as Blake, Wordsworth, and Coleridge and brought to America by Emerson, Thoreau, and others. Romanticism tends to glorify the poet as a prophet, to decry stylistic artificiality and value art that seems as artless and as spontaneous as nature, and to see art as personal expression. Whitman pushed each of these assumptions to its uttermost limit and in the process set the stage for much of modern American poetry, which has broken more quickly and more thoroughly with English poetic tradition than twentieth-century British poetry has done.

All writers have their limitations, of course, including Whitman, despite his aspiration to all-inclusiveness. Most of the defects are by-products of virtues. That thirst for all-inclusiveness, for example: At worst it led him to a fill-in-the-blanks approach to poetry, as in his undeservedly famous

> I hear America singing, the varied carols I hear,
> Those of mechanics, each one singing his as it should
> be blithe and strong,
> The carpenter singing his as he measures his plank
> or beam,
> The mason singing his as he makes ready for work,
> or leaves off work. .

Compare the sketchiness of the third line with the image of the carpenter quoted earlier. Here Whitman seems simply to be checking off a series of occupations out of a sense of duty. He wrote too much poetry like this. Poets who aspire to be prophets usually do. The young Henry James, attacking Whitman in 1865 (Document 5a), had a point when he observed that great art cannot come from literary incompetence or willful disregard for artistry.

It is true that Whitman *was* incompetent in some respects. His rhymed verse is terrible. "O Captain, My Captain," another undeservedly famous poem, is a prime example. It is true that Whitman often wrote carelessly. Worse, he sometimes wrote in a way that was both sloppy *and* pretentious, imitating the literary tinsel he was supposedly reacting against, as in "list to my morning's romanza." In mid-career he went back to earlier poems and changed his past participles from *ed* to the more "poetic" looking *'d* (*joined* to *join'd*, for example.) For a poet who aimed at capturing the immediate flow of experience, he had great trouble writing plain English. Lines like "the enclosing purport of us here is not a speculation or bon-mot or reconnoissance" came naturally to him.

Whitman's range of vision, moreover, was not so broad as he liked to think. His imagery goes thin when he moves his scenes too far from his native Long Island and Manhattan or from the army camps and hospitals he came to know in the 1860s. His globe-trotting poems, such as "Salut au Monde," too often read like the index of an atlas.

Like all the great classic American male writers from Cooper through Twain, Whitman wrote much more feelingly about male friendship than about relations between the sexes. His true love poems are the "Calamus" cluster; "Children of Adam" is mechanical by contrast. As D. H. Lawrence once said, Whitman might just as well have written "the femaleness waits for my maleness."

Whitman's sexism is a related problem. In the nineteenth century women readers shunned Whitman because they had been told, like Emily Dickinson, that he was "disgraceful." Contemporary women readers may also be moved to dismiss him too abruptly, since it is painfully clear that women often figure in his poetry as little more than bodies upon whom the ever-potent speaker is to beget the heroic American race of the future. This situation is ironic, since no nineteenth-century male poet proclaimed the theory of sexual equality more fervently (Whitman makes a point of referring to "workmen and workwomen," of addressing his reader as simultaneously male and female, even when it ruins the rhythm), and no male poet of the era tried harder to empathize with women's experience. (See especially the eleventh section of "Song of Myself.") Whitman's usual perceptiveness seems to have been overcome by cultural stereotypes, anxiety about his own sexuality, and reverence for the example of the person he most admired—his mother, who appears to have been the archetypal strong but domestic nineteenth-century American matriarch.

Such flaws as these, intertwined with Whitman's unusual innovativeness, make the highs and lows of his writing more pronounced than those of most major poets. Thus there are two different and equally valid ways of reading him. The reader for whom artistic technique is paramount will want to concentrate on the literary highlights, on the handful of poems where Whitman is at his best stylistically: such works as "Song of Myself," "Crossing Brooklyn Ferry," "Out of the Cradle," and "When Lilacs Last" among the longer poems; and "I Saw in Louisiana a Live-Oak Growing," "A Noiseless Patient Spider," "Come up from the Fields, Father," and "There Was a Child Went Forth" among the shorter poems. Those more willing to take Whitman on his own terms, however, will want to absorb as much of him as possible, reading for a sense of the complex personality and vision behind the printed page. Two sections of *Leaves* that particularly repay this approach are "Calamus" and "Drum-Taps" (including "Memories of President Lincoln"); both are more closely knit than most of the other sections. "Drum-Taps" should be read in conjunction with the Civil War portions of *Specimen Days*. But one should not stop here. To understand the giant one must survey him at full length. Whitman deserves readers as open-minded as he himself was. Such readers will find much more to praise than to blame.

Read this way, Whitman's writing tells two different stories of himself and his America. The first has a tragic plot. It starts with a mood of exuberant hope ("Song of Myself"), reflecting Whitman's and the nation's essential optimism during the antebellum years, and it ends in the slow twilight of decay, reflecting not only Whitman's old age but also, to some extent, the erosion of romantic optimism during the latter part of the nineteenth century. In the aging Whitman we see some of the melancholy and confusion characteristic of much twentieth-century American writing. The second story is much more affirmative. Whitman's writing can also be read as the literary record of some of the most distinctive and permanent traits of American culture—traits that Whitman was able to express because they were so ingrained in him. The use of the speaker who is both a single person and the voice of the people beautifully expresses the complementary American values of individualism and democratic consensus. The catalogue-of-images technique captures the boundlessness of American space and the feel of American diversity.

Through such techniques, Whitman managed to express the idea of America not only on the level of subject matter (by writing about Lincoln or about the transcontinental railroad) but on the level of style. For this reason, despite social changes between Whitman's time and ours, *Leaves of Grass* has a unique status as an American cultural document. In its very antitraditionalism it has helped to give expression and shape to the American cultural tradition as we understand it today.

Lawrence Buell
Oberlin, Ohio
October 1980

A NOTE ON THE TEXT

The text of *Leaves of Grass* printed here is the "deathbed edition" of 1891-92—the last that Whitman saw through the press. It concludes with his retrospective essay, "A Backward Glance O'er Travel'd Roads." Following *Leaves* in this volume is Whitman's last known poem, "A Thought of Columbus," far the best of the thirteen poems posthumously gathered and first published as "Old Age Echoes" in an 1897 edition of *Leaves*. The 1855 Preface is reprinted from the first edition of *Leaves*, in order to preserve Whitman's first and greatest manifesto and to enable the reader to compare it with his later transposition of many passages into the poem "By Blue Ontario's Shore." The other prose works printed here are taken from *Prose Works 1892*, which Whitman also prepared for the press. The present text attempts to correct the few scattered errors of the 1950 Modern Library edition. One or two revisions in Whitman's spelling have been made in the interest of intelligibility (e.g., correcting his "llamas" to "lamas"). The sources of the documents are given below.

SUGGESTED READINGS

Allen, Gay Wilson. *The Solitary Singer.* New York: Macmillan, 1955. Reprint. New York: New York University Press, 1967. By far the most detailed, authoritative, factual biography.

———. *The New Walt Whitman Handbook.* New York: New York University Press, 1975. A valuable summary of and guide to research about Whitman's life, the growth of *Leaves*, Whitman's ideas and poetic style, and his reputation and influence. See pp. 378-385 for an annotated list of the key editions and reprints of his works.

Asselineau, Roger. *The Evolution of Walt Whitman.* 2 vols. Trans. Asselineau and R. P. Adams. Cambridge: Harvard University Press, 1960, 1962. Particularly good for its first volume, which traces the development of Whitman's personality and the growth of *Leaves*.

Marki, Ivan. *The Trial of the Poet: An Interpretation of the First Edition of Leaves of Grass.* New York: Columbia University Press, 1976. The most detailed discussion of the argument and method of the 1855 edition.

Miller, Edwin Haviland. *Walt Whitman's Poetry: A Psychological Journey.* Boston: Houghton Mifflin, 1968; New York: New York University Press, 1968. A provocative psychobiographical study of Whitman's work.

Miller, James E., Jr. *The American Quest for a Supreme Fiction: Whitman's Legacy in the Personal Epic.* Chicago and London: University of Chicago Press, 1979. Discusses the "Whitman tradition" in American poetry.

———. *A Critical Guide to Leaves of Grass.* Chicago and London: University of Chicago Press, 1957. Useful for its attempt to describe the structure of *Leaves*.

Murphy, Francis, ed. *Walt Whitman: A Critical Anthology.* Middlesex, England: Penguin, 1969. An exceptionally comprehensive and well chosen collection of critical essays from 1855 to 1965.

Whitman, Walt. *The Collected Writings of Walt Whitman.* Edited by Gay Wilson Allen and Sculley Bradley. New York: New York University Press, 1961-. A multivolume scholarly edition, still in progress, of Whitman's complete works.

———. *Uncollected Poetry and Prose*. 2 vols. Edited by Emory Holloway. New York: Peter Smith, 1932. The most inclusive among a number of early gatherings of material Whitman omitted from his collected works. Partially but not yet wholly superseded by *The Collected Writings*.

———. *Whitman's Manuscripts: Leaves of Grass (1860)*. Edited by Fredson Bowers. Chicago and London: University of Chicago Press, 1955. Valuable for its technical but illuminating reconstruction of how one of the editions of *Leaves* was composed.

Walt Whitman Review. A quarterly journal, 1955-, that specializes in Whitman criticism. Through its bibliographies; through the annual bibliography issue of the *Publications of the Modern Language Association*, also a scholarly quarterly; and through the section on Whitman in the annual *American Literary Scholarship* (Durham, N.C.: Duke University Press), the interested student can keep abreast of ongoing Whitman research.

DOCUMENTS

1. Ralph Waldo Emerson's Letter to Whitman, 1855

This letter, one of the most significant in American literary history, was written as a thank-you note for a presentation copy of the first edition of Leaves. *Whitman published the letter in his second edition.*

Concord, Massachusetts, 21 July [1855]

Dear sir,

I am not blind to the worth of the wonderful gift of *Leaves of Grass*. I find it the most extraordinary piece of wit and and wisdom that America has yet contributed. I am very happy in reading it, as great power makes us happy. It meets the demand I am always making of what seemed the sterile and stingy nature, as if too much handiwork, or too much lymph in the temperature, were making our western wits fat and mean.

I give you joy of your free and brave thought. have great joy in it. I find incomparable things said incomparably well, as they must be. I find the courage of treatment which so delights us, and which large perception can only inspire.

I greet you at the beginning of a great career, which yet must have had a long foreground somewhere, for such a start. I rubbed my eyes a little, to see if this sunbeam were no illusion; but the solid sense of the book is a sober certainty.

I did not know until I last night saw the book advertised in a newspaper that I could trust the name as real and available for a post-office. I wish to see my benefactor, and have felt much like striking my tasks, and visiting New York to pay you my respects.

R. W. Emerson

2. Whitman's Response to Emerson, 1856

This is the opening of Whitman's long open letter to Emerson, printed (along with Emerson's letter) in the second edition of Leaves. *Note the exaggerations.*

Brooklyn, August, 1856

Here are thirty-two Poems, which I send you, dear Friend and Master, not having found how I could satisfy myself with sending any usual acknowledgment of your letter. The first edition, on which you mailed me that till now unanswered letter, was twelve poems—I printed a thousand copies, and they readily sold; these thirty-two Poems I stereotype, to print several thousand copies of. I much enjoy making poems. Other work I have set for myself to do, to meet people and The States face to face, to confront them with an American rude tongue; but the work of my life is making poems. I keep on till I make a hundred, and then several hundred—perhaps a thousand. The way is clear to me. A few years, and the average annual call for my Poems is ten or twenty thousand copies—more, quite likely. Why should I hurry or compromise? In poems or in speeches I say the word or two that has got to be said, adhere to the body, step with the countless common footsteps...

3. Early Reviews of *Leaves of Grass* (1855—56)

The first of the following three pieces appeared in what was then the nation's most prestigious intellectual magazine. The second appeared in the most literary of American religious journals, a publication of the Unitarians, the most liberal Protestant sect in America, the church to which most of the transcendentalists were at least loosely attached. The third, written by Whitman himself, was printed in America's leading literary magazine of Democratic persuasion. The first two reviews illustrate the early controversy over Leaves, *centering around the obscenity issue. The last is interesting both as self-advertisement and as a statement of poetic purpose.*

(a)

Edward Everett Hale, review of 1855 edition in North American Review, *82 (1856) 275, 277.*

Everything about the external arrangement of this book was odd and out of the way. The author printed it himself, and it seems to have been left to the winds of heaven to publish it.... It bears no publisher's name, and, if the reader goes to a bookstore for it, he may expect to be told at first, as we were, that there is no such book, and has not been. Nevertheless, there is such a book, and it is well worth going twice to the bookstore to buy it. Walter Whitman, an American,—one of the roughs,—no sentimentalist,—no stander above men and women, or apart from them,—no more modest than immodest,—has tried to write down here, in a sort of prose poetry, a good deal of what he has seen, felt, and guessed at in a pilgrimage of some thirty-five years. He has a horror of conventional language of any kind. His theory of expression is, that, "to speak in literature with the perfect rectitude and *insouciance* of the movements of animals, is the flawless triumph of art." Now a great many men have said this before. But generally it is the introduction to something more artistic than ever,—more conventional and strained. Antony began by saying he was no orator, but none the less did an oration follow. In this book, however, the prophecy is fairly fulfilled in the accomplishment.

° ° °

Claiming... a personal interest in every thing that has ever happened in the world, and, by the wonderful sharpness and distinctness of his imagination, making the claim effective and reasonable, Mr. "Walt Whitman" leaves it a matter of doubt where he has been in this world, and where not. It is very clear, that with him, as with most other effective writers, a keen, absolute memory, which takes in and holds every detail of the past,—as they say the exaggerated power of the memory does when a man is drowning,—is a gift of his organization as remarkable as his vivid imagination. What he has seen once, he has seen for ever. And thus there are in this curious book little thumb-nail sketches of life in the prairie, life in California, life at school, life in the nursery,—life, indeed, we know not where not,—which as they are unfolded one after another, strike us as real,—so real that we wonder how they came on paper.

For the purpose of showing that he is above every conventionalism, Mr. Whitman puts into the book one or two lines which he would not address to a woman nor to a company of men. There is not anything, perhaps, which modern usage would stamp as more indelicate than are some passages in Homer. There is not a word in it meant to attract readers by its grossness, as there is in half the literature of the last century, which holds its place unchallenged on the tables of our drawing-rooms. For all that, it is a pity that a book where everything else is natural should go out of the way to avoid the suspicion of being prudish.

(b)

Anonymous review of 1855 and 1856 editions in Christian Examiner, *61 (1856), 471-473.*

So, then, these rank "Leaves" have sprouted afresh, and in still greater abundance. We hoped that they had dropped, and we should hear no more of them. But since they thrust themselves upon us again...we can no longer refrain from speaking of them as we think they deserve. For here is not a question of literary opinion principally, but of the very essence of religion and morality....We are bound in conscience to call it impious and obscene.... Both its language and thought seem to have just broken out of Bedlam. It sets off upon a sort of distracted philosophy, and openly deifies the bodily organs, senses, and appetites, in terms that admit of no double sense. To its pantheism and libidinousness it adds the most ridiculous swell of self-applause...

...Indeed, we should even now hardly be tempted to make the slightest allusion to this crazy outbreak of conceit and vulgarity, if a sister Review [the *North American*] had not praised it, and even undertaken to set up a plea in apology for its indecencies. We must be allowed to say, that it is not good to confound the blots upon great compositions with the compositions that are nothing but a blot. It is not good to confound the occasional ebullitions of too loose a fancy or too wanton a wit with a profession and "illustrated" doctrine of licentiousness.... it is specially desirable to be able to discern the difference between the nudity of a statue and the gestures of a satyr; between ... the Iliad and the Odyssey, and an ithyphallic audacity that insults what is most sacred and decent among men.

(c)

Whitman's self-review of the 1855 edition, United States Review, 36 (1855), 205-206, 208-210.

An American bard at last! One of the roughs, large, proud, affectionate, eating, drinking, and breeding, his costume manly and free, his face sunburnt and bearded, his postures strong and erect, his voice bringing hope and prophecy to the generous races of young and old.

...

Self-reliant, with haughty eyes, assuming to himself all the attributes of his country, steps Walt Whitman into literature, talking like a man unaware that there was ever hitherto such a production as a book, or such a being as a writer. Every move of him has the free play of the muscle of one who never knew what it was to feel that he stood in the presence of a superior.... Not a whisper comes out of him of the old stock talk and rhyme of poetry—not the first recognition of gods or goddesses, or Greece or Rome. No breath of Europe, or her monarchies, or priestly conventions, or her notions of gentlemen and ladies founded on the idea of caste, seems ever to have fanned his face or been inhaled into his lungs.

...

No sniveller, or tea-drinking poet, no puny clawback or prude, is Walt Whitman. He will bring poems fit to fill the days and nights—fit for men and women with the attributes of throbbing blood and flesh. The body, he teaches, is beautiful. Sex is also beautiful.... Nature he proclaims inherently pure. Sex will not be put aside; it is a great ordination of the universe.

Doubtless in the scheme this man has built for himself, the writing of poems is but a proportionate part of the whole. It is plain that public and private performance, politics, love, friendship, behavior, the art of conversation, science, society, the American people, the reception of the great novelties of city and country, all have their equal call upon him, and receive equal attention. In politics he could enter with the freedom and reality he shows in poetry. His scope of life is the amplest of any yet in philosophy. He is the true spiritualist. He recognizes no annihilation, or death, or loss of identity. He is the largest lover and sympathizer that has appeared in literature.... Every one, he seems to say, appears excellent to me, every employment is adorned, and every male and female glorious.

4. Two Transcendentalists' Impressions of Whitman, 1855-56

The following selections were written by two of Emerson's friends who were prompted by him to read and to visit Whitman. Both express some skittishness and skeptecism, but also considerable admiration and fascination for Whitman's charisma.

(a)

Moncure Conway, 17 September 1855 letter to Emerson, in Conway's Autobiography *(Boston and New York: Houghton, 1904), 1, 215-216.*

I found him revising some proof. A man you would not have marked in a thousand; blue striped shirt, opening from a red throat; and sitting on a chair without a back, which, being the only one, he offered me, and sat down on a round of the printer's desk himself. His manner was blunt enough also, without being disagreeably so.

. . .

The likeness in the book is fair. His beard and hair are greyer than is usual with a man of thirty-six. His face and eye are interesting, and his head rather narrow behind the eyes; but a thick brow looks as if it might have absorbed much. He walked with me and crossed the Ferry; he seemed "hail fellow" with every man he met, all apparently in the labouring class. He says he is one of that class by choice; that he is personally dear to some thousands of such in New York, who "love him but cannot make head or tail of his book." He rides on the stage with the driver. Stops to talk with the old man or woman selling fruit at the street corner. And his dress, etc., is consistent with that.

I am quite sure after talking with him that there is much in all this of what you might call "playing Providence a little with the baser sort"...But I came off delighted with him. His eye can kindle strangely; and his words are ruddy with health. He is clearly his Book,—and I went off impressed with the sense of a new city on my map, viz., Brooklyn, just as if it had suddenly risen through the boiling sea.

(b)

A. Bronson Alcott, Journals, *edited by Odell Shepard (Boston: Little, Brown, 1938), pp. 286-287, 289-291.*

October 4 [1856]   New York City

P.M. To Brooklyn, and see Walt Whitman. I pass a couple of hours, and find him to be an extraordinary person, full of brute power, certainly of genius and audacity, and likely to make his mark on Young America—he affirming himself to be its representative man and poet....

A nondescript, he is not so easily described, nor seen to be described. Broad-shouldered, rouge-fleshed, Bacchus-browed, bearded like a satyr, and rank...Red flannel undershirt, open-breasted, exposing his brawny neck; striped calico jacket over this, the collar Byroneal, with coarse cloth overalls buttoned to it; cowhide boots; a heavy round-about, with huge outside pockets and buttons to match; and a slouched hat, for house and street alike. Eyes gray, unimaginative, cautious yet sagacious; his voice deep, sharp, tender sometimes and almost melting. When talking will recline upon the couch at length, pillowing his head upon his bended arm, and informing you naively how lazy he is, and slow. Listens well; asks you to repeat what he has failed to catch at once, yet hesitates in speaking often, or gives over as if fearing to come short of the sharp, full, concrete meaning of his thought. Inquisitive, very; over-curious even; inviting criticisms on himself, on his poems—pronouncing it "pomes."—In fine, an egoist, incapable of omitting, or suffering any one long to omit, noting Walt Whitman in discourse. Swaggy in his walk, burying both hands in his outside pockets Has never been sick, he says, nor taken medicine, nor sinned; and so is quite innocent of repentance and man's fall. A bachelor, he professes great respect for women.

November 10

This morning we [Alcott, Thoreau, and a third party] call on Whitman... He receives us kindly, yet awkwardly, and takes us up two narrow flights of stairs to sit or stand as we might in his attic study—also the bedchamber of himself and his feeble brother, the pressure of whose bodies was still apparent in the unmade bed standing in one corner, and the vessel [the chamberpot] scarcely hidden underneath. A few books were piled disorderly over the mantel-piece, and some characteristic pictures—a Hercules, a Bacchus, and a satyr—were pasted, unframed, upon the rude walls.

. . .

He had told me on my former visit of his being a house-builder, but I learned from his mother that his brother was the house-builder, and not Walt, who, she said, had no business but going out and coming in to eat, drink, write, and sleep. And she told how all the common folks loved him. He had his faults, she knew, and was not a perfect man, but meant us to understand that she thought him an extraordinary son of a fond mother.

I said, while looking at the pictures in his study: "Which,

now, of the three, particularly, is the new poet here—this Hercules, the Bacchus, or the satyr?" On which he begged me not to put my questions too close, meaning to take, as I inferred, the virtues of the three to himself unreservedly....

He is very curious of criticism on himself or his book, inviting it from all quarters, nor suffering the conversation to stray very wide away from Walt's godhead without recalling it to that high mark. I hoped to put him in communication direct with Thoreau, and tried my hand a little after we came down stairs and sat in the parlour below; but each seemed planted fast in reserves, surveying the other curiously,—like two beasts, each wondering what the other would do, whether to snap or run; and it came to no more than cold compliments between them. Whether Thoreau was meditating the possibility of Walt's stealing away his "out-of-doors" for some sinister ends, poetic or pecuniary, I could not well divine ... or whether Walt suspected or not that he had here, for once, and the first time, found his match and more at smelling out "all Nature," a sagacity potent, penetrating and peerless as his own, if indeed not more piercing and profound, finer and more formidable.

5. Two Contrasting Estimates of Whitman at Mid-Career

The following selections are from reviews of Drum-Taps, *the first a pugnacious dismissal by Henry James, the second an equally partisan defense by John Burroughs. James, in later years, mellowed toward Whitman and took pleasure in reading his poetry aloud to friends. The contrast between the reviews, however, illustrates a fundamental difference in approach to literature that is still very much alive in Whitman criticism today.*

(a)

Henry James, review in The Nation, *1 (1865), 625-626.*

It has been a melancholy task to read this book; and it is a still more melancholy one to write about it.... It exhibits the effort of an essentially prosaic mind to lift itself, by a prolonged muscular strain, into poetry. Like hundreds of other good patriots, during the last four years, Mr. Walt Whitman has imagined that a certain amount of violent sympathy with the great deeds and sufferings of our soldiers, and of admiration for our national energy, together with a ready command of picturesque language, are sufficient inspiration for a poet. If this were the case, we had been a nation of poets.

...

...Mr. Whitman prides himself especially on the substance— the life—of his poetry. It may be rough, it may be grim, it may be clumsy—such we take to be the author's argument—but it is sincere, it is sublime, it appeals to the soul of man, it is the voice of a people. He tells us... that the words of his book are nothing. To our perception they are everything, and very little at that.... no triumph, however small, is won but through the exercise of art, and... this volume is an offense against art.... [Whitman's attitude] is monstrous because it pretends to persuade the soul while it slights the intellect; because it pretends to gratify the feelings while it outrages the taste.... Our hearts are often touched through a compromise with the artistic sense, but never in direct violation with it.

(b)

John Burroughs, review in The Galaxy, *2 (1866), 606, 615.*

Considering the amount of adverse criticism that has been aimed at Walt Whitman for the last ten years, and the apparent security with which the public rests in the justness of its verdict concerning him, it certainly cannot be damaging to the cause of literature in America... for us to set up a claim, in a mild way... more favorable to this rejected and misinterpreted poet.

...

It seems to us that Walt Whitman possesses almost in excess, a quality in which every current poet is lacking. We mean the faculty of being in entire sympathy with nature, and the objects and shows of nature, and of rude, abysmal man; and appalling directness of utterance therefrom, without any intermediate agency or modification.

The influence of books and works of art upon an author may be seen in all respectable writers. If knowledge alone made literature, or culture genius, there would be no dearth of these things among the moderns. But we feel bound to say that there is something higher and deeper than the influence or perusal of any or all books, or all other productions of genius—a quality of information which the masters can never impart, and which all the libraries do not hold. This is the absorption by an author, previous to becoming so, of the spirit of nature, through the visible objects of the universe, and his affiliation with them subjectively and objectively.... Without it, literary productions may have the superb beauty of statues, but with it only can they have the beauty of life.

6. Acceptance

The following two selections reflect American critical acceptance of Whitman as a crucial literary figure for better or for worse. The author of the first, William D. Howells, a friend of Henry James, was widely regarded as the Dean of American letters at the turn of the twentieth century. Randall Jarrell, the author of the second, was a poet-critic whose style shows Whitman's mark. Note the similarities between Jarrell's estimate and Hale's (3a).

(a)

William Dean Howells, review of Whitman's November Boughs, Harper's Monthly, *78 (1889), 488.*

For the poet the long fight is over; he rests his cause with what he has done; and we think no one now would like to consider the result without respect, without deference, even if one cannot approach it with entire submission. It is time,

568

certainly, while such a poet is still with us, to own that his
literary intention was as generous as his spirit was bold, and
that if he has not accomplished all he intended, he has been
a force that is by no means spent.... He dealt literary con-
ventionality one of those blows which eventually show as
internal injuries, whatever the immediate effect seems to be.
He made it possible for poetry hereafter to be more direct
and natural than hitherto; the hearing which he has braved
nearly half a century of contumely and mockery to win
would now be granted on very different terms to a man of
his greatness. This is always the way...

(b)

*Randall Jarrell, "Some Lines from Whitman," Poetry and the
Age (New York: Knopf, 1953), pp. 114, 117-118, 126, 130-
131.*

To show Whitman for what he is one does not need to
praise or explain or argue, one needs simply to quote....
Even a few of his phrases are enough to show us that
Whitman was no sweeping rhetorician, but a poet of the
greatest and oddest delicacy and originality and sensitivity,
so far as words are concerned. This is, after all, the poet who
said, "Blind loving wrestling touch, sheath'd hooded
sharp-tooth'd touch"; who said, "Smartly attired,
countenance smiling, form upright, death under the
breast-bones, hell under the skull-bones"; who said, "Agonies
are one of my changes of garments"; who saw grass as the
"flag of my disposition," saw "the sharp-peak'd farmhouse,
with its scallop'd scum and slender shoots from the gutters,"
heard a plane's "wild ascending lisp," and saw and heard how
at the amputation "what is removed drops horribly in a
pail."

...

The interesting thing about Whitman's worst language (for,
just as few poets have ever written better, few poets have
ever written worse) is how unusually absurd, how really in-
geniously bad, such language is. I will quote none of the most

famous examples; but even a line like "*O culpable! I acknowl-edge. I exposé!*" is not anything that you and I could do—only a man with the most extraordinary feel for language, or none whatsoever, could have cooked up Whitman's worst messes.... And the queerly bad and merely queer and queerly good will often change into one another without warning: "Hefts of the moving world, at innocent gambols silently rising, freshly exuding, / Scooting obliquely high and low"—not good, but *queer*!—suddenly becomes "Something I cannot see puts up libidinous prongs, / Seas of bright juice suffuse heaven" and it is sunrise.

· · ·

... Whitman is a world, a waste with, here and there, systems blazing at random out of the darkness. Only an innocent and rigidly methodical mind will reject it for this disorganization, particularly since there are in it, here and there, little systems as beautifully and astonishingly organized as the rings and satellites of Saturn...

· · ·

Whitman is more coordinate and parallel than anybody, is *the* poet of parallel present participles, of twenty verbs joined by a single subject: all this helps to give his work its feeling of raw hypnotic reality, of being that world which also streams over us joined only by *ands*, until we supply the subordinating conjuctions; and since as children we see the *ands* and not the *becauses*, this method helps to give Whitman some of the freshness of childhood. How inexhaustibly interesting the world is in Whitman! [Matthew] Arnold all his life kept wishing that he could see the world "with a plainness as near, as flashing" as that with which Moses and Rebekah and the Argonauts saw it. He asked with elegiac nostalgia, "Who can see the green earth any more / As she was by the sources of Time?"—and all the time there was somebody alive who saw it so, as plain and near and flashing, and with a kind of calm, pastoral, Biblical dignity and elegance as well, sometimes. The *thereness* and *suchness* of the world are incarnate in Whitman as they are in few other writers.

I have said so little about Whitman's faults because they are so plain: baby critics who have barely learned to complain of the lack of ambiguity in *Peter Rabbit* can tell you all that is wrong with *Leaves of Grass*. But a good many of my readers must have felt that it is ridiculous to write an essay about the obvious fact that Whitman is a great poet.

Leaves of Grass
and
Selected Prose

Modern Library
College Editions

✒ Leaves of Grass

COME, said my Soul,
Such verses for my Body let us write,
  (for we are one,)
That should I after death invisibly return,
Or, long, long hence, in other spheres,
There to some group of mates
  the chants resuming,
(Tallying Earth's soil, trees, winds,
  tumultuous waves,)
Ever with pleas'd smile I may keep on,
Ever and ever yet the verses owning—
  as, first, I here and now,
Signing for Soul and Body,
  set to them my name,

Walt Whitman

[The following note by Walt Whitman appeared on the copyright page of the 1891-2 edition of *Leaves of Grass*.]

☛ As there are now several editions of L. of G., different texts and dates, I wish to say that I prefer and recommend this present one, complete, for future printing, if there should be any; a copy and fac-simile, indeed, of the text of these 438 pages. The subsequent adjusting interval which is so important to form'd and launch'd work, books especially, has pass'd; and waiting till fully after that, I have given (pages 423–438) my concluding words.

W. W.

Inscriptions

ONE'S-SELF I SING

ONE'S-SELF I sing, a simple separate person,
Yet utter the word Democratic, the word En-Masse.

Of physiology from top to toe I sing,
Not physiognomy alone nor brain alone is worthy for the Muse, I
    say the Form complete is worthier far,
The Female equally with the Male I sing.

Of Life immense in passion, pulse, and power,
Cheerful, for freest action form'd under the laws divine,
The Modern Man I sing.

AS I PONDER'D IN SILENCE

As I ponder'd in silence,
Returning upon my poems, considering, lingering long,
A Phantom arose before me with distrustful aspect,
Terrible in beauty, age, and power,
The genius of poets of old lands,
As to me directing like flame its eyes,
With finger pointing to many immortal songs,
And menacing voice, *What singest thou?* it said,
Know'st thou not there is but one theme for ever-enduring bards?
And that is the theme of War, the fortune of battles,
The making of perfect soldiers.

Be it so, then I answer'd,
I too haughty Shade also sing war, and a longer and greater one
    than any,
Waged in my book with varying fortune, with flight, advance and
    retreat, victory deferr'd and wavering,
(Yet methinks certain, or as good as certain, at the last,) the field
    the world,

3

For life and death, for the Body and for the eternal Soul,
Lo, I too am come, chanting the chant of battles,
I above all promote brave soldiers.

IN CABIN'D SHIPS AT SEA

IN cabin'd ships at sea,
The boundless blue on every side expanding,
With whistling winds and music of the waves, the large imperious
  waves,
Or some lone bark buoy'd on the dense marine,
Where joyous full of faith, spreading white sails,
She cleaves the ether mid the sparkle and the foam of day, or
  under many a star at night,
By sailors young and old haply will I, a reminiscence of the land,
  be read,
In full rapport at last.

Here are our thoughts, voyagers' thoughts,
Here not the land, firm land, alone appears, may then by them be
  said,
The sky o'erarches here, we feel the undulating deck beneath our
  feet,
We feel the long pulsation, ebb and flow of endless motion,
The tones of unseen mystery, the vague and vast suggestions of the
  briny world, the liquid-flowing syllables,
The perfume, the faint creaking of the cordage, the melancholy
  rhythm,
The boundless vista and the horizon far and dim are all here,
And this is ocean's poem.

Then falter not O book, fulfil your destiny,
You not a reminiscence of the land alone,
You too as a lone bark cleaving the ether, purpos'd I know not
  whither, yet ever full of faith,
Consort to every ship that sails, sail you!
Bear forth to them folded my love, (dear mariners, for you I fold
  it here in every leaf;)
Speed on my book! spread your white sails my little bark athwart
  the imperious waves,
Chant on, sail on, bear o'er the boundless blue from me to every
  sea,
This song for mariners and all their ships.

TO FOREIGN LANDS

I HEARD that you ask'd for something to prove this puzzle the New
World,
And to define America, her athletic Democracy,
Therefore I send you my poems that you behold in them what you
wanted.

TO A HISTORIAN

YOU who celebrate bygones,
Who have explored the outward, the surfaces of the races, the life
that has exhibited itself,
Who have treated of man as the creature of politics, aggregates,
rulers and priests,
I, habitan of the Alleghanies, treating of him as he is in himself
in his own rights,
Pressing the pulse of the life that has seldom exhibited itself, (the
great pride of man in himself,)
Chanter of Personality, outlining what is yet to be,
I project the history of the future.

TO THEE OLD CAUSE

To thee old cause!
Thou peerless, passionate, good cause,
Thou stern, remorseless, sweet idea,
Deathless throughout the ages, races, lands,
After a strange sad war, great war for thee,
(I think all war through time was really fought, and ever will be
really fought, for thee,)
These chants for thee, the eternal march of thee.

(A war O soldiers not for itself alone,
Far, far more stood silently waiting behind, now to advance in
this book.)

Thou orb of many orbs!
Thou seething principle! thou well-kept, latent germ! thou centre!
Around the idea of thee the war revolving,
With all its angry and vehement play of causes,
(With vast results to come for thrice a thousand years,)
These recitatives for thee,—my book and the war are one,
Merged in its spirit I and mine, as the contest hinged on thee,

As a wheel on its axis turns, this book unwitting to itself,
Around the idea of thee.

EIDÓLONS

    I MET a seer,
Passing the hues and objects of the world,
The fields of art and learning, pleasure, sense,
      To glean eidólons.

    Put in thy chants said he,
No more the puzzling hour nor day, nor segments, parts, put in,
Put first before the rest as light for all and entrance-song of all,
      That of eidólons.

    Ever the dim beginning,
Ever the growth, the rounding of the circle,
Ever the summit and the merge at last, (to surely start again,)
      Eidólons! eidólons!

    Ever the mutable,
Ever materials, changing, crumbling, re-cohering,
Ever the ateliers, the factories divine,
      Issuing eidólons.

    Lo, I or you,
Or woman, man, or state, known or unknown,
We seeming solid wealth, strength, beauty build,
      But really build eidólons.

    The ostent evanescent,
The substance of an artist's mood or savan's studies long,
Or warrior's, martyr's, hero's toils,
      To fashion his eidólon.

    Of every human life,
(The units gather'd, posted, not a thought, emotion, deed, left out,)
The whole or large or small summ'd, added up,
      In its eidólon.

    The old, old urge,
Based on the ancient pinnacles, lo, newer, higher pinnacles,
From science and the modern still impell'd,
      The old, old urge, eidólons.

The present now and here,
America's busy, teeming, intricate whirl,
Of aggregate and segregate for only thence releasing,
    To-day's eidólons.

These with the past,
Of vanish'd lands, of all the reigns of kings across the sea,
Old conquerors, old campaigns, old sailors' voyages,
    Joining eidólons.

Densities, growth, façades,
Strata of mountains, soils, rocks, giant trees,
Far-born, far-dying, living long, to leave,
    Eidólons everlasting.

Exalté, rapt, ecstatic,
The visible but their womb of birth,
Of orbic tendencies to shape and shape and shape,
    The mighty earth-eidólon.

All space, all time,
(The stars, the terrible perturbations of the suns,
Swelling, collapsing, ending, serving their longer, shorter use,)
    Fill'd with eidólons only.

The noiseless myriads,
The infinite oceans where the rivers empty,
The separate countless free identities, like eyesight,
    The true realities, eidólons.

Not this the world,
Nor these the universes, they the universes,
Purport and end, ever the permanent life of life,
    Eidólons, eidólons.

Beyond thy lectures learn'd professor,
Beyond thy telescope or spectroscope observer keen, beyond all
    mathematics,
Beyond the doctor's surgery, anatomy, beyond the chemist with
    his chemistry,
    The entities of entities, eidólons.

Unfix'd yet fix'd,
Ever shall be, ever have been and are,
Sweeping the present to the infinite future,
    Eidólons, eidólons, eidolons.

The prophet and the bard,
Shall yet maintain themselves, in higher stages yet,
Shall mediate to the Modern, to democracy, interpret yet to them,
    God and eidólóns.

And thee my soul,
Joys, ceaseless exercises, exaltations,
Thy yearning amply fed at last, prepared to meet,
    Thy mates, eidólons.

Thy body permanent,
The body lurking there within thy body,
The only purport of the form thou art, the real I myself,
    An image, an eidólon.

Thy very songs not in thy songs,
No special strains to sing, none for itself,
But from the whole resulting, rising at last and floating,
    A round full-orb'd eidólon.

FOR HIM I SING

FOR him I sing,
I raise the present on the past,
(As some perennial tree out of its roots, the present on the past,)
With time and space I him dilate and fuse the immortal laws,
To make himself by them the law unto himself.

WHEN I READ THE BOOK

WHEN I read the book, the biography famous,
And is this then (said I) what the author calls a man's life?
And so will some one when I am dead and gone write my life?
(As if any man really knew aught of my life,
Why even I myself I often think know little or nothing of my real
    life,
Only a few hints, a few diffused faint clews and indirections
I seek for my own use to trace out here.)

BEGINNING MY STUDIES

BEGINNING my studies the first step pleas'd me so much,
The mere fact consciousness, these forms, the power of motion,
The least insect or animal, the senses, eyesight, love,
The first step I say awed me and pleas'd me so much,
I have hardly gone and hardly wish'd to go any farther,
But stop and loiter all the time to sing it in ecstatic songs.

BEGINNERS

How they are provided for upon the earth, (appearing at intervals,)
How dear and dreadful they are to the earth,
How they inure to themselves as much as to any—what a paradox
    appears their age,
How people respond to them, yet know them not,
How there is something relentless in their fate all times,
How all times mischoose the objects of their adulation and reward,
And how the same inexorable price must still be paid for the same
    great purchase.

TO THE STATES

To the States or any one of them, or any city of the States, *Resist
    much, obey little,*
Once unquestioning obedience, once fully enslaved,
Once fully enslaved, no nation, state, city of this earth, ever after-
    ward resumes its liberty.

ON JOURNEYS THROUGH THE STATES

On journeys through the States we start,
(Ay through the world, urged by these songs,
Sailing henceforth to every land, to every sea,)
We willing learners of all, teachers of all, and lovers of all.

We have watch'd the seasons dispensing themselves and passing on,
And have said, Why should not a man or woman do as much as
    the seasons, and effuse as much?

We dwell a while in every city and town,
We pass through Kanada, the North-east, the vast valley of the
    Mississippi, and the Southern States,

We confer on equal terms with each of the States,
We make trial of ourselves and invite men and women to hear,
We say to ourselves, Remember, fear not, be candid, promulge the
    body and the soul.
Dwell a while and pass on, be copious, temperate, chaste, magnetic,
And what you effuse may then return as the seasons return,
And may be just as much as the seasons.

TO A CERTAIN CANTATRICE

HERE, take this gift,
I was reserving it for some hero, speaker, or general,
One who should serve the good old cause, the great idea, the prog-
    ress and freedom of the race,
Some brave confronter of despots, some daring rebel;
But I see that what I was reserving belongs to you just as much as
    to any.

ME IMPERTURBE

ME imperturbe, standing at ease in Nature,
Master of all or mistress of all, aplomb in the midst of irrational
    things,
Imbued as they, passive, receptive, silent as they,
Finding my occupation, poverty, notoriety, foibles, crimes, less im-
    portant than I thought,
Me toward the Mexican sea, or in the Mannahatta or the Tennes-
    see, or far north or inland,
A river man, or a man of the woods or of any farm-life of these
    States or of the coast, or the lakes or Kanada,
Me wherever my life is lived, O to be self-balanced for contingencies,
To confront night, storms, hunger, ridicule, accidents, rebuffs, as
    the trees and animals do.

SAVANTISM

THITHER as I look I see each result and glory retracing itself and
    nestling close, always obligated,
Thither hours, months, years—thither trades, compacts, establish-
    ments, even the most minute,
Thither every-day life, speech, utensils, politics, persons, estates;
Thither we also, I with my leaves and songs, trustful, admirant,
As a father to his father going takes his children along with him.

THE SHIP STARTING

Lo, the unbounded sea,
On its breast a ship starting, spreading all sails, carrying even her
    moonsails,
The pennant is flying aloft as she speeds she speeds so stately—
    below emulous waves press forward,
They surround the ship with shining curving motions and foam.

I HEAR AMERICA SINGING

I hear America singing, the varied carols I hear,
Those of mechanics, each one singing his as it should be blithe
    and strong,
The carpenter singing his as he measures his plank or beam,
The mason singing his as he makes ready for work, or leaves off
    work,
The boatman singing what belongs to him in his boat, the deckhand
    singing on the steamboat deck,
The shoemaker singing as he sits on his bench, the hatter singing
    as he stands,
The wood-cutter's song, the ploughboy's on his way in the morn-
    ing, or at noon intermission or at sundown,
The delicious singing of the mother, or of the young wife at work,
    or of the girl sewing or washing,
Each singing what belongs to him or her and to none else,
The day what belongs to the day—at night the party of young
    fellows, robust, friendly,
Singing with open mouths their strong melodious songs.

WHAT PLACE IS BESIEGED?

What place is besieged, and vainly tries to raise the siege?
Lo, I send to that place a commander, swift, brave, immortal,
And with him horse and foot, and parks of artillery,
And artillery-men, the deadliest that ever fired gun.

STILL THOUGH THE ONE I SING

Still though the one I sing,
(One, yet of contradictions made,) I dedicate to Nationality,
I leave in him revolt, (O latent right of insurrection! O quenchless,
    indispensable fire!)

SHUT NOT YOUR DOORS

SHUT not your doors to me proud libraries,
For that which was lacking on all your well-fill'd shelves, yet needed
    most, I bring,
Forth from the war emerging, a book I have made,
The words of my book nothing, the drift of it every thing,
A book separate, not link'd with the rest nor felt by the intellect,
But you ye untold latencies will thrill to every page.

POETS TO COME

POETS to come! orators, singers, musicians to come!
Not to-day is to justify me and answer what I am for,
But you, a new brood, native, athletic, continental, greater than
    before known,
Arouse! for you must justify me.

I myself but write one or two indicative words for the future,
I but advance a moment only to wheel and hurry back in the
    darkness.

I am a man who, sauntering along without fully stopping, turns a
    casual look upon you and then averts his face,
Leaving it to you to prove and define it,
Expecting the main things from you.

TO YOU

STRANGER, if you passing meet me and desire to speak to me, why
    should you not speak to me?
And why should I not speak to you?

THOU READER

THOU reader throbbest life and pride and love the same as I,
Therefore for thee the following chants.

Starting from Paumanok

1

STARTING from fish-shape Paumanok where I was born,
Well-begotten, and rais'd by a perfect mother,
After roaming many lands, lover of populous pavements,

Dweller in Mannahatta my city, or on southern savannas,
Or a soldier camp'd or carrying my knapsack and gun, or a miner
  in California,
Or rude in my home in Dakota's woods, my diet meat, my drink
  from the spring,
Or withdrawn to muse and meditate in some deep recess,
Far from the clank of crowds intervals passing rapt and happy,
Aware of the fresh free giver the flowing Missouri, aware of mighty
  Niagara,
Aware of the buffalo herds grazing the plains, the hirsute and
  strong-breasted bull,
Of earth, rocks, Fifth-month flowers experienced, stars, rain, snow,
  my amaze,
Having studied the mocking-bird's tones and the flight of the
  mountain-hawk,
And heard at dusk the unrivall'd one, the hermit thrush from the
  swamp-cedars,
Solitary, singing in the West, I strike up for a New World.

2

Victory, union, faith, identity, time,
The indissoluble compacts, riches, mystery,
Eternal progress, the Kosmos, and the modern reports.

This then is life,
Here is what has come to the surface after so many throes and
  convulsions.

How curious! how real!
Underfoot the divine soil, overhead the sun.

See revolving the globe,
The ancestor-continents away group'd together,
The present and future continents north and south, with the
  isthmus between.

See, vast trackless spaces,
As in a dream they change, they swiftly fill,
Countless masses debouch upon them,
They are now cover'd with the foremost people, arts, institutions,
  known.

See, projected through time,
For me an audience interminable.

With firm and regular step they wend, they never stop,
Successions of men, Americanos, a hundred millions,
One generation playing its part and passing on,
Another generation playing its part and passing on in its turn,
With faces turn'd sideways or backward towards me to listen,
With eyes retrospective towards me.

3

Americanos! conquerors! marches humanitarian!
Foremost! century marches! Libertad! masses!
For you a programme of chants.

Chants of the prairies,
Chants of the long-running Mississippi, and down to the Mexican
    sea,
Chants of Ohio, Indiana, Illinois, Iowa, Wisconsin and Minnesota,
Chants going forth from the centre from Kansas, and thence equi-
    distant,
Shooting in pulses of fire ceaseless to vivify all.

4

Take my leaves America, take them South, and take them North,
Make welcome for them everywhere, for they are your own off-
    spring,
Surround them East and West, for they would surround you,
And you precedents, connect lovingly with them, for they connect
    lovingly with you.

I conn'd old times,
I sat studying at the feet of the great masters,
Now if eligible O that the great masters might return and study me.

In the name of these States shall I scorn the antique?
Why these are the children of the antique to justify it.

5

Dead poets, philosophs, priests,
Martyrs, artists, inventors, governments long since,

Language-shapers on other shores,
Nations once powerful, now reduced, withdrawn, or desolate,
I dare not proceed till I respectfully credit what you have left
    wafted hither,
I have perused it, own it is admirable, (moving awhile among it,)
Think nothing can ever be greater, nothing can ever deserve more
    than it deserves,
Regarding it all intently a long while, then dismissing it,
I stand in my place with my own day here.

Here lands female and male,
Here the heir-ship and heiress-ship of the world, here the flame of
    materials,
Here spirituality the translatress, the openly-avow'd,
The ever-tending, the finalè of visible forms,
The satisfier, after due long-waiting now advancing,
Yes here comes my mistress the soul.

6

The soul,
Forever and forever—longer than soil is brown and solid—longer
    than water ebbs and flows.

I will make the poems of materials, for I think they are to be the
    most spiritual poems,
And I will make the poems of my body and of mortality,
For I think I shall then supply myself with the poems of my soul
    and of immortality.

I will make a song for these States that no one State may under
    any circumstances be subjected to another State,
And I will make a song that there shall be comity by day and by
    night between all the States, and between any two of them,
And I will make a song for the ears of the President, full of weap-
    ons with menacing points,
And behind the weapons countless dissatisfied faces;
And a song make I of the One form'd out of all,
The fang'd and glittering One whose head is over all,
Resolute warlike One including and over all,
(However high the head of any else that head is over all.)

I will acknowledge contemporary lands,
I will trail the whole geography of the globe and salute courte-
    ously every city large and small,

And employments! I will put in my poems that with you is hero-
    ism upon land and sea,
And I will report all heroism from an American point of view.

I will sing the song of companionship,
I will show what alone must finally compact these,
I believe these are to found their own ideal of manly love, indi-
    cating it in me,
I will therefore let flame from me the burning fires that were
    threatening to consume me,
I will lift what has too long kept down those smouldering fires,
I will give them complete abandonment,
I will write the evangel-poem of comrades and of love,
For who but I should understand love with all its sorrow and joy?
And who but I should be the poet of comrades?

7

I am the credulous man of qualities, ages, races,
I advance from the people in their own spirit,
Here is what sings unrestricted faith.

Omnes! omnes! let others ignore what they may,
I make the poem of evil also, I commemorate that part also,
I am myself just as much evil as good, and my nation is—and I
    say there is in fact no evil,
(Or if there is I say it is just as important to you, to the land or
    to me, as anything else.)

I too, following many and follow'd by many, inaugurate a religion,
    I descend into the arena,
(It may be I am destin'd to utter the loudest cries there, the win-
    ner's pealing shouts,
Who knows? they may rise from me yet, and soar above every thing.)

Each is not for its own sake,
I say the whole earth and all the stars in the sky are for religions
    sake.

I say no man has ever yet been half devout enough,
None has ever yet adored or worship'd half enough,
None has begun to think how divine he himself is, and how cer-
    tain the future is.

I say that the real and permanent grandeur of these States must
    be their religion,
Otherwise there is no real and permanent grandeur;
(Nor character nor life worthy the name without religion,
Nor land nor man or woman without religion.)

8

What are you doing young man?
Are you so earnest, so given up to literature, science, art, amours?
These ostensible realities, politics, points?
Your ambition or business whatever it may be?

It is well—against such I say not a word, I am their poet also,
But behold! such swiftly subside, burnt up for religion's sake,
For not all matter is fuel to heat, impalpable flame, the essential
    life of the earth,
Any more than such are to religion.

9

What do you seek so pensive and silent?
What do you need camerado?
Dear son do you think it is love?

Listen dear son—listen America, daughter or son,
It is a painful thing to love a man or woman to excess, and yet it
    satisfies, it is great,
But there is something else very great, it makes the whole coin-
    cide,
It, magnificent, beyond materials, with continuous hands sweeps
    and provides for all.

10

Know you, solely to drop in the earth the germs of a greater
    religion,
The following chants each for its kind I sing.

My comrade!
For you to share with me two greatnesses, and a third one rising
    inclusive and more resplendent,
The greatness of Love and Democracy, and the greatness of Reli-
    gion.

Melange mine own, the unseen and the seen,
Mysterious ocean where the streams empty,
Prophetic spirit of materials shifting and flickering around me,
Living beings, identities now doubtless near us in the air that we
    know not of,
Contact daily and hourly that will not release me,
These selecting, these in hints demanded of me.

Not he with a daily kiss onward from childhood kissing me,
Has winded and twisted around me that which holds me to him,
Any more than I am held to the heavens and all the spiritual
    world,
After what they have done to me, suggesting themes.

O such themes—equalities! O divine average!
Warblings under the sun, usher'd as now, or at noon, or setting,
Strains musical flowing through ages, now reaching hither,
I take to your reckless and composite chords, add to them, and
    cheerfully pass them forward.

11

As I have walk'd in Alabama my morning walk,
I have seen where the she-bird the mocking-bird sat on her nest
    in the briers hatching her brood.

I have seen the he-bird also,
I have paus'd to hear him near at hand inflating his throat and
    joyfully singing.

And while I paus'd it came to me that what he really sang for was
    not there only,
Nor for his mate nor himself only, nor all sent back by the echoes,
But subtle, clandestine, away beyond,
A charge transmitted and gift occult for those being born.

12

Democracy! near at hand to you a throat is now inflating itself
    and joyfully singing.

Ma femme! for the brood beyond us and of us,
For those who belong here and those to come,

I exultant to be ready for them will now shake out carols stronger
and haughtier than have ever yet been heard upon earth.

I will make the songs of passion to give them their way,
And your songs outlaw'd offenders, for I scan you with kindred
eyes, and carry you with me the same as any.

I will make the true poem of riches,
To earn for the body and the mind whatever adheres and goes
forward and is not dropt by death;
I will effuse egotism and show it underlying all, and I will be the
bard of personality,
And I will show of male and female that either is but the equal
of the other.
And sexual organs and acts! do you concentrate in me, for I am
determin'd to tell you with courageous clear voice to prove
you illustrious.
And I will show that there is no imperfection in the present, and
can be none in the future,
And I will show that whatever happens to anybody it may be
turn'd to beautiful results,
And I will show that nothing can happen more beautiful than
death,
And I will thread a thread through my poems that time and events
are compact,
And that all the things of the universe are perfect miracles, each
as profound as any.

I will not make poems with reference to parts,
But I will make poems, songs, thoughts, with reference to ensemble,
And I will not sing with reference to a day, but with reference to
all days,
And I will not make a poem nor the least part of a poem but has
reference to the soul,
Because having look'd at the objects of the universe, I find there
is no one nor any particle of one but has reference to the soul.

13

Was somebody asking to see the soul?
See, your own shape and countenance, persons, substances, beasts,
the trees, the running rivers, the rocks and sands.

All hold spiritual joys and afterwards loosen them;
How can the real body ever die and be buried?

Of your real body and any man's or woman's real body,
Item for item it will elude the hands of the corpse-cleaners and
    pass to fitting spheres,
Carrying what has accrued to it from the moment of birth to the
    moment of death.

Not the types set up by the printer return their impression, the
    meaning, the main concern,
Any more than a man's substance and life or a woman's substance
    and life return in the body and the soul,
Indifferently before death and after death.

Behold, the body includes and is the meaning, the main concern,
    and includes and is the soul;
Whoever you are, how superb and how divine is your body, or any part
of it!

14

Whoever you are, to you endless announcements!

Daughter of the lands did you wait for your poet?
Did you wait for one with a flowing mouth and indicative hand?
Toward the male of the States, and toward the female of the States,
Exulting words, words to Democracy's lands.

Interlink'd, food-yielding lands!
Land of coal and iron! land of gold! land of cotton, sugar, rice!
Land of wheat, beef, pork! land of wool ahd hemp! land of the
    apple and the grape!
Land of the pastoral plains, the grass-fields of the world! land of
    those sweet-air'd interminable plateaus!
Land of the herd, the garden, the healthy house of adobie!
Lands where the north-west Columbia winds, and where the south-
    west Colorado winds!
Land of the eastern Chesapeake! land of the Delaware!
Land of Ontario, Erie, Huron, Michigan!
Land of the Old Thirteen! Massachusetts land! land of Vermont
    and Connecticut!
Land of the ocean shores! land of sierras and peaks!
Land of boatmen and sailors! fishermen's land!
Inextricable lands! the clutch'd together! the passionate ones!

The side by side! the elder and younger brothers! the bony-limbed!
The great women's land! the feminine! the experienced sisters
    and the inexperienced sisters!
Far breath'd land! Arctic braced! Mexican breez'd! the diverse!
    the compact!
The Pennsylvanian! the Virginian! the double Carolinian!
O all and each well-loved by me! my intrepid nations! O I at
    any rate include you all with perfect love!
I cannot be discharged from you! not from one any sooner than
    another!
O death! O for all that, I am yet of you unseen this hour with
    irrepressible love,
Walking New England, a friend, a traveller,
Splashing my bare feet in the edge of the summer ripples on Pau-
    manok's sands,
Crossing the prairies, dwelling again in Chicago, dwelling in every
    town,
Observing shows, births, improvements, structures, arts,
Listening to orators and oratresses in public halls,
Of and through the States as during life, each man and woman
    my neighbor,
The Louisianian, the Georgian, as near to me, and I as near to
    him and her,
The Mississippian and Arkansian yet with me, and I yet with any
    of them,
Yet upon the plains west of the spinal river, yet in my house of
    adobie,
Yet returning eastward, yet in the Seaside State or in Maryland,
Yet Kanadian cheerily braving the winter, the snow and ice wel-
    come to me,
Yet a true son either of Maine or of the Granite State, or the
    Narragansett Bay State, or the Empire State,
Yet sailing to other shores to annex the same, yet welcoming every
    new brother,
Hereby applying these leaves to the new ones from the hour they
    unite with the old ones,
Coming among the new ones myself to be their companion and
    equal, coming personally to you now,
Enjoining you to acts, characters, spectacles, with me.

15

With me with firm holding, yet haste, haste on.

For your life adhere to me,
(I may have to be persuaded many times before I consent to give
    myself really to you, but what of that?
Must not Nature be persuaded many times?)

No dainty dolce affettuoso I,
Bearded, sun-burnt, gray-neck'd, forbidding, I have arrived,
To be wrestled with as I pass for the solid prizes of the universe,
For such I afford whoever can persevere to win them.

16

On my way a moment I pause,
Here for you! and here for America!
Still the present I raise aloft, still the future of the States I
    harbinge glad and sublime,
And for the past I pronounce what the air holds of the red
    aborigines.

The red aborigines,
Leaving natural breaths, sounds of rain and winds, calls as of birds
    and animals in the woods, syllabled to us for names,
Okonee, Koosa, Ottawa, Monongahela, Sauk, Natchez, Chatta-
    hoochee, Kaqueta, Oronoco,
Wabash, Miami, Saginaw, Chippewa, Oshkosh, Walla-Walla,
Leaving such to the States they melt, they depart, charging the
    water and the land with names.

17

Expanding and swift, henceforth,
Elements, breeds, adjustments, turbulent, quick and audacious,
A world primal again, vistas of glory incessant and branching,
A new race dominating previous ones and grander far, with new
    contests,
New politics, new literatures and religions, new inventions and arts.

These, my voice announcing—I will sleep no more but arise,
You oceans that have been calm within me! how I feel you, fathom-
    less, stirring, preparing unprecedented waves and storms.

18

See, steamers steaming through my poems,
See, in my poems immigrants continually coming and landing,

See, in arriere, the wigwam, the trail, the hunter's hut, the flat-boat, the maize-leaf, the claim, the rude fence, and the backwoods village,

See, on the one side the Western Sea and on the other the Eastern Sea, how they advance and retreat upon my poems as upon their own shores,

See, pastures and forests in my poems—see, animals wild and tame—see, beyond the Kaw, countless herds of buffalo feeding on short curly grass,

See, in my poems, cities, solid, vast, inland, with paved streets, with iron and stone edifices, ceaseless vehicles, and commerce,

See, the many-cylinder'd steam printing-press—see, the electric telegraph stretching across the continent,

See, through Atlantica's depths pulses American Europe reaching, pulses of Europe duly return'd,

See, the strong and quick locomotive as it departs, panting, blowing the steam-whistle,

See, ploughmen ploughing farms—see, miners digging mines—see, the numberless factories,

See, mechanics busy at their benches with tools—see from among them superior judges, philosophs, Presidents, emerge, drest in working dresses,

See, lounging through the shops and fields of the States, me well-belov'd, close-held by day and night,

Hear the loud echoes of my songs there—read the hints come at last.

19

O camerado close! O you and me at last, and us two only.
O a word to clear one's path ahead endlessly!
O something ecstatic and undemonstrable! O music wild!
O now I triumph—and you shall also;
O hand in hand—O wholesome pleasure—O one more desirer and lover!
O to haste firm holding—to haste, haste on with me.

Song of Myself

1

I CELEBRATE myself, and sing myself,
And what I assume you shall assume,
For every atom belonging to me as good belongs to you.

I loafe and invite my soul,
I lean and loafe at my ease observing a spear of summer grass.

My tongue, every atom of my blood, form'd from this soil, this
    air,
Born here of parents born here from parents the same, and their
    parents the same,
I, now thirty-seven years old in perfect health begin,
Hoping to cease not till death.

Creeds and schools in abeyance,
Retiring back a while suffced at what they are, but never forgotten
I harbor for good or bad, I permit to speak at every hazard,
Nature without check with original energy.

2

Houses and rooms are full of perfumes, the shelves are crowded
    with perfumes,
I breathe the fragrance myself and know it and like it,
The distillation would intoxicate me also, but I shall not let it.

The atmosphere is not a perfume, it has no taste of the distillation,
    it is odorless,
It is for my mouth forever, I am in love with it,
I will go to the bank by the wood and become undisguised and
    naked,
I am mad for it to be in contact with me.

The smoke of my own breath,
Echoes, ripples, buzz'd whispers, love-root, silk-thread, crotch and
    vine,
My respiration and inspiration, the beating of my heart, the passing
    of blood and air through my lungs,
The sniff of green leaves and dry leaves, and of the shore and
    dark-color'd sea-rocks, and of hay in the barn,
The sound of the belch'd words in my voice loos'd to the eddies
    of the wind,
A few light kisses, a few embraces, a reaching around of arms,
The play of shine and shade on the trees as the supple boughs
    wag,
The delight alone or in the rush of the streets, or along the fields
    and hill-sides,

The feeling of health, the full-noon trill, the song of me rising from
  bed and meeting the sun.

Have you reckon'd a thousand acres much? have you reckon'd
  the earth much?
Have you practis'd so long to learn to read?
Have you felt so proud to get at the meaning of poems?

Stop this day and night with me and you shall possess the origin
  of all poems,
You shall possess the good of the earth and sun, (there are millions
  of suns left,)
You shall no longer take things at second or third hand, nor look
  through the eyes of the dead, nor feed on the spectres in books,
You shall not look through my eyes either, nor take things from me,
You shall listen to all sides and filter them from your self.

3

I have heard what the talkers were talking, the talk of the beginning and the end,
But I do not talk of the beginning or the end.

There was never any more inception than there is now,
Nor any more youth or age than there is now,
And will never be any more perfection than there is now,
Nor any more heaven or hell than there is now.

Urge and urge and urge,
Always the procreant urge of the world.

Out of the dimness opposite equals advance, always substance and
  increase, always sex,
Always a knit of identity, always distinction, always a breed of life.

To elaborate is no avail, learn'd and unlearn'd feel that it is so.

Sure as the most certain sure, plumb in the uprights, well entretied,
  braced in the beams,
Stout as a horse, affectionate, haughty, electrical,
I and this mystery here we stand.

Clear and sweet is my soul, and clear and sweet is all that is not
  my soul.

Lack one lacks both, and the unseen is proved by the seen,
Till that becomes unseen and receives proof in its turn.

Showing the best and dividing it from the worst age vexes age,
Knowing the perfect fitness and equanimity of things, while they
    discuss I am silent, and go bathe and admire myself.

Welcome is every organ and attribute of me, and of any man
    hearty and clean,
Not an inch nor a particle of an inch is vile, and none shall be less
    familiar than the rest.

I am satisfied—I see, dance, laugh, sing;
As the hugging and loving bed-fellow sleeps at my side through
    the night, and withdraws at the peep of the day with stealthy
    tread,
Leaving me baskets cover'd with white towels swelling the house
    with their plenty,
Shall I postpone my acceptation and realization and scream at my
    eyes,
That they turn from gazing after and down the road,
And forthwith cipher and show to me a cent,
Exactly the value of one and exactly the value of two, and which
    is ahead?

4

Trippers and askers surround me,
People I meet, the effect upon me of my early life or the ward and
    city I live in, or the nation,
The latest dates, discoveries, inventions, societies, authors old and
    new,
My dinner, dress, associates, looks, compliments, dues,
The real or fancied indifference of some man or woman I love,
The sickness of one of my folks or of myself, or ill-doing or loss or
    lack of money, or depressions or exaltations,
Battles, the horrors of fratricidal war, the fever of doubtful news,
    the fitful events;
These come to me days and nights and go from me again,
But they are not the Me myself.

Apart from the pulling and hauling stands what I am,
Stands amused, complacent, compassionating, idle, unitary,
Looks down, is erect, or bends an arm on an impalpable certain rest,

Looking with side-curved head curious what will come next,
Both in and out of the game and watching and wondering at it.

Backward I see in my own days where I sweated through fog with
   linguists and contenders,
I have no mockings or arguments, I witness and wait.

5

I believe in you my soul, the other I am must not abase itself to you,
And you must not be abased to the other.

Loafe with me on the grass, loose the stop from your throat,
Not words, not music or rhyme I want, not custom or lecture, not
   even the best,
Only the lull I like, the hum of your valvèd voice.

I mind how once we lay such a transparent summer morning,
How you settled your head athwart my hips and gently turn'd over
   upon me,
And parted the shirt from my bosom-bone, and plunged your
   tongue to my bare-stript heart,
And reach'd till you felt my beard, and reach'd till you held my feet.

Swiftly arose and spread around me the peace and knowledge that
   pass all the argument of the earth,
And I know that the hand of God is the promise of my own,
And I know that the spirit of God is the brother of my own,
And that all the men ever born are also my brothers, and the women
   my sisters and lovers,
And that a kelson of the creation is love,
And limitless are leaves stiff or drooping in the fields,
And brown ants in the little wells beneath them,
And mossy scabs of the worm fence, heap'd stones, elder, mullein
   and poke-weed.

6

A child said *What is the grass?* fetching it to me with full hands;
How could I answer the child? I do not know what it is any more
   than he.

I guess it must be the flag of my disposition, out of hopeful green
   stuff woven.

Or I guess it is the handkerchief of the Lord,
A scented gift and remembrancer designedly dropt,
Bearing the owner's name someway in the corners, that we may
    see and remark, and say *Whose?*

Or I guess the grass is itself a child, the produced babe of the vegeta-
    tion.

Or I guess it is a uniform hieroglyphic,
And it means, Sprouting alike in broad zones and narrow zones,
Growing among black folks as among white,
Kanuck, Tuckahoe, Congressman, Cuff, I give them the same, I
    receive them the same.

And now it seems to me the beautiful uncut hair of graves.

Tenderly will I use your curling grass,
It may be you transpire from the breasts of young men,
It may be if I had known them I would have loved them,
It may be you are from old people, or from offspring taken soon
    out of their mothers' laps,
And here you are the mothers' laps.

This grass is very dark to be from the white heads of old mothers,
Darker than the colorless beards of old men,
Dark to come from under the faint red roofs of mouths.

O I perceive after all so many uttering tongues,
And I perceive they do not come from the roofs of mouths for
    nothing.

I wish I could translate the hints about the dead young men and
    women,
And the hints about old men and mothers, and the offspring taken
    soon out of their laps.

What do you think has become of the young and old men?
And what do you think has become of the women and children?

They are alive and well somewhere,
The smallest sprout shows there is really no death,
And if ever there was it led forward life, and does not wait at the
    end to arrest it,
And ceas'd the moment life appear'd.

All goes onward and outward, nothing collapses,
And to die is different from what any one supposed, and luckier.

7

Has any one supposed it lucky to be born?
I hasten to inform him or her it is just as lucky to die, and I know it.

I pass death with the dying and birth with the new-wash'd babe,
    and am not contain'd between my hat and boots,
And peruse manifold objects, no two alike and every one good,
The earth good and the stars good, and their adjuncts all good.

I am not an earth nor an adjunct of an earth,
I am the mate and companion of people, all just as immortal and
    fathomless as myself,
(They do not know how immortal, but I know.)

Every kind for itself and its own, for me mine male and female,
For me those that have been boys and that love women,
For me the man that is proud and feels how it stings to be slighted,
For me the sweet-heart and the old maid, for me mothers and the
    mothers of mothers,
For me lips that have smiled, eyes that have shed tears,
For me children and the begetters of children.

Undrape! you are not guilty to me, nor stale nor discarded,
I see through the broadcloth and gingham whether or no,
And am around, tenacious, acquisitive, tireless, and cannot be
    shaken away.

8

The little one sleeps in its cradle,
I lift the gauze and look a long time, and silently brush away flies
    with my hand.

The youngster and the red-faced girl turn aside up the bushy hill,
I peeringly view them from the top.

The suicide sprawls on the bloody floor of the bedroom,
I witness the corpse with its dabbled hair, I note where the pistol
    has fallen.

The blab of the pave, tires of carts, sluff of boot-soles, talk of the
      promenaders,
The heavy omnibus, the driver with his interrogating thumb, the
      clank of the shod horses on the granite floor,
The snow-sleighs, clinking, shouted jokes, pelts of snow-balls,
The hurrahs for popular favorites, the fury of rous'd mobs,
The flap of the curtain'd litter, a sick man inside borne to the
      hospital,
The meeting of enemies, the sudden oath, the blows and fall,
The excited crowd, the policeman with his star quickly working
      his passage to the centre of the crowd,
The impassive stones that receive and return so many echoes,
What groans of over-fed or half-starv'd who fall sunstruck or in fits,
What exclamations of women taken suddenly who hurry home and
      give birth to babes,
What living and buried speech is always vibrating here, what howls
      restrain'd by decorum,
Arrests of criminals, slights, adulterous offers made, acceptances,
      rejections with convex lips,
I mind them or the show or resonance of them—I come and I
      depart.

                                    9

The big doors of the country barn stand open and ready,
The dried grass of the harvest-time loads the slow-drawn wagon,
The clear light plays on the brown gray and green intertinged,
The armfuls are pack'd to the sagging mow.

I am there, I help, I came stretch'd atop of the load,
I felt its soft jolts, one leg reclined on the other,
I jump from the cross-beams and seize the clover and timothy,
And roll head over heels and tangle my hair full of wisps.

                                    10

Alone far in the wilds and mountains I hunt,
Wandering amazed at my own lightness and glee,
In the late afternoon choosing a safe spot to pass the night,
Kindling a fire and broiling the fresh-kill'd game,
Falling asleep on the gather'd leaves with my dog and gun by my
      side.

The Yankee clipper is under her sky-sails, she cuts the sparkle and
      scud,

My eyes settle the land, I bend at her prow or shout joyously from
the deck.

The boatmen and clam-diggers arose early and stopt for me,
I tuck'd my trowser-ends in my boots and went and had a good
time;
You should have been with us that day round the chowder-kettle.

I saw the marriage of the trapper in the open air in the far west,
the bride was a red girl,
Her father and his friends sat near cross-legged and dumbly smoking,
they had moccasins to their feet and large thick blankets hanging from their shoulders,
On a bank lounged the trapper, he was drest mostly in skins, his
luxuriant beard and curls protected his neck, he held his bride
by the hand,
She had long eyelashes, her head was bare, her coarse straight locks
descended upon her voluptuous limbs and reach'd to her feet.

The runaway slave came to my house and stopt outside,
I heard his motions crackling the twigs of the woodpile,
Through the swung half-door of the kitchen I saw him limpsy and
weak,
And went where he sat on a log and led him in and assured him,
And brought water and fill'd a tub for his sweated body and bruis'd
feet,
And gave him a room that enter'd from my own, and gave him
some coarse clean clothes,
And remember perfectly well his revolving eyes and his awkwardness,
And remember putting plasters on the galls of his neck and ankles;
He staid with me a week before he was recuperated and pass'd
north,
I had him sit next me at table, my fire-lock lean'd in the corner.

11

Twenty-eight young men bathe by the shore,
Twenty-eight young men and all so friendly;
Twenty-eight years of womanly life and all so lonesome.

She owns the fine house by the rise of the bank,
She hides handsome and richly drest aft the blinds of the window.

Which of the young men does she like the best?
Ah the homeliest of them is beautiful to her.

Where are you off to, lady? for I see you,
You splash in the water there, yet stay stock still in your room.

Dancing and laughing along the beach came the twenty-ninth bather,
The rest did not see her, but she saw them and loved them.

The beards of the young men glisten'd with wet, it ran from their
    long hair,
Little streams pass'd all over their bodies.

An unseen hand also pass'd over their bodies,
It descended tremblingly from their temples and ribs.

The young men float on their backs, their white bellies bulge to
    the sun, they do not ask who seizes fast to them,
They do not know who puffs and declines with pendant and bend-
    ing arch,
They do not think whom they souse with spray.

                                  12

The butcher-boy puts off his killing-clothes, or sharpens his knife
    at the stall in the market,
I loiter enjoying his repartee and his shuffle and break-down.

Blacksmiths with grimed and hairy chests environ the anvil,
Each has his main-sledge, they are all out, there is a great heat in
    the fire.

From the cinder-strew'd threshold I follow their movements,
The lithe sheer of their waists plays even with their massive arms,
Overhand the hammers swing, overhand so slow, overhand so sure,
They do not hasten, each man hits in his place.

                                  13

The negro holds firmly the reins of his four horses, the block swags
    underneath on its tied-over chain,
The negro that drives the long dray of the stone-yard, steady and
    tall he stands pois'd on one leg on the string-piece,

His blue shirt exposes his ample neck and breast and loosens over
his hip-band,
His glance is calm and commanding, he tosses the slouch of his
hat away from his forehead,
The sun falls on his crispy hair and mustache, falls on the black of
his polish'd and perfect limbs.

I behold the picturesque giant and love him, and I do not stop
there,
I go with the team also.

In me the caresser of life wherever moving, backward as well as
forward sluing,
To niches aside and junior bending, not a person or object missing,
Absorbing all to myself and for this song.

Oxen that rattle the yoke and chain or halt in the leafy shade, what
is that you express in your eyes?
It seems to me more than all the print I have read in my life.

My tread scares the wood-drake and wood-duck on my distant and
day-long ramble,
They rise together, they slowly circle around.

I believe in those wing'd purposes,
And acknowledge red, yellow, white, playing within me,
And consider green and violet and the tufted crown intentional,
And do not call the tortoise unworthy because she is not something
else,
And the jay in the woods never studied the gamut, yet trills pretty
well to me,
And the look of the bay mare shames silliness out, of me.

14

The wild gander leads his flock through the cool night,
Ya-honk he says, and sounds it down to me like an invitation,
The pert may suppose it meaningless, but I listening close,
Find its purpose and place up there toward the wintry sky.

The sharp-hoof'd moose of the north, the cat on the house-sill,
the chickadee, the prairie-dog,
The litter of the grunting sow as they tug at her teats,

The brood of the turkey-hen and she with her half-spread wings,
I see in them and myself the same old law.

The press of my foot to the earth springs a hundred affections,
They scorn the best I can do to relate them.

I am enamour'd of growing out-doors,
Of men that live among cattle or taste of the ocean or woods,
Of the builders and steerers of ships and the wielders of axes and
    mauls, and the drivers of horses,
I can eat and sleep with them week in and week out.

What is commonest, cheapest, nearest, easiest, is Me.
Me going in for my chances, spending for vast returns,
Adorning myself to bestow myself on the first that will take me,
Not asking the sky to come down to my good will,
Scattering it freely forever.

15

The pure contralto sings in the organ loft,
The carpenter dresses his plank, the tongue of his foreplane whistles
    its wild ascending lisp,
The married and unmarried children ride home to their Thanks-
    giving dinner,
The pilot seizes the king-pin, he heaves down with a strong arm,
The mate stands braced in the whale-boat, lance and harpoon are
    ready,
The duck-shooter walks by silent and cautious stretches,
The deacons are ordain'd with cross'd hands at the altar,
The spinning-girl retreats and advances to the hum of the big wheel,
The farmer stops by the bars as he walks on a First-day loafe and
    looks at the oats and rye,
The lunatic is carried at last to the asylum a confirm'd case,
(He will never sleep any more as he did in the cot in his mother's
    bed-room;)
The jour printer with gray head and gaunt jaws works at his case,
He turns his quid of tobacco while his eyes blurr with the manu-
    script;
The malform'd limbs are tied to the surgeon's table,
What is removed drops horribly in a pail;
The quadroon girl is sold at the auction-stand, the drunkard nods
    by the bar-room stove,

The machinist rolls up his sleeves, the policeman travels his beat, the gate-keeper marks who pass,

The young fellow drives the express-wagon, (I love him, though I do not know him;)

The half-breed straps on his light boots to compete in the race,

The western turkey-shooting draws old and young, some lean on their rifles, some sit on logs,

Out from the crowd steps the marksman, takes his position, levels his piece;

The groups of newly-come immigrants cover the wharf or levee,

As the woolly-pates hoe in the sugar-field, the overseer views them from his saddle,

The bugle calls in the ball-room, the gentlemen run for their partners, the dancers bow to each other,

The youth lies awake in the cedar-roof'd garret and harks to the musical rain,

The Wolverine sets traps on the creek that helps fill the Huron,

The squaw wrapt in her yellow-hemm'd cloth is offering moccasins and bead-bags for sale,

The connoisseur peers along the exhibition-gallery with half-shut eyes bent sideways,

As the deck-hands make fast the steamboat the plank is thrown for the shore-going passengers,

The young sister holds out the skein while the elder sister winds it off in a ball, and stops now and then for the knots,

The one-year wife is recovering and happy having a week ago borne her first child,

The clean-hair'd Yankee girl works with her sewing-machine or in the factory or mill,

The paving-man leans on his two-handed rammer, the reporter's lead flies swiftly over the note-book, the sign-painter is lettering with blue and gold,

The canal boy trots on the tow-path, the book-keeper counts at his desk, the shoemaker waxes his thread,

The conductor beats time for the band and all the performers follow him,

The child is baptized, the convert is making his first professions,

The regatta is spread on the bay, the race is begun, (how the white sails sparkle!)

The drover watching his drove sings out to them that would stray,

The pedler sweats with his pack on his back, (the purchaser higgling about the odd cent;)

The bride unrumples her white dress, the minute-hand of the clock
    moves slowly,
The opium-eater reclines with rigid head and just-open'd lips,
The prostitute draggles her shawl, her bonnet bobs on her tipsy
    and pimpled neck,
The crowd laugh at her blackguard oaths, the men jeer and wink
    to each other,
(Miserable! I do not laugh at your oaths nor jeer you;)
The President holding a cabinet council is surrounded by the great
    Secretaries,
On the piazza walk three matrons stately and friendly with twined
    arms,
The crew of the fish-smack pack repeated layers of halibut in the hold,
The Missourian crosses the plains toting his wares and his cattle,
As the fare-collector goes through the train he gives notice by the
    jingling of loose change,
The floor-men are laying the floor, the tinners are tinning the roof,
    the masons are calling for mortar,
In single file each shouldering his hod pass onward the laborers;
Seasons pursuing each other the indescribable crowd is gather'd,
    it is the fourth of Seventh-month, (what salutes of cannon and
    small arms!)
Seasons pursuing each other the plougher ploughs, the mower mows,
    and the winter-grain falls in the ground;
Off on the lakes the pike-fisher watches and waits by the hole in
    the frozen surface,
The stumps stand thick round the clearing, the squatter strikes
    deep with his axe,
Flatboatmen make fast towards dusk near the cotton-wood or
    pecan-trees,
Coon-seekers go through the regions of the Red river or through
    those drain'd by the Tennessee, or through those of the Ar-
    kansas,
Torches shine in the dark that hangs on the Chattahooche or
    Altamahaw,
Patriarchs sit at supper with sons and grandsons and great-grand-
    sons around them,
In walls of adobie, in canvas tents, rest hunters and trappers after
    their day's sport,
The city sleeps and the country sleeps,
The living sleep for their time, the dead sleep for their time,
The old husband sleeps by his wife and the young husband sleeps
    by his wife;

And these tend inward to me, and I tend outward to them,
And such as it is to be of these more or less I am,
And of these one and all I weave the song of myself.

16

I am of old and young, of the foolish as much as the wise,
Regardless of others, ever regardful of others,
Maternal as well as paternal, a child as well as a man,
Stuff'd with the stuff that is coarse and stuff'd with the stuff that
is fine,
One of the Nation of many nations, the smallest the same and the
largest the same,
A Southerner soon as a Northerner, a planter nonchalant and
hospitable down by the Oconee I live,
A Yankee bound my own way ready for trade, my joints the lim-
berest joints on earth and the sternest joints on earth,
A Kentuckian walking the vale of the Elkhorn in my deer-skin
leggings, a Louisianian or Georgian,
A boatman over lakes or bays or along coasts, a Hoosier, Badger,
Buckeye;
At home on Kanadian snow-shoes or up in the bush, or with fisher-
men off Newfoundland,
At home in the fleet of ice-boats, sailing with the rest and tacking,
At home on the hills of Vermont or in the woods of Maine, or the
Texan ranch,
Comrade of Californians, comrade of free North-Westerners, (lov-
ing their big proportions,)
Comrade of raftsmen and coalmen, comrade of all who shake
hands and welcome to drink and meat,
A learner with the simplest, a teacher of the thoughtfullest,
A novice beginning yet experient of myriads of seasons,
Of every hue and caste am I, of every rank and religion,
A farmer, mechanic, artist, gentleman, sailor, quaker,
Prisoner, fancy-man, rowdy, lawyer, physician, priest.

I resist any thing better than my own diversity,
Breathe the air but leave plenty after me,
And am not stuck up, and am in my place.

(The moth and the fish-eggs are in their place,
The bright suns I see and the dark suns I cannot see are in their
place,
The palpable is in its place and the impalpable is in its place.)

17

These are really the thoughts of all men in all ages and lands, they
    are not original with me,
If they are not yours as much as mine they are nothing, or next
    to nothing,
If they are not the riddle and the untying of the riddle they are
    nothing,
If they are not just as close as they are distant they are nothing.

This is the grass that grows wherever the land is and the water is,
This the common air that bathes the globe.

18

With music strong I come, with my cornets and my drums,
I play not marches for accepted victors only, I play marches for
    conquer'd and slain persons.

Have you heard that it was good to gain the day?
I also say it is good to fall, battles are lost in the same spirit in
    which they are won.

I beat and pound for the dead,
I blow through my embouchures my loudest and gayest for them.

Vivas to those who have fail'd!
And to those whose war-vessels sank in the sea!
And to those themselves who sank in the sea!
And to all generals that lost engagements, and all overcome heroes!
And the numberless unknown heroes equal to the greatest heroes
    known!

19

This is the meal equally set, this the meat for natural hunger,
It is for the wicked just the same as the righteous, I make appoint-
    ments with all.
I will not have a single person slighted or left away,
The kept-woman, sponger, thief, are hereby invited,
The heavy-lipp'd slave is invited, the venerealee is invited;
There shall be no difference between them and the rest.

This is the press of a bashful hand, this the float and odor of hair,
This the toucn of my lips to yours, this the murmur of yearning,

This the far-off depth and height reflecting my own face,
This the thoughtful merge of myself, and the outlet again.

Do you guess I have some intricate purpose?
Well I have, for the Fourth-month showers have, and the mica on
 the side of a rock has.

Do you take it I would astonish?
Does the daylight astonish? does the early redstart twittering
 through the woods?
Do I astonish more than they?

This hour I tell things in confidence,
I might not tell everybody, but I will tell you.

20

Who goes there? hankering, gross, mystical, nude;
How is it I extract strength from the beef I eat?

What is a man anyhow? what am I? what are you?

All I mark as my own you shall offset it with your own,
Else it were time lost listening to me.

I do not snivel that snivel the world over,
That months are vacuums and the ground but wallow and filth.

Whimpering and truckling fold with powders for invalids, conformity goes to the fourth-remov'd,
I wear my hat as I please indoors or out.

Why should I pray? why should I venerate and be ceremonious?

Having pried through the strata, analyzed to a hair, counsel'd with
 doctors and calculated close,
I find no sweeter fat than sticks to my own bones.

In all people I see myself, none more and not one a barley-corn
 less,
And the good or bad I say of myself I say of them.

I know I am solid and sound,
To me the converging objects of the universe perpetually flow,
All are written to me, and I must get what the writing means.

I know I am deathless,
I know this orbit of mine cannot be swept by a carpenter's compass,
I know I shall not pass like a child's carlacue cut with a burnt
    stick at night.

I know I am august,
I do not trouble my spirit to vindicate itself or be understood,
I see that the elementary laws never apologize,
(I reckon I behave no prouder than the level I plant my house by,
    after all.)

I exist as I am, that is enough,
If no other in the world be aware I sit content,
And if each and all be aware I sit content.

One world is aware and by far the largest to me, and that is
    myself,
And whether I come to my own to-day or in ten thousand or ten
    million years,
I can cheerfully take it now, or with equal cheerfulness I can wait.

My foothold is tenon'd and mortis'd in granite,
I laugh at what you call dissolution,
And I know the amplitude of time.

21

I am the poet of the Body and I am the poet of the Soul,
The pleasures of heaven are with me and the pains of hell are
    with me,
The first I graft and increase upon myself, the latter I translate
    into a new tongue.

I am the poet of the woman the same as the man,
And I say it is as great to be a woman as to be a man,
And I say there is nothing greater than the mother of men.

I chant the chant of dilation or pride,
We have had ducking and deprecating about enough,
I show that size is only development.

Have you outstript the rest? are you the President?
It is a trifle, they will more than arrive there every one, and still
    pass on.

I am he that walks with the tender and growing night,
I call to the earth and sea half-held by the night.

Press close bare-bosom'd night—press close magnetic nourishing
    night!
Night of south winds—night of the large few stars!
Still nodding night—mad naked summer night.

Smile O voluptuous cool-breath'd earth!
Earth of the slumbering and liquid trees!
Earth of departed sunset—earth of the mountains misty-topt!
Earth of the vitreous pour of the full moon just tinged with blue!
Earth of shine and dark mottling the tide of the river!
Earth of the limpid gray of clouds brighter and clearer for my
    sake!
Far-swooping elbow'd earth—rich apple-blossom'd earth!
Smile, for your lover comes.

Prodigal, you have given me love—therefore I to you give love!
O unspeakable passionate love.

22

You sea! I resign myself to you also—I guess what you mean,
I behold from the beach your crooked inviting fingers,
I believe you refuse to go back without feeling of me,
We must have a turn together, I undress, hurry me out of sight of
    the land,
Cushion me soft, rock me in billowy drowse,
Dash me with amorous wet, I can repay you.

Sea of stretch'd ground-swells,
Sea breathing broad and convulsive breaths,
Sea of the brine of life and of unshovell'd yet always-ready graves,
Howler and scooper of storms, capricious and dainty sea,
I am integral with you, I too am of one phase and of all phases.

Partaker of influx and efflux I, extoller of hate and conciliation,
Extoller of amies and those that sleep in each others' arms.

I am he attesting sympathy,
(Shall I make my list of things in the house and skip the house
    that supports them?)

I am not the poet of goodness only, I do not decline to be the poet of wickedness also.

What blurt is this about virtue and about vice?
Evil propels me and reform of evil propels me, I stand indifferent,
My gait is no fault-finder's or rejecter's gait,
I moisten the roots of all that has grown.

Did you fear some scrofula out of the unflagging pregnancy?
Did you guess the celestial laws are yet to be work'd over and rectified?

I find one side a balance and the antipodal side a balance,
Soft doctrine as steady help as stable doctrine,
Thoughts and deeds of the present our rouse and early start.

This minute that comes to me over the past decillions,
There is no better than it and now.

What behaved well in the past or behaves well to-day is not such a wonder,
The wonder is always and always how there can be a mean man or an infidel.

23

Endless unfolding of words of ages!
And mine a word of the modern, the word En-Masse.

A word of the faith that never balks,
Here or henceforward it is all the same to me, I accept Time absolutely.

It alone is without flaw, it alone rounds and completes all,
That mystic baffling wonder alone completes all.

I accept Reality and dare not question it,
Materialism first and last imbuing.

Hurrah for positive science! long live exact demonstration!
Fetch stonecrop mixt with cedar and branches of lilac,
This is the lexicographer, this the chemist, this made a grammar of the old cartouches,
These mariners put the ship through dangerous unknown seas,

This is the geologist, this works with the scalpel, and this is a mathematician.

Gentlemen, to you the first honors always!
Your facts are useful, and yet they are not my dwelling,
I but enter by them to an area of my dwelling.

Less the reminders of properties told my words,
And more the reminders they of life untold, and of freedom and extrication,
And make short account of neuters and geldings, and favor men and women fully equipt,
And beat the gong of revolt, and stop with fugitives and them that plot and conspire.

24

Walt Whitman, a kosmos, of Manhattan the son,
Turbulent, fleshy, sensual, eating, drinking and breeding,
No sentimentalist, no stander above men and women or apart from them,
No more modest than immodest.

Unscrew the locks from the doors!
Unscrew the doors themselves from their jambs!

Whoever degrades another degrades me,
And whatever is done or said returns at last to me.

Through me the afflatus surging and surging, through me the current and index.

I speak the pass-word primeval, I give the sign of democracy,
By God! I will accept nothing which all cannot have their counterpart of on the same terms.

Through me many long dumb voices,
Voices of the interminable generations of prisoners and slaves,
Voices of the diseas'd and despairing and of thieves and dwarfs,
Voices of cycles of preparation and accretion,
And of the threads that connect the stars, and of wombs and of the father-stuff,
And of the rights of them the others are down upon,
Of the deform'd, trivial, flat, foolish, despised,
Fog in the air, beetles rolling balls of dung.

Through me forbidden voices,
Voices of sexes and lusts, voices veil'd and I remove the veil,
Voices indecent by me clarified and transfigur'd.

I do not press my fingers across my mouth
I keep as delicate around the bowels as around the head and heart,
Copulation is no more rank to me than death is.

I believe in the flesh and the appetites,
Seeing, hearing, feeling, are miracles, and each part and tag of me
    is a miracle.

Divine am I inside and out, and I make holy whatever I touch or
    am touch'd from,
The scent of these arm-pits aroma finer than prayer,
This head more than churches, bibles, and all the creeds.

If I worship one thing more than another it shall be the spread of
    my own body, or any part of it,
Translucent mould of me it shall be you!
Shaded ledges and rests it shall be you!
Firm masculine colter it shall be you!
Whatever goes to the tilth of me it shall be you!
You my rich blood! your milky stream pale strippings of my life!
Breast that presses against other breasts it shall be you!
My brain it shall be your occult convolutions!
Root of wash'd sweet-flag! timorous pond-snipe! nest of guarded
    duplicate eggs! it shall be you!
Mix'd tussled hay of head, beard, brawn, it shall be you!
Trickling sap of maple, fibre of manly wheat, it shall be you!
Sun so generous it shall be you!
Vapors lighting and shading my face it shall be you!
You sweaty brooks and dews it shall be you!
Winds whose soft-tickling genitals rub against me it shall be you!
Broad muscular fields, branches of live oak, loving lounger in my
    winding paths, it shall be you!
Hands I have taken, face I have kiss'd, mortal I have ever
    touch'd it shall be you.

I dote on myself, there is that lot of me and all so luscious,
Each moment and whatever happens thrills me with joy,
I cannot tell how my ankles bend, nor whence the cause of my
    faintest wish,

Nor the cause of the friendship I emit, nor the cause of the friendship I take again.

That I walk up my stoop, I pause to consider if it really be,
A morning-glory at my window satisfies me more than the metaphysics of books.

To behold the day-break!
The little light fades the immense and diaphanous shadows,
The air tastes good to my palate.

Hefts of the moving world at innocent gambols silently rising,
freshly exuding,
Scooting obliquely high and low.

Something I cannot see puts upward libidinous prongs,
Seas of bright juice suffuse heaven.

The earth by the sky staid with, the daily close of their junction,
The heav'd challenge from the east that moment over my head,
The mocking taunt, See then whether you shall be master!

25

Dazzling and tremendous how quick the sun-rise would kill me,
If I could not now and always send sun-rise out of me.

We also ascend dazzling and tremendous as the sun,
We found our own O my soul in the calm and cool of the daybreak.

My voice goes after what my eyes cannot reach,
With the twirl of my tongue I encompass worlds and volumes of
worlds.

Speech is the twin of my vision, it is unequal to measure itself,
It provokes me forever, it says sarcastically,
Walt you contain enough, why don't you let it out then?

Come now I will not be tantalized, you conceive too much of
articulation,
Do you not know O speech how the buds beneath you are folded?
Waiting in gloom, protected by frost,

The dirt receding before my prophetical screams,
I underlying causes to balance them at last,
My knowledge my live parts, it keeping tally with the meaning of
    all things,
Happiness, (which whoever hears me let him or her set out in
    search of this day.)

My final merit I refuse you, I refuse putting from me what I really
    am,
Encompass worlds, but never try to encompass me,
I crowd your sleekest and best by simply looking toward you.

Writing and talk do not prove me,
I carry the plenum of proof and every thing else in my face,
With the hush of my lips I wholly confound the skeptic.

26

Now I will do nothing but listen,
To accrue what I hear into this song, to let sounds contribute
    toward it.

I hear bravuras of birds, bustle of growing wheat, gossip of flames,
    clack of sticks cooking my meals,
I hear the sound I love, the sound of the human voice,
I hear all sounds running together, combined, fused or following,
Sounds of the city and sounds out of the city, sounds of the day
    and night,
Talkative young ones to those that like them, the loud laugh of
    work-people at their meals,
The angry base of disjointed friendship, the faint tones of the sick,
The judge with hands tight to the desk, his pallid lips pronouncing
    a death-sentence,
The heave'e'yo of stevedores unlading ships by the wharves, the
    refrain of the anchor-lifters,
The ring of alarm-bells, the cry of fire, the whirr of swift-streaking
    engines and hose-carts with premonitory tinkles and color'd
    lights,
The steam-whistle, the solid roll of the train of approaching cars,
The slow march play'd at the head of the association marching
    two and two,
(They go to guard some corpse, the flag-tops are draped with
    black muslin.)

I hear the violoncello, ('tis the young man's heart's complaint,)
I hear the key'd cornet, it glides quickly in through my ears,
It shakes mad-sweet pangs through my belly and breast.

I hear the chorus, it is a grand opera,
Ah this indeed is music—this suits me.

A tenor large and fresh as the creation fills me,
The orbic flex of his mouth is pouring and filling me full.

I hear the train'd soprano (what work with hers is this?)
The orchestra whirls me wider than Uranus flies,
It wrenches such ardors from me I did not know I possess'd them,
It sails me, I dab with bare feet, they are lick'd by the indolent
    waves,
I am cut by bitter and angry hail, I lose my breath,
Steep'd amid honey'd morphine, my windpipe throttled in fakes
    of death,
At length let up again to feel the puzzle of puzzles,
And that we call Being.

27

To be in any form, what is that?
(Round and round we go, all of us, and ever come back thither,)
If nothing lay more develop'd the quahaug in its callous shell were
    enough.

Mine is no callous shell,
I have instant conductors all over me whether I pass or stop,
They seize every object and lead it harmlessly through me.

I merely stir, press, feel with my fingers, and am happy,
To touch my person to some one else's is about as much as I can
    stand.

28

Is this then a touch? quivering me to a new identity,
Flames and ether making a rush for my veins,
Treacherous tip of me reaching and crowding to help them,
My flesh and blood playing out lightning to strike what is hardly
    different from myself,
On all sides prurient provokers stiffening my limbs,
Straining the udder of my heart for its withheld drip,

Behaving licentious toward me, taking no denial,
Depriving me of my best as for a purpose,
Unbuttoning my clothes, holding me by the bare waist,
Deluding my confusion with the calm of the sunlight and pasture-
   fields,
Immodestly sliding the fellow-senses away,
They bribed to swap off with touch and go and graze at the edges
   of me,
No consideration, no regard for my draining strength or my anger,
Fetching the rest of the herd around to enjoy them a while,
Then all uniting to stand on a headland and worry me.

The sentries desert every other part of me,
They have left me helpless to a red marauder,
They all come to the headland to witness and assist against me.

I am given up by traitors,
I talk wildly, I have lost my wits, I and nobody else am the greatest
   traitor,
I went myself first to the headland, my own hands carried me
   there.

You villain touch! what are you doing? my breath is tight in its
   throat,
Unclench your floodgates, you are too much for me.

                              29

Blind loving wrestling touch, sheath'd hooded sharp-tooth'd touch!
Did it make you ache so, leaving me?

Parting track'd by arriving, perpetual payment of perpetual loan,
Rich showering rain, and recompense richer afterward.

Sprouts take and accumulate, stand by the curb prolific and vital,
Landscapes projected masculine, full-sized and golden.

                              30

All truths wait in all things,
They neither hasten their own delivery nor resist it,
They do not need the obstetric forceps of the surgeon,
The insignificant is as big to me as any,
(What is less or more than a touch?)

Logic and sermons never convince,
The damp of the night drives deeper into my soul.

(Only what proves itself to every man and woman is so,
Only what nobody denies is so.)

A minute and a drop of me settle my brain,
I believe the soggy clods shall become lovers and lamps,
And a compend of compends is the meat of a man or woman,
And a summit and flower there is the feeling they have for each
other,
And they are to branch boundlessly out of that lesson until it
becomes omnific,
And until one and all shall delight us, and we them.

31

I believe a leaf of grass is no less than the journey-work of the stars,
And the pismire is equally perfect, and a grain of sand, and the
egg of the wren,
And the tree-toad is a chef-d'œuvre for the highest,
And the running blackberry would adorn the parlors of heaven,
And the narrowest hinge in my hand puts to scorn all machinery,
And the cow crunching with depress'd head surpasses any statue,
And a mouse is miracle enough to stagger sextillions of infidels.

I find I incorporate gneiss, coal, long-threaded moss, fruits, grains,
esculent roots,
And am stucco'd with quadrupeds and birds all over,
And have distanced what is behind me for good reasons,
But call any thing back again when I desire it.

In vain the speeding or shyness,
In vain the plutonic rocks send their old heat against my approach,
In vain the mastodon retreats beneath its own powder'd bones,
In vain objects stand leagues off and assume manifold shapes,
In vain the ocean settling in hollows and the great monsters lying
low,
In vain the buzzard houses herself with the sky,
In vain the snake slides through the creepers and logs,
In vain the elk takes to the inner passes of the woods,
In vain the razor-bill'd auk sails far north to Labrador,
I follow quickly, I ascend to the nest in the fissure of the cliff.

32

I think I could turn, and live with animals, they are so placid and
    self-contain'd,
I stand and look at them long and long.

They do not sweat and whine about their condition,
They do not lie awake in the dark and weep for their sins,
They do not make me sick discussing their duty to God,
Not one is dissatisfied, not one is demented with the mania of
    owning things,
Not one kneels to another, nor to his kind that lived thousands of
    years ago,
Not one is respectable or unhappy over the whole earth.

So they show their relations to me and I accept them,
They bring me tokens of myself, they evince them plainly in their
    possession.

I wonder where they get those tokens,
Did I pass that way huge times ago and negligently drop them?
Myself moving forward then and now and forever,
Gathering and showing more always and with velocity,
Infinite and omnigenous, and the like of these among them,
Not too exclusive toward the reachers of my remembrancers,
Picking out here one that I love, and now go with him on brotherly
    terms.

A gigantic beauty of a stallion, fresh and responsive to my caresses,
Head high in the forehead, wide between the ears,
Limbs glossy and supple, tail dusting the ground,
Eyes full of sparkling wickedness, ears finely cut, flexibly moving.

His nostrils dilate as my heels embrace him,
His well-built limbs tremble with pleasure as we race around and
    return.

I but use you a minute, then I resign you, stallion,
Why do I need your paces when I myself out-gallop them?
Even as I stand or sit passing faster than you.

33

Space and Time! now I see it is true, what I guessed at,
What I guess'd when I loaf'd on the grass,

What I guess'd while I lay alone in my bed,
And again as I walk'd the beach under the paling stars of the
morning.

My ties and ballasts leave me, my elbows rest in sea-gaps,
I skirt sierras, my palms cover continents,
I am afoot with my vision.

By the city's quadrangular houses—in log huts, camping with
lumbermen,
Along the ruts of the turnpike, along the dry gulch and rivulet bed,
Weeding my onion-patch or hoeing rows of carrots and parsnips,
crossing savannas, trailing in forests,
Prospecting, gold-digging, girdling the trees of a new purchase,
Scorch'd ankle-deep by the hot sand, hauling my boat down the
shallow river,
Where the panther walks to and fro on a limb overhead, where
the buck turns furiously at the hunter,
Where the rattlesnake suns his flabby length on a rock, where the
otter is feeding on fish,
Where the alligator in his tough pimples sleeps by the bayou,
Where the black bear is searching for roots or honey, where the
beaver pats the mud with his paddle-shaped tail;
Over the growing sugar, over the yellow-flower'd cotton plant, over
the rice in its low moist field,
Over the sharp-peak'd farm house, with its scallop'd scum and
slender shoots from the gutters,
Over the western persimmon, over the long-leav'd corn, over the
delicate blue-flower flax,
Over the white and brown buckwheat, a hummer and buzzer there
with the rest,
Over the dusky green of the rye as it ripples and shades in the
breeze;
Scaling mountains, pulling myself cautiously up, holding on by low
scragged limbs,
Walking the path worn in the grass and beat through the leaves of
the brush,
Where the quail is whistling betwixt the woods and the wheat-lot,
Where the bat flies in the Seventh-month eve, where the great gold-
bug drops through the dark,
Where the brook puts out of the roots of the old tree and flows to
the meadow,

Where cattle stand and shake away flies with the tremulous shud-
     dering of their hides,
Where the cheese-cloth hangs in the kitchen, where andirons
     straddle the hearth-slab, where cobwebs fall in festoons from
     the rafters;
Where trip-hammers crash, where the press is whirling its cylinders,
Wherever the human heart beats with terrible throes under its ribs,
Where the pear-shaped balloon is floating aloft, (floating in it my-
     self and looking composedly down,)
Where the life-car is drawn on the slip-noose, where the heat
     hatches pale-green eggs in the dented sand,
Where the she-whale swims with her calf and never forsakes it,
Where the steam-ship trails hind-ways its long pennant of smoke,
Where the fin of the shark cuts like a black chip out of the water,
Where the half-burn'd brig is riding on unknown currents,
Where shells grow to her slimy deck, where the dead are corrupting
     below;
Where the dense-starr'd flag is borne at the head of the regiments,
Approaching Manhattan up by the long-stretching island,
Under Niagara, the cataract falling like a veil over my countenance,
Upon a door-step, upon the horse-block of hard wood outside,
Upon the race-course, or enjoying picnics or jigs or a good game of
     base-ball,
At he-festivals, with blackguard gibes, ironical license, bull-dances,
     drinking, laughter,
At the cider-mill tasting the sweets of the brown mash, sucking the
     juice through a straw,
At apple-peelings wanting kisses for all the red fruit I find,
At musters, beach-parties, friendly bees, huskings, house-raisings;
Where the mocking-bird sounds his delicious gurgles, cackles,
     screams, weeps,
Where the hay-rick stands in the barn-yard, where the dry-stalks
     are scatter'd, where the brood-cow waits in the hovel,
Where the bull advances to do his masculine work, where the stud
     to the mare, where the cock is treading the hen,
Where the heifers browse, where geese nip their food with short
     jerks,
Where sun-down shadows lengthen over the limitless and lonesome
     prairie,
Where herds of buffalo make a crawling spread of the square miles
     far and near,
Where the humming-bird shimmers, where the neck of the long-
     lived swan is curving and winding,

Where the laughing-gull scoots by the shore, where she laughs her
near-human laugh,

Where bee-hives range on a gray bench in the garden half hid by
the high weeds,

Where band-neck'd partridges roost in a ring on the ground with
their heads out,

Where burial coaches enter the arch'd gates of a cemetery,

Where winter wolves bark amid wastes of snow and icicled trees,

Where the yellow-crown'd heron comes to the edge of the marsh
at night and feeds upon small crabs,

Where the splash of swimmers and divers cools the warm noon,

Where the katy-did works her chromatic reed on the walnut-tree
over the well,

Through patches of citrons and cucumbers with silver-wired leaves,

Through the salt-lick or orange glade, or under conical firs,

Through the gymnasium, through the curtain'd saloon, through the
office or public hall;

Pleas'd with the native and pleas'd with the foreign, pleas'd with
the new and old,

Pleas'd with the homely woman as well as the handsome,

Pleas'd with the quakeress as she puts off her bonnet and talks
melodiously,

Pleas'd with the tune of the choir of the whitewash'd church,

Pleas'd with the earnest words of the sweating Methodist preacher,
impress'd seriously at the camp-meeting;

Looking in at the shop-windows of Broadway the whole forenoon,
flatting the flesh of my nose on the thick plate-glass,

Wandering the same afternoon with my face turn'd up to the
clouds, or down a lane or along the beach,

My right and left arms round the sides of two friends, and I in the
middle;

Coming home with the silent and dark-cheek'd bush-boy, (behind
me he rides at the drape of the day,)

Far from the settlements studying the print of animals' feet, or
the moccasin print,

By the cot in the hospital reaching lemonade to a feverish patient,

Nigh the coffin'd corpse when all is still, examining with a candle;

Voyaging to every port to dicker and adventure,

Hurrying with the modern crowd as eager and fickle as any,

Hot toward one I hate, ready in my madness to knife him,

Solitary at midnight in my back yard, my thoughts gone from me
a long while,

Walking the old hills of Judæa with the beautiful gentle God by
    my side,
Speeding through space, speeding through heaven and the stars,
Speeding amid the seven satellites and the broad ring, and the
    diameter of eighty thousand miles,
Speeding with tail'd meteors, throwing fire-balls like the rest,
Carrying the crescent child that carries its own full mother in its
    belly,
Storming, enjoying, planning, loving, cautioning,
Backing and filling, appearing and disappearing,
I tread day and night such roads.

I visit the orchards of spheres and look at the product,
And look at quintillions ripen'd and look at quintillions green.

I fly those flights of a fluid and swallowing soul,
My course runs below the soundings of plummets.

I help myself to material and immaterial,
No guard can shut me off, no law prevent me.

I anchor my ship for a little while only,
My messengers continually cruise away or bring their returns to me.

I go hunting polar furs and the seal, leaping chasms with a pike-
    pointed staff, clinging to topples of brittle and blue.

I ascend to the foretruck,
I take my place late at night in the crow's-nest,
We sail the arctic sea, it is plenty light enough,
Through the clear atmosphere I stretch around on the wonderful
    beauty,
The enormous masses of ice pass me and I pass them, the scenery
    is plain in all directions,
The white-topt mountains show in the distance, I fling out my
    fancies toward them,
We are approaching some great battle-field in which we are soon
    to be engaged,
We pass the colossal outposts of the encampment, we pass with still
    feet and caution,
Or we are entering by the suburbs some vast and ruin'd city,
The blocks and fallen architecture more than all the living cities
    of the globe.

I am a free companion, I bivouac by invading watchfires,
I turn the bridegroom out of bed and stay with the bride myself,
    I tighten her all night to my thighs and lips.

My voice is the wife's voice, the screech by the rail of the stairs,
They fetch my man's body up dripping and drown'd.

I understand the large hearts of heroes,
The courage of present times and all times,
How the skipper saw the crowded and rudderless wreck of the
    steam-ship, and Death chasing it up and down the storm,
How he knuckled tight and gave not back an inch, and was faith-
    ful of days and faithful of nights,
And chalk'd in large letters on a board, *Be of good cheer, we will
    not desert you;*
How he follow'd with them and tack'd with them three days and
    would not give it up,
How he saved the drifting company at last,
How the lank loose-gown'd women look'd when boated from the
    side of their prepared graves,
How the silent old-faced infants and the lifted sick, and the sharp-
    lipp'd unshaved men;
All this I swallow, it tastes good, I like it well, it becomes mine,
I am the man, I suffer'd, I was there.

The disdain and calmness of martyrs,
The mother of old, condemn'd for a witch, burnt with dry wood,
    her children gazing on,
The hounded slave that flags in the race, leans by the fence, blow-
    ing, cover'd with sweat,
The twinges that sting like needles his legs and neck, the mur-
    derous buckshot and the bullets,
All these I feel or am.

I am the hounded slave, I wince at the bite of the dogs,
Hell and despair are upon me, crack and again crack the marksmen,
I clutch the rails of the fence, my gore dribs, thinn'd with the ooze
    of my skin,
I fall on the weeds and stones,
The riders spur their unwilling horses, haul close,
Taunt my dizzy ears and beat me violently over the head with
    whip-stocks.

Agonies are one of my changes of garments,
I do not ask the wounded person how he feels, I myself become
the wounded person,
My hurts turn livid upon me as I lean on a cane and observe.

I am the mash'd fireman with breast-bone broken,
Tumbling walls buried me in their debris,
Heat and smoke I inspired, I heard the yelling shouts of my com-
rades,
I heard the distant click of their picks and shovels,
They have clear'd the beams away, they tenderly lift me forth.

I lie in the night air in my red shirt, the pervading hush is for my
sake,
Painless after all I lie exhausted but not so unhappy,
White and beautiful are the faces around me, the heads are bared
of their fire-caps,
The kneeling crowd fades with the light of the torches.

Distant and dead resuscitate,
They show as the dial or move as the hands of me, I am the clock
myself.

I am an old artillerist, I tell of my fort's bombardment,
I am there again.

Again the long roll of the drummers,
Again the attacking cannon, mortars,
Again to my listening ears the cannon responsive.

I take part, I see and hear the whole,
The cries, curses, roar, the plaudits for well-aim'd shots,
The ambulanza slowly passing trailing its red drip,
Workmen searching after damages, making indispensable repairs,
The fall of grenades through the rent roof, the fan-shaped explo-
sion,
The whizz of limbs, heads, stone, wood, iron, high in the air.

Again gurgles the mouth of my dying general, he furiously waves
with his hand,
He gasps through the clot *Mind not me—mind—the entrenchments.*

34

Now I tell what I knew in Texas in my early youth,
(I tell not the fall of Alamo,
Not one escaped to tell the fall of Alamo,
The hundred and fifty are dumb yet at Alamo,)
'Tis the tale of the murder in cold blood of four hundred and
    twelve young men.

Retreating they had form'd in a hollow square with their baggage
    for breastworks,
Nine hundred lives out of the surrounding enemy's, nine times
    their number, was the price they took in advance,
Their colonel was wounded and their ammunition gone,
They treated for an honorable capitulation, receiv'd writing and
    seal, gave up their arms and march'd back prisoners of war.

They were the glory of the race of rangers,
Matchless with horse, rifle, song, supper, courtship,
Large, turbulent, generous, handsome, proud, and affectionate,
Bearded, sunburnt, drest in the free costume of hunters,
Not a single one over thirty years of age.

The second First-day morning they were brought out in squads
    and massacred, it was beautiful early summer,
The work commenced about five o'clock and was over by eight.

None obey'd the command to kneel,
Some made a mad and helpless rush, some stood stark and straight,
A few fell at once, shot in the temple or heart, the living and dead
    lay together,
The maim'd and mangled dug in the dirt, the new-comers saw
    them there,
Some half-kill'd attempted to crawl away,
These were dispatch'd with bayonets or batter'd with the blunts
    of muskets,
A youth not seventeen years old seiz'd his assassin till two more
    came to release him,
The three were all torn and cover'd with the boy's blood.

At eleven o'clock began the burning of the bodies;
That is the tale of the murder of the four hundred and twelve
    young men.

35

Would you hear of an old-time sea-fight?
Would you learn who won by the light of the moon and stars?
List to the yarn, as my grandmother's father the sailor told it to me.

Our foe was no skulk in his ship I tell you, (said he,)
His was the surly English pluck, and there is no tougher or truer,
    and never was, and never will be;
Along the lower'd eve he came horribly raking us.

We closed with him, the yards entangled, the cannon touch'd,
My captain lash'd fast with his own hands.

We had receiv'd some eighteen pound shots under the water,
On our lower-gun-deck two large pieces had burst at the first fire,
    killing all around and blowing up overhead.

Fighting at sun-down, fighting at dark,
Ten o'clock at night, the full moon well up, our leaks on the gain,
    and five feet of water reported,
The master-at-arms loosing the prisoners confined in the after-hold
    to give them a chance for themselves.

The transit to and from the magazine is now stopt by the sentinels,
They see so many strange faces they do not know whom to trust.

Our frigate takes fire,
The other asks if we demand quarter?
If our colors are struck and the fighting done?

Now I laugh content, for I hear the voice of my little captain,
We have not struck, he composedly cries, *we have just begun our
    part of the fighting.*

Only three guns are in use,
One is directed by the captain himself against the enemy's main-
    mast,
Two well serv'd with grape and canister silence his musketry and
    clear his decks.

The tops alone second the fire of this little battery, especially the
    main-top,
They hold out bravely during the whole of the action.

Not a moment's cease,
The leaks gain fast on the pumps, the fire eats toward the powder-
    magazine.

One of the pumps has been shot away, it is generally thought we
    are sinking.

Serene stands the little captain,
He is not hurried, his voice is neither high nor low,
His eyes give more light to us than our battle-lanterns.

Toward twelve there in the beams of the moon they surrender to us.

                                    36

Stretch'd and still lies the midnight,
Two great hulls motionless on the breast of the darkness,
Our vessel riddled and slowly sinking, preparations to pass to the
    one we have conquer'd,
The captain on the quarter-deck coldly giving his orders through
    a countenance white as a sheet,
Near by the corpse of the child that serv'd in the cabin,
The dead face of an old salt with long white hair and carefully
    curl'd whiskers,
The flames spite of all that can be done flickering aloft and below,
The husky voices of the two or three officers yet fit for duty,
Formless stacks of bodies and bodies by themselves, dabs of flesh
    upon the masts and spars,
Cut of cordage, dangle of rigging, slight shock of the soothe of
    waves,
Black and impassive guns, litter of powder-parcels, strong scent,
A few large stars overhead, silent and mournful shining,
Delicate sniffs of sea-breeze, smells of sedgy grass and fields by the
    shore, death-messages given in charge to survivors,
The hiss of the surgeon's knife, the gnawing teeth of his saw
Wheeze, cluck, swash of falling blood, short wild scream, and long,
    dull, tapering groan,
These so, these irretrievable.

                                    37

You laggards there on guard! look to your arms!
In at the conquer'd doors they crowd! I am possess'd!

Embody all presences outlaw'd or suffering,
See myself in prison shaped like another man,
And feel the dull unintermitted pain.

For me the keepers of convicts shoulder their carbines and keep
    watch,
It is I let out in the morning and barr'd at night.

Not a mutineer walks handcuff'd to jail but I am handcuff'd to
    him and walk by his side,
(I am less the jolly one there, and more the silent one with sweat
    on my twitching lips.)

Not a youngster is taken for larceny but I go up too, and am tried
    and sentenced.

Not a cholera patient lies at the last gasp but I also lie at the last
    gasp,
My face is ash-color'd, my sinews gnarl, away from me people
    retreat.

Askers embody themselves in me and I am embodied in them,
I project my hat, sit shame-faced, and beg.

38

Enough! enough! enough!
Somehow I have been stunn'd. Stand back!
Give me a little time beyond my cuff'd head, slumbers, dreams,
    gaping,
I discover myself on the verge of a usual mistake.

That I could forget the mockers and insults!
That I could forget the trickling tears and the blows of the bludg-
    eons and hammers!
That I could look with a separate look on my own crucifixion and
    bloody crowning.

I remember now,
I resume the overstaid fraction,
The grave of rock multiplies what has been confided to it, or to
    any graves,
Corpses rise, gashes heal, fastenings roll from me.

I troop forth replenish'd with supreme power, one of an average
    unending procession,
Inland and sea-coast we go, and pass all boundary lines,
Our swift ordinances on their way over the whole earth,
The blossoms we wear in our hats the growth of thousands of
    years.

Eleves, I salute you! come forward!
Continue your annotations, continue your questionings.

39

The friendly and flowing savage, who is he?
Is he waiting for civilization, or past it and mastering it?

Is he some Southwesterner rais'd out-doors? is he Kanadian?
Is he from the Mississippi country? Iowa, Oregon, California?
The mountains? prairie-life, bush-life? or sailor from the sea?

Wherever he goes men and women accept and desire him,
They desire he should like them, touch them, speak to them, stay
    with them.

Behavior lawless as snow-flakes, words simple as grass, uncomb'd
    head, laughter, and naiveté,
Slow-stepping feet, common features, common modes and ema-
    nations,
They descend in new forms from the tips of his fingers,
They are wafted with the odor of his body or breath, they fly out
    of the glance of his eyes.

40

Flaunt of the sunshine I need not your bask—lie over!
You light surfaces only, I force surfaces and depths also.

Earth! you seem to look for something at my hands,
Say, old top-knot, what do you want?

Man or woman, I might tell how I like you, but cannot,
And might tell what it is in me and what it is in you, but cannot,
And might tell that pining I have, that pulse of my nights and days.

Behold, I do not give lectures or a little charity,
When I give I give myself.

You there, impotent, loose in the knees,
Open your scarf'd chops till I blow grit within you,
Spread your palms and lift the flaps of your pockets,
I am not to be denied, I compel, I have stores plenty and to spare,
And any thing I have I bestow.

I do not ask who you are, that is not important to me,
You can do nothing and be nothing but what I will infold you.

To cotton-field drudge or cleaner of privies I lean,
On his right cheek I put the family kiss,
And in my soul I swear I never will deny him.

On women fit for conception I start bigger and nimbler babes,
(This day I am jetting the stuff of far more arrogant republics.)

To any one dying, thither I speed and twist the knob of the door,
Turn the bed-clothes toward the foot of the bed,
Let the physician and the priest go home.

I seize the descending man and raise him with resistless will,
O despairer, here is my neck,
By God, you shall not go down! hang your whole weight upon me.

I dilate you with tremendous breath, I buoy you up,
Every room of the house do I fill with an arm'd force,
Lovers of me, bafflers of graves.

Sleep—I and they keep guard all night,
Not doubt, not decease shall dare to lay finger upon you,
I have embraced you, and henceforth possess you to myself,
And when you rise in the morning you will find what I tell you is so.

41

I am he bringing help for the sick as they pant on their backs,
And for strong upright men I bring yet more needed help.

I heard what was said of the universe,
Heard it and heard it of several thousand years;
It is middling well as far as it goes—but is that all?

Magnifying and applying come I,

Outbidding at the start the old cautious hucksters,

Taking myself the exact dimensions of Jehovah,

Lithographing Kronos, Zeus his son, and Hercules his grandson,

Buying drafts of Osiris, Isis, Belus, Brahma, Buddha,

In my portfolio placing Manito loose, Allah on a leaf, the crucifix
engraved,

With Odin and the hideous-faced Mexitli and every idol and image,

Taking them all for what they are worth and not a cent more,

Admitting they were alive and did the work of their days,

(They bore mites as for unfledg'd birds who have now to rise and
fly and sing for themselves,)

Accepting the rough deific sketches to fill out better in myself,
bestowing them freely on each man and woman I see,

Discovering as much or more in a framer framing a house,

Putting higher claims for him there with his roll'd-up sleeves driving
the mallet and chisel,

Not objecting to special revelations, considering a curl of smoke
or a hair on the back of my hand just as curious as any revelation,

Lads ahold of fire-engines and hook-and-ladder ropes no less to
me than the gods of the antique wars,

Minding their voices peal through the crash of destruction,

Their brawny limbs passing safe over charr'd laths, their white
foreheads whole and unhurt out of the flames;

By the mechanic's wife with her babe at her nipple interceding for
every person born,

Three scythes at harvest whizzing in a row from three lusty angels
with shirts bagg'd out at their waists,

The snag-tooth'd hostler with red hair redeeming sins past and to
come,

Selling all he possesses, traveling on foot to fee lawyers for his
brother and sit by him while he is tried for forgery;

What was strewn in the amplest strewing the square rod about
me, and not filling the square rod then,

The bull and the bug never worshipp'd half enough,

Dung and dirt more admirable than was dream'd,

The supernatural of no account, myself waiting my time to be one
of the supremes,

The day getting ready for me when I shall do as much good as
the best, and be as prodigious;

By my life-lumps! becoming already a creator,

Putting myself here and now to the ambush'd womb of the shadows.

42

A call in the midst of the crowd,
My own voice, orotund sweeping and final.

Come my children,
Come my boys and girls, my women, household and intimates,
Now the performer launches his nerve, he has pass'd his prelude
    on the reeds within.

Easily written loose-finger'd chords—I feel the thrum of your
    climax and close.

My head slues round on my neck,
Music rolls, but not from the organ,
Folks are around me, but they are no household of mine.

Ever the hard unsunk ground,
Ever the eaters and drinkers, ever the upward and downward sun,
    ever the air and the ceaseless tides,
Ever myself and my neighbors, refreshing, wicked, real,
Ever the old inexplicable query, ever that thorn'd thumb, that
    breath of itches and thirsts,
Ever the vexer's *hoot! hoot!* till we find where the sly one hides
    and bring him forth,
Ever love, ever the sobbing liquid of life,
Ever the bandage under the chin, ever the trestles of death.

Here and there with dimes on the eyes walking,
To feed the greed of the belly the brains liberally spooning,
Tickets buying, taking, selling, but in to the feast never once going,
Many sweating, ploughing, thrashing, and then the chaff for pay-
    ment receiving,
A few idly owning, and they the wheat continually claiming.

This is the city and I am one of the citizens,
Whatever interests the rest interests me, politics, wars, markets,
    newspapers, schools,
The mayor and councils, banks, tariffs, steamships, factories, stocks,
    stores, real estate and personal estate.

The little plentiful manikins skipping around in collars and tail'd
    coats,

I am aware who they are, (they are positively not worms or fleas,)
I acknowledge the duplicates of myself, the weakest and shallowest
　　is deathless with me,
What I do and say the same waits for them,
Every thought that flounders in me the same flounders in them.

I know perfectly well my own egotism,
Know my omnivorous lines and must not write any less,
And would fetch you whoever you are flush with myself.

Not words of routine this song of mine,
But abruptly to question, to leap beyond yet nearer bring;
This printed and bound book—but the printer and the printing-
　　office boy?
The well-taken photographs—but your wife or friend close and
　　solid in your arms?
The black ship mail'd with iron, her mighty guns in her turrets—
　　but the pluck of the captain and engineers?
In the houses the dishes and fare and furniture—but the host and
　　hostess, and the look out of their eyes?
The sky up there—yet here or next door, or across the way?
The saints and sages in history—but you yourself?
Sermons, creeds, theology—but the fathomless human brain,
And what is reason? and what is love? and what is life?

43

I do not despise you priests, all time, the world over,
My faith is the greatest of faiths and the least of faiths,
Enclosing worship ancient and modern and all between ancient
　　and modern,
Believing I shall come again upon the earth after five thousand
　　years,
Waiting responses from oracles, honoring the gods, saluting the
　　sun,
Making a fetich of the first rock or stump, powowing with sticks in
　　the circle of obis,
Helping the lama or brahmin as he trims the lamps of the idols,
Dancing yet through the streets in a phallic procession, rapt and
　　austere in the woods a gymnosophist,
Drinking mead from the skull-cup, to Shastas and Vedas admirant,
　　minding the Koran,
Walking the teokallis, spotted with gore from the stone and knife,
　　beating the serpent-skin drum,

Accepting the Gospels, accepting him that was crucified, knowing
assuredly that he is divine
To the mass kneeling or the puritan's prayer rising, or sitting
patiently in a pew,
Ranting and frothing in my insane crisis, or waiting dead-like till
my spirit arouses me,
Looking forth on pavement and land, or outside of pavement and
land,
Belonging to the winders of the circuit of circuits.

One of that centripetal and centrifugal gang I turn and talk like a
man leaving charges before a journey.

Down-hearted doubters dull and excluded,
Frivolous, sullen, moping, angry, affected, dishearten'd, atheistical,
I know every one of you, I know the sea of torment, doubt, despair
and unbelief.

How the flukes splash!
How they contort rapid as lightning, with spasms and spouts of
blood!

Be at peace bloody flukes of doubters and sullen mopers,
I take my place among you as much as among any,
The past is the push of you, me, all, precisely the same,
And what is yet untried and afterward is for you, me, all, precisely
the same.

I do not know what is untried and afterward,
But I know it will in its turn prove sufficient, and cannot fail.

Each who passes is consider'd, each who stops is consider'd, not
a single one can it fail.

It cannot fail the young man who died and was buried,
Nor the young woman who died and was put by his side,
Nor the little child that peep'd in at the door, and then drew back
and was never seen again,
Nor the old man who has lived without purpose, and feels it with
bitterness worse than gall,
Nor him in the poor house tubercled by rum and the bad disorder,
Nor the numberless slaughter'd and wreck'd, nor the brutish koboo
call'd the ordure of humanity,

Nor the sacs merely floating with open mouths for food to slip in,
Nor any thing in the earth, or down in the oldest graves of the earth,
Nor any thing in the myriads of spheres, nor the myriads of myriads that inhabit them,
Nor the present, nor the least wisp that is known.

44

It is time to explain myself—let us stand up.

What is known I strip away,
I launch all men and women forward with me into the Unknown.

The clock indicates the moment—but what does eternity indicate?

We have thus far exhausted trillions of winters and summers,
There are trillions ahead, and trillions ahead of them.

Births have brought us richness and variety,
And other births will bring us richness and variety.

I do not call one greater and one smaller,
That which fills its period and place is equal to any.

Were mankind murderous or jealous upon you, my brother, my sister?
I am sorry for you, they are not murderous or jealous upon me,
All has been gentle with me, I keep no account with lamentation,
(What have I to do with lamentation?)

I am an acme of things accomplish'd, and I an encloser of things to be.

My feet strike an apex of the apices of the stairs,
On every step bunches of ages, and larger bunches between the steps,
All below duly travel'd, and still I mount and mount.

Rise after rise bow the phantoms behind me,
Afar down I see the huge first Nothing, I know I was even there,
I waited unseen and always, and slept through the lethargic mist,
And took my time, and took no hurt from the fetid carbon.

Long I was hugg'd close—long and long.

Immense have been the preparations for me,
Faithful and friendly the arms that have help'd me.

Cycles ferried my cradle, rowing and rowing like cheerful boatmen,
For room to me stars kept aside in their own rings,
They sent influences to look after what was to hold me.

Before I was born out of my mother generations guided me,
My embryo has never been torpid, nothing could overlay it.

For it the nebula cohered to an orb,
The long slow strata piled to rest it on,
Vast vegetables gave it sustenance,
Monstrous sauroids transported it in their mouths and deposited
    it with care.

All forces have been steadily employ'd to complete and delight me,
Now on this spot I stand with my robust soul.

45

O span of youth! ever-push'd elasticity!
O manhood, balanced, florid and full.

My lovers suffocate me,
Crowding my lips, thick in the pores of my skin,
Jostling me through streets and public halls, coming naked to me
    at night,
Crying by day *Ahoy!* from the rocks of the river, swinging and
    chirping over my head,
Calling my name from flower-beds, vines, tangled underbrush,
Lighting on every moment of my life,
Bussing my body with soft balsamic busses,
Noiselessly passing handfuls out of their hearts and giving them
    to be mine.

Old age superbly rising! O welcome, ineffable grace of dying days!

Every condition promulges not only itself, it promulges what grows
    after and out of itself,
And the dark hush promulges as much as any.

I open my scuttle at night and see the far-sprinkled systems,
And all I see multiplied as high as I can cipher edge but the rim
    of the farther systems.

Wider and wider they spread, expanding, always expanding,
Outward and outward and forever outward.

My sun has his sun and round him obediently wheels,
He joins with his partners a group of superior circuit,
And greater sets follow, making specks of the greatest inside them.

There is no stoppage and never can be stoppage,
If I, you, and the worlds, and all beneath or upon their surfaces,
    were this moment reduced back to a pallid float, it would not
    avail in the long run,
We should surely bring up again where we now stand,
And surely go as much farther, and then farther and farther.

A few quadrillions of eras, a few octillions of cubic leagues, do not
    hazard the span or make it impatient,
They are but parts, any thing is but a part.

See ever so far, there is limitless space outside of that,
Count ever so much, there is limitless time around that.

My rendezvous is appointed, it is certain,
The Lord will be there and wait till I come on perfect terms,
The great Camerado, the lover true for whom I pine will be there.

46

I know I have the best of time and space, and was never measured
    and never will be measured.

I tramp a perpetual journey, (come listen all!)
My signs are a rain-proof coat, good shoes, and a staff cut from
    the woods,
No friend of mine takes his ease in my chair,
I have no chair, no church, no philosophy,
I lead no man to a dinner-table, library, exchange,
But each man and each woman of you I lead upon a knoll,
My left hand hooking you round the waist,
My right hand pointing to landscapes of continents and the public
    road.

Not I, not any one else can travel that road for you,
You must travel it for yourself.

It is not far, it is within reach,
Perhaps you have been on it since you were born and did not
    know,
Perhaps it is everywhere on water and on land.

Shoulder your duds dear son, and I will mine, and let us hasten
    forth,
Wonderful cities and free nations we shall fetch as we go.

If you tire, give me both burdens, and rest the chuff of your hand
    on my hip,
And in due time you shall repay the same service to me,
For after we start we never lie by again.

This day before dawn I ascended a hill and look'd at the crowded
    heaven,
And I said to my spirit *When we become the enfolders of those
    orbs, and the pleasure and knowledge of every thing in them,
    shall we be fill'd and satisfied then?*
And my spirit said *No, we but level that lift to pass and continue
    beyond.*

You are also asking me questions and I hear you,
I answer that I cannot answer, you must find out for yourself.

Sit a while dear son,
Here are biscuits to eat and here is milk to drink,
But as soon as you sleep and renew yourself in sweet clothes, I
    kiss you with a good-by kiss and open the gate for your egress
    hence.

Long enough have you dream'd contemptible dreams,
Now I wash the gum from your eyes,
You must habit yourself to the dazzle of the light and of every
    moment of your life.

Long have you timidly waded holding a plank by the shore,
Now I will you to be a bold swimmer,
To jump off in the midst of the sea, rise again, nod to me, shout,
    and laughingly dash with your hair.

47

I am the teacher of athletes,
He that by me spreads a wider breast than my own proves the width of my own,
He most honors my style who learns under it to destroy the teacher.

The boy I love, the same becomes a man not through derived power, but in his own right,
Wicked rather than virtuous out of conformity or fear,
Fond of his sweetheart, relishing well his steak,
Unrequited love or a slight cutting him worse than sharp steel cuts,
First-rate to ride, to fight, to hit the bull's eye, to sail a skiff, to sing a song or play on the banjo,
Preferring scars and the beard and faces pitted with small-pox over all latherers,
And those well-tann'd to those that keep out of the sun.

I teach straying from me, yet who can stray from me?
I follow you whoever you are from the present hour,
My words itch at your ears till you understand them.

I do not say these things for a dollar or to fill up the time while I wait for a boat,
(It is you talking just as much as myself, I act as the tongue of you,
Tied in your mouth, in mine it begins to be loosen'd.)

I swear I will never again mention love or death inside a house,
And I swear I will never translate myself at all, only to him or her who privately stays with me in the open air.

If you would understand me go to the heights or water-shore,
The nearest gnat is an explanation, and a drop or motion of waves a key,
The maul, the oar, the hand-saw, second my words.

No shutter'd room or school can commune with me,
But roughs and little children better than they.

The young mechanic is closest to me, he knows me well,
The woodman that takes his axe and jug with him shall take me with him all day,

The farm-boy ploughing in the field feels good at the sound of my
    voice,
In vessels that sail my words sail, I go with fishermen and seamen
    and love them.

The soldier camp'd or upon the march is mine,
On the night ere the pending battle many seek me, and I do not
    fail them,
On that solemn night (it may be their last) those that know me
    seek me.

My face rubs to the hunter's face when he lies down alone in his
    blanket,
The driver thinking of me does not mind the jolt of his wagon,
The young mother and old mother comprehend me,
The girl and the wife rest the needle a moment and forget where
    they are,
They and all would resume what I have told them.

48

I have said that the soul is not more than the body,
And I have said that the body is not more than the soul,
And nothing, not God, is greater to one than one's self is,
And whoever walks a furlong without sympathy walks to his own
    funeral drest in his shroud,
And I or you pocketless of a dime may purchase the pick of the
    earth,
And to glance with an eye or show a bean in its pod confounds
    the learning of all times,
And there is no trade or employment but the young man following
    it may become a hero,
And there is no object so soft but it makes a hub for the wheel'd
    universe,
And I say to any man or woman, Let your soul stand cool and
    composed before a million universes.

And I say to mankind, Be not curious about God,
For I who am curious about each am not curious about God,
(No array of terms can say how much I am at peace about God
    and about death.)

I hear and behold God in every object, yet understand God not
    in the least,

Nor do I understand who there can be more wonderful than myself.

Why should I wish to see God better than this day?
I see something of God each hour of the twenty-four, and each
moment then,
In the faces of men and women I see God, and in my own face in
the glass,
I find letters from God dropt in the street, and every one is sign'd
by God's name,
And I leave them where they are, for I know that wheresoe'er I go,
Others will punctually come for ever and ever.

49

And as to you Death, and you bitter hug of mortality, it is idle to
try to alarm me.

To his work without flinching the accoucheur comes,
I see the elder-hand pressing receiving supporting,
I recline by the sills of the exquisite flexible doors,
And mark the outlet, and mark the relief and escape.

And as to you Corpse I think you are good manure, but that does
not offend me,
I smell the white roses sweet-scented and growing,
I reach to the leafy lips, I reach to the polish'd breasts of melons.

And as to you Life I reckon you are the leavings of many deaths,
(No doubt I have died myself ten thousand times before.)

I hear you whispering there O stars of heaven,
O suns—O grass of graves—O perpetual transfers and promotions,
If you do not say any thing how can I say any thing?

Of the turbid pool that lies in the autumn forest,
Of the moon that descends the steeps of the soughing twilight,
Toss, sparkles of day and dusk—toss on the black stems that
decay in the muck,
Toss to the moaning gibberish of the dry limbs.

I ascend from the moon, I ascend from the night,
I perceive that the ghastly glimmer is noonday sunbeams reflected,
And debouch to the steady and central from the offspring great or
small.

50

There is that in me—I do not know what it is—but I know it is
   in me.

Wrench'd and sweaty—calm and cool then my body becomes,
I sleep—I sleep long.

I do not know it—it is without name—it is a word unsaid,
It is not in any dictionary, utterance, symbol.

Something it swings on more than the earth I swing on,
To it the creation is the friend whose embracing awakes me.

Perhaps I might tell more. Outlines! I plead for my brothers and
   sisters.

Do you see O my brothers and sisters?
It is not chaos or death—it is form, union, plan—it is eternal
   life—it is Happiness.

51

The past and present wilt—I have fill'd them, emptied them,
And proceed to fill my next fold of the future.

Listener up there! what have you to confide to me?
Look in my face while I snuff the sidle of evening,
(Talk honestly, no one else hears you, and I stay only a minute
   longer.)

Do I contradict myself?
Very well then I contradict myself,
(I am large, I contain multitudes.)

I concentrate toward them that are nigh, I wait on the door-slab.

Who has done his day's work? who will soonest be through with
   his supper?
Who wishes to walk with me?

Will you speak before I am gone? will you prove already too late?

52

The spotted hawk swoops by and accuses me, he complains of my
    gab and my loitering.

I too am not a bit tamed, I too am untranslatable,
I sound my barbaric yawp over the roofs of the world.

The last scud of day holds back for me,
It flings my likeness after the rest and true as any on the shadow'd
    wilds,
It coaxes me to the vapor and the dusk.

I depart as air, I shake my white locks at the runaway sun,
I effuse my flesh in eddies, and drift it in lacy jags.

I bequeath myself to the dirt to grow from the grass I love,
If you want me again look for me under your boot-soles.

You will hardly know who I am or what I mean,
But I shall be good health to you nevertheless,
And filter and fibre your blood.

Failing to fetch me at first keep encouraged,
Missing me one place search another,
I stop somewhere waiting for you.

Children of Adam

TO THE GARDEN THE WORLD

To the garden the world anew ascending,
Potent mates, daughters, sons, preluding,
The love, the life of their bodies, meaning and being,
Curious here behold my resurrection after slumber,
The revolving cycles in their wide sweep having brought me again,
Amorous, mature, all beautiful to me, all wondrous,
My limbs and the quivering fire that ever plays through them, for
    reasons, most wondrous,
Existing I peer and penetrate still,
Content with the present, content with the past,
By my side or back of me Eve following,
Or in front, and I following her just the same.

FROM PENT-UP ACHING RIVERS

From pent-up aching rivers,
From that of myself without which I were nothing,
From what I am determin'd to make illustrious, even if I stand
    sole among men,
From my own voice resonant, singing the phallus,
Singing the song of procreation,
Singing the need of superb children and therein · superb grown
    people,
Singing the muscular urge and the blending,
Singing the bedfellow's song, (O resistless yearning!
O for any and each the body correlative attracting!
O for you whoever you are your correlative body! O it, more than
    all else, you delighting!)
From the hungry gnaw that eats me night and day,
From native moments, from bashful pains, singing them,
Seeking something yet unfound though I have diligently sought it
    many a long year,
Singing the true song of the soul fitful at random,

Renascent with grossest Nature or among animals,
Of that, of them and what goes with them my poems informing,
Of the smell of apples and lemons, of the pairing of birds,
Of the wet of woods, of the lapping of waves,
Of the mad pushes of waves upon the land, I them chanting,
The overture lightly sounding, the strain anticipating,
The welcome nearness, the sight of the perfect body,
The swimmer swimming naked in the bath, or motionless on his
    back lying and floating,
The female form approaching, I pensive, love-flesh tremulous
    aching,
The divine list for myself or you or for any one making,
The face, the limbs, the index from head to foot, and what it arouses,
The mystic deliria, the madness amorous, the utter abandonment,
(Hark close and still what I now whisper to you,
I love you, O you entirely possess me,
O that you and I escape from the rest and go utterly off, free and
    lawless,
Two hawks in the air, two fishes swimming in the sea not more
    lawless than we;)
The furious storm through me careering, I passionately trembling,
The oath of the inseparableness of two together, of the woman
    that loves me and whom I love more than my life, that oath
    swearing,
(O I willingly stake all for you,
O let me be lost if it must be so!
O you and I! what is it to us what the rest do or think?
What is all else to us? only that we enjoy each other and exhaust
    each other if it must be so;)
From the master, the pilot I yield the vessel to,
The general commanding me, commanding all, from him permis-
    sion taking,
From time the programme hastening, (I have loiter'd too long as it
    is,)
From sex, from the warp and from the woof,
From privacy, from frequent repinings alone,
From plenty of persons near and yet the right person not near,
From the soft sliding of hands over me and thrusting of fingers
    through my hair and beard,
From the long sustain'd kiss upon the mouth or bosom,
From the close pressure that makes me or any man drunk, fainting
    with excess,
From what the divine husband knows, from the work of fatherhood,

From exultation, victory and relief, from the bedfellow's embrace
    in the night,
From the act-poems of eyes, hands, hips and bosoms,
From the cling of the trembling arm,
From the bending curve and the clinch,
From side by side the pliant coverlet off-throwing,
From the one so unwilling to have me leave, and me just as un-
    willing to leave,
(Yet a moment O tender waiter, and I return,)
From the hour of shining stars and dropping dews,
From the night a moment I emerging flitting out,
Celebrate you act divine and you children prepared for,
And you stalwart loins.

I SING THE BODY ELECTRIC

1

I SING the body electric,
The armies of those I love engirth me and I engirth them,
They will not let me off till I go with them, respond to them,
And discorrupt them, and charge them full with the charge of the
    soul.

Was it doubted that those who corrupt their own bodies conceal
    themselves?
And if those who defile the living are as bad as they who defile
    the dead?
And if the body does not do fully as much as the soul?
And if the body were not the soul, what is the soul?

2

The love of the body of man or woman balks account, the body
    itself balks account,
That of the male is perfect, and that of the female is perfect.

The expression of the face balks account,
But the expression of a well-made man appears not only in his face,
It is in his limbs and joints also, it is curiously in the joints of his
    hips and wrists,
It is in his walk, the carriage of his neck, the flex of his waist and
    knees, dress does not hide him,

The strong sweet quality he has strikes through the cotton and
 broadcloth,
To see him pass conveys as much as the best poem, perhaps more,
You linger to see his back, and the back of his neck and shoul-
 der-side.

The sprawl and fulness of babes, the bosoms and heads of women,
 the folds of their dress, their style as we pass in the street, the
 contour of their shape downwards,
The swimmer naked in the swimming-bath, seen as he swims
 through the transparent green-shine, or lies with his face up
 and rolls silently to and fro in the heave of the water,
The bending forward and backward of rowers in row-boats, the
 horseman in his saddle,
Girls, mothers, house-keepers, in all their performances,
The group of laborers seated at noon-time with their open dinner-
 kettles, and their wives waiting,
The female soothing a child, the farmer's daughter in the garden
 or cow-yard,
The young fellow hoeing corn, the sleigh-driver driving his six
 horses through the crowd,
The wrestle of wrestlers, two apprentice-boys, quite grown, lusty,
 good-natured, native-born, out on the vacant lot at sundown
 after work,
The coats and caps thrown down, the embrace of love and resistance,
The upper-hold and under-hold, the hair rumpled over and blind-
 ing the eyes;
The march of firemen in their own costumes, the play of masculine muscle through clean-setting trowsers and waist-straps,
The slow return from the fire, the pause when the bell strikes suddenly again, and the listening on the alert,
The natural, perfect, varied attitudes, the bent head, the curv'd
 neck and the counting;
Such-like I love—I loosen myself, pass freely, am at the mother's
 breast with the little child,
Swim with the swimmers, wrestle with wrestlers, march in line with
 the firemen, and pause, listen, count.

3

I knew a man, a common farmer, the father of five sons,
And in them the fathers of sons, and in them the fathers of sons.

This man was of wonderful vigor, calmness, beauty of person,
The shape of his head, the pale yellow and white of his hair and
    beard, the immeasurable meaning of his black eyes, the richness
    and breadth of his manners,
These I used to go and visit him to see, he was wise also,
He was six feet tall, he was over eighty years old, his sons were
    massive, clean, bearded, tan-faced, handsome,
They and his daughters loved him, all who saw him loved him,
They did not love him by allowance, they loved him with personal
    love,
He drank water only, the blood show'd like scarlet through the
    clear-brown skin of his face,
He was a frequent gunner and fisher, he sail'd his boat himself,
    he had a fine one presented to him by a ship-joiner, he had
    fowling-pieces presented to him by men that loved him,
When he went with his five sons and many grand-sons to hunt or
    fish, you would pick him out as the most beautiful and vigorous
    of the gang,
You would wish long and long to be with him, you would wish to
    sit by him in the boat that you and he might touch each other.

4

I have perceiv'd that to be with those I like is enough,
To stop in company with the rest at evening is enough,
To be surrounded by beautiful, curious, breathing, laughing flesh
    is enough,
To pass among them or touch any one, or rest my arm ever so
    lightly round his or her neck for a moment, what is this then?
I do not ask any more delight, I swim in it as in a sea.

There is something in staying close to men and women and looking
    on them, and in the contact and odor of them, that pleases
    the soul well,
All things please the soul, but these please the soul well.

5

This is the female form,
A divine nimbus exhales from it from head to foot,
It attracts with fierce undeniable attraction,
I am drawn by its breath as if I were no more than a helpless vapor,
    all falls aside but myself and it,

Books, art, religion, time, the visible and solid earth, and what was
  expected of heaven or fear'd of hell, are now consumed,
Mad filaments, ungovernable shoots play out of it, the response
  likewise ungovernable,
Hair, bosom, hips, bend of legs, negligent falling hands all dif-
  fused, mine too diffused,
Ebb stung by the flow and flow stung by the ebb, love-flesh swelling
  and deliciously aching,
Limitless limpid jets of love hot and enormous, quivering jelly of
  love, white-blow and delirious juice,
Bridegroom night of love working surely and softly into the pros-
  trate dawn,
Undulating into the willing and yielding day,
Lost in the cleave of the clasping and sweet-flesh'd day.

This is the nucleus—after the child is born of woman, man is born
  of woman,
This the bath of birth, this the merge of small and large, and the
  outlet again.

Be not ashamed women, your privilege encloses the rest, and is the
  exit of the rest,
You are the gates of the body, and you are the gates of the soul.

The female contains all qualities and tempers them,
She is in her place and moves with perfect balance,
She is all things duly veil'd, she is both passive and active,
She is to conceive daughters as well as sons, and sons as well as
  daughters.

As I see my soul reflected in Nature,
As I see through a mist, One with inexpressible completeness,
  sanity, beauty,
See the bent head and arms folded over the breast, the Female
  I see.

6

The male is not less the soul nor more, he too is in his place,
He too is all qualities, he is action and power,
The flush of the known universe is in him,
Scorn becomes him well, and appetite and defiance become him
  well,

The wildest largest passions, bliss that is utmost, sorrow that is
    utmost become him well, pride is for him,
The full-spread pride of man is calming and excellent to the soul,
Knowledge becomes him, he likes it always, he brings every thing
    to the test of himself,
Whatever the survey, whatever the sea and the sail he strikes
    soundings at last only here,
(Where else does he strike soundings except here?)

The man's body is sacred and the woman's body is sacred,
No matter who it is, it is sacred—is it the meanest one in the la-
    borers' gang?
Is it one of the dull-faced immigrants just landed on the wharf?
Each belongs here or anywhere just as much as the well-off, just
    as much as you,
Each has his or her place in the procession.

(All is a procession,
The universe is a procession with measured and perfect motion.)

Do you know so much yourself that you call the meanest ignorant?
Do you suppose you have a right to a good sight, and he or she
    has no right to a sight?
Do you think matter has cohered together from its diffuse float,
    and the soil is on the surface, and water runs and vegetation
    sprouts,
For you only, and not for him and her?

7

A man's body at auction,
(For before the war I often go to the slave-mart and watch the sale,)
I help the auctioneer, the sloven does not half know his business.

Gentlemen look on this wonder,
Whatever the bids of the bidders they cannot be high enough for it,
For it the globe lay preparing quintillions of years without one
    animal or plant,
For it the revolving cycles truly and steadily roll'd.

In this head the all-baffling brain,
In it and below it the makings of heroes.

Examine these limbs, red, black, or white, they are cunning in
tendon and nerve,
They shall be stript that you may see them.

Exquisite senses, life-lit eyes, pluck, volition,
Flakes of breast-muscle, pliant backbone and neck, flesh not flabby,
good-sized arms and legs,
And wonders within there yet.

Within there runs blood,
The same old blood! the same red-running blood!
There swells and jets a heart, there all passions, desires, reachings,
aspirations,
(Do you think they are not there because they are not express'd in
parlors and lecture-rooms?)

This is not only one man, this the father of those who shall be
fathers in their turns,
In him the start of populous states and rich republics,
Of him countless immortal lives with countless embodiments and
enjoyments.

How do you know who shall come from the offspring of his offspring through the centuries?
(Who might you find you have come from yourself, if you could
trace back through the centuries?)

8

A woman's body at auction,
She too is not only herself, she is the teeming mother of mothers,
She is the bearer of them that shall grow and be mates to the
mothers.

Have you ever loved the body of a woman?
Have you ever loved the body of a man?
Do you not see that these are exactly the same to all in all nations
and times all over the earth?

If any thing is sacred the human body is sacred,
And the glory and sweet of a man is the token of manhood un-
tainted,
And in man or woman a clean, strong, firm-fibred body, is more
beautiful than the most beautiful face.

Have you seen the fool that corrupted his own live body? or the
    fool that corrupted her own live body?
For they do not conceal themselves, and cannot conceal themselves.

9

O my body! I dare not desert the likes of you in other men and
    women, nor the likes of the parts of you,
I believe the likes of you are to stand or fall with the likes of the
    soul, (and that they are the soul,)
I believe the likes of you shall stand or fall with my poems, and
    that they are my poems,
Man's, woman's, child's, youth's, wife's, husband's, mother's,
    father's, young man's, young woman's poems,
Head, neck, hair, ears, drop and tympan of the ears,
Eyes, eye-fringes, iris of the eye, eyebrows, and the waking or
    sleeping of the lids,
Mouth, tongue, lips, teeth, roof of the mouth, jaws, and the jaw-
    hinges,
Nose, nostrils of the nose, and the partition,
Cheeks, temples, forehead, chin, throat, back of the neck, neck-
    slue,
Strong shoulders, manly beard, scapula, hind-shoulders, and the
    ample side-round of the chest,
Upper-arm, armpit, elbow-socket, lower-arm, arm-sinews, arm-
    bones,
Wrist and wrist-joints, hand, palm, knuckles, thumb, forefinger,
    finger-joints, finger-nails,
Broad breast-front, curling hair of the breast, breast-bone, breast-
    side,
Ribs, belly, backbone, joints of the backbone,
Hips, hip-sockets, hip-strength, inward and outward round, man-
    balls, man-root,
Strong set of thighs, well carrying the trunk above,
Leg-fibres, knee, knee-pan, upper-leg, under-leg,
Ankles, instep, foot-ball, toes, toe-joints, the heel;
All attitudes, all the shapeliness, all the belongings of my or your
    body or of any one's body, male or female,
The lung-sponges, the stomach-sac, the bowels sweet and clean,
The brain in its folds inside the skull-frame,
Sympathies, heart-valves, palate-valves, sexuality, maternity,
Womanhood, and all that is a woman, and the man that comes
    from woman,

The womb, the teats, nipples, breast-milk, tears, laughter, weeping,
 love-looks, love-perturbations and risings,
The voice, articulation, language, whispering, shouting aloud,
Food, drink, pulse, digestion, sweat, sleep, walking, swimming,
Poise on the hips, leaping, reclining, embracing, arm-curving and
 tightening,
The continual changes of the flex of the mouth, and around the eyes,
The skin, the sunburnt shade, freckles, hair,
The curious sympathy one feels when feeling with the hand the
 naked meat of the body,
The circling rivers the breath, and breathing it in and out,
The beauty of the waist, and thence of the hips, and thence down-
 ward toward the knees,
The thin red jellies within you or within me, the bones and the
 marrow in the bones,
The exquisite realization of health;
O I say these are not the parts and poems of the body only, but
 of the soul,
O I say now these are the soul!

A WOMAN WAITS FOR ME

A WOMAN waits for me, she contains all, nothing is lacking,
Yet all were lacking if sex were lacking, or if the moisture of the
 right man were lacking.

Sex contains all, bodies, souls,
Meanings, proofs, purities, delicacies, results, promulgations,
Songs, commands, health, pride, the maternal mystery, the seminal
 milk,
All hopes, benefactions, bestowals, all the passions, loves, beauties,
 delights of the earth,
All the governments, judges, gods, follow'd persons of the earth,
These are contain'd in sex as parts of itself and justifications of
 itself.

Without shame the man I like knows and avows the deliciousness
 of his sex,
Without shame the woman I like knows and avows hers.

Now I will dismiss myself from impassive women,
I will go stay with her who waits for me, and with those women
 that are warm-blooded and sufficient for me,

I see that they understand me and do not deny me,
I see that they are worthy of me, I will be the robust husband of
those women.

They are not one jot less than I am,
They are tann'd in the face by shining suns and blowing winds,
Their flesh has the old divine suppleness and strength,
They know how to swim, row, ride, wrestle, shoot, run, strike,
retreat, advance, resist, defend themselves,
They are ultimate in their own right—they are calm, clear, well-
possess'd of themselves.

I draw you close to me, you women,
I cannot let you go, I would do you good,
I am for you, and you are for me, not only for our own sake, but
for others' sakes,
Envelop'd in you sleep greater heroes and bards,
They refuse to awake at the touch of any man but me.

It is I, you women, I make my way,
I am stern, acrid, large, undissuadable, but I love you,
I do not hurt you any more than is necessary for you,
I pour the stuff to start sons and daughters fit for these States, I
press with slow rude muscle,
I brace myself effectually, I listen to no entreaties,
I dare not withdraw till I deposit what has so long accumulated
within me.

Through you I drain the pent-up rivers of myself,
In you I wrap a thousand onward years,
On you I graft the grafts of the best-beloved of me and America,
The drops I distil upon you shall grow fierce and athletic girls,
new artists, musicians, and singers,
The babes I beget upon you are to beget babes in their turn,
I shall demand perfect men and women out of my love-spendings,
I shall expect them to interpenetrate with others, as I and you
interpenetrate now,
I shall count on the fruits of the gushing showers of them, as I
count on the fruits of the gushing showers I give now,
I shall look for loving crops from the birth, life, death, immortality,
I plant so lovingly now.

SPONTANEOUS ME

SPONTANEOUS me, Nature,
The loving day, the mounting sun, the friend I am happy with,
The arm of my friend hanging idly over my shoulder,
The hillside whiten'd with blossoms of the mountain ash,
The same late in autumn, the hues of red, yellow, drab, purple,
and light and dark green,
The rich coverlet of the grass, animals and birds, the private
untrimm'd bank, the primitive apples, the pebble-stones,
Beautiful dripping fragments, the negligent list of one after an-
other as I happen to call them to me or think of them,
The real poems, (what we call poems being merely pictures,)
The poems of the privacy of the night, and of men like me,
This poem drooping shy and unseen that I always carry, and that
all men carry,
(Know once for all, avow'd on purpose, wherever are men like
me, are our lusty lurking masculine poems,)
Love-thoughts, love-juice, love-odor, love-yielding, love-climbers,
and the climbing sap,
Arms and hand of love, lips of love, phallic thumb of love, breasts
of love, bellies press'd and glued together with love,
Earth of chaste love, life that is only life after love,
The body of my love, the body of the woman I love, the body
of the man, the body of the earth,
Soft forenoon airs that blow from the south-west,
The hairy wild-bee that murmurs and hankers up and down, that
gripes the full-grown lady-flower, curves upon her with amorous firm legs, takes his will of her, and holds himself tremulous
and tight till he is satisfied;
The wet of woods through the early hours,
Two sleepers at night lying close together as they sleep, one with an
arm slanting down across and below the waist of the other,
The smell of apples, aromas from crush'd sage-plant, mint, birch-
bark,
The boy's longings, the glow and pressure as he confides to me what
he was dreaming,
The dead leaf whirling its spiral whirl and falling still and content
to the ground,
The no-form'd stings that sights, people, objects, sting me with,
The hubb'd sting of myself, stinging me as much as it ever can
any one,
The sensitive, orbic, underlapp'd brothers, that only privileged
feelers may be intimate where they are,

The curious roamer the hand roaming all over the body, the bash-
    ful withdrawing of flesh where the fingers soothingly pause and
    edge themselves,
The limpid liquid within the young man,
The vex'd corrosion so pensive and so painful,
The torment, the irritable tide that will not be at rest,
The like of the same I feel, the like of the same in others,
The young man that flushes and flushes, and the young woman
    that flushes and flushes,
The young man that wakes deep at night, the hot hand seeking to
    repress what would master him,
The mystic amorous night, the strange half-welcome pangs, visions,
    sweats,
The pulse pounding through palms and trembling encircling fin-
    gers, the young man all color'd, red, ashamed, angry;
The souse upon me of my lover the sea, as I lie willing and naked,
The merriment of the twin babes that crawl over the grass in the
    sun, the mother never turning her vigilant eyes from them,
The walnut-trunk, the walnut-husks, and the ripening or ripen'd
    long-round walnuts,
The continence of vegetables, birds, animals,
The consequent meanness of me should I skulk or find myself
    indecent, while birds and animals never once skulk or find
    themselves indecent,
The great chastity of paternity, to match the great chastity of
    maternity,
The oath of procreation I have sworn, my Adamic and fresh
    daughters,
The greed that eats me day and night with hungry gnaw, till I
    saturate what shall produce boys to fill my place when I am
    through,
The wholesome relief, repose, content,
And this bunch pluck'd at random from myself,
It has done its work—I toss it carelessly to fall where it may.

ONE HOUR TO MADNESS AND JOY

ONE hour to madness and joy! O furious! O confine me not!
(What is this that frees me so in storms?
What do my shouts amid lightnings and raging winds mean?)

O to drink the mystic deliria deeper than any other man!
O savage and tender achings! (I bequeath them to you my children,
I tell them to you, for reasons, O bridegroom and bride.)

O to be yielded to you whoever you are, and you to be yielded to
    me in defiance of the world!
O to return to Paradise! O bashful and feminine!
O to draw you to me, to plant on you for the first time the lips of
    a determin'd man.

O the puzzle, the thrice-tied knot, the deep and dark pool, all
    untied and illumin'd!
O to speed where there is space enough and air enough at last!
To be absolv'd from previous ties and conventions, I from mine
    and you from yours!
To find a new unthought-of nonchalance with the best of Nature!
To have the gag remov'd from one's mouth!
To have the feeling to-day or any day I am sufficient as I am.

O something unprov'd! something in a trance!
To escape utterly from others' anchors and holds!
To drive free! to love free! to dash reckless and dangerous!
To court destruction with taunts, with invitations!
To ascend, to leap to the heavens of the love indicated to me!
To rise thither with my inebriate soul!
To be lost if it must be so!
To feed the remainder of life with one hour of fulness and freedom!
With one brief hour of madness and joy.

OUT OF THE ROLLING OCEAN THE CROWD

OUT of the rolling ocean the crowd came a drop gently to me,
Whispering *I love you, before long I die,*
I have travel'd a long way merely to look on you to touch you,
For I could not die till I once look'd on you,
For I fear'd I might afterward lose you.

Now we have met, we have look'd, we are safe,
Return in peace to the ocean my love,
I too am part of that ocean my love, we are not so much sepa-
    rated,
Behold the great rondure, the cohesion of all, how perfect!
But as for me, for you, the irresistible sea is to separate us,
As for an hour carrying us diverse, yet cannot carry us diverse for-
    ever;
Be not impatient—a little space—know you I salute the air, the
    ocean and the land,
Everyday at sundown for your dear sake my love.

AGES AND AGES RETURNING AT INTERVALS

AGES and ages returning at intervals,
Undestroy'd, wandering immortal,
Lusty, phallic, with the potent original loins, perfectly sweet,
I, chanter of Adamic songs,
Through the new garden the West, the great cities calling,
Deliriate, thus prelude what is generated, offering these, offering
     myself,
Bathing myself, bathing my songs in Sex,
Offspring of my loins.

WE TWO, HOW LONG WE WERE FOOL'D

WE two, how long we were fool'd,
Now transmuted, we swiftly escape as Nature escapes,
We are Nature, long have we been absent, but now we return,
We become plants, trunks, foliage, roots, bark,
We are bedded in the ground, we are rocks,
We are oaks, we grow in the openings side by side,
We browse, we are two among the wild herds spontaneous as any,
We are two fishes swimming in the sea together,
We are what locust blossoms are, we drop scent around lanes
     mornings and evenings,
We are also the coarse smut of beasts, vegetables, minerals,
We are two predatory hawks, we soar above and look down,
We are two resplendent suns, we it is who balance ourselves orbic
     and stellar, we are as two comets,
We prowl fang'd and four-footed in the woods, we spring on
     prey,
We are two clouds forenoons and afternoons driving overhead,
We are seas mingling, we are two of those cheerful waves rolling
     over each other and interwetting each other,
We are what the atmosphere is, transparent, receptive, pervious,
     impervious,
We are snow, rain, cold, darkness, we are each product and in-
     fluence of the globe,
We have circled and circled till we have arrived home again, we
     two,
We have voided all but freedom and all but our own joy.

O HYMEN! O HYMENEE!

O HYMEN! O hymenee! why do you tantalize me thus?
O why sting me for a swift moment only?

Why can you not continue? O why do you now cease?
Is it because if you continued beyond the swift moment you would
    soon certainly kill me?

I AM HE THAT ACHES WITH LOVE

I AM he that aches with amorous love;
Does the earth gravitate? does not all matter, aching, attract all
    matter?
So the body of me to all I meet or know.

NATIVE MOMENTS

NATIVE moments—when you come upon me—ah you are here
    now,
Give me now libidinous joys only,
Give me the drench of my passions, give me life coarse and rank,
To-day I go consort with Nature's darlings, to-night too,
I am for those who believe in loose delights, I share the midnight
    orgies of young men,
I dance with the dancers and drink with the drinkers,
The echoes ring with our indecent calls, I pick out some low person
    for my dearest friend,
He shall be lawless, rude, illiterate, he shall be one condemn'd by
    others for deeds done,
I will play a part no longer, why should I exile myself from my
    companions?
O you shunned persons, I at least do not shun you,
I come forthwith in your midst, I will be your poet,
I will be more to you than to any of the rest.

ONCE I PASS'D THROUGH A POPULOUS CITY

ONCE I pass'd through a populous city imprinting my brain for
    future use with its shows, architecture, customs, traditions,
Yet now of all that city I remember only a woman I casually met
    there who detain'd me for love of me,
Day by day and night by night we were together—all else has
    long been forgotten by me,
I remember I say only that woman who passionately clung to me,
Again we wander, we love, we separate again,
Again she holds me by the hand, I must not go,
I see her close beside me with silent lips sad and tremulous.

I HEARD YOU SOLEMN-SWEET PIPES OF THE ORGAN

I HEARD you solemn-sweet pipes of the organ as last Sunday morn
  I pass'd the church
Winds of autumn, as I walk'd the woods at dusk I heard your
  long-stretch'd sighs up above so mournful,
I heard the perfect Italian tenor singing at the opera, I heard the
  soprano in the midst of the quartet singing;
Heart of my love! you too I heard murmuring low through one
  of the wrists around my head,
Heard the pulse of you when all was still ringing little bells last
  night under my ear.

FACING WEST FROM CALIFORNIA'S SHORES

FACING west from California's shores,
Inquiring, tireless, seeking what is yet unfound,
I, a child, very old, over waves, towards the house of maternity,
  the land of migrations, look afar,
Look off the shores of my Western sea, the circle almost circled;
For starting westward from Hindustan, from the vales of Kash-
  mere,
From Asia, from the north, from the God, the sage, and the hero,
From the south, from the flowery peninsulas and the spice islands,
Long having wander'd since, round the earth having wander'd,
Now I face home again, very pleas'd and joyous,
(But where is what I started for so long ago?
Any why is it yet unfound?)

AS ADAM EARLY IN THE MORNING

As Adam early in the morning,
Walking forth from the bower refresh'd with sleep,
Behold me where I pass, hear my voice, approach,
Touch me, touch the palm of your hand to my body as I pass,
Be not afraid of my body.

Calamus

IN PATHS UNTRODDEN

In paths untrodden,
In the growth by margins of pond-waters,
Escaped from the life that exhibits itself,
From all the standards hitherto publish'd, from the pleasures,
    profits, conformities,
Which too long I was offering to feed my soul,
Clear to me now standards not yet publish'd, clear to me that my
    soul,
That the soul of the man I speak for rejoices in comrades,
Here by myself away from the clank of the world,
Tallying and talk'd to here by tongues aromatic,
No longer abash'd, (for in this secluded spot I can respond as I
    would not dare elsewhere,)
Strong upon me the life that does not exhibit itself, yet contains
    all the rest,
Resolv'd to sing no songs to-day but those of manly attachment,
Projecting them along that substantial life,
Bequeathing hence types of athletic love,
Afternoon this delicious Ninth-month in my forty-first year,
I proceed for all who are or have been young men,
To tell the secret of my nights and days,
To celebrate the need of comrades.

SCENTED HERBAGE OF MY BREAST

Scented herbage of my breast,
Leaves from you I glean, I write, to be perused best afterwards,
Tomb-leaves, body-leaves growing up above me above death,
Perennial roots, tall leaves, O the winter shall not freeze you delicate
    leaves,
Every year shall you bloom again, out from where you retired you
    shall emerge again;

O I do not know whether many passing by will discover you or
    inhale your faint odor, but I believe a few will;
O slender leaves! O blossoms of my blood! I permit you to tell
    in your own way of the heart that is under you,
O I do not know what you mean there underneath yourselves, you
    are not happiness,
You are often more bitter than I can bear, you burn and sting me,
Yet you are beautiful to me you faint tinged roots, you make me
    think of death,
Death is beautiful from you, (what indeed is finally beautiful except
    death and love?)
O I think it is not for life I am chanting here my chant of lovers,
    I think it must be for death,
For how calm, how solemn it grows to ascend to the atmosphere
    of lovers,
Death or life I am then indifferent, my soul declines to prefer,
(I am not sure but the high soul of lovers welcomes death most,)
Indeed O death, I think now these leaves mean precisely the same
    as you mean,
Grow up taller sweet leaves that I may see! grow up out of my
    breast!
Spring away from the conceal'd heart there!
Do not fold yourself so in your pink-tinged roots timid leaves,
Do not remain down there so ashamed, herbage of my breast!
Come I am determin'd to unbare this broad breast of mine, I
    have long enough stifled and choked;
Emblematic and capricious blades I leave you, now you serve me
    not,
I will say what I have to say by itself,
I will sound myself and comrades only, I will never again utter a
    call only their call,
I will raise with it immortal reverberations through the States,
I will give an example to lovers to take permanent shape and will
    through the States,
Through me shall the words be said to make death exhilarating,
Give me your tone therefore O death, that I may accord with it,
Give me yourself, for I see that you belong to me now above all,
    and are folded inseparably together, you love and death are,
Nor will I allow you to balk me any more with what I was calling life,
For now it is convey'd to me that you are the purports essential,
That you hide in these shifting forms of life, for reasons, and that
    they are mainly for you,
That you beyond them come forth to remain, the real reality,

That behind the mask of materials you patiently wait, no matter
        how long,
That you will one day perhaps take control of all,
That you will perhaps dissipate this entire show of appearance,
That may-be you are what it is all for, but it does not last so very
        long,
But you will last very long.

WHOEVER YOU ARE HOLDING ME NOW IN HAND

WHOEVER you are holding me now in hand,
Without one thing all will be useless,
I give you fair warning before you attempt me further,
I am not what you supposed, but far different.

Who is he that would become my follower?
Who would sign himself a candidate for my affections?

The way is suspicious, the result uncertain, perhaps destructive,
You would have to give up all else, I alone would expect to be
        your sole and exclusive standard,
Your novitiate would even then be long and exhausting,
The whole past theory of your life and all conformity to the lives
        around you would have to be abandon'd,
Therefore release me now before troubling yourself any further, let
        go your hand from my shoulders,
Put me down and depart on your way.

Or else by stealth in some wood for trial,
Or back of a rock in the open air,
(For in any roof'd room of a house I emerge not, nor in company,
And in libraries I lie as one dumb, a gawk, or unborn, or dead,)
But just possibly with you on a high hill, first watching lest any
        person for miles around approach unawares,
Or possibly with you sailing at sea, or on the beach of the sea or
        some quiet island,
Here to put your lips upon mine I permit you,
With the comrade's long-dwelling kiss or the new husband's kiss,
For I am the new husband and I am the comrade.

Or if you will, thrusting me beneath your clothing,
Where I may fell the throbs of your heart or rest upon your hip,
Carry me when you go forth over land or sea;

For thus merely touching you is enough, is best,
And thus touching you would I silently sleep and be carried eter-
    nally.

But these leaves conning you con at peril,
For these leaves and me you will not understand,
They will elude you at first and still more afterward, I will certainly
    elude you,
Even while you should think you had unquestionably caught me,
    behold!
Already you see I have escaped from you.

For it is not for what I have put into it that I have written this
    book,
Nor is it by reading it you will acquire it,
Nor do those know me best who admire me and vauntingly praise
    me,
Nor will the candidates for my love (unless at most a very few)
    prove victorious,
Nor will my poems do good only, they will do just as much evil,
    perhaps more,
For all is useless without that which you may guess at many times
    and not hit, that which I hinted at;
Therefore release me and depart on your way.

FOR YOU O DEMOCRACY

COME, I will make the continent indissoluble,
I will make the most splendid race the sun ever shone upon,
I will make divine magnetic lands,
            With the love of comrades,
                With the life-long love of comrades.

I will plant companionship thick as trees along all the rivers of
    America, and along the shores of the great lakes, and all over
    the prairies,
I will make inseparable cities with their arms about each other's
    necks,
            By the love of comrades,
                By the manly love of comrades.

For you these from me, O Democracy, to serve you ma femme!
For you, for you I am trilling these songs.

THESE I SINGING IN SPRING

THESE I singing in spring collect for lovers,
(For who but I should understand lovers and all their sorrow and
    joy?
And who but I should be the poet of comrades?)
Collecting I traverse the garden the world, but soon I pass the
    gates,
Now along the pond-side, now wading in a little, fearing not the
    wet,
Now by the post-and-rail fences where the old stones thrown there,
    pick'd from the fields, have accumulated,
(Wild-flowers and vines and weeds come up through the stones
    and partly cover them, beyond these I pass,)
Far, far in the forest, or sauntering later in summer, before I think
    where I go,
Solitary, smelling the earthy smell, stopping now and then in the
    silence,
Alone I had thought, yet soon a troop gathers around me,
Some walk by my side and some behind, and some embrace my
    arms or neck,
They the spirits of dear friends dead or alive, thicker they come,
    a great crowd, and I in the middle,
Collecting, dispensing, singing, there I wander with them,
Plucking something for tokens, tossing toward whoever is near me,
Here, lilac, with a branch of pine,
Here, out of my pocket, some moss which I pull'd off a live-oak
    in Florida as it hung trailing down,
Here, some pinks and laurel leaves, and a handful of sage,
And here what I now draw from the water, wading in the pond-
    side,
(O here I last saw him that tenderly loves me, and returns again
    never to separate from me,
And this, O this shall henceforth be the token of comrades, this
    calamus-root shall,
Interchange it youths with each other! let none render it back!)
And twigs of maple and a bunch of wild orange and chestnut,
And stems of currants and plum-blows, and the aromatic cedar,
These I compass'd around by a thick cloud of spirits,
Wandering, point to or touch as I pass, or throw them loosely
    from me,
Indicating to each one what he shall have, giving something to
    each;

But what I drew from the water by the pond-side, that I reserve,
I will give of it, but only to them that love as I myself am capable
    of loving.

NOT HEAVING FROM MY RIBB'D BREAST ONLY

NOT heaving from my ribb'd breast only,
Not in sighs at night in rage dissatisfied with myself,
Not in those long-drawn, ill-supprest sighs,
Not in many an oath and promise broken,
Not in my wilful and savage soul's volition,
Not in the subtle nourishment of the air,
Not in this beating and pounding at my temples and wrists,
Not in the curious systole and diastole within which will one day
    cease,
Not in many a hungry wish told to the skies only,
Not in cries, laughter, defiances, thrown from me when alone far
    in the wilds,
Not in husky pantings through clinch'd teeth,
Not in sounded and resounded words, chattering words, echoes,
    dead words,
Not in the murmurs of my dreams while I sleep,
Nor the other murmurs of these incredible dreams of every day,
Nor in the limbs and senses of my body that take you and dismiss
    you continually—not there,
Not in any or all of them O adhesiveness! O pulse of my life!
Need I that you exist and show yourself any more than in these
    songs.

OF THE TERRIBLE DOUBT OF APPEARANCES

OF the terrible doubt of appearances,
Of the uncertainty after all, that we may be deluded,
That may-be reliance and hope are but speculations after all,
That may-be identity beyond the grave is a beautiful fable only,
May-be the things I perceive, the animals, plants, men, hills, shining
    and flowing waters,
The skies of day and night, colors, densities, forms, may-be these
    are (as doubtless they are) only apparitions, and the real
    something has yet to be known,
(How often they dart out of themselves as if to confound me and
    mock me!
How often I think neither I know, nor any man knows, aught of
    them,)

May-be seeming to me what they are (as doubtless they indeed
    but seem) as from my present point of view, and might prove
    (as of course they would) nought of what they appear, or
    nought anyhow, from entirely changed points of view;
To me these and the like of these are curiously answer'd by my
    lovers, my dear friends,
When he whom I love travels with me or sits a long while holding
    me by the hand,
When the subtle air, the impalpable, the sense that words and
    reason hold not, surround us and pervade us,
Then I am charged with untold and untellable wisdom, I am silent,
    I require nothing further,
I cannot answer the question of appearances or that of identity
    beyond the grave,
But I walk or sit indifferent, I am satisfied,
He ahold of my hand has completely satisfied me.

THE BASE OF ALL METAPHYSICS

AND now gentlemen,
A word I give to remain in your memories and minds,
As base and finale too for all metaphysics.

(So to the students the old professor,
At the close of his crowded course.)

Having studied the new and antique, the Greek and Germanic
    systems,
Kant having studied and stated, Fichte and Schelling and Hegel,
Stated the lore of Plato, and Socrates greater than Plato,
And greater than Socrates sought and stated, Christ divine having
    studied long,
I see reminiscent to-day those Greek and Germanic systems,
See the philosophies all, Christian churches and tenets see,
Yet underneath Socrates clearly see, and underneath Christ the
    divine I see,
The dear love of man for his comrade, the attraction of friend to
    friend,
Of the well-married husband and wife, of children and parents,
Of city for city and land for land.

RECORDERS AGES HENCE

RECORDERS ages hence,
Come, I will take you down underneath this impassive exterior, I
    will tell you what to say of me,

Publish my name and hang up my picture as that of the tenderest
   lover,
The friend the lover's portrait, of whom his friend his lover was
   fondest,
Who was not proud of his songs, but of the measureless ocean of
   love within him, and freely pour'd it forth,
Who often walk'd lonesome walks thinking of his dear friends, his
   lovers,
Who pensive away from one he lov'd often lay sleepless and dissatisfied at night,
Who knew too well the sick, sick dread lest the one he lov'd might
   secretly be indifferent to him,
Whose happiest days were far away through fields, in woods, on
   hills, he and another wandering hand in hand, they twain
   apart from other men,
Who oft as he saunter'd the streets curv'd with his arm the shoulder
   of his friend, while the arm of his friend rested upon him also.

WHEN I HEARD AT THE CLOSE OF THE DAY

WHEN I heard at the close of the day how my name had been
   receiv'd with plaudits in the capitol, still it was not a happy
   night for me that follow'd,
And else when I carous'd, or when my plans were accomplish'd,
   still I was not happy,
But the day when I rose at dawn from the bed of perfect health,
   refresh'd, singing, inhaling the ripe breath of autumn,
When I saw the full moon in the west grow pale and disappear in
   the morning light,
When I wander'd alone over the beach, and undressing bathed,
   laughing with the cool waters, and saw the sun rise,
And when I thought how my dear friend my lover was on his way
   coming, O then I was happy,
O then each breath tasted sweeter, and all that day my food nourish'd me more, and the beautiful day pass'd well,
And the next came with equal joy, and with the next at evening
   came my friend,
And that night while all was still I heard the waters roll slowly continually up the shores,
I heard the hssing rustle of the liquid and sands as directed to me
   whispering to congratulate me,
For the one I love most lay sleeping by me under the same cover
   in the cool night,

In the stillness in the autumn moonbeams his face was inclined
    toward me,
And his arm lay lightly around my breast—and that night I was
    happy.

ARE YOU THE NEW PERSON DRAWN TOWARD ME?

ARE you the new person drawn toward me?
To begin with take warning, I am surely far different from what
    you suppose;
Do you suppose you will find in me your ideal?
Do you think it so easy to have me become your lover?
Do you think the friendship of me would be unalloy'd satisfaction?
Do you think I am trusty and faithful?
Do you see no further than this façade, this smooth and tolerant
    manner of me?
Do you suppose yourself advancing on real ground toward a real
    heroic man?
Have you no thought O dreamer that it may be all maya, illusion?

ROOTS AND LEAVES THEMSELVES ALONE

ROOTS and leaves themselves alone are these,
Scents brought to men and women from the wild woods and
    pond-side,
Breast-sorrel and pinks of love, fingers that wind around tighter
    than vines,
Gushes from the throats of birds hid in the foliage of trees as the
    sun is risen,
Breezes of land and love set from living shores to you on the living
    sea, to you O sailors!
Frost-mellow'd berries and Third-month twigs offer'd fresh to
    young persons wandering out in the fields when the winter
    breaks up,
Love-buds put before you and within you whoever you are,
Buds to be unfolded on the old terms,
If you bring the warmth of the sun to them they will open and
    bring form, color, perfume, to you,
If you become the aliment and the wet they will become flowers,
    fruits, tall branches and trees.

NOT HEAT FLAMES UP AND CONSUMES

NOT heat flames up and consumes,
Not sea-waves hurry in and out,

Not the air delicious and dry, the air of ripe summer, bears lightly
    along white down-balls of myriads of seeds,
Wafted, sailing gracefully, to drop where they may;
Not these, O none of these more than the flames of me, consum-
    ing, burning for his love whom I love,
O none more than I hurrying in and out;
Does the tide hurry, seeking something, and never give up? O I
    the same,
O nor down-balls nor perfumes, nor the high rain-emitting clouds,
    are borne through the open air,
Any more than my soul is borne through the open air,
Wafted in all directions O love, for friendship, for you.

TRICKLE DROPS

TRICKLE drops! my blue veins leaving!
O drops of me! trickle, slow drops,
Candid from me falling, drip, bleeding drops,
From wounds made to free you whence you were prison'd,
From my face, from my forehead and lips,
From my breast, from within where I was conceal'd, press forth
    red drops, confession drops,
Stain every page, stain every song I sing, every word I say, bloody
    drops,
Let them know your scarlet heat, let them glisten,
Saturate them with yourself all ashamed and wet,
Glow upon all I have written or shall write, bleeding drops,
Let it all be seen in your light, blushing drops.

CITY OF ORGIES

CITY of orgies, walks and joys,
City whom that I have lived and sung in your midst will one day
    make you illustrious,
Not the pageants of you, not your shifting tableaus, your specta-
    cles, repay me,
Not the interminable rows of your houses, nor the ships at the
    wharves,
Nor the processions in the streets, nor the bright windows with
    goods in them,
Nor to converse with learn'd persons, or bear my share in the soiree
    or feast;
Not those, but as I pass O Manhattan, your frequent and swift
    flash of eyes offering me love,

Offering response to my own—these repay me,
Lovers, continual lovers, only repay me.

BEHOLD THIS SWARTHY FACE

BEHOLD this swarthy face, these gray eyes,
This beard, the white wool unclipt upon my neck,
My brown hands and the silent manner of me without charm;
Yet comes one a Manhattanese and ever at parting kisses me
    lightly on the lips with robust love,
And I on the crossing of the street or on the ship's deck give a
    kiss in return,
We observe that salute of American comrades land and sea,
We are those two natural and nonchalant persons.

I SAW IN LOUISIANA A LIVE-OAK GROWING

I saw in Louisiana a live-oak growing,
All alone stood it and the moss hung down from the branches,
Without any companion it grew there uttering joyous leaves of
    dark green,
And its look, rude, unbending, lusty, made me think of myself,
But I wonder'd how it could utter joyous leaves standing alone
    there without its friend near, for I knew I could not,
And I broke off a twig with a certain number of leaves upon it,
    and twined around it a little moss,
And brought it away, and I have placed it in sight in my room,
It is not needed to remind me as of my own dear friends,
(For I believe lately I think of little else than of them,)
Yet it remains to me a curious token, it makes me think of manly
    love;
For all that, and though the live-oak glistens there in Louisiana
    solitary in a wide flat space,
Uttering joyous leaves all its life without a friend a lover near,
I know very well I could not.

TO A STRANGER

PASSING stranger! you do not know how longingly I look upon
    you,
You must be he I was seeking, or she I was seeking, (it comes to
    me as of a dream,)
I have somewhere surely lived a life of joy with you,

All is recall'd as we flit by each other, fluid, affectionate, chaste,
    matured,
You grew up with me, were a boy with me or a girl with me,
I ate with you and slept with you, your body has become not yours
    only nor left my body mine only,
You give me the pleasure of your eyes, face, flesh, as we pass, you
    take of my beard, breast, hands, in return,
I am not to speak to you, I am to think of you when I sit alone
    or wake at night alone,
I am to wait, I do not doubt I am to meet you again,
I am to see to it that I do not lose you.

THIS MOMENT YEARNING AND THOUGHTFUL

THIS moment yearning and thoughtful sitting alone,
It seems to me there are other men in other lands yearning and
    thoughtful,
It seems to me I can look over and behold them in Germany,
    Italy, France, Spain,
Or far, far away, in China, or in Russia or Japan, talking other
    dialects,
And it seems to me if I could know those men I should become
    attached to them as I do to men in my own lands,
O I know we should be brethren and lovers,
I know I should be happy with them.

I HEAR IT WAS CHARGED AGAINST ME

I HEAR it was charged against me that I sought to destroy institu-
    tions,
But really I am neither for nor against institutions,
(What indeed have I in common with them? or what with the
    destruction of them?)
Only I will establish in the Mannahatta and in every city of these
    States inland and seaboard,
And in the fields and woods, and above every keel little or large
    that dents the water,
Without edifices or rules or trustees or any argument,
The institution of the dear love of comrades.

THE PRAIRIE-GRASS DIVIDING

THE prairie-grass dividing, its special odor breathing,
I demand of it the spiritual corresponding,

Demand the most copious and close companionship of men,
Demand the blades to rise of words, acts, beings,
Those of the open atmosphere, coarse, sunlit, fresh, nutritious,
Those that go their own gait, erect, stepping with freedom and
    command, leading not following,
Those with a never-quell'd audacity, those with sweet and lusty
    flesh clear of taint,
Those that look carelessly in the faces of Presidents and governors,
    as to say *Who are you?*
Those of earth-born passion, simple, never constrain'd, never
    obedient
Those of inland America.

WHEN I PERUSE THE CONQUER'D FAME

WHEN I peruse the conquer'd fame of heroes and the victories
    of mighty generals, I do not envy the generals,
Nor the President in his Presidency, nor the rich in his great house,
But when I hear of the brotherhood of lovers, how it was with
    them,
How together through life, through dangers, odium, unchanging,
    long and long,
Through youth and through middle and old age, how unfaltering,
    how affectionate and faithful they were,
Then I am pensive—I hastily walk away fill'd with the bitterest
    envy.

WE TWO BOYS TOGETHER CLINGING

WE two boys together clinging,
One the other never leaving,
Up and down the roads going, North and South excursions making,
Power enjoying, elbows stretching, fingers clutching,
Arm'd and fearless, eating, drinking, sleeping, loving,
No law less than ourselves owning, sailing, soldiering, thieving,
    threatening,
Misers, menials, priests alarming, air breathing, water drinking, on
    the turf or the sea-beach dancing,
Cities wrenching, ease scorning, statutes mocking, feebleness chas-
    ing,
Fulfilling our foray.

A PROMISE TO CALIFORNIA

A PROMISE to California,
Or inland to the great pastoral Plains, and on to Puget sound and
    Oregon;
Sojourning east a while longer, soon I travel toward you, to remain,
    to teach robust American love,
For I know very well that I and robust love belong among you,
    inland, and along the Western sea;
For these States tend inland and toward the Western sea, and I
    will also.

HERE THE FRAILEST LEAVES OF ME

HERE the frailest leaves of me and yet my strongest lasting,
Here I shade and hide my thoughts, I myself do not expose them,
And yet they expose me more than all my other poems.

NO LABOR-SAVING MACHINE

No labor-saving machine,
Nor discovery have I made,
Nor will I be able to leave behind me any wealthy bequest to found
    a hospital or library,
Nor reminiscence of any deed of courage for America,
Nor literary success nor intellect, nor book for the book-shelf,
But a few carols vibrating through the air I leave,
For comrades and lovers.

A GLIMPSE

A GLIMPSE through an interstice caught,
Of a crowd of workmen and drivers in a bar-room around the
    stove late of a winter night, and I unremark'd seated in a
    corner,
Of a youth who loves me and whom I love, silently approaching
    and seating himself near, that he may hold me by the hand,
A long while amid the noises of coming and going, of drinking
    and oath and smutty jest,
There we two, content, happy in being together, speaking little,
    perhaps not a word.

A LEAF FOR HAND IN HAND

A LEAF for hand in hand;
You natural persons old and young!

You on the Mississippi and on all the branches and bayous of the
    Mississippi!
You friendly boatmen and mechanics! you roughs!
You twain! and all processions moving along the streets!
I wish to infuse myself among you till I see it common for you to
    walk hand in hand.

EARTH, MY LIKENESS

EARTH, my likeness,
Though you look so impassive, ample and spheric there,
I now suspect that is not all;
I now suspect there is something fierce in you eligible to burst forth,
For an athlete is enamour'd of me, and I of him,
But toward him there is something fierce and terrible in me eligi-
    ble to burst forth,
I dare not tell it in words, not even in these songs.

I DREAM'D IN A DREAM

I DREAM'D in a dream I saw a city invincible to the attacks of the
    whole of the rest of the earth,
I dream'd that was the new city of Friends,
Nothing was greater there than the quality of robust love, it led
    the rest,
It was seen every hour in the actions of the men of that city,
And in all their looks and words.

WHAT THINK YOU I TAKE MY PEN IN HAND?

WHAT think you I take my pen in hand to record?
The battle-ship, perfect-model'd, majestic, that I saw pass the
    offing to-day under full sail?
The splendors of the past day? or the splendor of the night that
    envelops me?
Or the vaunted glory and growth of the great city spread around
    me?—no;
But merely of two simple men I saw to-day on the pier in the midst
    of the crowd, parting the parting of dear friends,
The one to remain hung on the other's neck and passionately
    kiss'd him,
While the one to depart tightly prest the one to remain in his arms.

TO THE EAST AND TO THE WEST

To the East and to the West,
To the man of the Seaside State and of Pennsylvania,
To the Kanadian of the north, to the Southerner I love,
These with perfect trust to depict you as myself, the germs are in all men,
I believe the main purport of these States is to found a superb friendship, exaltè, previously unknown,
Because I perceive it waits and has been always waiting, latent in all men.

SOMETIMES WITH ONE I LOVE

SOMETIMES with one I love I fill myself with rage for fear I effuse unreturn'd love,
But now I think there is no unreturn'd love, the pay is certain one way or another,
(I loved a certain person ardently and my love was not return'd,
Yet out of that I have written these songs.)

TO A WESTERN BOY

MANY things to absorb I teach to help you become eleve of mine;
Yet if blood like mine circle not in your veins,
If you be not silently selected by lovers and do not silently select lovers,
Of what use is it that you seek to become eleve of mine?

FAST ANCHOR'D ETERNAL O LOVE!

FAST-ANCHOR'D eternal O love! O woman I love!
O bride! O wife! more resistless than I can tell, the thought of you!
Then separate, as disembodied or another born,
Ethereal, the last athletic reality, my consolation,
I ascend, I float in the regions of your love O man,
O sharer of my roving life.

AMONG THE MULTITUDE

AMONG the men and women the multitude,
I perceive one picking me out by secret and divine signs,
Acknowledging none else, not parent, wife, husband, brother, child, any nearer than I am,
Some are baffled, but that one is not—that one knows me.

Ah lover and perfect equal,
I meant that you should discover me so by faint indirections,
And I when I meet you mean to discover you by the like in you.

O YOU WHOM I OFTEN AND SILENTLY COME

O YOU whom I often and silently come where you are that I may
   be with you,
As I walk by your side or sit near, or remain in the same room
   with you,
Little you know the subtle electric fire that for your sake is playing within me.

THAT SHADOW MY LIKENESS

THAT shadow my likeness that goes to and fro seeking a liveli-
   hood, chattering, chaffering,
How often I find myself standing and looking at it where it flits,
How often I question and doubt whether that is really me;
But among my lovers and caroling these songs,
O I never doubt whether that is really me.

FULL OF LIFE NOW

FULL of life now, compact, visible,
I, forty years old the eighty-third year of the States,
To one a century hence or any number of centuries hence,
To you yet unborn these, seeking you.

When you read these I that was visible am become invisible,
Now it is you, compact, visible, realizing my poems, seeking me,
Fancying how happy you were if I could be with you and become
   your comrade;
Be it as if I were with you. (Be not too certain but I am now with
   you.)

Salut au Monde!

1

O TAKE my hand Walt Whitman!
Such gliding wonders! such sights and sounds!
Such join'd unended links, each hook'd to the next,
Each answering all, each sharing the earth with all.

What widens within you Walt Whitman?
What waves and soils exuding?
What climes? what persons and cities are here?
Who are the infants, some playing, some slumbering?
Who are the girls? who are the married women?
Who are the groups of old men going slowly with their arms about
     each other's necks?
What rivers are these? what forests and fruits are these?
What are the mountains call'd that rise so high in the mists?
What myriads of dwellings are they fill'd with dwellers?

2

Within me latitude widens, longitude lengthens,
Asia, Africa, Europe, are to the east—America is provided for in
     the west,
Banding the bulge of the earth winds the hot equator,
Curiously north and south turn the axis-ends,
Within me is the longest day, the sun wheels in slanting rings, it
     does not set for months,
Stretch'd in due time within me the midnight sun just rises above
     the horizon and sinks again,
Within me zones, seas, cataracts, forests, volcanoes, groups,
Malaysia, Polynesia, and the great West Indian islands.

3

What do you hear Walt Whitman?

I hear the workman singing and the farmer's wife singing,
I hear in the distance the sounds of children and of animals early
     in the day,
I hear emulous shouts of Australians pursuing the wild horse,
I hear the Spanish dance with castanets in the chestnut shade, to
     the rebeck and guitar,
I hear continual echoes from the Thames,
I hear fierce French liberty songs,
I hear of the Italian boat-sculler the musical recitative of old poems,
I hear the locusts in Syria as they strike the grain and grass with
     the showers of their terrible clouds,
I hear the Coptic refrain toward sundown, pensively falling on the
     breast of the black venerable vast mother the Nile,
I hear the chirp of the Mexican muleteer, and the bells of the
     mule,

I hear the Arab muezzin calling from the top of the mosque,
I hear the Christian priests at the altars of their churches, I hear
the responsive base and soprano,
I hear the cry of the Cossack, and the sailor's voice putting to sea
at Okotsk,
I hear the wheeze of the slave-coffle as the slaves march on, as the
husky gangs pass on by twos and threes, fasten'd together with
wrist-chains and ankle-chains,
I hear the Hebrew reading his records and psalms,
I hear the rhythmic myths of the Greeks, and the strong legends
of the Romans,
I hear the tale of the divine life and bloody death of the beautiful
God the Christ,
I hear the Hindoo teaching his favorite pupil the loves, wars,
adages, transmitted safely to this day from poets who wrote
three thousand years ago.

4

What do you see Walt Whitman?
Who are they you salute, and that one after another salute you?

I see a great round wonder rolling through space,
I see diminute farms, hamlets, ruins, graveyards, jails, factories,
palaces, hovels, huts of barbarians, tents of nomads upon
the surface,
I see the shaded part on one side where the sleepers are sleeping,
and the sunlit part on the other side,
I see the curious rapid change of the light and shade,
I see distant lands, as real and near to the inhabitants of them as
my land is to me.

I see plenteous waters,
I see mountain peaks, I see the sierras of Andes where they range,
I see plainly the Himalayas, Chian Shahs, Altays, Ghauts,
I see the giant pinnacles of Elbruz, Kazbek, Bazardjusi,
I see the Styrian Alps, and the Karnac Alps,
I see the Pyrenees, Balks, Carpathians, and to the north the Dofra-
fields, and off at sea mount Hecla,
I see Vesuvius and Etna, the mountains of the Moon, and the
Red mountains of Madagascar,
I see the Lybian, Arabian, and Asiatic deserts,
I see huge dreadful Arctic and Antarctic icebergs,

I see the superior oceans and the inferior ones, the Atlantic and
    Pacific, the sea of Mexico, the Brazilian sea, and the sea of
    Peru,
The waters of Hindustan, the China sea, and the gulf of Guinea,
The Japan waters, the beautiful bay of Nagasaki land-lock'd in its
    mountains,
The spread of the Baltic, Caspian, Bothnia, the British shores, and
    the bay of Biscay,
The clear-sunn'd Mediterranean, and from one to another of its
    islands,
The White sea, and the sea around Greenland.

I behold the mariners of the world,
Some are in storms, some in the night with the watch on the look-
    out,
Some drifting helplessly, some with contagious diseases.

I behold the sail and steamships of the world, some in clusters in
    port, some on their voyages,
Some double the cape of Storms, some cape Verde, others capes
    Guardafui, Bon, or Bajadore,
Others Dondra head, others pass the straits of Sunda, others cape
    Lopatka, others Behring's straits,
Others cape Horn, others sail the gulf of Mexico or along Cuba
    or Hayti, others Hudson's bay or Baffin's bay,
Others pass the straits of Dover, others enter the Wash, others the
    firth of Solway, others round cape Clear, others the Land's
    End,
Others traverse the Zuyder Zee or the Scheld,
Others as comers and goers at Gibraltar or the Dardanelles,
Others sternly push their way through the northern winter-packs,
Others descend or ascend the Obi or the Lena,
Others the Niger or the Congo, others the Indus, the Burampooter
    and Cambodia,
Others wait steam'd up ready to start in the ports of Australia,
Wait at Liverpool, Glasgow, Dublin, Marseilles, Lisbon, Naples,
    Hamburg, Bremen, Bordeaux, the Hague, Copenhagen,
Wait at Valparaiso, Rio Janeiro, Panama.

5

I see the tracks of the railroads of the earth,
I see them in Great Britain, I see them in Europe,
I see them in Asia and in Africa.

I see the electric telegraphs of the earth,
I see the filaments of the news of the wars, deaths, losses, gains,
  passions, of my race.

I see the long river-stripes of the earth,
I see the Amazon and the Paraguay,
I see the four great rivers of China, the Amour, the Yellow River,
  the Yiang-tse, and the Pearl,
I see where the Seine flows, and where the Danube, the Loire, the
  Rhone, and the Guadalquiver flow,
I see the windings of the Volga, the Dnieper, the Oder,
I see the Tuscan going down the Arno, and the Venetian along
  the Po,
I see the Greek seaman sailing out of Egina bay.

6

I see the site of the old empire of Assyria, and that of Persia, and
  that of India,
I see the falling of the Ganges over the high rim of Saukara.

I see the place of the idea of the Deity incarnated by avatars in
  human forms,
I see the spots of the successions of priests on the earth, oracles,
  sacrificers, brahmins, sabians, lamas, monks, muftis, ex-
  horters,
I see where druids walk'd the groves of Mona, I see the mistletoe
  and vervain.
I see the temples of the deaths of the bodies of Gods, I see the
  old signifiers.

I see Christ eating the bread of his last supper in the midst of
  youths and old persons,
I see where the strong divine young man the Hercules toil'd faithfully and long and then died,
I see the place of the innocent rich life and hapless fate of the
  beautiful nocturnal son, the full-limb'd Bacchus,
I see Kneph, blooming, drest in blue, with the crown of feathers
  on his head,
I see Hermes, unsuspected, dying, well-belov'd, saying to the
  people *Do not weep for me,*
*This is not my true country, I have lived banish'd from my true
  country, I now go back there,*
I return to the celestial sphere where every one goes in his turn.

7

I see the battle-fields of the earth, grass grows upon them and
    blossoms and corn,
I see the tracks of ancient and modern expeditions.

I see the nameless masonries, venerable messages of the unknown
    events, heroes, records of the earth.

I see the places of the sagas,
I see pine-trees and fir-trees torn by northern blasts,
I see granite bowlders and cliffs, I see green meadows and lakes,
I see the burial-cairns of Scandinavian warriors,
I see them raised high with stones by the marge of restless oceans,
    that the dead men's spirits when they wearied of their quiet
    graves might rise up through the mounds and gaze on the
    tossing billows, and be refresh'd by storms, immensity, liberty,
    action.

I see the steppes of Asia,
I see the tumuli of Mongolia, I see the tents of Kalmucks and
    Baskirs,
I see the nomadic tribes with herds of oxen and cows,
I see the table-lands notch'd with ravines, I see the jungles and
    deserts,
I see the camel, the wild steed, the bustard, the fat-tail'd sheep,
    the antelope, and the burrowing wolf.

I see the highlands of Abyssinia,
I see flocks of goats feeding, and see the fig-tree, tamarind, date,
And see fields of teff-wheat and places of verdure and gold.

I see the Brazilian vaquero,
I see the Bolivian ascending mount Sorata,
I see the Wacho crossing the plains, I see the incomparable rider
    of horses with his lasso on his arm,
I see over the pampas the pursuit of wild cattle for their hides.

8

I see the regions of snow and ice,
I see the sharp-eyed Samoiede and the Finn,
I see the seal-seeker in his boat poising his lance,
I see the Siberian on his slight-built sledge drawn by dogs,

I see the porpoise-hunters, I see the whale-crews of the south
 Pacific and the north Atlantic,
I see the cliffs, glaciers, torrents, valleys, of Switzerland—I mark
 the long winters and the isolation.

9

I see the cities of the earth and make myself at random a part of
 them,
I am a real Parisian,
I am a habitan of Vienna, St. Petersburg, Berlin, Constantinople,
I am of Adelaide, Sidney, Melbourne,
I am of London, Manchester, Bristol, Edinburgh, Limerick,
I am of Madrid, Cadiz, Barcelona, Oporto, Lyons, Brussels, Berne,
 Frankfort, Stuttgart, Turin, Florence,
I belong in Moscow, Cracow, Warsaw, or northward in Christiania
 or Stockholm, or in Siberian Irkutsk, or in some street in
 Iceland,
I descend upon all those cities, and rise from them again.

10

I see vapors exhaling from unexplored countries,
I see the savage types, the bow and arrow, the poison'd splint, the
 fetich, and the obi.

I see African and Asiatic towns,
I see Algiers, Tripoli, Derne, Mogadore, Timbuctoo, Monrovia,
I see the swarms of Pekin, Canton, Benares, Delhi, Calcutta, Tokio,
I see the Kruman in his hut, and the Dahoman and Ashantee-man
 in their huts,
I see the Turk smoking opium in Aleppo,
I see the picturesque crowds at the fairs of Khiva and those of
 Herat,
I see Teheran, I see Muscat and Medina and the intervening sands,
I see the caravans toiling onward,
I see Egypt and the Egyptians, I see the pyramids and obelisks,
I look on chisell'd histories, records of conquering kings, dynasties,
 cut in slabs of sand-stone, or on granite-blocks,
I see at Memphis mummy-pits containing mummies embalm'd,
 swathed in linen cloth, lying there many centuries,
I look on the fall'n Theban, the large-ball'd eyes, the side-drooping
 neck, the hands folded across the breast.

I see all the menials of the earth, laboring,
I see all the prisoners in the prisons,

I see the defective human bodies of the earth,
The blind, the deaf and dumb, idiots, hunchbacks, lunatics,
The pirates, thieves, betrayers, murderers, slave-makers of the earth,
The helpless infants, and the helpless old men and women.

I see male and female everywhere,
I see the serene brotherhood of philosophs,
I see the constructiveness of my race,
I see the results of the perseverance and industry of my race,
I see ranks, colors, barbarisms, civilizations, I go among them, I
    mix indiscriminately,
And I salute all the inhabitants of the earth.

11

You whoever you are!
You daughter or son of England!
You of the mighty Slavic tribes and empires! you Russ in Russia!
You dim-descended, black, divine-soul'd African, large, fine-
    headed, nobly-form'd, superbly destin'd, on equal terms with
    me!
You Norwegian! Swede! Dane! Icelander! you Prussian!
You Spaniard of Spain! you Portuguese!
You Frenchwoman and Frenchman of France!
You Belge! you liberty-lover of the Netherlands! (you stock whence
    I myself have descended;)
You sturdy Austrian! you Lombard! Hun! Bohemian! farmer of
    Styria!
You neighbor of the Danube!
You working-man of the Rhine, the Elbe, or the Weser! you
    working-woman too!
You Sardinian! you Bavarian! Swabian! Saxon! Wallachian!
    Bulgarian!
You Roman! Neapolitan! you Greek!
You lithe matador in the arena at Seville!
You mountaineer living lawlessly on the Taurus or Caucasus!
You Bokh horse-herd watching your mares and stallions feeding!
You beautiful-bodied Persian at full speed in the saddle shooting
    arrows to the mark!
You Chinaman and Chinawoman of China! you Tartar of Tartary!
You women of the earth subordinated at your tasks!
You Jew journeying in your old age through every risk to stand
    once on Syrian ground!

You other Jews waiting in all lands for your Messiah!

You thoughtful Armenian pondering by some stream of the Euphrates! you peering amid the ruins of Nineveh! you ascending mount Ararat!

You foot-worn pilgrim welcoming the far-away sparkle of the minarets of Mecca!

You sheiks along the stretch from Suez to Bab-el-mandeb ruling your families and tribes!

You olive-grower tending your fruit on fields of Nazareth, Damascus, or lake Tiberias!

You Thibet trader on the wide inland or bargaining in the shops of Lassa!

You Japanese man or woman! you liver in Madagascar, Ceylon, Sumatra, Borneo!

All you continentals of Asia, Africa, Europe, Australia, indifferent of place!

All you on the numberless islands of the archipelagoes of the sea!

All you of centuries hence when you listen to me!

And you each and everywhere whom I specify not, but include just the same!

Health to you! good will to you all, from me and America sent!

Each of us inevitable,

Each of us limitless—each of us with his or her right upon the earth,

Each of us allow'd the eternal purports of the earth,

Each of us here as divinely as any is here.

12

You Hottentot with clicking palate! you woolly-hair'd hordes!

You own'd persons dropping sweat-drops or blood-drops!

You human forms with the fathomless ever-impressive countenances of brutes!

You poor koboo whom the meanest of the rest look down upon for all your glimmering language and spirituality!

You dwarf'd Kamtschatkan, Greenlander, Lapp!

You Austral negro, naked, red, sooty, with protrusive lip, groveling, seeking your food!

You Caffre, Berber, Soudanese!

You haggard, uncouth, untutor'd Bedowee!

You plague-swarms in Madras, Nankin, Kaubul, Cairo!

You benighted roamer of Amazonia! you Patagonian! you Feejee-man!

I do not prefer others so very much before you either,
I do not say one word against you, away back there where you
    stand,
(You will come forward in due time to my side.)

13

My spirit has pass'd in compassion and determination around the
    whole earth,
I have look'd for equals and lovers and found them ready for me
    in all lands,
I think some divine rapport has equalized me with them.

You vapors, I think I have risen with you, moved away to distant
    continents, and fallen down there, for reasons,
I think I have blown with you you winds;
You waters I have finger'd every shore with you,
I have run through what any river or strait of the globe has run
    through,
I have taken my stand on the bases of peninsulas and on the high
    embedded rocks, to cry thence:

Salut au monde!
What cities the light or warmth penetrates I penetrate those cities
    myself,
All islands to which birds wing their way I wing my way myself.

Toward you all, in America's name,
I raise high the perpendicular hand, I make the signal,
To remain after me in sight forever,
For all the haunts and homes of men.

Song of the Open Road

1

AFOOT and light-hearted I take to the open road,
Healthy, free, the world before me,
The long brown path before me leading wherever I choose.

Henceforth I ask not good-fortune, I myself am good-fortune,
Henceforth I whimper no more, postpone no more, need nothing,
Done with indoor complaints, libraries, querulous criticisms,
Strong and content I travel the open road.

The earth, that is sufficient,
I do not want the constellations any nearer,
I know they are very well where they are,
I know they suffice for those who belong to them.

(Still here I carry my old delicious burdens,
I carry them, men and women, I carry them with me wherever I go,
I swear it is impossible for me to get rid of them,
I am fill'd with them, and I will fill them in return.)

2

You road I enter upon and look around, I believe you are not all
    that is here,
I believe that much unseen is also here.

Here the profound lesson of reception, nor preference nor denial,
The black with his woolly head, the felon, the diseas'd, the illiterate
    person, are not denied;
The birth, the hasting after the physician, the beggar's tramp, the
    drunkard's stagger, the laughing party of mechanics,
The escaped youth, the rich person's carriage, the fop, the eloping
    couple,
The early market-man, the hearse, the moving of furniture into the
    town, the return back from the town,
They pass, I also pass, any thing passes, none can be interdicted,
None but are accepted, none but shall be dear to me.

3

You air that serves me with breath to speak!
You objects that call from diffusion my meanings and give them
    shape!
You light that wraps me and all things in delicate equable showers!
You paths worn in the irregular hollows by the roadsides!
I believe you are latent with unseen existences, you are so dear
    to me.

You flagg'd walks of the cities! you strong curbs at the edges!
You ferries! you planks and posts of wharves! you timber-lined
    sides! you distant ships!
You rows of houses! you window-pierc'd façades! you roofs!
You porches and entrances! you copings and iron guards!

You windows whose transparent shells might expose so much!
You doors and ascending steps! you arches!
You gray stones of interminable pavements! you trodden crossings!
From all that has touch'd you I believe you have imparted to
      yourselves, and now would impart the same secretly to me,
From the living and the dead you have peopled your impassive
      surfaces, and the spirits thereof would be evident and amicable
      with me.

4

The earth expanding right hand and left hand,
The picture alive, every part in its best light,
The music falling in where it is wanted, and stopping where it is
      not wanted,
The cheerful voice of the public road, the gay fresh sentiment of
      the road.

O highway I travel, do you say to me *Do not leave me?*
Do you say *Venture not—if you leave me you are lost?*
Do you say *I am already prepared, I am well-beaten and undenied,
      adhere to me?*

O public road, I say back I am not afraid to leave you, yet I love
      you,
You express me better than I can express myself,
You shall be more to me than my poem.

I think heroic deeds were all conceiv'd in the open air, and all
      free poems also,
I think I could stop here myself and do miracles,
I think whatever I shall meet on the road I shall like, and whoever
      beholds me shall like me,
I think whoever I see must be happy.

5

From this hour I ordain myself loos'd of limits and imaginary
      lines,
Going where I list, my own master total and absolute,
Listening to others, considering well what they say,
Pausing, searching, receiving, contemplating,
Gently, but with undeniable will, divesting myself of the holds
      that would hold me.

I inhale great draughts of space,
The east and the west are mine, and the north and the south are
      mine.

I am larger, better than I thought,
I did not know I held so much goodness.

All seems beautiful to me,
I can repeat over to men and women You have done such good
      to me I would do the same to you,
I will recruit for myself and you as I go,
I will scatter myself among men and women as I go,
I will toss a new gladness and roughness among them,
Whoever denies me it shall not trouble me,
Whoever accepts me he or she shall be blessed and shall bless me.

6

Now if a thousand perfect men were to appear it would not amaze
      me,
Now if a thousand beautiful forms of women appear'd it would
      not astonish me.

Now I see the secret of the making of the best persons,
It is to grow in the open air and to eat and sleep with the earth.

Here a great personal deed has room,
(Such a deed seizes upon the hearts of the whole race of men,
Its effusion of strength and will overwhelms law and mocks all
      authority and all argument against it.)

Here is the test of wisdom,
Wisdom is not finally tested in schools,
Wisdom cannot be pass'd from one having it to another not having
      it,
Wisdom is of the soul, is not suspectible of proof, is its own proof,
Applies to all stages and objects and qualities and is content,
Is the certainty of the reality and immortality of things, and the
      excellence of things;
Something there is in the float of the sight of things that provokes
      it out of the soul.

Now I re-examine philosophies and religions,
They may prove well in lecture-rooms, yet not prove at all under
     the spacious clouds and along the landscape and flowing
     currents.

Here is realization,
Here is a man tallied—he realizes here what he has in him,
The past, the future, majesty, love—if they are vacant of you, you
     are vacant of them.

Only the kernel of every object nourishes;
Where is he who tears off the husks for you and me?
Where is he that undoes stratagems and envelopes for you and me?

Here is adhesiveness, it is not previously fashion'd, it is apropos;
Do you know what it is as you pass to be loved by strangers?
Do you know the talk of those turning eye-balls?

7

Here is the efflux of the soul,
The efflux of the soul comes from within through embower'd gates,
     ever provoking questions,
These yearnings why are they? these thoughts in the darkness why
     are they?
Why are there men and women that while they are nigh me the
     sunlight expands my blood?
Why when they leave me do my pennants of joy sink flat and lank?
Why are there trees I never walk under but large and melodious
     thoughts descend upon me?
(I think they hang there winter and summer on those trees and
     always drop fruit as I pass;)
What is it I interchange so suddenly with strangers?
What with some driver as I ride on the seat by his side?
What with some fisherman drawing his seine by the shore as I
     walk by and pause?
What gives me to be free to a woman's and man's good-will? what
     gives them to be free to mine?

8

The efflux of the soul is happiness, here is happiness,
I think it pervades the open air, waiting at all times,
Now it flows unto us, we are rightly charged.

Here rises the fluid and attaching character,
The fluid and attaching character is the freshness and sweetness
    of man and woman,
(The herbs of the morning sprout no fresher and sweeter every
    day out of the roots of themselves, than it sprouts fresh and
    sweet continually out of itself.)
Toward the fluid and attaching character exudes the sweat of the
    love of young and old,
From it falls distill'd the charm that mocks beauty and attainments,
Toward it heaves the shuddering longing ache of contact.

9

Allons! whoever you are come travel with me!
Traveling with me you find what never tires.

The earth never tires,
The earth is rude, silent, incomprehensible at first, Nature is rude
    and incomprehensible at first,
Be not discouraged, keep on, there are divine things well envelop'd,
I swear to you there are divine things more beautiful than words
    can tell.

Allons! we must not stop here,
However sweet these laid-up stores, however convenient this dwell-
    ing we cannot remain here,
However shelter'd this port and however calm these waters we
    must not anchor here,
However welcome the hospitality that surrounds us we are per-
    mitted to receive it but a little while.

10

Allons! the inducements shall be greater,
We will sail pathless and wild seas,
We will go where winds blow, waves dash, and the Yankee clipper
    speeds by under full sail.

Allons! with power, liberty, the earth, the elements,
Health, defiance, gayety, self-esteem, curiosity;
Allons! from all formules!
From your formules, O bat-eyed and materialistic priests.

The stale cadaver blocks up the passage—the burial waits no
    longer.

Allons! yet take warning!
He traveling with me needs the best blood, thews, endurance.
None may come to the trial till he or she bring courage and health,
Come not here if you have already spent the best of yourself,
Only those may come who come in sweet and determin'd bodies,
No diseas'd person, no rum-drinker or veneral taint is permitted
    here.

(I and mine do not convince by arguments, similes, rhymes,
We convince by our presence.)

11

Listen! I will be honest with you,
I do not offer the old smooth prizes, but offer rough new prizes,
These are the days that must happen to you:
You shall not heap up what is call'd riches,
You shall scatter with lavish hand all that you earn or achieve,
You but arrive at the city to which you were destin'd, you hardly
    settle yourself to satisfaction before you are call'd by an
    irresistible call to depart,
You shall be treated to the ironical smiles and mockings of those
    who remain behind you,
What beckonings of love you receive you shall only answer with
    passionate kisses of parting,
You shall not allow the hold of those who spread their reach'd
    hands toward you.

12

Allons! after the great Companions, and to belong to them!
They too are on the road—they are the swift and majestic men—
    they are the greatest women,
Enjoyers of calms of seas and storms of seas,
Sailors of many a ship, walkers of many a mile of land,
Habituès of many distant countries, habituès of far-distant dwellings,
Trusters of men and women, observers of cities, solitary toilers,
Pausers and contemplators of tufts, blossoms, shells of the shore,
Dancers at wedding-dances, kissers of brides, tender helpers of
    children, bearers of children,

Soldiers of revolts, standers by gaping graves, lowerers-down of
    coffins,
Journeyers over consecutive seasons, over the years, the curious
    years each emerging from that which preceded it,
Journeyers as with companions, namely their own diverse phases,
Forth-steppers from the latent unrealized baby-days,
Journeyers gayly with their own youth, journeyers with their
    bearded and well-grain'd manhood,
Journeyers with their womanhood, ample, unsurpass'd, content,
Journeyers with their own sublime old age of manhood or woman-
    hood,
Old age, calm, expanded, broad with the haughty breadth of the
    universe,
Old age, flowing free with the delicious near-by freedom of death.

13

Allons! to that which is endless as it was beginningless,
To undergo much, tramps of days, rests of nights,
To merge all in the travel they tend to, and the days and nights
    they tend to,
Again to merge them in the start of superior journeys,
To see nothing anywhere but what you may reach it and pass it,
To conceive no time, however distant, but what you may reach it
    and pass it,
To look up or down no road but it stretches and waits for you,
    however long but it stretches and waits for you,
To see no being, not God's or any, but you also go thither,
To see no possession but you may possess it, enjoying all without
    labor or purchase, abstracting the feast yet not abstracting
    one particle of it,
To take the best of the farmer's farm and the rich man's elegant
    villa, and the chaste blessing of the well-married couple, and
    the fruits of orchards and flowers of gardens,
To take to your use out of the compact cities as you pass through,
To carry buildings and streets with you afterward wherever you go,
To gather the minds of men out of their brains as you encounter
    them, to gather the love out of their hearts,
To take your lovers on the road with you, for all that you leave
    them behind you,
To know the universe itself as a road, as many roads, as roads for
    traveling souls.

All parts away for the progress of souls,
All religion, all solid things, arts, governments—all that was or is
    apparent upon this globe or any globe, falls into niches and
    corners before the procession of souls along the grand roads
    of the universe.

Of the progress of the souls of men and women along the grand
    roads of the universe, all other progress is the needed emblem
    and sustenance.

Forever alive, forever forward,
Stately, solemn, sad, withdrawn, baffled, mad, turbulent, feeble,
    dissatisfied,
Desperate, proud, fond, sick, accepted by men, rejected by men,
They go! they go! I know that they go, but I know not where
    they go,
But I know that they go toward the best—toward something
    great.

Whoever you are, come forth! or man or woman come forth!
You must not stay sleeping and dallying there in the house, though
    you built it, or though it has been built for you.

Out of the dark confinement! out from behind the screen!
It is useless to protest, I know all and expose it.

Behold through you as bad as the rest,
Through the laughter, dancing, dining, supping, of people,
Inside of dresses and ornaments, inside of those wash'd and
    trimm'd faces,
Behold a secret silent loathing and despair.

No husband, no wife, no friend, trusted to hear the confession,
Another self, a duplicate of every one, skulking and hiding it goes,
Formless and wordless through the streets of the cities, polite and
    bland in the parlors,
In the cars of railroads, in steamboats, in the public assembly,
Home to the houses of men and women, at the table, in the bed-
    room, everywhere,
Smartly attired, countenance smiling, form upright, death under
    the breast-bones, hell under the skull-bones,
Under the broadcloth and gloves, under the ribbons and artificial
    flowers,

Keeping fair with the customs, speaking not a syllable of itself,
Speaking of any thing else but never of itself.

14

Allons! through struggles and wars!
The goal that was named cannot be countermanded.

Have the past struggles succeeded?
What has succeeded? yourself? your nation? Nature?
Now understand me well—it is provided in the essence of things
    that from any fruition of success, no matter what, shall come
    forth something to make a greater struggle necessary.

My call is the call of battle, I nourish active rebellion,
He going with me must go well arm'd
He going with me goes often with spare diet, poverty, angry ene-
    mies, desertions.

15

Allons! the road is before us!
It is safe—I have tried it—my own feet have tried it well—be
    not detain'd!
Let the paper remain on the desk unwritten, and the book on the
    shelf unopen'd!
Let the tools remain in the workshop! let the money remain un-
    earn'd!
Let the school stand! mind not the cry of the teacher!
Let the preacher preach in his pulpit! let the lawyer plead in the
    court, and the judge expound the law.

Camerado, I give you my hand!
I give you my love more precious than money,
I give you myself before preaching or law;
Will you give me yourself? will you come travel with me?
Shall we stick by each other as long as we live?

Crossing Brooklyn Ferry

1

FLOOD-TIDE below me! I see you face to face!
Clouds of the west—sun there half an hour high—I see you also
    face to face.

Crowds of men and women attired in the usual costumes, how
    curious you are to me!
On the ferry-boats the hundreds and hundreds that cross, return-
    ing home, are more curious to me than you suppose,
And you that shall cross from shore to shore years hence are more
    to me, and more in my meditations, than you might suppose.

2

The impalpable sustenance of me from all things at all hours of
    the day,
The simple, compact, well-join'd scheme, myself disintegrated,
    every one disintegrated yet part of the scheme,
The similitudes of the past and those of the future,
The glories strung like beads on my smallest sights and hearings,
    on the walk in the street and the passage over the river,
The current rushing so swiftly and swimming with me far away,
The others that are to follow me, the ties between me and them,
The certainty of others, the life, love, sight, hearing of others.

Others will enter the gates of the ferry and cross from shore to
    shore,
Others will watch the run of the flood-tide,
Others will see the shipping of Manhattan north and west, and
    the heights of Brooklyn to the south and east,
Others will see the islands large and small;
Fifty years hence, others will see them as they cross, the sun half
    an hour high,
A hundred years hence, or ever so many hundred years hence,
    others will see them,
Will enjoy the sunset, the pouring-in of the flood-tide, the falling-
    back to the sea of the ebb-tide.

3

It avails not, time nor place—distance avails not,
I am with you, you men and women of a generation, or ever so
    many generations hence,
Just as you feel when you look on the river and sky, so I felt,
Just as any of you is one of a living crowd, I was one of a crowd,
Just as you are refresh'd by the gladness of the river and the bright
    flow, I was refresh'd,
Just as you stand and lean on the rail, yet hurry with the swift
    current, I stood yet was hurried,

Just as you look on the numberless masts of ships and the thick-
    stemm'd pipes of steamboats, I look'd.

I too many and many a time cross'd the river of old,
Watched the Twelfth-month sea-gulls, saw them high in the air
    floating with motionless wings, oscillating their bodies,
Saw how the glistening yellow lit up parts of their bodies and left
    the rest in strong shadow,
Saw the slow-wheeling circles and the gradual edging toward the
    south,
Saw the reflection of the summer sky in the water,
Had my eyes dazzled by the shimmering track of beams,
Look'd at the fine centrifugal spokes of light round the shape of
    my head in the sunlit water,
Look'd on the haze on the hills southward and south-westward,
Look'd on the vapor as it flew in fleeces tinged with violet,
Look'd toward the lower bay to notice the vessels arriving,
Saw their approach, saw aboard those that were near me,
Saw the white sails of schooners and sloops, saw the ships at anchor,
The sailors at work in the rigging or out astride the spars,
The round masts, the swinging motion of the hulls, the slender
    serpentine pennants,
The large and small steamers in motion, the pilots in their pilot-
    houses,
The white wake left by the passage, the quick tremulous whirl of
    the wheels,
The flags of all nations, the falling of them at sunset,
The scallop-edged waves in the twilight, the ladled cups, the frolic-
    some crests and glistening,
The stretch afar growing dimmer and dimmer, the gray walls of
    the granite storehouses by the docks,
On the river the shadowy group, the big steam-tug closely flank'd
    on each side by the barges, the hay-boat, the belated lighter,
On the neighboring shore the fires from the foundry chimneys
    burning high and glaringly into the night,
Casting their flicker of black contrasted with wild red and yellow
    light over the tops of houses, and down into the clefts of streets.

4

These and all else were to me the same as they are to you,
I loved well those cities, loved well the stately and rapid river,
The men and women I saw were all near to me,

Others the same—others who look back on me because I look'd
    forward to them,
(The time will come, though I stop here to-day and to-night.)

5

What is it then between us?
What is the count of the scores or hundreds of years between us?

Whatever it is, it avails not—distance avails not, and place avails
    not,
I too lived, Brooklyn of ample hills was mine,
I too walk'd the streets of Manhattan island, and bathed in the
    waters around it,
I too felt the curious abrupt questionings stir within me,
In the day among crowds of people sometimes they came upon me,
In my walks home late at night or as I lay in my bed they came
    upon me,
I too had been struck from the float forever held in solution,
I too had receiv'd identity by my body,
That I was I knew was of my body, and what I should be I knew
    I should be of my body.

6

It is not upon you alone the dark patches fall,
The dark threw its patches down upon me also,
The best I had done seem'd to me blank and suspicious,
My great thoughts as I supposed them, were they not in reality
    meagre?
Nor is it you alone who know what it is to be evil,
I am he who knew what it was to be evil,
I too knitted the old knot of contrariety,
Blabb'd, blush'd, resented, lied, stole, grudg'd,
Had guile, anger, lust, hot wishes I dared not speak,
Was wayward, vain, greedy, shallow, sly, cowardly, malignant,
The wolf, the snake, the hog, not wanting in me,
The cheating look, the frivolous word, the adulterous wish, not
    wanting,
Refusals, hates, postponements, meanness, laziness, none of these
    wanting,
Was one with the rest, the days and haps of the rest,
Was call'd by my nighest name by clear loud voices of young men
    as they saw me approaching or passing,

Felt their arms on my neck as I stood, or the negligent leaning of
    their flesh against me as I sat,
Saw many I loved in the street or ferry-boat or public assembly,
    yet never told them a word,
Lived the same life with the rest, the same old laughing, gnawing,
    sleeping,
Play'd the part that still looks back on the actor or actress,
The same old role, the role that is what we make it, as great as we
    like,
Or as small as we like, or both great and small.

7

Closer yet I approach you,
What thought you have of me now, I had as much of you—I laid
    in my stores in advance,
I consider'd long and seriously of you before you were born.

Who was to know what should come home to me?
Who knows but I am enjoying this?
Who knows, for all the distance, but I am as good as looking at
    you now, for all you cannot see me?

8

Ah, what can ever be more stately and admirable to me than mast-
    hemm'd Manhattan?
River and sunset and scallop-edg'd waves of flood-tide?
The sea-gulls oscillating their bodies, the hay-boat in the twilight,
    and the belated lighter?

What gods can exceed these that clasp me by the hand, and with
    voices I love call me promptly and loudly by my nighest name
    as I approach?
What is more subtle than this which ties me to the woman or man
    that looks in my face?
Which fuses me into you now, and pours my meaning into you?

We understand then do we not?
What I promis'd without mentioning it, have you not accepted?
What the study could not teach—what the preaching could not
    accomplish is accomplish'd, is it not?

9

Flow on, river! flow with the flood-tide, and ebb with the ebb-tide!
Frolic on, crested and scallop-edg'd waves!

Gorgeous clouds of the sunset! drench with your splendor me, or
    the men and women generations after me!
Cross from shore to shore, countless crowds of passengers!
Stand up, tall masts of Mannahatta! stand up, beautiful hills of
    Brooklyn!
Throb, baffled and curious brain! throw out questions and answers!
Suspend here and everywhere, eternal float of solution!
Gaze, loving and thirsting eyes, in the house or street or public
    assembly!
Sound out, voices of young men! loudly and musically call me by
    my nighest name!
Live, old life! play the part that looks back on the actor or actress!
Play the old role, the role that is great or small according as one
    makes it!
Consider, you who peruse me, whether I may not in unknown
    ways be looking upon you;
Be firm, rail over the river, to support those who lean idly, yet
    haste with the hasting current;
Fly on, sea-birds! fly sideways, or wheel in large circles high in
    the air;
Receive the summer sky, you water, and faithfully hold it till all
    downcast eyes have time to take it from you!
Diverge, fine spokes of light, from the shape of my head, or any
    one's head, in the sunlit water!
Come on, ships from the lower bay! pass up or down, white-sail'd
    schooners, sloops, lighters!
Flaunt away, flags of all nations! be duly lower'd at sunset!
Burn high your fires, foundry chimneys! cast black shadows at
    nightfall! cast red and yellow light over the tops of the houses!
Appearances, now or henceforth, indicate what you are,
You necessary film, continue to envelop the soul,
About my body for me, and your body for you, be hung our di-
    vinest aromas,
Thrive, cities—bring your freight, bring your shows, ample and
    sufficient rivers,
Expand, being than which none else is perhaps more spiritual,
Keep your places, objects than which none else is more lasting.

You have waited, you always wait, you dumb, beautiful ministers,
We receive you with free sense at last, and are insatiate hence-
    forward,
Not you any more shall be able to foil us, or withhold yourselves
    from us,

We use you, and do not cast you aside—we plant you permanently within us,
We fathom you not—we love you—there is perfection in you also,
You furnish your parts toward eternity,
Great or small, you furnish your parts toward the soul.

Song of the Answerer

1

Now list to my morning's romanza, I tell the signs of the Answerer,
To the cities and farms I sing as they spread in the sunshine before me.

A young man comes to me bearing a message from his brother,
How shall the young man know the whether and when of his brother?
Tell him to send me the signs.

And I stand before the young man face to face, and take his right hand in my left hand and his left hand in my right hand,
And I answer for his brother and for men, and I answer for him that answers for all, and send these signs.

Him all wait for, him all yield up to, his word is decisive and final,
Him they accept, in him lave, in him perceive themselves as amid light,
Him they immerse and he immerses them.

Beautiful women, the haughtiest nations, laws, the landscape, people, animals,
The profound earth and its attributes and the unquiet ocean, (so tell I my morning's romanza,)
All enjoyments and properties and money, and whatever money will buy,
The best farms, others toiling and planting and he unavoidably reaps,
The noblest and costliest cities, others grading and building and he domiciles there,
Nothing for any one but what is for him, near and far are for him, the ships in the offing,
The perpetual shows and marches on land are for him if they are for anybody.

He puts things in their attitudes,
He puts to-day out of himself with plasticity and love,
He places his own times, reminiscences, parents, brothers and
    sisters, associations, employment, politics, so that the rest never
    shame them afterward, nor assume to command them.

He is the Answerer,
What can be answer'd he answers, and what cannot be answer'd
    he shows how it cannot be answer'd.

A man is a summons and challenge,
(It is vain to skulk—do you hear that mocking and laughter? do
    you hear the ironical echoes?)

Books, friendships, philosophers, priests, action, pleasure, pride,
    beat up and down seeking to give satisfaction,
He indicates the satisfaction, and indicates them that beat up and
    down also.

Whichever the sex, whatever the season or place, he may go freshly
    and gently and safely by day or by night,
He has the pass-key of hearts, to him the response of the prying
    of hands on the knobs.

His welcome is universal, the flow of beauty is not more welcome
    or universal than he is,
The person he favors by day or sleeps with at night is blessed.

Every existence has its idiom, every thing has an idiom and tongue,
He resolves all tongues into his own and bestows it upon men, and
    any man translates, and any man translates himself also,
One part does not counteract another part, he is the joiner, he
    sees how they join.

He says indifferently and alike *How are you friend?* to the President
    at his levee,
And he says *Good-day my brother*, to Cudge that hoes in the sugar-
    field,
And both understand him and know that his speech is right.

He walks with perfect ease in the capitol,
He walks among the Congress, and one Representative says to
    another, *Here is our equal appearing and new.*

Then the mechanics take him for a mechanic,
And the soldiers suppose him to be a soldier, and the sailors that
 he has follow'd the sea,
And the authors take him for an author, and the artists for an
 artist,
And the laborers perceive he could labor with them and love them,
No matter what the work is, that he is the one to follow it or has
 follow'd it,
No matter what the nation, that he might find his brothers and
 sisters there.

The English believe he comes of their English stock,
A Jew to the Jew he seems, a Russ to the Russ, usual and near,
 removed from none.

Whoever he looks at in the traveler's coffee-house claims him,
The Italian or Frenchman is sure, the German is sure, the Spaniard
 is sure, and the island Cuban is sure,
The engineer, the deck-hand on the great lakes, or on the Mississippi or St. Lawrence or Sacramento, or Hudson or Paumanok sound, claims him.

The gentleman of perfect blood acknowledges his perfect blood,
The insulter, the prostitute, the angry person, the beggar, see themselves in the ways of him, he strangely transmutes them,
They are not vile any more, they hardly know themselves they are
 so grown.

2

The indications and tally of time,
Perfect sanity shows the master among philosophs,
Time, always without break, indicates itself in parts,
What always indicates the poet is the crowd of the pleasant com-
 pany of singers, and their words,
The words of the singers are the hours or minutes of the light or
 dark, but the words of the maker of poems are the general
 light and dark,
The maker of poems settles justice, reality, immortality,
His insight and power encircle things and the human race,
He is the glory and extract thus far of things and of the human race.

The singers do not beget, only the Poet begets,
The singers are welcom'd, understood, appear often enough, but
 rare has the day been, likewise the spot, of the birth of the
 maker of poems, the Answerer,

(Not every century nor every five centuries has contain'd such a
    day, for all its names.)

The singers of successive hours of centuries may have ostensible
    names, but the name of each of them is one of the singers,
The name of each is, eye-singer, ear-singer, head-singer, sweet-
    singer, night-singer, parlor-singer, love-singer, weird-singer, or
    something else.

All this time and at all times wait the words of true poems,
The words of true poems do not merely please,
The true poets are not followers of beauty but the august masters of
    beauty;
The greatness of sons is the exuding of the greatness of mothers and
    fathers,
The words of true poems are the tuft and final applause of science.

Divine instinct, breadth of vision, the law of reason, health, rudeness
    of body, withdrawnness,
Gayety, sun-tan, air-sweetness, such are some of the words of poems.

The sailor and traveler underlie the maker of poems, the Answerer,
The builder, geometer, chemist, anatomist, phrenologist, artist, all
    these underlie the maker of poems, the Answerer.

The words of the true poems give you more than poems,
They give you to form for yourself poems, religions, politics, war,
    peace, behavior, histories, essays, daily life, and every thing
    else,
They balance ranks, colors, races, creeds, and the sexes,
They do not seek beauty, they are sought,
Forever touching them or close upon them follows beauty, longing,
    fain, love-sick.

They prepare for death, yet are they not the finish, but rather the
    outset,
They bring none to his or her terminus or to be content and full,
Whom they take they take into space to behold the birth of stars,
    to learn one of the meanings,
To launch off with absolute faith, to sweep through the ceaseless
    rings and never be quiet again.

Our Old Feuillage

ALWAYS our old feuillage!

Always Florida's green peninsula—always the priceless delta of Louisiana—always the cotton-fields of Alabama and Texas,

Always California's golden hills and hollows, and the silver mountains of New Mexico—always soft-breath'd Cuba,

Always the vast slope drain'd by the Southern sea, inseparable with the slopes drain'd by the Eastern and Western seas,

The area the eighty-third year of these States, the three and a half millions of square miles,

The eighteen thousand miles of sea-coast and bay-coast on the main, the thirty thousand miles of river navigation,

The seven millions of distinct families and the same number of dwellings—always these, and more, branching forth into numberless branches,

Always the free range and diversity—always the continent of Democracy;

Always the prairies, pastures, forests, vast cities, travelers, Kanada, the snows;

Always these compact lands tied at the hips with the belt stringing the huge oval lakes;

Always the West with strong native persons, the increasing density there, the habitans, friendly, threatening, ironical, scorning invaders;

All sights, South, North, East—all deeds, promiscuously done at all times,

All characters, movements, growths, a few noticed, myriads unnoticed,

Through Mannahatta's streets I walking, these things gathering,

On interior rivers by night in the glare of pine knots, steamboats wooding up,

Sunlight by day on the valley of the Susquehanna, and on the valleys of the Potomac and Rappahannock, and the valleys of the Roanoke and Delaware,

In their northerly wilds beasts of prey haunting the Adirondacks the hills, or lapping the Saginaw waters to drink,

In a lonesome inlet a sheldrake lost from the flock, sitting on the water rocking silently,

In farmers' barns oxen in the stable, their harvest labor done, they rest standing, they are too tired,

Afar on arctic ice the she-walrus lying drowsily while her cubs play around,

137

The hawk sailing where men have not yet sail'd, the farthest polar
    sea, ripply, crystalline, open, beyond the floes,
White drift spooning ahead where the ship in the tempest dashes,
On solid land what is done in cities as the bells strike midnight
    together,
In primitive woods the sounds there also sounding, the howl of the
    wolf, the scream of the panther, and the hoarse bellow of the
    elk,
In winter beneath the hard blue ice of Moosehead lake, in summer
    visible through the clear waters, the great trout swimming,
In lower latitudes in warmer air in the Carolinas the large black
    buzzard floating slowly high beyond the tree tops,
Below, the red cedar festoon'd with tylandria, the pines and
    cypresses growing out of the white sand that spreads far and
    flat,
Rude boats descending the big Pedee, climbing plants, parasites
    with color'd flowers and berries enveloping huge trees,
The waving drapery on the live-oak trailing long and low, noise-
    lessly waved by the wind,
The camp of Georgia wagoners just after dark, the supper-fires
    and the cooking and eating by whites and negroes,
Thirty or forty great wagons, the mules, cattle, horses, feeding
    from troughs,
The shadows, gleams, up under the leaves of the old sycamore-
    trees, the flames with the black smoke from the pitch-pine
    curling and rising;
Southern fishermen fishing, the sounds and inlets of North Caro-
    lina's coast, the shad-fishery and the herring-fishery, the large
    sweep-seines the windlasses on shore work'd by horses, the
    clearing, curing, and packing-houses;
Deep in the forest in piney woods turpentine dropping from the
    incisions in the trees, there are the turpentine works,
There are the negroes at work in good health, the ground in all
    directions is cover'd with pine straw;
In Tennessee and Kentucky slaves busy in the coalings, at the
    forge, by the furnace-blaze, or at the corn-shucking,
In Virginia, the planter's son returning after a long absence, joy-
    fully welcom'd and kiss'd by the aged mulatto nurse,
On rivers boatmen safely moor'd at nightfall in their boats under
    shelter of high banks,
Some of the younger men dance to the sound of the banjo or
    fiddle, others sit on the gunwale smoking and talking;

Late in the afternoon the mocking-bird, the American mimic,
singing in the Great Dismal Swamp,
There are the greenish waters, the resinous odor, the plenteous
moss, the cypress-tree, and the juniper-tree;
Northward, young men of Mannahatta, the target company from
an excursion returning home at evening, the musket-muzzles
all bear bunches of flowers presented by women;
Children at play, or on his father's lap a young boy fallen asleep,
(how his lips move! how he smiles in his sleep!)
The scout riding on horseback over the plains west of the Mississippi, he ascends a knoll and sweeps his eyes around;
California life, the miner, bearded, dress'd in his rude costume,
the stanch California friendship, the sweet air, the graves one
in passing meets solitary just aside the horse-path;
Down in Texas the cotton-field, the negro-cabins, drivers driving
mules or oxen before rude carts, cotton bales piled on banks
and wharves;
Encircling all, vast-darting up and wide, the American Soul, with
equal hemispheres, one Love, one Dilation or Pride;
In arriere the peace-talk with the Iroquois the aborigines, the
calumet, the pipe of good-will, arbitration, and indorsement,
The sachem blowing the smoke first toward the sun and then
toward the earth,
The drama of the scalp-dance enacted with painted faces and
guttural exclamations,
The setting out of the war-party, the long and stealthy march,
The single file, the swinging hatchets, the surprise and slaughter
of enemies;
All the acts, scenes, ways, persons, attitudes of these States, remi-
niscences, institutions,
All these States compact, every square mile of these States without
excepting a particle;
Me pleas'd, rambling in lanes and country fields, Paumanok's
fields,
Observing the spiral flight of two little yellow butterflies shuffling
between each other, ascending high in the air,
The darting swallow, the destroyer of insects, the fall traveler
southward but returning northward early in the spring,
The country boy at the close of the day driving the herd of cows
and shouting to them as they loiter to browse by the road-side,
The city wharf, Boston, Philadelphia, Baltimore, Charleston, New
Orleans, San Francisco,

The departing ships when the sailors heave at the capstan;
Evening—me in my room—the setting sun,
The setting summer sun shining in my open window, showing the
    swarm of flies, suspended, balancing in the air in the centre of
    the room, darting athwart, up and down, casting swift shadows
    in specks on the opposite wall where the shine is;
The athletic American matron speaking in public to crowds of
    listeners,
Males, females, immigrants, combinations, the copiousness, the
    individuality of the States, each for itself—the money-makers,
Factories, machinery, the mechanical forces, the windlass, lever,
    pulley, all certainties,
The certainty of space, increase, freedom, futurity,
In space the sporades, the scatter'd islands, the stars—on the firm
    earth, the lands, my lands,
O lands! all so dear to me—what you are, (whatever it is,) I putting
    it at random in these songs, become a part of that, whatever
    it is,
Southward there, I screaming, with wings slow flapping, with the
    myriads of gulls wintering along the coasts of Florida,
Otherways there atwixt the banks of the Arkansaw, the Rio
    Grande, the Nueces, the Brazos, the Tombigbee, the Red
    River, the Saskatchawan, or the Osage I with the spring waters
    laughing and skipping and running,
Northward, on the sands, on some shallow bay of Paumanok, I
    with parties of snowy herons wading in the wet to seek worms
    and aquatic plants,
Retreating, triumphantly twittering, the king-bird, from piercing
    the crow with its bill, for amusement—and I triumphantly
    twittering,
The migrating flock of wild geese alighting in autumn to refresh
    themselves, the body of the flock feed, the sentinels outside
    move around with erect heads watching, and are from time
    to time reliev'd by other sentinels—and I feeding and taking
    turns with the rest,
In Kanadian forests the moose, large as an ox, corner'd by hunters,
    rising desperately on his hind-feet, and plunging with his
    fore-feet, the hoofs as sharp as knives—and I, plunging at
    the hunters, corner'd and desperate,
In the Mannahatta, streets, piers, shipping, store-houses, and the
    countless workmen working in the shops,
And I too of the Mannahatta, singing thereof—and no less in
    myself than the whole of the Mannahatta in itself,

Singing the song of These, my ever-united lands—my body no more inevitably united, part to part, and made out of a thousand diverse contributions one identity, any more than my lands are inevitably united and made ONE IDENTITY;

Nativities, climates, the grass of the great pastoral Plains,

Cities, labors, death, animals, products, war, good and evil—these me,

These affording, in all their particulars, the old feuillage to me and to America, how can I do less than pass the clew of the union of them, to afford the like to you?

Whoever you are! how can I but offer you divine leaves, that you also be eligible as I am?

How can I but as here chanting, invite you for yourself to collect bouquets of the incomparable feuillage of these States?

A Song of Joys

O TO make the most jubilant song!
Full of music—full of manhood, womanhood, infancy!
Full of common employments—full of grain and trees.

O for the voices of animals—O for the swiftness and balance of fishes!
O for the dropping of raindrops in a song!
O for the sunshine and motion of waves in a song!

O the joy of my spirit—it is uncaged—it darts like lightning!
It is not enough to have this globe or a certain time,
I will have thousands of globes and all time.

O the engineer's joys! to go with a locomotive!
To hear the hiss of steam, the merry shriek, the steam-whistle, the laughing locomotive!
To push with resistless way and speed off in the distance.

O the gleesome saunter over fields and hillsides!
The leaves and flowers of the commonest weeds, the moist fresh stillness of the woods,
The exquisite smell of the earth at daybreak, and all through the forenoon.

O the horseman's and horsewoman's joys!
The saddle, the gallop, the pressure upon the seat, the cool gurgling by the ears and hair.

O the fireman's joys!
I hear the alarm at dead of night,
I hear bells, shouts! I pass the crowd, I run!
The sight of the flames maddens me with pleasure.

O the joy of the strong-brawn'd fighter, towering in the arena in
    perfect condition, conscious of power, thirsting to meet his
    opponent.

O the joy of that vast elemental sympathy which only the human
    soul is capable of generating and emitting in steady and limit-
    less floods.

O the mother's joys!
The watching, the endurance, the precious love, the anguish, the
    patiently yielded life.

O the joy of increase, growth, recuperation,
The joy of soothing and pacifying, the joy of concord and harmony.

O to go back to the place where I was born,
To hear the birds sing once more,
To ramble about the house and barn and over the fields once more,
And through the orchard and along the old lanes once more.

O to have been brought up on bays, lagoons, creeks, or along the
    coast,
To continue and be employ'd there all my life,
The briny and damp smell, the shore, the salt weeds exposed at
    low water,
The work of fishermen, the work of the eel-fisher and clam-fisher;
I come with my clam-rake and spade, I come with my eel-spear,
Is the tide out? I join the group of clam-diggers on the flats,
I laugh and work with them, I joke at my work like a mettlesome
    young man;
In winter I take my eel-basket and eel-spear and travel out on foot
    on the ice—I have a small axe to cut holes in the ice,
Behold me well-clothed going gayly or returning in the afternoon,
    my brood of tough boys accompanying me,
My brood of grown and part-grown boys, who love to be with no
    one else so well as they love to be with me,
By day to work with me, and by night to sleep with me.

Another time in warm weather out in a boat, to lift the lobster-pots
 where they are sunk with heavy stones, (I know the buoys,)
O the sweetness of the Fifth-month morning upon the water as I
 row just before sunrise toward the buoys,
I pull the wicker pots up slantingly, the dark green lobsters are
 desperate with their claws as I take them out, I insert wooden
 pegs in the joints of their pincers,
I go to all the places one after another, and then row back to the
 shore,
There in a huge kettle of boiling water the lobsters shall be boil'd
 till their color becomes scarlet.

Another time mackerel-taking,
Voracious, mad for the hook, near the surface, they seem to fill the
 water for miles;
Another time fishing for rock-fish in Chesapeake bay, I one of the
 brown-faced crew;
Another time trailing for blue-fish off Paumanok, I stand with
 braced body,
My left foot is on the gunwale, my right arm throws far out the
 coils of slender rope,
In sight around me the quick veering and darting of fifty skiffs,
 my companions.

O boating on the rivers,
The voyage down the St. Lawrence, the superb scenery, the
 steamers,
The ships sailing, the Thousand Islands, the occasional timber-raft
 and the raftsmen with long-reaching sweep-oars,
The little huts on the rafts, and the stream of smoke when they
 cook supper at evening.

(O something pernicious and dread!
Something far away from a puny and pious life!
Something unproved! something in a trance!
Something escaped from the anchorage and driving free.)

O to work in mines, or forging iron,
Foundry casting, the foundry itself, the rude high roof, the ample
 and shadow'd space,
The furnace, the hot liquid pour'd out and running.

O to resume the joys of the soldier!

To feel the presence of a brave commanding officer—to feel his
    sympathy!
To behold his calmness—to be warm'd in the rays of his smile!
To go to battle—to hear the bugles play and the drums beat!
To hear the crash of artillery—to see the glittering of the bayonets
    and musket-barrels in the sun!
To see men fall and die and not complain!
To taste the savage taste of blood—to be so devilish!
To gloat so over the wounds and deaths of the enemy.

O the whaleman's joys! O I cruise my old cruise again!
I feel the ship's motion under me, I feel the Atlantic breezes fan-
    ning me,
I hear the cry again sent down from the mast-head, *There—she*
    blows!
Again I spring up the rigging to look with the rest—we descend,
    wild with excitement,
I leap in the lower'd boat, we row toward our prey where he lies,
We approach stealthy and silent, I see the mountainous mass,
    lethargic, basking,
I see the harpooneer standing up, I see the weapon dart from his
    vigorous arm;
O swift again far out in the ocean the wounded whale, settling,
    running to windward, tows me,
Again I see him rise to breathe, we row close again,
I see a lance driven through his side, press'd deep, turn'd in the
    wound,
Again we back off, I see him settle again, the life is leaving him
    fast,
As he rises he spouts blood, I see him swim in circles narrower
    and narrower, swiftly cutting the water—I see him die,
He gives one convulsive leap in the centre of the circle, and then
    falls flat and still in the bloody foam.

O the old manhood of me, my noblest joy of all!
My children and grand-children, my white hair and beard,
My largeness, calmness, majesty, out of the long stretch of my life.

O ripen'd joy of womanhood! O happiness at last!
I am more than eighty years of age, I am the most venerable mother,
How clear is my mind—how all people draw nigh to me!
What attractions are these beyond any before? what bloom more
    than the bloom of youth?
What beauty is this that descends upon me and rises out of me?

O the orator's joys!
To inflate the chest, to roll the thunder of the voice out from the
    ribs and throat,
To make the people rage, weep, hate, desire, with yourself,
To lead America—to quell America with a great tongue.

O the joy of my soul leaning pois'd on itself, receiving identity
    through materials and loving them, observing characters and
    absorbing them,
My soul vibrated back to me from them, from sight, hearing, touch,
    reason, articulation, comparison, memory, and the like,
The real life of my senses and flesh transcending my senses and flesh,
My body done with materials, my sight done with my material eyes,
Proved to me this day beyond cavil that it is not my material eyes
    which finally see,
Nor my material body which finally loves, walks, laughs, shouts,
    embraces, procreates.

O the farmer's joys!
Ohioan's, Illinoisian's, Wisconsinese', Kanadian's, Iowan's, Kan-
    sian's, Missourian's, Oregonese' joys!
To rise at peep of day and pass forth nimbly to work,
To plough land in the fall for winter-sown crops,
To plough land in the spring for maize,
To train orchards, to graft the trees, to gather apples in the fall.

O to bathe in the swimming-bath, or in a good place along shore,
To splash the water! to walk ankle-deep, or race naked along the
    shore.

O to realize space!
The plenteousness of all, that there are no bounds,
To emerge and be of the sky, of the sun and moon and flying clouds,
    as one with them.

O the joy of a manly self-hood!
To be servile to none, to defer to none, not to any tyrant known
    or unknown,
To walk with erect carriage, a step springy and elastic,
To look with calm gaze or with a flashing eye,
To speak with a full and sonorous voice out of a broad chest,
To confront with your personality all the other personalities of the
    earth.

Know'st thou the excellent joys of youth?
Joys of the dear companions and of the merry word and laughing
    face?
Joy of the glad light-beaming day, joy of the wild-breath'd games?
Joy of sweet music, joy of the lighted ball-room and the dancers?
Joy of the plenteous dinner, strong carouse and drinking?

Yet O my soul supreme!
Know'st thou the joys of pensive thought?
Joys of the free and lonesome heart, the tender, gloomy heart?
Joys of the solitary walk, the spirit bow'd yet proud, the suffering
    and the struggle?
The agonistic throes, the ecstasies, joys of the solemn musings day
    or night?
Joys of the thought of Death, the great spheres Time and Space?
Prophetic joys of better, loftier love's ideals, the divine wife, the
    sweet, eternal, perfect comrade?
Joys all thine own undying one, joys worthy thee O soul.

O while I live to be the ruler of life, not a slave,
To meet life as a powerful conqueror,
No fumes, no ennui, no more complaints or scornful criticisms,
To these proud laws of the air, the water and the ground, proving
    my interior soul impregnable,
And nothing exterior shall ever take command of me.

For not life's joys alone I sing, repeating—the joy of death!
The beautiful touch of Death, soothing and benumbing a few
    moments, for reasons,
Myself discharging my excrementitious body to be burn'd, or
    render'd to powder, or buried,
My real body doubtless left to me for other spheres,
My voided body nothing more to me, returning to the purifications,
    further offices, eternal uses of the earth.

O to attract by more than attraction!
How it is I know not—yet behold! the something which obeys
    none of the rest,
It is offensive, never defensive—yet how magnetic it draws.

O to struggle against great odds, to meet enemies undaunted!
To be entirely alone with them, to find how much one can stand!
To look strife, torture, prison, popular odium, face to face!

To mount the scaffold, to advance to the muzzles of guns with
  perfect nonchalance!
To be indeed a God!

O to sail to sea in a ship!
To leave this steady unendurable land,
To leave the tiresome sameness of the streets, the sidewalks and
  the houses,
To leave you O you solid motionless land, and entering a ship,
To sail and sail and sail!

O to have life henceforth a poem of new joys!
To dance, clap hands, exult, shout, skip, leap, roll on, float on!
To be a sailor of the world bound for all ports,
A ship itself, (see indeed these sails I spread to the sun and air,)
A swift and swelling ship full of rich words, full of joys.

Song of the Broad-Axe

1

WEAPON shapely, naked, wan,
Head from the mother's bowels drawn,
Wooded flesh and metal bone, limb only one and lip only one,
Gray-blue leaf by red-heat grown, helve produced from a little
  seed sown,
Resting the grass amid and upon,
To be lean'd and to lean on.

Strong shapes and attributes of strong shapes, masculine trades,
  sights and sounds,
Long varied train of an emblem, dabs of music,
Fingers of the organist skipping staccato over the keys of the
  great organ.

2

Welcome are all earth's lands, each for its kind,
Welcome are lands of pine and oak,
Welcome are lands of the lemon and fig,
Welcome are lands of gold,
Welcome are lands of wheat and maize, welcome those of the
  grape,
Welcome are lands of sugar and rice,

Welcome the cotton-lands, welcome those of the white potato and
    sweet potato,
Welcome are mountains, flats, sands, forests, prairies,
Welcome the rich borders of rivers, table-lands, openings,
Welcome the measureless grazing-lands, welcome the teeming soil
    of orchards, flax, honey, hemp;
Welcome just as much the other more hard-faced lands,
Lands rich as lands of gold or wheat and fruit lands,
Lands of mines, lands of the manly and rugged ores,
Lands of coal, copper, lead, tin, zinc,
Lands of iron—lands of the make of the axe.

3

The log at the wood-pile, the axe supported by it,
The sylvan hut, the vine over the doorway, the space clear'd for a
    garden,
The irregular tapping of rain down on the leaves after the storm
    is lull'd,
The wailing and moaning at intervals, the thought of the sea,
The thought of ships struck in the storm and put on their beam
    ends, and the cutting away of masts,
The sentiment of the huge timbers of old-fashion'd houses and
    barns,
The remember'd print or narrative, the voyage at a venture of
    men, families, goods,
The disembarkation, the founding of a new city,
The voyage of those who sought a New England and found it, the
    outset anywhere,
The settlements of the Arkansas, Colorado, Ottawa, Willamette,
The slow progress, the scant fare, the axe, rifle, saddle-bags;
The beauty of all adventurous and daring persons,
The beauty of wood-boys and wood-men with their clear un-
    trimm'd faces,
The beauty of independence, departure, actions that rely on them-
    selves,
The American contempt for statutes and ceremonies, the boundless
    impatience of restraint,
The loose drift of character, the inkling through random types,
    the solidification;
The butcher in the slaughter-house, the hands aboard schooners
    and sloops, the raftsman, the pioneer,
Lumbermen in their winter camp, daybreak in the woods, stripes
    of snow on the limbs of trees, the occasional snapping,

The glad clear sound of one's own voice, the merry song, the natural life of the woods, the strong day's work,

The blazing fire at night, the sweet taste of supper, the talk, the bed of hemlock-boughs and the bear-skin;

The house-builder at work in cities or anywhere,

The preparatory jointing, squaring, sawing, mortising,

The hoist-up of beams, the push of them in their places, laying them regular,

Setting the studs by their tenons in the mortises according as they were prepared,

The blows of mallets and hammers, the attitudes of the men, their curv'd limbs,

Bending, standing, astride the beams, driving in pins, holding on by posts and braces,

The hook'd arm over the plate, the other arm wielding the axe,

The floor-men forcing the planks close to be nail'd,

Their postures bringing their weapons downward on the bearers,

The echoes resounding through the vacant building;

The huge storehouse carried up in the city well under way,

The six framing-men, two in the middle and two at each end, carefully bearing on their shoulders a heavy stick for a cross-beam,

The crowded line of masons with trowels in their right hands rapidly laying the long side-wall, two hundred feet from front to rear,

The flexible rise and fall of backs, the continual click of the trowels striking the bricks,

The bricks one after another each laid so workmanlike in its place, and set with a knock of the trowel-handle,

The piles of materials, the mortar on the mortar-boards, and the steady replenishing by the hod-men;

Spar-makers in the spar-yard, the swarming row of well-grown apprentices,

The swing of their axes on the square-hew'd log shaping it toward the shape of a mast,

The brisk short crackle of the steel driven slantingly into the pine,

The butter-color'd chips flying off in great flakes and slivers,

The limber motion of brawny young arms and hips in easy costumes,

The constructor of wharves, bridges, piers, bulk-heads, floats, stays against the sea;

The city fireman, the fire that suddenly bursts forth in the close-pack'd square,

The arriving engines, the hoarse shouts, the nimble stepping and
    daring,
The strong command through the fire-trumpets, the falling in line,
    the rise and fall of the arms forcing the water,
The slender, spasmic, blue-white jets, the bringing to bear of the
    hooks and ladders and their execution,
The crash and cut away of connecting wood-work, or through
    floors if the fire smoulders under them,
The crowd with their lit faces watching, the glare and dense shadows;
The forger at his forge-furnace and the user of iron after him,
The maker of the axe large and small, and the welder and tem-
    perer,
The chooser breathing his breath on the cold steel and trying the
    edge with his thumb,
The one who clean-shapes the handle and sets it firmly in the
    socket;
The shadowy processions of the portraits of the past users also,
The primal patient mechanics, the architects and engineers,
The far-off Assyrian edifice and Mizra edifice,
The Roman lictors preceding the consuls,
The antique European warrior with his axe in combat,
The uplifted arm, the clatter of blows on the helmeted head,
The death-howl, the limpsy tumbling body, the rush of friend and
    foe thither,
The siege of revolted lieges determin'd for liberty,
The summons to surrender, the battering at castle gates, the truce
    and parley,
The sack of an old city in its time,
The bursting in of mercenaries and bigots tumultuously and dis-
    orderly,
Roar, flames, blood, drunkenness, madness,
Goods freely rifled from houses and temples, screams of women in
    the gripe of brigands,
Craft and thievery of camp-followers, men running, old persons
    despairing,
The hell of war, the cruelties of creeds,
The list of all executive deeds and words just or unjust,
The power of personality just or unjust.

4

Muscle and pluck forever!
What invigorates life invigorates death,

And the dead advance as much as the living advance,
And the future is no more uncertain than the present,
For the roughness of the earth and of man encloses as much as
    the delicatesse of the earth and of man,
And nothing endures but personal qualities.

What do you think endures?
Do you think a great city endures?
Or a teeming manufacturing state? or a prepared constitution? or
    the best built steamships?
Or hotels of granite and iron? or any chef-d'œuvres of engineering,
    forts, armaments?

Away! these are not to be cherish'd for themselves,
They fill their hour, the dancers dance, the musicians play for
    them,
The show passes, all does well enough of course,
All does very well till one flash of defiance.

A great city is that which has the greatest men and women,
If it be a few ragged huts it is still the greatest city in the whole
    world.

5

The place where a great city stands is not the place of stretch'd
    wharves, docks, manufactures, deposits of produce merely,
Nor the place of ceaseless salutes of new-comers or the anchor-
    lifters of the departing,
Nor the place of the tallest and costliest buildings or shops selling
    goods from the rest of the earth,
Nor the place of the best libraries and schools, nor the place where
    money is plentiest,
Nor the place of the most numerous population.

Where the city stands with the brawniest breed of orators and
    bards,
Where the city stands that is belov'd by these, and loves them in
    return and understands them,
Where no monuments exist to heroes but in the common words
    and deeds,
Where thrift is in its place, and prudence is in its place,
Where the men and women think lightly of the laws,
Where the slave ceases, and the master of slaves ceases,

Where the populace rise at once against the never-ending audacity
    of elected persons,
Where fierce men and women pour forth as the sea to the whistle
    of death pours its sweeping and unript waves,
Where outside authority enters always after the precedence of
    inside authority,
Where the citizen is always the head and ideal, and President,
    Mayor, Governor and what not, are agents for pay,
Where children are taught to be laws to themselves, and to depend
    on themselves,
Where equanimity is illustrated in affairs,
Where speculations on the soul are encouraged,
Where women walk in public processions in the streets the same
    as the men,
Where they enter the public assembly and take places the same as
    the men;
Where the city of the faithfulest friends stands,
Where the city of the cleanliness of the sexes stands,
Where the city of the healthiest fathers stands,
Where the city of the best-bodied mothers stands,
There the great city stands.

6

How beggarly appear arguments before a defiant deed!
How the floridness of the materials of cities shrivels before a man's
    or woman's look!

All waits or goes by default till a strong being appears;
A strong being is the proof of the race and of the ability of the
    universe,
When he or she appears materials are overaw'd,
The dispute on the soul stops,
The old customs and phrases are confronted, turn'd back, or laid
    away.

What is your money-making now? what can it do now?
What is your respectability now?
What are your theology, tuition, society, traditions, statute-books,
    now?
Where are your jibes of being now?
Where are your cavils about the soul now?

7

A sterile landscape covers the ore, there is as good as the best for
all the forbidding appearance,
There is the mine, there are the miners,
The forge-furnace is there, the melt is accomplish'd, the hammers-
men are at hand with their tongs and hammers,
What always served and always serves is at hand.

Than this nothing has better served, it has served all,
Served the fluent-tongued and subtle-sensed Greek, and long ere
the Greek,
Served in building the buildings that last longer than any,
Served the Hebrew, the Persian, the most ancient Hindustanee,
Served the mound-raiser on the Mississippi, served those whose
relics remain in Central America,
Served Albic temples in woods or on plains, with unhewn pillars
and the druids,
Served the artificial clefts, vast, high, silent, on the snow-cover'd
hills of Scandinavia,
Served those who time out of mind made on the granite walls
rough sketches of the sun, moon, stars, ships, ocean waves,
Served the paths of the irruptions of the Goths, served the pastoral
tribes and nomads,
Served the long distant Kelt, served the hardy pirates of the Baltic,
Served before any of those the venerable and harmless men of
Ethiopia,
Served the making of helms for the galleys of pleasure and the
making of those for war,
Served all great works on land and all great works on the sea,
For the mediæval ages and before the mediæval ages,
Served not the living only then as now, but served the dead.

8

I see the European headsman,
He stands mask'd, clothed in red, with huge legs and strong naked
arms,
And leans on a ponderous axe.

(Whom have you slaughter'd lately European headsman?
Whose is that blood upon you so wet and sticky?)

I see the clear sunsets of the martyrs,
I see from the scaffolds the descending ghosts,

Ghosts of dead lords, uncrown'd ladies, impeach'd ministers,
     rejected kings,
Rivals, traitors, poisoners, disgraced chieftains and the rest.

I see those who in any land have died for the good cause,
The seed is spare, nevertheless the crop shall never run out,
(Mind you O foreign kings, O priests, the crop shall never run out.)

I see the blood wash'd entirely away from the axe,
Both blade and helve are clean,
They spirt no more the blood of European nobles, they clasp no
     more the necks of queens.

I see the headsman withdraw and become useless,
I see the scaffold untrodden and mouldy, I see no longer any axe
     upon it,
I see the mighty and friendly emblem of the power of my own
     race, the newest, largest race.

9

(America! I do not vaunt my love for you,
I have what I have.)

The axe leaps!
The solid forest gives fluid utterances,
They tumble forth, they rise and form,
Hut, tent, landing, survey,
Flail, plough, pick, crowbar, spade,
Shingle, rail, prop, wainscot, jamb, lath, panel, gable,
Citadel, ceiling, saloon, academy, organ, exhibition-house, li-
     brary,
Cornice, trellis, pilaster, balcony, window, turret, porch,
Hoe, rake, pitchfork, pencil, wagon, staff, saw, jack-plane, mallet,
     wedge, rounce,
Chair, tub, hoop, table, wicket, vane, sash, floor,
Work-box, chest, string'd instrument, boat, frame, and what not,
Capitols of States, and capitol of the nation of States,
Long stately rows in avenues, hospitals for orphans or for the poor
     or sick,
Manhattan steamboats and clippers taking the measure of all seas.

The shapes arise!
Shapes of the using of axes anyhow, and the users and all that neigh-
     bors them,

Cutters down of wood and haulers of it to the Penobscot or Ken-
nebec,

Dwellers in cabins among the Californian mountains or by the little
lakes, or on the Columbia,

Dwellers south on the banks of the Gila or Rio Grande, friendly
gatherings, the characters and fun,

Dwellers along the St. Lawrence, or north in Kanada, or down by
the Yellowstone, dwellers on coasts and off coasts,

Seal-fishers, whalers, arctic seamen breaking passages through the
ice.

The shapes arise!

Shapes of factories, arsenals, foundries, markets,

Shapes of the two-threaded tracks of railroads,

Shapes of the sleepers of bridges, vast frameworks, girders, arches,

Shapes of the fleets of barges, tows, lake and canal craft, river craft,

Ship-yards and dry-docks along the Eastern and Western seas, and
in many a bay and by-place,

The live-oak kelsons, the pine planks, the spars, the hackmatack-
roots for knees,

The ships themselves on their ways, the tiers of scaffolds, the
workmen busy outside and inside,

The tools lying around, the great auger and the little auger, the adze,
bolt, line, square gouge, and bead-plane.

10

The shapes arise!

The shape measur'd, saw'd, jack'd, join'd, stain'd,

The coffin-shape for the dead to lie within in his shroud,

The shape got out in posts, in the bedstead posts, in the posts of
the bride's bed,

The shape of the little trough, the shape of the rockers beneath,
the shape of the babe's cradle,

The shape of the floor-planks, the floor-planks for dancers' feet,

The shape of the planks of the family home, the home of the
friendly parents and children,

The shape of the roof of the home of the happy young man and
woman, the roof over the well-married young man and woman,

The roof over the supper joyously cook'd by the chaste wife, and
joyously eaten by the chaste husband, content after his day's
work.

The shapes arise!
The shape of the prisoner's place in the court-room, and of him
    or her seated in the place,
The shape of the liquor-bar lean'd against by the young rum-
    drinker and the old rum-drinker,
The shape of the shamed and angry stairs trod by sneaking foot-
    steps,
The shape of the sly settee, and the adulterous unwholesome couple,
The shape of the gambling-board with its devilish winnings and
    losings,
The shape of the step-ladder for the convicted and sentenced
    murderer, the murderer with haggard face and pinion'd arms,
The sheriff at hand with his deputies, the silent and white-lipp'd
    crowd, the dangling of the rope.

The shapes arise!
Shapes of doors giving many exits and entrances,
The door passing the dissever'd friend flush'd and in haste,
The door that admits good news and bad news,
The door whence the son left home confident and puff'd up,
The door he enter'd again from a long and scandalous absence,
    diseas'd, broken down, without innocence, without means.

11

Her shape arises,
She less guarded than ever, yet more guarded than ever,
The gross and soil'd she moves among do not make her gross and
    soil'd,
She knows the thoughts as she passes, nothing is conceal'd from her,
She is none the less considerate or friendly therefor,
She is the best belov'd, it is without exception, she has no reason
    to fear and she does not fear,
Oaths, quarrels, hiccupp'd songs, smutty expressions, are idle to
    her as she passes,
She is silent, she is possess'd of herself, they do not offend her,
She receives them as the laws of Nature receive them, she is strong,
She too is a law of Nature—there is no law stronger than she is.

12

The main shapes arise!
Shapes of Democracy total, result of centuries,

Shapes ever projecting other shapes,
Shapes of turbulent manly cities,
Shapes of the friends and home-givers of the whole earth,
Shapes bracing the earth and braced with the whole earth.

Song of the Exposition

1

(Ah little recks the laborer,
How near his work is holding him to God,
The loving Laborer through space and time.)

After all not to create only, or found only,
But to bring perhaps from afar what is already founded,
To give it our own identity, average, limitless, free,
To fill the gross the torpid bulk with vital religious fire,
Not to repel or destroy so much as accept, fuse, rehabilitate,
To obey as well as command, to follow more than to lead,
These also are the lessons of our New World;
While how little the New after all, how much the Old, Old World!

Long and long has the grass been growing,
Long and long has the rain been falling,
Long has the globe been rolling round.

2

Come Muse migrate from Greece and Ionia,
Cross out please those immensely overpaid accounts,
That matter of Troy and Achilles' wrath, and Æneas', Odysseus'
    wanderings,
Placard "Removed" and "To Let" on the rocks of your snowy
    Parnassus,
Repeat at Jerusalem, place the notice high on Jaffa's gate and on
    Mount Moriah,
The same on the walls of your German, French and Spanish castles,
    and Italian collections,
For know a better, fresher, busier sphere, a wide, untried domain
    awaits, demands you.

3

Responsive to our summons,
Or rather to her long-nurs'd inclination,

Join'd with an irresistible, natural gravitation,
She comes! I hear the rustling of her gown,
I scent the odor of her breath's delicious fragrance,
I mark her step divine, her curious eyes a-turning, rolling,
Upon this very scene.

The dame of dames! can I believe then,
Those ancient temples, sculptures classic, could none of them
    retain her?
Nor shades of Virgil and Dante, nor myriad memories, poems,
    old associations, magnetize and hold on to her?
But that she's left them all—and here?

Yes, if you will allow me to say so,
I, my friends, if you do not, can plainly see her,
The same undying soul of earth's, activity's, beauty's, heroism's
    expression,
Out from her evolutions hither come, ended the strata of her
    former themes,
Hidden and cover'd by to-day's, foundation of to-day's,
Ended, deceas'd through time, her voice by Castaly's fountain,
Silent the broken-lipp'd Sphynx in Egypt, silent all those century-
    baffling tombs,
Ended for aye the epics of Asia's, Europe's helmeted warriors,
    ended the primitive call of the muses,
Calliope's call forever closed, Clio, Melpomene, Thalia dead,
Ended the stately rhythmus of Una and Oriana, ended the quest
    of the holy Graal,
Jerusalem a handful of ashes blown by the wind, extinct,
The Crusaders' streams of shadowy midnight troops sped with the
    sunrise,
Amadis, Tancred, utterly gone, Charlemagne, Roland, Oliver gone,
Palmerin, ogre, departed, vanish'd the turrets that Usk from its
    waters reflected,
Arthur vanish'd with all his knights, Merlin and Lancelot and
    Galahad, all gone, dissolv'd utterly like an exhalation;
Pass'd! pass'd! for us, forever pass'd, that once so mighty world,
    now void, inanimate, phantom world,
Embroider'd, dazzling, foreign world, with all its gorgeous legends,
    myths,
Its kings and castles proud, its priests and warlike lords and courtly
    dames,
Pass'd to its charnel vault, coffin'd with crown and armor on,

Blazon'd with Shakspere's purple page,
And dirged by Tennyson's sweet sad rhyme.

I say I see, my friends, if you do not, the illustrious emigré, (having
    it is true in her day, although the same, changed, journey'd
    considerable,)
Making directly for this rendezvous, vigorously clearing a path for
    herself, striding through the confusion,
By thud of machinery and shrill steam-whistle undismay'd,
Bluff'd not a bit by drain-pipe, gasometers, artificial fertilizers,
Smiling and pleas'd with palpable intent to stay,
She's here, install'd amid the kitchen ware!

4

But hold—don't I forget my manners?
To introduce the stranger, (what else indeed do I live to chant
    for?) to thee Columbia;
In liberty's name welcome immortal! clasp hands,
And ever henceforth sisters dear be both.

Fear not O Muse! truly new ways and days receive, surround you,
I candidly confess a queer, queer race, of novel fashion,
And yet the same old human race, the same within, without,
Faces and hearts the same, feelings the same, yearnings the same,
The same old love, beauty and use the same.

5

We do not blame thee elder World, nor really separate ourselves
    from thee,
(Would the son separate himself from the father?)
Looking back on thee, seeing thee to thy duties, grandeurs, through
    past ages bending, building,
We build to ours to-day.

Mightier than Egypt's tombs,
Fairer than Grecia's, Roma's temples,
Prouder than Milan's statued, spired cathedral,
More picturesque than Rhenish castle-keeps,
We plan even now to raise, beyond them all,
Thy great cathedral sacred industry, no tomb,
A keep for life for practical invention.

As in a waking vision,
E'en while I chant I see it rise, I scan and prophesy outside and in,
Its manifold ensemble.

Around a palace, loftier, fairer, ampler than any yet,
Earth's modern wonder, history's seven outstripping,
High rising tier on tier with glass and iron façades,
Gladdening the sun and sky, enhued in cheerfulest hues,
Bronze, lilac, robin's-egg, marine and crimson,
Over whose golden roof shall flaunt, beneath thy banner Freedom,
The banners of the States and flags of every land,
A brood of lofty, fair, but lesser palaces shall cluster.

Somewhere within their walls shall all that forwards perfect human
    life be started,
Tried, taught, advanced, visibly exhibited.

Not only all the world of works, trade, products,
But all the workmen of the world here to be represented.

Here shall you trace in flowing operation,
In every state of practical, busy movement, the rills of civilization,
Materials here under your eye shall change their shape as if by
    magic,
The cotton shall be pick'd almost in the very field,
Shall be dried, clean'd, ginn'd, baled, spun into thread and cloth
    before you,
You shall see hands at work at all the old processes and all the
    new ones,
You shall see the various grains and how flour is made and then
    bread baked by the bakers,
You shall see the crude ores of California and Nevada passing on
    and on till they become bullion,
You shall watch how the printer sets type, and learn what a com-
    posing-stick is,
You shall mark in amazement the Hoe press whirling its cylinders,
    shedding the printed leaves steady and fast,
The photograph, model, watch, pin, nail, shall be created before
    you.

In large calm halls, a stately museum shall teach you the infinite
    lessons of minerals,
In another, woods, plants, vegetation shall be illustrated—in
    another animals, animal life and development.

One stately house shall be the music house,
Others for other arts—learning, the sciences, shall all be here,
None shall be slighted, none but shall here be honor'd, help'd,
    exampled.

6

(This, this and these, America, shall be *your* pyramids and obelisks,
Your Alexandrian Pharos, gardens of Babylon,
Your temple at Olympia.)

The male and female many laboring not,
Shall ever here confront the laboring many,
With precious benefits to both, glory to all,
To thee America, and thee eternal Muse.

And here shall ye inhabit powerful Matrons!
In your vast state vaster than all the old,
Echoed through long, long centuries to come,
To sound of different, prouder songs, with stronger themes,
Practical, peaceful life, the people's life, the People themselves,
Lifted, illumin'd, bathed in peace—elate, secure in peace.

7

Away with themes of war! away with war itself!
Hence from my shuddering sight to never more return that show
    of blacken'd, mutilated corpses!
That hell unpent and raid of blood, fit for wild tigers or for lop-
    tongued wolves, not reasoning men,
And in its stead speed industry's campaigns,
With thy undaunted armies, engineering,
Thy pennants labor, loosen'd to the breeze,
Thy bugles sounding loud and clear.

Away with old romance!
Away with novels, plots and plays of foreign courts,
Away with love-verses sugar'd in rhyme, the intrigues, amours of
    idlers,
Fitted for only banquets of the night where dancers to late music
    slide,
The unhealthy pleasures, extravagant dissipations of the few,
With perfumes, heat and wine, beneath the dazzling chandeliers.

To you ye reverent sane sisters,
I raise a voice for far superber themes for poets and for art,
To exalt the present and the real,
To teach the average man the glory of his daily walk and trade,
To sing in songs how exercise and chemical life are never to be
    baffled,
To manual work for each and all, to plough, hoe, dig,
To plant and tend the tree, the berry, vegetables, flowers,
For every man to see to it that he really do something, for every
    woman too;
To use the hammer and the saw, (rip, or cross-cut),
To cultivate a turn for carpentering, plastering, painting,
To work as tailor, tailoress, nurse, hostler, porter,
To invent a little, something ingenious, to aid the washing, cooking,
    cleaning,
And hold it no disgrace to take a hand at them themselves.

I say I bring thee Muse to-day and here,
All occupations, duties broad and close,
Toil, healthy toil and sweat, endless, without cessation,
The old, old practical burdens, interests, joys,
The family, parentage, childhood, husband and wife,
The house-comforts, the house itself and all its belongings,
Food and its preservation, chemistry applied to it,
Whatever forms the average, strong, complete, sweet-blooded man
    or woman, the perfect longeve personality,
And helps its present life to health and happiness, and shapes its soul,
For the eternal real life to come.

With latest connections, works, the inter-transportation of the world,
Steam-power, the great express lines, gas, petroleum,
These triumphs of our time, the Atlantic's delicate cable,
The Pacific railroad, the Suez canal, the Mont Cenis and Gothard
    and Hoosac tunnels, the Brooklyn bridge,
This earth all spann'd with iron rails, with lines of steamships
    threading every sea,
Our own rondure, the current globe I bring.

8

And thou America,
Thy offspring towering e'er so high, yet higher Thee above all
    towering,

With Victory on thy left, and at thy right hand Law;
Thou Union holding all, fusing, absorbing, tolerating all,
Thee, ever thee, I sing.

Thou, also thou, a World,
With all thy wide geographies, manifold, different, distant,
Rounded by thee in one—one common orbic language,
One common indivisible destiny for All.

And by the spells which ye vouchsafe to those your ministers in
        earnest,
I here personify and call my themes, to make them pass before ye.

Behold, America! (and thou, ineffable guest and sister!)
For thee come trooping up thy waters and thy lands;
Behold! thy fields and farms, thy far-off woods and mountains,
As in procession coming.

Behold, the sea itself,
And on its limitless, heaving breast, the ships;
See, where their white sails, bellying in the wind, speckle the green
        and blue,
See, the steamers coming and going, steaming in or out of port,
See, dusky and undulating, the long pennants of smoke.

Behold, in Oregon, far in the north and west,
Or in Maine, far in the north and east, thy cheerful axemen,
Wielding all day their axes.

Behold, on the lakes, thy pilots at their wheels, thy oarsmen,
How the ash writhes under those muscular arms!

There by the furnace, and there by the anvil,
Behold thy sturdy blacksmiths swinging their sledges,
Overhand so steady, overhand they turn and fall with joyous clank,
Like a tumult of laughter.

Mark the spirit of invention everywhere, thy rapid patents,
Thy continual workshops, foundries, risen or rising,
See, from their chimneys how the tall flame-fires stream.

Mark, thy interminable farms, North, South,
Thy wealthy daughter-states, Eastern and Western,

The varied products of Ohio, Pennsylvania, Missouri, Georgia,
     Texas, and the rest,
Thy limitless crops, grass, wheat, sugar, oil, corn, rice, hemp, hops,
Thy barns all fill'd, the endless freight-train and the bulging store-
     house,
The grapes that ripen on thy vines, the apples in thy orchards,
Thy incalculable lumber, beef, pork, potatoes, thy coal, thy gold
     and silver,
The inexhaustible iron in thy mines.

All thine O sacred Union!
Ships, farms, shops, barns, factories, mines,
City and State, North, South, item and aggregate,
We dedicate, dread Mother, all to thee!

Protectress absolute, thou! bulwark of all!
For well we know that while thou givest each and all, (generous
     as God,)
Without thee neither all nor each, nor land, home,
Nor ship, nor mine, nor any here this day secure,
Nor aught, nor any day secure.

9

And thou, the Emblem waving over all!
Delicate beauty, a word to thee, (it may be salutary,)
Remember thou hast not always been as here to-day so comfortably
     ensovereign'd,
In other scenes than these have I observed thee flag,
Not quite so trim and whole and freshly blooming in folds of stain-
     less silk,
But I have seen thee bunting, to tatters torn upon thy splinter'd staff,
Or clutch'd to some young color-bearer's breast with desperate hands,
Savagely struggled for, for life or death, fought over long,
'Mid cannons' thunder-crash and many a curse and groan and yell,
     and rifle-volleys cracking sharp,
And moving masses as wild demons surging, and lives as nothing
     risk'd,
For thy mere remnant grimed with dirt and smoke and sopp'd in
     blood,
For sake of that, my beauty, and that thou might'st dally as now
     secure up there,
Many a good man have I seen go under.

Now here and these and hence in peace, all thine O Flag!
And here and hence for thee, O universal Muse! and thou for them!
And here and hence O Union, all the work and workmen thine!
None separate from thee—henceforth One only, we and thou,
(For the blood of the children, what is it, only the blood maternal?
And lives and works, what are they all at last, except the roads to
    faith and death?)

While we rehearse our measureless wealth, it is for thee, dear
    Mother,
We own it all and several to-day indissoluble in thee;
Think not our chant, our show, merely for products gross or lucre
    —it is for thee, the soul in thee, electric, spiritual!
Our farms, inventions, crops, we own in thee! cities and States in
    thee!
Our freedom all in thee! our very lives in thee!

Song of the Redwood-Tree

1

A CALIFORNIA song,
A prophecy and indirection, a thought impalpable to breathe as air
A chorus of dryads, fading, departing, or hamadryads departing,
A murmuring, fateful, giant voice, out of the earth and sky,
Voice of a mighty dying tree in the redwood forest dense.

Farewell my brethren,
Farewell O earth and sky, farewell ye neighboring waters,
My time has ended, my term has come.

Along the northern coast,
Just back from the rock-bound shore and the caves,
In the saline air from the sea in the Mendocino country,
With the surge for base and accompaniment low and hoarse,
With crackling blows of axes sounding musically driven by strong
    arms,
Riven deep by the sharp tongues of the axes, there in the redwood
    forest dense,
I heard the mighty tree its death-chant chanting.

The choppers heard not, the camp shanties echoed not,
The quick-ear'd teamsters and chain and jack-screw men heard
    not,

As the wood-spirits came from their haunts of a thousand years to
    join the refrain,
But in my soul I plainly heard.

Murmuring out of its myriad leaves,
Down from its lofty top rising two hundred feet high,
Out of its stalwart trunk and limbs, out of its foot-thick bark,
That chant of the seasons and time, chant not of the past only
    but the future.

You untold life of me,
And all you venerable and innocent joys,
Perennial hardy life of me with joys 'mid rain and many a summer
    sun,
And the white snows and night and the wild winds;
O the great patient rugged joys, my soul's strong joys unreck'd by
    man,
(For know I bear the soul befitting me, I too have consciousness,
    identity,
And all the rocks and mountains have, and all the earth,)
Joys of the life befitting me and brothers mine,
Our time, our term has come.

Nor yield we mournfully majestic brothers,
We who have grandly fill'd our time;
With Nature's calm content, with tacit huge delight,
We welcome what we wrought for through the past,
And leave the field for them.

For them predicted long,
For a superber race, they too to grandly fill their time,
For them we abdicate, in them ourselves ye forest kings!
In them these skies and airs, these mountain peaks, Shasta,
    Nevadas,
These huge precipitous cliffs, this amplitude, these valleys, far
    Yosemite,
To be in them absorb'd, assimilated.

Then to a loftier strain,
Still prouder, more ecstatic rose the chant,
As if the heirs, the deities of the West,
Joining with master-tongue bore part.

Not wan from Asia's fetiches,
Nor red from Europe's old dynastic slaughter-house,
(Area of murder-plots of thrones, with scent left yet of wars and
*   scaffolds everywhere,)*
But come from Nature's long and harmless throes, peacefully builded
*   thence,*
These virgin lands, lands of the Western shore,
To the new culminating man, to you, the empire new,
You promis'd long, we pledge, we dedicate.

You occult deep volitions,
You average spiritual manhood, purpose of all, pois'd on yourself,
*   giving not taking law,*
You womanhood divine, mistress and source of all, whence life and
*   love and aught that comes from life and love,*
You unseen moral essence of all the vast materials of America, (age
*   upon age working in death the same as life,)*
You that, sometimes known, oftener unknown, really shape and
*   mould the New World, adjusting it to Time and Space,*
You hidden national will lying in your abysms, conceal'd but ever
*   alert,*
You past and present purposes tenaciously pursued, may-be uncon-
*   scious of yourselves,*
Unswerv'd by all the passing errors, perturbations of the surface;
You vital, universal, deathless germs, beneath all creeds, arts,
*   statutes, literatures,*
Here build your homes for good, establish here, these areas entire,
*   lands of the Western shore,*
We pledge, we dedicate to you.

For man of you, your characteristic race,
Here may he hardy, sweet, gigantic grow, here tower proportionate
*   to Nature,*
Here climb the vast pure spaces unconfined, uncheck'd by wall or
*   roof,*
Here laugh with storm or sun, here joy, here patiently inure,
Here heed himself, unfold himself, (not others' formulas heed,) here
*   fill his time,*
To duly fall, to aid, unreck'd at last,
To disappear, to serve.

Thus on the northern coast,
In the echo of teamsters' calls and the clinking chains, and the
    music of choppers' axes,

The falling trunk and limbs, the crash, the muffled shriek, the
    groan,
Such words combined from the redwood-tree, as of voices ecstatic,
    ancient and rustling,
The century-lasting, unseen dryads, singing, withdrawing,
All their recesses of forests and mountains leaving,
From the Cascade range to the Wahsatch, or Idaho far, or Utah,
To the deities of the modern henceforth yielding,
The chorus and indications, the vistas of coming humanity, the
    settlements, features all,
In the Mendocino woods I caught.

2

The flashing and golden pageant of California,
The sudden and gorgeous drama, the sunny and ample lands,
The long and varied stretch from Puget sound to Colorado south,
Lands bathed in sweeter, rarer, healthier air, valleys and mountain
    cliffs,
The fields of Nature long prepared and fallow, the silent, cyclic
    chemistry,
The slow and steady ages plodding, the unoccupied surface ripen-
    ing, the rich ores forming beneath;
At last the New arriving, assuming, taking possession,
A swarming and busy race settling and organizing everywhere,
Ships coming in from the whole round world, and going out to
    the whole world,
To India and China and Australia and the thousand island para-
    dises of the Pacific,
Populous cities, the latest inventions, the steamers on the rivers,
    the railroads, with many a thrifty farm, with machinery,
And wool and wheat and the grape, and diggings of yellow gold.

3

But more in you than these, lands of the Western shore,
(These but the means, the implements, the standing-ground,)
I see in you, certain to come, the promise of thousands of years,
    till now deferr'd,
Promis'd to be fulfill'd, our common kind, the race.

The new society at last, proportionate to Nature,
In man of you, more than your mountain peaks or stalwart trees
    imperial,

In woman more, far more, than all your gold or vines, or even
    vital air.

Fresh come, to a new world indeed, yet long prepared,
I see the genius of the modern, child of the real and ideal,
Clearing the ground for broad humanity, the true America, heir
    of the past so grand,
To build a grander future.

A Song for Occupations

1

A SONG for occupations!
In the labor of engines and trades and the labor of fields I find
    the developments,
And find the eternal meanings.

Workmen and Workwomen!
Were all educations practical and ornamental well display'd out
    of me, what would it amount to?
Were I as the head teacher, charitable proprietor, wise statesman,
    what would it amount to?
Were I to you as the boss employing and paying you, would that
    satisfy you?

The learn'd, virtuous, benevolent, and the usual terms,
A man like me and never the usual terms.

Neither a servant nor a master I,
I take no sooner a large price than a small price, I will have my
    own whoever enjoys me,
I will be even with you and you shall be even with me.
If you stand at work in a shop I stand as nigh as the nighest in
    the same shop,
If you bestow gifts on your brother or dearest friend I demand as
    good as your brother or dearest friend,
If your lover, husband, wife, is welcome by day or night, I must
    be personally as welcome,
If you become degraded, criminal, ill, then I become so for your
    sake,

If you remember your foolish and outlaw'd deeds, do you think
    I cannot remember my own foolish and outlaw'd deeds?
If you carouse at the table I carouse at the opposite side of the
    table,
If you meet some stranger in the streets and love him or her, why
    I often meet strangers in the street and love them.

Why what have you thought of yourself?
Is it you then that thought yourself less?
Is it you that thought the President greater than you?
Or the rich better off than you? or the educated wiser than you?

Because you are greasy or pimpled, or were once drunk, or a
    thief,
Or that you are diseas'd, or rheumatic, or a prostitute,
Or from frivolity or impotence, or that you are no scholar and
    never saw your name in print,
Do you give in that you are any less immortal?)

2

Souls of men and women! it is not you I call unseen, unheard,
    untouchable and untouching,
It is not you I go argue pro and con about, and to settle whether
    you are alive or no,
I own publicly who you are if nobody else owns.

Grown, half-grown and babe, of this country and every country, in-
    doors and out-doors, one just as much as the other, I see,
And all else behind or through them.

The wife, and she is not one jot less than the husband,
The daughter, and she is just as good as the son,
The mother, and she is every bit as much as the father.

Offspring of ignorant and poor, boys apprenticed to trades,
Young fellows working on farms and old fellows working on farms,
Sailor-men, merchant-men, coasters, immigrants,
All these I see, but nigher and farther the same I see,
None shall escape me and none shall wish to escape me.

I bring what you much need yet always have,
Not money, amours, dress, eating, erudition, but as good,

I send no agent or medium, offer no representative of value, but offer the value itself.

There is something that comes to one now and perpetually,
It is not what is printed, preach'd, discussed, it eludes discussion and print,
It is not to be put in a book, it is not in this book,
It is for you whoever you are, it is no farther from you than your hearing and sight are from you,
It is hinted by nearest, commonest, readiest, it is ever provoked by them.

You may read in many languages, yet read nothing about it,
You may read the President's message and read nothing about it there,
Nothing in the reports from the State department or Treasury department, or in the daily papers or weekly papers,
Or in the census or revenue returns, prices current, or any accounts of stock.

3

The sun and stars that float in the open air,
The apple-shaped earth and we upon it, surely the drift of them is something grand,
I do not know what it is except that it is grand, and that it is happiness,
And that the enclosing purport of us here is not a speculation or bon-mot or reconnoissance,
And that it is not something which by luck may turn out well for us, and without luck must be a failure for us,
And not something which may yet be retracted in a certain contingency.

The light and shade, the curious sense of body and identity, the greed that with perfect complaisance devours all things,
The endless pride and outstretching of man, unspeakable joys and sorrows,
The wonder every one sees in every one else he sees, and the wonders that fill each minute of time forever,
What have you reckon'd them for, camerado?
Have you reckon'd them for your trade or farm-work? or for the profits of your store?
Or to achieve yourself a position? or to fill a gentleman's leisure, or a lady's leisure?

Have you reckon'd that the landscape took substance and form
    that it might be painted in a picture?
Or men and women that they might be written of, and songs sung?
Or the attraction of gravity, and the great laws and harmonious
    combinations and the fluids of the air, as subjects for the
    savans?
Or the brown land and the blue sea for maps and charts?
Or the stars to be put in constellations and named fancy names?
Or that the growth of seeds is for agricultural tables, or agriculture
    itself?

Old institutions, these arts, libraries, legends, collections, and the
    practice handed along in manufactures, will we rate them so
    high?
Will we rate our cash and business high? I have no objection,
I rate them as high as the highest—then a child born of a woman
    and man I rate beyond all rate.

We thought our Union grand, and our Constitution grand,
I do not say they are not grand and good, for they are,
I am this day just as much in love with them as you,
Then I am in love with You, and with all my fellows upon the
    earth.

We consider bibles and religions divine—I do not say they are not
    divine,
I say they have all grown out of you, and may grow out of you
    still,
It is not they who give the life, it is you who give the life,
Leaves are not more shed from the trees, or trees from the earth,
    than they are shed out of you.

4

The sum of all known reverence I add up in you whoever you are,
The President is there in the White House for you, it is not you
    who are here for him,
The Secretaries act in their bureaus for you, not you here for them,
The Congress convenes every Twelfth-month for you,
Laws, courts, the forming of States, the charters of cities, the going
    and coming of commerce and mails, are all for you.

List close my scholars dear,
Doctrines, politics and civilization exurge from you,

Sculpture and monuments and any thing inscribed anywhere are
tallied in you,
The gist of histories and statistics as far back as the records reach
is in you this hour and myths and tales the same,
If you were not breathing and walking here, where would they all
be?
The most renown'd poems would be ashes, orations and plays
would be vacuums.

All architecture is what you do to it when you look upon it,
(Did you think it was in the white or gray stone? or the lines of
the arches and cornices?)

All music is what awakes from you when you are reminded by the
instruments,
It is not the violins and the cornets, it is not the oboe nor the beating
drums, nor the score of the baritone singer singing his sweet
romanza, nor that of the men's chorus, nor that of the women's
chorus,
It is nearer and farther than they.

5

Will the whole come back then?
Can each see signs of the best by a look in the looking-glass? is
there nothing greater or more?
Does all sit there with you, with the mystic unseen soul?

Strange and hard that paradox true I give,
Objects gross and the unseen soul are one.

House-building, measuring, sawing the boards, .
Blacksmithing, glass-blowing, nail-making, coopering, tin-roofing,
shingle-dressing,
Ship-joining, dock-building, fish-curing, flagging of sidewalks by
flaggers,
The pump, the pile-driver, the great derrick, the coal-kiln and
brick-kiln,
Coal-mines and all that is down there, the lamps in the darkness,
echoes, songs, what meditations, what vast native thoughts
looking through smutch'd faces,
Iron-works, forge-fires in the mountains or by river-banks, men
around feeling the melt with huge crowbars, lumps of ore, the
due combining of ore, limestone, coal,

The blast-furnace and the puddling-furnace, the loup-lump at the
bottom of the melt at last, the rolling-mill, the stumpy bars of
pig-iron, the strong clean-shaped T-rail for railroads,

Oil-works, silk-works, white-lead-works, the sugar-house, steam-
saws, the great mills and factories,

Stone-cutting, shapely trimmings for façades or window or door-
lintels, the mallet, the tooth-chisel, the jib to protect the thumb,

The calking-iron, the kettle of boiling vault-cement, and the fire
under the kettle,

The cotton-bale, the stevedore's hook, the saw and buck of the
sawyer, the mould of the moulder, the working-knife of the
butcher, the ice-saw, and all the work with ice,

The work and tools of the rigger, grappler, sail-maker, block-
maker,

Goods of gutta-percha, papier-maché, colors, brushes, brush-
making, glazier's implements,

The veneer and glue-pot, the confectioner's ornaments, the decanter
and glasses, the shears and flat-iron,

The awl and knee-strap, the pint measure and quart measure, the
counter and stool, the writing-pen of quill or metal, the making
of all sorts of edged tools,

The brewery, brewing, the malt, the vats, every thing that is done
by brewers, wine-makers, vinegar-makers,

Leather-dressing, coach-making, boiler-making, rope-twisting, dis-
tilling, sign-painting, lime-burning, cotton-picking, electro-
plating, electrotyping, stereotyping,

Stave-machines, planing-machines, reaping-machines, ploughing-
machines, thrashing-machines, steam wagons,

The cart of the carman, the omnibus, the ponderous dray,

Pyrotechny, letting off color'd fireworks at night, fancy figures and
jets;

Beef on the butcher's stall, the slaughter-house of the butcher, the
butcher in his killing-clothes,

The pens of live pork, the killing-hammer, the hog-hook, the
scalder's tub, gutting, the cutter's cleaver, the packer's maul,
and the plenteous winterwork of pork-packing,

Flour-works, grinding of wheat, rye, maize, rice, the barrels and
the half and quarter barrels, the loaded barges, the high piles
on wharves and levees,

The men and the work of the men on ferries, railroads, coasters,
fish-boats, canals;

The hourly routine of your own or any man's life, the shop, yard,
store, or factory,

These shows all near you by day and night—workman! whoever you
    are, your daily life!
In that and them the heft of the heaviest—in that and them far more
    than you estimated, (and far less also,)
In them realities for you and me, in them poems for you and me,
In them, not yourself—you and your soul enclose all things, regard-
    less of estimation,
In them the development good—in them all themes, hints, possi-
    bilities.

I do not affirm that what you see beyond is futile, I do not advise
    you to stop,
I do not say leadings you thought great are not great,
But I say that none lead to greater than these lead to.

6

Will you seek afar off? you surely come back at last,
In things best known to you finding the best, or as good as the best,
In folks nearest to you finding the sweetest, strongest, lovingest,
Happiness, knowledge, not in another place but this place, not for
    another hour but this hour,
Man in the first you see or touch, always in friend, brother, nighest
    neighbor—woman in mother, sister, wife,
The popular tastes and employments taking precedence in poems or
    anywhere,
You workwomen and workmen of these States having your own
    divine and strong life,
And all else giving place to men and women like you.

When the psalm sings instead of the singer,
When the script preaches instead of the preacher,
When the pulpit descends and goes instead of the carver that carved
    ·the supporting desk,
When I can touch the body of books by night or by day, and when
    they touch my body back again,
When a university course convinces like a slumbering woman and
    child convince,
When the minted gold in the vault smiles like the night-watchman's
    daughter,
When warrantee deeds loafe in chairs opposite and are my friendly
    companions,
I intend to reach them my hand, and make as much of them as I do
    of men and women like you.

A Song of the Rolling Earth

1

A SONG of the rolling earth, and of words according,
Were you thinking that those were the words, those upright lines?
    those curves, angles, dots?
No, those are not the words, the substantial words are in the ground
    and sea,
They are in the air, they are in you.

Were you thinking that those were the words, those delicious sounds
    out of your friends' mouths?
No, the real words are more delicious than they.

Human bodies are words, myriads of words,
(In the best poems re-appears the body, man's or woman's, well-
    shaped, natural, gay,
Every part able, active, receptive, without shame or the need of
    shame.)

Air, soil, water, fire—those are words,
I myself am a word with them—my qualities interpenetrate with
    theirs—my name is nothing to them,
Though it were told in the three thousand languages, what would
    air, soil, water, fire, know of my name?

A healthy presence, a friendly or commanding gesture, are words,
    sayings, meanings,
The charms that go with the mere looks of some men and women,
    are sayings and meanings also.

The workmanship of souls is by those inaudible words of the earth,
The masters know the earth's words and use them more than audible
    words.

Amelioration is one of the earth's words,
The earth neither lags nor hastens,
It has all attributes, growths, effects, latent in itself from the jump,
It is not half beautiful only, defects and excrescenses show just as
    much as perfections show.

The earth does not withhold, it is generous enough,
The truths of the earth continually wait, they are not so conceal'd
    either,

They are calm, subtle, untransmissible by print,
They are imbued through all things conveying themselves willingly,
Conveying a sentiment and invitation, I utter and utter,
I speak not, yet if you hear me not of what avail am I to you?
To bear, to better, lacking these of what avail am I?

(Accouche! accouchez!
Will you rot your own fruit in yourself there?
Will you squat and stifle there?)

The earth does not argue,
Is not pathetic, has no arrangements,
Does not scream, haste, persuade, threaten, promise,
Makes no discriminations, has no conceivable failures,
Closes nothing, refuses nothing, shuts none out,
Of all the powers, objects, states, it notifies, shuts none out.

The earth does not exhibit itself nor refuse to exhibit itself, possesses
    still underneath,
Underneath the ostensible sounds, the august chorus of heroes, the
    wail of slaves,
Persuasions of lovers, curses, gasps of the dying, laughter of young
    people, accents of bargainers,
Underneath these possessing words that never fail.

To her children the words of the eloquent dumb great mother never
    fail,
The true words do not fail, for motion does not fail and reflection
    does not fail,
Also the day and night do not fail, and the voyage we pursue does
    not fail.

Of the interminable sisters,
Of the ceaseless cotillons of sisters,
Of the centripetal and centrifugal sisters, the elder and younger
    sisters,
The beautiful sister we know dances on with the rest.

With her ample back towards every beholder,
With the fascinations of youth and the equal fascinations of age,
Sits she whom I too love like the rest, sits undisturb'd,
Holding up in her hand what has the character of a mirror, while
    her eyes glance back from it,

Glance as she sits, inviting none, denying none,
Holding a mirror day and night tirelessly before her own face.

Seen at hand or seen at a distance,
Duly the twenty-four appear in public every day,
Duly approach and pass with their companions or a companion,
Looking from no countenances of their own, but from the countenances of those who are with them,
From the countenances of children or women or the manly countenance,
From the open countenances of animals or from inanimate things,
From the landscape or waters or from the exquisite apparition of the sky,
From our countenances, mine and yours, faithfully returning them,
Every day in public appearing without fail, but never twice with the same companions.

Embracing man, embracing all, proceed the three hundred and sixty-five resistlessly round the sun;
Embracing all, soothing, supporting, follow close three hundred and sixty-five offsets of the first, sure and necessary as they.

Tumbling on steadily, nothing dreading,
Sunshine, storm, cold, heat, forever withstanding, passing, carrying,
The soul's realization and determination still inheriting,
The fluid vacuum around and ahead still entering and dividing,
No balk retarding, no anchor anchoring, on no rock striking,
Swift, glad, content, unbereav'd, nothing losing,
Of all able and ready at any time to give strict account,
The divine ship sails the divine sea.

2

Whoever you are! motion and reflection are especially for you,
The divine ship sails the divine sea for you.

Whoever you are! you are he or she for whom the earth is solid and liquid,
You are he or she for whom the sun and moon hang in the sky,
For none more than you are the present and the past,
For none more than you is immortality.

Each man to himself and each woman to herself, is the word of the past and present, and the true word of immortality;

No one can acquire for another—not one,
Not one can grow for another—not one.

The song is to the singer, and comes back most to him,
The teaching is to the teacher, and comes back most to him,
The murder is to the murderer, and comes back most to him,
The theft is to the thief, and comes back most to him,
The love is to the lover, and comes back most to him,
The gift is to the giver, and comes back most to him—it cannot fail,
The oration is to the orator, the acting is to the actor and actress not
    to the audience,
And no man understands any greatness or goodness but his own, or
    the indication of his own.

3

I swear the earth shall surely be complete to him or her who shall be
    complete,
The earth remains jagged and broken only to him or her who re-
    mains jagged and broken.

I swear there is no greatness or power that does not emulate those
    of the earth,
There can be no theory of any account unless it corroborate the
    theory of the earth,
No politics, song, religion, behavior, or what not, is of account, unless
    it compare with the amplitude of the earth,
Unless it face the exactness, vitality, impartiality, rectitude of the
    earth.

I swear I begin to see love with sweeter spasms than that which
    responds love,
It is that which contains itself, which never invites and never refuses.

I swear I begin to see little or nothing in audible words,
All merges toward the presentation of the unspoken meanings of the
    earth,
Toward him who sings the songs of the body and of the truths of the
    earth,
Toward him who makes the dictionaries of words that print cannot
    touch.

I swear I see what is better than to tell the best,
It is always to leave the best untold.

When I undertake to tell the best I find I cannot,
My tongue is ineffectual on its pivots,
My breath will not be obedient to its organs,
I become a dumb man.

The best of the earth cannot be told anyhow, all or any is best,
It is not what you anticipated, it is cheaper, easier, nearer,
Things are not dismiss'd from the places they held before,
The earth is just as positive and direct as it was before,
Facts, religions, improvements, politics, trades, are as real as before,
But the soul is also real, it too is positive and direct,
No reasoning, no proof has establish'd it,
Undeniable growth has establish'd it.

4

These to echo the tones of souls and the phrases of souls,
(If they did not echo the phrases of souls what were they then?
If they had not reference to you in especial what were they then?)

I swear I will never henceforth have to do with the faith that tells
    the best,
I will have to do only with that faith that leaves the best untold.

Say on, sayers! sing on, singers!
Delve! mould! pile the words of the earth!
Work on, age after age, nothing is to be lost,
It may have to wait long, but it will certainly come in use,
When the materials are all prepared and ready, the architects shall
    appear.

I swear to you the architects shall appear without fail,
I swear to you they will understand you and justify you,
The greatest among them shall be he who best knows you, and en-
    closes all and is faithful to all,
He and the rest shall not forget you, they shall perceive that you are
    not an iota less than they,
You shall be fully glorified in them.

YOUTH, DAY, OLD AGE AND NIGHT

YOUTH, large, lusty, loving—youth full of grace, force, fascination,
Do you know that Old Age may come after you with equal grace,
    force, fascination?

Day full-blown and splendid—day of the immense sun, action,
    ambition, laughter,
The Night follows close with millions of suns, and sleep and restoring
    darkness.

Birds of Passage

SONG OF THE UNIVERSAL

1

COME said the Muse,
Sing me a song no poet yet has chanted,
Sing me the universal.

In this broad earth of ours,
Amid the measureless grossness and the slag,
Enclosed and safe within its central heart,
Nestles the seed perfection.

By every life a share or more or less,
None born but it is born, conceal'd or unconcear'd the seed is waiting.

2

Lo! keen-eyed towering science,
As from tall peaks the modern overlooking,
Successive absolute fiats issuing.

Yet again, lo! the soul, above all science,
For it has history gather'd like husks around the globe,
For it the entire star-myriads roll through the sky.

In spiral routes by long detours,
(As a much-tacking ship upon the sea,)
For it the partial to the permanent flowing,
For it the real to the ideal tends.

For it the mystic evolution,
Not the right only justified, what we call evil also justified.

Forth from their masks, no matter what,
From the huge festering trunk, from craft and guile and tears,
Health to emerge and joy, joy universal.

Out of the bulk, the morbid and the shallow,
Out of the bad majority, the varied countless frauds of men and
    states,
Electric, antiseptic yet, cleaving, suffusing all,
Only the good is universal.

3

Over the mountain-growths disease and sorrow,
An uncaught bird is ever hovering, hovering,
High in the purer, happier air.

From imperfection's murkiest cloud,
Darts always forth one ray of perfect light,
One flash of heaven's glory.

To fashion's, custom's discord,
To the mad Babel-din, the deafening orgies,
Soothing each lull a strain is heard, just heard,
From some far shore the final chorus sounding.

O the blest eyes, the happy hearts,
That see, that know the guiding thread so fine,
Along the mighty labyrinth.

4

And thou America,
For the scheme's culmination, its thought and its reality,
For these (not for thyself) thou hast arrived.

Thou too surroundest all,
Embracing carrying welcoming all, thou too by pathways broad and
    new,
To the ideal tendest.

The measur'd faiths of other lands, the grandeurs of the past,
Are not for thee, but grandeurs of thine own,
Deific faiths and amplitudes, absorbing, comprehending all,
All eligible to all.

All, all for immortality,
Love like the light silently wrapping all,
Nature's amelioration blessing all,
The blossoms, fruits of ages, orchards divine and certain,
Forms, objects, growths, humanities, to spiritual images ripening.

Give me O God to sing that thought,
Give me, give him or her I love this quenchless faith,
In Thy ensemble, whatever else withheld withhold not from us,
Belief in plan of Thee enclosed in Time and Space,
Health, peace, salvation universal.

Is it a dream?
Nay but the lack of it the dream,
And failing it life's lore and wealth a dream,
And all the world a dream.

PIONEERS! O PIONEERS!

COME my tan-faced children,
Follow well in order, get your weapons ready,
Have you your pistols? have you your sharp-edged axes?
    Pioneers! O pioneers!

For we cannot tarry here,
We must march my darlings, we must bear the brunt of danger,
We the youthful sinewy races, all the rest on us depend,
    Pioneers! O pioneers!

O you youths, Western youths,
So impatient, full of action, full of manly pride and friendship,
Plain I see you Western youths, see you tramping with the foremost,
    Pioneers! O pioneers!

Have the elder races halted?
Do they droop and end their lesson, wearied over there beyond the
        seas?
We take up the task eternal, and the burden and the lesson,
    Pioneers! O pioneers!

All the past we leave behind,
We debouch upon a newer mightier world, varied world,
Fresh and strong the world we seize, world of labor and the march,
    Pioneers! O pioneers!

We detachments steady throwing,
Down the edges, through the passes, up the mountains steep,
Conquering, holding, daring, venturing as we go the unknown ways,
    Pioneers! O pioneers!

We primeval forests felling,
We the rivers stemming, vexing we and piercing deep the mines
    within,
We the surface broad surveying, we the virgin soil upheaving,
    Pioneers! O pioneers!

Colorado men are we,
From the peaks gigantic, from the great sierras and the high plateaus,
From the mine and from the gully, from the hunting trail we come,
    Pioneers! O pioneers!

From Nebraska, from Arkansas,
Central inland race are we, from Missouri, with the continental
    blood intervein'd,
All the hands of comrades clasping, all the Southern, all the North-
    ern,
    Pioneers! O pioneers!

O resistless restless race!
O beloved race in all! O my breast aches with tender love for all!
O I mourn and yet exult, I am rapt with love for all,
    Pioneers! O pioneers!

Raise the mighty mother mistress,
Waving high the delicate mistress, over all the starry mistress, (bend
    your heads all,)
Raise the fang'd and warlike mistress, stern, impassive, weapon'd
    mistress,
    Pioneers! O pioneers!

See my children, resolute children,
By those swarms upon our rear we must never yield or falter,
Ages back in ghostly millions frowning there behind us urging,
    Pioneers! O pioneers!

On and on the compact ranks,
With accessions ever waiting, with the places of the dead quickly
    fill'd,

Through the battle, through defeat, moving yet and never stopping,
    Pioneers! O pioneers!

  O to die advancing on!
Are there some of us to droop and die? has the hour come?
Then upon the march we fittest die, soon and sure the gap is fill'd,
    Pioneers! O pioneers!

  All the pulses of the world,
Falling in they beat for us, with the Western movement beat,
Holding single or together, steady moving to the front, all for us,
    Pioneers! O pioneers!

  Life's involv'd and varied pageants,
All the forms and shows, all the workmen at their work,
All the seamen and the landsmen, all the masters with their slaves,
    Pioneers! O pioneers!

  All the hapless silent lovers,
All the prisoners in the prisons, all the righteous and the wicked,
All the joyous, all the sorrowing, all the living, all the dying,
    Pioneers! O pioneers!

  I too with my soul and body,
We, a curious trio, picking, wandering on our way,
Through these shores amid the shadows, with the apparitions press-
    ing,
    Pioneers! O pioneers!

  Lo, the darting bowling orb!
Lo, the brother orbs around, all the clustering suns and planets,
All the dazzling days, all the mystic nights with dreams,
    Pioneers! O pioneers!

  These are of us, they are with us,
All for primal needed work, while the followers there in embryo wait
    behind,
We to-day's procession heading, we the route for travel clearing,
    Pioneers! O pioneers!

  O you daughters of the West!
O you young and elder daughters! O you mothers and you wives!
Never must you be divided, in our ranks you move united,
    Pioneers! O pioneers!

Minstrels latent on the prairies!
(Shrouded bards of other lands, you may rest, you have done your
    work,)
Soon I hear you coming warbling, soon you rise and tramp amid us,
    Pioneers! O pioneers!

Not for delectations sweet,
Not the cushion and the slipper, not the peaceful and the studious,
Not the riches safe and palling, not for us the tame enjoyment,
    Pioneers! O pioneers!

Do the feasters gluttonous feast?
Do the corpulent sleepers sleep? have they lock'd and bolted doors?
Still be ours the diet hard, and the blanket on the ground,
    Pioneers! O pioneers!

Has the night descended?
Was the road of late so toilsome? did we stop discouraged nodding
    on our way?
Yet a passing hour I yield you in your tracks to pause oblivious,
    Pioneers! O pioneers!

Till with sound of trumpet,
Far, far off the daybreak call—hark! how loud and clear I hear it
    wind,
Swift! to the head of the army!—swift! spring to your places,
    Pioneers! O pioneers!

TO YOU

WHOEVER you are, I fear you are walking the walks of dreams,
I fear these supposed realities are to melt from under your feet and
    hands,
Even now your features, joys, speech, house, trade, manners,
    troubles, follies, costume, crimes, dissipate away from you,
Your true soul and body appear before me,
They stand forth out of affairs, out of commerce, shops, work,
    farms, clothes, the house, buying, selling, eating, drinking,
    suffering, dying.

Whoever you are, now I place my hand upon you, that you be my
    poem,

I whisper with my lips close to your ear,
I have loved many women and men, but I love none better than you.

O I have been dilatory and dumb,
I should have made my way straight to you long ago,
I should have blabb'd nothing but you, I should have chanted noth-
    ing but you.

I will leave all and come and make the hymns of you,
None has understood you, but I understand you,
None has done justice to you, you have not done justice to yourself,
None but has found you imperfect, I only find no imperfection in you,
None but would subordinate you, I only am he who will never con-
    sent to subordinate you,
I only am he who places over you no master, owner, better, God,
    beyond what waits intrinsically in yourself.

Painters have painted their swarming groups and the centre-figure
    of all,
From the head of the centre-figure spreading a nimbus of gold-
    color'd light,
But I paint myriads of heads, but paint no head without its nim-
    bus of gold-color'd light,
From my hand from the brain of every man and woman it streams,
    effulgently flowing forever.

O I could sing such grandeurs and glories about you!
You have not known what you are, you have slumber'd upon
    yourself all your life,
Your eyelids have been the same as closed most of the time,
What you have done returns already in mockeries,
(Your thrift, knowledge, prayers, if they do not return in mockeries,
    what is their return?)

The mockeries are not you,
Underneath them and within them I see you lurk,
I pursue you where none else has pursued you,
Silence, the desk, the flippant expression, the night, the accustom'd
    routine, if these conceal you from others or from yourself,
    they do not conceal you from me,
The shaved face, the unsteady eye, the impure complexion, if these
    balk others they do not balk me,
The pert apparel, the deform'd attitude, drunkenness, greed, pre-
    mature death, all these I part aside.

There is no endowment in man or woman that is not tallied in
you,
There is no virtue, no beauty in man or woman, but as good is in
you,
No pluck, no endurance in others, but as good is in you,
No pleasure wating for others, but an equal pleasure waits for you.

As for me, I give nothing to any one except I give the like carefully to you,
I sing the songs of the glory of none, not God, sooner than I sing
the songs of the glory of you.

Whoever you are! claim your own at any hazard!
These shows of the East and West are tame compared to you,
These immense meadows, these interminable rivers, you are immense and interminable as they,
These furies, elements, storms, motions of Nature, throes of apparent dissolution, you are he or she who is master or mistress
over them,
Master or mistress in your own right over Nature, elements, pain,
passion, dissolution.

The hopples fall from your ankles, you find an unfailing sufficiency,
Old or young, male or female, rude, low, rejected by the rest,
whatever you are promulges itself,
Through birth, life, death, burial, the means are provided, nothing
is scanted,
Through angers, losses, ambition, ignorance, ennui, what you are
picks its way.

FRANCE,
The 18th Year of these States

A GREAT year and place,
A harsh discordant natal scream out-sounding, to touch the mother's
heart closer than any yet.

I walk'd the shores of my Eastern sea,
Heard over the waves the little voice,
Saw the divine infant where she woke mournfully wailing, amid the
roar of cannon, curses, shouts, crash of falling buildings,
Was not so sick from the blood in the gutters running, nor from
the single corpses, nor those in heaps, nor those borne away
in the tumbrils,
Was not so desperate at the battues of death—was not so shock'd
at the repeated fusillades of the guns.

Pale, silent, stern, what could I say to that long-accrued retribution?
Could I wish humanity different?
Could I wish the people made of wood and stone?
Or that there be no justice in destiny or time?

O Liberty! O mate for me!
Here too the blaze, the grape-shot and the axe, in reserve, to fetch
    them out in case of need,
Here too, though long represt, can never be destroy'd,
Here too could rise at last murdering and ecstatic,
Here too demanding full arrears of vengeance.

Hence I sign this salute over the sea,
And I do not deny that terrible red birth and baptism,
But remember the little voice that I heard wailing and wait with
    perfect trust, no matter how long,
And from to-day sad and cogent I maintain the bequeath'd cause,
    as for all lands,
And I send these words to Paris with my love,
And I guess some chansonniers there will understand them,
For I guess there is latent music yet in France, floods of it,
O I hear already the bustle of instruments, they will soon be
    drowning all that would interrupt them,
O I think the east wind brings a triumphal and free march,
It reaches hither, it swells me to joyful madness,
I will run transpose it in words, to justify it,
I will yet sing a song for you ma femme.

MYSELF AND MINE

MYSELF and mine gymnastic ever,
To stand the cold or heat, to take good aim with a gun, to sail a
    boat, to manage horses, to beget superb children,
To speak readily and clearly, to feel at home among common
    people,
And to hold our own in terrible positions on land and sea.

Not for an embroiderer,
(There will always be plenty of embroiderers, I welcome them also,)
But for the fibre of things and for inherent men and women.

Not to chisel ornaments,
But to chisel with free stroke the heads and limbs of plenteous
    supreme Gods, that the States may realize them walking and
    talking.

Let me have my own way,
Let others promulge the laws, I will make no account of the laws,
Let others praise eminent men and hold up peace, I hold up agitation and conflict,
I praise no eminent man, I rebuke to his face the one that was thought most worthy.

(Who are you? and what are you secretly guilty of all your life?
Will you turn aside all your life? will you grub and chatter all your life?
And who are you, blabbing by rote, years, pages, languages, reminiscences,
Unwitting to-day that you do not know how to speak properly a single word?)

Let others finish specimens, I never finish specimens,
I start them by exhaustless laws as Nature does, fresh, and modern continually.

I give nothing as duties,
What others give as duties I give as living impulses,
(Shall I give the heart's action as a duty?)

Let others dispose of questions, I dispose of nothing, I arouse unanswerable questions,
Who are they I see and touch, and what about them?
What about these likes of myself that draw me so close by tender directions and indirections?

I call to the world to distrust the accounts of my friends, but listen to my enemies, as I myself do,
I charge you forever reject those who would expound me, for I cannot expound myself,
I charge that there be no theory or school founded out of me,
I charge you to leave all free, as I have left all free.

After me, vista!
O I see life is not short, but immeasurably long,
I henceforth tread the world chaste, temperate, an early riser, a steady grower,
Every hour the semen of centuries, and still of centuries.

I must follow up these continual lessons of the air, water, earth,
I perceive I have no time to lose.

YEAR OF METEORS

(1859-60)

YEAR of meteors! brooding year!
I would bind in words retrospective some of your deeds and signs,
I would sing your contest for the 19th Presidentiad,
I would sing how an old man, tall, with white hair, mounted the
    scaffold in Virginia,
(I was at hand, silent I stood with teeth shut close, I watch'd,
I stood very near you old man when cool and indifferent, but
    trembling with age and your unheal'd wounds you mounted
    the scaffold;)
I would sing in my copious song your census returns of the States,
The tables of population and products, I would sing of your ships
    and their cargoes,
The proud black ships of Manhattan arriving, some fill'd with
    immigrants, some from the isthmus with cargoes of gold,
Songs thereof would I sing, to all that hitherward comes would I
    welcome give,
And you would I sing, fair stripling! welcome to you from me,
    young prince of England!
(Remember you surging Manhattan's crowds as you pass'd with
    your cortege of nobles?
There in the crowds stood I, and singled you out with attachment;)
Nor forget I to sing of the wonder, the ship as she swam up my
    bay,
Well-shaped and stately the Great Eastern swam up my bay, she
    was 600 feet long,
Her moving swiftly surrounded by myriads of small craft I forget
    not to sing;
Nor the comet that came unannounced out of the north flaring in
    heaven,
Nor the strange huge meteor-procession dazzling and clear shooting
    over our heads,
(A moment, a moment long it sail'd its balls of unearthly light
    over our heads,
Then departed, dropt in the night, and was gone;)
Of such, and fitful as they, I sing—with gleams from them would
    I gleam and patch these chants,
Your chants, O year all mottled with evil and good—year of fore-
    bodings!
Year of comets and meteors transient and strange—lo! even here
    one equally transient and strange!

As I flit through you hastily, soon to fall and be gone, what is this
  chant,
What am I myself but one of your meteors?

WITH ANTECEDENTS

1

WITH antecedents,
With my fathers and mothers and the accumulations of past ages,
With all which had it not been, I would not now be here, as I am,
With Egypt, India, Phenicia, Greece and Rome,
With the Kelt, the Scandinavian, the Alb and the Saxon,
With antique maritime ventures, laws, artisanship, wars and jour-
  neys,
With the poet, the skald, the saga, the myth, and the oracle,
With the sale of slaves, with enthusiasts, with the troubadour, the
  crusader, and the monk,
With those old continents whence we have come to this new
  continent,
With the fading kingdoms and kings over there,
With the fading religions and priests,
With the small shores we look back to from our own large and
  present shores,
With countless years drawing themselves onward and arrived at
  these years,
You and me arrived—America arrived and making this year,
This year! sending itself ahead countless years to come.

2

O but it is not the years—it is I, it is You,
We touch all laws and tally all antecedents,
We are the skald, the oracle, the monk and the knight, we easily
  include them and more,
We stand amid time beginningless and endless, we stand amid evil
  and good,
All swings around us, there is as much darkness as light,
The very sun swings itself and its system of planets around us,
Its sun, and its again, all swing around us.

As for me, (torn, stormy, amid these vehement days,)
I have the idea of all, and am all and believe in all,

I believe materialism is true and spiritualism is true, I reject no
    part.

(Have I forgotten any part? any thing in the past?
Come to me whoever and whatever, till I give you recognition.)

I respect Assyria, China, Teutonia, and the Hebrews,
I adopt each theory, myth, god, and demi-god,
I see that the old accounts, bibles, genealogies, are true, without
    exception,
I assert that all past days were what they must have been,
And that they could no-how have been better than they were,
And that to-day is what it must be, and that America is,
And that to-day and America could no-how be better than they
    are.

3

In the name of these States and in your and my name, the Past,
And in the name of these States and in your and my name, the
    Present time.

I know that the past was great and the future will be great,
And I know that both curiously conjoint in the present time,
(For the sake of him I typify, for the common average man's sake,
    your sake if you are he,)
And that where I am or you are this present day, there is the centre
    of all days, all races,
And there is the meaning to us of all that has ever come of races
    and days, or ever will come.

A Broadway Pageant

1

OVER the Western sea hither from Niphon come,
Courteous, the swart-cheek'd two-sworded envoys,
Leaning back in their open barouches, bare-headed, impassive,
Ride to-day through Manhattan.

Libertad! I do not know whether others behold what I behold,
In the procession along with the nobles of Niphon, the errand-
    bearers,

Bringing up the rear, hovering above, around, or in the ranks
    marching,
But I will sing you a song of what I behold Libertad.

When million-footed Manhattan unpent descends to her pavements,
When the thunder-cracking guns arouse me with the proud roar
    I love,
When the round-mouth'd guns out of the smoke and smell I love
    spit their salutes,
When the fire-flashing guns have fully alerted me, and heaven-
    clouds canopy my city with a delicate thin haze,
When gorgeous the countless straight stems, the forests at the
    wharves, thicken with colors,
When every ship richly drest carries her flag at the peak,
When pennants trail and street-festoons hang from the windows,
When Broadway is entirely given up to foot-passengers and foot-
    standers, when the mass is densest,
When the façades of the houses are alive with people, when eyes
    gaze riveted tens of thousands at a time,
When the guests from the islands advance, when the pageant moves
    forward visible,
When the summons is made, when the answer that waited thou-
    sands of years answers,
I too arising, answering, descend to the pavements, merge with
    the crowd, and gaze with them.

2

Superb-faced Manhattan!
Comrade Americanos! to us, then at last the Orient comes.

To us, my city,
Where our tall-topt marble and iron beauties range on opposite
    sides, to walk in the space between,
To-day our Antipodes comes.

The Originatress comes,
The nest of languages, the bequeather of poems, the race of eld,
Florid with blood, pensive, rapt with musings, hot with passion,
Sultry with perfume, with ample and flowing garments,
With sunburnt visage, with intense soul and glittering eyes,
The race of Brahma comes.

See my cantabile! these and more are flashing to us from the
    procession,
As it moves changing, a kaleidoscope divine it moves changing
    before us.

For not the envoys nor the tann'd Japanee from his island only,
Lithe and silent the Hindoo appears, the Asiatic continent itself
    appears, the past, the dead,
The murky night-morning of wonder and fable inscrutable,
The envelop'd mysteries, the old and unknown hive-bees,
The north, the sweltering south, eastern Assyria, the Hebrews, the
    ancient of ancients,
Vast desolated cities, the gliding present, all of these and more are
    in the pageant-procession.

Geography, the world, is in it,
The Great Sea, the brood of islands, Polynesia, the coast beyond,
The coast you henceforth are facing—you Libertad! from your
    Western golden shores,
The countries there with their populations, the millions en-masse
    are curiously here,
The swarming market-places, the temples with idols ranged along
    the sides or at the end, bonze, brahmin, and lama,
Mandarin, farmer, merchant, mechanic, and fisherman,
The singing-girl and the dancing-girl, the ecstatic persons, the
    secluded emperors,
Confucius himself, the great poets and heroes, the warriors, the
    castes, all,
Trooping up, crowding from all directions, from the Altay moun-
    tains,
From Thibet, from the four winding and far-flowing rivers of
    China,
From the southern peninsulas and the demi-continental islands,
    from Malaysia,
These and whatever belongs to them palpable show forth to me,
    and are seiz'd by me,
And I am seiz'd by them, and friendlily held by them,
Till as here them all I chant, Libertad! for themselves and for you.

For I too raising my voice join the ranks of this pageant,
I am the chanter, I chant aloud over the pageant,
I chant the world on my Western sea,
I chant copious the islands beyond, thick as stars in the sky,

I chant the new empire grander than any before, as in a vision it
    comes to me,
I chant America the mistress, I chant a greater supremacy,
I chant projected a thousand blooming cities yet in time on those
    groups of sea-islands,
My sail-ships and steam-ships threading the archipelagoes,
My stars and stripes fluttering in the wind,
Commerce opening, the sleep of ages having done its work, races
    reborn, refresh'd,
Lives, works resumed—the object I know not—but the old, the
    Asiatic renew'd as it must be,
Commencing from this day surrounded by the world.

3

And you Libertad of the world!
You shall sit in the middle well-pois'd thousands and thousands of
    years,
As to-day from one side the nobles of Asia come to you,
As to-morrow from the other side the queen of England sends her
    eldest son to you.

The sign is reversing, the orb is enclosed,
The ring is circled, the journey is done,
The box-lid is but perceptibly open'd, nevertheless the perfume
    pours copiously out of the whole box.

Young Libertad! with the venerable Asia, the all-mother,
Be considerate with her now and ever hot Libertad, for you are all,
Bend your proud neck to the long-off mother now sending mes-
    sages over the archipelagoes to you,
Bend your proud neck low for once, young Libertad.

Were the children straying westward so long? so wide the tramping?
Were the precedent dim ages debouching westward from Paradise
    so long?
Were the centuries steadily footing it that way, all the while un-
    known, for you, for reasons?

They are justified, they are accomplish'd, they shall now be turn'd
    the other way also, to travel toward you thence.
They shall now also march obediently eastward for your sake
    Libertad.

Sea-Drift

OUT OF THE CRADLE ENDLESSLY ROCKING

Out of the cradle endlessly rocking,
Out of the mocking-bird's throat, the musical shuttle,
Out of the Ninth-month midnight,
Over the sterile sands and the fields beyond, where the child leaving
    his bed wander'd alone, bareheaded, barefoot,
Down from the shower'd halo,
Up from the mystic play of shadows twining and twisting as if
    they were alive,
Out from the patches of briers and blackberries,
From the memories of the bird that chanted to me,
From your memories sad brother, from the fitful risings and fall-
    ings I heard,
From under that yellow half-moon late-risen and swollen as if with
    tears,
From those beginning notes of yearning and love there in the mist,
From the thousand responses of my heart never to cease,
From the myriad thence-arous'd words,
From the word stronger and more delicious than any,
From such as now they start the scene revisiting,
As a flock, twittering, rising, or overhead passing,
Borne hither, ere all eludes me, hurriedly,
A man, yet by these tears a little boy again,
Throwing myself on the sand, confronting the waves,
I, chanter of pains and joys, uniter of here and hereafter,
Taking all hints to use them, but swiftly leaping beyond them,
A reminiscence sing.

Once Paumanok,
When the lilac-scent was in the air and Fifth-month grass was
    growing,
Up this seashore in some briers,
Two feather'd guests from Alabama, two together,

And their nest, and four light-green eggs spotted with brown,
And every day the he-bird to and fro near at hand,
And every day the she-bird crouch'd on her nest, silent, with bright
    eyes,
And every day I, a curious boy, never too close, never disturbing
    them,
Cautiously peering, absorbing, translating.

Shine! shine! shine!
Pour down your warmth, great sun!
While we bask, we two together.

Two together!
Winds blow south, or winds blow north,
Day come white, or night come black,
Home, or rivers and mountains from home,
Singing all time, minding no time,
While we two keep together.

Till of a sudden,
May-be kill'd, unknown to her mate,
One forenoon the she-bird crouch'd not on the nest,
Nor return'd that afternoon, nor the next
Nor ever appear'd again.

And thenceforward all summer in the sound of the sea,
And at night under the full of the moon in calmer weather,
Over the hoarse surging of the sea,
Or flitting from brier to brier by day,
I saw, I heard at intervals the remaining one, the he-bird,
The solitary guest from Alabama.

Blow! blow! blow!
Blow up sea-winds along Paumanok's shore;
I wait and I wait till you blow my mate to me.

Yes, when the stars glisten'd,
All night long on the prong of a moss-scallop'd stake,
Down almost amid the slapping waves,
Sat the lone singer wonderful causing tears.

He call'd on his mate,
He pour'd forth the meanings which I of all men know.

Yes my brother I know,
The rest might not, but I have treasur'd every note,
For more than once dimly down to the beach gliding,
Silent, avoiding the moonbeams, blending myself with the shadows,
Recalling now the obscure shapes, the echoes, the sounds and
    sights after their sorts,
The white arms out in the breakers tirelessly tossing,
I, with bare feet, a child, the wind wafting my hair,
Listen'd long and long.

Listen'd to keep, to sing, now translating the notes,
Following you my brother.

Soothe! soothe! soothe!
Close on its wave soothes the wave behind,
And again another behind embracing and lapping, every one close,
But my love soothes not me, not me.

Low hangs the moon, it rose late,
It is lagging—O I think it is heavy with love, with love.

O madly the sea pushes upon the land,
With love, with love.

O night! do I not see my love fluttering out among the breakers?
What is that little black thing I see there in the white?

Loud! loud! loud!
Loud I call to you, my love!

High and clear I shoot my voice over the waves,
Surely you must know who is here, is here,
You must know who I am, my love.

Low-hanging moon!
What is that dusky spot in your brown yellow?
O it is the shape, the shape of my mate!
O moon do not keep her from me any longer.

Land! land! O land!
Whichever way I turn, O I think you could give me my mate back
    again if you only would,
For I am almost sure I see her dimly whichever way I look.

O rising stars!
Perhaps the one I want so much will rise, will rise with some of you.

O throat! O trembling throat!
Sound clearer through the atmosphere!
Pierce the woods, the earth,
Somewhere listening to catch you must be the one I want.

Shake out carols!
Solitary here, the night's carols!
Carols of lonesome love! death's carols!
Carols under that lagging, yellow, waning moon!
O under that moon where she droops almost down into the sea!
O reckless despairing carols.

But soft! sink low!
Soft! let me just murmur,
And do you wait a moment you husky-nois'd sea,
For somewhere I believe I heard my mate responding to me,
So faint, I must be still, be still to listen,
But not altogether still, for then she might not come immediately to me.

Hither my love!
Here I am! here!
With this just-sustain'd note, I announce myself to you,
This gentle call is for you my love, for you.

Do not be decoy'd elsewhere,
That is the whistle of the wind, it is not my voice,
That is the fluttering, the fluttering of the spray,
Those are the shadows of leaves.

O darkness! O in vain!
O I am very sick and sorrowful.

O brown halo in the sky near the moon, drooping upon the sea!
O troubled reflection in the sea!
O throat! O throbbing heart!
And I singing uselessly, uselessly all the night.

O past! O happy life! O songs of joy!
In the air, in the woods, over fields,
Loved! loved! loved! loved! loved!

But my mate no more, no more with me!
We two together no more.

The aria sinking,
All else continuing, the stars shining,
The winds blowing, the notes of the bird continuous echoing,
With angry moans the fierce old mother incessantly moaning,
On the sands of Paumanok's shore gray and rustling,
The yellow half-moon enlarged, sagging down, drooping, the face of
    the sea almost touching,
The boy ecstatic, with his bare feet the waves, with his hair the
    atmosphere dallying,
The love in the heart long pent, now loose, now at last tumultuously
    bursting,
The aria's meaning, the ears, the soul, swiftly depositing,
The strange tears down the cheeks coursing,
The colloquy there, the trio, each uttering,
The undertone, the savage old mother incessantly crying,
To the boy's soul's questions sullenly timing, some drown'd secret
    hissing,
To the outsetting bard.

Demon or bird! (said the boy's soul,)
Is it indeed toward your mate you sing? or is it really to me?
For I, that was a child, my tongue's use sleeping, now I have heard
    you,
Now in a moment I know what I am for, I awake,
And already a thousand singers, a thousand songs, clearer, louder
    and more sorrowful than yours,
A thousand warbling echoes have started to life within me, never
    to die.

O you singer solitary, singing by yourself, projecting me,
O solitary me listening, never more shall I cease perpetuating you,
Never more shall I escape, never more the reverberations,
Never more the cries of unsatisfied love be absent from me,
Never again leave me to be the peaceful child I was before what there
    in the night,
By the sea under the yellow and sagging moon,
The messenger there arous'd, the fire, the sweet hell within,
The unknown want, the destiny of me.

O give me the clew! (it lurks in the night here somewhere,)
O if I am to have so much, let me have more!

A word then, (for I will conquer it,)
The word final, superior to all,
Subtle, sent up—what is it?—I listen;
Are you whispering it, and have been all the time, you sea-waves?
Is that it from your liquid rims and wet sands?

Whereto answering, the sea,
Delaying not, hurrying not,
Whisper'd me through the night, and very plainly before daybreak,
Lisp'd to me the low and delicious word death,
And again death, death, death, death,
Hissing melodious, neither like the bird nor like my arous'd child's
    heart,
But edging near as privately for me rustling at my feet,
Creeping thence steadily up to my ears and laving me softly all over,
Death, death, death, death, death.

Which I do not forget,
But fuse the song of my dusky demon and brother,
That he sang to me in the moonlight on Paumanok's gray beach,
With the thousand responsive songs at random,
My own songs awaked from that hour,
And with them the key, the word up from the waves,
The word of the sweetest song and all songs,
That strong and delicious word which, creeping to my feet,
(Or like some old crone rocking the cradle, swathed in sweet gar-
    ments, bending aside,)
The sea whisper'd me.

AS I EBB'D WITH THE OCEAN OF LIFE

1

As I ebb'd with the ocean of life,
As I wended the shores I know,
As I walk'd where the ripples continually wash you Paumanok,
Where they rustle up hoarse and sibilant,
Where the fierce old mother endlessly cries for her castaways,
I musing late in the autumn day, gazing off southward,
Held by this electric self out of the pride of which I utter poems,
Was seiz'd by the spirit that trails in the lines underfoot,
The rim, the sediment that stands for all the water and all the land
    of the globe.

Fascinated, my eyes reverting from the south, dropt, to follow those
    slender windrows,
Chaff, straw, splinters of wood, weeds, and the sea-gluten,
Scum, scales from shining rocks, leaves of salt-lettuce, left by the
    tide,
Miles walking, the sound of breaking waves the other side of me,
Paumanok there and then as I thought the old thought of likenesses,
These you presented to me you fish-shaped island,
As I wended the shores I know,
As I walk'd with that electric self seeking types.

2

As I wend to the shores I know not,
As I list to the dirge, the voices of men and women wreck'd,
As I inhale the impalpable breezes that set in upon me,
As the ocean so mysterious rolls toward me closer and closer,
I too but signify at the utmost a little wash'd-up drift,
A few sands and dead leaves to gather,
Gather, and merge myself as part of the sands and drift.

O baffled, balk'd, bent to the very earth,
Oppress'd with myself that I have dared to open my mouth,
Aware now that amid all that blab whose echoes recoil upon me I
    have not once had the least idea who or what I am,
But that before all my arrogant poems the real Me stands yet un-
    touch'd, untold, altogether unreach'd,
Withdrawn far, mocking me with mock-congratulatory signs and
    bows,
With peals of distant ironical laughter at every word I have written,
Pointing in silence to these songs, and then to the sand beneath.
I perceive I have not really understood any thing, not a single object,
    and that no man ever can,
Nature here in sight of the sea taking advantage of me to dart upon
    me and sting me,
Because I have dared to open my mouth to sing at all.

3

You oceans both, I close with you,
We murmur alike reproachfully rolling sands and drift, knowing not
    why,
These little shreds indeed standing for you and me and all.

You friable shore with trails of debris,
You fish-shaped island, I take what is underfoot,
What is yours is mine my father.

I too Paumanok,
I too have bubbled up, floated the measureless float, and been wash'd
    on your shores,
I too am but a trail of drift and debris,
I too leave little wrecks upon you, you fish-shaped island.

I throw myself upon your breast my father,
I cling to you so that you cannot unloose me,
I hold you so firm till you answer me something.

Kiss me my father,
Touch me with your lips as I touch those I love,
Breathe to me while I hold you close the secret of the murmuring
    I envy.

4

Ebb, ocean of life, (the flow will return,)
Cease not your moaning you fierce old mother,
Endlessly cry for your castaways, but fear not, deny not me,
Rustle not up so hoarse and angry against my feet as I touch you or
    gather from you.

I mean tenderly by you and all,
I gather for myself and for this phantom looking down where we
    lead, and following me and mine.

Me and mine, loose windrows, little corpses,
Froth, snowy white, and bubbles,
(See, from my dead lips the ooze exuding at last,
See, the prismatic colors glistening and rolling,)
Tufts of straw, sands, fragments,
Buoy'd hither from many moods, one contradicting another,
From the storm, the long calm, the darkness, the swell,
Musing, pondering, a breath, a briny tear, a dab of liquid or soil,
Up just as much out of fathomless workings fermented and thrown,
A limp blossom or two, torn, just as much over waves floating,
    drifted at random,
Just as much for us that sobbing dirge of Nature,
Just as much whence we come that blare of the cloud-trumpets,

We, capricious, brought hither we know not whence, spread out
    before you,
You up there walking or sitting,
Whoever you are, we too lie in drifts at your feet.

TEARS

TEARS! tears! tears!
In the night, in solitude, tears,
On the white shore dripping, dripping, suck'd in by the sand,
Tears, not a star shining, all dark and desolate,
Moist tears from the eyes of a muffled head;
O who is that ghost? that form in the dark, with tears?
What shapeless lump is that, bent, crouch'd there on the sand?
Streaming tears, sobbing tears, throes, choked with wild cries;
O storm, embodied, rising, careering with swift steps along the
    beach!
O wild and dismal night storm, with wind—O belching and des-
    perate!
O shade so sedate and decorous by day, with calm countenance and
    regulated pace,
But away at night as you fly, none looking—O then the unloosen'd
    ocean,
Of tears! tears! tears!

TO THE MAN-OF-WAR-BIRD

THOU who hast slept all night upon the storm,
Waking renew'd on thy prodigious pinions,
(Burst the wild storm? above it thou ascended'st,
And rested on the sky, thy slave that cradled thee,)
Now a blue point, far, far in heaven floating,
As to the light emerging here on deck I watch thee,
(Myself a speck, a point on the world's floating vast.)

Far, far at sea,
After the night's fierce drifts have strewn the shore with wrecks,
With re-appearing day as now so happy and serene,
The rosy and elastic dawn, the flashing sun,
The limpid spread of air cerulean,
Thou also re-appearest.

Thou born to match the gale, (thou art all wings,)
To cope with heaven and earth and sea and hurricane,

Thou ship of air that never furl'st thy sails,
Days, even weeks untired and onward, through spaces, realms gyrating,
At dusk that look'st on Senegal, at morn America,
That sport'st amid the lightning-flash and thunder-cloud,
In them, in thy experiences, had'st thou my soul,
What joys! what joys were thine!

ABOARD AT A SHIP'S HELM

ABOARD at a ship's helm,
A young steersman steering with care.

Through fog on a sea-coast dolefully ringing,
An ocean-bell—O a warning bell, rock'd by the waves.

O you give good notice indeed, you bell by the sea-reefs ringing,
Ringing, ringing, to warn the ship from its wreck-place.

For as on the alert O steersman, you mind the loud admonition,
The bows turn, the freighted ship tacking speeds away under her gray sails,
The beautiful and noble ship with all her precious wealth speeds away gayly and safe.

But O the ship, the immortal ship! O ship aboard the ship!
Ship of the body, ship of the soul, voyaging, voyaging, voyaging.

ON THE BEACH AT NIGHT

ON the beach at night,
Stands a child with her father,
Watching the east, the autumn sky.

Up through the darkness,
While ravening clouds, the burial clouds, in black masses spreading,
Lower sullen and fast athwart and down the sky,
Amid a transparent clear belt of ether yet left in the east,
Ascends large and calm the lord-star Jupiter,
And nigh at hand, only a very little above,
Swim the delicate sisters the Pleiades.

From the beach the child holding the hand of her father,
Those burial-clouds that lower victorious soon to devour all,
Watching, silently weeps.

Weep not, child,
Weep not, my darling,
With these kisses let me remove your tears,
The ravening clouds shall not long be victorious,
They shall not long possess the sky, they devour the stars only in
    apparition,
Jupiter shall emerge, be patient, watch again another night, the
    Pleiades shall emerge,
They are immortal, all those stars both silvery and golden shall shine
    out again,
The great stars and the little ones shall shine out again, they endure,
The vast immortal suns and the long-enduring pensive moons shall
    again shine.

Then dearest child mournest thou only for Jupiter?
Considerest thou alone the burial of the stars?

Something there is,
(With my lips soothing thee, adding I whisper,
I give thee the first suggestion, the problem and indirection,)
Something there is more immortal even than the stars,
(Many the burials, many the days and nights, passing away,)
Something that shall endure longer even than lustrous Jupiter,
Longer than sun or any revolving satellite,
Or the radiant sisters the Pleiades.

THE WORLD BELOW THE BRINE

THE world below the brine,
Forests at the bottom of the sea, the branches and leaves,
Sea-lettuce, vast lichens, strange flowers and seeds, the thick tangle,
    openings, and pink turf,
Different colors, pale gray and green, purple, white, and gold, the
    play of light through the water,
Dumb swimmers there among the rocks, coral, gluten, grass, rushes,
    and the aliment of the swimmers,
Sluggish existences grazing there suspended, or slowly crawling close
    to the bottom,
The sperm-whale at the surface blowing air and spray, or disporting
    with his flukes,
The leaden-eyed shark, the walrus, the turtle, the hairy sea-leopard,
    and the sting-ray,
Passions there, wars, pursuits, tribes, sight in those ocean-depths,
    breathing that thick-breathing air, as so many do,

The change thence to the sight here, and to the subtle air breathed
    by beings like us who walk this sphere,
The change onward from ours to that of beings who walk other
    spheres.

ON THE BEACH AT NIGHT ALONE

ON the beach at night alone,
As the old mother sways her to and fro singing her husky song,
As I watch the bright stars shining, I think a thought of the clef of
    the universes and of the future.

A vast similitude interlocks all,
All spheres, grown, ungrown, small, large, suns, moons, planets,
All distances of place however wide,
All distances of time, all inanimate forms,
All souls, all living bodies though they be ever so different, or in
    different worlds,
All gaseous, watery, vegetable, mineral processes, the fishes, the
    brutes,
All nations, colors, barbarisms, civilizations, languages,
All identities that have existed or may exist on this globe, or any
    globe,
All lives and deaths, all of the past, present, future,
This vast similitude spans them, and always has spann'd,
And shall forever span them and compactly hold and enclose them.

SONG FOR ALL SEAS, ALL SHIPS

1

TO-DAY a rude brief recitative,
Of ships sailing the seas, each with its special flag or ship-signal,
Of unnamed heroes in the ships—of waves spreading and spreading
    far as the eye can reach,
Of dashing spray, and the winds piping and blowing,
And out of these a chant for the sailors of all nations.
Fitful, like a surge.

Of sea-captains young or old, and the mates, and of all intrepid
    sailors,
Of the few, very choice, taciturn, whom fate can never surprise nor
    death dismay,
Pick'd sparingly without noise by thee old ocean, chosen by thee,

Thou sea that pickest and cullest the race in time, and unitest
      nations,
Suckled by thee, old husky nurse, embodying thee,
Indomitable, untamed as thee.

(Ever the heroes on water or on land, by ones or twos appearing,
Ever the stock preserv'd and never lost, though rare, enough for seed
      preserv'd.)

2

Flaunt out O sea your separate flags of nations!
Flaunt out visible as ever the various ship-signals!
But do you reserve especially for yourself and for the soul of man
      one flag above all the rest,
A spiritual woven signal for all nations, emblem of man elate above
      death,
Token of all brave captains and all intrepid sailors and mates,
And all that went down doing their duty,
Reminiscent of them, twined from all intrepid captains young or old,
A pennant universal, subtly waving all time, o'er all brave sailors,
All seas, all ships.

PATROLING BARNEGAT

WILD, wild the storm, and the sea high running,
Steady the roar of the gale, with incessant undertone muttering,
Shouts of demoniac laughter fitfully piercing and pealing,
Waves, air, midnight, their savagest trinity lashing,
Out in the shadows there milk-white combs careering,
On beachy slush and sand spirts of snow fierce slanting,
Where through the murk the easterly death-wind breasting,
Through cutting swirl and spray watchful and firm advancing,
(That in the distance! is that a wreck? is the red signal flaring?)
Slush and sand of the beach tireless till daylight wending,
Steadily, slowly, through hoarse roar never remitting,
Along the midnight edge by those milk-white combs careering,
A group of dim, weird forms, struggling, the night confronting,
That savage trinity warily watching.

AFTER THE SEA-SHIP

AFTER the sea-ship, after the whistling winds,
After the white-gray sails taut to their spars and ropes,

Below, a myriad myriad waves hastening, lifting up their necks,
Tending in ceaseless flow toward the track of the ship,
Waves of the ocean bubbling and gurgling, blithely prying,
Waves, undulating waves, liquid, uneven, emulous waves,
Toward that whirling current, laughing and buoyant, with curves,
Where the great vessel sailing and tacking displaced the surface,
Larger and smaller waves in the spread of the ocean yearnfully flow-
     ing,
The wake of the sea-ship after she passes, flashing and frolicsome
     under the sun,
A motley procession with many a fleck of foam and many fragments,
Following the stately and rapid ship, in the wake following.

By the Roadside

A BOSTON BALLAD
(1854)

To get betimes in Boston town I rose this morning early
Here's a good place at the corner, I must stand and see the show.

Clear the way there Jonathan!
Way for the President's marshal—way for the government cannon!
Way for the Federal foot and dragoons, (and the apparitions co-
    piously tumbling.)

I love to look on the Stars and Stripes, I hope the fifes will play
    Yankee Doodle.
How bright shine the cutlasses of the foremost troops!
Every man holds his revolver, marching stiff through Boston town.

A fog follows, antiques of the same come limping,
Some appear wooden-legged, and some appear bandaged and blood-
    less.

Why this is indeed a show—it has called the dead out of the earth!
The old graveyards of the hills have hurried to see!
Phantoms! phantoms countless by flank and rear!
Cock'd hats of mothy mould—crutches made of mist!
Arms in slings—old men leaning on young men's shoulders.

What troubles you Yankee phantoms? what is all this chattering of
    bare gums?
Does the ague convulse your limbs? do you mistake your crutches
    for firelocks and level them?

If you blind your eyes with tears you will not see the President's
    marshal,
If you groan such groans you might balk the government cannon.

For shame old maniacs—bring down those toss'd arms, and let your
   white hair be,
Here gape your great-grandsons, their wives gaze at them from the
   windows,
See how well dress'd, see how orderly they conduct themselves.

Worse and worse—can't you stand it? are you retreating?
Is this hour with the living too dead for you?

Retreat then—pell-mell!
To your graves—back—back to the hills old limpers!
I do not think you belong here anyhow.

But there is one thing that belongs here—shall I tell you what it is,
   gentlemen of Boston?

I will whisper it to the Mayor, he shall send a committee to England,
They shall get a grant from the Parliament, go with a cart to the
   royal vault,
Dig out King George's coffin, unwrap him quick from the grave-
   clothes, box up his bones for a journey,
Find a swift Yankee clipper—here is freight for you, black-bellied
   clipper,
Up with your anchor—shake out your sails—steer straight toward
   Boston bay.

Now call for the President's marshal again, bring out the government cannon,
Fetch home the roarers from Congress, make another procession,
   guard it with foot and dragoons.

This centre-piece for them;
Look, all orderly citizens—look from the windows, women!

The committee open the box, set up the regal ribs, glue those that
   will not stay,
Clap the skull on top of the ribs, and clap a crown on top of the
   skull.

You have got your revenge, old buster—the crown is come to its
   own, and more than its own.

Stick your hands in your pockets, Jonathan—you are a made man
   from this day,
You are mighty cute—and here is one of your bargains.

EUROPE

The 72d and 73d Years of These States

SUDDENLY out of its stale and drowsy lair, the lair of slaves,
Like lightning it le'pt forth half startled at itself,
Its feet upon the ashes and the rags, its hands tight to the throats
    of kings.

O hope and faith!
O aching close of exiled patriot's lives!
O many a sicken'd heart!
Turn back unto this day and make yourselves afresh.

And you, paid to defile the People—you liars, mark!
Not for numberless agonies, murders, lusts,
For court thieving in its manifold mean forms, worming from his
    simplicity the poor man's wages,
For many a promise sworn by royal lips and broken and laugh'd
    at in the breaking.

Then in their power not for all these did the blows strike revenge,
    or the heads of the nobles fall;
The People scorn'd the ferocity of kings.

But the sweetness of mercy brew'd bitter destruction, and the
    frighten'd monarchs come back,
Each comes in state with his train, hangman, priest, tax-gatherer,
Soldier, lawyer, lord, jailer, and sycophant.

Yet behind all lowering stealing, lo, a shape,
Vague as the night, draped interminably, head, front and form, in
    scarlet folds,
Whose face and eyes none may see,
Out of its robes only this, the red robes lifted by the arm,
One finger crook'd pointed high over the top, like the head of a
    snake appears.

Meanwhile corpses lie in new-made graves, bloody corpses of
    young men,
The rope of the gibbet hangs heavily, the bullets of princes are
    flying, the creatures of power laugh aloud,
And all these things bear fruits, and they are good.

Those corpses of young men,
Those martyrs that hang from the gibbets, those hearts pierc'd by
    the gray lead,

Cold and motionless as they seem live elsewhere with unslaughter'd
    vitality.

They live in other young men O kings!
They live in brothers again ready to defy you,
They were purified by death, they were taught and exalted.

Not a grave of the murder'd for freedom but grows seed for free-
    dom, in its turn to bear seed,
Which the winds carry afar and re-sow, and the rains and the
    snows nourish.

Not a disembodied spirit can the weapons of tyrants let loose,
But it stalks invisibly over the earth, whispering, counseling,
    cautioning.

Liberty, let others despair of you—I never despair of you.

Is the house shut? is the master away?
Nevertheless, be ready, be not weary of watching,
He will soon return, his messengers come anon.

A HAND-MIRROR

HOLD it up sternly—see this it sends back, (who is it? is it you?)
Outside fair costume, within ashes and filth,
No more a flashing eye, no more a sonorous voice or springy step,
Now some slave's eye, voice, hands, step,
A drunkard's breath, unwholesome eater's face, venerealee's flesh,
Lungs rotting away piecemeal, stomach sour and cankerous,
Joints rheumatic, bowels clogged with abomination,
Blood circulating dark and poisonous streams,
Words babble, hearing and touch callous,
No brain, no heart left, no magnetism of sex;
Such from one look in this looking-glass ere you go hence,
Such a result so soon—and from such a beginning!

GODS

LOVER divine and perfect Comrade,
Waiting content, invisible yet, but certain,
Be thou my God.

Thou, thou, the Ideal Man,
Fair, able, beautiful, content, and loving,
Complete in body and dilate in spirit,
Be thou my God.

O Death, (for Life has served its turn,)
Opener and usher to the heavenly mansion,
Be thou my God.

Aught, aught of mightiest, best I see, conceive, or know,
(To break the stagnant tie—thee, thee to free, O soul,)
Be thou my God.

All great ideas, the races' aspirations,
All heroisms, deeds of rapt enthusiasts,
Be ye my Gods.

Or Time and Space,
Or shape of Earth divine and wondrous,
Or some fair shape I viewing, worship,
Or lustrous orb of sun or star by night,
Be ye my Gods.

GERMS

FORMS, qualities, lives, humanity, language, thoughts,
The ones known, and the ones unknown, the ones on the stars,
The stars themselves, some shaped, others unshaped,
Wonders as of those countries, the soil, trees, cities, inhabitants,
    whatever they may be,
Splendid suns, the moons and rings, the countless combinations
    and effects,
Such-like, and as good as such-like, visible here or anywhere,
    stand provided for in a handful of space, which I extend my
    arm and half enclose with my hand,
That containing the start of each and all, the virtue, the germs
    of all.

THOUGHTS

OF ownership—as if one fit to own things could not at pleasure
    enter upon all, and incorporate them into himself or herself;
Of vista—suppose some sight in arriere through the formative
    chaos, presuming the growth, fulness, life, now attain'd on
    the journey,

(But I see the road continued, and the journey ever continued;)
Of what was once lacking on earth, and in due time has become
supplied—and of what will yet be supplied,
Because all I see and know I believe to have its main purport in
what will yet be supplied.

WHEN I HEARD THE LEARN'D ASTRONOMER

WHEN I heard the learn'd astronomer,
When the proofs, the figures, were ranged in columns before me,
When I was shown the charts and diagrams, to add, divide, and
measure them,
When I sitting heard the astronomer where he lectured with much
applause in the lecture-room,
How soon unaccountable I became tired and sick,
Till rising and gliding out I wander'd off by myself,
In the mystical moist night-air, and from time to time,
Look'd up in perfect silence at the stars.

PERFECTIONS

ONLY themselves understand themselves and the like of themselves,
As souls only understand souls.

O ME! O LIFE!

O ME! O life! of the questions of these recurring,
Of the endless trains of the faithless, of cities fill'd with the foolish,
Of myself forever reproaching myself, (for who more foolish than
I, and who more faithless?)
Of eyes that vainly crave the light, of the objects mean, of the
struggle ever renew'd,
Of the poor results of all, of the plodding and sordid crowds I see
around me,
Of the empty and useless years of the rest, with the rest me inter-
twined,
The question, O me! so sad, recurring—What good amid these,
O me, O life?

Answer

That you are here—that life exists and identity,
That the powerful play goes on, and you may contribute a verse.

TO A PRESIDENT

ALL you are doing and saying is to America dangled mirages,
You have not learn'd of Nature—of the politics of Nature you
  have not learn'd the great amplitude, rectitude, impartiality,
You have not seen that only such as they are for these States,
And that what is less than they must sooner or later lift off from
  these States.

I SIT AND LOOK OUT

I SIT and look out upon all the sorrows of the world, and upon all
  oppression and shame,
I hear secret convulsive sobs from young men at anguish with
  themselves, remorseful after deeds done,
I see in low life the mother misused by her children, dying,
  neglected, gaunt, desperate,
I see the wife misused by her husband, I see the treacherous
  seducer of young women,
I mark the ranklings of jealousy and unrequited love attempted to
  be hid, I see these sights on the earth,
I see the workings of battle, pestilence, tyranny, I see martyrs and
  prisoners,
I observe a famine at sea, I observe the sailors casting lots who
  shall be kill'd to preserve the lives of the rest,
I observe the slights and degradations cast by arrogant persons
  upon laborers, the poor, and upon negroes, and the like;
All these—all the meanness and agony without end I sitting look
  out upon,
See, hear, and am silent.

TO RICH GIVERS

WHAT you give me I cheerfully accept,
A little sustenance, a hut and garden, a little money, as I rendezvous
  with my poems,
A traveler's lodging and breakfast as I journey through the States,
  —why should I be ashamed to own such gifts? why to advertise
  for them?
For I myself am not one who bestows nothing upon man and
  woman,
For I bestow upon any man or woman the entrance to all the gifts
  of the universe.

THE DALLIANCE OF THE EAGLES

SKIRTING the river road, (my forenoon walk, my rest,)
Skyward in air a sudden muffled sound, the dalliance of the eagles,
The rushing amorous contact high in space together,
The clinching interlocking claws, a living, fierce, gyrating wheel,
Four beating wings, two beaks, a swirling mass tight grappling,
In tumbling turning clustering loops, straight downward falling,
Till o'er the river pois'd, the twain yet one, a moment's lull,
A motionless still balance in the air, then parting, talons loosing,
Upward again on slow-firm pinions slanting, their separate diverse
    flight,
She hers, he his, pursuing.

ROAMING IN THOUGHT
(*After reading* HEGEL)

ROAMING in thought over the Universe, I saw the little that is
    Good steadily hastening towards immortality,
And the vast all that is call'd Evil I saw hastening to merge itself
    and become lost and dead.

A FARM PICTURE

THROUGH the ample open door of the peaceful country barn,
A sunlit pasture field with cattle and horses feeding,
And haze and vista, and the far horizon fading away.

A CHILD'S AMAZE

SILENT and amazed even when a little boy,
I remember I heard the preacher every Sunday put God in his
    statements,
As contending against some being or influence.

THE RUNNER

ON a flat road runs the well-train'd runner,
He is lean and sinewy with muscular legs,
He is thinly clothed, he leans forward as he runs,
With lightly closed fists and arms partially rais'd.

BEAUTIFUL WOMEN

WOMEN sit or move to and fro, some old, some young,
The young are beautiful—but the old are more beautiful than the
    young.

MOTHER AND BABE

I SEE the sleeping babe nestling the breast of its mother,
The sleeping mother and babe—hush'd, I study them long and
long.

THOUGHT

OF obedience, faith, adhesiveness;
As I stand aloof and look there is to me something profoundly
affecting in large masses of men following the lead of those
who do not believe in men.

VISOR'D

A MASK, a perpetual natural disguiser of herself,
Concealing her face, concealing her form,
Changes and transformations every hour, every moment,
Falling upon her even when she sleeps.

THOUGHT

OF Justice—as if Justice could be any thing but the same ample
law, expounded by natural judges and saviors,
As if it might be this thing or that thing, according to decisions.

GLIDING O'ER ALL

GLIDING o'er all, through all,
Through Nature, Time, and Space,
As a ship on the waters advancing,
The voyage of the soul—not life alone,
Death, many deaths I'll sing.

HAST NEVER COME TO THEE AN HOUR

HAST never come to thee an hour,
A sudden gleam divine, precipitating, bursting all these bubbles,
fashions, wealth?
These eager business aims—books, politics, art, amours,
To utter nothingness?

THOUGHT

OF Equality—as if it harm'd me, giving others the same chances
and rights as myself—as if it were not indispensable to my
own rights that others possess the same.

TO OLD AGE

I SEE in you the estuary that enlarges and spreads itself grandly as
it pours in the great sea.

LOCATIONS AND TIMES

LOCATIONS and times—what is it in me that meets them all, whenever and wherever, and makes me at home?
Forms, colors, densities, odors—what is it in me that corresponds
with them?

OFFERINGS

A THOUSAND perfect men and women appear,
Around each gathers a cluster of friends, and gay children and
youths, with offerings.

TO THE STATES,
To Identify the 16th, 17th, or 18th Presidentiad

WHY reclining, interrogating? why myself and all drowsing?
What deepening twilight—scum floating atop of the waters,
Who are they as bats and night-dogs askant in the capitol?
What a filthy Presidentiad! (O South, your torrid suns! O North,
your arctic freezings!)
Are those really Congressmen? are those the great Judges? is that
the President?
Then I will sleep awhile yet, for I see that these States sleep, for
reasons;
(With gathering murk, with muttering thunder and lambent shoots
we all duly awake,
South, North, East, West, inland and seaboard, we will surely
awake.)

Drum-Taps

FIRST O SONGS FOR A PRELUDE

FIRST O songs for a prelude,
Lightly strike on the stretch'd tympanum pride and joy in my city,
How she led the rest to arms, how she gave the cue,
How at once with lithe limbs unwaiting a moment she sprang,
(O superb! O Manhattan, my own, my peerless!
O strongest you in the hour of danger, in crisis! O truer than steel!)
How you sprang—how you threw off the costumes of peace with
    indifferent hand,
How your soft opera-music changed, and the drum and fife were
    heard in their stead,
How you led to the war, (that shall serve for our prelude, songs
    of soldiers,)
How Manhattan drum-taps led.

Forty years had I in my city seen soldiers parading,
Forty years as a pageant, till unawares the lady of this teeming
    and turbulent city,
Sleepless amid her ships, her houses, her incalculable wealth,
With her million children around her, suddenly,
At dead of night, at news from the south,
Incens'd struck with clinch'd hand the pavement.
A shock electric, the night sustain'd it,
Till with ominous hum our hive at daybreak pour'd out its myriads.

From the houses then and the workshops, and through all the
    doorways,
Leapt they tumultuous, and lo! Manhattan arming.

To the drum-taps prompt,
The young men falling in and arming,

The mechanics arming, (the trowel, the jack-plane, the black-
smith's hammer, tost aside with precipitation,)

The lawyer leaving his office and arming, the judge leaving the
court,

The driver deserting his wagon in the street, jumping down, throwing
the reins abruptly down on the horses' backs,

The salesman leaving the store, the boss, book-keeper, porter, all
leaving;

Squads gather everywhere by common consent and arm,

The new recruits, even boys, the old men show them how to wear
their accoutrements, they buckle the straps carefully,

Outdoors arming, indoors arming, the flash of the musket-barrels,

The white tents cluster in camps, the arm'd sentries around, the
sunrise cannon and again at sunset,

Arm'd regiments arrive every day, pass through the city, and
embark from the wharves,

(How good they look as they tramp down to the river, sweaty,
with their guns on their shoulders!

How I love them! how I could hug them, with their brown faces
and their clothes and knapsacks cover'd with dust!)

The blood of the city up—arm'd! arm'd! the cry everywhere,

The flags flung out from the steeples of churches and from all the
public buildings and stores,

The tearful parting, the mother kisses her son, the son kisses his
mother,

(Loth is the mother to part, yet not a word does she speak to detain
him,)

The tumultuous escort, the ranks of policemen preceding, clearing
the way,

The unpent enthusiasm, the wild cheers of the crowd for their
favorites,

The artillery, the silent cannons bright as gold, drawn along,
rumble lightly over the stones,

(Silent cannons, soon to cease your silence,

Soon unlimber'd to begin the red business;)

All the mutter of preparation, all the determin'd arming,

The hospital service, the lint, bandages, and medicines,

The women volunteering for nurses, the work begun for in earnest,
no mere parade now;

War! an arm'd race is advancing! the welcome for battle, no
turning away;

War! be it weeks, months, or years, an arm'd race is advancing
to welcome it.

Mannahatta a-march—and it's O to sing it well!
It's O for a manly life in the camp.

And the sturdy artillery,
The guns bright as gold, the work for giants, to serve well the guns,
Unlimber them! (no more as the past forty years for salutes for
    courtesies merely,
Put in something now besides powder and wadding.)

And you lady of ships, you Mannahatta,
Old matron of this proud, friendly, turbulent city,
Often in peace and wealth you were pensive or covertly frown'd
    amid all your children,
But now you smile with joy exulting old Mannahatta.

EIGHTEEN SIXTY-ONE

ARM'D year—year of the struggle,
No dainty rhymes or sentimental love verses for you terrible year,
Not you as some pale poetling seated at a desk lisping cadenzas
    piano,
But as a strong man erect, clothed in blue clothes, advancing,
    carrying a rifle on your shoulder,
With well-gristled body and sunburnt face and hands, with a knife
    in the belt at your side,
As I heard you shouting loud, your sonorous voice ringing across
    the continent,
Your masculine voice O year, as rising amid the great cities,
Amid the men of Manhattan I saw you as one of the workmen,
    the dwellers in Manhattan,
Or with large steps crossing the prairies out of Illinois and
    Indiana,
Rapidly crossing the West with springy gait and descending the
    Alleghanies,
Or down from the great lakes or in Pennsylvania, or on deck along
    the Ohio river,
Or southward along the Tennessee or Cumberland rivers, or at
    Chattanooga on the mountain top,
Saw I your gait and saw I your sinewy limbs clothed in blue, bearing
    weapons, robust year,
Heard your determin'd voice launch'd forth again and again,
Year that suddenly sang by the mouths of the round-lipp'd cannon,
I repeat you, hurrying, crashing, sad, distracted year.

BEAT! BEAT! DRUMS!

BEAT! beat! drums!—blow! bugles! blow!
Through the windows—through doors—burst like a ruthless force,
Into the solemn church, and scatter the congregation,
Into the school where the scholar is studying;
Leave not the bridegroom quiet—no happiness must he have now with his bride,
Nor the peaceful farmer any peace, ploughing his field or gathering his grain,
So fierce you whirr and pound you drums—so shrill you bugles blow.

Beat! beat! drums!—blow! bugles! blow!
Over the traffic of cities—over the rumble of wheels in the streets;
Are beds prepared for sleepers at night in the houses? no sleepers must sleep in those beds,
No bargainers' bargains by day—no brokers or speculators—would they continue?
Would the talkers be talking? would the singer attempt to sing?
Would the lawyer rise in the court to state his case before the judge?
Then rattle quicker, heavier drums—you bugles wilder blow.

Beat! beat! drums!—blow! bugles! blow!
Make no parley—stop for no expostulation,
Mind not the timid—mind not the weeper or prayer,
Mind not the old man beseeching the young man,
Let not the child's voice be heard, nor the mother's entreaties,
Make even the trestles to shake the dead where they lie awaiting the hearses,
So strong you thump O terrible drums—so loud you bugles blow.

FROM PAUMANOK STARTING I FLY LIKE A BIRD

FROM Paumanok starting I fly like a bird,
Around and around to soar to sing the idea of all,
To the north betaking myself to sing there arctic songs,
To Kanada till I absorb Kanada in myself, to Michigan then,
To Wisconsin, Iowa, Minnesota, to sing their songs, (they are inimitable;)

Then to Ohio and Indiana to sing theirs, to Missouri and Kansas
 and Arkansas to sing theirs,
To Tennessee and Kentucky, to the Carolinas and Georgia to sing
 heirs,
To Texas and so along up toward California, to roam accepted
 everywhere;
To sing first, (to the tap of the war-drum if need be,)
The idea of all, of the Western world one and inseparable,
And then the song of each member of these States.

SONG OF THE BANNER AT DAYBREAK
Poet

O A new song, a free song,
Flapping, flapping, flapping, flapping, by sounds, by voices clearer,
By the wind's voice and that of the drum,
By the banner's voice and child's voice and sea's voice and father's
 voice,
Low on the ground and high in the air
On the ground where father and child stand,
In the upward air where their eyes turn,
Where the banner at daybreak is flapping

Words! book-words! what are you?
Words no more, for hearken and see,
My song is there in the open air, and I must sing,
With the banner and pennant a-flapping.

I'll weave the chord and twine in,
Man's desire and babe's desire, I'll twine them in, I'll put in life,
I'll put the bayonet's flashing point, I'll let bullets and slugs whizz,
(As one carrying a symbol and menace far into the future,
Crying with trumpet voice, Arouse and beware! Beware and arouse!)
I'll pour the verse with streams of blood, full of volition, full of joy,
Then loosen, launch forth, to go and compete,
With the banner and pennant a-flapping.

Penant

Come up here, bard, bard,
Come up here, soul, soul
Come up here, dear little child,
To fly in the clouds and winds with me, and play with the measureless
 light.

Child

Father what is that in the sky beckoning to me with long finger?
And what does it say to me all the while?

Father

Nothing my babe you see in the sky,
And nothing at all to you it says—but look you my babe,
Look at these dazzling things in the houses and see you the money-
    shops opening,
And see you the vehicles preparing to crawl along the streets, with
    goods;
These, ah these, how valued and toil'd for these!
How envied by all the earth.

Poet

Fresh and rosy red the sun is mounting high,
On floats the sea in distant blue careering through its channels,
On floats the wind over the breast of the sea setting in toward land,
The great steady wind from west or west-by-south,
Floating so buoyant with milk-white foam on the waters.

But I am not the sea nor the red sun,
I am not the wind with girlish laughter,
Not the immense wind which strengthens, not the wind which lashes,
Not the spirit that ever lashes its own body to terror and death,
But I am that which unseen comes and sings, sings, sings,
Which babbles in brooks and scoots in showers on the land,
Which the birds know in the woods mornings and evenings,
And the shore-sands know and the hissing wave, and that banner
    and pennant,
Aloft there flapping and flapping.

Child

O father it is alive—it is full of people—it has children,
O now it seems to me it is talking to its children,
I hear it—it talks to me—O it is wonderful!
O it stretches—it spreads and runs so fast—O my father,
It is so broad it covers the whole sky.

Father

Cease, cease, my foolish babe,
What you are saying is sorrowful to me, much it displeases me;

Behold with the rest again I say, behold not banners and pennants
    aloft,
But the well-prepared pavements behold, and mark the solid-wall'd
    houses.

Banner and Pennant

Speak to the child O bard out of Manhattan,
To our children all, or north or south of Manhattan,
Point this day, leaving all the rest, to us over all—and yet we know
    not why,
For what are we, mere strips of cloth profiting nothing,
Only flapping in the wind?

Poet

I hear and see not strips of cloth alone,
I hear the tramp of armies, I hear the challenging sentry,
I hear the jubilant shouts of millions of men, I hear Liberty!
I hear the drums beat and the trumpets blowing,
I myself move abroad swift-rising flying then,
I use the wings of the land-bird and use the wings of the sea-bird,
    and look down as from a height,
I do not deny the precious results of peace, I see populous cities with
    wealth incalculable,
I see numberless farms, I see the farmers working in their fields or
    barns,
I see mechanics working, I see buildings everywhere founded, going
    up, or finish'd,
I see trains of cars swiftly speeding along railroad tracks drawn by
    the locomotives,
I see the stores, depots, of Boston, Baltimore, Charleston, New
    Orleans,
I see far in the West the immense area of grain, I dwell awhile hover-
    ing,
I pass to the lumber forests of the North, and again to the Southern
    plantation, and again to California;
Sweeping the whole I see the countless profit, the busy gatherings,
    earn'd wages,
See the Identity formed out of thirty-eight spacious and haughty
    States, (and many more to come,)
See forts on the shores of harbors, see ships sailing in and out;
Then over all, (aye! aye!) my little and lengthen'd pennant shaped
    like a sword.
Runs swiftly up indicating war and defiance—and now the halyards
    have rais'd it,

Side of my banner broad and blue, side of my starry banner,
Discarding peace over all the sea and land.

Banner and Pennant

Yet louder, higher, stronger, bard! yet farther, wider cleave!
No longer let our children deem us riches and peace alone,
We may be terror and carnage, and are so now,
Not now are we any one of these spacious and haughty States, (nor
any five, nor ten,)
Nor market nor depot we, nor money-bank in the city,
But these and all, and the brown and spreading land, and the mines
below, are ours,
And the shores of the sea are ours, and the rivers great and small,
And the fields they moisten, and the crops and the fruits are ours,
Bays and channels and ships sailing in and out are ours—while we
over all,
Over the area spread below, the three or four millions of square
miles, the capitals,
The forty millions of people,—O bard! in life and death supreme,
We, even we, henceforth flaunt out masterful, high up above,
Not for the present alone, for a thousand years chanting through
you,
This song to the soul of one poor little child.

Child

O my father I like not the houses,
They will never to me be any thing, nor do I like money,
But to mount up there I would like, O father dear, that banner I like,
That pennant I would be and must be.

Father

Child of mine you fill me with anguish,
To be that pennant would be too fearful,
Little you know what it is this day, and after this day, forever,
It is to gain nothing, but risk and defy every thing,
Forward to stand in front of wars—and O, such wars!—what have
you to do with them?
With passions of demons, slaughter, premature death?

Banner

Demons and death then I sing,
Put in all, aye all will I, sword-shaped pennant for war,

And a pleasure new and ecstatic, and the prattled yearning of chil-
  dren,
Blent with the sounds of the peaceful land and the liquid wash of the
  sea,
And the black ships fighting on the sea envelop'd in smoke,
And the icy cool of the far, far north, with rustling cedars and pines,
And the whirr of drums and the sound of soldiers marching, and the
  hot sun shining south,
And the beach-waves combing over the beach on my Eastern shore,
  and my Western shore the same,
And all between those shores, and my ever running Mississippi with
  bends and chutes,
And my Illinois fields, and my Kansas fields, and my fields of Mis-
  souri,
The Continent, devoting the whole identity without reserving an
  atom,
Pour in! whelm that which asks, which sings, with all and the yield
  of all,
Fusing and holding, claiming, devouring the whole,
No more with tender lip, nor musical labial sound,
But out of the night emerging for good, our voice persuasive no
  more,
Croaking like crows here in the wind.

Poet

My limbs, my veins dilate, my theme is clear at last,
Banner so broad advancing out of the night, I sing you haughty and
  resolute,
I burst through where I waited long, too long, deafen'd and blinded,
My hearing and tongue are come to me, (a little child taught me,)
I hear from above O pennant of war your ironical call and demand,
Insensate! insensate! (yet I at any rate chant you,) O banner!
Not houses of peace indeed are you, nor any nor all their prosperity,
  (if need be, you shall again have every one of those houses to
  destroy them,
You thought not to destroy those valuable houses, standing fast, full
  of comfort, built with money,
May they stand fast, then? not an hour except you above them and
  all stand fast;)
O banner, not money so precious are you, not farm produce you,
  nor the material good nutriment,
Nor excellent stores, nor landed on wharves from the ships,

Not the superb ships with sail-power or steam-power, fetching and
carrying cargoes,
Nor machinery, vehicles, trade, nor revenues—but you as henceforth
I see you,
Running up out of the night, bringing your cluster of stars, (ever-
enlarging stars,)
Divider of daybreak you, cutting the air, touch'd by the sun, measur-
ing the sky,
(Passionately seen and yearn'd for by one poor little child,
While others remain busy or smartly talking, forever teaching thrift,
thrift;)
O you up there! O pennant! where you undulate like a snake hissing
so curious,
Out of reach, an idea only, yet furiously fought for, risking bloody
death, loved by me,
So loved—O you banner leading the day with stars brought from the
night!
Valueless, object of eyes, over all and demanding all—(absolute
owner of all)—O banner and pennant!
I too leave the rest—great as it is, it is nothing—houses, machines
are nothing—I see them not,
I see but you, O warlike pennant! O banner so broad, with stripes,
I sing you only,
Flapping up there in the wind.

RISE O DAYS FROM YOUR FATHOMLESS DEEPS

1

RISE O days from your fathomless deeps, till you loftier, fiercer
sweep,
Long for my soul hungering gymnastic I devour'd what the earth
gave me,
Long I roam'd the woods of the north, long I watch'd Niagara
pouring,
I travel'd the prairies over and slept on their breast, I cross'd the
Nevadas, I cross'd the plateaus,
I ascended the towering rocks along the Pacific, I sail'd out to sea,
I sail'd through the storm, I was refresh'd by the storm,
I watch'd with joy the threatening maws of the waves,
I mark'd the white combs where they career'd so high, curling over,
I heard the wind piping, I saw the black clouds,
Saw from below what arose and mounted, (O superb! O wild as my
heart, and powerful!)

Heard the continuous thunder as it bellow'd after the lightning,
Noted the slender and jagged threads of lightning as sudden and fast
    amid the din they chased each other across the sky;
These, and such as these, I, elate, saw—saw with wonder, yet pensive
    and masterful,
All the menacing might of the globe uprisen around me,
Yet there with my soul I fed, I fed content, supercilious.

2

'Twas well, O soul—'twas a good preparation you gave me,
Now we advance our latent and ampler hunger to fill,
Now we go forth to receive what the earth and the sea never gave us,
Not through the mighty woods we go, but through the mightier
    cities,
Something for us is pouring now more than Niagara pouring,
Torrents of men, (sources and rills of the Northwest are you indeed
    inexhaustible?)
What, to pavements and homesteads here, what were those storms of
    the mountains and sea?
What, to passions I witness around me to-day? was the sea risen?
Was the wind piping the pipe of death under the black clouds?
Lo! from deeps more unfathomable, something more deadly and
    savage,
Manhattan rising, advancing with menacing front—Cincinnati,
    Chicago, unchain'd;
What was that swell I saw on the ocean? behold what comes here,
How it climbs with daring feet and hands—how it dashes!
How the true thunder bellows after the lightning—how bright the
    flashes of lightning!
How Democracy with desperate vengeful port strides on, shown
    through the dark by those flashes of lightning!
(Yet a mournful wail and low sob I fancied I heard through the dark,
In a lull of the deafening confusion.)

3

Thunder on! stride on, Democracy! strike with vengeful stroke!
And do you rise higher than ever yet O days, O cities!
Crash heavier, heavier yet O storms! you have done me good,
My soul prepared in the mountains absorbs your immortal strong
    nutriment,
Long had I walk'd my cities, my country roads through farms, only
    half satisfied,

One doubt nauseous undulating like a snake, crawl'd on the ground
    before me,
Continually preceding my steps, turning upon me oft, ironically
    hissing low;
The cities I loved so well I abandon'd and left, I sped to the certain-
    ties suitable to me,
Hungering, hungering, hungering, for primal energies and Nature's
    dauntlessness,
I refresh'd myself with it only, I could relish it only,
I waited the bursting forth of the pent fire—on the water and air I
    waited long;
But now I no longer wait, I am fully satisfied, I am glutted,
I have witness'd the true lightning, I have witness'd my cities electric,
I have lived to behold man burst forth and warlike America rise,
Hence I will seek no more the food of the northern solitary wilds,
No more the mountains roam or sail the stormy sea.

VIRGINIA—THE WEST

THE noble sire fallen on evil days,
I saw with hand uplifted, menacing, brandishing,
(Memories of old in abeyance, love and faith in abeyance,)
The insane knife toward the Mother of All.

The noble son on sinewy feet advancing,
I saw, out of the land of prairies, land of Ohio's waters and of Indi-
    ana,
To the rescue the stalwart giant hurry his plenteous offspring,
Drest in blue, bearing their trusty rifles on their shoulders.

Then the Mother of All with calm voice speaking,
As to you Rebellious, (I seemed to hear her say,) why strive against
    me, and why seek my life?
When you yourself forever provide to defend me?
For you provided me Washington—and now these also.

CITY OF SHIPS

CITY of ships!
(O the black ships! O the fierce ships!
O the beautiful sharp-bow'd steam-ships and sail-ships!)
City of the world! (for all races are here,
All the lands of the earth make contributions here;)

City of the sea! city of hurried and glittering tides!
City whose gleeful tides continually rush or recede, whirling in and
    out with eddies and foam!
City of wharves and stores—city of tall façades of marble and iron!
Proud and passionate city—mettlesome, mad, extravagant city!
Spring up O city— not for peace alone, but be indeed yourself, war-
    like!
Fear not—submit to no models but your own O city!
Behold me—incarnate me as I have incarnated you!
I have rejected nothing you offer'd me—whom you adopted I have
    adopted,
Good or bad I never question you—I love all—I do not condemn
    any thing,
I chant and celebrate all that is yours—yet peace no more,
In peace I chanted peace, but now the drum of war is mine,
War, red war is my song through your streets, O city!

THE CENTENARIAN'S STORY

Volunteer of 1861–2, (*at Washington Park, Brooklyn, assisting the Centenarian*)

GIVE me your hand old Revolutionary,
The hill-top is nigh, but a few steps, (make room gentlemen,)
Up the path you have follow'd me well, spite of your hundred and
    extra years,
You can walk old man, though your eyes are almost done,
Your faculties serve you, and presently I must have them serve me.

Rest, while I tell what the crowd around us means,
On the plain below recruits are drilling and exercising,
There is the camp, one regiment departs to-morrow,
Do you hear the officers giving their orders?
Do you hear the clank of the muskets?

Why what comes over you now old man?
Why do you tremble and clutch my hand so convulsively?
The troops are but drilling, they are yet surrounded with smiles,
Around them at hand the well-drest friends and the women,
While splendid and warm the afternoon sun shines down,
Green the midsummer verdure and fresh blows the dallying breeze,
O'er proud and peaceful cities and arm of the sea between.

But drill and parade are over, they march back to quarters,
Only hear that approval of hands! hear what a clapping!

As wending the crowds now part and disperse—but we old man,
Not for nothing have I brought you hither—we must remain,
You to speak in your turn, and I to listen and tell.

The Centenarian

When I clutch'd your hand it was not with terror,
But suddenly pouring about me here on every side,
And below there where the boys were drilling, and up the slopes they
    ran,
And where tents are pitch'd, and wherever you see south and south-
    east and south-west,
Over hills, across lowlands, and in the skirts of woods,
And along the shores, in mire (now fill'd over) came again and sud-
    denly raged,
As eighty-five years a-gone no mere parade receiv'd with applause
    of friends,
But a battle which I took part in myself—aye, long ago as it is, I took
    part in it,
Walking then this hilltop, this same ground.

Aye, this is the ground,
My blind eyes even as I speak behold it re-peopled from graves,
The years recede, pavements and stately houses disappear,
Rude forts appear again, the old hoop'd guns are mounted,
I see the lines of rais'd earth stretching from river to bay,
I mark the vista of waters, I mark the uplands and slopes;
Here we lay encamp'd, it was this time in summer also.

As I talk I remember all, I remember the Declaration,
It was read here, the whole army paraded, it was read to us here,
By his staff surrounded the General stood in the middle, he held up
    his unsheath'd sword,
It glitter'd in the sun in full sight of the army.

'Twas a bold act then—the English war-ships had just arrived,
We could watch down the lower bay where they lay at anchor,
And the transports swarming with soldiers.

A few days more and they landed, and then the battle.

Twenty thousand were brought against us,
A veteran force furnish'd with good artillery.

I tell not now the whole of the battle,
But one brigade early in the forenoon order'd forward to engage the
    red-coats,
Of that brigade I tell, and how steadily it march'd,
And how long and well it stood confronting death.

Who do you think that was marching steadily sternly confronting
    death?
It was the brigade of the youngest men, two thousand strong,
Rais'd in Virginia and Maryland, and most of them known person-
    ally to the General.

Jauntily forward they went with quick step toward Gowanus' waters,
Till of a sudden unlook'd for by defiles through the woods, gain'd at
    night,
The British advancing, rounding in from the east, fiercely playing
    their guns,
That brigade of the youngest was cut off and at the enemy's mercy.

The General watch'd them from this hill,
They made repeated desperate attempts to burst their environment,
Then drew close together, very compact, their flag flying in the
    middle,
But O from the hills how the cannon were thinning and thinning
    them!

It sickens me yet, that slaughter!
I saw the moisture gather in drops on the face of the General.
I saw how he wrung his hands in anguish.

Meanwhile the British manœuvr'd to draw us out for a pitch'd
    battle,
But we dared not trust the chances of a pitch'd battle.

We fought the fight in detachments,
Sallying forth we fought at several points, but in each the luck was
    against us,
Our foe advancing, steadily getting the best of it, push'd us back to
    the works on this hill,
Till we turn'd menacing here, and then he left us.

That was the going out of the brigade of the youngest men, two
    thousand strong,
Few return'd, nearly all remain in Brooklyn.

That and here my General's first battle,
No women looking on nor sunshine to bask in, it did not conclude
    with applause,
Nobody clapp'd hands here then.

But in darkness in mist on the ground under a chill rain,
Wearied that night we lay foil'd and sullen,
While scornfully laugh'd many an arrogant lord off against us en-
    camp'd,
Quite within hearing, feasting, clinking wineglasses together over
    their victory.

So dull and damp and another day,
But the night of that, mist lifting, rain ceasing,
Silent as a ghost while they thought they were sure of him, my Gen-
    eral retreated.

I saw him at the river-side,
Down by the ferry lit by torches, hastening the embarcation;
My General waited till the soldiers and wounded were all pass'd over,
And then, (it was just ere sunrise,) these eyes rested on him for the
    last time.

Every one else seem'd fill'd with gloom,
Many no doubt thought of capitulation.

But when my General pass'd me,
As he stood in his boat and look'd toward the coming sun,
I saw something different from capitulation.

Terminus

Enough, the Centenarian's story ends,
The two, the past and present, have interchanged,
I myself as connecter, as chansonnier of a great future, am now
    speaking.

And is this the ground Washington trod?
And these waters I listlessly daily cross, are these the waters he
    cross'd,
As resolute in defeat as other generals in their proudest triumphs?

I must copy the story, and send it eastward and westward,
I must preserve that look as it beam'd on you rivers of Brooklyn.

See—as the annual round returns the phantoms return,
It is the 27th of August and the British have landed,
The battle begins, and goes against us, behold through the smoke
    Washington's face,
The brigade of Virginia and Maryland have march'd forth to inter-
    cept the enemy,
They are cut off, murderous artillery from the hills plays upon
    them,
Rank after rank falls, while over them silently droops the flag,
Baptized that day in many a young man's bloody wounds,
In death, defeat, and sisters', mothers' tears.

Ah, hills and slopes of Brooklyn! I perceive you are more valuable
    than your owners supposed;
In the midst of you stands an encampment very old,
Stands forever the camp of that dead brigade.

CAVALRY CROSSING A FORD

A LINE in long array where they wind betwixt green islands,
They take a serpentine course, their arms flash in the sun—hark
    to the musical clank,
Behold the silvery river, in it the splashing horses loitering stop to
    drink,
Behold the brown-faced men, each group, each person, a picture,
    the negligent rest on the saddles,
Some emerge on the opposite bank, others are just entering the
    ford—while,
Scarlet and blue and snowy white,
The guidon flags flutter gayly in the wind.

BIVOUAC ON A MOUNTAIN SIDE

I SEE before me now a traveling army halting,
Below a fertile valley spread, with barns and the orchards of
    summer,
Behind, the terraced sides of a mountain, abrupt, in places rising
    high,
Broken, with rocks, with clinging cedars, with tall shapes dingily
    seen,
The numerous camp-fires scatter'd near and far, some away up on
    the mountain,
The shadowy forms of men and horses, looming, large-sized,
    flickering,

And over all the sky—the sky! far, far out of reach, studded,
    breaking out, the eternal stars.

AN ARMY CORPS ON THE MARCH

WITH its cloud of skirmishers in advance,
With now the sound of a single shot snapping like a whip, and
    now an irregular volley,
The swarming ranks press on and on, the dense brigades press
    on,
Glittering dimly, toiling under the sun—the dust-cover'd men,
In columns rise and fall to the undulations of the ground,
With artillery interspers'd—the wheels rumble, the horses sweat,
As the army corps advances.

BY THE BIVOUAC'S FITFUL FLAME

BY the bivouac's fitful flame,
A procession winding around me, solemn and sweet and slow—but
    first I note,
The tents of the sleeping army, the fields' and woods' dim
    outline,
The darkness lit by spots of kindled fire, the silence,
Like a phantom far or near an occasional figure moving,
The shrubs and trees, (as I lift my eyes they seem to be stealthily
    watching me,)
While wind in procession thoughts, O tender and wondrous
    thoughts,
Of life and death, of home and the past and loved, and of those
    that are far away;
A solemn and slow procession there as I sit on the ground,
By the bivouac's fitful flame.

COME UP FROM THE FIELDS FATHER

COME up from the fields father, here's a letter from our Pete,
And come to the front door mother, here's a letter from thy dear
    son.

Lo, 'tis autumn,
Lo, where the trees, deeper green, yellower and redder,
Cool and sweeten Ohio's villages with leaves fluttering in the
    moderate wind,

Where apples ripe in the orchards hang and grapes on the trellis'd
    vines,
(Smell you the smell of the grapes on the vines?
Smell you the buckwheat where the bees were lately buzzing?)

Above all, lo, the sky so calm, so transparent after the rain, and
    with wondrous clouds,
Below too, all calm, all vital and beautiful, and the farm prospers
    well.

Down in the fields all prospers well,
But now from the fields come father, come at the daughter's call,
And come to the entry mother, to the front door come right away.

Fast as she can she hurries, something ominous, her steps
    trembling,
She does not tarry to smooth her hair nor adjust her cap.

Open the envelope quickly,
O this is not our son's writing, yet his name is sign'd,
O a strange hand writes for our dear son, O stricken mother's soul!
All swims before her eyes, flashes with black, she catches the main
    words only,
Sentences broken, *gunshot wound in the breast, cavalry skirmish,
    taken to hospital,*
At present low, but will soon be better.

Ah now the single figure to me,
Amid all teeming and wealthy Ohio with all its cities and farms,
Sickly white in the face and dull in the head, very faint,
By the jamb of a door leans.

Grieve not so, dear mother, (the just-grown daughter speaks
    through her sobs,
The little sisters huddle around speechless and dismay'd,)
See, dearest mother, the letter says Pete will soon be better.

Alas poor boy, he will never be better, (nor may-be needs to be
    better, that brave and simple soul,)
While they stand at home at the door he is dead already,
The only son is dead.

But the mother needs to be better,
She with thin form presently drest in black,

By day her meals untouch'd, then at night fitfully sleeping, often waking,
In the midnight waking, weeping, longing with one deep longing,
O that she might withdraw unnoticed, silent from life escape and withdraw,
To follow, to seek, to be with her dear dead son.

VIGIL STRANGE I KEPT ON THE FIELD ONE NIGHT

VIGIL strange I kept on the field one night;
When you my son and my comrade dropt at my side that day,
One look I but gave which your dear eyes return'd with a look I shall never forget,
One touch of your hand to mine O boy, reach'd up as you lay on the ground,
Then onward I sped in the battle, the even-contested battle,
Till late in the night reliev'd to the place at last again I made my way,
Found you in death so cold dear comrade, found your body son of responding kisses, (never again on earth responding,)
Bared your face in the starlight, curious the scene, cool blew the moderate night-wind,
Long there and then in vigil I stood, dimly around me the battle-field spreading,
Vigil wondrous and vigil sweet there in the fragrant silent night,
Bu⁺ not a tear fell, not even a long-drawn sigh, long, long I gazed,
Then on the earth partially reclining sat by your side leaning my chin in my hands,
Passing sweet hours, immortal and mystic hours with you dearest comrade—not a tear, not a word,
Vigil of silence, love and death, vigil for you my son and my soldier,
As onward silently stars aloft, eastward new ones upward stole,
Vigil final for you brave boy, (I could not save you, swift was your death,
I faithfully loved you and cared for you living, I think we shall surely meet again,)
Till at latest lingering of the night, indeed just as the dawn appear'd,
My comrade I wrapt in his blanket, envelop'd well his form,
Folded the blanket well, tucking it carefully over head and carefully under feet,
And there and then and bathed by the rising sun, my son in his grave, in his rude-dug grave I deposited,

Ending my vigil strange with that, vigil of night and battle-field
     dim,
Vigil for boy of responding kisses, (never again on earth
     responding,)
Vigil for comrade swiftly slain, vigil I never forget, how as day
     brighten'd,
I rose from the chill ground and folded my soldier well in his
     blanket,
And buried him where he fell.

A MARCH IN THE RANKS HARD-PREST, AND THE ROAD UNKNOWN

A MARCH in the ranks hard-prest, and the road unknown,
A route through a heavy wood with muffled steps in the darkness,
Our army foil'd with loss severe, and the sullen remnant retreating,
Till after midnight glimmer upon us the lights of a dim-lighted
     building,
We come to an open space in the woods, and halt by the dim-
     lighted building,
'Tis a large old church at the crossing roads, now an impromptu
     hospital,
Entering but for a minute I see a sight beyond all the pictures and
     poems ever made,
Shadows of deepest, deepest black, just lit by moving candles and
     lamps,
And by one great pitchy torch stationary with wild red flame and
     clouds of smoke,
By these, crowds, groups of forms vaguely I see on the floor, some
     in the pews laid down,
At my feet more distinctly a soldier, a mere lad, in danger of
     bleeding to death, (he is shot in the abdomen,)
I stanch the blood temporarily, (the youngster's face is white as
     a lily,)
Then before I depart I sweep my eyes o'er the scene fain to
     absorb it all,
Faces, varieties, postures beyond description, most in obscurity,
     some of them dead,
Surgeons operating, attendants holding lights, the smell of ether,
     the odor of blood,
The crowd, O the crowd of the bloody forms, the yard outside
     also fill'd,
Some on the bare ground, some on planks or stretchers, some in
     the death-spasm sweating,

An occasional scream or cry, the doctor's shouted orders or calls,
The glisten of the little steel instruments catching the glint of the
    torches,
These I resume as I chant, I see again the forms, I smell the odor,
Then hear outside the orders given, *Fall in, my men, fall in;*
But first I bend to the dying lad, his eyes open, a half-smile gives
    he me,
Then the eyes close, calmly close, and I speed forth to the
    darkness,
Resuming, marching, ever in darkness marching, on in the ranks,
The unknown road still marching.

A SIGHT IN CAMP IN THE DAYBREAK GRAY AND DIM

A sight in camp in the daybreak gray and dim,
As from my tent I emerge so early sleepless,
As slow I walk in the cool fresh air the path near by the hospital
    tent,
Three forms I see on stretchers lying, brought out there untended
    lying,
Over each the blanket spread, ample brownish woolen blanket,
Gray and heavy blanket, folding, covering all.

Curious I halt and silent stand,
Then with light fingers I from the face of the nearest the first just
    lift the blanket;
Who are you elderly man so gaunt and grim, with well-gray'd
    hair, and flesh all sunken about the eyes?
Who are you my dear comrade?

Then to the second I step—and who are you my child and darling?
Who are you sweet boy with cheeks yet blooming?

Then to the third—a face nor child nor old, very calm, as of
    beautiful yellow-white ivory;
Young man I think I know you—I think this face is the face of
    the Christ himself,
Dead and divine and brother of all, and here again he lies.

AS TOILSOME I WANDER'D VIRGINIA'S WOODS

As toilsome I wander'd Virginia's woods,
To the music of rustling leaves kick'd by my feet, (for 'twas
    autumn,)

I mark'd at the foot of a tree the grave of a soldier;
Mortally wounded he and buried on the retreat, (easily all could
     I understand,)
The halt of a mid-day hour, when up! no time to lose—yet this
     sign left,
On a tablet scrawl'd and nail'd on the tree by the grave,
Bold, cautious, true, and my loving comrade.

Long, long I muse, then on my way go wandering,
Many a changeful season to follow, and many a scene of life,
Yet at times through changeful season and scene, abrupt, alone,
     or in the crowded street,
Comes before me the unknown soldier's grave, comes the inscrip-
     tion rude in Virginia's woods,
Bold, cautious, true, and my loving comrade.

NOT THE PILOT

NOT the pilot has charged himself to bring his ship into port,
     though beaten back and many times baffled;
Not the pathfinder penetrating inland weary and long,
By deserts, parch'd snows chill'd, rivers wet, perseveres till he
     reaches his destination,
More than I have charged myself, heeded or unheeded, to com-
     pose a march for these States,
For a battle-call, rousing to arms if need be, years, centuries hence.

YEAR THAT TREMBLED AND REEL'D BENEATH ME

YEAR that trembled and reel'd beneath me!
Your summer wind was warm enough, yet the air I breathed froze
     me,
A thick gloom fell through the sunshine and darken'd me,
Must I change my triumphant songs? said I to myself,
Must I indeed learn to chant the cold dirges of the baffled?
And sullen hymns of defeat?

THE WOUND-DRESSER

1

AN old man bending I come among new faces,
Years looking backward resuming in answer to children,
Come tell us old man, as from young men and maidens that love
     me,

(Arous'd and angry, I'd thought to beat the alarum, and urge relentless war,
But soon my fingers fail'd me, my face droop'd and I resign'd myself,
To sit by the wounded and soothe them, or silently watch the dead;)
Years hence of these scenes, of these furious passions, these chances,
Of unsurpass'd heroes, (was one side so brave? the other was equally brave;)
Now be witness again, paint the mightiest armies of earth,
Of those armies so rapid so wondrous what saw you to tell us?
What stays with you latest and deepest? of curious panics,
Of hard-fought engagements or sieges tremendous what deepest remains?

2

O maidens and young men I love and that love me,
What you ask of my days those the strangest and sudden your talking recalls,
Soldier alert I arrive after a long march cover'd with sweat and dust,
In the nick of time I come, plunge in the fight, loudly shout in the rush of successful charge,
Enter the captur'd works—yet lo, like a swift-running river they fade,
Pass and are gone they fade—I dwell not on soldiers' perils or soldiers' joys,
(Both I remember well—many the hardships, few the joys, yet I was content.)

But in silence, in dreams' projections,
While the world of gain and appearance and mirth goes on,
So soon what is over forgotten, and waves wash the imprints off the sand,
With hinged knees returning I enter the doors, (while for you up there,
Whoever you are, follow without noise and be of strong heart.)

Bearing the bandages, water and sponge,
Straight and swift to my wounded I go,
Where they lie on the ground after the battle brought in,
Where their priceless blood reddens the grass the ground,

Or to the rows of the hospital tent, or under the roof'd hospital,
To the long rows of cots up and down each side I return,
To each and all one after another I draw near, not one do I miss,
An attendant follows holding a tray, he carries a refuse pail,
Soon to be fill'd with clotted rags and blood, emptied, and fill'd
    again.

I onward go, I stop,
With hinged knees and steady hand to dress wounds,
I am firm with each, the pangs are sharp yet unavoidable,
One turns to me his appealing eyes—poor boy! I never knew you,
Yet I think I could not refuse this moment to die for you, if that
    would save you.

3

On, on I go, (open doors of time! open hospital doors!)
The crush'd head I dress, (poor crazed hand tear not the bandage
    away,)
The neck of the cavalry-man with the bullet through and through
    I examine,
Hard the breathing rattles, quite glazed already the eye, yet life
    struggles hard,
(Come sweet death! be persuaded O beautiful death!
In mercy come quickly.)

From the stump of the arm, the amputated hand,
I undo the clotted lint, remove the slough, wash off the matter
    and blood,
Back on his pillow the soldier bends with curv'd neck and side-
    falling head,
His eyes are closed, his face is pale, he dares not look on the bloody
    stump,
And has not yet look'd on it.

I dress a wound in the side, deep, deep,
But a day or two more, for see the frame all wasted and sinking,
And the yellow-blue countenance see.

I dress the perforated shoulder, the foot with the bullet-wound,
Cleanse the one with a gnawing and putrid gangrene, so sickening,
    so offensive,
While the attendant stands behind aside me holding the tray and
    pail.

I am faithful, I do not give out,
The fractur'd thigh, the knee, the wound in the abdomen,
These and more I dress with impassive hand, (yet deep in my
   breast a fire, a burning flame.)

4

Thus in silence in dreams' projections,
Returning, resuming, I thread my way through the hospitals,
The hurt and wounded I pacify with soothing hand,
I sit by the restless all the dark night, some are so young,
Some suffer so much, I recall the experience sweet and sad,
(Many a soldier's loving arms about this neck have cross'd and
   rested,
Many a soldier's kiss dwells on these bearded lips.)

LONG, TOO LONG AMERICA

LONG, too long America,
Traveling roads all even and peaceful you learn'd from joys and
   prosperity only,
But now, ah now, to learn from crises of anguish, advancing, grappling with direst fate and recoiling not,
And now to conceive and show to the world what your children
   en-masse really are,
(For who except myself has yet conceiv'd what your children
   en-masse really are?)

GIVE ME THE SPLENDID SILENT SUN

1

GIVE me the splendid silent sun with all his beams full-dazzling,
Give me juicy autumnal fruit ripe and red from the orchard,
Give me a field where the unmow'd grass grows,
Give me an arbor, give me the trellis'd grape,
Give me fresh corn and wheat, give me serene-moving animals
   teaching content,
Give me nights perfectly quiet as on high plateaus west of the
   Mississippi, and I looking up at the stars,
Give me odorous at sunrise a garden of beautiful flowers where I
   can walk undisturb'd,
Give me for marriage a sweet-breath'd woman of whom I should
   never tire,

Give me a perfect child, give me away aside from the noise of the
    world a rural domestic life,
Give me to warble spontaneous songs recluse by myself, for my
    own ears only,
Give me solitude, give me Nature, give me again O Nature your
    primal sanities!

These demanding to have them, (tired with ceaseless excitement,
    and rack'd by the war-strife,)
These to procure incessantly asking, rising in cries from my heart,
While yet incessantly asking still I adhere to my city,
Day upon day and year upon year O city, walking your streets,
Where you hold me enchain'd a certain time refusing to give me
    up,
Yet giving to make me glutted, enrich'd of soul, you give me forever
    faces;
(O I see what I sought to escape, confronting, reversing my cries,
I see my own soul trampling down what it ask'd for.)

2

Keep your splendid silent sun,
Keep your woods O Nature, and the quiet places by the woods,
Keep your fields of clover and timothy, and your corn-fields and
    orchards,
Keep the blossoming buckwheat fields where the Ninth-month
    bees hum;
Give me faces and streets—give me these phantoms incessant and
    endless along the trottoirs!
Give me interminable eyes—give me women—give me comrades
    and lovers by the thousand!
Let me see new ones every day—let me hold new ones by the hand
    every day!
Give me such shows—give me the streets of Manhattan!
Give me Broadway, with the soldiers marching—give me the
    sound of the trumpets and drums!
(The soldiers in companies or regiments—some starting away,
    flush'd and reckless,
Some, their time up, returning with thinn'd ranks, young, yet very
    old, worn, marching, noticing nothing;)
Give me the shores and wharves heavy-fringed with black ships!
O such for me! O an intense life, full to repletion and varied!
The life of the theatre, bar-room, huge hotel, for me!

The saloon of the steamer! the crowded excursion for me! the torchlight procession!
The dense brigade bound for the war, with high piled military wagons following;
People, endless, streaming, with strong voices, passions, pageants,
Manhattan streets with their powerful throbs, with beating drums as now,
The endless and noisy chorus, the rustle and clank of muskets, (even the sight of the wounded,)
Manhattan crowds, with their turbulent musical chorus!
Manhattan faces and eyes forever for me.

DIRGE FOR TWO VETERANS

THE last sunbeam
Lightly falls from the finish'd Sabbath,
On the pavement here, and there beyond it is looking,
Down a new-made double grave.

Lo, the moon ascending,
Up from the east the silvery round moon,
Beautiful over the house-tops, ghastly, phantom moon,
Immense and silent moon.

I see a sad procession,
And I hear the sound of coming full-key'd bugles,
All the channels of the city streets they're flooding,
As with voices and with tears.

I hear the great drums pounding,
And the small drums steady whirring,
And every blow of the great convulsive drums,
Strikes me through and through.

For the son is brought with the father,
(In the foremost ranks of the fierce assault they fell,
Two veterans son and father dropt together,
And the double grave awaits them.)

Now nearer blow the bugles,
And the drums strike more convulsive,
And the daylight o'er the pavement quite has faded,
And the strong dead-march enwraps me.

In the eastern sky up-buoying,
The sorrowful vast phantom moves illumin'd,
('Tis some mother's large transparent face,
    In heaven brighter growing.)

    O strong dead-march you please me!
O moon immense with your silvery face you soothe me!
O my soldiers twain! O my veterans passing to burial!
    What I have I also give you.

    The moon gives you light,
And the bugles and the drums give you music,
And my heart, O my soldiers, my veterans,
    My heart gives you love.

OVER THE CARNAGE ROSE PROPHETIC A VOICE

OVER the carnage rose prophetic a voice,
Be not dishearten'd, affection shall solve the problems of freedom
    yet,
Those who love each other shall become invincible,
They shall yet make Columbia victorious.

Sons of the Mother of All, you shall yet be victorious,
You shall yet laugh to scorn the attacks of all the remainder of the
    earth.

No danger shall balk Columbia's lovers,
If need be a thousand shall sternly immolate themselves for one.

One from Massachusetts shall be a Missourian's comrade,
From Maine and from hot Carolina, and another an Oregonese, shall
    be friends triune,
More precious to each other than all the riches of the earth.

To Michigan, Florida perfumes shall tenderly come,
Not the perfumes of flowers, but sweeter, and wafted beyond death.

It shall be customary in the houses and streets to see manly affection,
The most dauntless and rude shall touch face to face lightly,
The dependence of Liberty shall be lovers,
The continuance of Equality shall be comrades.

These shall tie you and band you stronger than hoops of iron,
I, ecstatic, O partners! O lands! with the love of lovers tie you.

(Were you looking to be held together by lawyers?
Or by an agreement on paper? or by arms?
Nay, nor the world, nor any living thing, will so cohere.)

I SAW OLD GENERAL AT BAY

I SAW old General at bay,
(Old as he was, his gray eyes yet shone out in battle like stars,)
His small force was now completely hemm'd in, in his works,
He call'd for volunteers to run the enemy's lines, a desperate emer-
gency,
I saw a hundred and more step forth from the ranks, but two or three
were selected,
I saw them receive their orders aside, they listen'd with care, the
m adjutant was very grave,
I saw them depart with cheerfulness, freely risking their lives.

THE ARTILLERYMAN'S VISION

WHILE my wife at my side was slumbering, and the wars are over long,
And my head on the pillow rests at home, and the vacant midnight
passes,
And through the stillness, through the dark, I hear, just hear, the
breath of my infant,
There in the room as I wake from sleep this vision presses upon me;
The engagement opens there and then in fantasy unreal,
The skirmishers begin, they crawl cautiously ahead, I hear the irregu-
lar snap! snap!
I hear the sounds of the different missiles, the short *t-h-t! t-h-t!* of
the rifle-balls,
I see the shells exploding leaving small white clouds, I hear the great
shells shrieking as they pass,
The grape like the hum and whirr of wind through the trees, (tumul-
tuous now the contest rages,)
All the scenes at the batteries rise in detail before me again,
The crashing and smoking, the pride of the men in their pieces,
The chief-gunner ranges and sights his piece and selects a fuse of the
right time,
After firing I see him lean aside and look eagerly off to note the effect;
Elsewhere I hear the cry of a regiment charging, (the young colonel
leads himself this time with brandish'd sword,)

I see the gaps cut by the enemy's volleys, (quickly fill'd up, no delay,)
I breathe the suffocating smoke, then the flat clouds hover low concealing all;
Now a strange lull for a few seconds, not a shot fired on either side,
Then resumed the chaos louder than ever, with eager calls and orders of officers,
While from some distant part of the field the wind wafts to my ears a shout of applause, (some special success,)
And ever the sound of the cannon far or near, (rousing even in dreams a devilish exultation and all the old mad joy in the depths of my soul,)
And ever the hastening of infantry shifting positions, batteries, cavalry, moving hither and thither,
(The falling, dying, I heed not, the wounded dripping and red I heed not, some to the rear are hobbling,)
Grime, heat, rush, aide-de-camps galloping by or on a full run,
With the patter of small arms, the warning s-s-t of the rifles, (these in my vision I hear or see,)
And bombs bursting in air, and at night the vari-color'd rockets.

ETHIOPIA SALUTING THE COLORS

WHO are you dusky woman, so ancient hardly human,
With your woolly-white and turban'd head, and bare bony feet?
Why rising by the roadside here, do you the colors greet?

('Tis while our army lines Carolina's sands and pines,
Forth from thy hovel door thou Ethiopia com'st to me,
As under doughty Sherman I march toward the sea.)

Me master years a hundred since from my parents sunder'd,
A little child, they caught me as the savage beast is caught,
Then hither me across the sea the cruel slaver brought.

No further does she say, but lingering all the day,
Her high-borne turban'd head she wags, and rolls her darkling eye,
And courtesies to the regiments, the guidons moving by.

What is it fateful woman, so blear, hardly human?
Why wag your head with turban bound, yellow, red and green?
Are the things so strange and marvelous you see or have seen?

NOT YOUTH PERTAINS TO ME

NOT youth pertains to me,
Nor delicatesse, I cannot beguile the time with talk,
Awkward in the parlor, neither a dancer nor elegant,
In the learn'd coterie sitting constrain'd and still, for learning inures
    not to me,
Beauty, knowledge, inure not to me—yet there are two or three
    things inure to me,
I have nourish'd the wounded and sooth'd many a dying soldier,
And at intervals waiting or in the midst of camp,
Composed these songs.

RACE OF VETERANS

RACE of veterans—race of victors!
Race of the soil, ready for conflict—race of the conquering march!
(No more credulity's race, abiding-temper'd race,)
Race henceforth owning no law but the law of itself,
Race of passion and the storm.

WORLD TAKE GOOD NOTICE

WORLD take good notice, silver stars fading,
Milky hue ript, weft of white detaching,
Coals thirty-eight, baleful and burning,
Scarlet, significant, hands off warning,
Now and henceforth flaunt from these shores.

O TAN-FACED PRAIRIE-BOY

O TAN-FACED prairie-boy,
Before you came to camp many a welcome gift,
Praises and presents came and nourishing food, till at last among the
    recruits,
You came, taciturn, with nothing to give—we but look'd on each
    other,
When lo! more than all the gifts of the world you gave me.

LOOK DOWN FAIR MOON

LOOK down fair moon and bathe this scene,
Pour softly down night's nimbus floods on faces ghastly, swollen,
    purple.

On the dead on their backs with arms toss'd wide,
Pour down your unstinted nimbus sacred moon.

RECONCILIATION

WORD over all, beautiful as the sky,
Beautiful that war and all its deeds of carnage must in time be utterly
     lost,
That the hands of the sisters Death and Night incessantly softly wash
     again, and ever again, this soil'd world;
For my enemy is dead, a man divine as myself is dead,
I look where he lies white-faced and still in the coffin—I draw near,
Bend down and touch lightly with my lips the white face in the coffin.

HOW SOLEMN AS ONE BY ONE

(*Washington City*, 1865)

How solemn as one by one,
As the ranks returning worn and sweaty, as the men file by where I
     stand,
As the faces the masks appear, as I glance at the faces studying the
     masks,
(As I glance upward out of this page studying you, dear friend, who-
     ever you are,)
How solemn the thought of my whispering soul to each in the ranks,
     and to you,
I see behind each mask that wonder a kindred soul,
O the bullet could never kill what you really are, dear friend,
Nor the bayonet stab what you really are;
The soul! yourself I see, great as any, good as the best,
Waiting secure and content, which the bullet could never kill,
Nor the bayonet stab O friend.

AS I LAY WITH MY HEAD IN YOUR LAP CAMERADO

As I lay with my head in your lap camerado,
The confession I made I resume, what I said to you and the open air
     I resume,
I know I am restless and make others so,
I know my words are weapons full of danger, full of death,
For I confront peace, security, and all the settled laws, to unsettle
     them,
I am more resolute because all have denied me than I could ever have
     been had all accepted me,

I heed not and have never heeded either experience, cautions, major-
    ities, nor ridicule,
And the threat of what is call'd hell is little or nothing to me,
And the lure of what is call'd heaven is little or nothing to me;
Dear camerado! I confess I have urged you onward with me, and
    still urge you, without the least idea what is our destination,
Or whether we shall be victorious, or utterly quell'd and defeated.

DELICATE CLUSTER

Delicate cluster! flag of teeming life!
Covering all my lands—all my seashores lining!
Flag of death! (how I watch'd you through the smoke of battle
    pressing!
How I heard you flap and rustle, cloth defiant!)
Flag cerulean—sunny flag, with the orbs of night dappled!
Ah my silvery beauty—ah my woolly white and crimson!
Ah to sing the song of you, my matron mighty!
My sacred one, my mother.

TO A CERTAIN CIVILIAN

Did you ask dulcet rhymes from me?
Did you seek the civilian's peaceful and languishing rhymes?
Did you find what I sang erewhile so hard to follow?
Why I was not singing erewhile for you to follow, to understand—
    nor am I now;
(I have been born of the same as the war was born,
The drum-corps' rattle is ever to me sweet music, I love well the
    martial dirge,
With slow wail and convulsive throb leading the officer's funeral;)
What to such as you anyhow such a poet as I? therefore leave my
    works,
And go lull yourself with what you can understand, and with piano-
    tunes,
For I lull nobody, and you will never understand me.

LO, VICTRESS ON THE PEAKS

Lo, Victress on the peaks,
Where thou with mighty brow regarding the world,
(The world O Libertad, that vainly conspired against thee,)
Out of its countless beleaguering toils, after thwarting them all,

Dominant, with the dazzling sun around thee,
Flauntest now unharm'd in immortal soundness and bloom—lo, in
    these hours supreme,
No poem proud, I chanting bring to thee, nor mastery's rapturous
    verse,
But a cluster containing night's darkness and blood-dripping
    wounds,
And psalms of the dead.

SPIRIT WHOSE WORK IS DONE

(*Washington City*, 1865)

SPIRIT whose work is done—spirit of dreadful hours!
Ere departing fade from my eyes your forests of bayonets;
Spirit of gloomiest fears and doubts, (yet onward ever unfaltering
    pressing,)
Spirit of many a solemn day and many a savage scene—electric
    spirit,
That with muttering voice through the war now closed, like a tireless
    phantom flitted,
Rousing the land with breath of flame, while you beat and beat the
    drum,
Now as the sound of the drum, hollow and harsh to the last, rever-
    berates round me,
As your ranks, your immortal ranks, return, return from the battles,
As the muskets of the young men yet lean over their shoulders,
As I look on the bayonets bristling over their shoulders,
As those slanted bayonets, whole forests of them appearing in the
    distance, approach and pass on, returning homeward,
Moving with steady motion, swaying to and fro to the right and left,
Evenly lightly rising and falling while the steps keep time;
Spirit of hours I knew, all hectic red one day, but pale as death next
    day,
Touch my mouth ere you depart, press my lips close,
Leave me your pulses of rage—bequeath them to me—fill me with
    currents convulsive,
Let them scorch and blister out of my chants when you are gone,
Let them identify you to the future in these songs.

ADIEU TO A SOLDIER

ADIEU O soldier,
You of the rude campaigning, (which we shared,)
The rapid march, the life of the camp,

The hot contention of opposing fronts, the long manœuvre,
Red battles with their slaughter, the stimulus, the strong terrific
    game,
Spell of all brave and manly hearts, the trains of time through you
    and like of you all fill'd,
With war and war's expression.

Adieu dear comrade,
Your mission is fulfill'd—but I, more warlike,
Myself and this contentious soul of mine,
Still on our own campaigning bound,
Through untried roads with ambushes opponents lined,
Through many a sharp defeat and many a crisis, often baffled,
Here marching, ever marching on, a war fight out—aye here,
To fiercer, weightier battles give expression.

TURN O LIBERTAD

Turn O Libertad, for the war is over,
From it and all henceforth expanding, doubting no more, resolute,
    sweeping the world,
Turn from lands retrospective recording proofs of the past,
From the singers that sing the trailing glories of the past,
From the chants of the feudal world, the triumphs of kings, slavery,
    caste,
Turn to the world, the triumphs reserv'd and to come—give up that
    backward world,
Leave to the singers of hitherto, give them the trailing past,
But what remains remains for singers for you—wars to come are for
    you,
(Lo, how the wars of the past have duly inured to you, and the wars
    of the present also inure;)
Then turn, and be not alarm'd O Libertad—turn your undying face,
To where the future, greater than all the past,
Is swiftly, surely preparing for you.

TO THE LEAVEN'D SOIL THEY TROD

To the leaven'd soil they trod calling I sing for the last,
(Forth from my tent emerging for good, loosing, untying the tent-
    ropes,)
In the freshness the forenoon air, in the far-stretching circuits and
    vistas again to peace restored,

To the fiery fields emanative and the endless vistas beyond, to the
    South and the North,
To the leaven'd soil of the general Western world to attest my songs,
To the Alleghanian hills and the tireless Mississippi,
To the rocks I calling sing, and all the trees in the woods,
To the plains of the poems of heroes, to the prairies spreading wide,
To the far-off sea and the unseen winds, and the sane impalpable air;
And responding they answer all, (but not in words,)
The average earth, the witness of war and peace, acknowledges
    mutely,
The prairie draws me close, as the father to bosom broad the son,
The Northern ice and rain that began me nourish me to the end,
But the hot sun of the South is to fully ripen my songs.

Memories of President Lincoln

WHEN LILACS LAST IN THE DOORYARD BLOOM'D

1

When lilacs last in the dooryard bloom'd,
And the great star early droop'd in the western sky in the night,
I mourn'd, and yet shall mourn with ever-returning spring.

Ever-returning spring, trinity sure to me you bring,
Lilac blooming perennial and drooping star in the west,
And thought of him I love.

2

O powerful western fallen star!
O shades of night—O moody, tearful night!
O great star disappear'd—O the black murk that hides the star!
O cruel hands that hold me powerless—O helpless soul of me!
O harsh surrounding cloud that will not free my soul.

3

In the dooryard fronting an old farm-house near the white-wash'd
 palings,
Stands the lilac-bush tall-growing with heart-shaped leaves of rich
 green,
With many a pointed blossom rising delicate, with the perfume strong
 I love,
With every leaf a miracle—and from this bush in the dooryard,
With delicate-color'd blossoms and heart-shaped leaves of rich green,
A sprig with its flower I break.

4

In the swamp in secluded recesses,
A shy and hidden bird is warbling a song.

Solitary the thrush,
The hermit withdrawn to himself, avoiding the settlements,
Sings by himself a song.

Song of the bleeding throat,
Death's outlet song of life, (for well dear brother I know,
If thou wast not granted to sing thou would'st surely die.)

5

Over the breast of the spring, the land, amid cities,
Amid lanes and through old woods, where lately the violets peep'd
    from the ground, spotting the gray debris,
Amid the grass in the fields each side of the lanes, passing the endless
    grass,
Passing the yellow-spear'd wheat, every grain from its shroud in the
    dark-brown fields uprisen,
Passing the apple-tree blows of white and pink in the orchards,
Carrying a corpse to where it shall rest in the grave,
Night and day journeys a coffin.

6

Coffin that passes through lanes and streets,
Through day and night with the great cloud darkening the land,
With the pomp of the inloop'd flags with the cities draped in black,
With the show of the States themselves as of crape-veil'd women
    standing,
With processions long and winding and the flambeaus of the night,
With the countless torches lit, with the silent sea of faces and the
    unbared heads,
With the waiting depot, the arriving coffin, and the sombre faces,
With dirges through the night, with the thousand voices rising strong
    and solemn,
With all the mournful voices of the dirges pour'd around the coffin,
The dim-lit churches and the shuddering organs—where amid these
    you journey,
With the tolling tolling bells' perpetual clang,
Here, coffin that slowly passes,
I give you my sprig of lilac.

7

(Nor for you, for one alone,
Blossoms and branches green to coffins all I bring,

For fresh as the morning, thus would I chant a song for you O sane
    and sacred death.

All over bouquets of roses,
O death, I cover you over with roses and early lilies,
But mostly and now the lilac that blooms the first,
Copious I break, I break the sprigs from the bushes,
With loaded arms I come, pouring for you,
For you and the coffins all of you O death.)

8

O western orb sailing the heaven,
Now I know what you must have meant as a month since I walk'd,
As I walk'd in silence the transparent shadowy night,
As I saw you had something to tell as you bent to me night after
    night,
As you droop'd from the sky low down as if to my side, (while the
    other stars all look'd on,)
As we wander'd together the solemn night, (for something I know
    not what kept me from sleep,)
As the night advanced, and I saw on the rim of the west how full
    you were of woe,
As I stood on the rising ground in the breeze in the cool transparent
    night,
As I watch'd where you pass'd and was lost in the netherward black
    of the night,
As my soul in its trouble dissatisfied sank, as where you sad orb,
Concluded, dropt in the night, and was gone.

9

Sing on there in the swamp,
O singer bashful and tender, I hear your notes, I hear your call,
I hear, I come presently, I understand you,
But a moment I linger, for the lustrous star has detain'd me,
The star my departing comrade holds and detains me.

10

O how shall I warble myself for the dead one there I loved?
And how shall I deck my song for the large sweet soul that has gone?
And what shall my perfume be for the grave of him I love?

Sea-winds blown from east and west,
Blown from the Eastern sea and blown from the Western sea, till
    there on the prairies meeting,
These and with these and the breath of my chant,
I'll perfume the grave of him I love.

11

O what shall I hang on the chamber walls?
And what shall the pictures be that I hang on the walls,
To adorn the burial-house of him I love?

Pictures of growing spring and farms and homes,
With the Fourth-month eve at sundown, and the gray smoke lucid
    and bright,
With floods of the yellow gold of the gorgeous, indolent, sinking sun,
    burning, expanding the air,
With the fresh sweet herbage under foot, and the pale green leaves
    of the trees prolific,
In the distance the flowing glaze, the breast of the river, with a wind-
    dapple here and there,
With ranging hills on the banks, with many a line against the sky,
    and shadows,
And the city at hand with dwellings so dense, and stacks of chimneys,
And all the scenes of life and the workshops, and the workmen home-
    ward returning.

12

Lo, body and soul—this land,
My own Manhattan with spires, and the sparkling and hurrying
    tides, and the ships,
The varied and ample land, the South and the North in the light,
    Ohio's shores and flashing Missouri,
And ever the far-spreading prairies cover'd with grass and corn.

Lo, the most excellent sun so calm and haughty,
The violet and purple morn with just-felt breezes,
The gentle soft-born measureless light,
The miracle spreading bathing all, the fulfill'd noon,
The coming eve delicious, the welcome night and the stars,
Over my cities shining all, enveloping man and land.

13

Sing on, sing on you gray-brown bird,
Sing from the swamps, the recesses, pour your chant from the
    bushes,
Limitless out of the dusk, out of the cedars and pines.

Sing on dearest brother, warble your reedy song,
Loud human song, with voice of uttermost woe.

O liquid and free and tender!
O wild and loose to my soul—O wondrous singer!
You only I hear—yet the star holds me, (but will soon depart,)
Yet the lilac with mastering odor holds me.

14

Now while I sat in the day and look'd forth,
In the close of the day with its light and the fields of spring, and
    the farmers preparing their crops,
In the large unconscious scenery of my land with its lakes and
    forests,
In the heavenly aerial beauty, (after the perturb'd winds and the
    storms,)
Under the arching heavens of the afternoon swift passing, and the
    voices of children and women,
The many-moving sea-tides, and I saw the ships how they sail'd,
And the summer approaching with richness, and the fields all busy
    with labor,
And the infinite separate houses, how they all went on, each with
    its meals and minutia of daily usages,
And the streets how their throbbings throbb'd, and the cities pent
    —lo, then and there,
Falling upon them all and among them all, enveloping me with the
    rest,
Appear'd the cloud, appear'd the long black trail,
And I knew death, its thought, and the sacred knowledge of death.

Then with the knowledge of death as walking one side of me,
And the thought of death close-walking the other side of me,
And I in the middle as with companions, and as holding the hands
    of companions,
I fled forth to the hiding receiving night that talks not,

Down to the shores of the water, the path by the swamp in the
    dimness,
To the solemn shadowy cedars and ghostly pines so still.

And the singer so shy to the rest receiv'd me,
The gray-brown bird I know receiv'd us comrades three,
And he sang the carol of death, and a verse for him I love.

From deep secluded recesses,
From the fragrant cedars and the ghostly pines so still,
Came the carol of the bird.

And the charm of the carol rapt me,
As I held as if by their hands my comrades in the night,
And the voice of my spirit tallied the song of the bird.

Comely lovely and soothing death,
Undulate round the world, serenely arriving, arriving,
In the day, in the night, to all, to each,
Sooner or later delicate death.

Prais'd be the fathomless universe,
For life and joy, and for objects and knowledge curious,
And for love, sweet love—but praise! praise! praise!
For the sure-enwinding arms of cool-enfolding death.

Dark mother always gliding near with soft feet,
Have none chanted for thee a chant of fullest welcome?
Then I chant it for thee, I glorify thee above all,
I bring thee a song that when thou must indeed come, come unfal-
    eringly.

Approach strong deliveress,
When it is so, when thou hast taken them I joyously sing the dead,
Lost in the loving floating ocean of thee,
Laved in the flood of thy bliss O death.

From me to thee glad serenades,
Dances for thee I propose saluting thee, adornments and feastings
    for thee,
And the sights of the open landscape and the high-spread sky are
    fitting,
And life and the fields, and the huge and thoughtful night.

The night in silence under many a star,
The ocean shore and the husky whispering wave whose voice I know,
And the soul turning to thee O vast well-veil'd death,
And the body gratefully nestling close to thee.

Over the tree-tops I float thee a song,
Over the rising and sinking waves, over the myriad fields and the
    prairies wide,
Over the dense-pack'd cities all and the teeming wharves and ways,
I float this carol with joy, with joy to thee O death.

                              15

To the tally of my soul,
Loud and strong kept up the gray-brown bird,
With pure deliberate notes spreading filling the night.

Loud in the pines and cedars dim,
Clear in the freshness moist and the swamp-perfume,
And I with my comrades there in the night.

While my sight that was bound in my eyes unclosed,
As to long panoramas of visions.

And I saw askant the armies,
I saw as in noiseless dreams hundred of battle-flags,
Borne through the smoke of the battles and pierc'd with missiles
    I saw them,
And carried hither and yon through the smoke, and torn and
    bloody,
And at last but a few shreds left on the staffs, (and all in silence,)
And the staffs all splinter'd and broken.

I saw battle-corpses, myriads of them,
And the white skeletons of young men, I saw them,
I saw the debris and debris of all the slain soldiers of the war,
But I saw they were not as was thought,
They themselves were fully at rest, they suffer'd not,
The living remain'd and suffer'd, the mother suffer'd,
And the wife and the child and the musing comrade suffer'd,
And the armies that remain'd suffer'd.

16

Passing the visions, passing the night,
Passing, unloosing the hold of my comrades' hands,
Passing the song of the hermit bird and the tallying song of my
     soul,
Victorious song, death's outlet song, yet varying ever-altering song,
As low and wailing, yet clear the notes, rising and falling, flooding
     the night,
Sadly sinking and fainting, as warning and warning, and yet again
     bursting with joy,
Covering the earth and filling the spread of the heaven,
As that powerful psalm in the night I heard from recesses,
Passing, I leave thee lilac with heart-shaped leaves,
I leave thee there in the door-yard, blooming, returning with
     spring.

I cease from my song for thee,
From my gaze on thee in the west, fronting the west, communing
     with thee,
O comrade lustrous with silver face in the night.

Yet each to keep and all, retrievements out of the night,
The song, the wondrous chant of the gray-brown bird,
And the tallying chant, the echo arous'd in my soul,
With the lustrous and drooping star with the countenance full of
     woe,
With the holders holding my hand nearing the call of the bird,
Comrades mine and I in the midst, and their memory ever to keep,
     for the dead I loved so well,
For the sweetest, wisest soul of all my days and lands—and this
     for his dear sake,
Lilac and star and bird twined with the chant of my soul,
There in the fragrant pines and the cedars dusk and dim.

O CAPTAIN! MY CAPTAIN!

O CAPTAIN! my Captain! our fearful trip is done,
The ship has weather'd every rack, the prize we sought is won,
The port is near, the bells I hear, the people all exulting,
While follow eyes the steady keel, the vessel grim and daring;
          But O heart! heart! heart!
               O the bleeding drops of red,
                    Where on the deck my Captain lies,
                         Fallen cold and dead.

O Captain! my Captain! rise up and hear the bells;
Rise up—for you the flag is flung—for you the bugle trills,
For you bouquets and ribbon'd wreaths—for you the shores
    a-crowding,
For you they call, the swaying mass, their eager faces turning;
    Here Captain! dear father!
        This arm beneath your head!
           It is some dream that on the deck,
              You've fallen cold and dead.

My Captain does not answer, his lips are pale and still,
My father does not feel my arm, he has no pulse nor will,
The ship is anchor'd safe and sound, its voyage closed and done,
From fearful trip the victor ship comes in with object won;
    Exult O shores, and ring O bells!
        But I with mournful tread,
           Walk the deck my Captain lies,
              Fallen cold and dead.

HUSH'D BE THE CAMPS TO-DAY

(*May* 4, 1865)

HUSH'D be the camps to-day,
And soldiers let us drape our war-worn weapons,
And each with musing soul retire to celebrate,
Our dear commander's death.

No more for him life's stormy conflicts,
Nor victory, nor defeat—no more time's dark events,
Charging like ceaseless clouds across the sky.

But sing poet in our name,
Sing of the love we bore him—because you, dweller in camps,
    know it truly.

As they invault the coffin there,
Sing—as they close the doors of earth upon him—one verse,
For the heavy hearts of soldiers.

THIS DUST WAS ONCE THE MAN

THIS dust was once the man,
Gentle, plain, just and resolute, under whose cautious hand,
Against the foulest crime in history known in any land or age,
Was saved the Union of these States.

By Blue Ontario's Shore

1

By blue Ontario's shore,
As I mused of these warlike days and of peace return'd, and the
dead that return no more,
A Phantom gigantic superb, with stern visage accosted me,
Chant me the poem, it said, *that comes from the soul of America,
chant me the carol of victory,
And strike up the marches of Libertad, marches more powerful yet,
And sing me before you go the song of the throes of Democracy.*

(Democracy, the destin'd conqueror, yet treacherous lip-smiles
everywhere,
And death and infidelity at every step.)

2

A Nation announcing itself,
I myself make the only growth by which I can be appreciated,
I reject none, accept all, then reproduce all in my own forms.

A breed whose proof is in time and deeds,
What we are we are, nativity is answer enough to objections,
We wield ourselves as a weapon is wielded,
We are powerful and tremendous in ourselves,
We are executive in ourselves, we are sufficient in the variety of
ourselves,
We are the most beautiful to ourselves and in ourselves,
We stand self-pois'd in the middle, branching thence over the
world,
From Missouri, Nebraska, or Kansas, laughing attacks to scorn.

Nothing is sinful to us outside of ourselves.
Whatever appears, whatever does not appear, we are beautiful or
sinful in ourselves only.

(O Mother—O Sisters dear!
If we are lost, no victor else has destroy'd us,
It is by ourselves we go down to eternal night.)

3

Have you thought there could be but a single supreme?
There can be any number of supremes—one does not countervail another any more than one eyesight countervails another, or one life countervails another.

All is eligible to all,
All is for individuals, all is for you,
No condition is prohibited, not God's or any.

All comes by the body, only health puts you rapport with the universe.

Produce great Persons, the rest follows.

4

Piety and conformity to them that like,
Peace, obesity, allegiance, to them that like,
I am he who tauntingly compels men, women, nations,
Crying, Leap from your seats and contend for your lives!

I am he who walks the States with a barb'd tongue, questioning every one I meet,
Who are you that wanted only to be told what you knew before?
Who are you that wanted only a book to join you in your nonsense?

(With pangs and cries as thine own O bearer of many children,
These clamors wild to a race of pride I give.)

O lands, would you be freer than all that has ever been before?
If you would be freer than all that has been before, come listen to me.

Fear grace, elegance, civilization, delicatesse,
Fear the mellow sweet, the sucking of honey-juice,
Beware the advancing mortal ripening of Nature,
Beware what precedes the decay of the ruggedness of states and men.

5

Ages, precedents, have long been accumulating undirected materials,
America brings builders, and brings its own styles.

The immortal poets of Asia and Europe have done their work and
     pass'd to other spheres,
A work remains, the work of surpassing all they have done.

America, curious toward foreign characters, stands by its own at
     all hazards,
Stands removed, spacious, composite, sound, initiates the true
     use of precedents,
Does not repel them or the past or what they have produced under
     their forms,
Takes the lesson with calmness, perceives the corpse slowly borne
     from the house,
Perceives that it waits a little while in the door, that it was fittest
     for its days,
That its life has descended to the stalwart and well-shaped heir
     who approaches,
And that he shall be fittest for his days.

Any period one nation must lead,
One land must be the promise and reliance of the future.

These States are the amplest poem,
Here is not merely a nation but a teeming Nation of nations,
Here the doings of men correspond with the broadcast doings of
     the day and night,
Here is what moves in magnificent masses careless of particulars,
Here are the roughs, beards, friendliness, combativeness, the soul
     loves,
Here the flowing trains, here the crowds, equality, diversity, the
     soul loves.

6

Land of lands and bards to corroborate!
Of them standing among them, one lifts to the light a west-bred
     face,
To him the hereditary countenance bequeath'd both mother's and
     father's,
His first parts substances, earth, water, animals, trees,
Built of the common stock, having room for far and near,
Used to dispense with other lands, incarnating this land,
Attracting it body and soul to himself, hanging on its neck with
     incomparable love,

Plunging his seminal muscle into its merits and demerits,
Making its cities, beginnings, events, diversities, wars, vocal in him,
Making its rivers, lakes, bays, embouchure in him,
Mississippi with yearly freshets and changing chutes, Columbia,
  Niagara, Hudson, spending themselves lovingly in him,
If the Atlantic coast stretch or the Pacific coast stretch, he stretch-
  ing with them North or South,
Spanning between them East and West, and touching whatever is
  between them,
Growths growing from him to offset the growths of pine, cedar,
  hemlock, live-oak, locust, chestnut, hickory, cottonwood,
  orange, magnolia,
Tangles as tangled in him as any canebrake or swamp,
He likening sides and peaks of mountains, forests coated with
  northern transparent ice,
Off him pasturage sweet and natural as savanna, upland, prairie,
Through him flights, whirls, screams, answering those of the fish-
  hawk, mocking-bird, night-heron, and eagle,
His spirit surrounding his country's spirit, unclosed to good and
  evil,
Surrounding the essences of real things, old times and present
  times,
Surrounding just found shores, islands, tribes of red aborigines,
Weather-beaten vessels, landings, settlements, embryo stature and
  muscle,
The haughty defiance of the Year One, war, peace, the formation
  of the Constitution,
The separate States, the simple elastic scheme, the immigrants,
The Union always swarming with blatherers and always sure and
  impregnable,
The unsurvey'd interior, log-houses, clearings, wild animals, hunt-
  ers, trappers,
Surrounding the multiform agriculture, mines, temperature, the
  gestation of new States,
Congress convening every Twelfth-month, the members duly
  coming up from the uttermost parts,
Surrounding the noble character of mechanics and farmers, especially the young men,
Responding their manners, speech, dress, friendships, the gait they
  have of persons who never knew how it felt to stand in the
  presence of superiors,
The freshness and candor of their physiognomy, the copiousness
  and decision of their phrenology,

The picturesque looseness of their carriage, their fierceness when
    wrong'd,
The fluency of their speech, their delight in music, their curiosity,
    good temper and open-handedness, the whole composite make,
The prevailing ardor and enterprise, the large amativeness,
The perfect equality of the female with the male, the fluid move-
    ment of the population,
The superior marine, free commerce, fisheries, whaling, gold-
    digging,
Wharf-hemm'd cities, railroad and steamboat lines intersecting all
    points,
Factories, mercantile life, labor-saving machinery, the Northeast,
    Northwest, Southwest,
Manhattan firemen, the Yankee swap, southern plantation life,
Slavery—the murderous, treacherous conspiracy to raise it upon the
    ruins of all the rest,
On and on to the grapple with it—Assassin! then your life or ours
    be the stake, and respite no more.

7

(Lo, high toward heaven, this day,
Libertad, from the conqueress' field return'd,
I mark the new aureola around your head,
No more of soft astral, but dazzling and fierce,
With war's flames and the lambent lightnings playing,
And your port immovable where you stand,
With still the inextinguishable glance and the clinch'd and lifted fist,
And your foot on the neck of the menacing one, the scorner utterly
    crush'd beneath you,
The menacing arrogant one that strode and advanced with his sense-
    less scorn, bearing the murderous knife,
The wide-swelling one, the braggart that would yesterday do so
    much,
To-day a carrion dead and damn'd, the despised of all the earth,
An offal rank, to the dunghill maggots spurn'd.)

8

Others take finish, but the Republic is ever constructive and ever
    keeps vista,
Others adorn the past, but you O days of the present, I adorn you,
O days of the future I believe in you—I isolate myself for your sake,
O America because you build for mankind I build for you,

O well-beloved stone-cutters, I lead them who plan with decision and
    science,
Lead the present with friendly hand toward the future.

(Bravas to all impulses sending sane children to the next age!
But damn that which spends itself with no thought of the stain, pains,
    dismay, feebleness, it is bequeathing.)

9

I listened to the Phantom by Ontario's shore,
I heard the voice arising demanding bards,
By them all native and grand, by them alone can these States be fused
    into the compact organism of a Nation.

To hold men together by paper and seal or by compulsion is no
    account,
That only holds men togeher which aggregates all in a living prin-
    ciple, as the hold of the limbs of the body or the fibres of plants.

Of all races and eras these States with veins full of poetical stuff most
    need poets, and are to have the greatest, and use them the
    greatest,
Their Presidents shall not be their common referee so much as their
    poets shall.

(Soul of love and tongue of fire!
Eye to pierce the deepest deeps and sweep the world!
Ah Mother, prolific and full in all besides, yet how long barren,
    barren?)

10

Of these States the poet is the equable man,
Not in him but off from him things are grotesque, eccentric, fail of
    their full returns,
Nothing out of its place is good, nothing in its place is bad,
He bestows on every object or quality its fit proportion, neither more
    nor less,
He is the arbiter of the diverse, he is the key,
He is the equalizer of his age and land,
He supplies what wants supplying, he checks what wants checking,
In peace out of him speaks the spirit of peace, large, rich, thrifty,
    building populous towns, encouraging agriculture, arts, com-
    merce, lighting the study of man, the soul, health, immortality,
    government,

In war he is the best backer of the war, he fetches artillery as good as
    the engineer's, he can make every word he speaks draw blood,
The years straying toward infidelity he withholds by his steady faith,
He is no arguer, he is judgment, (Nature accepts him absolutely,)
He judges not as the judge judges but as the sun falling round a help-
    less thing,
As he sees the farthest he has the most faith,
His thoughts are the hymns of the praise of things,
In the dispute on God and eternity he is silent,
He sees eternity less like a play with a prologue and denouement,
He sees eternity in men and women, he does not see men and women
    as dreams or dots.

For the great Idea, the idea of perfect and free individuals,
For that, the bard walks in advance, leader of leaders,
The attitude of him cheers up slaves and horrifies foreign despots.

Without extinction is Liberty, without retrograde is Equality,
They live in the feelings of young men and the best women,
(Not for nothing have the indomitable heads of the earth been
    always ready to fall for Liberty.)

11

For the great Idea,
That, O my brethren, that is the mission of poets.

Songs of stern defiance ever ready,
Songs of the rapid arming and the march,
The flag of peace quick-folded, and instead the flag we know,
Warlike flag of the great Idea.

(Angry cloth I saw there leaping!
I stand again in leaden rain your flapping folds saluting,
I sing you over all, flying beckoning through the fight—O the hard-
    contested fight!
The cannons ope their rosy-flashing muzzles—the hurtled balls
    scream,
The battle-front forms amid the smoke—the volleys pour incessant
    from the line,
Hark, the ringing word *Charge!*—now the tussle and the furious
    maddening yells,

Now the corpses tumble curl'd upon the ground,
Cold, cold in death, for precious life of you,
Angry cloth I saw there leaping.)

12

Are you he who would assume a place to teach or be a poet here in
    the States?
The place is august, the terms obdurate.

Who would assume to teach here may well prepare himself body and
    mind,
He may well survey, ponder, arm, fortify, harden, make lithe himself,
He shall surely be question'd beforehand by me with many and stern
    questions.

Who are you indeed who would talk or sing to America?
Have you studied out the land, its idioms and men?
Have you learn'd the physiology, phrenology, politics, geography,
    pride, freedom, friendship of the land? its substratums and
    objects?
Have you consider'd the organic compact of the first day of the first
    year of Independence, sign'd by the Commissioners, ratified by
    the States, and read by Washington at the head of the army?
Have you possess'd yourself of the Federal Constitution?
Do you see who have left all feudal processes and poems behind
    them, and assumed the poems and processes of Democracy?
Are you faithful to things? do you teach what the land and sea, the
    bodies of men, womanhood, amativeness, heroic angers, teach?
Have you sped through fleeting customs, popularities?
Can you hold your hand against all seductions, follies, whirls, fierce
    contentions? are you very strong? are you really of the whole
    People?
Are you not of some coterie? some school or mere religion?
Are you done with reviews and criticisms of life? animating now to
    life itself?
Have you vivified yourself from the maternity of these States?
Have you too the old ever-fresh forbearance and impartiality?
Do you hold the like love for those hardening to maturity? for the
    last-born? little and big? and for the errant?

What is this you bring my America?
Is it uniform with my country?

Is it not something that has been better told or done before?
Have you not imported this or the spirit of it in some ship?
Is it not a mere tale? a rhyme? a prettiness?—is the good old cause
    in it?
Has it not dangled long at the heels of the poets, politicians, literats,
    of enemies' lands?
Does it not assume that what is notoriously gone is still here?
Does it answer universal needs? will it improve manners?
Does it sound with trumpet-voice the proud victory of the Union in
    that secession war?
Can your performance face the open fields and the seaside?
Will it absorb into me as I absorb food, air, to appear again in my
    strength, gait, face?
Have real employments contributed to it? original makers, not mere
    amanuenses?
Does it meet modern discoveries, calibres, facts, face to face?
What does it mean to American persons, progresses, cities? Chicago,
    Kanada, Arkansas?
Does it see behind the apparent custodians the real custodians stand-
    ing, menacing, silent, the mechanics, Manhattanese, Western
    men, Southerners, significant alike in their apathy, and in the
    promptness of their love?
Does it see what finally befalls, and has always finally befallen, each
    temporizer, patcher, outsider, partialist, alarmist, infidel, who
    has ever ask'd any thing of America?
What mocking and scornful negligence?
The track strew'd with the dust of skeletons,
By the roadside others disdainfully toss'd.

ĭ

13

Rhymes and rhymers pass away, poems distill'd from poems pass
    away,
The swarms of reflectors and the polite pass, and leave ashes,
Admirers, importers, obedient persons, make but the soil of litera-
    ture,
America justifies itself, give it time, no disguise can deceive it or con-
    ceal from it, it is impassive enough,
Only toward the likes of itself will it advance to meet them,
If its poets appear it will in due time advance to meet them, there is
    no fear of mistake,
(The proof of a poet shall be sternly deferr'd till his country absorbs
    him as affectionately as he has absorb'd it.)

He masters whose spirit masters, he tastes sweetest who results
sweetest in the long run,
The blood of the brawn beloved of time is unconstraint;
In the need of songs, philosophy, an appropriate native grand-opera,
shipcraft, any craft,
He or she is greatest who contributes the greatest original practical
example.

Already a nonchalant breed, silently emerging, appears on the
streets,
People's lips salute only doers, lovers, satisfiers, positive knowers,
There will shortly be no more priests, I say their work is done,
Death is without emergencies here, but life is perpetual emergencies
here,
Are your body, days, manners, superb? after death you shall be
superb,
Justice, health, self-esteem, clear the way with irresistible power;
How dare you place any thing before a man?

14

Fall behind me States!
A man before all—myself, typical, before all.

Give me the pay I have served for,
Give me to sing the songs of the great Idea, take all the rest,
I have loved the earth, sun, animals, I have despised riches,
I have given alms to every one that ask'd, stood up for the stupid
and crazy, devo ed my income and labor to others,
Hated tyrants, argued not concerning God, had patience and indul-
gence toward the people, taken off my hat to nothing known or
unknown,
Gone freely with powerful uneducated persons and with the young,
and with the mothers of families,
Read these leaves to myself in the open air, tried them by trees, stars,
rivers,
Dismiss'd whatever insulted my own soul or defiled my body,
Claim'd nothing to myself which I have not carefully claim'd for
others on the same terms,
Sped to the camps, and comrades found and accepted from every
State,
(Upon this breast has many a dying soldier lean'd to breathe his last,
This arm, this hand, this voice, have nourish'd, rais'd, restored,
To life recalling many a prostrate form;

I am willing to wait to be understood by the growth of the taste of
    myself,
Rejecting none, permitting all.

(Say O Mother, have I not to your thought been faithful?
Have I not through life kept you and yours before me?)

15

I swear I begin to see the meaning of these things,
It is not the earth, it is not America who is so great,
It is I who am great or to be great, it is You up there, or any one,
It is to walk rapidly through civilizations, governments, theories,
Through poems, pageants, shows, to form individuals.

Underneath all, individuals,
I swear nothing is good to me now that ignores individuals,
The American compact is altogether with individuals,
The only government is that which makes minute of individuals,
The whole theory of the universe is directed unerringly to one single
    individual—namely to You.

(Mother! with subtle sense severe, with the naked sword in your
    hand,
I saw you at last refuse to treat but directly with individuals.)

16

Underneath all, Nativity,
I swear I will stand by my own nativity, pious or impious so be it;
I swear I am charm'd with nothing except nativity,
Men, women, cities, nations, are only beautiful from nativity.

Underneath all is the Expression of love for men and women,
(I swear I have seen enough of mean and impotent modes of express-
    ing love for men and women,
After this day I take my own modes of expressing love for men and
    women.)

I swear I will have each quality of my race in myself,
(Talk as you like, he only suits these States whose manners favor the
    audacity and sublime turbulence of the States.)

Underneath the lessons of things, spirits, Nature, governments,
    ownerships, I swear I perceive other lessons,

Underneath all to me is myself, to you yourself, (the same monoto-
    nous old song.)

17

O I see flashing that this America is only you and me,
Its power, weapons, testimony, are you and me,
Its crimes, lies, thefts, defections, are you and me,
Its Congress is you and me, the officers, capitols, armies, ships, are
    you and me,
Its endless gestations of new States are you and me,
The war, (that war so bloody and grim, the war I will henceforth
    forget), was you and me,
Natural and artificial are you and me,
Freedom, language, poems, employments, are you and me,
Past, present, future, are you and me.

I dare not shirk any part of myself,
Not any part of America good or bad,
Not to build for that which builds for mankind,
Not to balance ranks, complexions, creeds, and the sexes,
Not to justify science nor the march of equality,
Nor to feed the arrogant blood of the brawn belov'd of time.

I am for those that have never been master'd,
For men and women whose tempers have never been master'd,
For those whom laws, theories, conventions, can never master.

I am for those who walk abreast with the whole earth,
Who inaugurate one to inaugurate all.

I will not be outfaced by irrational things,
I will penetrate what it is in them that is sarcastic upon me,
I will make cities and civilizations defer to me,
This is what I have learnt from America—it is the amount, and it I
    teach again.

(Democracy, while weapons were everywhere aim'd at your breast,
I saw you serenely give birth to immortal children, saw in dreams
    your dilating form,
Saw you with spreading mantle covering the world.)

18

I will confront these shows of the day and night,
I will know if I am to be less than they,

I will see if I am not as majestic as they,
I will see if I am not as subtle and real as they,
I will see if I am to be less generous than they,
I will see if I have no meaning, while the houses and ships have
    meaning,
I will see if the fishes and birds are to be enough for themselves, and
    I am not to be enough for myself.

I match my spirit against yours you orbs, growths, mountains, brutes,
Copious as you are I absorb you all in myself, and become the
    master myself,
America isolated yet embodying all, what is it finally except myself?
These States, what are they except myself?

I know now why the earth is gross, tantalizing, wicked, it is for my
    sake,
I take you specially to be mine, you terrible, rude forms.

(Mother, bend down, bend close to me your face,
I know not what these plots and wars and deferments are for,
I know not fruition's success, but I know that through war and crime
    your work goes on, and must yet go on.)

19

Thus, by blue Ontario's shore,
While the winds fann'd me and the waves came trooping toward me,
I thrill'd with the power's pulsations, and the charm of my theme
    was upon me,
Till the tissues that held me parted their ties upon me.

And I saw the free souls of poets,
The loftiest bards of past ages strode before me,
Strange large men, long unwaked, undisclosed, were disclosed to me.

20

O my rapt verse, my call, mock me not!
Not for the bards of the past, not to invoke them have I launch'd
    you forth,
Not to call even those lofty bards here by Ontario's shores,
Have I sung so capricious and loud my savage song.

Bards for my own land only I invoke,
(For the war, the war is over, the field is clear'd,)

Till they strike up marches henceforth triumphant and onward,
To cheer O Mother your boundless expectant soul.

Bards of the great Idea! bards of the peaceful inventions! (for the
    war, the war is over!)
Yet bards of latent armies, a million soldiers waiting ever-ready,
Bards with songs as from burning coals or the lightning's fork'd
    stripes!
Ample Ohio's, Kanada's bards—bards of California! inland bards—
    bards of the war!
You by my charm I invoke.

REVERSALS

LET that which stood in front go behind,
Let that which was behind advance to the front,
Let bigots, fools, unclean persons, offer new propositions,
Let the old propositions be postponed,
Let a man seek pleasure everywhere except in himself,
Let a woman seek happiness everywhere except in herself.

Autumn Rivulets

AS CONSEQUENT, *Etc.*

As consequent from store of summer rains,
Or wayward rivulets in autumn flowing,
Or many a herb-lined brook's reticulations,
Or subterranean sea-rills making for the sea,
Songs of continued years I sing.

Life's ever-modern rapids first, (soon, soon to blend,
With the old streams of death.)

Some threading Ohio's farm-fields or the woods,
Some down Colorado's cañons from sources of perpetual snow,
Some half-hid in Oregon, or away southward in Texas,
Some in the north finding their way to Erie, Niagara, Ottawa,
Some to Atlantica's bays, and so to the great salt brine.

In you whoe'er you are my book perusing,
In I myself, in all the world, these currents flowing,
All, all toward the mystic ocean tending.

Currents for starting a continent new,
Overtures sent to the solid out of the liquid,
Fusion of ocean and land, tender and pensive waves,
(Not safe and peaceful only, waves rous'd and ominous too,
Out of the depths the storm's absymic waves, who knows whence?
Raging over the vast, with many a broken spar and tatter'd sail.)

Or from the sea of Time, collecting vasting all, I bring,
A windrow-drift of weeds and shells.

O little shells, so curious-convolute, so limpid-cold and voiceless,
Will you not little shells to the tympans of temples held,
Murmurs and echoes still call up, eternity's music faint and far,

Wafted inland, sent from Atlantica's rim, strains for the soul of the
     prairies,
Whisper'd reverberations, chords for the ear of the West joyously
     sounding,
Your tidings old, yet ever new and untranslatable,
Infinitesimals out of my life, and many a life,
(For not my life and years alone I give—all, all I give,)
These waifs from the deep, cast high and dry,
Wash'd on America's shores?

THE RETURN OF THE HEROES

1

For the lands and for these passionate days and for myself,
Now I awhile retire to thee O soil of autumn fields,
Reclining on thy breast, giving myself to thee,
Answering the pulses of thy sane and equable heart,
Tuning a verse for thee.

O earth that hast no voice, confide to me a voice,
O harvest of my lands—O boundless summer growths,
O lavish brown parturient earth—O infinite teeming womb,
A song to narrate thee.

2

Ever upon this stage,
Is acted God's calm annual drama,
Gorgeous processions, songs of birds,
Sunrise that fullest feeds and freshens most the soul,
The heaving sea, the waves upon the shore, the musical, strong
     waves,
The woods, the stalwart trees, the slender, tapering trees,
The liliput countless armies of the grass,
The heat, the showers, the measureless pasturages,
The scenery of the snows, the winds' free orchestra,
The stretching light-hung roof of clouds, the clear cerulean and the
     silvery fringes,
The high dilating stars, the placid beckoning stars,
The moving flocks and herds, the plains and emerald meadows,
The shows of all the varied lands and all the growths and products.

3

Fecund America—to-day,
Thou art all over set in births and joys!

Thou groan'st with riches, they wealth clothes thee as a swathing-
  garment
Thou laughest loud with ache of great possessions,
A myriad-twining life like interlacing vines binds all thy vast demesne,
As some huge ship freighted to water's edge thou ridest into port,
As rain falls from the heaven and vapors rise from earth, so have the
  precious values fallen upon thee and risen out of thee;
Thou envy of the globe! thou miracle!
Thou, bathed, choked, swimming in plenty,
Thou lucky Mistress of the tranquil barns,
Thou Prairie Dame that sittest in the middle and lookest out upon
  thy world, and lookest East and lookest West,
Dispensatress, that by a word givest a thousand miles, a million
  farms, and missest nothing,
Thou all-acceptress—thou hospitable, (thou only art hospitable as
  God is hospitable.)

4

When late I sang sad was my voice,
Sad were the shows around me with deafening noises of hatred and
  smoke of war
In the midst of the conflict, the heroes, I stood,
Or pass'd with slow step through the wounded and dying.

But now I sing not war,
Nor the measur'd march of soldiers, nor the tents of camps,
Nor the regiments hastily coming up deploying in line of battle;
No more the sad, unnatural shows of war.

Ask'd room those flush'd immortal ranks, the first forth-stepping
  armies?
Ask room alas the ghastly ranks, the armies dread that follow'd.

(Pass, pass, ye proud brigades, with your tramping sinewy legs,
With your shoulders young and strong, with your knapsacks and
  your muskets;
How elate I stood and watch'd you, where starting off you march'd.

Pass—then rattle drums again,
For an army heaves in sight, O another gathering army,
Swarming, trailing on the rear, O you dread accruing army,
O you regiments so piteous, with your mortal diarrhœa, with your
  fever,

O my land's maim'd darlings, with the plenteous bloody bandage
    and the crutch,
Lo, your pallid army follows.)

5

But on these days of brightness,
On the far-stretching beauteous landscape, the roads and lanes, the
    high-piled farm-wagons, and the fruits and barns,
Should the dead intrude?

Ah the dead to me mar not, they fit well in Nature,
They fit very well in the landscape under the trees and grass,
And along the edge of the sky in the horizon's far margin.

Nor do I forget you Departed,
Nor in winter or summer my lost ones,
But most in the open air as now when my soul is rapt and at peace,
    like pleasing phantoms,
Your memories rising glide silently by me.

6

I saw the day the return of the heroes,
(Yet the heroes never surpass'd shall never return,
Them that day I saw not.)

I saw the interminable corps, I saw the processions of armies,
I saw them approaching, defiling by with divisions,
Streaming northward, their work done, camping awhile in clusters
    of mighty camps.

No holiday soldiers—youthful, yet veterans,
Worn, swart, handsome, strong, of the stock of homestead and
    workshop,
Harden'd of many a long campaign and sweaty march,
Inured on many a hard-fought bloody field.

A pause—the armies wait,
A million flush'd embattled conquerors wait,
The world too waits, then soft as breaking night and sure as dawn,
They melt, they disappear.

Exult O lands! victorious lands!
Not there your victory on those red shuddering fields,
But here and hence your victory.

Melt, melt away ye armies—disperse ye blue-clad soldiers,
Resolve ye back again, give up for good your deadly arms,
Other the arms the fields henceforth for you, or South or North,
With saner wars, sweet wars, life-giving wars.

7

Loud O my throat, and clear O soul!
The season of thanks and the voice of full-yielding,
The chant of joy and power for boundless fertility.

All till'd and untill'd fields expand before me,
I see the true arenas of my race, or first or last,
Man's innocent and strong arenas.

I see the heroes at other toils,
I see well-wielded in their hands the better weapons.

I see where the Mother of All,
With full-spanning eye gazes forth, dwells long,
And counts the varied gathering of the products.

Busy the far, the sunlit panorama,
Prairie, orchard, and yellow grain of the North,
Cotton and rice of the South and Louisianian cane,
Open unseeded fallows, rich fields of clover and timothy,
Kine and horses feeding, and droves of sheep and swine,
And many a stately river flowing and many a jocund brook,
And healthy uplands with herby-perfumed breezes,
And the good green grass, that delicate miracle the ever-recurring
    grass.

8

Toil on heroes! harvest the products!
Not alone on those warlike fields the Mother of All,
With dilated form and lambent eyes watch'd you.

Toil on heroes! toil well! handle the weapons well!
The Mother of All, yet here as ever she watches you.

Well-pleased America thou beholdest,
Over the fields of the West those crawling monsters,
The human-divine inventions, the labor-saving implements;
Beholdest moving in every direction imbued as with life the revolving
    hay-rakes,
The steam-power reaping-machines and the horse-power machines,
The engines, thrashers of grain and cleaners of grain, well separating
    the straw, the nimble work of the patent pitchfork,
Beholdest the newer saw-mill, the southern cotton-gin, and the rice-
    cleanser.
Beneath thy look O Maternal,
With these and else and with their own strong hands the heroes
    harvest.

All gather and all harvest,
Yet but for thee O Powerful, not a scythe might swing as now in
    security,
Not a maize-stalk dangle as now its silken tassels in peace.

Under thee only they harvest, even but a wisp of hay under thy great
    face only,
Harvest the wheat of Ohio, Illinois, Wisconsin, every barbed spear
    under thee,
Harvest the maize of Missouri, Kentucky, Tennessee, each ear in its
    light-green sheath,
Gather the hay to its myriad mows in the odorous tranquil barns,
Oats to their bins, the white potato, the buckwheat of Michigan, to
    theirs;
Gather the cotton in Mississippi or Alabama, dig and hoard the
    golden the sweet potato of Georgia and the Carolinas,
Clip the wool of California or Pennsylvania,
Cut the flax in the Middle States, or hemp or tobacco in the Borders,
Pick the pea and the bean, or pull apples from the trees or bunches
    of grapes from the vines,
Or aught that ripens in all these States or North or South,
Under the beaming sun and under thee.

THERE WAS A CHILD WENT FORTH

THERE was child went forth every day,
And the first object he look'd upon, that object he became,
And that object became part of him for the day or a certain part of
    the day,
Or for many years or stretching cycles of years.

The early lilacs became part of this child,
And grass and white and red morning-glories, and white and red
    clover, and the song of the phœbe-bird,
And the Third-month lambs and the sow's pink-faint litter, and the
    mare's foal and the cow's calf,
And the noisy brood of the barnyard or by the mire of the pond-side,
And the fish suspending themselves so curiously below there, and
    the beautiful curious liquid,
And the water-plants with their graceful flat heads, all became part
    of him.

The field-sprouts of Fourth-month and Fifth-month became part
    of him,
Winter-grain sprouts and those of the light-yellow corn, and the
    esculent roots of the garden,
And the apple-trees cover'd with blossoms and the fruit afterward,
    and wood-berries, and the commonest weeds by the road,
And the old drunkard staggering home from the outhouse of the
    tavern whence he had lately risen,
And the schoolmistress that pass'd on her way to the school,
And the friendly boys that pass'd and the quarrelsome boys,
And the tidy and fresh-cheek'd girls, and the barefoot negro boy
    and girl,
And all the changes of city and country wherever he went.

His own parents, he that had father'd him and she that had con-
    ceiv'd him in her womb and birth'd him,
They gave this child more of themselves than that,
They gave him afterward every day, they became part of him.

The mother at home quietly placing the dishes on the supper-
    table,
The mother with mild words, clean her cap and gown, a whole-
    some odor falling off her person and clothes as she walks by,
The father, strong, self-sufficient, manly, mean, anger'd, unjust,
The blow, the quick loud word, the tight bargain, the crafty lure,
The family usages, the language, the company, the furniture, the
    yearning and swelling heart,
Affection that will not be gainsay'd, the sense of what is real, the
    thought if after all it should prove unreal,
The doubts of day-time and the doubts of night-time, the curious
    whether and how,
Whether that which appears so is so, or is it all flashes and specks?

Men and women crowding fast in the streets, if they are not flashes and specks what are they?

The streets themselves and the façades of houses, and goods in the windows,

Vehicles, teams, the heavy-plank'd wharves, the huge crossing at the ferries,

The village on the highland seen from afar at sunset, the river between,

Shadows, aureola and mist, the light falling on roofs and gables of white or brown two miles off,

The schooner near by sleepily dropping down the tide, the little boat slack-tow'd astern,

The hurrying tumbling waves, quick-broken crests, slapping,

The strata of color'd clouds, the long bar of maroon-tint away solitary by itself, the spread of purity it lies motionless in,

The horizon's edge, the flying sea-crow, the fragrance of salt marsh and shore mud,

These became part of that child who went forth every day, and who now goes, and will always go forth every day.

OLD IRELAND

FAR hence amid an isle of wondrous beauty,

Crouching over a grave an ancient sorrowful mother,

Once a queen, now lean and tatter'd seated on the ground,

Her old white hair drooping dishevel'd round her shoulders,

At her feet fallen an unused royal harp,

Long silent, she too long silent, mourning her shrouded hope and heir,

Of all the earth her heart most full of sorrow because most full of love.

Yet a word ancient mother,

You need crouch there no longer on the cold ground with forehead between your knees,·

O you need not sit there veil'd in your old white hair so dishevel'd,

For know you the one you mourn is not in that grave,

It was an illusion, the son you love was not really dead,

The Lord is not dead, he is risen again young and strong in another country,

Even while you wept there by your fallen harp by the grave,

What you wept for was translated, pass'd from the grave,

The winds favor'd and the sea sail'd it,

And now with rosy and new blood,
Moves to-day in a new country.

THE CITY DEAD-HOUSE

BY the city dead-house by the gate,
As idly sauntering wending my way from the clangor,
I curious pause, for lo, an outcast form, a poor dead prostitute
brought,
Her corpse they deposit unclaim'd, it lies on the damp brick
pavement,
The divine woman, her body, I see the body, I look on it alone,
That house once full of passion and beauty, all else I notice not,
Nor stillness so cold, nor running water from faucet, nor odors
morbific impress me,
But the house alone—that wondrous house—that delicate fair
house—that ruin!
That immortal house more than all the rows of dwellings ever built!
Or white-domed capitol with majestic figure surmounted, or all
the old high-spired cathedrals,
That little house alone more than them all—poor, desperate house!
Fair, fearful wreck—tenement of a soul—itself a soul,
Unclaim'd, avoided house—take one breath from my tremulous
lips,
Take one tear dropt aside as I go for thought of you,
Dead house of love—house of madness and sin, crumbled, crush'd,
House of life, erewhile talking and laughing—but ah, poor house,
dead even then,
Months, years, an echoing, garnish'd house—but dead, dead, dead.

THIS COMPOST

1

SOMETHING startles me where I thought I was safest,
I withdraw from the still woods I loved,
I will not go now on the pastures to walk,
I will not strip the clothes from my body to meet my lover the sea,
I will not touch my flesh to the earth as to other flesh to renew me.

O how can it be that the ground itself does not sicken?
How can you be alive you growths of spring?

How can you furnish health you blood of herbs, roots, orchards,
    grain?
Are they not continually putting distemper'd corpses within you?
Is not every continent work'd over and over with sour dead?

Where have you disposed of their carcasses?
Those drunkards and gluttons of so many generations?
Where have you drawn off all the foul liquid and meat?
I do not see any of it upon you to-day, or perhaps I am deceiv'd,
I will run a furrow with my plough, I will press my spade through
    the sod and turn it up underneath,
I am sure I shall expose some of the foul meat.

2

Behold this compost! behold it well!
Perhaps every mite has once form'd part of a sick person—yet
    behold!
The grass of spring covers the prairies,
The bean bursts noiselessly through the mould in the garden,
The delicate spear of the onion pierces upward,
The apple-buds cluster together on the apple-branches,
The resurrection of the wheat appears with pale visage out of its
    graves,
The tinge awakes over the willow-tree and the mulberry-tree,
The he-birds carol mornings and evenings while the she-birds sit
    on their nests,
The young of poultry break through the hatch'd eggs,
The new-born of animals appear, the calf is dropt from the cow,
    the colt from the mare,
Out of its little hill faithfully rise the potato's dark green leaves,
Out of its hill rises the yellow maize-stalk, the lilacs bloom in the
    dooryards,
The summer growth is innocent and disdainful above all those
    strata of sour dead.

What chemistry!
That the winds are really not infectious,
That this is no cheat, this transparent green-wash of the sea which
    is so amorous after me,
That it is safe to allow it to lick my naked body all over with its
    tongues,
That it will not endanger me with the fevers that have deposited
    themselves in it,

That all is clean forever and forever,
That the cool drink from the well tastes so good,
That blackberries are so flavorous and juicy,
That the fruits of the apple-orchard and the orange-orchard, that
    melons, grapes, peaches, plums, will none of them poison me,
That when I recline on the grass I do not catch any disease,
Though probably every spear of grass rises out of what was once
    a catching disease.

Now I am terrified at the Earth, it is that calm and patient,
It grows such sweet things out of such corruptions,
It turns harmless and stainless on its axis, with such endless succes-
    sions of diseas'd corpses,
It distills such exquisite winds out of such infused fetor,
It renews with such unwitting looks its prodigal, annual, sumptuous
    crops,
It gives such divine materials to men, and accepts such leavings
    from them at last.

TO A FOIL'D EUROPEAN REVOLUTIONAIRE

COURAGE yet, my brother or my sister!
Keep on—Liberty is to be subserv'd whatever occurs;
That is nothing that is quell'd by one or two failures, or any num-
    ber of failures,
Or by the indifference or ingratitude of the people, or by any
    unfaithfulness,
Or the show of the tushes of power, soldiers, cannon, penal statutes.

What we believe in waits latent forever through all the continents,
Invites no one, promises nothing, sits in calmness and light, is
    positive and composed, knows no discouragement,
Waiting patiently, waiting its time.

(Not songs of loyalty alone are these,
But songs of insurrection also,
For I am the sworn poet of every dauntless rebel the world over,
And he going with me leaves peace and routine behind him,
And stakes his life to be lost at any moment.)

The battle rages with many a loud alarm and frequent advance
    and retreat,
The infidel triumphs, or supposes he triumphs,

The prison, scaffold, garroté, handcuffs, iron necklace and leadballs do their work,
The named and unnamed heroes pass to other spheres,
The great speakers and writers are exiled, they lie sick in distant
lands,
The cause is asleep, the strongest throats are choked with their own
blood,
The young men droop their eyelashes toward the ground when they
meet;
But for all this Liberty has not gone out of the place, nor the infidel
enter'd into full possession.

When liberty goes out of a place it is not the first to go, nor the
second or third to go,
It waits for all the rest to go, it is the last.

When there are no more memories of heroes and martyrs,
And when all life and all the souls of men and women are dis-
charged from any part of the earth,
Then only shall liberty or the idea of liberty be discharged from
that part of the earth,
And the infidel come into full possession.

Then courage European revolter, revoltress!
For till all ceases neither must you cease.

I do not know what you are for, (I do not know what I am for
myself, nor what any thing is for,)
But I will search carefully for it even in being foil'd,
In defeat, poverty, misconception, imprisonment—for they too are
great.

Did we think victory great?
So it is—but now it seems to me, when it cannot be help'd, that
defeat is great,
And that death and dismay are great.

UNNAMED LANDS

NATIONS ten thousand years before these States, and many times
ten thousand years before these States,
Garner'd clusters of ages that men and women like us grew up and
travel'd their course and pass'd on,

What vast-built cities, what orderly republics, what pastoral tribes
    and nomads,
What histories, rulers, heroes, perhaps transcending all others,
What laws, customs, wealth, arts, traditions,
What sort of marriage, what costumes, what physiology and
    phrenology,
What of liberty and slavery among them, what they thought of
    death and the soul,
Who were witty and wise, who beautiful and poetic, who brutish
    and undevelop'd,
Not a mark, not a record remains—and yet all remains.

O I know that those men and women were not for nothing, any
    more than we are for nothing,
I know that they belong to the scheme of the world every bit as
    much as we now belong to it.

Afar they stand, yet near to me they stand,
Some with oval countenances learn'd and calm,
Some naked and savage, some like huge collections of insects,
Some in tents, herdsmen, patriarchs, tribes, horsemen,
Some prowling through woods, some living peaceably on farms,
    laboring, reaping, filling barns,
Some traversing paved avenues, amid temples, palaces, factories,
    libraries, shows, courts, theatres, wonderful monuments.

Are those billions of men really gone?
Are those women of the old experience of the earth gone?
Do their lives, cities, arts, rest only with us?
Did they achieve nothing for good for themselves?

I believe of all those men and women that fill'd the unnamed lands,
    every one exists this hour here or elsewhere, invisible to us,
In exact proportion to what he or she grew from in life, and out
    of what he or she did, felt, became, loved, sinn'd, in life.

I believe that was not the end of those nations or any person of
    them, any more than this shall be the end of my nation, or
    of me;
Of their languages, governments, marriage, literature, products,
    games, wars, manners, crimes, prisons, slaves, heroes, poets,
I suspect their results curiously await in the yet unseen world,
    counterparts of what accrued to them in the seen world,

I suspect I shall meet them there,
I suspect I shall there find each old particular of those unnamed
lands.

SONG OF PRUDENCE

MANHATTAN'S streets I saunter'd pondering,
On Time, Space, Reality—on such as these, and abreast with them
Prudence.

The last explanation always remains to be made about prudence,
Little and large alike drop quietly aside from the prudence that
suits immortality.

The soul is of itself,
All verges to it, all has reference to what ensues,
All that a person does, says, thinks, is of consequence,
Not a move can a man or woman make, that affect him or her in
a day, month, any part of the direct lifetime, or the hour of
death,
But the same affects him or her onward afterward through the in-
direct lifetime.

The indirect is just as much as the direct,
The spirit receives from the body just as much as it gives to the body,
if not more.

Not one word or deed, not venereal sore, discoloration, privacy
of the onanist,
Putridity of gluttons or rum-drinkers, peculation, cunning, betrayal,
murder, seduction, prostitution,
But has results beyond death as really as before death.

Charity and personal force are the only investments worth any
thing.

No specification is necessary, all that a male or female does, that is
vigorous, benevolent, clean, is so much profit to him or her,
In the unshakable order of the universe and through the whole
scope of it forever.

Who has been wise receives interest,
Savage, felon, President, judge, farmer, sailor, mechanic, literat,
young, old, it is the same,
The interest will come round—all will come round.

Singly, wholly, to affect now, affected their time, will forever affect,
    all of the past and all of the present and all of the future,
All the brave actions of war and peace,
All help given to relatives, strangers, the poor, old, sorrowful, young
    children, widows, the sick, and to shunn'd persons,
All self-denial that stood steady and aloof on wrecks, and saw others
    fill the seats of the boats,
All offering of substance or life for the good old cause, or for a
    friend's sake, or opinion's sake,
All pains of enthusiasts scoff'd at by their neighbors,
All the limitless sweet love and precious suffering of mothers,
All honest men baffled in strifes recorded or unrecorded,
All the grandeur and good of ancient nations whose fragments we
    inherit,
All the good of the dozens of ancient nations unknown to us by
    name, date, location,
All that was ever manfully begun, whether it succeeded or no,
All suggestions of the divine mind of man or the divinity of his
    mouth, or the shaping of his great hands,
All that is well thought or said this day on any part of the globe,
    or on any of the wandering stars, or on any of the fix'd stars,
    by those there as we are here,
All that is henceforth to be thought or done by you whoever you
    are, or by any one,
These inure, have inured, shall inure, to the identities from which
    they sprang, or shall spring.

Did you guess any thing lived only its moment?
The world does not so exist, no parts palpable or impalpable so
    exist,
No consummation exists without being from some long previous
    consummation, and that from some other,
Without the farthest conceivable one coming a bit nearer the be-
    ginning than any.

Whatever satisfies souls is true;
Prudence entirely satisfies the craving and glut of souls,
Itself only finally satisfies the soul,
The soul has that measureless pride which revolts from every lesson
    but its own.

Now I breathe the word of the prudence that walks abreast with
    time, space, reality,
That answers the pride which refuses every lesson but its own.

What is prudence is indivisible,
Declines to separate one part of life from every part,
Divides not the righteous from the unrighteous or the living from
    the dead,
Matches every thought or act by its correlative,
Knows no possible forgiveness or deputed atonement,
Knows that the young man who composedly peril'd his life and
    lost it has done exceedingly well for himself without doubt,
That he who never peril'd his life, but retains it to old age in riches
    and ease, has probably achiev'd nothing for himself worth
    mentioning,
Knows that only that person has really learn'd who has learn'd to
    prefer results,
Who favors body and soul the same,
Who perceives the indirect assuredly following the direct,
Who in his spirit in any emergency whatever neither hurries nor
    avoids death.

THE SINGER IN THE PRISON

1

O sight of pity, shame and dole!
O fearful thought—a convict soul.

RANG the refrain along the hall, the prison,
Rose to the roof, the vaults of heaven above,
Pouring in floods of melody in tones so pensive sweet and strong
    the like whereof was never heard,
Reaching the far-off sentry and the armed guards, who ceas'd their
    pacing,
Making the hearer's pulses stop for ecstasy and awe.

2

The sun was low in the west one winter day,
When down a narrow aisle amid the thieves and outlaws of the land
(There by the hundreds seated, sear-faced murderers, wily counter-
    feiters,
Gather'd to Sunday church in prison walls, the keepers round,
Plenteous, well-armed, watching with vigilant eyes,)
Calmly a lady walk'd holding a little innocent child by either hand,
Whom seating on their stools beside her on the platform,
She, first preluding with the instrument a low and musical prelude,
In voice surpassing all, sang forth a quaint old hymn.

A soul confined by bars and bands,
Cries, help! O help! and wrings her hands,
Blinded her eyes, bleeding her breast,
Nor pardon finds, nor balm of rest.

Ceaseless she paces to and fro,
O heart-sick days! O nights of woe!
Nor hand of friend, nor loving face,
Nor favor comes, nor word of grace.

It was not I that sinn'd the sin,
The ruthless body dragg'd me in;
Though long I strove courageously,
The body was too much for me.

Dear prison'd soul bear up a space,
For soon or late the certain grace;
To set thee free and bear thee home,
The heavenly pardoner death shall come.

> *Convict no more, nor shame, nor dole!*
> *Depart—a God-enfranchis'd soul!*

3

The singer ceas'd,
One glance swept from her clear calm eyes o'er all those upturn'd
    faces,
Strange sea of prison faces, a thousand varied, crafty, brutal,
    seam'd and beauteous faces,
Then rising, passing back along the narrow aisle between them,
While her gown touch'd them rustling in the silence,
She vanish'd with her children in the dusk.

While upon all, convicts and armed keepers ere they stirr'd,
(Convict forgetting prison, keeper his loaded pistol,)
A hush and pause fell down a wondrous minute,
With deep half-stifled sobs and sound of bad men bow'd and moved
    to weeping,
And youth's convulsive breathings, memories of home,
The mother's voice in lullaby, the sister's care, the happy childhood,
The long-pent spirit rous'd to reminiscence;
A wondrous minute then—but after in the solitary night, to many,
    many there,

Years after, even in the hour of death, the sad refrain, the tune,
    the voice, the words,
Resumed, the large calm lady walks the narrow aisle,
The wailing melody again, the singer in the prison sings,

> *O sight of pity, shame and dole!*
> *O fearful thought—a convict soul.*

WARBLE FOR LILAC-TIME

WARBLE me now for joy of lilac time, (returning in reminiscence,)
Sort me O tongue and lips for Nature's sake, souvenirs of earliest
    summer,
Gather the welcome signs, (as children with pebbles or stringing
    shells,)
Put in April and May, the hylas croaking in the ponds, the elastic
    air,
Bees, butterflies, the sparrow with its simple notes,
Blue-bird and darting swallow, nor forget the high-whole flashing
    his golden wings,
The tranquil sunny haze, the clinging smoke, the vapor,
Shimmer of waters with fish in them, the cerulean above,
All that is jocund and sparkling, the brooks running,
The maple woods, the crisp February days and the sugar-making,
The robin where he hops, bright-eyed, brown-breasted,
With musical clear call at sunrise, and again at sunset,
Or flitting among the trees of the apple-orchard, building the nest
    of his mate,
The melted snow of March, the willow sending forth its yellow-
    green sprouts,
For spring-time is here! the summer is here! and what is this in it
    and from it?
Thou, soul, unloosen'd—the restlessness after I know not what;
Come, let us lag here no longer, let us be up and away!
O if one could but fly like a bird!
O to escape, to sail forth as in a ship!
To glide with thee O soul, o'er all, in all, as a ship o'er the waters;
Gathering these hints, the preludes, the blue sky, the grass, the
    morning drops of dew,
The lilac-scent, the bushes with dark green heart-shaped leaves,
Wood-violets, the little delicate pale blossoms called innocence,

Samples and sorts not for themselves alone, but for their atmosphere,
To grace the bush I love—to sing with the birds,
A warble for joy of lilac-time, returning in reminiscence.

OUTLINES FOR A TOMB

(G.P., Buried 1870)

1

WHAT may we chant, O thou within this tomb?
What tablets, outlines, hang for thee, O millionnaire?
The life thou lived'st we know not,
But that thou walk'dst thy years in barter, 'mid the haunts of
    brokers,
Nor heroism thine, nor war, nor glory.

2

Silent, my soul,
With drooping lids, as waiting, ponder'd,
Turning from all the samples, monuments of heroes.

While through the interior vistas,
Noiseless uprose, phantasmic, (as by night Auroras of the north,)
Lambent tableaus, prophetic, bodiless scenes,
Spiritual projections.

In one, among the city streets a laborer's home appear'd,
After his day's work done, cleanly, sweet-air'd, the gaslight burning,
The carpet swept and a fire in the cheerful stove.

In one, the sacred parturition scene,
A happy painless mother birth'd a perfect child.

In one, at a bounteous morning meal,
Sat peaceful parents with contented sons.

In one, by twos and threes, young people,
Hundreds concentring, walk'd the paths and streets and roads,
Toward a tall-domed school.

In one a trio beautiful,
Grandmother, loving daughter, loving daughter's daughter, sat,
Chatting and sewing.

In one, along a suite of noble rooms,
'Mid plenteous books and journals, paintings on the walls, fine
    statuettes,
Were groups of friendly journeymen, mechanics young and old,
Reading, conversing.

All, all the shows of laboring life,
City and country, women's, men's and children's,
Their wants provided for, hued in the sun and tinged for once with
    joy,
Marriage, the street, the factory, farm, the house-room, lodging-
    room,
Labor and toil, the bath, gymnasium, playground, library, college,
The student, boy or girl, led forward to be taught,
The sick cared for, the shoeless shod, the orphan father'd and
    mother'd,
The hungry fed, the houseless housed;
(The intentions perfect and divine,
The workings, details, haply human.)

3

O thou within this tomb,
From thee such scenes, thou stintless, lavish giver,
Tallying the gifts of earth, large as the earth,
Thy name an earth, with mountains, fields and tides.

Nor by your streams alone, you rivers,
By you, your banks Connecticut,
By you and all your teeming life old Thames,
By you Potomac laving the ground Washington trod, by you
    Patapsco,
You Hudson, you endless Mississippi—nor you alone,
But to the high seas launch, my thought, his memory.

OUT FROM BEHIND THIS MASK

(To Confront a Portrait)

1

OUT from behind this bending rough-cut mask,
These lights and shades, this drama of the whole,
This common curtain of the face contain'd in me for me, in you for
    you, in each for each,

(Tragedies, sorrows, laughter, tears—O heaven!
The passionate teeming plays this curtain hid!)
This glaze of God's serenest purest sky,
This film of Satan's seething pit,
This heart's geography's map, this limitless small continent, this
    soundless sea;
Out from the convolutions of this globe,
This subtler astronomic orb than sun or moon, than Jupiter, Venus,
    Mars,
This condensation of the universe, (nay here the only universe,
Here the idea, all in this mystic handful wrapt;)
These burin'd eyes, flashing to you to pass to future time,
To launch and spin through space revolving sideling, from these to
    emanate,
To you whoe'er you are—a look.

2

A traveler of thoughts and years, of peace and war,
Of youth long sped and middle age declining,
(As the first volume of a tale perused and laid away, and this the
    second,
Songs, ventures, speculations, presently to close,)
Lingering a moment here and now, to you I opposite turn,
As on the road or at some crevice door by chance, or open'd window,
Pausing, inclining, baring my head, you specially I greet,
To draw and clinch your soul for once inseparably with mine,
Then travel travel on.

VOCALISM

1

VOCALISM, measure, concentration, determination, and the divine
    power to speak words;
Are you full-lung'd and limber-lipp'd from long trial? from vigorous
    practice? from physique?
Do you move in these broad lands as broad as they?
Come duly to the divine power to speak words?
For only at last after many years, after chastity, friendship, procrea-
    tion, prudence, and nakedness,
After treading ground and breasting river and lake,
After a loosen'd throat, after absorbing eras, temperaments, races,
    after knowledge, freedom, crimes,

After complete faith, after clarifyings, elevations, and removing
    obstructions,
After these and more, it is just possible there comes to a man, a
    woman, the divine power to speak words;
Then toward that man or that woman swiftly hasten all—none
    refuse, all attend,
Armies, ships, antiquities, libraries, paintings, machines, cities, hate,
    despair, amity, pain, theft, murder, aspiration, form in close
    ranks,
They debouch as they are wanted to march obediently through the
    mouth of that man or that woman.

2

O what is it in me that makes me tremble so at voices?
Surely whoever speaks to me in the right voice, him or her I shall
    follow,
As the water follows the moon, silently, with fluid steps, anywhere
    around the globe.

All waits for the right voices;
Where is the practis'd and perfect organ? where is the develop'd
    soul?
For I see every word utter'd thence has deeper, sweeter, new sounds,
    impossible on less terms.

I see brains and lips closed, tympans and temples unstruck,
Until that comes which has the quality to strike and to unclose,
Until that comes which has the quality to bring forth what lies slum-
    bering forever ready in all words.

TO HIM THAT WAS CRUCIFIED

My spirit to yours dear brother,
Do not mind because many sounding your name do not understand
    you,
I do not sound your name, but I understand you,
I specify you with joy O my comrade to salute you, and to salute
    those who are with you, before and since, and those to come
    also,
That we all labor together transmitting the same charge and suc-
    cession,
We few equals indifferent of lands, indifferent of times,
We, enclosers of all continents, all castes, allowers of all theologies,

Compassionaters, perceivers, rapport of men,
We walk silent among disputes and assertions, but reject not the
    disputers nor any thing that is asserted,
We hear the bawling and din, we are reach'd at by divisions, jealous-
    ies, recriminations on every side,
They close peremptorily upon us to surround us, my comrade,
Yet we walk unheld, free, the whole earth over, journeying up and
    down till we make our ineffaceable mark upon time and the
    diverse eras,
Till we saturate time and eras, that the men and women of races, ages
    to come, may prove brethren and lovers as we are.

YOU FELONS ON TRIAL IN COURTS

You felons on trial in courts,
You convicts in prison-cells, you sentenced assassins chain'd and
    handcuff'd with iron,
Who am I too that I am not on trial or in prison?
Me ruthless and devilish as any, that my wrists are not chain'd with
    iron, or my ankles with iron?

You prostitutes flaunting over the trottoirs or obscene in your rooms,
Who am I that I should call you more obscene than myself?
O culpable! I acknowledge—I exposé!

(O admirers, praise not me—compliment not me—you make me
    wince,
I see what you do not—I know what you do not.)

Inside these breast-bones I lie smutch'd and choked,
Beneath this face that appears so impassive hell's tides continually
    run,
Lusts and wickedness are acceptable to me,
I walk with delinquents with passionate love,
I feel I am of them—I belong to those convicts and prostitutes
    myself,
And henceforth I will not deny them—for how can I deny myself?

LAWS FOR CREATIONS

Laws for creations,
For strong artists and leaders, for fresh broods of teachers and per-
    fect literats for America,
For noble savans and coming musicians.

All must have reference to the ensemble of the world, and the compact truth of the world,
There shall be no subject too pronounced—all works shall illustrate the divine law of indirections.

What do you suppose creation is?
What do you suppose will satisfy the soul, except to walk free and own no superior?
What do you suppose I would intimate to you in a hundred ways, but that man or woman is as good as God?
And that there is no God any more divine than Yourself?
And that that is what the oldest and newest myths finally mean?
And that you or any one must approach creations through such laws?

TO A COMMON PROSTITUTE

BE composed—be at ease with me—I am Walt Whitman, liberal and lusty as Nature,
Not till the sun excludes you do I exclude you,
Not till the waters refuse to glisten for you and the leaves to rustle for you, do my words refuse to glisten and rustle for you.

My girl I appoint with you an appointment, and I charge you that you make preparation to be worthy to meet me,
And I charge you that you be patient and perfect till I come.

Till then I salute you with a significant look that you do not forget me.

I WAS LOOKING A LONG WHILE

I WAS looking a long while for Intentions,
For a clew to the history of the past for myself, and for these chants—and now I have found it,
It is not in those paged fables in the libraries, (them I neither accept nor reject,)
It is no more in the legends than in all else,
It is in the present—it is this earth to-day,
It is in Democracy—(the purport and aim of all the past,)
It is the life of one man or one woman to-day—the average man of to-day,
It is in languages, social customs, literatures, arts,
It is in the broad show of artificial things, ships, machinery, politics, creeds, modern improvements, and the interchange of nations,
All for the modern—all for the average man of to-day.

THOUGHT

OF persons arrived at high positions, ceremonies, wealth, scholar-
ships, and the like;
(To me all that those persons have arrived at sinks away from them,
except as it results to their bodies and souls,
So that often to me they appear gaunt and naked,
And often to me each one mocks the others, and mocks himself or
herself,
And of each one the core of life, namely happiness, is full of the
rotten excrement of maggots,
And often to me those men and women pass unwittingly the true
realities of life, and go toward false realities,
And often to me they are alive after what custom has served them,
but nothing more,
And often to me they are sad, hasty, unwaked sonnambules walking
the dusk.)

MIRACLES

WHY, who makes much of a miracle?
As to me I know of nothing else but miracles,
Whether I walk the streets of Manhattan,
Or dart my sight over the roofs of houses toward the sky,
Or wade with naked feet along the beach just in the edge of the
water,
Or stand under trees in the woods,
Or talk by day with any one I love, or sleep in the bed at night with
any one I love,
Or sit at table at dinner with the rest,
Or look at strangers opposite me riding in the car,
Or watch honey-bees busy around the hive of a summer forenoon,
Or animals feeding in the fields,
Or birds, or the wonderfulness of insects in the air,
Or the wonderfulness of the sundown, or of stars shining so quiet
and bright,
Or the exquisite delicate thin curve of the new moon in spring;
These with the rest, one and all, are to me miracles,
The whole referring, yet each distinct and in its place.

To me every hour of the light and dark is a miracle,
Every cubic inch of space is a miracle,
Every square yard of the surface of the earth is spread with the same,
Every foot of the interior swarms with the same.

To me the sea is a continual miracle,
The fishes that swim—the rocks—the motion of the waves—the ships
　　with men in them,
What stranger miracles are there?

SPARKLES FROM THE WHEEL

WHERE the city's ceaseless crowd moves on the livelong day,
Withdrawn I join a group of children watching, I pause aside with
　　them.

By the curb toward the edge of the flagging,
A knife-grinder works at his wheel sharpening a great knife,
Bending over he carefully holds it to the stone, by foot and knee,
With measur'd tread he turns rapidly, as he presses with light but
　　firm hand,
Forth issue then in copious golden jets,
Sparkles from the wheel.

The scene and all its belongings, how they seize and affect me,
The sad sharp-chinn'd old man with worn clothes and broad shoul-
　　der-band of leather,
Myself effusing and fluid, a phantom curiously floating, now here
　　absorb'd and arrested,
The group, (an unminded point set in a vast surrounding,)
The attentive, quiet children, the loud, proud, restive base of the
　　streets,
The low hoarse purr of the whirling stone, the light-press'd blade,
Diffusing, dropping, sideways-darting, in tiny showers of gold,
Sparkles from the wheel.

TO A PUPIL

Is reform needed? is it through you?
The greater the reform needed, the greater the Personality you need
　　to accomplish it.

You! do you not see how it would serve to have eyes, blood, com-
　　plexion, clean and sweet?
Do you not see how it would serve to have such a body and soul that
　　when you enter the crowd an atmosphere of desire and com-
　　mand enters with you, and every one is impress'd with your
　　Personality?

O the magnet! the flesh over and over!
Go, dear friend, if need be give up all else, and commence to-day
     to inure yourself to pluck, reality, self-esteem, definiteness,
     elevatedness,
Rest not till you rivet and publish yourself of your own Personality.

UNFOLDED OUT OF THE FOLDS

UNFOLDED out of the folds of the woman man comes unfolded, and
     is always to come unfolded,
Unfolded only out of the superbest woman of the earth is to come
     the superbest man of the earth,
Unfolded out of the friendliest woman is to come the friendliest man,
Unfolded only out of the perfect body of a woman can a man be
     form'd of perfect body,
Unfolded only out of the inimitable poems of woman can come the
     poems of man, (only thence have my poems come;)
Unfolded out of the strong and arrogant woman I love, only thence
     can appear the strong and arrogant man I love,
Unfolded by brawny embraces from the well-muscled woman I love,
     only thence come the brawny embraces of the man,
Unfolded out of the folds of the woman's brain come all the folds of
     the man's brain, duly obedient,
Unfolded out of the justice of the woman all justice is unfolded,
Unfolded out of the sympathy of the woman is all sympathy;
A man is a great thing upon the earth and through eternity, but every
     jot of the greatness of man is unfolded out of woman;
First the man is shaped in the woman, he can then be shaped in
     himself.

WHAT AM I AFTER ALL

WHAT am I after all but a child, pleas'd with the sound of my own
     name? repeating it over and over;
I stand apart to hear—it never tires me.

To you your name also;
Did you think there was nothing but two or three pronunciations in
     the sound of your name?

KOSMOS

WHO includes diversity and is Nature,
Who is the amplitude of the earth, and the coarseness and sexuality
     of the earth, and the great charity of the earth, and the equilib-
     rium also,

Who has not look'd forth from the windows the eyes for nothing,
  or whose brain held audience with messengers for nothing,
Who contains believers and disbelievers, who is the most majestio
  lover,
Who holds duly his or her triune proportion of realism, spiritualism,
  and of the æsthetic or intellectual,
Who having consider'd the body finds all its organs and parts good,
Who, out of the theory of the earth and of his or her body under-
  stands by subtle analogies all other theories,
The theory of a city, a poem, and of the large politics of these States;
Who believes not only in our globe with its sun and moon, but in
  other globes with their suns and moons,
Who, constructing the house of himself or herself, not for a day but
  for all time, sees races, eras, dates, generations,
The past, the future, dwelling there, like space, inseparable togethei.

OTHERS MAY PRAISE WHAT THEY LIKE

OTHERS may praise what they like;
But I, from the banks of the running Missouri, praise nothing in art
  or aught else,
Till it has well inhaled the atmosphere of this river, also the western
  prairie-scent,
And exudes it all again.

WHO LEARNS MY LESSON COMPLETE?

WHO learns my lesson complete?
Boss, journeyman, apprentice, churchman and atheist,
The stupid and the wise thinker, parents and offspring, merchant,
  clerk, porter and customer,
Editor, author, artist, and schoolboy—draw nigh and commence;
It is no lesson—it lets down the bars to a good lesson,
And that to another, and every one to another still.

The great laws take and effuse without argument,
I am of the same style, for I am their friend,
I love them quits and quits, I do not halt and make salaams.

I lie abstracted and hear beautiful tales of things and the reasons of
  things,
They are so beautiful I nudge myself to listen.

I cannot say to any person what I hear—I cannot say it to myself—
  it is very wonderful.

It is no small matter, this round and delicious globe moving so
    exactly in its orbit for ever and ever, without one jolt or the
    untruth of a single second,
I do not think it was made in six days, nor in ten thousand years,
    nor ten billions of years,
Nor plann'd and built one thing after another as an architect plans
    and builds a house.

I do not think seventy years is the time of a man or woman,
Nor that seventy millions of years is the time of a man or woman,
Nor that years will ever stop the existence of me, or any one else.

Is it wonderful that I should be immortal? as every one is immortal;
I know it is wonderful, but my eyesight is equally wonderful, and
    how I was conceived in my mother's womb is equally wonderful,
And pass'd from a babe in the creeping trance of a couple of summers
    and winters to articulate and walk—all this is equally wonderful.

And that my soul embraces you this hour, and we affect each
    other without ever seeing each other, and never perhaps to
    see each other, is every bit as wonderful.

And that I can think such thoughts as these is just as wonderful,
And that I can remind you, and you think them and know them to
    be true, is just as wonderful.

And that the moon spins round the earth and on with the earth, is
    equally wonderful,
And that they balance themselves with the sun and stars is equally
    wonderful.

TESTS

ALL submit to them where they sit, inner, secure, unapproachable to
    analysis in the soul,
Not traditions, not the outer authorities are the judges,
They are the judges of outer authorities and of all traditions,
They corroborate as they go only whatever corroborates themselves,
    and touches themselves;
For all that, they have it forever in themselves to corroborate far and
    near without one exception.

THE TORCH

ON my Northwest coast in the midst of the night a fishermen's group
    stands watching,

Out on the lake that expands before them, others are spearing
    salmon,
The canoe, a dim shadowy thing, moves across the black water,
Bearing a torch ablaze at the prow.

O STAR OF FRANCE

1870–71

O STAR of France,
The brightness of thy hope and strength and fame,
Like some proud ship that led the fleet so long,
Beseems to-day a wreck driven by the gale, a mastless hulk,
And 'mid its teeming madden'd half-drown'd crowds,
Nor helm nor helmsman.

Dim smitten star,
Orb not of France alone, pale symbol of my soul, its dearest hopes,
The struggle and the daring, rage divine for liberty,
Of aspirations toward the far ideal, enthusiast's dreams of brother-
    hood,
Of terror to the tyrant and the priest.

Star crucified—by traitors sold,
Star panting o'er a land of death, heroic land,
Strange, passionate, mocking, frivolous land.

Miserable! yet for thy errors, vanities, sins, I will not now rebuke
    thee,
Thy unexampled woes and pangs have quell'd them all,
And left thee sacred.

In that amid thy many faults thou ever aimedst highly,
In that thou wouldst not really sell thyself however great the price,
In that thou surely wakedst weeping from thy drugg'd sleep,
In that alone among thy sisters thou, giantess, didst rend the ones
    that shamed thee,
In that thou couldst not, wouldst not, wear the usual chains,
This cross, thy livid face, thy pierced hands and feet,
The spear thrust in thy side.

O star! O ship of France, beat back and baffled long!
Bear up O smitten orb! O ship continue on!

Sure as the ship of all, the Earth itself,
Product of deathly fire and turbulent chaos,
Forth from its spasms of fury and its poisons,
Issuing at last in perfect power and beauty,
Onward beneath the sun following its course,
So thee O ship of France!

Finish'd the days, the clouds dispel'd,
The travail o'er, the long-sought extrication,
When lo! reborn, high o'er the European world,
(In gladness answering thence, as face afar to face, reflecting ours
    Columbia,)
Again thy star O France, fair lustrous star,
In heavenly peace, clearer, more bright than ever,
Shall beam immortal.

THE OX-TAMER

In a far-away northern county in the placid pastoral region
Lives my farmer friend, the theme of my recitative, a famous tamer
    of oxen,
There they bring him the three-year-olds and the four-year-olds to
    break them,
He will take the wildest steer in the world and break him and tame
    him,
He will go fearless without any whip where the young bullock
    chafes up and down the yard,
The bullock's head tosses restless high in the air with raging eyes,
Yet see you! how soon his rage subsides—how soon this tamer
    tames him;
See you! on the farms hereabout a hundred oxen young and old,
    and he is the man who has tamed them,
They all know him, all are affectionate to him;
See you! some are such beautiful animals, so lofty looking;
Some are buff-color'd, some mottled, one has a white line running
    along his back, some are brindled,
Some have wide flaring horns (a good sign)—see you! the bright
    hides,
See, the two with stars on the foreheads—see, the round bodies
    and broad backs,
How straight and square they stand on their legs—what fine saga-
    cious eyes!

How they watch their tamer—they wish him near them—how they
  turn to look after him!
What yearning expression! how uneasy they are when he moves
  away from them;
Now I marvel what it can be he appears to them, (books, politics,
  poems, depart—all else departs,)
I confess I envy only his fascination—my silent, illiterate friend,
Whom a hundred oxen love there in his life on farms,
In the northern county far, in the placid pastoral region.

AN OLD MAN'S THOUGHT OF SCHOOL

For the Inauguration of a Public School, Camden, New Jersey, 1874

An old man's thought of school,
An old man gathering youthful memories and blooms that youth
  itself cannot.

Now only do I know you,
O fair auroral skies—O morning dew upon the grass!

And these I see, these sparkling eyes,
These stores of mystic meaning, these young lives,
Building, equipping like a fleet of ships, immortal ships,
Soon to sail out over the measureless seas,
On the soul's voyage.

Only a lot of boys and girls?
Only the tiresome spelling, writing, ciphering classes?
Only a public school?

Ah more, infinitely more;
(As George Fox rais'd his warning cry, "Is it this pile of brick
  and mortar, these dead floors, windows, rails, you call the
  church?
Why this is not the church at all—the church is living, ever living
  souls.")

And you America,
Cast you the real reckoning for your present?
The lights and shadows of your future, good or evil?
To girlhood, boyhood look, the teacher and the school.

WANDERING AT MORN

WANDERING at morn,
Emerging from the night from gloomy thoughts, thee in my thoughts,
Yearning for thee harmonious Union! thee, singing bird divine!
Thee coil'd in evil times my country, with craft and black dismay,
    with every meanness, treason thrust upon thee,
This common marvel I beheld—the parent thrush I watch'd feeding
    its young,
The singing thrush whose tones of joy and faith ecstatic,
Fail not to certify and cheer my soul.

There ponder'd, felt I,
If worms, snakes, loathsome grubs, may to sweet spiritual songs
    be turn'd,
If vermin so transposed, so used and bless'd may be,
Then may I trust in you, your fortunes, days, my country;
Who knows but these may be the lessons fit for you?
From these your future song may rise with joyous trills,
Destin'd to fill the world.

ITALIAN MUSIC IN DAKOTA

["The Seventeenth—the finest regimental Band I ever heard"]

THROUGH the soft evening air enwinding all,
Rocks, woods, fort, cannon, pacing sentries, endless wilds,
In dulcet streams, in flutes' and cornets' notes,
Electric, pensive, turbulent, artificial,
(Yet strangely fitting even here, meanings unknown before,
Subtler than ever, more harmony, as if born here, related here,
Not to the city's fresco'd rooms, not to the audience of the opera
    house,
Sounds, echoes, wandering strains, as really here at home,
Sonnambula's innocent love, trios with *Norma's* anguish,
And thy ecstatic chorus *Poliuto;)*
Ray'd in the limpid yellow slanting sundown,
Music, Italian music in Dakota.

While Nature, sovereign of this gnarl'd realm,
Lurking in hidden barbaric grim recesses,
Acknowledging rapport however far remov'd,
(As some old root or soil of earth its last-born flower or fruit,)
Listens well pleas'd.

WITH ALL THY GIFTS

WITH all thy gifts America,
Standing secure, rapidly tending, overlooking the world,
Power, wealth, extent, vouchsafed to thee—with these and like of
these vouchsafed to thee,
What if one gift thou lackest? (the ultimate human problem never
solving,)
The gift of perfect women fit for thee—what if that gift of gifts
thou lackest?
The towering feminine of thee? the beauty, health, completion,
fit for thee?
The mothers fit for thee?

MY PICTURE-GALLERY

IN a little house keep I pictures suspended, it is not a fix'd house,
It is round, it is only a few inches from one side to the other;
Yet behold, it has room for all the shows of the world, all memories!
Here the tableaus of life, and here the groupings of death;
Here, do you know this? this is cicerone himself,
With finger rais'd he points to the prodigal pictures.

THE PRAIRIE STATES

A NEWER garden of creation, no primal solitude,
Dense, joyous, modern, populous millions, cities and farms,
With iron interlaced, composite, tied, many in one,
By all the world contributed—freedom's and law's and thrift's
society,
The crown and teeming paradise, so far, of time's accumulations,
To justify the past.

Proud Music of the Storm

1

PROUD music of the storm,
Blast that careers so free, whistling across the prairies,
Strong hum of forest tree-tops—wind of the mountains,
Personified dim shapes—you hidden orchestras,
You serenades of phantoms with instruments alert,
Blending wih Nature's rhythmus all the tongues of nations;
You chords left as by vast composers—you choruses,

You formless, free, religious dances—you from the Orient,
You undertone of rivers, roar of pouring cataracts,
You sounds from distant guns with galloping cavalry,
Echoes of camps with all the different bugle-calls,
Trooping tumultuous, filling the midnight late, bending me power-
    less,
Entering my lonesome slumber-chamber, why have you seiz'd me?

2

Come forward O my soul, and let the rest retire,
Listen, lose not, it is toward thee they tend,
Parting the midnight, entering my slumber-chamber,
For thee they sing and dance O soul.

A festival song,
The duet of the bridegroom and the bride, a marriage-march,
With lips of love, and hearts of lovers fill'd to the brim with love,
The red-flush'd cheeks and perfumes, the cortege swarming full of
    friendly faces young and old,
To flutes' clear notes and sounding harps' cantabile.

Now loud approaching drums,
Victoria! see'st thou in powder-smoke the banners torn but flying?
    the rout of the baffled?
Hearest those shouts of a conquering army?

(Ah soul, the sobs of women, the wounded groaning in agony,
The hiss and crackle of flames, the blacken'd ruins, the embers
    of cities,
The dirge and desolation of mankind.)

Now airs antique and mediæval fill me,
I see and hear old harpers with their harps at Welsh festivals,
I hear the minnesingers singing their lays of love,
I hear the minstrels, gleemen, troubadours, of the middle ages.

Now the great organ sounds,
Tremulous, while underneath, (as the hid footholds of the earth,
On which arising rest, and leaping forth depend,
All shapes of beauty, grace and strength, all hues we know,
Green blades of grass and warbling birds, children that gambol
    and play, the clouds of heaven above,)
The strong base stands, and its pulsations intermits not,

Bathing, supporting, merging all the rest, maternity of all the rest,
And with it every instrument in multitudes,
The players playing, all the world's musicians,
The solemn hymns and masses rousing adoration,
All passionate heart-chants, sorrowful appeals,
The measureless sweet vocalists of ages,
And for their solvent setting earth's own diapason,
Of winds and woods and mighty ocean waves,
A new composite orchestra, binder of years and climes, ten-fold
    renewer,
As of the far-back days the poets tell, the Paradiso,
The straying thence, the separation long, but now the wandering
    done,
The journey done, the journeyman come home,
And man and art with Nature fused again.

Tutti! for earth and heaven;
(The Almighty leader now for once has signal'd with his wand.)

The manly strophe of the husbands of the world,
And all the wives responding.

The tongues of violins,
(I think O tongues ye tell this heart, that cannot tell itself,
This brooding yearning heart, that cannot tell itself.)

3

Ah from a little child,
Thou knowest soul how to me all sounds became music,
My mother's voice in lullaby or hymn,
(The voice, O tender voices, memory's loving voices,
Last miracle of all, O dearest mother's, sister's, voices;)
The rain, the growing corn, the breeze among the long-leav'd corn,
The measur'd sea-surf beating on the sand,
The twittering bird, the hawk's sharp scream,
The wild-fowl's notes at night as flying low migrating north or south,
The psalm in the country church or mid the clustering trees, the
    open air camp-meeting,
The fiddler in the tavern, the glee, the long-strung sailor-song,
The lowing cattle, bleating sheep, the crowing cock at dawn.

All songs of current lands come sounding round me,
The German airs of friendship, wine and love,

Irish ballads, merry jigs and dances, English warbles,
Chansons of France, Scotch tunes, and o'er the rest,
Italia's peerless compositions.

Across the stage with pallor on her face, yet lurid passion,
Stalks Norma brandishing the dagger in her hand.

I see poor crazed Lucia's eyes' unnatural gleam,
Her hair down her back falls loose and dishevel'd.

I see where Ernani walking the bridal garden,
Amid the scent of night-roses, radiant, holding his bride by the hand,
Hears the infernal call, the death-pledge of the horn.

To crossing swords and gray hairs bared to heaven,
The clear electric base and baritone of the world,
The trombone duo, Libertad forever!

From Spanish chestnut trees' dense shade,
By old and heavy convent walls a wailing song,
Song of lost love, the torch of youth and life quench'd in despair,
Song of the dying swan, Fernando's heart is breaking.

Awaking from her woes at last retriev'd Amina sings,
Copious as stars and glad as morning light the torrents of her joy.

(The teeming lady comes,
The lustrous orb, Venus contralto, the blooming mother,
Sister of loftiest gods, Alboni's self I hear.)

4

I hear those odes, symphonies, operas,
I hear in the *William Tell* the music of an arous'd and angry people,
I hear Meyerbeer's *Huguenots*, the *Prophet*, or *Robert*,
Gounod's *Faust*, or Mozart's *Don Juan*.

I hear the dance-music of all nations,
The waltz, some delicious measure, lapsing, bathing me in bliss,
The bolero to tinkling guitars and clattering castanets.

I see religious dances old and new,
I hear the sound of the Hebrew lyre,

I see the crusaders marching bearing the cross on high, to the
    martial clang of cymbals,
I hear dervishes monotonously chanting, interspers'd with frantic
    shouts, as they spin around turning always towards Mecca,
I see the rapt religious dances of the Persians and the Arabs,
Again, at Eleusis, home of Ceres, I see the modern Greeks dancing,
I hear them clapping their hands as they bend their bodies,
I hear the metrical shuffling of their feet.

I see again the wild old Corybantian dance, the performers wounding
    each other,
I see the Roman youth to the shrill sound of flageolets throwing
    and catching their weapons,
As they fall on their knees and rise again.

I hear from the Mussulman mosque the muezzin calling,
I see the worshippers within, nor form nor sermon, argument nor
    word,
But silent, strange, devout, rais'd, glowing heads, ecstatic faces.

I hear the Egyptian harp of many strings,
The primitive chants of the Nile boatmen,
The sacred imperial hymns of China,
To the delicate sounds of the king, (the stricken wood and stone,)
Or to Hindu flutes and the fretting twang of the vina,
A band of bayaderes.

5

Now Asia, Africa leave me, Europe seizing inflates me,
To organs huge and bands I hear as from vast concourses of voices,
Luther's strong hymn *Eine feste Burg ist unser Gott,*
Rossini's *Stabat Mater dolorosa,*
Or floating in some high cathedral dim with gorgeous color'd
    windows,
The passionate *Agnus Dei* or *Gloria in Excelsis.*

Composers! mighty maestros!
And you, sweet singers of old lands, soprani, tenori, bassi!
To you a new bard caroling in the West,
Obeisant sends his love.

(Such led to thee O soul,
All senses, shows and objects, lead to thee,
But now it seems to me sound leads o'er all the rest.)

I hear the annual singing of the children in St. Paul's cathedral
Or, under the high roof of some colossal hall, the symphonies,
      oratorios of Beethoven, Handel, or Haydn,
The *Creation* in billows of godhood laves me.

Give me to hold all sounds, (I madly struggling cry,)
Fill me with all the voices of the universe,
Endow me with their throbbings, Nature's also,
The tempests, waters, winds, operas and chants, marches and dances,
Utter, pour in, for I would take them all!

6

Then I woke softly,
And pausing, questioning awhile the music of my dream,
And questioning all those reminiscences, the tempest in its fury,
And all the songs of sopranos and tenors,
And those rapt oriental dances of religious fervor,
And the sweet varied instruments, and the diapason of organs,
And all the artless plaints of love and grief and death,
I said to my silent curious soul out of the bed of the slumber-
      chamber,
Come, for I have found the clew I sought so long,
Let us go forth refresh'd amid the day,
Cheerfully tallying life, walking the world, the real,
Nourish'd henceforth by our celestial dream.

And I said, moreover,
Haply what thou hast heard O soul was not the sounds of winds,
Nor dream of raging storm, nor sea-hawk's flapping wings nor
      harsh scream,
Nor vocalism of sun-bright Italy,
Nor German organ majestic, nor vast concourse of voices, nor
      layers of harmonies,
Nor strophes of husbands and wives, nor sound of marching
      soldiers,
Nor flutes, nor harps, nor the bugle-calls of camps,
But to a new rhythmus fitted for thee,

Poems bridging the way from Life to Death, vaguely wafted in
    night air, uncaught, unwritten,
Which let us go forth in the bold day and write.

Passage to India

1

SINGING my days,
Singing the great achievements of the present,
Singing the strong light works of engineers,
Our modern wonders, (the antique ponderous Seven outvied,)
In the Old World the east the Suez canal,
The New by its mighty railroad spann'd,
The seas inlaid with eloquent gentle wires;
Yet first to sound, and ever sound, the cry with thee O soul,
The Past! the Past! the Past!

The Past—the dark unfathom'd retrospect!
The teeming gulf—the sleepers and the shadows!
The past—the infinite greatness of the past!
For what is the present after all but a growth out of the past?
(As a projectile form'd, impell'd, passing a certain line, still keeps
    on,
So the present, utterly form'd, impell'd by the past.)

2

Passage O soul to India!
Eclaircise the myths Asiatic, the primitive fables.

Not you alone proud truths of the world,
Nor you alone ye facts of modern science,
But myths and fables of eld, Asia's, Africa's fables,
The far-darting beams of the spirit, the unloos'd dreams,
The deep diving bibles and legends,
The daring plots of the poets, the elder religions;
O you temples fairer than lilies pour'd over by the rising sun!
O you fables spurning the known, eluding the hold of the known,
    mounting to heaven!
You lofty and dazzling towers, pinnacled, red as roses, burnish'd
    with gold!
Towers of fables immortal fashion'd from mortal dreams!
You too I welcome and fully the same as the rest!
You too with joy I sing.

Passage to India!
Lo, soul, seest thou not God's purpose from the first?
The earth to be spann'd, connected by network,
The races, neighbors, to marry and be given in marriage,
The oceans to be cross'd, the distant brought near,
The lands to be welded together.

A worship new I sing,
You captains, voyagers, explorers, yours,
You engineers, you architects, machinists, yours,
You, not for trade or transportation only,
But in God's name, and for thy sake O soul.

3

Passage to India!
Lo soul for thee of tableaus twain,
I see in one the Suez canal initiated, open'd,
I see the procession of steamships, the Empress Eugenie's leading
    the van,
I mark from on deck the strange landscape, the pure sky, the
    level sand in the distance,
I pass swiftly the picturesque groups, the workmen gather'd,
The gigantic dredging machines.

In one again, different, (yet thine, all thine, O soul, the same,)
I see over my own continent the Pacific railroad surmounting every
    barrier,
I see continual trains of cars winding along the Platte carrying
    freight and passengers,
I hear the locomotives rushing and roaring, and the shrill steam-
    whistle,
I hear the echoes reverberate through the grandest scenery in the
    world,
I cross the Laramie plains, I note the rocks in grotesque shapes,
  · the buttes,
I see the plentiful larkspur and wild onions, the barren, colorless,
    sage-deserts,
I see in glimpses afar or towering immediately above me the great
    mountains, I see the Wind river and the Wahsatch mountains,
I see the Monument mountain and the Eagle's Nest, I pass the
    Promontory, I ascend the Nevadas,
I scan the noble Elk mountain and wind around its base,
I see the Humboldt range, I thread the valley and cross the river,
I see the clear waters of lake Tahoe, I see forests of majestic pines,

Or crossing the great desert, the alkaline plains, I behold enchanting
  mirages of waters and meadows,
Marking through these and after all, in duplicate slender lines,
Bridging the three or four thousand miles of land travel
Tying the Eastern to the Western sea,
The road between Europe and Asia.

(Ah Genoese thy dream! thy dream!
Centuries after thou art laid in thy grave,
The shore thou foundest verifies thy dream.)

4

Passage to India!
Struggles ot many a captain, tales of many a sailor dead,
Over my mood stealing and spreading they come,
Like clouds and cloudlets in the unreach'd sky.

Along all history, down the slopes,
As a rivulet running, sinking now, and now again to the surface
  rising,
A ceaseless thought, a varied train—lo, soul, to thee, thy sight,
  they rise,
The plans, the voyages again, the expeditions;
Again Vasco de Gama sails forth,
Again the knowledge gain'd, the mariner's compass,
Lands found and nations born, thou born America,
For purpose vast, man's long probation fill'd,
Thou rondure of the world at last accomplish'd.

5

O vast Rondure, swimming in space,
Cover'd all over with visible power and beauty,
Alternate light and day and the teeming spiritual darkness,
Unspeakable high processions of sun and moon and countless
  stars above,
Below, the manifold grass and waters, animals, mountains, trees,
With inscrutable purpose, some hidden prophetic intention,
Now first it seems my thought begins to span thee.

Down from the gardens of Asia descending radiating,
Adam and Eve appear, then their myriad progeny after them,
Wandering, yearning, curious, with restless explorations,

With questionings, baffled, formless, feverish, with never-happy
    hearts,
With that sad incessant refrain, *Wherefore unsatisfied soul?* and
    Whither O mocking life?

Ah who shall soothe these feverish children?
Who justify these restless explorations?
Who speak the secret of impassive earth?
Who bind it to us? what is this separate Nature so unnatural?
What is this earth to our affections? (unloving earth, without a throb
    to answer ours,
Cold earth, the place of graves.)

Yet soul be sure the first intent remains, and shall be carried out,
Perhaps even now the time has arrived.

After the seas are all cross'd, (as they seem already cross'd,)
After the great captains and engineers have accomplish'd their work,
After the noble inventors, after the scientists, the chemist, the
    geologist, ethnologist,
Finally shall come the poet worthy that name,
The true son of God shall come singing his songs.

Then not your deeds only O voyagers, O scientists and inventors,
    shall be justified,
All these hearts as of fretted children shall be sooth'd,
All affection shall be fully responded to, the secret shall be told,
All these separations and gaps shall be taken up and hook'd and
    link'd together,
The whole earth, this cold, impassive, voiceless earth, shall be com-
    pletely justified,
Trinitas divine shall be gloriously accomplish'd and compacted by
    the true son of God, the poet,
(He shall indeed pass the straits and conquer the mountains,
He shall double the cape of Good Hope to some purpose,)
Nature and Man shall be disjoin'd and diffused no more,
The true son of God shall absolutely fuse them.

6

Year at whose wide-flung door I sing!
Year of the purpose accomplish'd!
Year of the marriage of continents, climates and oceans!

(No mere doge of Venice now wedding the Adriatic,)
I see O year in you the vast terraqueous globe given and giving all,
Europe to Asia, Africa join'd, and they to the New World,
The lands, geographies, dancing before you, holding a festival gar-
    land,
As brides and bridegrooms hand in hand.

Passage to India!
Cooling airs from Caucasus far, soothing cradle of man,
The river Euphrates flowing, the past lit up again.

Lo soul, the retrospect brought forward,
The old, most populous, wealthiest of earth's lands,
The streams of the Indus and the Ganges and their many affluents,
(I my shores of America walking to-day behold, resuming all,)
The tale of Alexander on his warlike marches suddenly dying,
On one side China and on the other side Persia and Arabia,
To the south the great seas and the bay of Bengal,
The flowing literatures, tremendous epics, religions, castes,
Old occult Brahma interminably far back, the tender and junior
    Buddha,
Central and southern empires and all their belongings, possessors,
The wars of Tamerlane, the reign of Aurungzebe,
The traders, rulers, explorers, Moslems, Venetians, Byzantium, the
    Arabs, Portuguese,
The first travelers famous yet, Marco Polo, Batouta the Moor,
Doubts to be solv'd, the map incognita, blanks to be fill'd,
The foot of man unstay'd, the hands never at rest,
Thyself O soul that will not brook a challenge.

The mediæval navigators rise before me,
The world of 1492, with its awaken'd enterprise,
Something swelling in humanity now like the sap of the earth in
    spring,
The sunset splendor of chivalry declining.

And who art thou sad shade?
Gigantic, visionary, thyself a visionary,
With majestic limbs and pious beaming eyes,
Spreading around with every look of thine a golden world,
Enhuing it with gorgeous hues.

As the chief histrion,
Down to the footlights walks in some great scena,

Dominating the rest I see the Admiral himself,
(History's type of courage, action, faith,)
Behold him sail from Palos leading his little fleet,
His voyage behold, his return, his great fame,
His misfortunes, calumniators, behold him a prisoner, chain'd,
Behold his dejection, poverty, death.

(Curious in time I stand, noting the efforts of heroes,
Is the deferment long? bitter the slander, poverty, death?
Lies the seed unreck'd for centuries in the ground? lo, to God's due
    occasion,
Uprising in the night, it sprouts, blooms,
And fills the earth with use and beauty.)

7

Passage indeed O soul to primal thought,
Not lands and seas alone, thy own clear freshness,
The young maturity of brood and bloom,
To realms of budding bibles.

O soul, repressless, I with thee and thou with me,
Thy circumnavigation of the world begin,
Of man, the voyage of his mind's return,
To reason's early paradise,
Back, back to wisdom's birth, to innocent intuitions,
Again with fair creation.

8

O we can wait no longer,
We too take ship O soul,
Joyous we too launch out on trackless seas,
Fearless for unknown shores on waves of ecstasy to sail,
Amid the wafting winds, (thou pressing me to thee, I thee to me, O
    soul,)
Caroling free, singing our song of God,
Chanting our chant of pleasant exploration.

With laugh and many a kiss,
(Let others deprecate, let others weep for sin, remorse, humiliation,)
O soul thou pleasest me, I thee.

Ah more than any priest O soul we too believe in God,
But with the mystery of God we dare not dally.

O soul thou pleasest me, I thee,
Sailing these seas or on the hills, or waking in the night,
Thoughts, silent thoughts, of Time and Space and Death, like waters
 flowing,
Bear me indeed as through the regions infinite,
Whose air I breathe, whose ripples hear, lave me all over,
Bathe me O God in thee, mounting to thee,
I and my soul to range in range of thee.

O Thou transcendent,
Nameless, the fibre and the breath,
Light of the light, shedding forth universes, thou centre of them,
Thou mightier centre of the true, the good, the loving,
Thou moral, spiritual fountain—affection's source—thou reservoir,
(O pensive soul of me—O thirst unsatisfied—waitest not there?
Waitest not haply for us somewhere there the Comrade perfect?)
Thou pulse—thou motive of the stars, suns, systems,
That, circling, move in order, safe, harmonious,
Athwart the shapeless vastnesses of space,
How should I think, how breathe a single breath, how speak, if, out
 of myself,
I could not launch, to those, superior universes?

Swiftly I shrivel at the thought of God,
At Nature and its wonders, Time and Space and Death,
But that I, turning, call to thee O soul, thou actual Me,
And lo, thou gently masterest the orbs,
Thou matest Time, smilest content at Death,
And fillest, swellest full the vastnesses of Space.

Greater than stars or suns,
Bounding O soul thou journeyest forth;
What love than thine and ours could wider amplify?
What aspirations, wishes, outvie thine and ours O soul?
What dreams of the ideal? what plans of purity, perfection, strength?
What cheerful willingness for others' sake to give up all?
For others' sake to suffer all?

Reckoning ahead O soul, when thou, the time achiev'd,
The seas all cross'd, weather'd the capes, the voyage done,
Surrounded, copest, frontest God, yieldest, the aim attain'd,
As fill'd with friendship, love complete, the Elder Brother found,
The Younger melts in fondness in his arms.

9

Passage to more than India!
Are thy wings plumed indeed for such far flights?
O soul, voyagest thou indeed on voyages like those?
Disportest thou on waters such as those?
Soundest below the Sanscrit and the Vedas?
Then have thy bent unleash'd.

Passage to you, your shores, ye aged fierce enigmas!
Passage to you, to mastership of you, ye strangling problems!
You, strew'd with the wrecks of skeletons, that, living, never reach'd
    you.

Passage to more than India!
O secret of the earth and sky!
Of you O waters of the sea! O winding creeks and rivers!
Of you O woods and fields! of you strong mountains of my land!
Of you O prairies! of you gray rocks!
O morning red! O clouds! O rain and snows!
O day and night, passage to you!

O sun and moon and all you stars! Sirius and Jupiter!
Passage to you!

Passage, immediate passage! the blood burns in my veins!
Away O soul! hoist instantly the anchor!
Cut the hawsers—haul out—shake out every sail!
Have we not stood here like trees in the ground long enough?
Have we not grovel'd here long enough, eating and drinking like
    mere brutes?
Have we not darken'd and dazed ourselves with books long enough?

Sail forth—steer for the deep waters only,
Reckless O soul, exploring, I with thee, and thou with me,
For we are bound where mariner has not yet dared to go,
And we will risk the ship, ourselves and all.

O my brave soul!
O farther farther sail!
O daring joy, but safe! are they not all the seas of God?
O farther, farther, farther sail!

Prayer of Columbus

A BATTER'D, wreck'd old man,
Thrown on this savage shore, far, far from home,
Pent by the sea and dark rebellious brows, twelve dreary months,
Sore, stiff with many toils, sicken'd and nigh to death,
I take my way along the island's edge,
Venting a heavy heart.

I am too full of woe!
Haply I may not live another day;
I cannot rest O God, I cannot eat or drink or sleep,
Till I put forth myself, my prayer, once more to Thee,
Breathe, bathe myself once more in Thee, commune with Thee,
Report myself once more to Thee.

Thou knowest my years entire, my life,
My long and crowded life of active work, not adoration merely;
Thou knowest the prayers and vigils of my youth,
Thou knowest my manhood's solemn and visionary meditations,
Thou knowest how before I commenced I devoted all to come to
      Thee,
Thou knowest I have in age ratified all those vows and strictly kept
      them,
Thou knowest I have not once lost nor faith nor ecstasy in Thee,
In shackles, prison'd, in disgrace, repining not,
Accepting all from Thee, as duly come from Thee.

All my emprises have been fill'd with Thee,
My speculations, plans, begun and carried on in thoughts of Thee,
Sailing the deep or journeying the land for Thee;
Intentions, purports, aspirations mine, leaving results to Thee.

O I am sure they really came from Thee,
The urge, the ardor, the unconquerable will,
The potent, felt, interior command, stronger than words,
A message from the Heavens whispering to me even in sleep,
These sped me on.

By me and these the work so far accomplish'd,
By me earth's elder cloy'd and stifled lands uncloy'd, unloos'd,
By me the hemispheres rounded and tied, the unknown to the known.

The end I know not, it is all in Thee,
Or small or great I know not—haply what broad fields, what lands,
Haply the brutish measureless human undergrowth I know,
Transplanted there may rise to stature, knowledge worthy Thee,
Haply the swords I know may there indeed be turn'd to reaping-tools,
Haply the lifeless cross I know, Europe's dead cross, may bud and
    blossom there.

One effort more, my altar this bleak sand;
That thou O God my life hast lighted,
With ray of light, steady, ineffable, vouchsafed of Thee,
Light rare untellable, lighting the very light,
Beyond all signs, descriptions, languages;
For that O God, be it my latest word, here on my knees,
Old, poor, and paralyzed, I thank Thee.

My terminus near,
The clouds already closing in upon me,
The voyage balk'd, the course disputed, lost,
I yield my ships to Thee.

My hands, my limbs grow nerveless,
My brain feels rack'd, bewilder'd,
Let the old timbers part, I will not part,
I will cling fast to Thee, O God, though the waves buffet me,
Thee, Thee at least I know.

Is it the prophet's thought I speak, or am I raving?
What do I know of life? What of myself?
I know not even my own work past or present,
Dim ever-shifting guesses of it spread before me,
Of newer better worlds, their mighty parturition,
Mocking, perplexing me.

And these things I see suddenly, what mean they?
As if some miracle, some hand divine unseal'd my eyes,
Shadowy vast shapes smile through the air and sky,
And on the distant waves sail countless ships,
And anthems in new tongues I hear saluting me.

The Sleepers
1

I WANDER all night in my vision,
Stepping with light feet, swiftly and noiselessly stepping and stop-
    ping,

Bending with open eyes over the shut eyes of sleepers,
Wandering and confused, lost to myself, ill-assorted, contradictory,
Pausing, gazing, bending, and stopping.

How solemn they look there, stretch'd and still,
How quiet they breathe, the little children in their cradles.

The wretched features of ennuyés, the white features of corpses, the
    livid faces of drunkards, the sick-gray faces of onanists,
The gash'd bodies on battle-fields, the insane in their strong-door'd
    rooms, the sacred idiots, the new-born emerging from gates, and
    the dying emerging from gates,
The night pervades them and infolds them.

The married couple sleep calmly in their bed, he with his palm on the
    hip of the wife, and she with her palm on the hip of the husband,
The sisters sleep lovingly side by side in their bed,
The men sleep lovingly side by side in theirs,
And the mother sleeps with her little child carefully wrapt.

The blind sleep, and the deaf and dumb sleep,
The prisoner sleeps well in the prison, the runaway son sleeps,
The murderer that is to be hung next day, how does he sleep?
And the murder'd person, how does he sleep?

The female that loves unrequited sleeps,
And the male that loves unrequited sleeps,
The head of the money-maker that plotted all day sleeps,
And the enraged and treacherous dispositions, all, all sleep.

I stand in the dark with drooping eyes by the worst-suffering and the
    most restless,
I pass my hands soothingly to and fro a few inches from them,
The restless sink in their beds, they fitfully sleep.

Now I pierce the darkness, new beings appear,
The earth recedes from me into the night,
I saw that it was beautiful, and I see that what is not the earth is
    beautiful.

I go from bedside to bedside, I sleep close with the other sleepers
    each in turn,

I dream in my dream all the dreams of the other dreamers,
And I become the other dreamers.

I am a dance—play up there! the fit is whirling me fast!

I am the ever-laughing—it is new moon and twilight,
I see the hiding of douceurs, I see nimble ghosts whichever way I
    look,
Cache and cache again deep in the ground and sea, and where it is
    neither ground nor sea.

Well do they do their jobs those journeymen divine,
Only from me can they hide nothing, and would not if they could,
I reckon I am their boss and they make me a pet besides,
And surround me and lead me and run ahead when I walk,
To lift their cunning covers to signify me with stretch'd arms, and
    resume the way;
Onward we move, a gay gang of blackguards! with mirth-shouting
    music and wild-flapping pennants of joy!

I am the actor, the actress, the voter, the politician,
The emigrant and the exile, the criminal that stood in the box,
He who has been famous and he who shall be famous after to-day,
The stammerer, the well-form'd person, the wasted or feeble person.

I am she who adorn'd herself and folded her hair expectantly,
My truant lover has come, and it is dark.

Double yourself and receive me darkness,
Receive me and my lover too, he will not let me go without him.

I roll myself upon you as upon a bed, I resign myself to the dusk.

He whom I call answers me and takes the place of my lover,
He rises with me silently from the bed.

Darkness, you are gentler than my lover, his flesh was sweaty and
    panting,
I feel the hot moisture yet that he left me.

My hands are spread forth, I pass them in all directions,
I would sound up the shadowy shore to which you are journeying.

Be careful darkness! already what was it touch'd me?
I thought my lover had gone, else darkness and he are one,
I hear the heart-beat, I follow, I fade away.

2

I descend my western course, my sinews are flaccid,
Perfume and youth course through me and I am their wake.

It is my face yellow and wrinkled instead of the old woman's,
I sit low in a straw-bottom chair and carefully darn my grandson's
    stockings.

It is I too, the sleepless widow looking out on the winter midnight,
I see the sparkles of starshine on the icy and pallid earth.

A shroud I see and I am the shroud, I wrap a body and lie in the
    coffin,
It is dark here under ground, it is not evil or pain here, it is blank
    here, for reasons.

(It seems to me that every thing in the light and air ought to be
    happy,
Whoever is not in his coffin and the dark grave let him know he has
    enough.)

3

I see a beautiful gigantic swimmer swimming naked through the
    eddies of the sea,
His brown hair lies close and even to his head, he strikes out with
    courageous arms, he urges himself with his legs,
I see his white body, I see his undaunted eyes,
I hate the swift-running eddies that would dash him head-foremost
    on the rocks.

What are you doing you ruffianly red-trickled waves?
Will you kill the courageous giant? will you kill him in the prime of
    his middle age?

Steady and long he struggles,
He is baffled, bang'd, bruis'd, he holds out while his strength holds
    out,

The slapping eddies are spotted with his blood, they bear him away,
    they roll him, swing him, turn him,
His beautiful body is borne in the circling eddies, it is continually
    bruis'd on rocks,
Swiftly and out of sight is borne the brave corpse.

4

I turn but do not extricate myself,
Confused, a past-reading, another, but with darkness yet.

The beach is cut by the razory ice-wind, the wreck-guns sound,
The tempest lulls, the moon comes floundering through the drifts.

I look where the ship helplessly heads end on, I hear the burst as she
    strikes, I hear the howls of dismay, they grow fainter and fainter.

I cannot aid with my wringing fingers,
I can but rush to the surf and let it drench me and freeze upon me.

I search with the crowd, not one of the company is wash'd to us alive,
In the morning I help pick up the dead and lay them in rows in a barn.

5

Now of the older war-days, the defeat at Brooklyn,
Washington stands inside the lines, he stands on the intrench'd hills
    amid a crowd of officers,
His face is cold and damp, he cannot repress the weeping drops,
He lifts the glass perpetually to his eyes, the color is blanch'd from
    his cheeks,
He sees the slaughter of the southern braves confided to him by their
    parents.

The same at last and at last when peace is declared,
He stands in the room of the old tavern, the well-belov'd soldiers all
    pass through,
The officers speechless and slow draw near in their turns,
The chief encircles their necks with his arm and kisses them on the
    cheek,
He kisses lightly the wet cheeks one after another, he shakes hands
    and bids good-by to the army.

6

Now what my mother told me one day as we sat at dinner together,
Of when she was a nearly grown girl living home with her parents on
 the old homestead.

A red squaw came one breakfast-time to the old homestead,
On her back she carried a bundle of rushes for rush-bottoming chairs,
Her hair, straight, shiny, coarse, black, profuse, half-envelop'd her
 face,
Her step was free and elastic, and her voice sounded exquisitely as
 she spoke.

My mother look'd in delight and amazement at the stranger,
She look'd at the freshness of her tall-borne face and full and pliant
 limbs,
The more she look'd upon her she loved her,
Never before had she seen such wonderful beauty and purity,
She made her sit on a bench by the jamb of the fireplace, she cook'd
 food for her,
She had no work to give her, but she gave her remembrance and
 fondness.

The red squaw staid all the forenoon, and toward the middle of the
 afternoon she went away,
O my mother was loth to have her go away,
All the week she thought of her, she watch'd for her many a month,
She remember'd her many a winter and many a summer,
But the red squaw never came nor was heard of there again.

7

A show of the summer softness—a contact of something unseen—an
 amour of the light and air,
I am jealous and overwhelm'd with friendliness,
And will go gallivant with the light and air myself.

O love and summer, you are in the dreams and in me,
Autumn and winter are in the dreams, the farmer goes with his thrift,
The droves and crops increase, the barns are well-fill'd.

Elements merge in the night, ships make tacks in the dreams,
The sailor sails, the exile returns home,

The fugitive returns unharm'd, the immigrant is back beyond months
    and years,
The poor Irishman lives in the simple house of his childhood with
    the well-known neighbors and faces,
They warmly welcome him, he is barefoot again, he forgets he is well
    off,
The Dutchman voyages home, and the Scotchman and Welshman
    voyage home, and the native of the Mediterranean voyages
    home,
To every port of England, France, Spain, enter well-fill'd ships,
The Swiss foots it toward his hills, the Prussian goes his way, the
    Hungarian his way, and the Pole his way,
The Swede returns, and the Dane and Norwegian return.

The homeward bound and the outward bound,
The beautiful lost swimmer, the ennuyé, the onanist, the female that
    loves unrequited, the money-maker,
The actor and actress, those through with their parts and those wait-
    ing to commence,
The affectionate boy, the husband and wife, the voter, the nominee
    that is chosen and the nominee that has fail'd,
The great already known and the great any time after to-day,
The stammerer, the sick, the perfect-form'd, the homely,
The criminal that stood in the box, the judge that sat and sentenced
    him, the fluent lawyers, the jury, the audience,
The laugher and weeper, the dancer, the midnight widow, the red
    squaw,
The consumptive, the erysipalite, the idiot, he that is wrong'd,
The antipodes, and every one between this and them in the dark,
I swear they are averaged now—one is no better than the other,
The night and sleep have liken'd them and restored them.

I swear they are all beautiful,
Every one that sleeps is beautiful, every thing in the dim light is
    beautiful,
The wildest and bloodiest is over, and all is peace.

Peace is always beautiful,
The myth of heaven indicates peace and night.

The myth of heaven indicates the soul,
The soul is always beautiful, it appears more or it appears less, it
    comes or it lags behind,

It comes from its embower'd garden and looks pleasantly on itself
    and encloses the world,
Perfect and clean the genitals previously jetting, and perfect and
    clean the womb cohering,
The head well-grown proportion'd and plumb, and the bowels and
    joints proportion'd and plumb.

The soul is always beautiful,
The universe is duly in order, every thing is in its place,
What has arrived is in its place and what waits shall be in its place,
The twisted skull waits, the watery or rotten blood waits,
The child of the glutton or venerealee waits long, and the child
    of the drunkard waits long, and the drunkard himself waits
    long,
The sleepers that lived and died wait, the far advanced are to go
    on in their turns, and the far behind are to come on in their
    turns,
The diverse shall be no less diverse, but they shall flow and unite—
    they unite now.

8

The sleepers are very beautiful as they lie unclothed,
They flow hand in hand over the whole earth from east to west as
    they lie unclothed,
The Asiatic and African are hand in hand, the European and
    American are hand in hand,
Learn'd and unlearn'd are hand in hand, and male and female are
    hand in hand,
The bare arm of the girl crosses the bare breast of her lover, they
    press close without lust, his lips press her neck,
The father holds his grown or ungrown son in his arms with meas-
    ureless love, and the son holds the father in his arms with
    measureless love,
The white hair of the mother shines on the white wrist of the
    daughter,
The breath of the boy goes with the breath of the man, friend is
    inarm'd by friend,
The scholar kisses the teacher and the teacher kisses the scholar,
    the wrong'd is made right,
The call of the slave is one with the master's call, and the master
    salutes the slave,
The felon steps forth from the prison, the insane becomes sane,
    the suffering of sick persons is reliev'd,

The sweatings and fevers stop, the throat that was unsound is
    sound, the lungs of the consumptive are resumed, the poor
    distress'd head is free,
The joints of the rheumatic move as smoothly as ever, and smoother
    than ever,
Stiflings and passages open, the paralyzed become supple,
The swell'd and convuls'd and congested awake to themselves in
    condition,
They pass the invigoration of the night and the chemistry of the
    night, and awake.

I too pass from the night,
I stay a while away O night, but I return to you again and love you.

Why should I be afraid to trust myself to you?
I am not afraid, I have been well brought forward by you,
I love the rich running day, but I do not desert her in whom I lay
    so long,
I know not how I came of you and I know not where I go with
    you, but I know I came well and shall go well.

I will stop only a time with the night, and rise betimes,
I will duly pass the day O my mother, and duly return to you.

TRANSPOSITIONS

LET the reformers descend from the stands where they are forever
    bawling—let an idiot or insane person appear on each of the
    stands;
Let judges and criminals be transposed—let the prison-keepers be
    put in prison—let those that were prisoners take the keys;
Let them that distrust birth and death lead the rest.

To Think of Time

1

To think of time—of all that retrospection,
To think of to-day, and the ages continued henceforward.

Have you guess'd you yourself would not continue?
Have you dreaded these earth-beetles?
Have you fear'd the future would be nothing to you?

Is to-day nothing? is the beginningless past nothing?
If the future is nothing they are just as surely nothing.

To think that the sun rose in the east—that men and women were
    flexible, real, alive—that every thing was alive,
To think that you and I did not see, feel, think, nor bear our part,
To think that we are now here and bear our part.

2

Not a day passes, not a minute or second without an accouchement,
Not a day passes, not a minute or second without a corpse.

The dull nights go over and the dull days also,
The soreness of lying so much in bed goes over,
The physician after long putting off gives the silent and terrible
    look for an answer,
The children come hurried and weeping, and the brothers and
    sisters are sent for,
Medicines stand unused on the shelf, (the camphor-smell has long
    pervaded the rooms,)
The faithful hand of the living does not desert the hand of the dying,
The twitching lips press lightly on the forehead of the dying,
The breath ceases and the pulse of the heart ceases,
The corpse stretches on the bed and the living look upon it,
It is palpable as the living are palpable.

The living look upon the corpse with their eyesight,
But without eyesight lingers a different living and looks curiously
    on the corpse.

3

To think the thought of death merged in the thought of materials,
To think of all these wonders of city and country, and others taking
    great interest in them, and we taking no interest in them.

To think how eager we are in building our houses,
To think others shall be just as eager, and we quite indifferent.

(I see one building the house that serves him a few years, or seventy
    or eighty years at most,
I see one building the house that serves him longer than that.)

Slow-moving and black lines creep over the whole earth—they
    never cease—they are the burial lines,
He that was President was buried, and he that is now President
    shall surely be buried.

4

A reminiscence of the vulgar fate,
A frequent sample of the life and death of workmen,
Each after his kind.

Cold dash of waves at the ferry-wharf, posh and ice in the river,
    half-frozen mud in the streets,
A gray discouraged sky overhead, the short last daylight of
    December,
A hearse and stages, the funeral of an old Broadway stage-driver,
    the cortege mostly drivers.

Steady the trot to the cemetery, duly rattles the death-bell,
The gate is pass'd, the new-dug grave is halted at, the living alight,
    the hearse uncloses,
The coffin is pass'd out, lower'd and settled, the whip is laid on
    the coffin, the earth is swiftly shovel'd in,
The mound above is flatted with the spades—silence,
A minute—no one moves or speaks—it is done,
He is decently put away—is there any thing more?

He was a good fellow, free-mouth'd, quick-temper'd, not bad-
    looking,
Ready with life or death for a friend, fond of women, gambled,
    ate hearty, drank hearty,
Had known what it was to be flush, grew low-spirited toward the
    last, sicken'd, was help'd by a contribution,
Died, aged forty-one years—and that was his funeral.

Thumb extended, finger uplifted, apron, cape, gloves, strap, wet-
    weather clothes, whip carefully chosen,
Boss, spotter, starter, hostler, somebody loafing on you, you loafing
    on somebody, headway, man before and man behind,
Good day's work, bad day's work, pet stock, mean stock, first out,
    last out, turning-in at night,
To think that these are so much and so nigh to other drivers, and
    he there takes no interest in them.

5

The markets, the government, the working-man's wages, to think
what account they are through our nights and days,
To think that other working-men will make just as great account
of them, yet we make little or no account.

The vulgar and the refined, what you call sin and what you call
goodness, to think how wide a difference,
To think the difference will still continue to others, yet we lie
beyond the difference.

To think how much pleasure there is,
Do you enjoy yourself in the city? or engaged in business? or
planning a nomination and election? or with your wife and
family?
Or with your mother and sisters? or in womanly housework? or
the beautiful maternal cares?
These also flow onward to others, you and I flow onward,
But in due time you and I shall take less interest in them.

Your farm, profits, crops—to think how engross'd you are,
To think there will still be farms, profits, crops, yet for you of
what avail?

6

What will be will be well, for what is is well,
To take interest is well, and not to take interest shall be well.

The domestic joys, the daily housework or business, the building
of houses, are not phantasms, they have weight, form, location,
Farms, profits, crops, markets, wages, government, are none of
them phantasms,
The difference between sin and goodness is no delusion,
The earth is not an echo, man and his life and all the things of
his life are well-consider'd.

You are not thrown to the winds, you gather certainly and safely
around yourself,
Yourself! yourself! yourself, for ever and ever!

7

It is not to diffuse you that you were born of your mother and
father, it is to identify you,

It is not that you should be undecided, but that you should be
    decided,
Something long preparing and formless is arrived and form'd in you,
You are henceforth secure, whatever comes or goes.

The threads that were spun are gather'd, the weft crosses the warp,
    the pattern is systematic.

The preparations have every one been justified,
The orchestra have sufficiently tuned their instruments, the baton
    has given the signal.

The guest that was coming, he waited long, he is now housed,
He is one of those who are beautiful and happy, he is one of those
    that to look upon and be with is enough.

The law of the past cannot be eluded,
The law of the present and future cannot be eluded,
The law of the living cannot be eluded, it is eternal,
The law of promotion and transformation cannot be eluded,
The law of heroes and good-doers cannot be eluded,
The law of drunkards, informers, mean persons, not one iota thereof
    can be eluded.

8

Slow moving and black lines go ceaselessly over the earth,
Northerner goes carried and Southerner goes carried, and they on
    the Atlantic side and they on the Pacific,
And they between, and all through the Mississippi country, and
    all over the earth.

The great masters and kosmos are well as they go, the heroes and
    good-doers are well,
The known leaders and inventors and the rich owners and pious
    and distinguish'd may be well,
But there is more account than that, there is strict account of all.

The interminable hordes of the ignorant and wicked are not nothing,
The barbarians of Africa and Asia are not nothing,
The perpetual successions of shallow people are not nothing as
    they go.

Of and in all these things,
I have dream'd that we are not to be changed so much, nor the
law of us changed,
I have dream'd that heroes and good-doers shall be under the
present and past law,
And that murderers, drunkards, liars, shall be under the present
and past law,
For I have dream'd that the law they are under now is enough.

And I have dream'd that the purpose and essence of the known
life, the transient,
Is to form and decide identity for the unknown life, the permanent.

If all came but to ashes of dung,
If maggots and rats ended us, then Alarum! for we are betray'd,
Then indeed suspicion of death.

Do you suspect death? If I were to suspect death I should die
now,
Do you think I could walk pleasantly and well-suited toward
annihilation?

Pleasantly and well-suited I walk,
Whither I walk I cannot define, but I know it is good,
The whole universe indicates that it is good,
The past and the present indicate that it is good.

How beautiful and perfect are the animals!
How perfect the earth, and the minutest thing upon it!
What is called good is perfect, and what is called bad is just as
perfect,
The vegetables and minerals are all perfect, and the imponderable
fluids perfect;
Slowly and surely they have pass'd on to this, and slowly and surely
they yet pass on.

9

I swear I think now that every thing without exception has an
eternal soul!
The trees have, rooted in the ground! the weeds of the sea have!
the animals!

I swear I think there is nothing but immortality!
That the exquisite scheme is for it, and the nebulous float is for it,
    and the cohering is for it!
And all preparation is for it—and identity is for it—and life and
    materials are altogether for it!

Whispers of Heavenly Death

DAREST THOU NOW O SOUL

DAREST thou now O soul,
Walk out with me toward the unknown region,
Where neither ground is for the feet nor any path to follow?

No map there, nor guide,
Nor voice sounding, nor touch of human hand,
Nor face with blooming flesh, nor lips, nor eyes, are in that land.

I know it not O soul,
Nor dost thou, all is a blank before us,
All waits undream'd of in that region, that inaccessible land.

Till when the ties loosen,
All but the ties eternal, Time and Space,
Nor darkness, gravitation, sense, nor any bounds bounding us.

Then we burst forth, we float,
In Time and Space O soul, prepared for them,
Equal, equipt at last, (O joy! O fruit of all!) them to fulfil O soul.

WHISPERS OF HEAVENLY DEATH

WHISPERS of heavenly death murmur'd I hear,
Labial gossip of night, sibilant chorals,
Footsteps gently ascending, mystical breezes wafted soft and low,
Ripples of unseen rivers, tides of a current flowing, forever flowing,
(Or is it the plashing of tears? the measureless waters of human
    tears?)

I see, just see skyward, great cloud-masses,
Mournfully slowly they roll, silently swelling and mixing,
With at times a half-dimm'd sadden'd far-off star,
Appearing and disappearing.

(Some parturition rather, some solemn immortal birth;
On the frontiers to eyes impenetrable,
Some soul is passing over.)

CHANTING THE SQUARE DEIFIC

1

CHANTING the square deific, out of the One advancing, out of the
    sides,
Out of the old and new, out of the square entirely divine,
Solid, four-sided, (all the sides needed,) from this side Jehovah
    am I,
Old Brahm I, and I Saturnius am;
Not Time affects me—I am Time, old, modern as any,
Unpersuadable, relentless, executing righteous judgments,
As the Earth, the Father, the brown old Kronos, with laws,
Aged beyong computation, yet ever new, ever with those mighty
    laws rolling,
Relentless I forgive no man—whoever sins dies—I will have that
    man's life;
Therefore let none expect mercy—have the seasons, gravitation,
    the appointed days, mercy? no more have I,
But as the seasons and gravitation, and as all the appointed days
    that forgive not,
I dispense from this side judgments inexorable without the least
    remorse.

2

Consolator most mild, the promis'd one advancing,
With gentle hand extended, the mightier God am I,
Foretold by prophets and poets in their most rapt prophecies and
    poems,
From this side, lo! the Lord Christ gazes—lo! Hermes I—lo!
    mine is Hercules' face,
All sorrow, labor, suffering, I, tallying it, absorb in myself,
Many times have I been rejected, taunted, put in prison, and cruci-
    fied, and many times shall be again,
All the world have I given up for my dear brothers' and sisters'
    sake, for the soul's sake,
Wending my way through the homes of men, rich or poor, with
    the kiss of affection,
For I am affection, I am the cheer-bringing God, with hope and
    all-enclosing charity,

With indulgent words as to children, with fresh and sane words,
    mine only,
Young and strong I pass knowing well I am destin'd myself to an
    early death;
But my charity has no death—my wisdom dies not, neither early
    nor late,
And my sweet love bequeath'd here and elsewhere never dies.

3

Aloof, dissatisfied, plotting revolt,
Comrade of criminals, brother of slaves,
Crafty, despised, a drudge, ignorant,
With sudra face and worn brow, black, but in the depths of my
    heart, proud as any,
Lifted now and always against whoever scorning assumes to rule me,
Morose, full of guile, full of reminiscences, brooding, with many
    wiles,
(Though it was thought I was baffled and dispel'd, and my wiles
    done, but that will never be,)
Defiant, I, Satan, still live, still utter words, in new lands duly
    appearing, (and old ones also,)
Permanent here from my side, warlike, equal with any, real as any,
Nor time nor change shall ever change me or my words.

4

Santa Spirita, breather, life,
Beyond the light, lighter than light,
Beyond the flame of hell, joyous, leaping easily above hell,
Beyond Paradise, perfumed solely with mine own perfume,
Including all life on earth, touching, including God, including
    Saviour and Satan,
Ethereal, pervading all, (for without me what were all? what were
    God?)
Essence of forms, life of the real identities, permanent, positive,
    (namely the unseen,)
Life of the great round world, the sun and stars, and of man,
    I, the general soul,
Here the square finishing, the solid, I the most solid,
Breathe my breath also through these songs.

OF HIM I LOVE DAY AND NIGHT

OF him I love day and night I dream'd I heard he was dead,
And I dream'd I went where they had buried him I love, but he
  was not in that place,
And I dream'd I wander'd searching among burial-places to find
  him,
And I found that every place was a burial-place;
The houses full of life were equally full of death, (this house is
  now,)
The streets, the shipping, the places of amusement, the Chicago,
  Boston, Philadelphia, the Mannahatta, were as full of the
  dead as of the living,
And fuller, O vastly fuller of the dead than of the living;
And what I dream'd I will henceforth tell to every person and age,
And I stand henceforth bound to what I dream'd,
And now I am willing to disregard burial-places and dispense with
  them,
And if the memorials of the dead were put up indifferently every-
  where, even in the room where I eat or sleep, I should be
  satisfied,
And if the corpse of any one I love, or if my own corpse, be duly
  render'd to powder and pour'd in the sea, I shall be satisfied,
Or if it be distributed to the winds I shall be satisfied.

YET, YET, YE DOWNCAST HOURS

YET, yet, ye downcast hours, I know ye also,
Weights of lead, how ye clog and cling at my ankles,
Earth to a chamber of mourning turns—I hear the o'erweening,
  mocking voice,
Matter is conqueror—matter, triumphant only, continues onward.

Despairing cries float ceaselessly toward me,
The call of my nearest lover, putting forth, alarm'd, uncertain,
The sea I am quickly to sail, come tell me,
Come tell me where I am speeding, tell me my destination.

I understand your anguish, but I cannot help you,
I approach, hear, behold, the sad mouth, the look out of the eyes,
  your mute inquiry,
Whither I go from the bed I recline on, come tell me;

Old age, alarm'd, uncertain—a young woman's voice, appealing
    to me for comfort;
A young man's voice, *Shall I not escape?*

AS IF A PHANTOM CARESS'D ME

As if a phantom caress'd me,
I thought I was not alone walking here by the shore;
But the one I thought was with me as now I walk by the shore,
    the one I loved that caress'd me,
As I lean and look through the glimmering light, that one has
    utterly disappear'd,
And those appear that are hateful to me and mock me.

ASSURANCES

I NEED no assurances, I am a man who is pre-occupied of his own
    soul;
I do not doubt that from under the feet and beside the hands and
    face I am cognizant of, are now looking faces I am not cognizant
    of, calm and actual faces,
I do not doubt but the majesty and beauty of the world are latent
    in any iota of the world,
I do not doubt I am limitless, and that the universes are limitless,
    in vain I try to think how limitless,
I do not doubt that the orbs and the systems of orbs play their
    swift sports through the air on purpose, and that I shall one
    day be eligible to do as much as they, and more than they,
I do not doubt that temporary affairs keep on and on millions of
    years,
I do not doubt interiors have their interiors, and exteriors have
    their exteriors, and that the eyesight has another eyesight,
    and the hearing another hearing, and the voice another voice,
I do not doubt that the passionately-wept deaths of young men
    are provided for, and that the deaths of young women and
    the deaths of little children are provided for,
(Did you think Life was so well provided for, and Death, the purport
    of all Life, is not well provided for?)
I do not doubt that wrecks at sea, no matter what the horrors of
    them, no matter whose wife, child, husband, father, lover, has
    gone down, are provided for, to the minutest points,
I do not doubt that whatever can possibly happen anywhere at
    any time, is provided for in the inherences of things,

I do not think Life provides for all and for Time and Space, but I
  believe Heavenly Death provides for all.

QUICKSAND YEARS

QUICKSAND years that whirl me I know not whither,
Your schemes, politics, fail, lines give way, substances mock and
  elude me,
Only the theme I sing, the great and strong-possess'd soul, eludes
  not,
One's-self must never give way—that is the final substance—that
  out of all is sure,
Out of politics, triumphs, battles, life, what at last finally remains?
When shows break up what but One's-Self is sure?

THAT MUSIC ALWAYS ROUND ME

THAT music always round me, unceasing, unbeginning, yet long
  untaught I did not hear,
But now the chorus I hear and am elated,
A tenor, strong, ascending with power and health, with glad notes of
  daybreak I hear,
A soprano at intervals sailing buoyantly over the tops of immense
  waves,
A transparent base shuddering lusciously under and through the
  universe,
The triumphant tutti, the funeral wailings with sweet flutes and
  violins, all these I fill myself with,
I hear not the volumes of sound merely, I am moved by the exquisite
  meanings,
I listen to the different voices winding in and out, striving, contending
  with fiery vehemence to excel each other in emotion;
I do not think the performers know themselves—but now I think I
  begin to know them.

WHAT SHIP PUZZLED AT SEA

WHAT ship puzzled at sea, cons for the true reckoning?
Or coming in, to avoid the bars and follow the channel a perfect pilot
  needs?
Here, sailor! here, ship! take aboard the most perfect pilot,
Whom, in a little boat, putting off and rowing, I hailing you offer.

A NOISELESS PATIENT SPIDER

A NOISELESS patient spider,
I mark'd where on a little promontory it stood isolated,
Mark'd how to explore the vacant vast surrounding,
It launch'd forth filament, filament, filament, out of itself,
Ever unreeling them, ever tirelessly speeding them.

And you O my soul where you stand,
Surrounded, detached, in measureless oceans of space,
Ceaselessly musing, venturing, throwing, seeking the spheres to con-
    nect them,
Till the bridge you will need be form'd, till the ductile anchor hold,
Till the gossamer thread you fling catch somewhere, O my soul.

O LIVING ALWAYS, ALWAYS DYING

O LIVING always, always dying!
O the burials of me past and present,
O me while I stride ahead, material, visible, imperious as ever;
O me, what I was for years, now dead, (I lament not, I am content;)
O to disengage myself from those corpses of me, which I turn and
    look at where I cast them,
To pass on, (O living! always living!) and leave the corpses behind.

TO ONE SHORTLY TO DIE

FROM all the rest I single out you, having a message for you,
You are to die—let others tell you what they please, I cannot pre-
    varicate,
I am exact and merciless, but I love you—there is no escape for you.

Softly I lay my right hand upon you, you just feel it,
I do not argue, I bend my head close and half envelop it,
I sit quietly by, I remain faithful,
I am more than nurse, more than parent or neighbor,
I absolve you from all except yourself spiritual bodily, that is eternal,
    you yourself will surely escape,
The corpse you will leave will be but excrementitious.

The sun bursts through in unlooked-for directions,
Strong thoughts fill you and confidence, you smile,
You forget you are sick, as I forget you are sick,

You do not see the medicines, you do not mind the weeping friends,
    I am with you,
I exclude others from you, there is nothing to be commiserated,
I do not commiserate, I congratulate you.

NIGHT ON THE PRAIRIES

NIGHT on the prairies,
The supper is over, the fire on the ground burns low,
The wearied emigrants sleep, wrapt in their blankets;
I walk by myself—I stand and look at the stars, which I think now I
    never realized before.

Now I absorb immortality and peace,
I admire death and test propositions.

How plenteous! how spiritual! how resumé!
The same old man and soul—the same old aspirations, and the same
    content.

I was thinking the day most splendid till I saw what the not-day
    exhibited,
I was thinking this globe enough till there sprang out so noiseless
    around me myriads of other globes.

Now while the great thoughts of space and eternity fill me I will
    measure myself by them,
And now touch'd with the lives of other globes arrived as far along
    as those of the earth,
Or waiting to arrive, or pass'd on farther than those of the earth,
I henceforth no more ignore them than I ignore my own life,
Or the lives of the earth arrived as far as mine, or waiting to arrive.

O I see now that life cannot exhibit all to me, as the day cannot,
I see that I am to wait for what will be exhibited by death.

THOUGHT

As I sit with others at a great feast, suddenly while the music is
    playing,
To my mind, (whence it comes I know not,) spectral in mist of a
    wreck at sea,
Of certain ships, how they sail from port with flying streamers and
    wafted kisses, and that is the last of them,

Of the solemn and murky mystery about the fate of the President,
Of the flower of the marine science of fifty generations founder'd off
    the Northeast coast and going down—of the steamship Arctic
    going down,
Of the veil'd tableau—women gather'd together on deck, pale, heroic,
    waiting the moment that draws so close—O the moment!
A huge sob—a few bubbles—the white foam spirting up—and then
    the women gone,
Sinking there while the passionless wet flows on—and I now ponder-
    ing, Are those women indeed gone?
Are souls drown'd and destroy'd so?
Is only matter triumphant?

THE LAST INVOCATION

At the last, tenderly,
From the walls of the powerful fortress'd house,
From the clasp of the knitted locks, from the keep of the well-closed
    doors,
Let me be wafted.

Let me glide noiselessly forth;
With the key of softness unlock the locks—with a whisper,
Set ope the doors O soul.

Tenderly—be not impatient,
(Strong is your hold O mortal flesh,
Strong is your hold O love.)

AS I WATCH'D THE PLOUGHMAN PLOUGHING

As I watch'd the ploughman ploughing,
Or the sower sowing in the fields, or the harvester harvesting,
I saw there too, O life and death, your analogies;
(Life, life is the tillage, and Death is the harvest according.)

PENSIVE AND FALTERING

Pensive and faltering,
The words *the Dead* I write,
For living are the Dead,
(Haply the only living, only real,
And I the apparition, I the spectre.)

Thou Mother with Thy Equal Brood

1

THOU Mother with thy equal brood,
Thou varied chain of different States, yet one identity only,
A special song before I go I'd sing o'er all the rest,
For thee, the future.

I'd sow a seed for thee of endless Nationality,
I'd fashion thy ensemble including body and soul,
I'd show away ahead thy real Union, and how it may be accomplish'd.

The paths to the house I seek to make,
But leave to those to come the house itself.

Belief I sing, and preparation;
As Life and Nature are not great with reference to the present only,
But greater still from what is yet to come,
Out of that formula for thee I sing.

2

As a strong bird on pinions free,
Joyous, the amplest spaces heavenward cleaving,
Such be the thought I'd think of thee America,
Such be the recitative I'd bring for thee.

The conceits of the poets of other lands I'd bring thee not,
Nor the compliments that have served their turn so long,
Nor rhyme, nor the classics, nor perfume of foreign court or indoor
    library;
But an odor I'd bring as from forests of pine in Maine, or breath of
    an Illinois prairie,
With open airs of Virginia or Georgia or Tennessee, or from Texas
    uplands, or Florida's glades,
Or the Saguenay's black stream, or the wide blue spread of Huron,
With presentment of Yellowstone's scenes, or Yosemite,
And murmuring under, pervading all, I'd bring the rustling sea-sound,
That endlessly sounds from the two Great Seas of the world.

And for thy subtler sense subtler refrains dread Mother,
Preludes of intellect tallying these and thee, mind-formulas fitted for
    thee, real and sane and large as these and thee,

Thou! mounting higher, diving deeper than we knew, thou trans-
cendental Union!
By thee fact to be justified, blended with thought,
Thought of man justified, blended with God,
Through thy idea, lo, the immortal reality!
Through thy reality, lo, the immortal idea!

3

Brain of the New World, what a task is thine,
To formulate the Modern—out of the peerless grandeur of the
modern,
Out of thyself, comprising science, to recast poems, churches, art,
(Recast, may-be discard them, end them—may-be their work is done,
who knows?)
By vision, hand, conception, on the background of the mighty past,
the dead,
To limn with absolute faith the mighty living present.

And yet thou living present brain, heir of the dead, the Old World
brain,
Thou that lay folded like an unborn babe within its folds so long,
Thou carefully prepared by it so long—haply thou but unfoldest it,
only maturest it,
It to eventuate in thee—the essence of the by-gone time contain'd in
thee,
Its poems, churches, arts, unwitting to themselves, destined with
reference to thee;
Thou but the apples, long, long, long a-growing,
The fruit of all the Old ripening to-day in thee.

4

Sail, sail thy best, ship of Democracy,
Of value is thy freight, 'tis not the Present only,
The Past is also stored in thee,
Thou holdest not the venture of thyself alone, not of the Western
continent alone,
Earth's *résumé* entire floats on thy keel O ship, is steadied by thy
spars,
With thee Time voyages in trust, the antecedent nations sink or swim
with thee,
With all their ancient struggles, martyrs, heroes, epics, wars, thou
bear'st the other continents,

Theirs, theirs as much as thine, the destination-port triumphant;
Steer then with good strong hand and wary eye O helmsman, thou
    carriest great companions,
Venerable priestly Asia sails this day with thee,
And royal feudal Europe sails with thee.

5

Beautiful world of new superber birth that rises to my eyes,
Like a limitless golden cloud filling the western sky,
Emblem of general maternity lifted above all,
Sacred shape of the bearer of daughters and sons,
Out of thy teeming womb thy giant babes in ceaseless procession
    issuing,
Acceding from such gestation, taking and giving continual strength
    and life,
World of the real—world of the twain in one,
World of the soul, born by the world of the real alone, led to identity,
    body, by it alone,
Yet in beginning only, incalculable masses of composite precious
    materials,
By history's cycles forwarded, by every nation, language, hither sent,
Ready, collected here, a freer, vast, electric world, to be constructed
    here,
(The true New World, the world of orbic science, morals, literatures
    to come,)
Thou wonder world yet undefined, unform'd, neither do I define thee,
How can I pierce the impenetrable blank of the future?
I feel thy ominous greatness evil as well as good,
I watch thee advancing, absorbing the present, transcending the past,
I see thy light lighting, and thy shadow shadowing, as if the entire
    globe,
But I do not undertake to define thee, hardly to comprehend thee,
I but thee name, thee prophesy, as now,
I merely thee ejaculate!

Thee in thy future,
Thee in thy only permanent life, career, thy own unloosen'd mind,
    thy soaring spirit,
Thee as another equally needed sun, radiant, ablaze, swift-moving,
    fructifying all,
Thee risen in potent cheerfulness and joy, in endless great hilarity,
Scattering for good the cloud that hung so long, that weigh'd so long
    upon the mind of man,

The doubt, suspicion, dread, of gradual, certain decadence of man;
Thee in thy larger, saner brood of female, male—thee in thy athletes,
   moral, spiritual, South, North, West, East,
(To thy immortal breasts, Mother of All, thy every daughter, son,
   endear'd alike, forever equal,)
Thee in thy own musicians, singers, artists, unborn yet, but certain,
Thee in thy moral wealth and civilization, (until which thy proudest
   material civilization must remain in vain,)
Thee in thy all-supplying, all-enclosing worship—thee in no single
   bible, saviour, merely,
Thy saviours countless, latent within thyself, thy bibles incessant
   within thyself, equal to any, divine as any,
(Thy soaring course thee formulating, not in thy two great wars, nor
   in thy century's visible growth,
But far more in these leaves and chants, thy chants, great Mother!)
Thee in an education grown of thee, in teachers, studies, students,
   born of thee,
Thee in thy democratic fêtes en-masse, thy high original festivals,
   operas, lecturers, preachers,
Thee in thy ultimata, (the preparations only now completed, the
   edifice on sure foundations tied,)
Thee in thy pinnacles, intellect, thought, thy topmost rational joys,
   thy love and godlike aspiration,
In thy resplendent coming literati, thy full-lung'd orators, thy sacer-
   dotal bards, kosmic savans,
These! these in thee, (certain to come,) to-day I prophesy.

6

Land tolerating all, accepting all, not for the good alone, all good for
   thee,
Land in the realms of God to be a realm unto thyself,
Under the rule of God to be a rule unto thyself.

(Lo, where arise three peerless stars,
To be thy natal stars my country, Ensemble, Evolution, Freedom,
Set in the sky of Law.)

Land of unprecedented faith, God's faith,
Thy soil, thy very subsoil, all upheav'd,
The general inner earth so long so sedulously draped over, now hence
   for what it is boldly laid bare,
Open'd by thee to heaven's light for benefit or bale.

Not for success alone,
Not to fair-sail unintermitted always,
The storm shall dash thy face, the murk of war and worse than war
    shall cover thee all over,
(Wert capable of war, its tug and trials? be capable of peace, its trials,
For the tug and mortal strain of nations come at last in prosperous
    peace, not war;)
In many a smiling mask death shall approach beguiling thee, thou
    in disease shalt swelter,
The livid cancer spread its hideous claws, clinging upon thy breasts,
    seeking to strike thee deep within,
Consumption of the worst, moral consumption, shall rouge thy face
    with hectic,
But thou shalt face thy fortunes, thy diseases, and surmount them all,
Whatever they are to-day and whatever through time they may be,
They each and all shall lift and pass away and cease from thee,
While thou, Time's spirals rounding, out of thyself, thyself still extri-
    cating, fusing,
Equable, natural, mystical Union thou, (the mortal with immortal
    blent,)
Shalt soar toward the fulfilment of the future, the spirit of the body
    and the mind,
The soul, its destinies.

The soul, its destinies, the real real,
(Purport of all these apparitions of the real;)
In thee America, the soul, its destinies,
Thou globe of globes! thou wonder nebulous!
By many a throe of heat and cold convuls'd, (by these thyself solidi-
    fying,)
Thou mental, moral orb—thou New, indeed new, Spiritual World!
The Present holds thee not—for such vast growth as thine,
For such unparallel'd flight as thine, such brood as thine,
The FUTURE only holds thee and can hold thee.

A PAUMANOK PICTURE

Two boats with nets lying off the sea-beach, quite still,
Ten fishermen waiting—they discover a thick school of mossbonkers
    —they drop the join'd seine-ends in the water,
The boats separate and row off, each on its rounding course to the
    beach, enclosing the mossbonkers,
The net is drawn in by a windlass by those who stop ashore,

Some of the fishermen lounge in their boats, others stand ankle-deep
    in the water, pois'd on strong legs,
The boats partly drawn up, the water slapping against them,
Strew'd on the sand in heaps and windrows, well out from the water,
    the green-back'd spotted mossbonkers.

From Noon to Starry Night

THOU ORB ALOFT FULL-DAZZLING

THOU orb aloft full-dazzling! thou hot October noon!
Flooding with sheeny light the gray beach sand,
The sibilant near sea with vistas far and foam,
And tawny streaks and shades and spreading blue;
O sun of noon refulgent! my special word to thee.

Hear me illustrious!
Thy lover me, for always I have loved thee,
Even as basking babe, then happy boy alone by some wood edge, thy
    touching-distant beams enough,
Or man matured, or young or old, as now to thee I launch my invo-
    cation.

(Thou canst not with thy dumbness me deceive,
I know before the fitting man all Nature yields,
Though answering not in words, the skies, trees, hear his voice—and
    thou O sun,
As for thy throes, thy perturbations, sudden breaks and shafts of
    flame gigantic,
I understand them, I know those flames, those perturbations well.)

Thou that with fructifying heat and light,
O'er myriad farms, o'er lands and waters North and South,
O'er Mississippi's endless course, o'er Texas' grassy plains, Kanada's
    woods,
O'er all the globe that turns its face to thee shining in space,
Thou that impartially infoldest all, not only continents, seas,
Thou that to grapes and weeds and little wild flowers givest so
    liberally,
Shed, shed thyself on mine and me, with but a fleeting ray out of thy
    million millions,
Strike through these chants.

Nor only launch thy subtle dazzle and thy strength for these,
Prepare the later afternoon of me myself—prepare my lengthening
    shadows,
Prepare my starry nights.

FACES

1

SAUNTERING the pavement or riding the country by-road, lo, such
    faces!
Faces of friendship, precision, caution, suavity, ideality,
The spiritual-prescient face, the always welcome common benevolent
    face,
The face of the singing of music, the grand faces of natural lawyers
    and judges broad at the back-top,
The faces of hunters and fishers bulged at the brows, the shaved
    blanch'd faces of orthodox citizens,
The pure, extravagant, yearning, questioning artist's face,
The ugly face of some beautiful soul, the handsome detested or
    despised face,
The sacred faces of infants, the illuminated face of the mother of
    many children,
The face of an amour, the face of veneration.
The face as of a dream, the face of an immobile rock,
The face withdrawn of its good and bad, a castrated face,
A wild hawk, his wings clipp'd by the clipper,
A stallion that yielded at last to the thongs and knife of the gelder.

Sauntering the pavement thus, or crossing the ceaseless ferry, faces
    and faces and faces,
I see them and complain not, and am content with all.

2

Do you suppose I could be content with all if I thought them their
    own finalè?

This now is too lamentable a face for a man,
Some abject louse asking leave to be, cringing for it,
Some milk-nosed maggot blessing what lets it wrig to its hole.

This face is a dog's snout sniffing for garbage,
Snakes nest in that mouth, I hear the sibilant threat.

This face is a haze more chill than the arctic sea,
Its sleepy and wabbling icebergs crunch as they go.

This is a face of bitter herbs, this an emetic, they need no label,
And more of the drug-shelf, laudanum, caoutchouc, or hog's lard.

This face is an epilepsy, its wordless tongue gives out the unearthly
     cry,
Its veins down the neck distend, its eyes roll till they show nothing
     but their whites,
Its teeth grit, the palms of the hands are cut by the turn'd-in nails,
The man falls struggling and foaming to the ground, while he specu-
     lates well.

This face bitten by vermin and worms,
And this is some murderer's knife with a half-pull'd scabbard.

This face owes to the sexton his dismalest fee,
An unceasing death-bell tolls there.

3

Features of my equals would you trick me with your creas'd and
     cadaverous march?
Well, you cannot trick me.

I see your rounded never-erased flow,
I see 'neath the rims of your haggard and mean disguises.

Splay and twist as you like, poke with the tangling fores of fishes or
     rats,
You'll be unmuzzled, you certainly will.

I saw the face of the most smear'd and slobbering idiot they had at
     the asylum,
And I knew for my consolation what they knew not,
I knew of the agents that emptied and broke my brother,
The same wait to clear the rubbish from the fallen tenement,
And I shall look again in a score or two of ages,
And I shall meet the real landlord perfect and unharm'd, every inch
     as good as myself.

4

The Lord advances, and yet advances,
Always the shadow in front, always the reach'd hand bringing up the
    laggards.

Out of this face emerge banners and horses—O superb! I see what is
    coming,
I see the high pioneer-caps, see staves of runners clearing the way,
I hear victorious drums.

This face is a life-boat,
This is the face commanding and bearded, it asks no odds of the
    rest,
This face is flavor'd fruit ready for eating,
This face of a healthy honest boy is the programme of all good.

These faces bear testimony slumbering or awake,
They show their descent from the Master himself.

Off the word I have spoken I except not one—red, white, black,
    are all deific,
In each house is the ovum, it comes forth after a thousand years.

Spots or cracks at the windows do not disturb me,
Tall and sufficient stand behind and make signs to me,
I read the promise and patiently wait.

This is a full-grown lily's face,
She speaks to the limber-hipp'd man near the garden pickets,
Come here she blushingly cries, *Come nigh to me limber-hipp'd man,*
Stand at my side till I lean as high as I can upon you,
Fill me with albescent honey, bend down to me,
Rub to me with your chafing beard, rub to my breast and shoulders.

5

The old face of the mother of many children,
Whist! I am fully content.
Lull'd and late is the smoke of the First-day morning,

It hangs low over the rows of trees by the fences,
It hangs thin by the sassafras and wild-cherry and cat-brier under
    them.

I saw the rich ladies in full dress at the soiree,
I heard what the singers were singing so long,
Heard who sprang in crimson youth from the white froth and the
water-blue.

Behold a woman!
She looks out from her quaker cap, her face is clearer and more
beautiful than the sky.

She sits in an armchair under the shaded porch of the farmhouse,
The sun just shines on her old white head.

Her ample gown is of cream-hued linen,
Her grandsons raised the flax, and her grand-daughters spun it
with the distaff and the wheel.

The melodious character of the earth,
The finish beyond which philosophy cannot go and does not wish
to go,
The justified mother of men.

THE MYSTIC TRUMPETER

1

HARK, some wild trumpeter, some strange musician,
Hovering unseen in air, vibrates capricious tunes to-night.

I hear thee trumpeter, listening alert I catch thy notes,
Now pouring, whirling like a tempest round me,
Now low, subdued, now in the distance lost.

2

Come nearer bodiless one, haply in thee resounds
Some dead composer, haply thy pensive life
Was fill'd with aspirations high, unform'd ideals,
Waves, oceans musical, chaotically surging,
That now ecstatic ghost, close to me bending, thy cornet echoing,
pealing,
Gives out to no one's ears but mine, but freely gives to mine,
That I may thee translate.

3

Blow trumpeter free and clear, I follow thee,
While at thy liquid prelude, glad, serene,
The fretting world, the streets, the noisy hours of day withdraw,
A holy calm descends like dew upon me,
I walk in cool refreshing night the walks of Paradise,
I scent the grass, the moist air and the roses;
Thy song expands my numb'd imbonded spirit, thou freest, launchest
    me,
Floating and basking upon heaven's lake.

4

Blow again trumpeter! and for my sensuous eyes,
Bring the old pageants, show the feudal world.

What charm thy music works! thou makest pass before me,
Ladies and cavaliers long dead, barons are in their castle halls, the
    troubadours are singing,
Arm'd knights go forth to redress wrongs, some in quest of the
    holy Graal;
I see the tournament, I see the contestants incased in heavy armor
    seated on stately champing horses,
I hear the shouts, the sounds of blows and smiting steel;
I see the Crusaders' tumultuous armies—hark, how the cymbals
    clang,
Lo, where the monks walk in advance, bearing the cross on high.

5

Blow again trumpeter! and for thy theme,
Take now the enclosing theme of all, the solvent and the setting,
Love, that is pulse of all, the sustenance and the pang,
The heart of man and woman all for love,
No other theme but love—knitting, enclosing, all-diffusing love.

O how the immmortal phantoms crowd around me!
I see the vast alembic ever working, I see and know the flames
    that heat the world,
The glow, the blush, the beating hearts of lovers,
So blissful happy some, and some so silent, dark, and nigh to death;
Love, that is all the earth to lovers—love, that mocks time and
    space,
Love, that is day and night—love, that is sun and moon and stars,

Love, that is crimson, sumptuous, sick with perfume,
No other words but words of love, no other thought but love.

6

Blow again trumpeter—conjure war's alarums.

Swift to thy spell a shuddering hum like distant thunder rolls,
Lo, where the arm'd men hasten—lo, mid the clouds of dust the
    glint of bayonets,
I see the grime-faced cannoneers, I mark the rosy flash amid the
    smoke, I hear the cracking of the guns;
Nor war alone—thy fearful music-song, wild player, brings every
    sight of fear,
The deeds of ruthless brigands, rapine, murder—I hear the cries
    for help!
I see ships foundering at sea, I behold on deck and below deck
    the terrible tableaus.

7

O trumpeter, methinks I am myself the instrument thou playest,
Thou melt'st my heart, my brain—thou movest, drawest, changest
    them at will;
And now thy sullen notes send darkness through me,
Thou takest away all cheering light, all hope,
I see the enslaved, the overthrown, the hurt, the opprest of the
    whole earth,
I feel the measureless shame and humiliation of my race, it becomes
    all mine,
Mine too the revenges of humanity, the wrongs of ages, baffled
    feuds and hatreds,
Utter defeat upon me weighs—all lost—the foe victorious,
(Yet 'mid the ruins Pride colossal stands unshaken to the last,
Endurance, resolution to the last.)

8

Now trumpeter for thy close,
Vouchsafe a higher strain than any yet,
Sing to my soul, renew its languishing faith and hope,
Rouse up my slow belief, give me some vision of the future,
Give me for once its prophecy and joy.

O glad, exulting, culminating song!
A vigor more than earth's is in thy notes,
Marches of victory—man disenthral'd—the conqueror at last,
Hymns to the universal God from universal man—all joy!
A reborn race appears—a perfect world, all joy!
Women and men in wisdom innocence and health—all joy!
Riotous laughing bacchanals fill'd with joy!
War, sorrow, suffering gone—the rank earth purged—nothing but
      joy left!
The ocean fill'd with joy—the atmosphere all joy!
Joy! joy! in freedom, worship, love! joy in the ecstasy of life!
Enough to merely be! enough to breathe!
Joy! joy! all over joy!

TO A LOCOMOTIVE IN WINTER

THEE for my recitative,
Thee in the driving storm even as now, the snow, the winter-day
      declining,
Thee in thy panoply, thy measur'd dual throbbing and thy beat
      convulsive,
Thy black cylindric body, golden brass and silvery steel,
Thy ponderous side-bars, parallel and connecting rods, gyrating,
      shuttling at thy sides,
Thy metrical, now swelling pant and roar, now tapering in the
      distance,
Thy great protruding head-light fix'd in front,
Thy long, pale, floating vapor-pennants, tinged with delicate purple,
The dense and murky clouds out-belching from thy smoke-stack,
Thy knitted frame, thy springs and valves, the tremulous twinkle
      of thy wheels,
Thy train of cars behind, obedient, merrily following,
Through gale or calm, now swift, now slack, yet steadily careering;
Type of the modern—emblem of motion and power—pulse of the
      continent,
For once come serve the Muse and merge in verse, even as here
      I see thee,
With storm and buffeting gusts of wind and falling snow,
By day thy warning ringing bell to sound its notes,
By night thy silent signal lamps to swing.

Fierce-throated beauty!
Roll through my chant with all thy lawless music, thy swinging
lamps at night,
Thy madly-whistled laughter, echoing, rumbling like an earthquake,
rousing all,
Law of thyself complete, thine own track firmly holding,
(No sweetness debonair of tearful harp or glib piano thine,)
Thy thrills of shrieks by rocks and hills return'd,
Launch'd o'er the prairies wide, across the lakes,
To the free skies unpent and glad and strong.

O MAGNET-SOUTH

O MAGNET-SOUTH! O glistening perfumed South! my South!
O quick mettle, rich blood, impulse and love! good and evil! O
all dear to me!
O dear to me my birth-things—all moving things and the trees where
I was born—the grains, plants, rivers,
Dear to me my own slow sluggish rivers where they flow, distant,
over flats of silvery sands or through swamps,
Dear to me the Roanoke, the Savannah, the Altamahaw, the Pedee,
the Tombigbee, the Santee, the Coosa and the Sabine,
O pensive, far away wandering, I return with my soul to haunt
their banks again,
Again in Florida I float on transparent lakes, I float on the Okee-
chobee, I cross the hummock-land or through pleasant openings
or dense forests,
I see the parrots in the woods, I see the papaw-tree and the blossoming titi;
Again, sailing in my coaster on deck, I coast off Georgia, I coast
up the Carolinas,
I see where the live-oak is growing, I see where the yellow-pine,
the scented bay-tree, the lemon and orange, the cypress, the
graceful palmetto,
I pass the rude sea-headlands and enter Pamlico sound through an inlet,
and dart my vision inland;
O the cotton plant! the growing fields of rice, sugar, hemp!
The cactus guarded with thorns, the laurel-tree with large white
flowers,
The range afar, the richness and barrenness, the old woods charged
with mistletoe and trailing moss,
The piney odor and the gloom, the awful natural stillness, (here
in these dense swamps the freebooter carries his gun, and the
fugitive has his conceal'd hut;)

O the strange fascination of these half-known half-impassable swamps, infested by reptiles, resounding with the bellow of the alligator, the sad noises of the night-owl and the wild-cat, and the whirr of the rattlesnake,

The mocking-bird, the American mimic, singing all the forenoon, singing through the moon-lit night,

The humming-bird, the wild turkey, the raccoon, the opossum;

A Kentucky corn-field, the tall, graceful, long-leav'd corn, slender, flapping, bright green, with tassels, with beautiful ears each well-sheath'd in its husk;

O my heart! O tender and fierce pangs, I can stand them not, I will depart;

O to be a Virginian where I grew up! O to be a Carolinian!

O longings irrepressible! O I will go back to old Tennessee and never wander more.

MANNAHATTA

I was asking for something specific and perfect for my city,
Whereupon lo! upsprang the aboriginal name.

Now I see what there is in a name, a word, liquid, sane, unruly, musical, self-sufficient,
I see that the word of my city is that word from of old,
Because I see that word nested in nests of water-bays, superb,
Rich, hemm'd thick all around with sailships and steamships, an island sixteen miles long, solid-founded,
Numberless crowded streets, high growths of iron, slender, strong, light, splendidly uprising toward clear skies,
Tides swift and ample, well-loved by me, toward sundown,
The flowing sea-currents, the little islands, larger adjoining islands, the heights, the villas,
The countless masts, the white shore-steamers, the lighters, the ferry-boats, the black sea-steamers well-model'd,
The down-town streets, the jobbers' houses of business, the houses of business of the ship-merchants and money-brokers, the river-streets,
Immigrants arriving, fifteen or twenty thousand in a week,
The carts hauling goods, the manly race of drivers of horses, the brown-faced sailors,
The summer air, the bright sun shining, and the sailing clouds aloft,
The winter snows, the sleigh-bells, the broken ice in the river, passing along up or down with the flood-tide or ebb-tide,

The mechanics of the city, the masters, well-form'd, beautiful-
  faced, looking you straight in the eyes,
Trottoirs throng'd, vehicles, Broadway, the women, the shops and
  shows,
A million people—manners free and superb—open voices—
  hospitality—the most courageous and friendly young men,
City of hurried and sparkling waters! city of spires and masts!
City nested in bays! my city!

ALL IS TRUTH

O ME, man of slack faith so long,
Standing aloof, denying portions so long,
Only aware to-day of compact all-diffused truth,
Discovering to-day there is no lie or form of lie, and can be none,
  but grows as inevitably upon itself as the truth does upon
  itself,
Or as any law of the earth or any natural production of the earth
  does.

(This is curious and may not be realized immediately, but it must
  be realized,
I feel in myself that I represent falsehoods equally with the rest,
And that the universe does.)

Where has fail'd a perfect return indifferent of lies or the truth?
Is it upon the ground, or in water or fire? or in the spirit of man?
  or in the meat and blood?

Meditating among liars and retreating sternly into myself, I see
  that there are really no liars or lies after all,
And that nothing fails its perfect return, and that what are called
  lies are perfect returns,
And that each thing exactly represents itself and what has pre-
  ceded it,
And that the truth includes all, and is compact just as much as
  space is compact,
And that there is no flaw or vacuum in the amount of the truth—
  but that all is truth without exception;
And henceforth I will go celebrate any thing I see or am,
And sing and laugh and deny nothing.

A RIDDLE SONG

THAT which eludes this verse and any verse,
Unheard by sharpest ear, unform'd in clearest eye or cunningest
  mind,
Nor lore nor fame, nor happiness nor wealth,
And yet the pulse of every heart and life throughout the world
  incessantly,
Which you and I and all pursuing ever ever miss,
Open but still a secret, the real of the real, an illusion,
Costless, vouchsafed to each, yet never man the owner,
Which poets vainly seek to put in rhyme, historians in prose,
Which sculptor never chisel'd yet, nor painter painted,
Which vocalist never sung, nor orator nor actor ever utter'd,
Invoking here and now I challenge for my song.

Indifferently, 'mid public, private haunts, in solitude,
Behind the mountain and the wood,
Companion of the city's busiest streets, through the assemblage,
It and its radiations constantly glide.

In looks of fair unconscious babes,
Or strangely in the coffin'd dead,
Or show of breaking dawn or stars by night,
As some dissolving delicate film of dreams,
Hiding yet lingering.

Two little breaths of words comprising it,
Two words, yet all from first to last comprised in it.

How ardently for it!
How many ships have sail'd and sunk for it!
How many travelers started from their homes and ne'er return'd!
How much of genius boldly staked and lost for it!
What countless stores of beauty, love, ventur'd for it!
How all superbest deeds since Time began are traceable to it—and
  shall be to the end!
How all heroic martyrdoms to it!
How, justified by it, the horrors, evils, battles of the earth!
How the bright fascinating lambent flames of it, in every age and
  land, have drawn men's eyes,
Rich as a sunset on the Norway coast, the sky, the islands, and the
  cliffs,
Or midnight's silent glowing northern lights unreachable.

Haply God's riddle it, so vague and yet so certain,
The soul for it, and all the visible universe for it,
And heaven at last for it.

EXCELSIOR

WHO has gone farthest? for I would go farther,
And who has been just? for I would be the most just person of the
    earth,
And who most cautious? for I would be more cautious,
And who has been happiest? O I think it is I—I think no one was
    ever happier than I,
And who has lavish'd all? for I lavish constantly the best I have,
And who proudest? for I think I have reason to be the proudest son
    alive—for I am the son of the brawny and tall-topt city,
And who has been bold and true? for I would be the boldest and
    truest being of the universe,
And who benevolent? for I would show more benevolence than
    all the rest,
And who has receiv'd the love of the most friends? for I know
    what it is to receive the passionate love of many friends,
And who possesses a perfect and enamour'd body? for I do not
    believe any one possesses a more perfect or enamour'd body
    than mine,
And who thinks the amplest thoughts? for I would surround those
    thoughts,
And who has made hymns fit for the earth? for I am mad with de-
    vouring ecstasy to make joyous hymns for the whole earth.

AH POVERTIES, WINCINGS, AND SULKY RETREATS

AH poverties, wincings, and sulky retreats,
Ah you foes that in conflict have overcome me,
(For what is my life or any man's life but a conflict with foes, the
    old, the incessant war?)
You degradations, you tussle with passions and appetites,
You smarts from dissatisfied friendships, (ah wounds the sharpest
    of all!)
You toil of painful and choked articulations, you meannesses,
You shallow tongue-talks at tables, (my tongue the shallowest of
    any;)
You broken resolutions, you racking angers, you smother'd ennuis!
Ah think not you finally triumph, my real self has yet to come
    forth,

It shall yet march forth o'ermastering, till all lies beneath me,
It shall yet stand up the soldier of ultimate victory.

THOUGHTS

OF public opinion,
Of a calm and cool fiat sooner or later, (how impassive! how certain
    and final!)
Of the President with pale face asking secretly to himself, *What
    will the people say at last?*
Of the frivolous Judge—of the corrupt Congressman, Governor,
    Mayor—of such as these standing helpless and exposed,
Of the mumbling and screaming priest, (soon, soon deserted,)
Of the lessening year by year of venerableness, and of the dicta
    of officers, statutes, pulpits, schools,
Of the rising forever taller and stronger and broader of the intui-
    tions of men and women, and of Self-esteem and Personality;
Of the true New World—of the Democracies resplendent en-masse,
Of the conformity of politics, armies, navies, to them,
Of the shining sun by them—of the inherent light, greater than the
    rest,
Of the envelopment of all by them, and the effusion of all from them.

MEDIUMS

THEY shall arise in the States,
They shall report Nature, laws, physiology, and happiness,
They shall illustrate Democracy and the kosmos,
They shall be alimentive, amative, perceptive,
They shall be complete women and men, their pose brawny and
    supple, their drink water, their blood clean and clear,
They shall fully enjoy materialism and the sight of products, they
    shall enjoy the sight of the beef, lumber, bread-stuffs, of
    Chicago the great city,
They shall train themselves to go in public to become orators and
    oratresses,
Strong and sweet shall their tongues be, poems and materials of
    poems shall come from their lives, they shall be makers
    and finders,
Of them and of their works shall emerge divine conveyers, to convey
    gospels,
Characters, events, retrospections, shall be convey'd in gospels,
    trees, animals, waters, shall be convey'd,
Death, the future, the invisible faith, shall all be convey'd.

WEAVE IN, MY HARDY LIFE

WEAVE in, weave in, my hardy life,
Weave yet a soldier strong and full for great campaigns to come,
Weave in red blood, weave sinews in like ropes, the senses, sight
    weave in,
Weave lasting sure, weave day and night the weft, the warp, incessant
    weave, tire not,
(We know not what the use O life, nor know the aim, the end,
    nor really aught we know,
But know the work, the need goes on and shall go on, the death-
    envelop'd march of peace as well as war goes on,)
For great campaigns of peace the same the wiry threads to weave,
We know not why or what, yet weave, forever weave.

SPAIN, 1873–74

OUT of the murk of heaviest clouds,
Out of the feudal wrecks and heap'd-up skeletons of kings,
Out of that old entire European debris, the shatter'd mummeries,
Ruin'd cathedrals, crumble of palaces, tombs of priests,
Lo, Freedom's features fresh undimm'd look forth—the same
    immortal face looks forth;
(A glimpse as of thy Mother's face Columbia,
A flash significant as of a sword,
Beaming towards thee.)

Nor think we forget thee maternal;
Lag'd'st thou so long? shall the clouds close again upon thee?
Ah, but thou hast thyself now appear'd to us—we know thee,
Thou hast given us a sure proof, the glimpse of thyself,
Thou waitest there as everywhere thy time.

BY BROAD POTOMAC'S SHORE

BY broad Potomac's shore, again old tongue,
(Still uttering, still ejaculating, canst never cease this babble?)
Again old heart so gay, again to you, your sense, the full flush spring
    returning,
Again the freshness and the odors, again Virginia's summer sky,
    pellucid blue and silver,
Again the forenoon purple of the hills,
Again the deathless grass, so noiseless soft and green,
Again the blood-red roses blooming.

Perfume this book of mine O blood-red roses!
Lave subtly with your waters every line Potomac!
Give me of you O spring, before I close, to put between its pages!
O forenoon purple of the hills, before I close, of you!
O deathless grass, of you!

FROM FAR DAKOTA'S CAÑONS

June 25, 1876

FROM far Dakota's cañons,
Lands of the wild ravine, the dusky Sioux, the lonesome stretch, the silence,
Haply to-day a mournful wail, haply a trumpet-note for heroes.

The battle-bulletin,
The Indian ambuscade, the craft, the fatal environment,
The cavalry companies fighting to the last in sternest heroism,
In the midst of their little circle, with their slaughter'd horses for breastworks,
The fall of Custer and all his officers and men.

Continues yet the old, old legend of our race,
The loftiest of life upheld by death,
The ancient banner perfectly maintain'd,
O lesson opportune, O how I welcome thee!

As sitting in dark days,
Lone, sulky, through the time's thick murk looking in vain for light, for hope,
From unsuspected parts a fierce and momentary proof,
(The sun there at the centre though conceal'd,
Electric life forever at the centre,)
Breaks forth a lightning flash.

Thou of the tawny flowing hair in battle,
I erewhile saw, with erect head, pressing ever in front, bearing a bright sword in thy hand,
Now ending well in death the splendid fever of thy deeds,
(I bring no dirge for it or thee, I bring a glad triumphal sonnet,)
Desperate and glorious, aye in defeat most desperate, most glorious,
After thy many battles in which never yielding up a gun or a color,
Leaving behind thee a memory sweet to soldiers,
Thou yieldest up thyself.

OLD WAR-DREAMS

In midnight sleep of many a face of anguish,
Of the look at first of the mortally wounded, (of that indescribable look,)
Of the dead on their backs with arms extended wide,
     I dream, I dream, I dream.

Of scenes of Nature, fields and mountains,
Of skies so beauteous after a storm, and at night the moon so unearthly bright,
Shining sweetly, shining down, where we dig the trenches and gather the heaps,
     I dream, I dream, I dream.
Long have they pass'd, faces and trenches and fields,
Where through the carnage I moved with a callous composure, or away from the fallen,
Onward I sped at the time—but now of their forms at night,
     I dream, I dream, I dream.

THICK-SPRINKLED BUNTING

Thick-sprinkled bunting! flag of stars!
Long yet your road, fateful flag—long yet your road, and lined with bloody death,
For the prize I see at issue at last is the world,
All its ships and shores I see interwoven with your threads greedy banner;
Dream'd again the flags of kings, highest borne, to flaunt unrival'd?
O hasten flag of man—O with sure and steady step, passing highest flags of kings,
Walk supreme to the heavens mighty symbol—run up above them all,
Flag of stars! thick-sprinkled bunting!

WHAT BEST I SEE IN THEE
To U. S. G. return'd from his World's Tour

What best I see in thee,
Is not that where thou mov'st down history's great highways,
Ever undimm'd by time shoots warlike victory's dazzle,
Or that thou sat'st where Washington sat, ruling the land in peace,
Or thou the man whom feudal Europe feted, venerable Asia swarm'd upon,

Who walk'd with kings with even pace the round world's prome-
    nade;
But that in foreign lands, in all thy walks with kings,
Those prairie sovereigns of the West, Kansas, Missouri, Illinois,
Ohio's, Indiana's millions, comrades, farmers, soldiers, all to the
    front,
Invisibly with thee walking with kings with even pace the round
    world's promenade,
Were all so justified.

SPIRIT THAT FORM'D THIS SCENE

Written in Platte Cañon, Colorado

SPIRIT that form'd this scene,
These tumbled rock-piles grim and red,
These reckless heaven-ambitious peaks,
These gorges, turbulent-clear streams, this naked freshness,
These formless wild arrays, for reasons of their own,
I know thee, savage spirit—we have communed together,
Mine too such wild arrays, for reasons of their own;
Was't charged against my chants they had forgotten art?
To fuse within themselves its rules precise and delicatesse?
The lyrist's measur'd beat, the wrought-out temple's grace—column
    and polish'd arch forgot?
But thou that revelest here—spirit that form'd this scene,
They have remember'd thee.

AS I WALK THESE BROAD MAJESTIC DAYS

As I walk these broad majestic days of peace,
(For the war, the struggle of blood finish'd, wherein, O terrific
    Ideal,
Against vast odds erewhile having gloriously won,
Now thou stridest on, yet perhaps in time toward denser wars,
Perhaps to engage in time in still more dreadful contests, dangers,
Longer campaigns and crises, labors beyond all others,)
Around me I hear that eclat of the world, politics, produce,
The announcements of recognized things, science,
The approved growth of cities and the spread of inventions.

I see the ships, (they will last a few years,)
The vast factories with their foremen and workmen,
And hear the indorsement of all, and do not object to it.

But I too announce solid things,
Science, ships, politics, cities, factories, are not nothing,
Like a grand procession to music of distant bugles pouring, tri-
    umphantly moving, and grander heaving in sight,
They stand for realities—all is as it should be.

Then my realities;
What else is so real as mine?
Libertad and the divine average, freedom to every slave on the
    face of the earth,
The rapt promises and luminè of seers, the spiritual world, these
    centuries-lasting songs,
And our visions, the visions of poets, the most solid announcements
    of any.

A CLEAR MIDNIGHT

THIS is thy hour O Soul, thy free flight into the wordless,
Away from books, away from art, the day erased, the lesson done,
Thee fully forth emerging, silent, gazing, pondering the themes
    thou lovest best,
Night, sleep, death and the stars.

Songs of Parting

As the time draws nigh glooming a cloud,
A dread beyond of I know not what darkens me.

I shall go forth,
I shall traverse the States awhile, but I cannot tell whither or how
    long,
Perhaps soon some day or night while I am singing my voice will
    suddenly cease.

O book, O chants! must all then amount to but this?
Must we barely arrive at this beginning of us?—and yet it is enough,
    O soul;
O soul, we have positively appear'd—that is enough.

YEARS OF THE MODERN

YEARS of the modern! years of the unperform'd!
Your horizon rises, I see it parting away for more august dramas,
I see not America only, not only Liberty's nation but other nations
    preparing,
I see tremendous entrances and exits, new combinations, the soli-
    darity of races,
I see that force advancing with irresistible power on the world's stage,
(Have the old forces, the old wars, played their parts? are the acts
    suitable to them closed?)
I see Freedom, completely arm'd and victorious and very haughty,
    with Law on one side and Peace on the other,
A stupendous trio all issuing forth against the idea of caste;
What historic denouements are these we so rapidly approach?
I see men marching and countermarching by swift millions,
I see the frontiers and boundaries of the old aristocracies broken,
I see the landmarks of European kings removed,

I see this day the People beginning their landmarks, (all others
    give way;)
Never were such sharp questions ask'd as this day,
Never was average man, his soul, more energetic, more like a God,
Lo, how he urges and urges, leaving the masses no rest!
His daring foot is on land and sea everywhere, he colonizes the
    Pacific, the archipelagoes,
With the steamship, the electric telegraph, the newspaper, the
    wholesale engines of war,
With these and the world-spreading factories he interlinks all geog-
    raphy, all lands;
What whispers are these O lands, running ahead of you, passing
    under the seas?
Are all nations communing? is there going to be but one heart to
    the globe?
Is humanity forming en-masse? for lo, tyrants tremble, crowns
    grow dim,
The earth, restive, confronts a new era, perhaps a general divine war,
No one knows what will happen next, such portents fill the days
    and nights;
Years prophetical! the space ahead as I walk, as I vainly try to
    pierce it, is full of phantoms,
Unborn deeds, things soon to be, project their shapes around me,
This incredible rush and heat, this strange ecstatic fever of dreams
    O years!
Your dreams O years, how they penetrate through me! (I know
    not whether I sleep or wake;)
The perform'd America and Europe grow dim, retiring in shadow
    behind me,
The unperform'd, more gigantic than ever, advance, advance upon
    me.

ASHES OF SOLDIERS

ASHES of soldiers South or North,
As I muse retrospective murmuring a chant in thought,
The war resumes, again to my sense your shapes,
And again the advance of the armies.

Noiseless as mists and vapors,
From their graves in the trenches ascending,
From cemeteries all through Virginia and Tennessee,
From every point of the compass out of the countless graves,

In wafted clouds, in myriads large, or squads of twos or threes or
    single ones they come,
And silently gather round me.

Now sound no note O trumpeters,
Not at the head of my cavalry parading on spirited horses,
With sabres drawn and glistening, and carbines by their thighs, (ah
    my brave horsemen!
My handsome tan-faced horsemen! what life, what joy and pride,
With all the perils were yours.)

Nor you drummers, neither at reveillé at dawn,
Nor the long roll alarming the camp, nor even the muffled beat
    for a burial,
Nothing from you this time O drummers bearing my warlike drums.

But aside from these and the marts of wealth and the crowded
    promenade,
Admitting around me comrades close unseen by the rest and
    voiceless,
The slain elate and alive again, the dust and debris alive,
I chant this chant of my silent soul in the name of all dead soldiers.

Faces so pale with wondrous eyes, very dear, gather closer yet,
Draw close, but speak not.

Phantoms of countless lost,
Invisible to the rest henceforth become my companions,
Follow me ever—desert me not while I live.

Sweet are the blooming cheeks of the living—sweet are the musical
    voices sounding,
But sweet, ah sweet, are the dead with their silent eyes.

Dearest comrades, all is over and long gone,
But love is not over—and what love, O comrades!
Perfume from battle-fields rising, up from the fœtor arising.

Perfume therefore my chant, O love, immortal love,
Give me to bathe the memories of all dead soldiers,
Shroud them, embalm them, cover them all over with tender pride.

Perfume all—make all wholesome,
Make these ashes to nourish and blossom,
O love, solve all, fructify all with the last chemistry.

Give me exhaustless, make me a fountain,
That I exhale love from me wherever I go like a moist perennial dew,
For the ashes of all dead soldiers South or North.

THOUGHTS

1

OF these years I sing,
How they pass and have pass'd through convuls'd pains, as through
        parturitions,
How America illustrates birth, muscular youth, the promise, the
        sure fulfilment, the absolute success, despite of people—
        illustrates evil as well as good,
The vehement struggle so fierce for unity in one's-self;
How many hold despairingly yet to the models departed, caste,
        myths, obedience, compulsion, and to infidelity,
How few see the arrived models, the athletes, the Western States,
        or see freedom or spirituality, or hold any faith in results,
(But I see the athletes, and I see the results of the war glorious
        and inevitable, and they again leading to other results.)

How the great cities appear—how the Democratic masses, turbulent,
        wilful, as I love them,
How the whirl, the contest, the wrestle of evil with good, the sound-
        ing and resounding, keep on and on,
How society waits unform'd, and is for a while between things
        ended and things begun,
How America is the continent of glories, and of the triumph of
        freedom and of the Democracies, and of the fruits of society,
        and of all that is begun,
And how the States are complete in themselves—and how all
        triumphs and glories are complete in themselves, to lead onward,
And how these of mine and of the States will in their turn be con-
        vuls'd, and serve other parturitions and transitions,
And how all people, sights, combinations, the democratic masses
        too, serve—and how every fact, and war itself, with all its
        horrors, serves,
And how now or at any time each serves the exquisite transition
        of death.

2

Of seeds dropping into the ground, of births,
Of the steady concentration of America, inland, upward, to impregnable and swarming places,
Of what Indiana, Kentucky, Arkansas, and the rest, are to be,
Of what a few years will show there in Nebraska, Colorado, Nevada, and the rest,
(Or afar, mounting the Northern Pacific to Sitka or Aliaska,)
Of what the feuillage of America is the preparation for—and of what all sights, North, South, East and West, are,
Of this Union welded in blood, of the solemn price paid, of the unnamed lost ever present in my mind;
Of the temporary use of materials for identity's sake,
Of the present, passing, departing—of the growth of completer men than any yet,
Of all sloping down there where the fresh free giver the mother, the Mississippi flows,
Of mighty inland cities yet unsurvey'd and unsuspected,
Of the new and good names, of the modern developments, of inalienable homesteads,
Or a free and original life there, of simple diet and clean and sweet blood,
Of litheness, majestic faces, clear eyes, and perfect physique there,
Of immense spiritual results future years far West, each side of the Anahuacs,
Of these songs, well understood there, (being made for that area,)
Of the native scorn of grossness and gain there,
(O it lurks in me night and day—what is gain after all to savageness and freedom?)

SONG AT SUNSET

SPLENDOR of ended day floating and filling me,
Hour prophetic, hour resuming the past,
Inflating my throat, you divine average,
You earth and life till the last ray gleams I sing.

Open mouth of my soul uttering gladness,
Eyes of my soul seeing perfection,
Natural life of me faithfully praising things,
Corroborating forever the triumph of things.

Illustrious every one!
Illustrious what we name space, sphere of unnumber'd spirits,
Illustrious the mystery of motion in all beings, even the tiniest insect,
Illustrious the attribute of speech, the senses, the body,
Illustrious the passing light—illustrious the pale reflection on the
　　new moon in the western sky,
Illustrious whatever I see or hear or touch, to the last.

Good in all,
In the satisfaction and aplomb of animals,
In the annual return of the seasons,
In the hilarity of youth,
In the strength and flush of manhood,
In the grandeur and exquisiteness of old age,
In the superb vistas of death.

Wonderful to depart!
Wonderful to be here!
The heart, to jet the all-alike and innocent blood!
To breathe the air, how delicious!
To speak—to walk—to seize something by the hand!
To prepare for sleep, for bed, to look on my rose-color'd flesh!
To be conscious of my body, so satisfied, so large!
To be this incredible God I am!
To have gone forth among other Gods, these men and women I love.

Wonderful how I celebrate you and myself!
How my thoughts play subtly at the spectacles around!
How the clouds pass silently overhead!
How the earth darts on and on! and how the sun, moon, stars, dart
　　on and on!
How the water sports and sings! (surely it is alive!)
How the trees rise and stand up, with strong trunks, with branches
　　and leaves!
(Surely there is something more in each of the trees, some living
　　soul.)

O amazement of things—even the least particle!
O spirituality of things!
O strain musical flowing through ages and continents, now reaching
　　me and America!
I take your strong chords, intersperse them, and cheerfully pass
　　them forward.

I too carol the sun, usher'd or at noon, or as now, setting,
I too throb to the brain and beauty of the earth and of all the
    growths of the earth,
I too have felt the resistless call of myself.

As I steam'd down the Mississippi,
As I wander'd over the prairies,
As I have lived, as I have look'd through my windows my eyes,
As I went forth in the morning, as I beheld the light breaking in
    the east,
As I bathed on the beach of the Eastern Sea, and again on the
    beach of the Western Sea,
As I roam'd the streets of inland Chicago, whatever streets I have
    roam'd,
Or cities or silent woods, or even amid the sights of war,
Wherever I have been I have charged myself with contentment
    and triumph.

I sing to the last the equalities modern or old,
I sing the endless finales of things,
I say Nature continues, glory continues,
I praise with electric voice,
For I do not see one imperfection in the universe,
And I do not see one cause or result lamentable at last in the
    universe.

O setting sun! though the time has come,
I still warble under you, if none else does, unmitigated adoration.

AS AT THY PORTALS ALSO DEATH

As at thy portals also death,
Entering thy sovereign, dim, illimitable grounds,
To memories of my mother, to the divine blending, maternity,
To her, buried and gone, yet buried not, gone not from me,
(I see again the calm benignant face fresh and beautiful still,
I sit by the form in the coffin,
I kiss and kiss convulsively again the sweet old lips, the cheeks,
    the closed eyes in the coffin;)
To her, the ideal woman, practical, spiritual, of all of earth, life,
    love, to me the best,
I grave a monumental line, before I go, amid these songs,
And set a tombstone here.

MY LEGACY

THE business man the acquirer vast,
After assiduous years surveying results, preparing for departure,
Devises houses and lands to his children, bequeaths stocks, goods,
    funds for a school or hospital,
Leaves money to certain companions to buy tokens, souvenirs of
    gems and gold.

But I, my life surveying, closing,
With nothing to show to devise from its idle years,
Nor houses nor lands, nor tokens of gems or gold for my friends,
Yet certain remembrances of the war for you, and after you,
And little souvenirs of camps and soldiers, with my love,
I bind together and bequeath in this bundle of songs.

PENSIVE ON HER DEAD GAZING

PENSIVE on her dead gazing I heard the Mother of All,
Desperate on the torn bodies, on the forms covering the battle-
    fields gazing,
(As the last gun ceased, but the scent of the powder-smoke linger'd,)
As she call'd to her earth with mournful voice while she stalk'd,
Absorb them well O my earth, she cried, I charge you lose not
    my sons, lose not an atom,
And you streams absorb them well, taking their dear blood,
And you local spots, and you airs that swim above lightly impalpable,
And all you essences of soil and growth, and you my rivers' depths,
And you mountain sides, and the woods where my dear children's
    blood trickling redden'd,
And you trees down in your roots to bequeath to all future trees,
My dead absorb or South or North—my young men's bodies
    absorb, and their precious precious blood,
Which holding in trust for me faithfully back again give me many
    a year hence,
In unseen essence and odor of surface and grass, centuries hence,
In blowing airs from the fields back again give me my darlings,
    give my immortal heroes,
Exhale me them centuries hence, breathe me their breath, let not an
    atom be lost,
O years and graves! O air and soil! O my dead, an aroma sweet!
Exhale them perennial sweet death, years, centuries hence.

CAMPS OF GREEN

NOT alone those camps of white, old comrades of the wars,
When as order'd forward, after a long march,
Footsore and weary, soon as the light lessens we halt for the night,
Some of us so fatigued carrying the gun and knapsack, dropping
    asleep in our tracks,
Others pitching the little tents, and the fires lit up begin to sparkle,
Outposts of pickets posted surrounding alert through the dark,
And a word provided for countersign, careful for safety,
Till to the call of the drummers at daybreak loudly beating the
    drums,
We rise up refresh'd the night and sleep pass'd over, and resume
    our journey,
Or proceed to battle.

Lo, the camps of the tents of green,
Which the days of peace keep filling, and the days of war keep
    filling,
With a mystic army, (is it too order'd forward? is it too only halting
    awhile,
Till night and sleep pass over?)

Now in those camps of green, in their tents dotting the world,
In the parents, children, husbands, wives, in them, in the old and
    young,
Sleeping under the sunlight, sleeping under the moonlight, content
    and silent there at last,
Behold the mighty bivouac-field and waiting-camp of all,
Of the corps and generals all, and the President over the corps
    and generals all,
And of each of us O soldiers, and of each and all in the ranks we
    fought,
(There without hatred we all, all meet.)

For presently O soldiers, we too camp in our place in the bivouac-
    camps of green,
But we need not provide for outposts, nor word for the countersign,
Nor drummer to beat the morning drum.

THE SOBBING OF THE BELLS

(Midnight, Sept. 19-20, 1881)

THE sobbing of the bells, the sudden death-news everywhere,
The slumberers rouse, the rapport of the People,
(Full well they know that message in the darkness,
Full well return, respond within their breasts, their brains, the sad
    reverberations,)
The passionate toll and clang—city to city, joining, sounding,
    passing,
Those heart-beats of a Nation in the night.

AS THEY DRAW TO A CLOSE

As they draw to a close,
Of what underlies the precedent songs—of my aims in them,
Of the seed I have sought to plant in them,
Of joy, sweet joy, through many a year, in them,
(For them, for them have I lived, in them my work is done,)
Of many an aspiration fond, of many a dream and plan;
Through Space and Time fused in a chant, and the flowing eternal
    identity,
To Nature encompassing these, encompassing God—to the joyous,
    electric all,
To the sense of Death, and accepting exulting in Death in its turn
    the same as life,
The entrance of man to sing;
To compact you, ye parted, diverse lives,
To put rapport the mountains and rocks and streams,
And the winds of the north, and the forests of oak and pine,
With you O soul.

JOY, SHIPMATE, JOY!

JOY, shipmate, joy!
(Pleas'd to my soul at death I cry,)
Our life is closed, our life begins,
The long, long anchorage we leave,
The ship is clear at last, she leaps!
She swiftly courses from the shore,
Joy, shipmate, joy.

THE UNTOLD WANT

THE untold want by life and land ne'er granted,
Now voyager sail thou forth to seek and find.

PORTALS

WHAT are those of the known but to ascend and enter the Unknown?
And what are those of life but for Death?

THESE CAROLS

THESE carols sung to cheer my passage through the world I see,
For completion I dedicate to the Invisible World.

NOW FINALÈ TO THE SHORE

Now finalè to the shore,
Now, land and life finalè and farewell,
Now Voyager depart, (much, much for thee is yet in store,)
Often enough hast thou adventur'd o'er the seas,
Cautiously cruising, studying the charts,
Duly again to port and hawser's tie returning;
But now obey thy cherish'd secret wish,
Embrace thy friends, leave all in order,
To port and hawser's tie no more returning,
Depart upon thy endless cruise old Sailor.

SO LONG!

To conclude, I announce what comes after me.

I remember I said before my leaves sprang at all,
I would raise my voice jocund and strong with reference to con-
summations.

When America does what was promis'd,
When through these States walk a hundred millions of superb
persons,
When the rest part away for superb persons and contribute to them,
When breeds of the most perfect mothers denote America,
Then to me and mine our due fruition.

I have press'd through in my own right,
I have sung the body and the soul, war and peace have I sung,
and the songs of life and death,
And the songs of birth, and shown that there are many births.

I have offer'd my style to every one, I have journey'd with confident
   step;
While my pleasure is yet at the full I whisper *So long!*
And take the young woman's hand and the young man's hand for
   the last time.

I announce natural persons to arise,
I announce justice triumphant,
I announce uncompromising liberty and equality,
I announce the justification of candor and the justification of pride.

I announce that the identity of these States is a single identity only,
I announce the Union more and more compact, indissoluble,
I announce splendors and majesties to make all the previous politics
   of the earth insignificant.

I announce adhesiveness, I say it shall be limitless, unloosen'd,
I say you shall yet find the friend you were looking for.

I announce a man or woman coming, perhaps you are the one,
   (*So long!*)
I announce the great individual, fluid as Nature, chaste, affection-
   ate, compassionate, fully arm'd.

I announce a life that shall be copious, vehement, spiritual, bold,
I announce an end that shall lightly and joyfully meet its translation.

I announce myriads of youths, beautiful, gigantic, sweet-blooded,
I announce a race of splendid and savage old men.

O thicker and faster—(*So long!*)
O crowding too close upon me,
I foresee too much, it means more than I thought,
It appears to me I am dying.

Hasten throat and sound your last,
Salute me—salute the days once more. Peal the old cry once more.

Screaming electric, the atmosphere using,
At random glancing, each as I notice absorbing,
Swiftly on, but a little while alighting,
Curious envelop'd messages delivering,
Sparkles hot, seed ethereal down in the dirt dropping,

Myself unknowing, my commission obeying, to question it never
    daring,
To ages and ages yet the growth of the seed leaving,
To troops out of the war arising, they the tasks I have set promul-
    ging,
To women certain whispers of myself bequeathing, their affection
    me more clearly explaining,
To young men my problems offering—no dallier I—I the muscle of
    their brains trying,
So I pass, a little time vocal, visible, contrary,
Afterward a melodious echo, passionately bent for, (death making
    me really undying,)
The best of me then when no longer visible, for toward that I have
    been incessantly preparing.

What is there more, that I lag and pause and crouch extended with
    unshut mouth?
Is there a single final farewell?

My songs cease, I abandon them,
From behind the screen where I hid I advance personally solely
    to you.

Camerado, this is no book,
Who touches this touches a man,
(Is it night? are we here together alone?)
It is I you hold and who holds you,
I spring from the pages into your arms—decease calls me forth.

O how your fingers drowse me,
Your breath falls around me like dew, your pulse lulls the tympans
    of my ears,
I feel immerged from head to foot,
Delicious, enough.

Enough O deed impromptu and secret,
Enough O gliding present—enough O summ'd-up past.

Dear friend whoever you are take this kiss,
I give it especially to you, do not forget me,
I feel like one who has done work for the day to retire awhile,
I receive now again of my many translations, from my avataras as-
    cending, while others doubtless await me,

An unknown sphere more real than I dream'd, more direct, darts
    awakening rays about me, *So long!*
Remember my words, I may again return,
I love you, I depart from materials,
I am as one disembodied, triumphant, dead.

Sands at Seventy

MANNAHATTA

MY city's fit and noble name resumed,
Choice aboriginal name, with marvellous beauty, meaning,
A rocky founded island—shores where ever gayly dash the coming,
    going, hurrying sea waves.

PAUMANOK

SEA-BEAUTY! stretch'd and basking!
One side thy inland ocean laving, broad, with copious commerce,
    steamers, sails,
And one the Atlantic's wind caressing, fierce or gentle—mighty
    hulls dark-gliding in the distance.
Isle of sweet brooks of drinking-water—healthy air and soil!
Isle of the salty shore and breeze and brine!

FROM MONTAUK POINT

I STAND as on some mighty eagle's beak,
Eastward the sea absorbing, viewing, (nothing but sea and sky,)
The tossing waves, the foam, the ships in the distance,
The wild unrest, the snowy, curling caps—that inbound urge and
    urge of waves,
Seeking the shores forever.

TO THOSE WHO'VE FAIL'D

To those who've fail'd, in aspiration vast,
To unnam'd soldiers fallen in front on the lead,
To calm, devoted engineers—to over-ardent travelers—to pilots
    on their ships,

To many a lofty song and picture without recognition—I'd rear
    a laurel-cover'd monument,
High, high above the rest—To all cut off before their time,
Possess'd by some strange spirit of fire,
Quench'd by an early death.

A CAROL CLOSING SIXTY-NINE

A carol closing sixty-nine—a *résumé*—a repetition,
My lines in joy and hope continuing on the same,
Of ye, O God, Life, Nature, Freedom, Poetry;
Of you, my Land—your rivers, prairies, States—you, mottled
    Flag I love,
Your aggregate retain'd entire—Of north, south, east and west,
    your items all,
Of me myself—the jocund heart yet beating in my breast,
The body wreck'd, old, poor and paralyzed—the strange inertia
    falling pall-like round me,
The burning fires down in my sluggish blood not yet extinct,
The undiminish'd faith—the groups of loving friends.

THE BRAVEST SOLDIERS

Brave, brave were the soldiers (high named to-day) who lived
    through the fight;
But the bravest press'd to the front and fell, unnamed, unknown.

A FONT OF TYPE

This latent mine—these unlaunch'd voices—passionate powers,
Wrath, argument, or praise, or comic leer, or prayer devout,
(Not nonpareil, brevier, bourgeois, long primer merely,)
These ocean waves arousable to fury and to death,
Or sooth'd to ease and sheeny sun and sleep,
Within the pallid slivers slumbering.

AS I SIT WRITING HERE

As I sit writing here, sick and grown old,
Not my least burden is that dulness of the years, querilities,
Ungracious glooms, aches, lethargy, constipation, whimpering
    ennui,
May filter in my daily songs.

MY CANARY BIRD

DID we count great, O soul, to penetrate the themes of mighty
  books,
Absorbing deep and full from thoughts, plays, speculations?
But now from thee to me, caged bird, to feel thy joyous warble,
Filling the air, the lonesome room, the long forenoon,
Is it not just as great, O soul?

QUERIES TO MY SEVENTIETH YEAR

APPROACHING, nearing, curious,
Thou dim, uncertain spectre—bringest thou life or death?
Strength, weakness, blindness, more paralysis and heavier?
Or placid skies and sun? Wilt stir the waters yet?
Or haply cut me short for good? Or leave me here as now,
Dull, parrot-like and old, with crack'd voice harping, screeching?

THE WALLABOUT MARTYRS

[In Brooklyn, in an old vault, mark'd by no special recognition, lie huddled at
this moment the undoubtedly authentic remains of the stanchest and earliest
revolutionary patriots from the British prison ships and prisons of the times of
1776–83, in and around New York, and from all over Long Island; originally
buried—many thousands of them—in trenches in the Wallabout sands.]

GREATER than memory of Achilles or Ulysses,
More, more by far to thee than tomb of Alexander,
Those cart loads of old charnel ashes, scales and splints of mouldy
  bones,
Once living men—once resolute courage, aspiration, strength,
The stepping stones to thee to-day and here, America.

THE FIRST DANDELION

SIMPLE and fresh and fair from winter's close emerging,
As if no artifice of fashion, business, politics, had ever been,
Forth from its sunny nook of shelter'd grass—innocent, golden,
  calm as the dawn,
The spring's first dandelion shows its trustful face.

AMERICA

CENTRE of equal daughters, equal sons,
All, all alike endear'd, grown, ungrown, young or old,

Strong, ample, fair, enduring, capable, rich,
Perennial with the Earth, with Freedom, Law and Love,
A grand, sane, towering, seated Mother,
Chair'd in the adamant of Time.

MEMORIES

How sweet the silent backward tracings!
The wanderings as in dreams—the meditation of old times re-
    sumed—their loves, joys, persons, voyages.

TO-DAY AND THEE

THE appointed winners in a long-stretch'd game;
The course of Time and nations—Egypt, India, Greece and Rome;
The past entire, with all its heroes, histories, arts, experiments,
Its store of songs, inventions, voyages, teachers, books,
Garner'd for now and thee—To think of it!
The heirdom all converged in thee!

AFTER THE DAZZLE OF DAY

AFTER the dazzle of day is gone,
Only the dark, dark night shows to my eyes the stars;
After the clangor of organ majestic, or chorus, or perfect band,
Silent, athwart my soul, moves the symphony true.

ABRAHAM LINCOLN, BORN FEB. 12, 1809

TO-DAY, from each and all, a breath of prayer—a pulse of thought,
To memory of Him—to birth of Him.
    Publish'd Feb. 12, 1888.

OUT OF MAY'S SHOWS SELECTED

APPLE orchards, the trees all cover'd with blossoms;
Wheat fields carpeted far and near in vital emerald green;
The eternal, exhaustless freshness of each early morning;
The yellow, golden, transparent haze of the warm afternoon sun;
The aspiring lilac bushes with profuse purple or white flowers.

HALCYON DAYS

NOT from successful love alone,
Nor wealth, nor honor'd middle age, nor victories of politics or war;
But as life wanes, and all the turbulent passions calm,

As gorgeous, vapory, silent hues cover the evening sky,
As softness, fulness, rest, suffuse the frame, like fresher, balmier air,
As the days take on a mellower light, and the apple at last hangs
    really finish'd and indolent-ripe on the tree,
Then for the teeming quietest, happiest days of all!
The brooding and blissful halcyon days!

Fancies at Navesink

THE PILOT IN THE MIST

STEAMING the northern rapids—(an old St. Lawrence reminiscence,
A sudden memory-flash comes back, I know not why,
Here waiting for the sunrise, gazing from this hill;)*
Again 'tis just at morning—a heavy haze contends with daybreak,
Again the trembling, laboring vessel veers me—I press through
    foam-dash'd rocks that almost touch me,
Again I mark where aft the small thin Indian helmsman
Looms in the mist, with brow elate and governing hand.

HAD I THE CHOICE

HAD I the choice to tally greatest bards,
To limn their portraits, stately, beautiful, and emulate at will,
Homer with all his wars and warriors—Hector, Achilles, Ajax,
Or Shakspere's woe-entangled Hamlet, Lear, Othello—Tennyson's
    fair ladies,
Metre or wit the best, or choice conceit to wield in perfect rhyme,
    delight of singers;
These, these, O sea, all these I'd gladly barter,
Would you the undulation of one wave, its trick to me transfer,
Or breathe one breath of yours upon my verse,
And leave its odor there.

YOU TIDES WITH CEASELESS SWELL

YOU tides with ceaseless swell! you power that does this work!
You unseen force, centripetal, centrifugal, through space's spread,
Rapport of sun, moon, earth, and all the constellations,
What are the messages by you from distant stars to us? what
    Sirius' what Capella's?
What central heart—and you the pulse—vivifies all? what boundless
    aggregate of all?

---

* Navesink—a sea-side mountain, lower entrance of New York Bay.

What subtle indirection and significance in you? what clue to all in
    you? what fluid, vast identity,
Holding the universe with all its parts as one—as sailing in a ship?

LAST OF EBB, AND DAYLIGHT WANING

LAST of ebb, and daylight waning,
Scented sea-cool landward making, smells of sedge and salt in-
    coming,
With many a half-caught voice sent up from the eddies,
Many a muffled confession—many a sob and whisper'd word,
As of speakers far or hid.

How they sweep down and out! how they mutter!
Poets unnamed—artists greatest of any, with cherish'd lost designs,
Love's unresponse—a chorus of age's complaints—hope's last
    words,
Some suicide's despairing cry, *Away to the boundless waste, and
    never again return.*

On to oblivion then!
On, on, and do your part, ye burying, ebbing tide!
On for your time, ye furious debouché!

AND YET NOT YOU ALONE

AND yet not you alone, twilight and burying ebb,
Nor you, ye lost designs alone—nor failures, aspirations;
I know, divine deceitful ones, your glamour's seeming;
Duly by you, from you, the tide and light again—duly the hinges
    turning,
Duly the needed discord-parts offsetting, blending,
Weaving from you, from Sleep, Night, Death itself,
The rhythmus of Birth eternal.

PROUDLY THE FLOOD COMES IN

PROUDLY the flood comes in, shouting, foaming, advancing,
Long it holds at the high, with bosom broad outswelling,
All throbs, dilates—the farms, woods, streets of cities—workmen
    at work,
Mainsails, topsails, jibs, appear in the offing—steamers' pennants
    of smoke—and under the forenoon sun,

Freighted with human lives, gaily the outward bound, gaily the
    inward bound,
Flaunting from many a spar the flag I love.

BY THAT LONG SCAN OF WAVES

By that long scan of waves, myself call'd back, resumed upon
    myself,
In every crest some undulating light or shade—some retrospect,
Joys, travels, studies, silent panoramas—scenes ephemeral,
The long past war, the battles, hospital sights, the wounded and the
    dead,
Myself through every by-gone phase—my idle youth—old age at
    hand,
My three-score years of life summ'd up, and more, and past,
By any grand ideal tried, intentionless, the whole a nothing,
And haply yet some drop within God's scheme's ensemble—some
    wave, or part of wave,
Like one of yours, ye multitudinous ocean.

THEN LAST OF ALL

Then last of all, caught from these shores, this hill,
Of you O tides, the mystic human meaning:
Only by law of you, your swell and ebb, enclosing me the same,
The brain that shapes, the voice that chants this song.

ELECTION DAY, NOVEMBER, 1884

If I should need to name, O Western World, your powerfulest
    scene and show,
'Twould not be you, Niagara—nor you, ye limitless prairies—nor
    your huge rifts of canyons, Colorado,
Nor you, Yosemite—nor Yellowstone, with all its spasmic geyser-
    loops ascending to the skies, appearing and disappearing,
Nor Oregon's white cones—nor Huron's belt of mighty lakes—
    nor Mississippi's stream:
—This seething hemisphere's humanity, as now, I'd name—*the
    still small voice* vibrating—America's choosing day,
(The heart of it not in the chosen—the act itself the main, the
    quadriennial choosing,)
The stretch of North and South arous'd—sea-board and inland—
    Texas to Maine—the Prairie States—Vermont, Virginia, Cali-
    fornia,

The final ballot-shower from East to West—the paradox and conflict,
The countless snow-flakes falling—(a swordless conflict,
Yet more than all Rome's wars of old, or modern Napoleon's:)
    the peaceful choice of all,
Or good or ill humanity—welcoming the darker odds, the dross.
—Foams and ferments the wine? it serves to purify—while the
    heart pants, life glows:
These stormy gusts and winds waft precious ships,
Swell'd Washington's, Jefferson's, Lincoln's sails.

WITH HUSKY-HAUGHTY LIPS, O SEA!

WITH husky-haughty lips, O sea!
Where day and night I wend thy surf-beat shore,
Imaging to my sense thy varied strange suggestions,
(I see and plainly list thy talk and conference here,)
Thy troops of white-maned racers racing to the goal,
Thy ample, smiling face, dash'd with the sparkling dimples of the
    sun,
Thy brooding scowl and murk—thy unloos'd hurricanes,
Thy unsubduedness, caprices, wilfulness;
Great as thou art above the rest, thy many tears—a lack from all
    eternity in thy content,
(Naught but the greatest struggles, wrongs, defeats, could make
    thee greatest—no less could make thee,)
Thy lonely state—something thou ever seek'st and seek'st, yet
    never gain'st,
Surely some right withheld—some voice, in huge monotonous rage,
    of freedom-lover pent,
Some vast heart, like a planet's, chain'd and chafing in those
    breakers,
By lengthen'd swell, and spasm, and panting breath,
And rhythmic rasping of thy sands and waves,
And serpent hiss, and savage peals of laughter,
And undertones of distant lion roar,
(Sounding, appealing to the sky's deaf ear—but now, rapport for
    once,
A phantom in the night thy confidant for once,)
The first and last confession of the globe,
Outsurging, muttering from thy soul's abysms,
The tale of cosmic elemental passion,
Thou tellest to a kindred soul.

DEATH OF GENERAL GRANT

As one by one withdraw the lofty actors,
From that great play on history's stage eterne,
That lurid, partial act of war and peace—of old and new con-
  tending,
Fought out through wrath, fears, dark dismays, and many a long
  suspense;
All past—and since, in countless graves receding, mellowing,
Victor's and vanquish'd—Lincoln's and Lee's—now thou with
  them,
Man of the mighty days—and equal to the days!
Thou from the prairies!—tangled and many-vein'd and hard has
  been thy part,
To admiration has it been enacted!

RED JACKET (FROM ALOFT)

[Impromptu on Buffalo City's monument to, and re-burial of the old Iroquois
orator, October 9, 1884.]

Upon this scene, this show,
Yielded to-day by fashion, learning, wealth,
(Nor in caprice alone—some grains of deepest meaning,)
Haply, aloft, (who knows?) from distant sky-clouds' blended shapes,
As some old tree, or rock or cliff, thrill'd with its soul,
Product of Nature's sun, stars, earth direct—a towering human form,
In hunting-shirt of film, arm'd with the rifle, a half-ironical smile
  curving its phantom lips,
Like one of Ossian's ghosts looks down.

WASHINGTON'S MONUMENT, FEBRUARY, 1885

Ah, not this marble, dead and cold:
Far from its base and shaft expanding—the round zones circling,
  comprehending,
Thou, Washington, art all the world's, the continents' entire—
  not yours alone, America,
Europe's as well, in every part, castle of lord or laborer's cot,
Or frozen North, or sultry South—the African's—the Arab's in
  his tent,
Old Asia's there with venerable smile, seated amid her ruins;
(Greets the antique the hero new? 'tis but the same—the heir
  legitimate, continued ever,

The indomitable heart and arm—proofs of the never-broken line,
Courage, alertness, patience, faith, the same—e'en in defeat de-
    feated not, the same:)
Wherever sails a ship, or house is built on land, or day or night,
Through teeming cities' streets, indoors or out, factories or farms,
Now, or to come, or past—where patriot wills existed or exist,
Wherever Freedom, pois'd by Toleration, sway'd by Law,
Stands or is rising thy true monument.

OF THAT BLITHE THROAT OF THINE

[More than eighty-three degrees north—about a good day's steaming distance
to the Pole by one of our fast oceaners in clear water—Greely the explorer
heard the song of a single snow-bird merrily sounding over the desolation.]

OF that blithe throat of thine from arctic bleak and blank,
I'll mind the lesson, solitary bird—let me too welcome chilling
    drifts,
E'en the profoundest chill, as now—a torpid pulse, a brain unnerv'd,
Old age land-lock'd within its winter bay—(cold, cold, O cold!)
These snowy hairs, my feeble arm, my frozen feet,
For them thy faith, thy rule I take, and grave it to the last;
Not summer's zones alone—not chants of youth, or south's warm
    tides alone,
But held by sluggish floes, pack'd in the northern ice, the cumulus
    of years,
These with gay heart I also sing.

BROADWAY

WHAT hurrying human tides, or day or night!
What passions, winnings, losses, ardors, swim thy waters!
What whirls of evil, bliss and sorrow, stem thee!
What curious questioning glances—glints of love!
Leer, envy, scorn, contempt, hope, aspiration!
Thou portal—thou arena—thou of the myriad long-drawn lines
    and groups!
(Could but thy flagstones, curbs, façades, tell their inimitable tales;
Thy windows rich, and huge hotels—thy side-walks wide;)
Thou of the endless sliding, mincing, shuffling feet!
Thou, like the parti-colored world itself—like infinite, teeming,
    mocking life!
Thou visor'd, vast, unspeakable show and lesson!

TO GET THE FINAL LILT OF SONGS

To get the final lilt of songs,
To penetrate the inmost lore of poets—to know the mighty ones,
Job, Homer, Eschylus, Dante, Shakspere, Tennyson, Emerson;
To diagnose the shifting-delicate tints of love and pride and doubt—
    to truly understand,
To encompass these, the last keen faculty and entrance-price,
Old age, and what it brings from all its past experiences.

OLD SALT KOSSABONE

FAR back, related on my mother's side,
Old Salt Kossabone, I'll tell you how he died:
(Had been a sailor all his life—was nearly 90—lived with his married
    grandchild, Jenny;
House on a hill, with view of bay at hand, and distant cape, and
    stretch to open sea;)
The last of afternoons, the evening hours, for many a year his
    regular custom,
In his great arm chair by the window seated,
(Sometimes, indeed, through half the day,)
Watching the coming, going of the vessels, he mutters to himself—
    And now the close of all:
One struggling outbound brig, one day, baffled for long—cross-
    tides and much wrong going,
At last at nightfall strikes the breeze aright, her whole luck veering,
And swiftly bending round the cape, the darkness proudly entering,
    cleaving, as he watches,
"She's free—she's on her destination"—these the last words—
    when Jenny came, he sat there dead,
Dutch Kossabone, Old Salt, related on my mother's side, far back.

THE DEAD TENOR

As down the stage again,
With Spanish hat and plumes, and gait inimitable
Back from the fading lessons of the past, I'd call, I'd tell and own,
How much from thee! the revelation of the singing voice from thee!
(So firm—so liquid-soft—again that tremulous, manly timbre!
The perfect singing voice—deepest of all to me the lesson—trial
    and test of all:)
How through those strains distill'd—how the rapt ears, the soul
    of me, absorbing

Fernando's heart, *Manrico's* passionate call, *Ernani's*, sweet *Gen-
        naro's*,
I fold thenceforth, or seek to fold, within my chants transmuting,
Freedom's and Love's and Faith's unloos'd cantabile,
(As perfume's, color's, sunlight's correlation:)
From these, for these, with these, a hurried line, dead tenor,
A wafted autumn leaf, dropt in the closing grave, the shovel'd
        earth,
To memory of thee.

CONTINUITIES

[From a talk I had lately with a German spiritualist.]

NOTHING is ever really lost, or can be lost,
No birth, identity, form—no object of the world.
Nor life, nor force, nor any visible thing;
Appearance must not foil, nor shifted sphere confuse thy brain.
Ample are time and space—ample the fields of Nature.
The body, sluggish, aged, cold—the embers left from earlier fires,
The light in the eye grown dim, shall duly flame again;
The sun now low in the west rises for mornings and for noons
        continual;
To frozen clods ever the spring's invisible law returns,
With grass and flowers and summer fruits and corn.

YONNONDIO

[The sense of the word is *lament for the aborigines*. It is an Iroquois term;
and has been used for a personal name.]

A SONG, a poem of itself—the word itself a dirge,
Amid the wilds, the rocks, the storm and wintry night,
To me such misty, strange tableaux the syllables calling up;
Yonnondio—I see, far in the west or north, a limitless ravine, with
        plains and mountains dark,
I see swarms of stalwart chieftains, medicine-men, and warriors,
As flitting by like clouds of ghosts, they pass and are gone in the
        twilight,
(Race of the woods, the landscapes free, and the falls!
No picture, poem, statement, passing them to the future:)
Yonnondio! Yonnondio!—unlimn'd they disappear;
To-day gives place, and fades—the cities, farms, factories fade;

A muffled sonorous sound, a wailing word is borne through the
 air for a moment,
Then blank and gone and still, and utterly lost.

LIFE

EVER the undiscouraged, resolute, struggling soul of man;
(Have former armies fail'd? then we send fresh armies—and fresh
 again;)
Ever the grappled mystery of all earth's ages old or new;
Ever the eager eyes, hurrahs, the welcome-clapping hands, the loud
 applause;
Ever the soul dissatisfied, curious, unconvinced at last;
Struggling to-day the same—battling the same.

"GOING SOMEWHERE"

MY science-friend, my noblest woman-friend,
(Now buried in an English grave—and this a memory-leaf for her
 dear sake,)
Ended our talk—"The sum, concluding all we know of old or
 modern learning, intuitions deep,
"Of all Geologies—Histories—of all Astronomy—of Evolution,
 Metaphysics all,
"Is, that we all are onward, onward, speeding slowly, surely
 bettering,
"Life, life an endless march, an endless army, (no halt, but it is
 duly over,)
"The world, the race, the soul—in space and time the universes,
"All bound as is befitting each—all surely going somewhere."

From the 1867 edition L. of G.

SMALL THE THEME OF MY CHANT

SMALL the theme of my Chant, yet the greatest—namely, One's-
 Self—a simple, separate person. That, for the use of the New
 World, I sing.
Man's physiology complete, from top to toe, I sing. Not physi-
 ognomy alone, nor brain alone, is worthy for the Muse;—I
 say the Form complete is worthier far. The Female equally
 with the Male, I sing.
Nor cease at the theme of One's-Self. I speak the word of the modern,
 the word En-Masse.
My Days I sing, and the Lands—with interstice I knew of hapless
 War.

(O friend, whoe'er you are, at last arriving hither to commence,
    I feel through every leaf the pressure of your hand, which I
    return.
And thus upon our journey, footing the road, and more than
    once, and link'd together let us go.)

TRUE CONQUERORS

OLD farmers, travelers, workmen (no matter how crippled or bent,)
Old sailors, out of many a perilous voyage, storm and wreck,
Old soldiers from campaigns, with all their wounds, defeats and
    scars;
Enough that they've survived at all—long life's unflinching ones!
Forth from their struggles, trials, fights, to have emerged at all—
    in that alone,
True conquerors o'er all the rest.

THE UNITED STATES TO OLD WORLD CRITICS

HERE first the duties of to-day, the lessons of the concrete,
Wealth, order, travel, shelter, products, plenty;
As of the building of some varied, vast, perpetual edifice,
Whence to arise inevitable in time, the towering roofs, the lamps,
The solid-planted spires tall shooting to the stars.

THE CALMING THOUGHT OF ALL

THAT coursing on, whate'er men's speculations,
Amid the changing schools, theologies, philosophies,
Amid the bawling presentations new and old,
The round earth's silent vital laws, facts, modes continue.

THANKS IN OLD AGE

THANKS in old age—thanks ere I go,
For health, the midday sun, the impalpable air—for life, mere life,
For precious ever-lingering memories, (of you my mother dear—
    you, father—you, brothers, sisters, friends,)
For all my days—not those of peace alone—the days of war the same,
For gentle words, caresses, gifts from foreign lands,
For shelter, wine and meat—for sweet appreciation,
(You distant, dim unknown—or young or old—countless, un-
    specified, readers belov'd,

We never met, and ne'er shall meet—and yet our souls embrace,
    long, close and long;)
For beings, groups, love, deeds, words, books—for colors, forms,
For all the brave strong men—devoted, hardy men—who've for-
    ward sprung in freedom's help, all years, all lands,
For braver, stronger, more devoted men—(a special laurel ere I
    go, to life's war's chosen ones,
The cannoneers of song and thought—the great artillerists—the
    foremost leaders, captains of the soul:)
As soldier from an ended war return'd—As traveler out of myriads,
    to the long procession retrospective,
Thanks—joyful thanks!—a soldier's, traveler's thanks.

LIFE AND DEATH

THE two old, simple problems ever intertwined,
Close home, elusive, present, baffled, grappled.
By each successive age insoluble, pass'd on,
To ours to-day—and we pass on the same.

THE VOICE OF THE RAIN

AND who art thou? said I to the soft-falling shower,
Which, strange to tell, gave me an answer, as here translated:
I am the Poem of Earth, said the voice of the rain,
Eternal I rise impalpable out of the land and the bottomless sea,
Upward to heaven, whence, vaguely form'd, altogether changed,
    and yet the same,
I descend to lave the drouths, atomies, dust-layers of the globe,
And all that in them without me were seeds only, latent, unborn;
And forever, by day and night, I give back life to my own origin,
    and make pure and beautify it:
(For song, issuing from its birth-place, after fulfilment, wandering,
Reck'd or unreck'd, duly with love returns.)

SOON SHALL THE WINTER'S FOIL BE HERE

SOON shall the winter's foil be here;
Soon shall these icy ligatures unbind and melt—A little while,
And air, soil, wave, suffused shall be in softness, bloom and growth--
    a thousand forms shall rise
From these dead clods and chills as from low burial graves.

Thine eyes, ears—all thy best attributes—all that takes cognizance
    of natural beauty,
Shall wake and fill. Thou shalt perceive the simple shows, the delicate
    miracles of earth,
Dandelions, clover, the emerald grass, the early scents and flowers,
The arbutus under foot, the willow's yellow-green, the blossoming
    plum and cherry;
With these the robin, lark and thrush, singing their songs—the
    flitting bluebird;
For such the scenes the annual play brings on.

WHILE NOT THE PAST FORGETTING

WHILE not the past forgetting,
To-day, at least, contention sunk entire—peace, brotherhood up-
    risen;
For sign reciprocal our Northern, Southern hands,
Lay on the graves of all dead soldiers, North or South,
(Nor for the past alone—for meanings to the future,)
Wreaths of roses and branches of palm.
   Publish'd May 30, 1888

THE DYING VETERAN
[A Long Island incident—early part of the present century.]

AMID these days of order, ease, prosperity,
Amid the current songs of beauty, peace, decorum,
I cast a reminiscence—(likely 'twill offend you,
I heard it in my boyhood;)—More than a generation since,
A queer old savage man, a fighter under Washington himself,
Large, brave, cleanly, hot-blooded, no talker, rather spiritualistic,
Had fought in the ranks—fought well—had been all through the
    Revolutionary war,)
Lay dying—sons, daughters, church-deacons, lovingly tending him,
Sharping their sense, their ears, towards his murmuring, half-
    caught words:
"Let me return again to my war-days,
To the sights and scenes—to forming the line of battle,
To the scouts ahead reconnoitering,
To the cannons, the grim artillery,
To the galloping aids, carrying orders,
To the wounded, the fallen, the heat, the suspense,
The perfume strong, the smoke, the deafening noise;

Away with your life of peace!—your joys of peace!
Give me my old wild battle-life again!"

STRONGER LESSONS

HAVE you learn'd lessons only of those who admired you, and
were tender with you, and stood aside for you?
Have you not learn'd great lessons from those who reject you,
and brace themselves against you? or who treat you with
contempt, or dispute the passage with you?

A PRAIRIE SUNSET

SHOT gold, maroon and violet, dazzling silver, emerald, fawn,
The earth's whole amplitude and Nature's multiform power con-
sign'd for once to colors;
The light, the general air possess'd by them—colors till now un-
known,
No limit, confine—not the Western sky alone—the high meridian—
North, South, all,
Pure luminous color fighting the silent shadows to the last.

TWENTY YEARS

DOWN on the ancient wharf, the sand, I sit, with a new-comer
chatting:
He shipp'd as green-hand boy, and sail'd away, (took some sudden,
vehement notion;)
Since, twenty years and more have circled round and round,
While he the globe was circling round and round,—and now
returns:
How changed the place—all the old land-marks gone—the parents
dead;
(Yes, he comes back *to lay in port for good—to settle*—has a well-
fill'd purse—no spot will do but this;)
The little boat that scull'd him from the sloop, now held in leash
I see,
I hear the slapping waves, the restless keel, the rocking in the sand,
I see the sailor kit, the canvas bag, the great box bound with brass,
I scan the face all berry-brown and bearded—the stout-strong frame,
Dress'd in its russet suit of good Scotch cloth:
(Then what the told-out story of those twenty years? What of the
future?)

ORANGE BUDS BY MAIL FROM FLORIDA

[Voltaire closed a famous argument by claiming that a ship of war and the grand opera were proofs enough of civilization's and France's progress, in his day.]

A LESSER proof than old Voltaire's, yet greater,
Proof of this present time, and thee, thy broad expanse, America,
To my plain Northern hut, in outside clouds and snow,
Brought safely for a thousand miles o'er land and tide,
Some three days since on their own soil live-sprouting,
Now here their sweetness through my room unfolding,
A bunch of orange buds by mail from Florida.

TWILIGHT

THE soft voluptuous opiate shades,
The sun just gone, the eager light dispell'd—(I too will soon be gone dispell'd,)
A haze—nirwana—rest and night—oblivion.

YOU LINGERING SPARSE LEAVES OF ME

YOU lingering sparse leaves of me on winter-nearing boughs,
And I some well-shorn tree of field or orchard-row;
You tokens diminute and lorn—(not now the flush of May, or July clover-bloom—no grain of August now;)
You pallid banner-staves—you pennants valueless—you overstay'd of time,
Yet my soul-dearest leaves confirming all the rest,
The faithfulest—hardiest—last.

NOT MEAGRE, LATENT BOUGHS ALONE

NOT meagre, latent boughs alone, O songs! (scaly and bare, like eagles' talons,)
But haply for some sunny day (who knows?) some future spring, some summer—bursting forth,
To verdant leaves, or sheltering shade—to nourishing fruit,
Apples and grapes—the stalwart limbs of trees emerging—the fresh, free, open air,
And love and faith, like scented roses blooming.

THE DEAD EMPEROR

TO-DAY, with bending head and eyes, thou, too, Columbia,
Less for the mighty crown laid low in sorrow—less for the Emperor,
Thy true condolence breathest, sendest out o'er many a salt sea mile,
Mourning a good old man—a faithful shepherd, patriot.

Publish'd March 10, 1888.

AS THE GREEK'S SIGNAL FLAME

[For Whittier's eightieth birthday, December 17, 1887.]

As the Greek's signal flame, by antique records told,
Rose from the hill-top, like applause and glory,
Welcoming in fame some special veteran, hero,
With rosy tinge reddening the land he'd served,
So I aloft from Mannahatta's ship-fringed shore,
Lift high a kindled brand for thee, Old Poet.

THE DISMANTLED SHIP

IN some unused lagoon, some nameless bay,
On sluggish, lonesome waters, anchor'd near the shore,
An old, dismasted, gray and batter'd ship, disabled, done,
After free voyages to all the seas of earth, haul'd up at last and
    hawser'd tight,
Lies rusting, mouldering.

NOW PRECEDENT SONGS, FAREWELL

Now precedent songs, farewell—by every name farewell,
(Trains of a staggering line in many a strange procession, waggons,
From ups and downs—with intervals—from elder years, mid-age,
    or youth,)
"In Cabin'd Ships," or "Thee Old Cause" or "Poets to Come,"
Or "Paumanok," "Song of Myself," "Calamus," or "Adam,"
Or "Beat! Beat! Drums!" or "To the Leaven'd Soil they Trod,"
Or "Captain! My Captain!" "Kosmos," "Quicksand Years," or
    "Thoughts,"
"Thou Mother with thy Equal Brood," and many, many more
    unspecified,
From fibre heart of mine—from throat and tongue—(My life's
    hot pulsing blood,
The personal urge and form for me—not merely paper, automatic
    type and ink,)

Each song of mine—each utterance in the past—having its long,
   long history,
Of life or death, or soldier's wound, of country's loss or safety,
(O heaven! what flash and started endless train of all! compared
   indeed to that!
What wretched shred e'en at the best of all!)

AN EVENING LULL

AFTER a week of physical anguish,
Unrest and pain, and feverish heat,
Toward the ending day a calm and lull comes on,
Three hours of peace and soothing rest of brain.*

OLD AGE'S LAMBENT PEAKS

THE touch of flame—the illuminating fire—the loftiest look at
   last,
O'er city, passion, sea—o'er prairie, mountain, wood—the earth
   itself;
The airy, different, changing hues of all, in falling twilight,
Objects and groups, bearings, faces, reminiscences;
The calmer sight—the golden setting, clear and broad:
So much i' the atmosphere, the points of view, the situations whence
   we scan,
Bro't out by them alone—so much (perhaps the best) unreck'd
   before;
The lights indeed from them—old age's lambent peaks.

AFTER THE SUPPER AND TALK

AFTER the supper and talk—after the day is done,
As a friend from friends his final withdrawal prolonging,
Good-bye and Good-bye with emotional lips repeating,
(So hard for his hand to release those hands—no more will they
   meet,
No more for communion of sorrow and joy, of old and young,
A far-stretching journey awaits him, to return no more,)

---

* The two songs on this page [NOW PRECEDENT SONGS, FAREWELL and AN
EVENING LULL] are eked out during an afternoon, June, 1888, in my seventieth
year, at a critical spell of illness. Of course no reader and probably no
human being at any time will ever have such phases of emotional and solemn
action as these involve to me. I feel in them an end and close of all.

Shunning, postponing severance—seeking to ward off the last word
    ever so little,
E'en at the exit-door turning—charges superfluous calling back—
    e'en as he descends the steps,
Something to eke out a minute additional—shadows of nightfall
    deepening,
Farewells, messages lessening—dimmer the forthgoer's visage and
    form,
Soon to be lost for aye in the darkness—loth, O so loth to depart!
Garrulous to the very last.

Good-Bye My Fancy

PREFACE NOTE TO 2d ANNEX,

CONCLUDING L. OF G.—1891

HAD I not better withhold (in this old age and paralysis of me) such little tags and fringe-dots (maybe specks, stains,) as follow a long dusty journey, and witness it afterward? I have probably not been enough afraid of careless touches, from the first—and am not now—nor of parrot-like repetitions—nor platitudes and the commonplace. Perhaps I am too democratic for such avoidances. Besides, is not the verse-field, as originally plann'd by my theory, now sufficiently illustrated—and full time for me to silently retire?—(indeed amid no loud call or market for my sort of poetic utterance.)

In answer, or rather defiance, to that kind of well-put interrogation, here comes this little cluster, and conclusion of my preceding clusters. Though not at all clear that, as here collated, it is worth printing (certainly I have nothing fresh to write)—I while away the hours of my 72d year—hours of forced confinement in my den—by putting in shape this small old age collation:

> Last droplets of and after spontaneous rain,
> From many limpid distillations and past showers;
> (Will they germinate anything? mere exhalations as they all are—
>   the land's and sea's—America's;
> Will they filter to any deep emotion? any heart and brain?)

However that may be, I feel like improving to-day's opportunity and wind up. During the last two years I have sent out, in the lulls of illness and exhaustion, certain chirps—lingering-dying ones probably (undoubtedly)—which now I may as well gather and put in fair type while able to see correctly—(for my eyes plainly warn me they are dimming, and my brain more and more palpably neglects or refuses, month after month, even slight tasks or revisions.)

In fact, here I am these current years 1890 and '91, (each successive fortnight getting stiffer and stuck deeper) much like some hard-cased dilapidated grim ancient shell-fish or time-bang'd conch (no legs, utterly non-locomotive) cast up high and dry on the shore-sands, helpless to move anywhere—nothing left but behave myself quiet, and while away the days yet assign'd, and discover if there is anything for the said grim and time-bang'd conch to be got at last out of inherited good spirits and primal buoyant centre-pulses down there deep somewhere within his gray-blurr'd old shell ....(Reader, you must allow a little fun here—for one reason there are too many of the following poemets about death, &c., and for another the passing hours (July 5, 1890) are so sunny-fine. And old as I am I feel to-day almost a part of some frolicsome wave, or for sporting yet like a kid or kitten—probably a streak of physical adjustment and perfection here and now. I believe I have it in me perennially anyhow.)

Then behind all, the deep-down consolation (it is a glum one, but I dare not be sorry for the fact of it in the past, nor refrain from dwelling, even vaunting here at the end) that this late-years palsied old shorn and shell-fish condition of me is the indubitable outcome and growth, now near for 20 years along, of too over-zealous, over-continued bodily and emotional excitement and action through the times of 1862, '3, '4 and '5, visiting and waiting on wounded and sick army volunteers, both sides, in campaigns or contests, or after them, or in hospitals or fields south of Washington City, or in that place and elsewhere—those hot, sad, wrenching times—the army volunteers, all States,—or North or South—the wounded, suffering, dying—the exhausting, sweating summers, marches, battles, carnage—those trenches hurriedly heap'd by the corpse-thousands, mainly unknown—Will the America of the future—will this vast rich Union ever realize what itself cost, back there after all?—those hecatombs of battle-deaths—Those times of which, O far-off reader, this whole book is indeed finally but a reminiscent memorial from thence by me to you?

SAIL OUT FOR GOOD, EIDÓLON YACHT!

HEAVE the anchor short!
Raise main-sail and jib—steer forth,
O little white-hull'd sloop, now speed on really deep waters,
(I will not call it our concluding voyage,
But outset and sure entrance to the truest, best, maturest;)
Depart, depart from solid earth—no more returning to these shores,
Now on for aye our infinite free venture wending,
Spurning all yet tried ports, seas, hawsers, densities, gravitation,
Sail out for good, eidólon yacht of me!

LINGERING LAST DROPS

AND whence and why come you?

We know not whence, (was the answer,)
We only know that we drift here with the rest,
That we linger'd and lagg'd—but were wafted at last, and are
     now here,
To make the passing shower's concluding drops.

GOOD-BYE MY FANCY

GOOD-BYE* my fancy—(I had a word to say,
But 'tis not quite the time—The best of any man's word or say,
Is when its proper place arrives—and for its meaning,
I keep mine till the last.)

---

   * Behind a Good-bye there lurks much of the salutation of another beginning—to me, Development, Continuity, Immortality, Transformation, are
the chiefest life-meanings of Nature and Humanity, and are the *sine qua non*
of all facts, and each fact.
   Why do folks dwell so fondly on the last words, advice, appearance, of the
departing? Those last words are not samples of the best, which involve
vitality at its full, and balance, and perfect control and scope. But they are
valuable beyond measure to confirm and endorse the varied train, facts, theories
and faith of the whole preceding life.

ON, ON THE SAME, YE JOCUND TWAIN!

ON, on the same, ye jocund twain!
My life and recitative, containing birth, youth, mid-age years,
Fitful as motley-tongues of flame, inseparably twined and merged
    in one—combining all,
My single soul—aims, confirmations, failures, joys—Nor single
    soul alone,
I chant my nation's crucial stage, (America's, haply humanity's)
    —the trial great, the victory great,
A strange *eclaircissement* of all the masses past, the eastern world,
    the ancient, medieval,
Here, here from wanderings, strayings, lessons, wars, defeats—here
    at the west a voice triumphant—justifying all,
A gladsome pealing cry—a song for once of utmost pride and
    satisfaction;
I chant from it the common bulk, the general average horde, (the
    best no sooner than the worst)—And now I chant old age,
(My verses, written first for forenoon life, and for the summer's,
    autumn's spread,
I pass to snow-white hairs the same, and give to pulses winter-
    cool'd the same;)
As here in careless trill, I and my recitatives, with faith and love,
Wafting to other work, to unknown songs, conditions,
On, on, ye jocund twain! continue on the same!

MY 71ST YEAR

AFTER surmounting three-score and ten,
With all their chances, changes, losses, sorrows,
My parents' deaths, the vagaries of my life, the many tearing pas-
    sions of me, the war of '63 and '4,
As some old broken soldier, after a long, hot, wearying march, or
    haply after battle,
To-day at twilight, hobbling, answering company roll-call, *Here*,
    with vital voice,
Reporting yet, saluting yet the Officer over all.

APPARITIONS

A VAGUE mist hanging 'round half the pages:
(Sometimes how strange and clear to the soul,
That all these solid things are indeed but apparitions, concepts,
    non-realities.)

THE PALLID WREATH

SOMEHOW I cannot let it go yet, funeral though it is,
Let it remain back there on its nail suspended,
With pink, blue, yellow, all blanch'd, and the white now gray and
        ashy,
One wither'd rose put years ago for thee, dear friend;
But I do not forget thee. Hast thou then faded?
Is the odor exhaled? Are the colors, vitalities, dead?
No, while memories subtly play—the past vivid as ever;
For but last night I woke, and in that spectral ring saw thee,
Thy smile, eyes, face, calm, silent, loving as ever:
So let the wreath hang still awhile within my eye-reach,
It is not yet dead to me, nor even pallid.

AN ENDED DAY

THE soothing sanity and blitheness of completion,
The pomp and hurried contest-glare and rush are done;
Now triumph! transformation! jubilate!*

* NOTE.—*Summer country life.—Several years.*—In my rambles and explorations I found a woody place near the creek, where for some reason the birds
in happy mood seem'd to resort in unusual numbers. Especially at the beginning
of the day, and again at the ending, I was sure to get there the most copious bird-
concerts. I repair'd there frequently at sunrise—and also at sunset, or just
before . . . Once the question arose in me: Which is the best singing, the first or
the lattermost? The first always exhilarated, and perhaps seem'd more joyous
and stronger; but I always felt the sunset or late afternoon sounds more
penetrating and sweeter—seem'd to touch the soul—often the evening thrushes,
two or three of them, responding and perhaps blending. Though I miss'd some
of the mornings, I found myself getting to be quite strictly punctual at the evening utterances.

ANOTHER NOTE.—"He went out with the tide and the sunset," was a phrase
I heard from a surgeon describing an old sailor's death under peculiarly gentle
conditions.

During the Secession War, 1863 and '4, visiting the Army Hospitals around
Washington, I form'd the habit, and continued it to the end, whenever the ebb
or flood tide began the latter part of day, of punctually visiting those at that
time populous wards of suffering men. Somehow (or I thought so) the effect of
the hour was palpable. The badly wounded would get some ease, and would like
to talk a little, or be talk'd to. Intellectual and emotional natures would be at
their best: Deaths were always easier; medicines seem'd to have better effect
when given then, and a lulling atmosphere would pervade the wards.

Similar influences, similar circumstances and hours, day-close, after great
battles, even with all their horrors. I had more than once the same experience
on the fields cover'd with fallen or dead.

OLD AGE'S SHIP & CRAFTY DEATH'S

FROM east and west across the horizon's edge,
Two mighty masterful vessels sailers steal upon us:
But we 'll make race a-time upon the seas—a battle-contest yet!
    bear lively there!
(Our joys of strife and derring-do to the last!)
Put on the old ship all her power to-day!
Crowd top-sail, top-gallant and royal studding-sails,
Out challenge and defiance—flags and flaunting pennants added,
As we take to the open—take to the deepest, freest waters.

TO THE PENDING YEAR

HAVE I no weapon-word for thee—some message brief and fierce?
(Have I fought out and done indeed the battle?) Is there no shot
    left,
For all thy affectations, lisps, scorns, manifold silliness?
Nor for myself—my own rebellious self in thee?

Down, down, proud gorge!—though choking thee;
Thy bearded throat and high-borne forehead to the gutter;
Crouch low thy neck to eleemosynary gifts.

SHAKSPERE-BACON'S CIPHER

I DOUBT it not—then more, far more;
In each old song bequeath'd—in every noble page or text,
(Different—something unreck'd before—some unsuspected author,)
In every object, mountain, tree, and star—in every birth and life,
As part of each—evolv'd from each—meaning, behind the ostent,
A mystic cipher waits infolded.

LONG, LONG HENCE

AFTER a long, long course, hundreds of years, denials,
Accumulations, rous'd love and joy and thought,
Hopes, wishes, aspirations, ponderings, victories, myriads of
    readers,
Coating, compassing, covering—after ages' and ages' encrustations,
Then only may these songs reach fruition.

BRAVO, PARIS EXPOSITION!

ADD to your show, before you close it, France,
With all the rest, visible, concrete, temples, towers, goods, machines
    and ores,
Our sentiment wafted from many million heart-throbs, ethereal but
    solid,
(We grand-sons and great-grand-sons do not forget your grand-
    sires,)
From fifty Nations and nebulous Nations, compacted, sent over-
    sea to-day,
America's applause, love, memories and good-will.

INTERPOLATION SOUNDS

[General Philip Sheridan was buried at the Cathedral, Washington, D. C.,
August, 1888, with all the pomp, music and ceremonies of the Roman Catholic
service.]

OVER and through the burial chant,
Organ and solemn service, sermon, bending priests,
To me come interpolation sounds not in the show—plainly to me,
    crowding up the aisle and from the window,
Of sudden battle's hurry and harsh noises—war's grim game to
    sight and ear in earnest;
The scout call'd up and forward—the general mounted and his aids
    around him—the new-brought word—the instantaneous order
    issued;
The rifle crack—the cannon thud—the rushing forth of men from
    their tents;
The clank of cavalry—the strange celerity of forming ranks—the
    slender bugle note;
The sound of horses' hoofs departing—saddles, arms, accoutre-
    ments.

NOTE.—CAMDEN, N. J., August 7, 1888.—Walt Whitman asks the *New York
Herald* "to add his tribute to Sheridan:"

"In the grand constellation of five or six names, under Lincoln's Presidency,
that history will bear for ages in her firmament as marking the last life-throbs
of secession, and beaming on its dying gasps, Sheridan's will be bright. One
consideration rising out of the now dead soldier's example as it passes my mind,
is worth taking notice of. If the war had continued any long time these States,
in my opinion, would have shown and proved the most conclusive military
talents ever evinced by any nation on earth. That they possess'd a rank and file
ahead of all other known in points of quality and limitlessness of number are
easily admitted. But we have, too, the eligibility of organizing, handling and
officering equal to the other. These two, with modern arms, transportation,
and inventive American genius, would make the United States, with earnestness, not only able to stand the whole world, but conquer that world united
against us."

TO THE SUN-SET BREEZE

AH, whispering, something again, unseen,
Where late this heated day thou enterest at my window, door,
Thou, laving, tempering all, cool-freshing, gently vitalizing
Me, old, alone, sick, weak-down, melted-worn with sweat;
Thou, nestling, folding close and firm yet soft, companion better
    than talk, book, art,
(Thou hast, O Nature! elements! utterance to my heart beyond
    the rest—and this is of them,)
So sweet thy primitive taste to breathe within—thy soothing fingers
    on my face and hands,
Thou, messenger-magical strange bringer to body and spirit of me,
(Distances balk'd—occult medicines penetrating me from head to
    foot,)
I feel the sky, the prairies vast—I feel the mighty northern lakes,
I feel the ocean and the forest—somehow I feel the globe itself
    swift-swimming in space;
Thou blown from lips so loved, now gone—haply from endless
    store, God-sent,
(For thou art spiritual, Godly, most of all known to my sense,)
Minister to speak to me, here and now, what word has never told,
    and cannot tell,
Art thou not universal concrete's distillation? Law's, all Astron-
    omy's last refinement?
Hast thou no soul? Can I not know, identify thee?

OLD CHANTS

AN ancient song, reciting, ending,
Once gazing toward thee, Mother of All,
Musing, seeking themes fitted for thee,
Accept for me, thou saidst, *the elder ballads*,
And name for me before thou goest each ancient poet.

(Of many debts incalculable,
Haply our New World's chiefest debt is to old poems.)

Ever so far back, preluding thee, America,
Old chants, Egyptian priests, and those of Ethiopia,
The Hindu epics, the Grecian, Chinese, Persian,
The Biblic books and prophets, and deep idyls of the Nazarene,
The Iliad, Odyssey, plots, doings, wanderings of Eneas,

Hesiod, Eschylus, Sophocles, Merlin, Arthur,
The Cid, Roland at Roncesvalles, the Nibelungen,
The troubadours, minstrels, minnesingers, skalds,
Chaucer, Dante, flocks of singing birds,
The Border Minstrelsy, the bye-gone ballads, feudal tales, essays,
     plays,
Shakspere, Schiller, Walter Scott, Tennyson,
As some vast wondrous weird dream-presences,
The great shadowy groups gathering around,
Darting their mighty masterful eyes forward at thee,
Thou! with as now thy bending neck and head, with courteous
     hand and word, ascending,
Thou! pausing a moment, drooping thine eyes upon them, blent
     with their music,
Well pleased, accepting all, curiously prepared for by them,
Thou enterest at thy entrance porch.

A CHRISTMAS GREETING

From a Northern Star-Group to a Southern. 1889–'90

WELCOME, Brazilian brother—thy ample place is ready;
A loving hand—a smile from the north—a sunny instant hail!
(Let the future care for itself, where it reveals its troubles, impedi-
     mentas,
Ours, ours the present throe, the democratic aim, the acceptance
     and the faith;)
To thee to-day our reaching arm, our turning neck—to thee from
     us the expectant eye,
Thou cluster free! thou brilliant lustrous one! thou, learning well,
The true lesson of a nation's light in the sky,
(More shining than the Cross, more than the Crown,)
The height to be superb humanity.

SOUNDS OF THE WINTER

SOUNDS of the winter too,
Sunshine upon the mountains—many a distant strain
From cheery railroad train—from nearer field, barn, house,
The whispering air—even the mute crops, garner'd apples, corn,
Children's and women's tones—rhythm of many a farmer and of
     flail,
An old man's garrulous lips among the rest, *Think not we give
     out yet,*
Forth from these snowy hairs we keep up yet the lilt.

A TWILIGHT SONG

As I sit in twilight late alone by the flickering oak-flame,
Musing on long-pass'd war-scenes—of the countless buried un-
    known soldiers,
Of the vacant names, as unindented air's and sea's—the unreturn'd,
The brief truce after battle, with grim burial-squads, and the deep-
    fill'd trenches
Of gather'd dead from all America, North, South, East, West,
    whence they came up,
From wooded Maine, New-England's farms, from fertile Pennsyl-
    vania, Illinois, Ohio,
From the measureless West, Virginia, the South, the Carolinas,
    Texas,
(Even here in my room-shadows and half-lights in the noiseless
    flickering flames,
Again I see the stalwart ranks on-filing, rising—I hear the rhythmic
    tramp of the armies;)
You million unwrit names all, all—you dark bequest from all the
    war,
A special verse for you—a flash of duty long neglected—your
    mystic roll strangely gather'd here,
Each name recall'd by me from out the darkness and death's ashes,
Henceforth be, deep, deep within my heart recording, for many
    a future year,
Your mystic roll entire of unknown names, or North or South,
Embalm'd with love in this twilight song.

WHEN THE FULL-GROWN POET CAME

WHEN the full-grown poet came,
Out spake pleased Nature (the round impassive globe, with all its
    shows of day and night,) saying, *He is mine;*
But out spake too the Soul of man, proud, jealous and unrecon-
    ciled, *Nay, he is mine alone;*
—Then the full-grown poet stood between the two, and took each
    by the hand;
And to-day and ever so stands, as blender, uniter, tightly holding
    hands,
Which he will never release until he reconciles the two,
And wholly and joyously blends them.

OSCEOLA

[When I was nearly grown to manhood in Brooklyn, New York, (middle of 1838,) I met one of the return'd U. S. Marines from Fort Moultrie, S. C., and had long talks with him—learn'd the occurrence below described—death of Osceola. The latter was a young, brave, leading Seminole in the Florida war of that time—was surrender'd to our troops, imprison'd and literally died of "a broken heart," at Fort Moultrie. He sicken'd of his confinement—the doctor and officers made every allowance and kindness possible for him; then the close:]

WHEN his hour for death had come,
He slowly rais'd himself from the bed on the floor,
Drew on his war-dress, shirt, leggings, and girdled the belt around
    his waist,
Call'd for vermilion paint (his looking-glass was held before him,)
Painted half his face and neck, his wrists, and back-hands,
Put the scalp-knife carefully in his belt—then lying down, resting a
    moment,
Rose again, half sitting, smiled, gave in silence his extended hand
    to each and all,
Sank faintly low to the floor (tightly grasping the tomahawk handle,)
Fix'd his look on wife and little children—the last:

(And here a line in memory of his name and death.)

A VOICE FROM DEATH

(The Johnstown, Penn., cataclysm, May 31, 1889)

A VOICE from Death, solemn and strange, in all his sweep and
    power,
With sudden, indescribable blow—towns drown'd—humanity by
    thousands slain,
The vaunted work of thrift, goods, dwellings, forge, street, iron
    bridge,
Dash'd pell-mell by the blow—yet usher'd life continuing on,
(Amid the rest, amid the rushing, whirling, wild debris,
A suffering woman saved—a baby safely born!)

Although I come and unannounc'd, in horror and in pang,
In pouring flood and fire, and wholesale elemental crash, (this
    voice so solemn, strange,)
I too a minister of Deity.

Yea, Death, we bow our faces, veil our eyes to thee,
We mourn the old, the young untimely drawn to thee,
The fair, the strong, the good, the capable,
The household wreck'd, the husband and the wife, the engulf'd
    forger in his forge,
The corpses in the whelming waters and the mud,
The gather'd thousands to their funeral mounds, and thousands
    never found or gather'd.

Then after burying, mourning the dead,
(Faithful to them found or unfound, forgetting not, bearing the
    past, here new musing,)
A day—a passing moment or an hour—America itself bends low,
Silent, resign'd, submissive.

War, death, cataclysm like this, America,
Take deep to thy proud prosperous heart.

E'en as I chant, lo! out of death, and out of ooze and slime,
The blossoms rapidly blooming, sympathy, help, love,
From West and East, from South and North and over sea,
Its hot-spurr'd hearts and hands humanity to human aid moves on;
And from within a thought and lesson yet.

Thou ever-darting Globe! through Space and Air!
Thou waters that encompass us!
Thou that in all the life and death of us, in action or in sleep!
Thou laws invisible that permeate them and all,
Thou that in all, and over all, and through and under all, incessant!
Thou! thou! the vital, universal, giant force resistless, sleepless,
    calm,
Holding Humanity as in thy open hand, as some ephemeral toy,
How ill to e'er forget thee!

For I too have forgotten,
(Wrapt in these little potencies of progress, politics, culture, wealth,
    inventions, civilization,)
Have lost my recognition of your silent ever-swaying power, ye
    mighty, elemental throes,
In which and upon which we float, and every one of us is buoy'd.

A PERSIAN LESSON

FOR his o'erarching and last lesson the greybeard sufi,
In the fresh scent of the morning in the open air,

On the slope of a teeming Persian rose-garden,
Under an ancient chestnut-tree wide spreading its branches,
Spoke to the young priests and students.

"Finally my children, to envelop each word, each part of the rest,
Allah is all, all, all—is immanent in every life and object,
May-be at many and many-a-more removes—yet Allah, Allah,
    Allah is there.

"Has the estray wander'd far? Is the reason-why strangely hidden?
Would you sound below the restless ocean of the entire world?
Would you know the dissatisfaction? the urge and spur of every
    life;
The something never still'd—never entirely gone? the invisible need
    of every seed?

"It is the central urge in every atom,
(Often unconscious, often evil, downfallen,)
To return to its divine source and origin, however distant,
Latent the same in subject and in object, without one exception."

THE COMMONPLACE

THE commonplace I sing;
How cheap is health! how cheap nobility!
Abstinence, no falsehood, no gluttony, lust;
The open air I sing, freedom, toleration,
(Take here the mainest lesson—less from books—less from the
    schools,)
The common day and night—the common earth and waters,
Your farm—your work, trade, occupation,
The democratic wisdom underneath, like solid ground for all.

"THE ROUNDED CATALOGUE DIVINE COMPLETE"

[Sunday,___ __ ___.—Went this forenoon to church. A college professor,
Rev. Dr.___, gave us a fine sermon, during which I caught the above words;
but the minister included in his "rounded catalogue" letter and spirit, only the
esthetic things, and entirely ignored what I name in the following:]

The devilish and the dark, the dying and diseas'd,
The countless (nineteen-twentieths) low and evil, crude and savage,
The crazed, prisoners in jail, the horrible, rank, malignant,
Venom and filth, serpents, the ravenous sharks, liars, the dissolute;

(What is the part the wicked and the loathesome bear within earth's
　　orbic scheme?)
Newts, crawling things in slime and mud, poisons,
The barren soil, the evil men, the slag and hideous rot.

MIRAGES

(Noted verbatim after a supper-talk outdoors in Nevada with two old miners.)

MORE experiences and sights, stranger, than you'd think for;
Times again, now mostly just after sunrise or before sunset,
Sometimes in spring, oftener in autumn, perfectly clear weather, in
　　plain sight,
Camps far or near, the crowded streets of cities and the shop-fronts,
(Account for it or not—credit or not—it is all true,
And my mate there could tell you the like—we have often confab'd
　　about it,)
People and scenes, animals, trees, colors and lines, plain as could be,
Farms and dooryards of home, paths border'd with box, lilacs in
　　corners,
Weddings in churches, thanksgiving dinners, returns of long-absent
　　sons,
Glum funerals, the crape-veil'd mother and the daughters,
Trials in courts, jury and judge, the accused in the box,
Contestants, battles, crowds, bridges, wharves,
Now and then mark'd faces of sorrow or joy,
(I could pick them out this moment if I saw them again,)
Show'd to me just aloft to the right in the sky-edge,
Or plainly there to the left on the hill-tops.

L. OF G.'S PURPORT

NOT to exclude or demarcate, or pick out evils from their formid-
　　able masses (even to expose them,)
But add, fuse, complete, extend—and celebrate the immortal and
　　the good.

Haughty this song, its words and scope,
To span vast realms of space and time,
Evolution—the cumulative—growths and generations.

Begun in ripen'd youth and steadily pursued,
Wandering, peering, dallying with all—war, peace, day and night
　　absorbing,

Never even for one brief hour abandoning my task,
I end it here in sickness, poverty, and old age.

I sing of life, yet mind me well of death:
To-day shadowy Death dogs my steps, my seated shape, and has
    for years—
Draws sometimes close to me, as face to face.

THE UNEXPRESS'D

How dare one say it?
After the cycles, poems, singers, plays,
Vaunted Ionia's, India's—Homer, Shakspere—the long, long times'
    thick dotted roads, areas,
The shining clusters and the Milky Ways of stars—Nature's pulses
    reap'd,
All retrospective passions, heroes, war, love, adoration,
All ages' plummets dropt to their utmost depths,
All human lives, throats, wishes, brains—all experiences' utterance;
After the countless songs, or long or short, all tongues, all lands,
Still something not yet told in poesy's voice or print—something
    lacking,
(Who knows? the best yet unexpress'd and lacking.)

GRAND IS THE SEEN

GRAND is the seen, the light, to me—grand are the sky and stars,
Grand is the earth, and grand are lasting time and space,
And grand their laws, so multiform, puzzling, evolutionary;
But grander far the unseen soul of me, comprehending, endowing
    all those,
Lighting the light, the sky and stars, delving the earth, sailing the
    sea,
(What were all those, indeed, without thee, unseen soul? of what
    amount without thee?)
More evolutionary, vast, puzzling, O my soul!
More multiform far—more lasting thou than they.

UNSEEN BUDS

UNSEEN buds, infinite, hidden well,
Under the snow and ice, under the darkness, in every square or
    cubic inch,
Germinal, exquisite, in delicate lace, microscopic, unborn,

Like babes in wombs, latent, folded, compact, sleeping;
Billions of billions, and trillions of trillions of them waiting,
(On earth and in the sea—the universe—the stars there in the
    heavens,)
Urging slowly, surely forward, forming endless,
And waiting ever more, forever more behind.

GOOD-BYE MY FANCY!

GOOD-BYE my Fancy!
Farewell dear mate, dear love!
I'm going away, I know not where,
Or to what fortune, or whether I may ever see you again,
So Good-bye my Fancy.

Now for my last—let me look back a moment;
The slower fainter ticking of the clock is in me,
Exit, nightfall, and soon the heart-thud stopping.

Long have we lived, joy'd, caress'd together;
Delightful!—now separation—Good-bye my Fancy.

Yet let me not be too hasty,
Long indeed have we lived, slept, filter'd, become really blended
    into one;
Then if we die we die together, (yes, we'll remain one,)
If we go anywhere we'll go together to meet what happens,
May-be we'll be better off and blither, and learn something,
May-be it is yourself now really ushering me to the true songs,
    (who knows?)
May-be it is you the mortal knob really undoing, turning—so now
    finally,
Good-bye—and hail! my Fancy.

A Backward Glance O'er Travel'd Roads

PERHAPS the best of songs heard, or of any and all true love, or life's fairest episodes, or sailors', soldiers' trying scenes on land or sea, is the *résumé* of them, or any of them, long afterwards, looking at the actualities away back past, with all their practical excitations gone. How the soul loves to float amid such reminiscences!

So here I sit gossiping in the early candle-light of old age—I and my book—casting backward glances over our travel'd road. After completing, as it were, the journey—(a varied jaunt of years, with many halts and gaps of intervals—or some lengthen'd ship-voyage, wherein more than once the last hour had apparently arrived, and we seem'd certainly going down—yet reaching port in a sufficient way through all discomfitures at last)—After completing my poems, I am curious to review them in the light of their own (at the time unconscious, or mostly unconscious) intentions, with certain unfoldings of the thirty years they seek to embody. These lines, therefore, will probably blend the weft of first purposes and speculations, with the warp of that experience afterwards, always bringing strange developments.

Result of seven or eight stages and struggles extending through nearly thirty years, (as I nigh my three-score-and-ten I live largely on memory,) I look upon "Leaves of Grass," now finish'd to the end of its opportunities and powers, as my definitive *carte visite* to the coming generations of the New World,* if I may assume to say so. That I have not gain'd the acceptance of my own time, but have fallen back on fond dreams of the future—anticipations—("still lives the song, though Regnar dies")—That from a worldly and business point of view "Leaves of Grass" has been worse than a failure—that public criticism on the book and myself as author of

---

* When Champollion, on his death-bed, handed to the printer the revised proof of his "Egyptian Grammar," he said gayly, "Be careful of this—it is my *carte de visite* to posterity."

431

it yet shows mark'd anger and contempt more than anything else—
("I find a solid line of enemies to you everywhere,"—letter from
W. S. K., Boston, May 28, 1884)—And that solely for publishing it
I have been the object of two or three pretty serious special official
buffetings—is all probably no more than I ought to have expected.
I had my choice when I commenc'd. I bid neither for soft eulogies,
big money returns, nor the approbation of existing schools and conventions. As fulfill'd, or partially fulfill'd, the best comfort of the
whole business (after a small band of the dearest friends and up-
holders ever vouchsafed to man or cause—doubtless all the more
faithful and uncompromising—this little phalanx!—for being so
few) is that, unstopp'd and unwarp'd by any influence outside
the soul within me, I have had my say entirely my own way, and
put it unerringly on record—the value thereof to be decided by
time.

In calculating that decision, William O'Connor and Dr. Bucke
are far more peremptory than I am. Behind all else that can be
said, I consider "Leaves of Grass" and its theory experimental—
as, in the deepest sense, I consider our American republic itself to
be, with its theory. (I think I have at least enough philosophy not
to be too absolutely certain of any thing, or any results.) In the
second place, the volume is a *sortie*—whether to prove triumphant,
and conquer its field of aim and escape and construction, nothing
less than a hundred years from now can fully answer. I consider
the point that I have positively gain'd a hearing, to far more than
make up for any and all other lacks and withholdings. Essentially,
that was from the first, and has remain'd throughout, the main
object. Now it seems to be achiev'd, I am certainly contented to
waive any otherwise momentous drawbacks, as of little account.
Candidly and dispassionately reviewing all my intentions, I feel that
they were creditable—and I accept the result, whatever it may be.

After continued personal ambition and effort, as a young fellow,
to enter with the rest into competition for the usual rewards, business, political, literary, &c.—to take part in the great *mèlée*, both
for victory's prize itself and to do some good—After years of those
aims and pursuits, I found myself remaining possess'd, at the age
of thirty-one to thirty-three, with a special desire and conviction.
Or rather, to be quite exact, a desire that had been flitting through
my previous life, or hovering on the flanks, mostly indefinite hitherto,
had steadily advanced to the front, defined itself, and finally dominated everything else. This was a feeling or ambition to articulate
and faithfully express in literary or poetic form, and uncompromisingly, my own physical, emotional, moral, intellectual, and æsthetic

Personality, in the midst of, and tallying, the momentous spirit and facts of its immediate days, and of current America—and to exploit that Personality, identified with place and date, in a far more candid and comprehensive sense than any hitherto poem or book.

Perhaps this is in brief, or suggests, all I have sought to do. Given the Nineteenth Century, with the United States, and what they furnish as area and points of view, "Leaves of Grass" is, or seeks to be, simply a faithful and doubtless self-will'd record. In the midst of all, it gives one man's—the author's—identity, ardors, observations, faiths, and thoughts, color'd hardly at all with any decided coloring from other faiths or other identities. Plenty of songs had been sung—beautiful, matchless songs—adjusted to other lands than these—another spirit and stage of evolution; but I would sing, and leave out or put in, quite solely with reference to America and to-day. Modern science and democracy seem'd to be throwing out their challenge to poetry to put them in its statements in contradistinction to the songs and myths of the past. As I see it now (perhaps too late,) I have unwittingly taken up that challenge and made an attempt at such statements—which I certainly would not assume to do now, knowing more clearly what it means.

For grounds for "Leaves of Grass," as a poem, I abandon'd the conventional themes, which do not appear in it: none of the stock ornamentation, or choice plots of love or war, or high, exceptional personages of Old-World song; nothing, as I may say, for beauty's sake—no legend, or myth, or romance, nor euphemism, nor rhyme. But the broadest average of humanity and its identities in the now ripening Nineteenth Century, and especially in each of their countless examples and practical occupations in the United States to-day.

One main contrast of the ideas behind every page of my verses, compared with establish'd poems, is their different relative attitude towards God, towards the objective universe, and still more (by reflection, confession, assumption, &c.) the quite changed attitude of the ego, the one chanting or talking, towards himself and towards his fellow-humanity. It is certainly time for America, above all, to begin this readjustment in the scope and basic point of view of verse; for everything else has changed. As I write, I see in an article on Wordsworth, in one of the current English magazines, the lines, "A few weeks ago an eminent French critic said that, owing to the special tendency to science and to its all-devouring force, poetry would cease to be read in fifty years." But I anticipate the very contrary. Only a firmer, vastly broader, new era begins to

434

exist—nay, is already form'd—to which the poetic genius must emigrate. Whatever may have been the case in years gone by, the true use for the imaginative faculty of modern times is to give ultimate vivification to facts, to science, and to common lives, endowing them with the glows and glories and final illustriousness which belong to every real thing, and to real things only. Without that ultimate vivification—which the poet or other artist alone can give—reality would seem incomplete, and science, democracy, and life itself, finally in vain.

Few appreciate the moral revolutions, our age, which have been profounder far than the material or inventive or war-produced ones. The Nineteenth Century, now well towards its close (and ripening into fruit the seeds of the two preceding centuries*)—the uprisings of national masses and shiftings of boundary-lines—the historical and other prominent facts of the United States—the war of attempted Secession—the stormy rush and haste of nebulous forces—never can future years witness more excitement and din of action—never completer change of army front along the whole line, the whole civilized world. For all these new and evolutionary facts, meanings, purposes, new poetic messages, new forms and expresons, are inevitable.

My Book and I—what a period we have presumed to span! those thirty years from 1850 to '80—and America in them! Proud, proud indeed may we be, if we have cull'd enough of that period in its own spirit to worthily waft a few live breaths of it to the future!

Let me not dare, here or anywhere, for my own purposes, or any purposes, to attempt the definition of Poetry, nor answer the question what it is. Like Religion, Love, Nature, while those terms are indispensable, and we all give a sufficiently accurate meaning to them, in my opinion no definition that has ever been made sufficiently encloses the name Poetry; nor can any rule or convention ever so absolutely obtain but some great exception may arise and disregard and overturn it.

Also it must be carefully remember'd that first-class literature does not shine by any luminosity of its own; nor do its poems. They grow of circumstances, and are evolutionary. The actual living light is always curiously from elsewhere—follows unaccountable sources, and is lunar and relative at the best. There are, I know,

* The ferment and germination even of the United States to-day, dating back to, and in my opinion mainly founded on, the Elizabethan age in English history, the age of Francis Bacon and Shakspere. Indeed, when we pursue it, what growth or advent is there that does not date back, back, until lost—perhaps its most tantalizing clues lost—in the receded horizons of the past?

certain controlling themes that seem endlessly appropriated to the poets—as war, in the past—in the Bible, religious rapture and adoration—always love, beauty, some fine plot, or pensive or other emotion. But, strange as it may sound at first, I will say there is something striking far deeper and towering far higher than those themes for the best elements of modern song.

Just as all the old imaginative works rest, after their kind, on long trains of presuppositions, often entirely unmention'd by themselves, yet supplying the most important bases of them, and without which they could have had no reason for being, so "Leaves of Grass," before a line was written, presupposed something different from any other, and, as it stands, is the result of such presupposition. I should say, indeed, it were useless to attempt reading the book without first carefully tallying that preparatory background and quality in the mind. Think of the United States to-day—the facts of these thirty-eight or forty empires solder'd in one—sixty or seventy millions of equals, with their lives, their passions, their future—these incalculable, modern, American, seething multitudes around us, of which we are inseparable parts! Think, in comparison, of the petty environage and limited area of the poets of past or present Europe, no matter how great their genius. Think of the absence and ignorance, in all cases hitherto, of the multitudinous-ness, vitality, and the unprecedented stimulants of to-day and here. It almost seems as if a poetry with cosmic and dynamic features of magnitude and limitlessness suitable to the human soul, were never possible before. It is certain that a poetry of absolute faith and equality for the use of the democratic masses never was.

In estimating first-class song, a sufficient Nationality, or, on the other hand, what may be call'd the negative and lack of it, (as in Goethe's case, it sometimes seems to me,) is often, if not always, the first element. One needs only a little penetration to see, at more or less removes, the material facts of their country and radius, with the coloring of the moods of humanity at the time, and its gloomy or hopeful prospects, behind all poets and each poet, and forming their birth-marks. I know very well that my "Leaves" could not possibly have emerged or been fashion'd or completed, from any other era than the latter half of the Nineteenth Century, nor any other land than democratic America, and from the absolute triumph of the National Union arms.

And whether my friends claim it for me or not, I know well enough, too, that in respect to pictorial talent, dramatic situations, and especially in verbal melody and all the conventional technique of poetry, not only the divine works that to-day stand ahead in the world's reading, but dozens more, transcend (some of them immeasurably transcend) all I have done, or could do. But it seem'd to me, as the objects in Nature, the themes of æstheticism, and all special exploitations of the mind and soul, involve not only their own inherent quality, but the quality, just as inherent and important, of *their point of view*,* the time had come to reflect all themes and things, old and new, in the lights thrown on them by the advent of America and democracy—to chant those themes through the utterance of one, not only the grateful and reverent legatee of the past, but the born child of the New World—to illustrate all through the genesis and ensemble of to-day; and that such illustration and ensemble are the chief demands of America's prospective imaginative literature. Not to carry out, in the approved style, some choice plot of fortune or misfortune, or fancy, or fine thoughts, or incidents, or courtesies—all of which has been done overwhelmingly and well, probably never to be excell'd—but that while in such æsthetic presentation of objects, passions, plots, thoughts, &c., our lands and days do not want, and probably will never have, anything better than they already possess from the bequests of the past, it still remains to be said that there is even towards all those a subjective and contemporary point of view appropriate to ourselves alone, and to our new genius and environments, different from anything hitherto; and that such conception of current or gone-by life and art is for us the only means of their assimilation consistent with the Western world.

Indeed, and anyhow, to put it specifically, has not the time arrived when, (if it must be plainly said, for democratic America's sake, if for no other) there must imperatively come a readjustment of the whole theory and nature of Poetry? The question is important, and I may turn the argument over and repeat it: Does not the best thought of our day and Republic conceive of a birth and spirit of song superior to anything past or present? To the effectual and moral consolidation of our lands (already, as materially establish'd, the greatest factors in known history, and far, far greater through what they prelude and necessitate, and are to be in future)—to conform with and build on the concrete realities and theories of the universe furnish'd by science, and henceforth the only irrefragable basis for anything, verse included—to root both influences in the emotional and imaginative action of the modern time, and dominate all that precedes or opposes them—is not either a radical advance and step forward, or a new verteber of the best song indispensable?

* According to Immanuel Kant, the last essential reality, giving shape and significance to all the rest.

The New World receives with joy the poems of the antique, with European feudalism's rich fund of epics, plays, ballads—seeks not in the least to deaden or displace those voices from our ear and area —holds them indeed as indispensable studies, influences, records, comparisons. But though the dawn-dazzle of the sun of literature is in those poems for us of to-day—though perhaps the best parts of current character in nations, social groups, or any man's or woman's individuality, Old World or New, are from them—and though if I were ask'd to name the most precious bequest to current American civilization from all the hitherto ages, I am not sure but I would name those old and less old songs ferried hither from east and west—some serious words and debits remain; some acrid considerations demand a hearing. Of the great poems receiv'd from abroad and from the ages, and to-day enveloping and penetrating America, is there one that is consistent with these United States, or essentially applicable to them as they are and are to be? Is there one whose underlying basis is not a denial and insult to democracy? What a comment it forms, anyhow, on this era of literary fulfilment, with the splendid day-rise of science and resuscitation of history, that our chief religious and poetical works are not our own, nor adapted to our light, but have been furnish'd by far-back ages out of their arriere and darkness, or, at most, twilight dimness! What is there in those works that so imperiously and scornfully dominates all our advanced civilization, and culture?

Even Shakspere, who so suffuses current letters and art (which indeed have in most degrees grown out of him,) belongs essentially to the buried past. Only he holds the proud distinction for certain important phases of that past, of being the loftiest of the singers life has yet given voice to. All, however, relate to and rest upon conditions, standards, politics, sociologies, ranges of belief, that have been quite eliminated from the Eastern hemisphere, and never existed at all in the Western. As authoritative types of song they belong in America just about as much as the persons and institutes they depict. True, it may be said, the emotional, moral, and æsthetic natures of humanity have not radically changed—that in these old poems apply to our times and all times, irrespective of date; and that they are of incalculable value as pictures of the past. I willingly make those admissions, and to their fullest extent; then advance the points herewith as of serious, even paramount importance.

I have indeed put on record elsewhere my reverence and eulogy for those never-to-be-excell'd poetic bequests, and their indescribable preciousness as heirlooms for America. Another and separate point must now be candidly stated. If I had not stood before those poems with uncover'd head, fully aware of their colossal grandeur and beauty of form and spirit, I could not have written "Leaves of Grass." My verdict and conclusions as illustrated in its pages are arrived at through the temper and inculcation of the old works as much as through anything else—perhaps more than through anything else. As America fully and fairly construed is the legitimate result and evolutionary outcome of the past, so I would dare to claim for my verse. Without stopping to qualify the averment, the Old World has had the poems of myths, fictions, feudalism, conquest, caste, dynastic wars, and splendid exceptional characters and affairs, which have been great; but the New World needs the poems of realities and science and of the democratic average and basic equality, which shall be greater. In the centre of all, and object of all, stands the Human Being, towards whose heroic and spiritual evolution poems and everything directly or indirectly tend, Old World or New.

Continuing the subject, my friends have more than once suggested—or may be the garrulity of advancing age is possessing me—some further embryonic facts of "Leaves of Grass," and especially how I enter'd upon them. Dr. Bucke has, in his volume, already fully and fairly described the preparation of my poetic field, with the particular and general plowing, planting, seeding, and occupation of the ground, till everything was fertilized, rooted, and ready to start its own way for good or bad. Not till after all this, did I attempt any serious acquaintance with poetic literature. Along in my sixteenth year I had become possessor of a stout, well-cramm'd one thousand page octavo volume (I have it yet,) containing Walter Scott's poetry entire—an inexhaustible mine and treasury of poetic forage (especially the endless forests and jungles of notes)—has been so to me for fifty years, and remains so to this day.*

Later, at intervals, summers and falls, I used to go off, sometimes for a week at a stretch, down in the country, or to Long Island's seashores—there, in the presence of outdoor influences, I went over

---

*Sir Walter Scott's COMPLETE POEMS; especially including BORDER MINSTRELSY; then Sir Tristrem; Lay of the Last Minstrel; Ballads from the German; Marmion; Lady of the Lake; Vision of Don Roderick; Lord of the Isles; Rokeby; Bridal of Triermain; Field of Waterloo; Harold the Dauntless; all the Dramas; various Introductions, endless interesting Notes, and Essays on Poetry, Romance, &c.

Lockhart's 1833 (or '34) edition with Scott's latest and copious revisions and annotations. (All the poems were thoroughly read by me, but the ballads of the Border Minstrelsy over and over again.)

thoroughly the Old and New Testaments, and absorb'd (probably to better advantage for me than in any library or indoor room—it makes such difference *where* you read,) Shakspere, Ossian, the best translated versions I could get of Homer, Eschylus, Sophocles, the old German Nibelungen, the ancient Hindoo poems, and one or two other masterpieces, Dante's among them. As it happen'd, I read the latter mostly in an old wood. The Iliad (Buckley's prose version,) I read first thoroughly on the peninsula of Orient, northeast end of Long Island, in a shelter'd hollow of rocks and sand, with the sea on each side. (I have wonder'd since why I was not overwhelm'd by those mighty masters. Likely because I read them, as described, in the full presence of Nature, under the sun, with the far-spreading landscape and vistas, or the sea rolling in.)

Toward the last I had among much else look'd over Edgar Poe's poems—of which I was not an admirer, tho' I always saw that beyond their limited range of melody (like perpetual chimes of music bells, ringing from lower *b* flat up to *g*) they were melodious expressions, and perhaps never excell'd ones, of certain pronounc'd phases of human morbidity. (The Poetic area is very spacious—has room for all—has so many mansions!) But I was repaid in Poe's prose by the idea that (at any rate for our occasions, our day) there can be no such thing as a long poem. The same thought had been haunting my mind before, but Poe's argument, though short, work'd the sum out and proved it to me.

Another point had an early settlement, clearing the ground greatly. I saw, from the time my enterprise and questionings positively shaped themselves (how best can I express my own distinctive era and surroundings, America, Democracy?) that the trunk and centre whence the answer was to radiate, and to which all should return from straying however far a distance, must be an identical body and soul, a personality—which personality, after many considerations and ponderings I deliberately settled should be myself—indeed could not be any other. I also felt strongly (whether I have shown it or not) that to the true and full estimate of the Present both the Past and the Future are main considerations.

These, however, and much more might have gone on and come to naught (almost positively would have come to naught,) if a sudden, vast, terrible, direct and indirect stimulus for new and national declamatory expression had not been given to me. It is certain, I say, that, although I had made a start before, only from the occurrence of the Secession War, and what it show'd me as by flashes of lightning, with the emotional depths it sounded and arous'd (of course, I don't mean in my own heart only, I saw it just as plainly in others, in millions)—that only from the strong flare and provocation of that war's sights and scenes the final reasons-for-being of an autochthonic and passionate song definitely came forth.

I went down to the war fields in Virginia (end of 1862), lived thenceforward in camp—saw great battles and the days and nights afterward—partook of all the fluctuations, gloom, despair, hopes again arous'd, courage evoked—death readily risk'd—*the cause,* too—along and filling those agonistic and lurid following years, 1863–'64–'65—the real parturition years (more than 1776–'83) of this henceforth homogeneous Union. Without those three or four years and the experiences they gave, "Leaves of Grass" would not now be existing.

But I set out with the intention also of indicating or hinting some point-characteristics which I since see (though I did not then, at least not definitely) were bases and object-urgings toward those "Leaves" from the first. The word I myself put primarily for the description of them as they stand at last, is the word Suggestiveness. I round and finish little, if anything; and could not, consistently with my scheme. The reader will always have his or her part to do, just as much as I have had mine. I seek less to state or display any theme or thought, and more to bring you, reader, into the atmosphere of the theme or thought—there to pursue your own flight. Another impetus-word is Comradeship as for all lands, and in a more commanding and acknowledg'd sense than hitherto. Other word-signs would be Good Cheer, Content, and Hope.

The chief trait of any given poet is always the spirit he brings to the observation of Humanity and Nature—the mood out of which he contemplates his subjects. What kind of temper and what amount of faith report these things? Up to how recent a date is the song carried? What the equipment, and special raciness of the singer—what his tinge of coloring? The last value of artistic ex-pressers, past and present—Greek æsthetes, Shakspere—or in our own day Tennyson, Victor Hugo, Carlyle, Emerson—is certainly involv'd in such questions. I say the profoundest service that poems or any other writings can do for their reader is not merely to satisfy the intellect, or supply something polish'd and interesting, nor even to depict great passions, or persons or events, but to fill him with vigorous and clean manliness, religiousness, and give him *good heart* as a radical possession and habit. The educated world seems to have been growing more and more ennuyed for ages, leaving to our time the inheritance of it all. Fortunately there is the original inexhaustible fund of buoyancy, normally resident in the race, forever eligible to be appeal'd to and relied on.

As for native American individuality, though certain to come, and on a large scale, the distinctive and ideal type of Western character (as consistent with the operative political and even money-making features of United States' humanity in the Nineteenth Century as chosen knights, gentlemen and warriors were the ideals of the centuries of European feudalism) it has not yet appear'd. I have allow'd the stress of my poems from beginning to end to bear upon American individuality and assist it—not only because that is a great lesson in Nature, amid all her generalizing laws, but as counterpoise to the leveling tendencies of Democracy—and for other reasons. Defiant of ostensible literary and other conventions, I avowedly chant "the great pride of man in himself," and permit it to be more or less a *motif* of nearly all my verse. I think this pride indispensable to an American. I think it not inconsistent with obedience, humility, deference, and self-questioning.

Democracy has been so retarded and jeopardized by powerful personalities, that its first instincts are fain to clip, conform, bring in stragglers, and reduce everything to a dead level. While the ambitious thought of my song is to help the forming of a great aggregate Nation, it is, perhaps, altogether through the forming of myriads of fully develop'd and enclosing individuals. Welcome as are equality's and fraternity's doctrines and popular education, a certain liability accompanies them all, as we see. That primal and interior something in man, in his soul's abysms, coloring all, and, by exceptional fruitions, giving the last majesty to him—something continually touch'd upon and attain'd by the old poems and ballads of feudalism, and often the principal foundation of them—modern science and democracy appear to be endangering, perhaps eliminating. But that forms an appearance only; the reality is quite different. The new influences, upon the whole, are surely preparing the way for grander individualities than ever. To-day and here personal force is behind everything, just the same. The times and depictions from the Iliad to Shakspere inclusive can happily never again be realized—but the elements of courageous and lofty manhood are unchanged.

Without yielding an inch the working-man and working-woman were to be in my pages from first to last. The ranges of heroism and loftiness with which Greek and feudal poets endow'd their god-like or lordly born characters—indeed prouder and better based and with fuller ranges than those—I was to endow the democratic averages of America. I was to show that we, here and to-day, are eligible to the grandest and the best—more eligible now than any times of old were. I will also want my utterances (I said to myself before beginning) to be in spirit the poems of the morning. (They have been founded and mainly written in the sunny forenoon and early midday of my life.) I will want them to be the poems of women entirely as much as men. I have wish'd to put the complete Union of the States in my songs without any preference or partiality whatever. Henceforth, if they live and are read, it must be just as much South as North—just as much along the Pacific as Atlantic— in the valley of the Mississippi, in Canada, up in Maine, down in Texas, and on the shores of Puget Sound.

From another point of view "Leaves of Grass" is avowedly the song of Sex and Amativeness, and even Animality—though meanings that do not usually go along with those words are behind all, and will duly emerge; and all are sought to be lifted into a different light and atmosphere. Of this feature, intentionally palpable in a few lines, I shall only say the espousing principle of those lines so gives breath of life to my whole scheme that the bulk of the pieces might as well have been left unwritten were those lines omitted. Difficult as it will be, it has become, in my opinion, imperative to achieve a shifted attitude from superior men and women towards the thought and fact of sexuality, as an element in character, personality, the emotions, and a theme in literature. I am not going to argue the question by itself; it does not stand by itself. The vitality of it is altogether in its relations, bearings, significance—like the clef of a symphony. At last analogy the lines I allude to, and the spirit in which they are spoken, permeate all "Leaves of Grass," and the work must stand or fall with them, as the human body and soul must remain as an entirety.

Universal as are certain facts and symptoms of communities or individuals all times, there is nothing so rare in modern conventions and poetry as their normal recognizance. Literature is always calling in the doctor for consultation and confession, and always giving evasions and swathing suppressions in place of that "heroic nudity"* on which only a genuine diagnosis of serious cases can be built. And in respect to editions of "Leaves of Grass" in time to come (if there should be such) I take occasion now to confirm those lines with the settled convictions and deliberate renewals of thirty years, and to hereby prohibit, as far as word of mine can do so, any elision of them.

Then still a purpose enclosing all, and over and beneath all.

---

*"Nineteenth Century," July, 1883.

Ever since what might be call'd thought, or the budding of thought, fairly began in my youthful mind, I had had a desire to attempt some worthy record of that entire faith and acceptance ("to justify the ways of God to man" is Milton's well-known and ambitious phrase) which is the foundation of moral America. I felt it all as positively then in my young days as I do now in my old ones; to formulate a poem whose every thought or fact should directly or indirectly be or connive at an implicit belief in the wisdom, health, mystery, beauty of every process, every concrete object, every human or other existence, not only consider'd from the point of view of all, but of each.

While I can not understand it or argue it out, I fully believe in a clue and purpose in Nature, entire and several; and that invisible spiritual results, just as real and definite as the visible, eventuate all concrete life and all materialism, through Time. My book ought to emanate buoyancy and gladness legitimately enough, for it was grown out of those elements, and has been the comfort of my life since it was originally commenced.

One main genesis-motive of the "Leaves" was my conviction (just as strong to-day as ever) that the crowning growth of the United States is to be spiritual and heroic. To help start and favor that growth—or even to call attention to it, or the need of it—is the beginning, middle and final purpose of the poems. (In fact, when really cipher'd out and summ'd to the last, plowing up in earnest the interminable average fallows of humanity—not "good government" merely, in the common sense—is the justification and main purpose of these United States.)

Isolated advantages in any rank or grace or fortune—the direct or indirect threads of all the poetry of the past—are in my opinion distasteful to the republican genius, and offer no foundation for its fitting verse. Establish'd poems, I know, have the very great advantage of chanting the already perform'd, so full of glories, reminiscences dear to the minds of men. But my volume is a candidate for the future. "All original art," says Taine, anyhow, "is self-regulated, and no original art can be regulated from without; it carries its own counterpoise, and does not receive it from elsewhere—lives on its own blood"—a solace to my frequent bruises and sulky vanity.

As the present is perhaps mainly an attempt at personal statement or illustration, I will allow myself as further help to extract the following anecdote from a book, "Annals of Old Painters," conn'd by me in youth. Rubens, the Flemish painter, in one of his wanderings through the galleries of old convents, came across a singular work. After looking at it thoughtfully for a good while, and listening to the criticisms of his suite of students, he said to the latter, in answer to their questions (as to what school the work implied or belong'd,) "I do not believe the artist, unknown and perhaps no longer living, who has given the world this legacy, ever belong'd to any school, or ever painted anything but this one picture, which is a personal affair—a piece out of a man's life."

"Leaves of Grass" indeed (I cannot too often reiterate) has mainly been the outcropping of my own emotional and other personal nature—an attempt, from first to last, to put *a Person*, a human being (myself, in the latter half of the Nineteenth Century, in America,) freely, fully and truly on record. I could not find any similar personal record in current literature that satisfied me. But it is not on "Leaves of Grass" distinctively as *literature*, or a specimen thereof, that I feel to dwell, or advance claims. No one will get at my verses who insists upon viewing them as a literary performance, or attempt at such performance, or as aiming mainly toward art or æstheticism.

I say no land or people or circumstances ever existed so needing a race of singers and poems differing from all others, and rigidly their own, as the land and people and circumstances of our United States need such singers and poems to–day, and for the future. Still further, as long as the States continue to absorb and be dominated by the poetry of the Old World, and remain unsupplied with autochthonous song, to express, vitalize and give color to and define their material and political success, and minister to them distinctively, so long will they stop short of first–class Nationality and remain defective.

In the free evening of my day I give to you, reader, the foregoing garrulous talk, thoughts, reminiscences,

> As idly drifting down the ebb,
> Such ripples, half-caught voices, echo from the shore.

Concluding with two items for the imaginative genius of the West, when it worthily rises—First, what Herder taught to the young Goethe, that really great poetry is always (like the Homeric or Biblical canticles) the result of a national spirit, and not the privilege of a polish'd and select few; Second, that the strongest and sweetest songs yet remain to be sung.

EPILOGUE: Whitman's Last Completed Poem.

A THOUGHT OF COLUMBUS

THE mystery of mysteries, the crude and hurried ceaseless flame,
    spontaneous, bearing on itself.
The bubble and the huge, round, concrete orb!
A breath of Deity, as thence the bulging universe unfolding!
The many issuing cycles from their precedent minute!
The eras of the soul incepting in an hour,
Haply the widest, farthest evolutions of the world and man.

Thousands and thousands of miles hence, and now four centuries
    back,
A mortal impulse thrilling its brain cell,
Reck'd or unreck'd, the birth can no longer be postpon'd:
A phantom of the moment, mystic, stalking, sudden,
Only a silent thought, yet toppling down of more than walls of
    brass or stone.
(A flutter at the darkness' edge as if old Time's and Space's secret
    near revealing.)
A thought! a definite thought works out in shape.
Four hundred years roll on.
The rapid cumulus—trade, navigation, war, peace, democracy, roll
    on;
The restless armies and the fleets of time following their leader—
    the old camps of ages pitch'd in newer, larger areas,
The tangl'd, long-deferr'd eclaircissement of human life and hopes
    bodly begins untying,
As here to-day up-grows the Western World.

(An added word yet to my song, far Discoverer, as ne'er before
    sent back to son of earth—
If still thou hearest, hear me,
Voicing as now—lands, races, arts, bravas to thee,

O'er the long backward path to thee—one vast consensus, north
    south, east, west,
Soul plaudits! acclamation! reverent echoes!
One manifold, huge memory to thee! oceans and lands!
The modern world to thee and thought of thee!)

❦ Selected Prose

Preface, 1855

AMERICA does not repel the past or what it has produced under its forms or amid other politics or the idea of castes or the old religions . . . . accepts the lesson with calmness . . . is not so impatient as has been supposed that the slough still sticks to opinions and manners and literature while the life which served its requirements has passed into the new life of the new forms . . . perceives that the corpse is slowly borne from the eating and sleeping rooms of the house . . . perceives that it waits a little while in the door . . . that it was fittest for its days . . . that its action has descended to the stalwart and wellshaped heir who approaches . . . and that he shall be fittest for his days.

The Americans of all nations at any time upon the earth have probably the fullest poetical nature. The United States themselves are essentially the greatest poem. In the history of the earth hitherto the largest and most stirring appear tame and orderly to their ampler largeness and stir. Here at last is something in the doings of man that corresponds with the broadcast doings of the day and night. Here is not merely a nation but a teeming nation of nations. Here is action untied from strings necessarily blind to particulars and details magnificently moving in vast masses. Here is the hospitality which forever indicates heroes . . . . Here are the roughs and beards and space and ruggedness and nonchalance that the soul loves. Here the performance disdaining the trivial unapproached in the tremendous audacity of its crowds and groupings and the push of its perspective spreads with crampless and flowing breadth and showers its prolific and splendid extravagance. One sees it must indeed own the riches of the summer and winter, and need never be bankrupt while corn grows from the ground or the orchards drop apples or the bays contain fish or men beget children upon women.

Other states indicate themselves in their deputies . . . . but the

genius of the United States is not best or most in its executives or
legislatures, nor in its ambassadors or authors or colleges or churches
or parlors, nor even in its newspapers or inventors . . . but always
most in the common people. Their manners speech dress friendships
—the freshness and candor of their physiognomy—the picturesque
looseness of their carriage . . . their deathless attachment to freedom
—their aversion to anything indecorous or soft or mean—the
practical acknowledgment of the citizens of one state by the citizens
of all other states—the fierceness of their roused resentment—their
curiosity and welcome of novelty—their self-esteem and wonderful
sympathy—their susceptibility to a slight—the air they have of
persons who never knew how it felt to stand in the presence of
superiors—the fluency of their speech—their delight in music, the
sure symptom of manly tenderness and native elegance of soul . . .
their good temper and openhandedness—the terrible significance of
their elections—the President's taking off his hat to them not they
to him—these too are unrhymed poetry. It awaits the gigantic and
generous treatment worthy of it.

The largeness of nature or the nation were monstrous without a
corresponding largeness and generosity of the spirit of the citizen.
Not nature nor swarming states nor streets and steamships nor
prosperous business nor farms nor capital nor learning may suffice
for the ideal of man . . . nor suffice the poet. No reminiscences may
suffice either. A live nation can always cut a deep mark and can
have the best authority the cheapest . . . namely from its own soul.
This is the sum of the profitable uses of individuals or states and of
present action and grandeur and of the subjects of poets.—As if it
were necessary to trot back generation after generation to the eastern
records! As if the beauty and sacredness of the demonstrable must
fall behind that of the mythical! As if men do not make their mark
out of any times! As if the opening of the western continent by discovery and what has transpired since in North and South America
were less than the small theatre of the antique or the aimless sleep-
walking of the middle ages! The pride of the United States leaves
the wealth and finesse of the cities and all returns of commerce and
agriculture and all the magnitude of geography or shows of exterior
victory to enjoy the breed of fullsized men or one fullsized man
unconquerable and simple.

The American poets are to enclose old and new for America is
the race of races. Of them a bard is to be commensurate with a
people. To him the other continents arrive as contributions . . . he
gives them reception for their sake and his own sake. His spirit
responds to his country's spirit . . . . he incarnates its geography and

natural life and rivers and lakes. Mississippi with annual freshets and changing chutes, Missouri and Columbia and Ohio and Saint Lawrence with the falls and beautiful masculine Hudson, do not embouchure where they spend themselves more than they embouchure into him. The blue breadth over the inland sea of Virginia and Maryland and the sea off Massachusetts and Maine and over Manhattan bay and over Champlain and Erie and over Ontario and Huron and Michigan and Superior, and over the Texan and Mexican and Floridian and Cuban seas and over the seas off California and Oregon, is not tallied by the blue breadth of the waters below more than the breadth of above and below is tallied by him. When the long Atlantic coast stretches longer and the Pacific coast stretches longer he easily stretches with them north or south. He spans between them also from east to west and reflects what is between them. On him rise solid growths that offset the growths of pine and cedar and hemlock and liveoak and locust and chestnut and cypress and hickory and limetree and cottonwood and tuliptree and cactus and wildvine and tamarind and persimmon . . . . and tangles as tangled as any canebrake or swamp . . . . and forests coated with transparent ice and icicles hanging from the boughs and crackling in the wind . . . . and sides and peaks of mountains . . . . and pasturage sweet and free as savannah or upland or prairie . . . . with flights and songs and screams that answer those of the wild-pigeon and highhold and orchard-oriole and coot and surf-duck and redshouldered-hawk and fish-hawk and white-ibis and indian-hen and cat-owl and water-pheasant and qua-bird and pied-sheldrake and blackbird and mockingbird and buzzard and condor and night-heron and eagle. To him the hereditary countenance descends both mother's and father's. To him enter the essences of the real things and past and present events—of the enormous diversity of temperature and agriculture and mines—the tribes of red aborigines —the weatherbeaten vessels entering new ports or making landings on rocky coasts—the first settlements north or south—the rapid stature and muscle—the haughty defiance of '76, and the war and peace and formation of the constitution . . . . the union always surrounded by blatherers and always calm and impregnable—the perpetual coming of immigrants—the wharf hem'd cities and superior marine—the unsurveyed interior—the loghouses and clearings and wild animals and hunters and trappers . . . . the free commerce— the fisheries and whaling and gold-digging—the endless gestation of new states—the convening of Congress every December, the members duly coming up from all climates and the uttermost parts . . . . the noble character of the young mechanics and of all

free American workmen and workwomen . . . . the general ardor and
friendliness and enterprise—the perfect equality of the female with
the male . . . . the large amativeness—the fluid movement of the
population—the factories and mercantile life and laborsaving
machinery—the Yankee swap—the New-York firemen and the target
excursion—the southern plantation life—the character of the northeast and of the northwest and southwest—slavery and the tremulous
spreading of hands to protect it, and the stern opposition to it
which shall never cease till it ceases or the speaking of tongues and
the moving of lips cease. For such the expression of the American
poet is to be transcendant and new. It is to be indirect and not direct
or descriptive or epic. Its quality goes through these to much more.
Let the age and wars of other nations be chanted and their eras and
characters be illustrated and that finish the verse. Not so the great
psalm of the republic. Here the theme is creative and has vista.
Here comes one among the wellbeloved stonecutters and plans with
decision and science and sees the solid and beautiful forms of the
future where there are now no solid forms.

Of all nations the United States with veins full of poetical stuff
most need poets and will doubtless have the greatest and use them
the greatest. Their Presidents shall not be their common referee so
much as their poets shall. Of all mankind the great poet is the equable
man. Not in him but off from him things are grotesque or eccentric
or fail of their sanity. Nothing out of its place is good and nothing
in its place is bad. He bestows on every object or quality its fit proportions neither more nor less. He is the arbiter of the diverse and
he is the key. He is the equalizer of his age and land . . . . he supplies
what wants supplying and checks what wants checking. If peace is
the routine out of him speaks the spirit of peace, large, rich, thrifty,
building vast and populous cities, encouraging agriculture and the
arts and commerce—lighting the study of man, the soul, immortality
—federal, state or municipal government, marriage, health, free-
trade, intertravel by land and sea . . . . nothing too close, nothing too
far off . . . the stars not too far off. In war he is the most deadly force
of the war. Who recruits him recruits horse and foot . . . he fetches
parks of artillery the best that engineer ever knew. If the time becomes slothful and heavy he knows how to arouse it . . . he can make
every word he speaks draw blood. Whatever stagnates in the flat
of custom or obedience or legislation he never stagnates. Obedience
does not master him, he masters it. High up out of reach he stands
turning a concentrated light . . . he turns the pivot with his finger . . .
he baffles the swiftest runners as he stands and easily overtakes and
envelops them. The time straying toward infidelity and confections

and persiflage he withholds by his steady faith . . . he spreads out
his dishes . . . he offers the sweet firmfibred meat that grows men and
women. His brain is the ultimate brain. He is no arguer . . . he is
judgment. He judges not as the judge judges but as the sun falling
around a helpless thing. As he sees the farthest he has the most
faith. His thoughts are the hymns of the praise of things. In the
talk on the soul and eternity and God off of his equal plane he is
silent. He sees eternity less like a play with a prologue and denouement . . . . he sees eternity in men and women . . . he does not
see men and women as dreams or dots. Faith is the antiseptic of the
soul . . . it pervades the common people and preserves them . . . they
never give up believing and expecting and trusting. There is that
indescribable freshness and unconsciousness about an illiterate person that humbles and mocks the power of the noblest expressive
genius. The poet sees for a certainty how one not a great artist may
be just as sacred and perfect as the greatest artist. . . . . .The power
to destroy or remould is freely used by him but never the power of
attack. What is past is past. If he does not expose superior models
and prove himself by every step he takes he is not what is wanted.
The presence of the greatest poet conquers . . . not parleying
or struggling or any prepared attempts. Now he has passed that
way see after him! there is not left any vestige of despair or misan-
thropy or cunning or exclusiveness or the ignominy of a nativity
or color or delusion of hell or the necessity of hell . . . . . and no
man thenceforward shall be degraded for ignorance or weakness
or sin.

The greatest poet hardly knows pettiness or triviality. If he breathes
into any thing that was before thought small it dilates with the grandeur and life of the universe. He is a seer . . . . he is individual . . .
he is complete in himself . . . . the others are as good as he, only he
sees it and they do not. He is not one of the chorus . . . . he does not
stop for any regulation . . . he is the president of regulation. What
the eyesight does to the rest he does to the rest. Who knows the
curious mystery of the eyesight? The other senses corroborate
themselves, but this is removed from any proof but its own and
foreruns the identities of the spiritual world. A single glance of it
mocks all the investigations of man and all the instruments and books
of the earth and all reasoning. What is marvellous? what is unlikely?
what is impossible or baseless or vague? after you have once just
opened the space of a peachpit and given audience to far and near
and to the sunset and had all things enter with electric swiftness
softly and duly without confusion or jostling or jam.

The land and sea, the animals fishes and birds, the sky of heaven

and the orbs, the forests mountains and rivers, are not small themes
. . . but folks expect of the poet to indicate more than the beauty and
dignity which always attach to dumb real objects . . . . they expect
him to indicate the path between reality and their souls. Men and
women perceive the beauty well enough . . probably as well as he.
The passionate tenacity of hunters, woodmen, early risers, cultivators
of gardens and orchards and fields, the love of healthy women for
the manly form, seafaring persons, drivers of horses, the passion for
light and the open air, all is an old varied sign of the unfailing perception of beauty and of a residence of the poetic in outdoor people.
They can never be assisted by poets to perceive . . . some may but they
never can. The poetic quality is not marshalled in rhyme or uniformity or abstract addresses to things nor in melancholy complaints
or good precepts, but is the life of these and much else and is in the
soul. The profit of rhyme is that it drops seeds of a sweeter and more
luxuriant rhyme, and of uniformity that it conveys itself into its own
roots in the ground out of sight. The rhyme and uniformity of perfect
poems show the free growth of metrical laws and bud from them as
unerringly and loosely as lilacs or roses on a bush, and take shapes as
compact as the shapes of chestnuts and oranges and melons and
pears, and shed the perfume impalpable to form. The fluency and
ornaments of the finest poems or music or orations or recitations
are not independent but dependent. All beauty comes from beautiful
blood and a beautiful brain. If the greatnesses are in conjunction
in a man or woman it is enough . . . . the fact will prevail through the
universe . . . . but the gaggery and gilt of a million years will not
prevail. Who troubles himself about his ornaments or fluency is lost.
This is what you shall do: Love the earth and sun and the animals,
despise riches, give alms to every one that asks, stand up for the
stupid and crazy, devote your income and labor to others, hate
tyrants, argue not concerning God, have patience and indulgence
toward the people, take off your hat to nothing known or unknown
or to any man or number of men, go freely with powerful uneducated
persons and with the young and with the mothers of families, read
these leaves in the open air every season of every year of your life,
reexamine all you have been told at school or church or in any book,
dismiss whatever insults your own soul, and your very flesh shall
be a great poem and have the richest fluency not only in its words
but in the silent lines of its lips and face and between the lashes of
your eyes and in every motion and joint of your body. . . . . . . The
poet shall not spend his time in unneeded work. He shall know that
the ground is always ready ploughed and manured . . . . others
may not know it but he shall. He shall go directly to the creation.

His trust shall master the trust of everything he touches . . . . and shall master all attachment.

The known universe has one complete lover and that is the greatest poet. He consumes an eternal passion and is indifferent which chance happens and which possible contingency of fortune or misfortune and persuades daily and hourly his delicious pay. What balks or breaks others is fuel for his burning progress to contact and amorous joy. Other proportions of the reception of pleasure dwindle to nothing to his proportions. All expected from heaven or from the highest he is rapport with in the sight of the daybreak or a scene of the winter woods or the presence of children playing or with his arm round the neck of a man or woman. His love above all love has leisure and expanse . . . . he leaves room ahead of himself. He is no irresolute or suspicious lover . . . he is sure . . . he scorns intervals. His experience and the showers and thrills are not for nothing. Nothing can jar him . . . . suffering and darkness cannot—death and fear cannot. To him complaint and jealousy and envy are corpses buried and rotten in the earth . . . . he saw them buried. The sea is not surer of the shore or the shore of the sea than he is of the fruition of his love and of all perfection and beauty.

The fruition of beauty is no chance of hit or miss . . . it is inevitable as life . . . . it is exact and plumb as gravitation. From the eyesight proceeds another eyesight and from the hearing proceeds another hearing and from the voice proceeds another voice eternally curious of the harmony of things with man. To these respond perfections not only in the committees that were supposed to stand for the rest but in the rest themselves just the same. These understand the law of perfection in masses and floods . . . that its finish is to each for itself and onward from itself . . . that it is profuse and impartial . . . that there is not a minute of the light or dark nor an acre of the earth or sea without it—nor any direction of the sky nor any trade or employment nor, any turn of events. This is the reason that about the proper expression of beauty there is precision and balance . . . one part does not need to be thrust above another. The best singer is not the one who has the most lithe and powerful organ . . . the pleasure of poems is not in them that take the handsomest measure and similes and sound.

Without effort and without exposing in the least how it is done the greatest poet brings the spirit of any or all events and passions and scenes and persons some more and some less to bear on your individual character as you hear or read. To do this well is to compete with the laws that pursue and follow time. What is the purpose must surely be there and the clue of it must be there . . . . and the faintest indication is the indication of the best and then becomes the clearest indication. Past and present and future are not disjoined but joined. The greatest poet forms the consistence of what is to be from what has been and is. He drags the dead out of their coffins and stands them again on their feet . . . . he says to the past, Rise and walk before me that I may realize you. He learns the lesson . . . . he places himself where the future becomes present. The greatest poet does not only dazzle his rays over character and scenes and passions . . . he finally ascends and finishes all . . . he exhibits the pinnacles that no man can tell what they are for or what is beyond . . . . he glows a moment on the extremest verge. He is most wonderful in his last half-hidden smile or frown . . . by that flash of the moment of parting the one that sees it shall be encouraged or terrified afterward for many years. The greatest poet does not moralize or make applications of morals . . . he knows the soul. The soul has that measureless pride which consists in never acknowledging any lessons but its own. But it has sympathy as measureless as its pride and the one balances the other and neither can stretch too far while it stretches in company with the other. The inmost secrets of art sleep with the twain. The greatest poet has lain close betwixt both and they are vital in his style and thoughts.

The art of art, the glory of expression and the sunshine of the light of letters is simplicity. Nothing is better than simplicity . . . . nothing can make up for excess or for the lack of definiteness. To carry on the heave of impulse and pierce intellectual depths and give all subjects their articulations are powers neither common nor very uncommon. But to speak in literature with the perfect rectitude and insouciance of the movements of animals and the unimpeachableness of the sentiment of trees in the woods and grass by the roadside is the flawless triumph of art. If you have looked on him who has achieved it you have looked on one of the masters of the artists of all nations and times. You shall not contemplate the flight of the graygull over the bay or the mettlesome action of the blood horse or the tall leaning of sunflowers on their stalk or the appearance of the sun journeying through heaven or the appearance of the moon afterward with any more satisfaction than you shall contemplate him. The greatest poet has less a marked style and is more the channel of thoughts and things without increase or diminution, and is the free channel of himself. He swears to his art, I will not be meddlesome, I will not have in my writing any elegance or effect or originality to hang in the way between me and the rest like curtains. I will have nothing hang in the way, not the richest curtains. What I tell I tell for precisely what it is. Let who may exalt or startle or fascinate or sooth I will have purposes as health or heat or snow has and be as regardless of observation. What I experience or portray shall go from my composition without a shred of my composition. You shall stand by my side and look in the mirror with me.

The old red blood and stainless gentility of great poets will be proved by their unconstraint. A heroic person walks at his ease through and out of that custom or precedent or authority that suits him not. Of the traits of the brotherhood of writers savans musicians inventors and artists nothing is finer than silent defiance advancing from new free forms. In the need of poems philosophy politics mechanism science behaviour, the craft of art, an appropriate native grand-opera, shipcraft, or any craft, he is greatest forever and forever who contributes the greatest original practical example. The cleanest expression is that which finds no sphere worthy of itself and makes one.

The messages of great poets to each man and woman are, Come to us on equal terms, Only then can you understand us, We are no better than you, What we enclose you enclose, What we enjoy you may enjoy. Did you suppose there could be only one Supreme? We affirm there can be unnumbered Supremes, and that one does not countervail another any more than one eyesight countervails another . . and that men can be good or grand only of the consciousness of their supremacy within them. What do you think is the grandeur of storms and dismemberments and the deadliest battles and wrecks and the wildest fury of the elements and the power of the sea and the motion of nature and of the throes of human desires and dignity and hate and love? It is that something in the soul which says, Rage on, Whirl on, I tread master here and everywhere, Master of the spasms of the sky and of the shatter of the sea, Master of nature and passion and death, And of all terror and all pain.

The American bards shall be marked for generosity and affection and for encouraging competitors . . They shall be kosmos . . without monopoly or secresy . . glad to pass any thing to any one . . hungry for equals night and day. They shall not be careful of riches and privilege . . . . they shall be riches and privilege . . . . they shall perceive who the most affluent man is. The most affluent man is he that confronts all the shows he sees by equivalents out of the stronger wealth of himself. The American bard shall delineate no class of persons nor one or two out of the strata of interests nor love most nor truth most nor the soul most nor the body most . . . . and not be for the eastern states more than the western or the northern states more than the southern.

Exact science and its practical movements are no checks on the greatest poet but always his encouragement and support. The outset and remembrance are there . . there the arms that lifted him first and brace him best . . . . there he returns after all his goings and comings. The sailor and traveler . . the anatomist chemist astronomer geologist phrenologist spiritualist mathematician historian and lexicographer are not poets, but they are the lawgivers of poets and their construction underlies the structure of every perfect poem. No matter what rises or is uttered they sent the seed of the conception of it . . . of them and by them stand the visible proofs of souls . . . . . always of their fatherstuff must be begotten the sinewy races of bards. If there shall be love and content between the father and the son and if the greatness of the son is the exuding of the greatness of the father there shall be love between the poet and the man of demonstrable science. In the beauty of poems are the tuft and final applause of science.

Great is the faith of the flush of knowledge and of the investigation of the depths of qualities and things. Cleaving and circling here swells the soul of the poet yet it president of itself always. The depths are fathomless and therefore calm. The innocence and nakedness are resumed . . . they are neither modest nor immodest. The whole theory of the special and supernatural and all that was twined with it or educed out of it departs as a dream. What has ever happened . . . . what happens and whatever may or shall happen, the vital laws enclose all . . . . they are sufficient for any case and for all cases . . . none to be hurried or retarded . . . . any miracle of affairs or persons inadmissible in the vast clear scheme where every motion and every spear of grass and the frames and spirits of men and women and all that concerns them are unspeakably perfect miracles all referring to all and each distinct and in its place. It is also not consistent with the reality of the soul to admit that there is anything in the known universe more divine than men and women.

Men and women and the earth and all upon it are simply to be taken as they are, and the investigation of their past and present and future shall be unintermitted and shall be done with perfect candor. Upon this basis philosophy speculates ever looking toward the poet, ever regarding the eternal tendencies of all toward happiness never inconsistent with what is clear to the senses and to the soul. For the eternal tendencies of all toward happiness make the only point of sane philosophy. Whatever comprehends less than that . . . whatever is less than the laws of light and of astronomical motion . . . or less than the laws that follow the thief the liar the glutton and the drunkard through this life and doubtless afterward

...... or less than vast stretches of time or the slow formation of density or the patient upheaving of strata—is of no account. Whatever would put God in a poem or system of philosophy as contending against some being or influence is also of no account. Sanity and ensemble characterise the great master ... spoilt in one principle all is spoilt. The great master has nothing to do with miracles. He sees health for himself in being one of the mass .... he sees the hiatus in singular eminence. To the perfect shape comes common ground. To be under the general law is great for that is to correspond with it. The master knows that he is unspeakably great and that all are unspeakably great .... that nothing for instance is greater than to conceive children and bring them up well ... that to be is just as great as to perceive or tell.

In the make of the great masters the idea of political liberty is indispensable. Liberty takes the adherence of heroes wherever men and women exist .... but never takes any adherence or welcome from the rest more than from poets. They are the voice and exposition of liberty. They out of ages are worthy the grand idea .. to them it is confided and they must sustain it. Nothing has precedence of it and nothing can warp or degrade it. The attitude of great poets is to cheer up slaves and horrify despots. The turn of their necks, the sound of their feet, the motions of their wrists, are full of hazard to the one and hope to the other. Come nigh them awhile and though they neither speak or advise you shall learn the faithful American lesson. Liberty is poorly served by men whose good intent is quelled from one failure or two failures or any number of failures, or from the casual indifference or ingratitude of the people, or from the sharp show of the tushes of power, or the bringing to bear soldiers and cannon or any penal statutes. Liberty relies upon itself, invites no one, promises nothing, sits in calmness and light, is positive and composed, and knows no discouragement. The battle rages with many a loud alarm and frequent advance and retreat .... the enemy triumphs .... the prison, the handcuffs, the iron necklace and anklet, the scaffold, garrote and leadballs do their work .... the cause is asleep .... the strong throats are choked with their own blood .... the young men drop their eyelashes toward the ground when they pass each other .... and is liberty gone out of that place? No never. When liberty goes it is not the first to go nor the second or third to go .. it waits for all the rest to go .. it is the last. .. When the memories of the old martyrs are faded utterly away .... when the large names of patriots are laughed at in the public halls from the lips of the orators .... when the boys are no more christened after the same but christened after tyrants and traitors instead . . . . when the laws of the free are grudgingly permitted and laws for informers and bloodmoney are sweet to the taste of the people . . . . when I and you walk abroad upon the earth stung with compassion at the sight of numberless brothers answering our equal friendship and calling no man master—and when we are elated with noble joy at the sight of slaves . . . . when the soul retires in the cool communion of the night and surveys its experience and has much extasy over the word and deed that put back a helpless innocent person into the gripe of the gripers or into any cruel inferiority . . . . when those in all parts of these states who could easier realize the true American character but do not yet—when the swarms of cringers, suckers, doughfaces, lice of politics, planners of sly involutions for their own preferment to city officers or state legislatures or the judiciary or congress or the presidency, obtain a response of love and natural deference from the people whether they get the offices or no . . . . when it is better to be a bound booby and rogue in office at a high salary than the poorest free mechanic or farmer with his hat unmoved from his head and firm eyes and a candid and generous heart . . . . and when servility by town or state or the federal government or any oppression on a large scale or small scale can be tried on without its own punishment following duly after in exact proportion against the smallest chance of escape . . . . or rather when all life and all the souls of men and women are discharged from any part of the earth—then only shall the instinct of liberty be dischargeed from that part of the earth.

As the attributes of the poets of the kosmos concentre in the real body and soul and in the pleasure of things they possess the superiority of genuineness over all fiction and romance. As they emit themselves facts are showered over with light . . . . the daylight is lit with more volatile light . . . . also the deep between the setting and rising sun goes deeper many fold. Each precise object or condition or combination or process exhibits a beauty . . . . . the multiplication table its—old age its—the carpenter's trade its—the grand-opera its . . . . the hugehulled cleanshaped New-York clipper at sea under steam or full sail gleams with unmatched beauty . . . . the American circles and large harmonies of government gleam with theirs . . . . and the commonest definite intentions and actions with theirs. The poets of the kosmos advance through all interpositions and coverings and turmoils and stratagems to first principles. They are of use . . . . they dissolve poverty from its need and riches from its conceit. You large proprietor they say shall not realize or perceive more than any one else. The owner of the library is not he who holds a legal title to it having bought and paid for it. Any one and every one is owner of the library who can read the same through all the varieties of tongues and subjects and styles, and in whom they enter with ease and take residence and force toward paternity and maternity, and make supple and powerful and rich and large. . . . . These American states strong and healthy and accomplished shall receive no pleasure from violations of natural models and must not permit them. In paintings or mouldings or carvings in mineral or wood, or in the illustrations of books or newspapers, or in any comic or tragic prints, or in the patterns of woven stuffs or any thing to beautify rooms or furniture or costumes, or to put upon cornices or monuments or on the prows or sterns of ships, or to put anywhere before the human eye indoors or out, that which distorts honest shapes or which creates unearthly beings or places or contingencies is a nuisance and revolt. Of the human form especially it is so great it must never be made ridiculous. Of ornaments to a work nothing outre can be allowed . . but those ornaments can be allowed that conform to the perfect facts of the open air and that flow out of the nature of the work and come irrepressibly from it and are necessary to the completion of the work. Most works are most beautiful without ornament. . . Exaggerations will be revenged in human physiology. Clean and vigorous children are jetted and conceived only in those communities where the models of natural forms are public every day. . . . . Great genius and the people of these states must never be demeaned to romances. As soon as histories are properly told there is no more need of romances.

The great poets are also to be known by the absence in them of tricks and by the justification of perfect personal candor. Then folks echo a new cheap joy and a divine voice leaping from their brains: How beautiful is candor! All faults may be forgiven of him who has perfect candor. Henceforth let no man of us lie, for we have seen that openness wins the inner and outer world and that there is no single exception, and that never since our earth gathered itself in a mass have deceit or subterfuge or prevarication attracted its smallest particle or the faintest tinge of a shade—and that through the enveloping wealth and rank of a state or the whole republic of states a sneak or sly person shall be discovered and despised . . . . and that the soul has never been once fooled and never can be fooled . . . . and thrift without the loving nod of the soul is only a fœtid puff . . . . and there never grew up in any of the continents of the globe nor upon any planet or satellite or star, nor upon the asteroids, nor in any part of ethereal space, nor in the midst of density, nor under the fluid wet of the sea, nor in that condition which precedes the birth of babes, nor at any time during the changes of life, nor in that condition that follows what we term death, nor in any stretch of abeyance or action afterward of vitality, nor in any process of formation or reformation anywhere, a being whose instinct hated the truth.

Extreme caution or prudence, the soundest organic health, large hope and comparison and fondness for women and children, large alimentiveness and destructiveness and causality, with a perfect sense of the oneness of nature and the propriety of the same spirit applied to human affairs . . these are called up of the float of the brain of the world to be parts of the greatest poet from his birth out of his mother's womb and from her birth out of her mother's. Caution seldom goes far enough. It has been thought that the prudent citizen was the citizen who applied himself to solid gains and did well for himself and his family and completed a lawful life without debt or crime. The greatest poet sees and admits these economies as he sees the economies of food and sleep, but has higher notions of prudence than to think he gives much when he gives a few slight attentions at the latch of the gate. The premises of the prudence of life are not the hospitality of it or the ripeness and harvest of it. Beyond the independence of a little sum laid aside for burial-money, and of a few clapboards around and shingles overhead on a lot of American soil owned, and the easy dollars that supply the year's plain clothing and meals, the melancholy prudence of the abandonment of such a great being as a man is to the toss and pallor of years of moneymaking with all their scorching days and icy nights and all their stifling deceits and underhanded dodgings, or infinitesimals of parlors, or shameless stuffing while others starve . . and all the loss of the bloom and odor of the earth and of the flowers and atmosphere and of the sea and of the true taste of the women and men you pass or have to do with in youth or middle age, and the issuing sickness and desperate revolt at the close of a life without elevation or naivete, and the ghastly chatter of a death without serenity or majesty, is the great fraud upon modern civilization and forethought, blotching the surface and system which civilization undeniably drafts, and moistening with tears the immense features it spreads and spreads with such velocity before the reached kisses of the soul. . . Still the right explanation remains to be made about prudence. The prudence of the mere wealth and respectability of the most esteemed life appears too faint for the eye to observe at all when little and large alike drop quietly aside at the thought of the prudence suitable for immortality What is wisdom that fills the thinness of a year or seventy or eighty years to wisdom spaced out by ages and coming back at a certain time with strong reinforcements and rich presents and the clear faces of wedding-guests as far as you can look in every direction running gaily toward you? Only the soul is of itself . . . . all else has reference to what ensues. All that a person does or thinks is of consequence. Not a move can a man or woman make that affects him or her in a day or a month or any part of the direct lifetime or the hour of death but the same affects him or her onward afterward through the indirect lifetime. The indirect is always as great and real as the direct. The spirit receives from the body just as much as it gives to the body. Not one name of word or deed . . not of venereal sores or discolorations . . not the privacy of the onanist . . not of the putrid veins of gluttons or rumdrinkers . . . not peculation or cunning or betrayal or murder . . no serpentine poison of those that seduce women . . not the foolish yielding of women . . not prostitution . . not of any depravity of young men . . not of the attainment of gain by discreditable means . . not any nastiness of appetite . . not any harshness of officers to men or judges to prisoners or fathers to sons or sons to fathers or of husbands to wives or bosses to their boys . . not of greedy looks or malignant wishes . . . nor any of the wiles practised by people upon themselves . . . ever is or ever can be stamped on the programme but it is duly realized and returned, and that returned in further performances . . . and they returned again. Nor can the push of charity or personal force ever be any thing else than the profoundest reason, whether it bring arguments to hand or no. No specification is necessary . . to add or subtract or divide is in vain. Little or big, learned or unlearned, white or black, legal or illegal, sick or well, from the first inspiration down the windpipe to the last expiration out of it, all that a male or female does that is vigorous and benevolent and clean is so much sure profit to him or her in the unshakable order of the universe and through the whole scope of it forever. If the savage or felon is wise it is well . . . . if the greatest poet or savan is wise it is simply the same . . if the President or chief justice is wise it is the same . . . if the young mechanic or farmer is wise it is no more or less . . if the prostitute is wise it is no more nor less. The interest will come round . . all will come round. All the best actions of war and peace . . . all help given to relatives and strangers and the poor and old and sorrowful and young children and widows and the sick, and to all shunned persons . . all further-ance of fugitives and of the escape of slaves . . all the self-denial that stood steady and aloof on wrecks and saw others take the seats of the boats . . . all offering of substance or life for the good old cause, or for a friend's sake or opinion's sake . . . all pains of enthusiasts scoffed at by their neighbors . . all the vast sweet love and precious suffering of mothers . . . all honest men baffled in strifes recorded or unrecorded . . . . all the grandeur and good of the few ancient nations whose fragments of annals we inherit . . and all the good of the hundreds of far mightier and more ancient nations unknown to us by name or date or location . . . . all that was ever manfully begun, whether it succeeded or no . . . . all that has at any time been well suggested out of the divine heart of man or by the divinity of his mouth or by the shaping of his great hands . . and all that is well thought or done this day on any part of the surface of the globe . . or on any of the wandering stars or fixed stars by those there as we are here . . or that is henceforth to be well thought or done by you whoever you are, or by any one—these singly and wholly inured at their time and inure now and will inure always to the identities from which they sprung or shall spring. . . Did you guess any of them lived only its moment? The world does not so exist . . no parts palpable or impalpable so exist . . . no result exists now without being from its long antecedent result, and that from its antecedent, and so backward without the farthest mentionable spot coming a bit nearer the beginning than any other spot. . . . . Whatever satisfies the soul is truth. The prudence of the greatest poet answers at last the craving and glut of the soul, is not contemptuous of less ways of prudence if they conform to its ways, puts off nothing, permits no let-up for its own case or any case, has no particular sabbath or judgment-day, divides not the living from the dead or the righteous from the unrighteous, is satisfied with the present, matches every thought or act by its correlative, knows no possible forgiveness or deputed atonement . . knows that the young man who composedly periled his life and lost it has done exceeding well for himself, while the man who has not periled his life and retains it to old age in riches and ease has perhaps achieved nothing for himself worth mentioning . . and that only that person has no great prudence to learn who has learnt to prefer real longlived things, and favors body and soul the same, and perceives the indirect assuredly following the direct, and what evil or good he does leaping onward and waiting to meet him again—and who in his spirit in any emergency whatever neither hurries or avoids death.

The direct trial of him who would be the greatest poet is today. If he does not flood himself with the immediate age as with vast oceanic tides . . . . . and if he does not attract his own land body and soul to himself and hang on its neck with incomparable love and plunge his semitic muscle into its merits and demerits . . . and if he be not himself the age transfigured . . . . and if to him is not opened the eternity which gives similitude to all periods and locations and processes and animate and inanimate forms, and which is the bond of time, and rises up from its inconceivable vagueness and infiniteness in the swimming shape of today, and is held by the ductile anchors of life, and makes the present spot the passage from what was to what shall be, and commits itself to the representation of this wave of an hour and this one of the sixty beautiful children of the wave—let him merge in the general run and wait his development. . . . Still the final test of poems or any character or work remains. The prescient poet projects himself centuries ahead and judges performer or performance after the changes of time. Does it live through them? Does it still hold on untired? Will the same style and the direction of genius to similar points be satisfactory now? Has no new discovery in science or arrival at superior planes of thought and judgment and behavior fixed him or his so that either can be looked down upon? Have the marches of tens and hundreds and thousands of years made willing detours to the right hand and the left hand for his sake? Is he beloved long and long after he is buried? Does the young man think often of him? and the young woman think often of him? and do the middleaged and the old think of him?

A great poem is for ages and ages in common and for all degrees and complexions and all departments and sects and for a woman as much as a man and a man as much as a woman. A great poem is no finish to a man or woman but rather a beginning. Has any once fancied he could sit at last under some due authority and rest satisfied with explanations and realize and be content and full? To no such terminus does the greatest poet bring . . . he brings neither cessation or sheltered fatness and ease. The touch of him tells in action. Whom he takes he takes with firm sure grasp into live regions previously unattained . . . . thenceforward is no rest . . . . they see the space and ineffable sheen that turn the old spots and lights into dead vacuums. The companion of him beholds the birth and progress of stars and learns one of the meanings. Now there shall be a man cohered out of tumult and chaos . . . . the elder encourages the younger and shows him how . . . they two shall launch off fearlessly together till the new world fits an orbit for itself and looks unabashed on the lesser orbits of the stars and sweeps through the ceaseless rings and shall never be quiet again.

There will soon be no more priests. Their work is done. They may wait a while . . perhaps a generation or two . . dropping off by degrees. A superior breed shall take their place . . . . the gangs of kosmos and prophets en masse shall take their place. A new order shall arise and they shall be the priests of man, and every man shall be his own priest. The churches built under their umbrage shall be the churches of men and women. Through the divinity of themselves shall the kosmos and the new breed of poets be interpreters of men and women and of all events and things. They shall find their inspiration in real objects today, symptoms of the past and future .... They shall not deign to defend immortality or God or the perfection of things or liberty or the exquisite beauty and reality of the soul. They shall arise in America and be responded to from the remainder of the earth.

The English language befriends the grand American expression .... it is brawny enough and limber and full enough. On the tough stock of a race who through all change of circumstance was never without the idea of political liberty, which is the animus of all liberty, it has attracted the terms of daintier and gayer and subtler and more elegant tongues. It is the powerful language of resistance ... it is the dialect of common sense. It is the speech of the proud and melancholy races and of all who aspire. It is the chosen tongue to express growth faith self-esteem freedom justice equality friendliness amplitude prudence decision and courage. It is the medium that shall well nigh express the inexpressible.

No great literature nor any like style of behaviour or oratory or social intercourse or household arrangements or public institutions or the treatment by bosses of employed people, nor executive detail or detail of the army or navy, nor spirit of legislation or courts or police or tuition or architecture or songs or amusements or the costumes of young men, can long elude the jealous and passionate instinct of American standards. Whether or no the sign appears from the mouths of the people, it throbs a live interrogation in every freeman's and freewoman's heart after that which passes by or this built to remain. Is it uniform with my country? Are its disposals without ignominious distinctions? Is it for the evergrowing communes of brothers and lovers, large, well-united, proud beyond the old models, generous beyond all models? Is it something grown fresh out of the fields or drawn from the sea for use to me today here? I know that what answers for me an American must answer for any individual or nation that serves for a part of my materials. Does this answer? or is it without reference to universal needs? or sprung of the needs of the less developed society of special ranks? or old needs of pleasure overlaid by modern science and forms? Does this acknowledge liberty with audible and absolute acknowledgement, and set slavery at nought for life and death? Will it help breed one good-shaped and wellhung man, and a woman to be his perfect and independent mate? Does it improve manners? Is it for the nursing of the young of the republic? Does it solve readily with the sweet milk of the nipples of the breasts of the mother of many children? Has it too the old ever-fresh forbearance and impartiality? Does it look with the same love on the last born and on those hardening toward stature, and on the errant, and on those who disdain all strength of assault outside of their own?

The poems distilled from other poems will probably pass away. The coward will surely pass away. The expectation of the vital and great can only be satisfied by the demeanor of the vital and great. The swarms of the polished deprecating and reflectors and the polite float off and leave no remembrance. America prepares with composure and goodwill for the visitors that have sent word. It is not intellect that is to be their warrant and welcome. The talented, the artist, the ingenious, the editor, the statesman, the erudite . . they are not unappreciated . . they fall in their place and do their work. The soul of the nation also does its work. No disguise can pass on it . . no disguise can conceal from it. It rejects none, it permits all. Only toward as good as itself and toward the like of itself will it advance half-way. An individual is as superb as a nation when he has the qualities which make a superb nation. The soul of the largest and wealthiest and proudest nation may well go half-way to meet that of its poets. The signs are effectual. There is no fear of mistake. If the one is true the other is true. The proof of a poet is that his country absorbs him as affectionately as he has absorbed it.

Democratic Vistas

As the greatest lessons of Nature through the universe are perhaps the lessons of variety and freedom, the same present the greatest lessons also in New World politics and progress. If a man were ask'd, for instance, the distinctive points contrasting modern European and American political and other life with the old Asiatic cultus, as lingering-bequeath'd yet in China and Turkey, he might find the amount of them in John Stuart Mill's profound essay on Liberty in the future, where he demands two main constituents, or substrata, for a truly grand nationality—1st, a large variety of character—and 2d, full play for human nature to expand itself in numberless and even conflicting directions—(seems to be for general humanity much like the influences that make up, in their limitless field, that perennial health-action of the air we call the weather—an infinite number of currents and forces, and contributions, and temperatures, and cross purposes, whose ceaseless play of counterpart upon counterpart brings constant restoration and vitality.) With this thought—and not for itself alone, but all it necessitates, and draws after it—let me begin my speculations.

America, filling the present with greatest deeds and problems, cheerfully accepting the past, including feudalism, (as, indeed, the present is but the legitimate birth of the past, including feudalism,) counts, as I reckon, for her justification and success, (for who, as yet, dare claim success?) almost entirely on the future. Nor is that hope unwarranted. To-day, ahead, though dimly yet, we see, in vistas, a copious, sane gigantic offspring. For our New World I consider far less important for what it has done, or what it is, than for results to come. Sole among nationalities, these States have assumed the task to put in forms of lasting power and practicality, on areas of amplitude rivaling the operations of the physical kosmos, the moral political speculations of ages, long, long deferr'd, the democratic republican principle, and the theory of development and perfection by voluntary standards, and self-reliance. Who else, indeed, except the United States, in history, so far, have accepted in unwitting faith, and, as we now see, stand, act upon, and go security for, these things?

But preluding no longer, let me strike the key-note of the following strain. First premising that, though the passages of it have been written at widely different times, (it is, in fact, a collection of memoranda, perhaps for future designers, comprehenders,) and though it may be open to the charge of one part contradicting another—for there are opposite sides to the great question of democracy, as to every great question—I feel the parts harmoniously blended in my own realization and convictions, and present them to be read only in such oneness, each page and each claim and assertion modified and temper'd by the others. Bear in mind, too, that they are not the result of studying up in political economy, but of the ordinary sense, observing, wandering among men, these States, these stirring years of war and peace. I will not gloss over the appalling dangers of universal suffrage in the United States. In fact, it is to admit and face these dangers I am writing. To him or her within whose thought rages the battle, advancing, retreating, between democracy's convictions, aspirations, and the people's crudeness, vice, caprices, I mainly write this essay. I shall use the words America and democracy as convertible terms. Not an ordinary one is the issue. The United States are destined either to surmount the gorgeous history of feudalism, or else prove the most tremendous failure of time. Not the least doubtful am I on any prospects of their material success. The triumphant future of their business, geographic and productive departments, on larger scales and in more varieties than ever, is certain. In those respects the republic must soon (if she does not already) outstrip all examples hitherto afforded, and dominate the world.*

---

*"From a territorial area of less than nine hundred thousand square miles, the Union has expanded into over four millions and a half—fifteen times larger than that of Great Britain and France combined—with a shore-line, including Alaska, equal to the entire circumference of the earth, and with a domain within these lines far wider than that of the Romans in their proudest days of conquest and renown. With a river, lake, and coastwise commerce estimated at over two thousand millions of dollars per year; with a railway traffic of four to six thousand millions per year, and the annual domestic exchanges of the country running up to nearly ten thousand millions per year; with over two thousand millions of dollars invested in manufacturing, mechanical, and mining industry; with over five hundred millions of acres of land in actual occupancy, valued, with their appurtenances, at over seven thousand millions of dollars, and producing annually crops valued at over three thousand millions of dollars; with a realm which, if the density of Belgium's population were possible, would be vast enough to include all the present inhabitants of the world; and with equal rights guaranteed to even the poorest and humblest of

Admitting all this, with the priceless value of our political institutions, general suffrage, (and fully acknowledging the latest, widest
opening of the doors,) I say that, far deeper than these, what finally
and only is to make of our western world a nationality superior
to any hither known, and outtopping the past, must be vigorous,
yet unsuspected Literatures, perfect personalities and sociologies,
original, transcendental, and expressing (what, in highest sense, are
not yet express'd at all,) democracy and the modern. With these,
and out of these, I promulge new races of Teachers, and of perfect
Women, indispensable to endow the birth-stock of a New World.
For feudalism, caste, the ecclesiastic traditions, though palpably
retreating from political institutions, still hold essentially, by their
spirit, even in this country, entire possession of the more important
fields, indeed the very subsoil, of education, and of social standards
and literature.

I say that democracy can never prove itself beyond cavil, until it
founds and luxuriantly grows its own forms of art, poems, schools,
theology, displacing all that exists, or that has been produced anywhere in the past, under opposite influences. It is curious to me that
while so many voices, pens, minds, in the press, lecture-rooms, in
our Congress, &c., are discussing intellectual topics, pecuniary dangers, legislative problems, the suffrage, tariff and labor questions,
and the various business and benevolent needs of America, with
propositions, remedies, often worth deep attention, there is one
need, a hiatus the profoundest, that no eye seems to perceive, no
voice to state. Our fundamental want to-day in the United States,

---

our forty millions of people—we can, with a manly pride akin to that which
distinguish'd the palmiest days of Rome, claim," &c., &c., &c.—*Vice-President
Colfax's Speech, July 4, 1870.*

LATER—*London "Times," (Weekly,) June 23, '82*
"The wonderful wealth-producing power of the United States defies and
sets at naught the grave drawbacks of a mischievous protective tariff, and has
already obliterated, almost wholly, the traces of the greatest of modern civil
wars. What is especially remarkable in the present development of American
energy and success is its wide and equable distribution. North and south,
east and west, on the shores of the Atlantic and the Pacific, along the chain
of the great lakes, in the valley of the Mississippi, and on the coasts of the
gulf of Mexico, the creation of wealth and the increase of population are
signally exhibited. It is quite true, as has been shown by the recent apportion-
ment of population in the House of Representatives, that some sections of the
Union have advanced, relatively to the rest, in an extraordinary and unexpected
degree. But this does not imply that the States which have gain'd no additional
representatives or have actually lost some have been stationary or have receded.
The fact is that the present tide of prosperity has risen so high that it has overflow'd all barriers, and has fill'd up the back-waters, and establish'd something
like an approach to uniform success."

with closest, amplest reference to present conditions, and to the future, is of a class, and the clear idea of a class, of native authors, literatuses, far different, far higher in grade than any yet known, sacerdotal, modern, fit to cope with our occasions, lands, permeating the whole mass of American mentality, taste, belief, breathing into it a new breath of life, giving it decision, affecting politics far more than the popular superficial suffrage, with results inside and underneath the elections of Presidents or Congresses—radiating, begetting appropriate teachers, schools, manners, and, as its grandest result, accomplishing, (what neither the schools nor the churches and their clergy have hitherto accomplish'd, and without which this nation will no more stand, permanently, soundly, than a house will stand without a substratum,) a religious and moral character beneath the political and productive and intellectual bases of the States. For know you not, dear, earnest reader, that the people of our land may all read and write, and may all possess the right to vote—and yet the main things may be entirely lacking?—(and this to suggest them.)

View'd, to-day, from a point of view sufficiently over-arching, the problem of humanity all over the civilized world is social and religious, and is to be finally met and treated by literature. The priest departs, the divine literatus comes. Never was anything more wanted than, to-day, and here in the States, the poet of the modern is wanted, or the great literatus of the modern. At all times, perhaps, the central point in any nation, and that whence it is itself really sway'd the most, and whence it sways others, is its national literature, especially its archetypal poems. Above all previous lands, a great original literature is surely to become the justification and reliance, (in some respects the sole reliance,) of American democracy.

Few are aware how the great literature penetrates all, gives hue to all, shapes aggregates and individuals, and, after subtle ways, with irresistible power, constructs, sustains, demolishes at will. Why tower, in reminiscence, above all the nations of the earth, two special lands, petty in themselves, yet inexpressibly gigantic, beautiful, columnar? Immortal Judah lives, and Greece immortal lives, in a couple of poems.

Nearer than this. It is not generally realized, but it is true, as the genius of Greece, and all the sociology, personality, politics and religion of those wonderful states, resided in their literature or esthetics, that what was afterwards the main support of European chivalry, the feudal, ecclesiastical, dynastic world over there—forming its osseous structure, holding it together for hundreds, thousands of years, preserving its flesh and bloom, giving it form, decision, rounding it out, and so saturating it in the conscious and unconscious blood, breed, belief, and intuitions of men, that it still prevails powerful to this day, in defiance of the mighty changes of time—was its literature, permeating to the very marrow, especially that major part, its enchanting songs, ballads, and poems.*

To the ostent of the senses and eyes, I know, the influences which stamp the world's history are wars, uprisings or downfalls of dynasties, changeful movements of trade, important inventions, navigation, military or civil governments, advent of powerful personalities, conquerors, &c. These of course play their part; yet, it may be, a single new thought, imagination, abstract principle, even literary style, fit for the time, put in shape by some great literatus, and projected among mankind, may duly cause changes, growths, removals, greater than the longest and bloodiest war, or the most stupendous merely political, dynastic, or commercial overturn.

In short, as, though it may not be realized, it is strictly true, that a few first-class poets, philosophs, and authors, have substantially settled and given status to the entire religion, education, law, sociology, &c., of the hitherto civilized world, by tinging and often creating the atmospheres out of which they have arisen, such also must stamp, and more than ever stamp, the interior and real democratic construction of this American continent, to-day, and days to come. Remember also this fact of difference, that, while through the antique and through the mediæval ages, highest thoughts and ideals realized themselves, and their expression made its way by other arts, as much as, or even more than by, technical literature, (not open to the mass of persons, or even to the majority of eminent persons,) such literature in our day and for current purposes, is not only more eligible than all the other arts put together, but has become the only general means of morally influencing the world. Painting, sculpture, and the dramatic theatre, it would seem, no

---

* See, for hereditaments, specimens, Walter Scott's Border Minstrelsy, Percy's collection, Ellis's early English Metrical Romances, the European continental poems of Walter of Aquitania, and the Nibelungen, of pagan stock, but monkish-feudal redaction; the history of the Troubadours, by Fauriel; even the far-back cumbrous old Hindu epics, as indicating the Asian eggs out of which European chivalry was hatch'd; Ticknor's chapters on the Cid, and on the Spanish poems and poets of Calderon's time. Then always, and, of course, as the superbest poetic culmination-expression of feudalism, the Shaksperean dramas, in the attitudes, dialogue, characters, &c., of the princes, lords and gentlemen, the pervading atmosphere, the implied and express'd standard of manners, the high port and proud stomach, the regal embroidery of style, &c.

longer play an indispensable or even important part in the workings and mediumship of intellect, utility, or even high esthetics.
Architecture remains, doubtless with capacities, and a real future.
Then music, the combiner, nothing more spiritual, nothing more
sensuous, a god, yet completely human, advances, prevails, holds
highest place; supplying in certain wants and quarters what nothing
else could supply. Yet in the civilization of to-day it is undeniable
that, over all the arts, literature dominates, serves beyond all—
shapes the character of church and school—or, at any rate, is capable of doing so. Including the literature of science, its scope is
indeed unparallel'd.

Before proceeding further, it were perhaps well to discriminate
on certain points. Literature tills its crops in many fields, and some
may flourish, while others lag. What I say in these Vistas has its
main bearing on imaginative literature, especially poetry, the stock
of all. In the department of science, and the specialty of journalism,
there appear, in these States, promises, perhaps fulfilments, of highest earnestness, reality, and life. These, of course, are modern. But
in the region of imaginative, spinal and essential attributes, something equivalent to creation is, for our age and lands, imperatively
demanded. For not only is it not enough that the new blood, new
frame of democracy shall be vivified and held together merely by
political means, superficial suffrage, legislation, &c., but it is clear
to me that, unless it goes deeper, gets at least as firm and as warm
a hold in men's hearts, emotions and belief, as, in their days, feudalism or ecclesiasticism, and inaugurates its own perennial sources,
welling from the centre forever, its strength will be defective, its
growth doubtful, and its main charm wanting. I suggest, therefore,
the possibility, should some two or three really original American
poets, (perhaps artists or lecturers,) arise, mounting the horizon
like planets, stars of the first magnitude, that, from their eminence,
fusing contributions, races, far localities, &c., together, they would
give more compaction and more moral identity, (the quality to-day
most needed,) to these States, than all its Constitutions, legislative
and judicial ties, and all its hitherto political, warlike, or materialistic experiences. As, for instance, there could hardly happen anything that would more serve the States, with all their variety of
origins, their diverse climes, cities, standards, &c., than possessing
an aggregate of heroes, characters, exploits, sufferings, prosperity
or misfortune, glory or disgrace, common to all, typical of all—no
less, but even greater would it be to possess the aggregation of a
cluster of mighty poets, artists, teachers, fit for us, national expressers, comprehending and effusing for the men and women of the

States, what is universal, native, common to all, inland and sea-board, northern and southern. The historians say of ancient Greece, with her ever-jealous autonomies, cities, and states, that the only positive unity she ever own'd or receiv'd, was the sad unity of a common subjection, at the last, to foreign conquerors. Subjection, aggregation of that sort, is impossible to America; but the fear of conflicting and irreconcilable interiors, and the lack of a common skeleton, knitting all close, continually haunts me. Or, if it does not, nothing is plainer than the need, a long period to come, of a fusion of the States into the only reliable identity, the moral and artistic one. For, I say, the true nationality of the States, the genu-ine union, when we come to a mortal crisis, is, and is to be, after all, neither the written law, nor, (as is generally supposed,) either self-interest, or common pecuniary or material objects—but the fervid and tremendous IDEA, melting everything else with resist-less heat, and solving all lesser and definite distinctions in vast, indefinite, spiritual, emotional power.

It may be claim'd, (and I admit the weight of the claim,) that common and general worldly prosperity, and a populace well-to-do, and with all life's material comforts, is the main thing, and is enough. It may be argued that our republic is, in performance, really enact-ing to-day the grandest arts, poems, &c., by beating up the wilder-ness into fertile farms, and in her railroads, ships, machinery, &c. And it may be ask'd, Are these not better, indeed, for America, than any utterances even of greatest rhapsode, artist, or literatus?

I too hail those achievements with pride and joy: then answer that the soul of man will not with such only—nay, not with such at all—be finally satisfied; but needs what, (standing on these and on all things, as the feet stand on the ground,) is address'd to the loftiest, to itself alone.

Out of such considerations, such truths, arises for treatment in these Vistas the important question of character, of an American stock-personality, with literatures and arts for outlets and return-expressions, and, of course, to correspond, within outlines com-mon to all. To these, the main affair, the thinkers of the United States, in general so acute, have either given feeblest attention, or have remain'd, and remain, in a state of somnolence.

For my part, I would alarm and caution even the political and business reader, and to the utmost extent, against the prevailing delusion that the establishment of free political institutions, and plentiful intellectual smartness, with general good order, physical plenty, industry, &c., (desirable and precious advantages as they all are,) do, of themselves, determine and yield to our experiment of democracy the fruitage of success. With such advantages at present fully, or almost fully, possess'd—the Union just issued, victorious, from the struggle with the only foes it need ever fear, (namely, those within itself, the interior ones,) and with unprecedented materialistic advancement—society, in these States, is canker'd, crude, superstitious, and rotten. Political, or law-made society is, and private, or voluntary society, is also. In any vigor, the element of the moral conscience, the most important, the verteber to State or man, seems to me either entirely lacking, or seriously enfeebled or ungrown.

I say we had best look our times and lands searchingly in the face, like a physician diagnosing some deep disease. Never was there, perhaps, more hollowness at heart than at present, and here in the United States. Genuine belief seems to have left us. The underlying principles of the States are not honestly believ'd in, (for all this hectic glow, and these melo-dramatic screamings,) nor is humanity itself believ'd in. What penetrating eye does not everywhere see through the mask? The spectacle is appalling. We live in an atmosphere of hypocrisy throughout. The men believe not in the women, nor the women in the men. A scornful superciliousness rules in literature. The aim of all the *littérateurs* is to find something to make fun of. A lot of churches, sects, &c., the most dismal phantasms I know, usurp the name of religion. Conversation is a mass of badinage. From deceit in the spirit, the mother of all false deeds, the offspring is already incalculable. An acute and candid person, in the revenue department in Washington, who is led by the course of his employment to regularly visit the cities, north, south and west, to investigate frauds, has talk'd much with me about his discoveries. The depravity of the business classes of our country is not less than has been supposed, but infinitely greater. The official services of America, national, state, and municipal, in all their branches and departments, except the judiciary, are saturated in corruption, bribery, falsehood, mal-administration; and the judiciary is tainted. The great cities reek with respectable as much as non-respectable robbery and scoundrelism. In fashionable life, flippancy, tepid amours, weak infidelism, small aims, or no aims at all, only to kill time. In business, (this all-devouring modern word, business,) the one sole object is, by any means, pecuniary gain. The magician's serpent in the fable ate up all the other serpents; and money-making is our magician's serpent, remaining to-day sole master of the field. The best class we show, is but a mob of fashionably dress'd speculators and vulgarians. True, indeed, behind this fantastic farce, enacted on the visible stage of society, solid things and stupendous labors are to be discover'd, existing crudely and going on in the background, to advance and tell themselves in time. Yet the truths are none the less terrible. I say that our New World democracy, however great a success in uplifting the masses out of their sloughs, in materialistic development, products, and in a certain highly-deceptive superficial popular intellectuality, is, so far, an almost complete failure in its social aspects, and in really grand religious, moral, literary, and esthetic results. In vain do we march with unprecedented strides to empire so colossal, outvying the antique, beyond Alexander's, beyond the proudest sway of Rome. In vain have we annex'd Texas, California, Alaska, and reach north for Canada and south for Cuba. It is as if we were somehow being endow'd with a vast and more and more thoroughly-appointed body, and then left with little or no soul.

Let me illustrate further, as I write, with current observations, localities, &c. The subject is important, and will bear repetition. After an absence, I am now again (September, 1870) in New York city and Brooklyn, on a few weeks' vacation. The splendor, picturesqueness, and oceanic amplitude and rush of these great cities, the unsurpass'd situation, rivers and bay, sparkling sea-tides, costly and lofty new buildings, façades of marble and iron, of original grandeur and elegance of design, with the masses of gay color, the preponderance of white and blue, the flags flying, the endless ships, the tumultuous streets, Broadway, the heavy, low, musical roar, hardly ever intermitted, even at night; the jobbers' houses, the rich shops, the wharves, the great Central Park, and the Brooklyn Park of hills, (as I wander among them this beautiful fall weather, musing, watching, absorbing)—the assemblages of the citizens in their groups, conversations, trades, evening amusements, or along the by-quarters—these, I say, and the like of these, completely satisfy my senses of power, fulness, motion, &c., and give me, through such senses and appetites, and through my esthetic conscience, a continued exaltation and absolute fulfilment. Always and more and more, as I cross the East and North rivers, the ferries, or with the pilots in their pilot-houses, or pass an hour in Wall street, or the gold exchange, I realize, (if we must admit such partialisms,) that not Nature alone is great in her fields of freedom and the open air, in her storms, the shows of night and day, the mountains, forests, seas—but in the artificial, the work of man too is equally great—

in this profusion of teeming humanity—in these ingenuities, streets, goods, houses, ships—these hurrying, feverish, electric crowds of men, their complicated business genius, (not least among the geniuses,) and all this mighty, many-threaded wealth and industry concentrated here.

But sternly discarding, shutting our eyes to the glow and grandeur of the general superficial effect, coming down to what is of the only real importance, Personalities, and examining minutely, we question, we ask, Are there, indeed, *men* here worthy the name? Are there athletes? Are there perfect women, to match the generous material luxuriance? Is there a pervading atmosphere of beautiful manners? Are there crops of fine youths, and majestic old persons? Are there arts worthy freedom and a rich people? Is there a great moral and religious civilization—the only justification of a great material one? Confess that to severe eyes, using the moral microscope upon humanity, a sort of dry and flat Sahara appears, these cities, crowded with petty grotesques, malformations, phantoms, playing meaningless antics. Confess that everywhere, in shop, street, church, theatre, bar-room, official chair, are pervading flippancy and vulgarity, low cunning, infidelity—everywhere the youth puny, impudent, foppish, prematurely ripe—everywhere an abnormal libidinousness, unhealthy forms, male, female, painted, padded, dyed, chignon'd, muddy complexions, bad blood, the capacity for good motherhood deceasing or deceas'd, shallow notions of beauty, with a range of manners, or rather lack of manners, (considering the advantages enjoy'd,) probably the meanest to be seen in the world.*

Of all this, and these lamentable conditions, to breathe into them the breath recuperative of sane and heroic life, I say a new founded literature, not merely to copy and reflect existing surfaces, or pander to what is called taste—not only to amuse, pass away time, celebrate the beautiful, the refined, the past, or exhibit technical, rhythmic, or grammatical dexterity—but a literature underlying life,

---

* Of these rapidly-sketch'd hiatuses, the two which seem to me most serious are, for one, the condition, absence, or perhaps the singular abeyance, of moral conscientious fibre all through American society; and, for another, the appalling depletion of women in their powers of sane athletic maternity, their crowning attribute, and ever making the woman, in loftiest spheres, superior to the man.

I have sometimes thought, indeed, that the sole avenue and means of a reconstructed sociology depended, primarily, on a new birth, elevation, expansion, invigoration of woman, affording, for races to come, (as the conditions that antedate birth are indispensable,) a perfect motherhood. Great, great, indeed, far greater than they know, is the sphere of women. But doubtless the question of such new sociology all goes together, includes many varied and complex influences and premises, and the man as well as the woman, and the woman as well as the man.

religious, consistent with science, handling the elements and forces with competent power, teaching and training men—and, as perhaps the most precious of its results, achieving the entire redemption of woman out of these incredible holds and webs of silliness, millinery, and every kind of dyspeptic depletion—and thus insuring to the States a strong and sweet Female Race, a race of perfect Mothers—is what is needed.

And now, in the full conception of these facts and points, and all that they infer, pro and con—with yet unshaken faith in the elements of the American masses, the composites, of both sexes, and even consider'd as individuals—and ever recognizing in them the broadest bases of the best literary and esthetic appreciation—I proceed with my speculations, Vistas.

First, let us see what we can make out of a brief, general, sentimental consideration of political democracy, and whence it has arisen, with regard to some of its current features, as an aggregate, and as the basic structure of our future literature and authorship. We shall, it is true, quickly and continually find the origin-idea of the singleness of man, individualism, asserting itself, and cropping forth, even from the opposite ideas. But the mass, or lump character, for imperative reasons, is to be ever carefully weigh'd, borne in mind, and provided for. Only from it, and from its proper regulation and potency, comes the other, comes the chance of individualism. The two are contradictory, but our task is to reconcile them.*

The political history of the past may be summ'd up as having grown out of what underlies the words, order, safety, caste, and especially out of the need of some prompt deciding authority, and of cohesion at all cost. Leaping time, we come to the period within the memory of people now living, when, as from some lair where they had slumber'd long, accumulating wrath, sprang up and are yet active, (1790, and on even to the present, 1870,) those noisy eructations, destructive iconoclasms, a fierce sense of wrongs, amid which moves the form, well known in modern history, in the old world, stain'd with much blood, and mark'd by savage reactionary

---

* The question hinted here is one which time only can answer. Must not the virtue of modern Individualism, continually enlarging, usurping all, seriously affect, perhaps keep down entirely, in America, the like of the ancient virtue of Patriotism, the fervid and absorbing love of general country? I have no doubt myself that the two will merge, and will mutually profit and brace each other, and that from them a greater product, a third, will arise. But I feel that at present they and their oppositions form a serious problem and paradox in the United States.

clamors and demands. These bear, mostly, as on one inclosing point of need.

For after the rest is said—after the many time-honor'd and really true things for subordination, experience, rights of property, &c., have been listen'd to and acquiesced in—after the valuable and well-settled statement of our duties and relations in society is thoroughly conn'd over and exhausted—it remains to bring forward and modify everything else with the idea of that Something a man is, (last precious consolation of the drudging poor,) standing apart from all else, divine in his own right, and a woman in hers, sole and untouchable by any canons of authority, or any rule derived from precedent, state-safety, the acts of legislatures, or even from what is called religion, modesty, or art. The radiation of this truth is the key of the most significant doings of our immediately preceding three centuries, and has been the political genesis and life of America. Advancing visibly, it still more advances invisibly. Underneath the fluctuations of the expressions of society, as well as the movements of the politics of the leading nations of the world, we see steadily pressing ahead and strengthening itself, even in the midst of immense tendencies toward aggregation, this image of completeness in separatism, of individual personal dignity, of a single person, either male or female, characterized in the main, not from extrinsic acquirements or position, but in the pride of himself or herself alone; and, as an eventual conclusion and summing up, (or else the entire scheme of things is aimless, a cheat, a crash,) the simple idea that the last, best dependence is to be upon humanity itself, and its own inherent, normal, full-grown qualities, without any superstitious support whatever. This idea of perfect individualism it is indeed that deepest tinges and gives character to the idea of the aggregate. For it is mainly or altogether to serve independent separatism that we favor a strong generalization, consolidation. As it is to give the best vitality and freedom to the rights of the States, (every bit as important as the right of nationality, the union,) that we insist on the identity of the Union at all hazards.

The purpose of democracy—supplanting old belief in the necessary absoluteness of establish'd dynastic rulership, temporal, ecclesiastical, and scholastic, as furnishing the only security against chaos, crime, and ignorance—is, through many transmigrations, and amid endless ridicules, arguments, and ostensible failures, to illustrate, at all hazards, this doctrine or theory that man, properly train'd in sanest, highest freedom, may and must become a law, and series of laws, unto himself, surrounding and providing for, not only his own personal control, but all his relations to other individuals, and to the State; and that, while other theories, as in the past histories of nations, have proved wise enough, and indispensable perhaps for their conditions, *this*, as matters now stand in our civilized world, is the only scheme worth working from, as warranting results like those of Nature's laws, reliable, when once establish'd, to carry on themselves.

The argument of the matter is extensive, and, we admit, by no means all on one side. What we shall offer will be far, far from sufficient. But while leaving unsaid much that should properly even prepare the way for the treatment of this many-sided question of political liberty, equality, or republicanism—leaving the whole history and consideration of the feudal plan and its products, embodying humanity, its politics and civilization, through the retrospect of past time, (which plan and products, indeed, make up all of the past, and a large part of the present)—leaving unanswer'd, at least by any specific and local answer, many a well-wrought argument and instance, and many a conscientious declamatory cry and warning— as, very lately, from an eminent and venerable person abroad*— things, problems, full of doubt, dread, suspense, (not new to me, but old occupiers of many an anxious hour in city's din, or night's silence,) we still may give a page or so, whose drift is opportune. Time alone can finally answer these things. But as a substitute in passing, let us, even if fragmentarily, throw forth a short direct or indirect suggestion of the premises of that other plan, in the new spirit, under the new forms, started here in our America.

As to the political section of Democracy, which introduces and breaks ground for further and vaster sections, few probably are the minds, even in these republican States, that fully comprehend the aptness of that phrase, "THE GOVERNMENT OF THE PEOPLE, BY THE PEOPLE, FOR THE PEOPLE," which we inherit from the lips of Abraham Lincoln; a formula whose verbal shape is homely wit, but whose scope includes both the totality and all minutiæ of the lesson.

The People! Like our huge earth itself, which, to ordinary scan-

---

*"SHOOTING NIAGARA.."—I was at first roused to much anger and abuse by this essay from Mr. Carlyle, so insulting to the theory of America—but happening to think afterwards how I had more than once been in the like mood, during which his essay was evidently cast, and seen persons and things in the same light, (indeed some might say there are signs of the same feeling in these Vistas)—I have since read it again, not only as a study, expressing as it does certain judgments from the highest feudal point of view, but have read it with respect as coming from an earnest soul, and as contributing certain sharp-cutting metallic grains, which, if not gold or silver, may be good hard, honest iron.

sion, is full of vulgar contradictions and offence, man, viewed in the lump, displeases, and is a constant puzzle and affront to the merely educated classes. The rare, cosmical, artist-mind, lit with the Infinite, alone confronts his manifold and oceanic qualities—but taste, intelligence and culture, (so-called,) have been against the masses, and remain so. There is plenty of glamour about the most damnable crimes and hoggish meannesses, special and general, of the feudal and dynastic world over there, with its *personnel* of lords and queens and courts, so well-dress'd and so handsome. But the People are ungrammatical, untidy, and their sins gaunt and ill-bred.

Literature, strictly consider'd, has never recognized the People, and, whatever may be said, does not to-day. Speaking generally, the tendencies of literature, as hitherto pursued, have been to make mostly critical and querulous men. It seems as if, so far, there were some natural repugnance between a literary and professional life, and the rude rank spirit of the democracies. There is, in later literature, a treatment of benevolence, a charity business, rife enough it is true; but I know nothing more rare, even in this country, than a fit scientific estimate and reverent appreciation of the People—of their measureless wealth of latent power and capacity, their vast, artistic contrasts of lights and shades—with, in America, their entire reliability in emergencies, and a certain breadth of historic grandeur, of peace or war, far surpassing all the vaunted samples of book-heroes, or any *haut ton* coteries, in all the records of the world.

The movements of the late secession war, and their results, to any sense that studies well and comprehends them, show that popular democracy, whatever its faults and dangers, practically justifies itself beyond the proudest claims and wildest hopes of its enthusiasts. Probably no future age can know, but I well know, how the gist of this fiercest and most resolute of the world's warlike contentions resided exclusively in the unnamed, unknown rank and file; and how the brunt of its labor of death was, to all essential purposes, volunteer'd. The People, of their own choice, fighting, dying for their own idea, insolently attack'd by the secession-slave-power, and its very existence imperil'd. Descending to detail, entering any of the armies, and mixing with the private soldiers, we see and have seen august spectacles. We have seen the alacrity with which the American-born populace, the peaceablest and most good-natured race in the world, and the most personally independent and intelligent, and the least fitted to submit to the irksomeness and exasperation of regimental discipline, sprang, at the

first tap of the drum, to arms—not for gain, nor even glory, nor
to repel invasion—but for an emblem, a mere abstraction—for the
life, *the safety of the flag*. We have seen the unequal'd docility and
obedience of these soldiers. We have seen them tried long and long
by hopelessness, mismanagement, and by defeat; have seen the incredible slaughter toward or through which the armies, (as at first
Fredericksburg, and afterward at the Wilderness,) still unhesitatingly
obey'd orders to advance. We have seen them in trench, or crouching behind breastwork, or tramping in deep mud, or amid pouring
rain or thick-falling snow, or under forced marches in hottest summer (as on the road to get to Gettysburg)—vast suffocating swarms,
divisions, corps, with every single man so grimed and black with
sweat and dust, his own mother would not have known him—his
clothes all dirty, stain'd and torn, with sour, accumulated sweat for
perfume—many a comrade, perhaps a brother, sun-struck, staggering out, dying, by the roadside, of exhaustion—yet the great bulk
bearing steadily on, cheery enough, hollow-bellied from hunger, but
sinewy with unconquerable resolution.

We have seen this race proved by wholesale by drearier, yet more
fearful tests—the wound, the amputation, the shatter'd face or
limb, the slow hot fever, long impatient anchorage in bed, and all
the forms of maiming, operation and disease. Alas! America have
we seen, though only in her early youth, already to hospital brought.
There have we watch'd these soldiers, many of them only boys in
years—mark'd their decorum, their religious nature and fortitude,
and their sweet affection. Wholesale, truly. For at the front, and
through the camps, in countless tents, stood the regimental, brigade
and division hospitals; while everywhere amid the land, in or near
cities, rose clusters of huge, white-wash'd, crowded, one-story
wooden barracks; and there ruled agony with bitter scourge, yet
seldom brought a cry; and there stalk'd death by day and night
along the narrow aisles between the rows of cots, or by the blankets
on the ground, and touch'd lightly many a poor sufferer, often with
blessed, welcome touch.

I know not whether I shall be understood, but I realize that it
is finally from what I learn'd personally mixing in such scenes that
I am now penning these pages. One night in the gloomiest period
of the war, in the Patent office hospital in Washington city, as I
stood by the bedside of a Pennsylvania soldier, who lay, conscious
of quick approaching death, yet perfectly calm, and with noble,
spiritual manner, the veteran surgeon, turning aside, said to me,
that though he had witness'd many, many deaths of soldiers, and
had been a worker at Bull Run, Antietam, Fredericksburg, &c., he

had not seen yet the first case of man or boy that met the approach of dissolution with cowardly qualms or terror. My own observation fully bears out the remark.

What have we here, if not, towering above all talk and argument, the plentifully-supplied, last-needed proof of democracy, in its personalities? Curiously enough, too, the proof on this point comes, I should say, every bit as much from the south, as from the north. Although I have spoken only of the latter, yet I deliberately include all. Grand, common stock! to me the accomplish'd and convincing growth, prophetic of the future; proof undeniable to sharpest sense, of perfect beauty, tenderness and pluck, that never feudal lord, nor Greek, nor Roman breed, yet rival'd. Let no tongue ever speak in disparagement of the American races, north or south, to one who has been through the war in the great army hospitals.

Meantime, general humanity, (for to that we return, as, for our purposes, what it really is, to bear in mind,) has always, in every department, been full of perverse maleficence, and is so yet. In downcast hours the soul thinks it always will be—but soon recovers from such sickly moods. I myself see clearly enough the crude, defective streaks in all the strata of the common people; the specimens and vast collections of the ignorant, the credulous, the unfit and uncouth, the incapable, and the very low and poor. The eminent person just mention'd sneeringly asks whether we expect to elevate and improve a nation's politics by absorbing such morbid collections and qualities therein. The point is a formidable one, and there will doubtless always be numbers of solid and reflective citizens who will never get over it. Our answer is general, and is involved in the scope and letter of this essay. We believe the ulterior object of political and all other government, (having of, course, provided for the police, the safety of life, property, and for the basic statute and common law, and their administration, always first in order,) to be among the rest, not merely to rule, to repress disorder, &c., but to develop, to open up to cultivation, to encourage the possibilities of all beneficent and manly outcroppage, and of that aspiration for independence, and the pride and self-respect latent in all characters. (Or, if there be exceptions, we cannot, fixing our eyes on them alone, make theirs the rule for all.)

I say the mission of government, henceforth, in civilized lands, is not repression alone, and not authority alone, not even of law, nor by that favorite standard of the eminent writer, the rule of the best men, the born heroes and captains of the race, (as if such ever, or one time out of a hundred, get into the big places, elective or dynastic)—but higher than the highest arbitrary rule, to train communities through all their grades, beginning with individuals and ending there again, to rule themselves. What Christ appear'd for in the moral-spiritual field for human-kind, namely, that in respect to the absolute soul, there is in the possession of such by each single individual, something so transcendent, so incapable of gradations, (like life,) that, to that extent, it places all beings on a common level, utterly regardless of the distinctions of intellect, virtue, station, or any height or lowliness whatever—is tallied in like manner, in this other field, by democracy's rule that men, the nation, as a common aggregate of living identities, affording in each a separate and complete subject for freedom, worldly thrift and happiness, and for a fair chance for growth, and for protection in citizenship, &c., must, to the political extent of the suffrage or vote, if no further, be placed, in each and in the whole, on one broad, primary, universal, common platform.

The purpose is not altogether direct; perhaps it is more indirect. For it is not that democracy is of exhaustive account, in itself. Perhaps, indeed, it is, (like Nature,) of no account in itself. It is that, as we see, it is the best, perhaps only, fit and full means, formulater, general caller-forth, trainer, for the million, not for grand material personalities only, but for immortal souls. To be a voter with the rest is not so much; and this, like every institute, will have its imperfections. But to become an enfranchised man, and now, impediments removed, to stand and start without humiliation, and equal with the rest; to commence, or have the road clear'd to commence, the grand experiment of development, whose end, (perhaps requiring several generations,) may be the forming of a full-grown man or woman—that *is* something. To ballast the State is also secured, and in our times is to be secured, in no other way.

We do not, (at any rate I do not), put it either on the ground that the People, the masses, even the best of them, are, in their latent or exhibited qualities, essentially sensible and good—nor on the ground of their rights; but that good or bad, rights or no rights, the democratic formula is the only safe and preservative one for coming times. We endow the masses with the suffrage for their own sake, no doubt; then, perhaps still more, from another point of view, for community's sake. Leaving the rest to the sentimentalists, we present freedom as sufficient in its scientific aspect, cold as ice, reasoning, deductive, clear and passionless as crystal.

Democracy too is law, and of the strictest, amplest kind. Many suppose, (and often in its own ranks the error,) that it means a throwing aside of law, and running riot. But, briefly, it is the superior law, not alone that of physical force, the body, which, adding to, it supersedes with that of the spirit. Law is the unshakable order of the universe forever; and the law over all, and law of laws, is the law of successions; that of the superior law, in time, gradually supplanting and overwhelming the inferior one. (While, for myself, I would cheerfully agree—first covenanting that the formative tendencies shall be administer'd in favor, or at least not against it, and that this reservation be closely construed—that until the individual or community show due signs, or be so minor and fractional as not to endanger the State, the condition of authoritative tutelage may continue, and self-government must abide its time.) Nor is the esthetic point, always an important one, without fascination for highest aiming souls. The common ambition strains for elevations, to become some privileged exclusive. The master sees greatness and health in being part of the mass; nothing will do as well as common ground. Would you have in yourself the divine, vast, general law? Then merge yourself in it.

And, topping democracy, this most alluring record, that it alone can bind, and ever seeks to bind, all nations, all men, of however various and distant lands, into a brotherhood, a family. It is the old, yet ever-modern dream of earth, out of her eldest and her youngest, her fond philosophers and poets. Not that half only, individualism, which isolates. There is another half, which is adhesiveness or love, that fuses, ties and aggregates, making the races comrades, and fraternizing all. Both are to be vitalized by religion, (sole worthiest elevator of man or State,) breathing into the proud, material tissues, the breath of life. For I say at the core of democracy, finally, is the religious element. All the religions, old and new, are there. Nor may the scheme step forth, clothed in resplendent beauty and command, till these, bearing the best, the latest fruit, the spiritual, shall fully appear.

A portion of our pages we might indite with reference toward Europe, especially the British part of it, more than our own land, perhaps not absolutely needed for the home reader. But the whole question hangs together, and fastens and links all peoples. The liberalist of to-day has this advantage over antique or medieval times, that his doctrine seeks not only to individualize but to universalize. The great word Solidarity has arisen. Of all dangers to a nation, as things exist in our day, there can be no greater one than having certain portions of the people set off from the rest by a line drawn—they not privileged as others, but degraded, humiliated, made of no account. Much quackery teems, of course, even on democracy's side, yet does not really affect the orbic quality of the matter. To work in, if we may so term it, and justify God, his divine aggregate, the People, (or, the veritable horn'd and sharp-tail'd Devil, *his* aggregate, if there be who convulsively insist upon it)—this, I say, is what democracy is for; and this is what our America means, and is doing—may I not say, has done? If not, she means nothing more, and does nothing more, than any other land. And as, by virtue of its kosmical, antiseptic power, Nature's stomach is fully strong enough not only to digest the morbific matter always presented, not to be turn'd aside, and perhaps, indeed, intuitively gravitating thither—but even to change such contributions into nutriment for highest use and life—so American democracy's. That is the lesson we, these days, send over to European lands by every western breeze.

And, truly, whatever may be said in the way of abstract argument, for or against the theory of a wider democratizing of institutions in any civilized country, much trouble might well be saved to all European lands by recognizing this palpable fact, (for a palpable fact it is,) that some form of such democratizing is about the only resource now left. *That*, to chronic dissatisfaction continued, mutterings which grow annually louder and louder, till, in due course, and pretty swiftly in most cases, the inevitable crisis, crash, dynastic ruin. Anything worthy to be call'd statesmanship in the Old World, I should say, among the advanced students, adepts, or men of any brains, does not debate to-day whether to hold on, attempting to lean back and monarchize, or to look forward and democratize—but *how*, and in what degree and part, most prudently to democratize.

The eager and often inconsiderate appeals of reformers and revolutionists are indispensable, to counterbalance the inertness and fossilism making so large a part of human institutions. The latter will always take care of themselves—the danger being that they rapidly tend to ossify us. The former is to be treated with indulgence, and even with respect. As circulation to air, so is agitation and a plentiful degree of speculative license to political and moral sanity. Indirectly, but surely, goodness, virtue, law, (of the very best,) follow freedom. These, to democracy, are what the keel is to the ship, or saltness to the ocean.

The true gravitation-hold of liberalism in the United States will be a more universal ownership of property, general homesteads, general comfort—a vast, intertwining reticulation of wealth. As the human frame, or, indeed, any object in this manifold universe, is best kept together by the simple miracle of its own cohesion, and the necessity, exercise and profit thereof, so a great and varied nationality, occupying millions of square miles, were firmest held and knit by the principle of the safety and endurance of the aggregate of its middling property owners. So that, from another point of view, ungracious as it may sound, and a paradox after what we have been saying, democracy looks with suspicious, ill-satisfied eye upon the very poor, the ignorant, and on those out of business. She asks for men and women with occupations, well-off, owners of houses and acres, and with cash in the bank—and with some cravings for literature, too; and must have them, and hastens to make them. Luckily, the seed is already well-sown, and has taken ineradicable root.*

Huge and mighty are our days, our republican lands—and most in their rapid shiftings, their changes, all in the interest of the cause. As I write this particular passage, (November, 1868,) the din of disputation rages around me. Acrid the temper of the parties, vital the pending questions. Congress convenes; the President sends his message; reconstruction is still in abeyance; the nomination and the contest for the twenty-first Presidentiad draw close, with loudest threat and bustle. Of these, and all the like of these, the eventuations I know not; but well I know that behind them, and whatever their eventuations, the vital things remain safe and certain, and all the needed work goes on. Time, with soon or later superciliousness, disposes of Presidents, Congressmen, party platforms, and such. Anon, it clears the stage of each and any mortal shred that thinks itself so potent to its day; and at and after which, (with precious, golden exceptions once or twice in a century,) all that relates to sir potency is flung to moulder in a burial-vault, and no one bothers himself the least bit about it afterward. But the People ever remain, tendencies continue, and all the idiocratic transfers in unbroken chain go on.

---

* For fear of mistake, I may as well distinctly specify, as cheerfully included in the model and standard of these Vistas, a practical, stirring, worldly, money-making, even materialistic character. It is undeniable that our farms, stores, offices, dry-goods, coal and groceries, enginery, cash-accounts, trades, earnings, markets, &c., should be attended to in earnest, and actively pursued, just as if they had a real and permanent existence. I perceive clearly that the extreme business energy, and this almost maniacal appetite for wealth prevalent in the United States, are parts of amelioration and progress, indispensably needed to prepare the very results I demand. My theory includes riches, and the getting of riches, and the amplest products, power, activity, inventions, movements, &c. Upon them, as upon substrata, I raise the edifice design'd in these Vistas.

In a few years the dominion-heart of America will be far inland, toward the West. Our future national capital may not be where the present one is. It is possible, nay likely, that in less than fifty years, it will migrate a thousand or two miles, will be re-founded, and every thing belonging to it made on a different plan, original, far more superb. The main social, political, spine-character of the States will probably run along the Ohio, Missouri and Mississippi rivers, and west and north of them, including Canada. Those regions, with the group of powerful brothers toward the Pacific, (destined to the mastership of that sea and its countless paradises of islands,) will compact and settle the traits of America, with all the old retain'd, but more expanded, grafted on newer, hardier, purely native stock. A giant growth, composite from the rest, getting their contribution, absorbing it, to make it more illustrious. From the north, intellect, the sun of things, also the idea of unswayable justice, anchor amid the last, the wildest tempests. From the south the living soul, the animus of good and bad, haughtily admitting no demonstration but its own. While from the west itself comes solid personality, with blood and brawn, and the deep quality of all-accepting fusion.

Political democracy, as it exists and practically works in America, with all its threatening evils, supplies a training-school for making first-class men. It is life's gymnasium, not of good only, but of all. We try often, though we fall back often. A brave delight, fit for freedom's athletes, fills these arenas, and fully satisfies, out of the action in them, irrespective of success. Whatever we do not attain, we at any rate attain the experiences of the fight, the hardening of the strong campaign, and throb with currents of attempt at least. Time is ample. Let the victors come after us. Not for nothing does evil play its part among us. Judging from the main portions of the history of the world, so far, justice is always in jeopardy, peace walks amid hourly pitfalls, and of slavery, misery, meanness, the craft of tyrants and the credulity of the populace, in some of their protean forms, no voice can at any time say, They are not. The clouds break a little, and the sun shines out—but soon and certain the lowering darkness falls again, as if to last forever. Yet is there an immortal courage and prophecy in every sane soul that cannot, must not, under any circumstances, capitulate. *Vive*, the attack—the perennial assault! *Vive*, the unpopular cause—the spirit that audaciously aims—the never-abandon'd efforts, pursued the same amid opposing proofs and precedents.

Once, before the war, (Alas! I dare not say how many times the mood has come!) I, too, was fill'd with doubt and gloom. A foreigner, an acute and good man, had impressively said to me, that day—putting in form, indeed, my own observations: "I have trav-el'd much in the United States, and watch'd their politicians, and listen'd to the speeches of the candidates, and read the journals, and gone into the public houses, and heard the unguarded talk of men. And I have found your vaunted America honeycomb'd from top to toe with infidelism, even to itself and its own programme. I have mark'd the brazen hell-faces of secession and slavery gazing defiantly from all the windows and doorways. I have everywhere found, primarily, thieves and scalliwags arranging the nominations to offices, and sometimes filling the offices themselves. I have found the north just as full of bad stuff as the south. Of the holders of public office in the Nation or the States or their municipalities, I have found that not one in a hundred has been chosen by any spontaneous selection of the outsiders, the people, but all have been nominated and put through by little or large caucuses of the politicians, and have got in by corrupt rings and electioneering, not capacity or desert. I have noticed how the millions of sturdy farm-ers and mechanics are thus the helpless supple-jacks of compara-tively few politicians. And I have noticed more and more, the alarming spectacle of parties usurping the government, and openly and shamelessly wielding it for party purposes."

Sad, serious, deep truths. Yet are there other, still deeper, amply confronting, dominating truths. Over those politicians and great and little rings, and over all their insolence and wiles, and over the powerfulest parties, looms a power, too sluggish may-be, but ever holding decisions and decrees in hand, ready, with stern process, to execute them as soon as plainly needed—and at times, indeed, summarily crushing to atoms the mightiest parties, even in the hour of their pride.

In saner hours far different are the amounts of these things from what, at first sight, they appear. Though it is no doubt important who is elected governor, mayor, or legislator, (and full of dismay when incompetent or vile ones get elected, as they sometimes do,) there are other, quieter contingencies, infinitely more important. Shams, &c., will always be the show, like ocean's scum; enough, if waters deep and clear make up the rest. Enough, that while the piled embroider'd shoddy gaud and fraud spreads to the superficial eye, the hidden warp and weft are genuine, and will wear forever. Enough, in short, that the race, the land which could raise such as the late rebellion, could also put it down.

The average man of a land at last only is important. He, in these States, remains immortal owner and boss, deriving good uses somehow, out of any sort of servant in office, even the basest; (certain universal requisites, and their settled regularity and protection, being first secured,) a nation like ours, in a sort of geological formation state, trying continually new experiments, choosing new delegations, is not served by the best men only, but sometimes more by those that provoke it—by the combats they arouse. Thus national rage, fury, discussion, &c., better than content. Thus, also, the warning signals, invaluable for after times.

What is more dramatic than the spectacle we have seen repeated, and doubtless long shall see—the popular judgment taking the successful candidates on trial in the offices—standing off, as it were, and observing them and their doings for a while, and always giving, finally, the fit, exactly due reward? I think, after all, the sublimest part of political history, and its culmination, is currently issuing from the American people. I know nothing grander, better exercise, better digestion, more positive proof of the past, the triumphant result of faith in human kind, than a well-contested American national election.

Then still the thought returns, (like the thread-passage in overtures,) giving the key and echo to these pages. When I pass to and fro, different latitudes, different seasons, beholding the crowds of the great cities, New York, Boston, Philadelphia, Cincinnati, Chicago, St. Louis, San Francisco, New Orleans, Baltimore—when I mix with these interminable swarms of alert, turbulent, good-natured, independent citizens, mechanics, clerks, young persons—at the idea of this mass of men, so fresh and free, so loving and so proud, a singular awe falls upon me. I feel, with dejection and amazement, that among our geniuses and talented writers or speakers, few or none have yet really spoken to this people, created a single image-making work for them, or absorb'd the central spirit and the idiosyncrasies which are theirs—and which, thus, in highest ranges, so far remain entirely uncelebrated, unexpress'd.

Dominion strong is the body's; dominion stronger is the mind's. What has fill'd, and fills to-day our intellect, our fancy, furnishing the standards therein, is yet foreign. The great poems, Shakspere included, are poisonous to the idea of the pride and dignity of the common people, the life-blood of democracy. The models of our literature, as we get it from other lands, ultramarine, have had their birth in courts, and bask'd and grown in castle sunshine; all smells of princes' favors. Of workers of a certain sort, we have, indeed, plenty, contributing after their kind; many elegant, many learn'd, all complacent. But touch'd by the national test, or tried by the standards of democratic personality, they wither to ashes. I say I have not seen a single writer, artist, lecturer, or what not, that has confronted the voiceless but ever erect and active, pervading, underlying will and typic aspiration of the land, in a spirit kindred to itself. Do you call those genteel little creatures American poets? Do you term that perpetual, pistareen, paste-pot work, American art, American drama, taste, verse? I think I hear, echoed as from some mountain-top afar in the west, the scornful laugh of the Genius of these States.

Democracy, in silence, biding its time, ponders its own ideals, not of literature and art only—not of men only, but of women. The idea of the women of America, (extricated from this daze, this fossil and unhealthy air which hangs about the word *lady*,) develop'd, raised to become the robust equals, workers, and, it may be, even practical and political deciders with the men—greater than man, we may admit, through their divine maternity, always their towering, emblematical attribute—but great, at any rate, as man, in all departments; or, rather, capable of being so, soon as they realize it, and can bring themselves to give up toys and fictions, and launch forth, as men do, amid real, independent, stormy life.

Then, as towards our thought's finalè, (and, in that, overarching the true scholar's lesson,) we have to say there can be no complete or epical presentation of democracy in the aggregate, or anything like it, at this day, because its doctrines will only be effectually incarnated in any one branch, when, in all, their spirit is at the root and centre. Far, far, indeed, stretch, in distance, our Vistas! How much is still to be disentangled, freed! How long it takes to make this American world see that it is, in itself, the final authority and reliance!

Did you, too, O friend, suppose democracy was only for elections, for politics, and for a party name? I say democracy is only of use there that it may pass on and come to its flower and fruits in manners, in the highest forms of interaction between men, and their beliefs—in religion, literature, colleges, and schools—democracy in all public and private life, and in the army and navy.* I

---

* The whole present system of the officering and personnel of the army and navy of these States, and the spirit and letter of their trebly-aristocratic rules and regulations, is a monstrous exotic, a nuisance and revolt, and belong here just as much as orders of nobility, or the Pope's council of cardinals. I say if the present theory of our army and navy is sensible and true, then the rest of America is an unmitigated fraud.

have intimated that, as a paramount scheme, it has yet few or no full realizers and believers. I do not see, either, that it owes any serious thanks to noted propagandists or champions, or has been essentially help'd, though often harm'd, by them. It has been and is carried on by all the moral forces, and by trade, finance, machinery, intercommunications, and, in fact, by all the developments of history, and can no more be stopp'd than the tides, or the earth in its orbit. Doubtless, also, it resides, crude and latent, well down in the hearts of the fair average of the American-born people, mainly in the agricultural regions. But it is not yet, there or anywhere, the fully-receiv'd, the fervid, the absolute faith.

I submit, therefore, that the fruition of democracy, on aught like a grand scale, resides altogether in the future. As, under any profound and comprehensive view of the gorgeous-composite feudal world, we see in it, through the long ages and cycles of ages, the results of a deep, integral, human and divine principle, or fountain, from which issued laws, ecclesia, manners, institutes, costumes, personalities, poems, (hitherto unequall'd,) faithfully partaking of their source, and indeed only arising either to betoken it, or to furnish parts of that varied-flowing display, whose centre was one and absolute—so, long ages hence, shall the due historian or critic make at least an equal retrospect, an equal history for the democratic principle. It too must be adorn'd, credited with its results—then, when it, with imperial power, through amplest time, has dominated mankind—has been the source and test of all the moral, esthetic, social, political, and religious expressions and institutes of the civilized world—has begotten them in spirit and in form, and has carried them to its own unprecedented heights—has had, (it is possible,) monastics and ascetics, more numerous, more devout than the monks and priests of all previous creeds—has sway'd the ages with a breadth and rectitude tallying Nature's own—has fashion'd, systematized, and triumphantly finish'd and carried out, in its own interest, and with unparallel'd success, a new earth and a new man.

Thus we presume to write, as it were, upon things that exist not, and travel by maps yet unmade, and a blank. But the throes of birth are upon us; and we have something of this advantage in seasons of strong formations, doubts, suspense—for then the afflatus of such themes haply may fall upon us, more or less; and then, hot from surrounding war and revolution, our speech, though without polish'd coherence, and a failure by the standard called criticism, comes forth, real at least as the lightnings.

And may-be we, these days, have, too, our own reward—(for there are yet some, in all lands, worthy to be so encouraged.) Though not for us the joy of entering at the last the conquer'd city—not ours the chance ever to see with our own eyes the peerless power and splendid *eclat* of the democratic principle, arriv'd at meridian, filling the world with effulgence and majesty far beyond those of past history's kings, or all dynastic sway—there is yet, to whoever is eligible among us, the prophetic vision, the joy of being toss'd in the brave turmoil of these times—the promulgation and the path, obedient, lowly reverent to the voice, the gesture of the god, or holy ghost, which others see not, hear not—with the proud consciousness that amid whatever clouds, seductions, or heart-wearying postponements, we have never deserted, never despair'd, never abandon'd the faith.

So much contributed, to be conn'd well, to help prepare and brace our edifice, our plann'd Idea—we still proceed to give it in another of its aspects—perhaps the main, the high façade of all. For to democracy, the leveler, the unyielding principle of the average, is surely join'd another principle, equally unyielding, closely tracking the first, indispensable to it, opposite, (as the sexes are opposite,) and whose existence, confronting and ever modifying the other, often clashing, paradoxical, yet neither of highest avail without the other, plainly supplies to these grand cosmic politics of ours, and to the launch'd forth mortal dangers of republicanism, to-day or any day, the counterpart and offset whereby Nature restrains the deadly original relentlessness of all her first-class laws. This second principle is individuality, the pride and centripetal isolation of a human being in himself—identity—personalism. Whatever the name, its acceptance and thorough infusion through the organizations of political commonalty now shooting Aurora-like about the world, are of utmost importance, as the principle itself is needed for very life's sake. It forms, in a sort, or is to form, the compensating balance-wheel of the successful working machinery of aggregate America.

And, if we think of it, what does civilization itself rest upon—and what object has it, with its religions, arts, schools, &c., but rich, luxuriant, varied personalism? To that, all bends; and it is because toward such result democracy alone, on anything like Nature's scale, breaks up the limitless fallows of humankind, and plants the seed, and gives fair play, that its claims now precede the rest. The literature, songs, esthetics, &c., of a country are of importance principally because they furnish the materials and suggestions of personality for the women and men of that country, and enforce them in a thousand effective ways.* As the topmost claim of a strong consolidating of the nationality of these States, is, that only by such powerful compaction can the separate States secure that full and free swing within their spheres, which is becoming to them, each after its kind, so will individuality, with unimpeded branchings, flourish best under imperial republican forms.

Assuming Democracy to be at present in its embryo condition, and that the only large and satisfactory justification of it resides in the future, mainly through the copious production of perfect characters among the people, and through the advent of a sane and pervading religiousness, it is with regard to the atmosphere and spaciousness fit for such characters, and of certain nutriment and cartoon-draftings proper for them, and indicating them for New World purposes, that I continue the present statement—an exploration, as of new ground, wherein, like other primitive surveyors, I must do the best I can, leaving it to those who come after me to do much better. (The service, in fact, if any, must be to break a sort of first path or track, no matter how rude and ungeometrical.)

We have frequently printed the word Democracy. Yet I cannot too often repeat that it is a word the real gist of which still sleeps,

---

* After the rest is satiated, all interest culminates in the field of persons, and never flags there. Accordingly in this field have the great poets and literatuses signally toil'd. They too, in all ages, all lands, have been creators, fashioning, making types of men and women, as Adam and Eve are made in the divine fable. Behold, shaped, bred by orientalism, feudalism, through their long growth and culmination, and breeding back in return—(when shall we have an equal series, typical of democracy?)—behold, commencing in primal Asia, (apparently formulated, in what beginning we know, in the gods of the mythologies, and coming down thence,) a few samples out of the countless product, bequeath'd to the moderns, bequeath'd to America as studies. For the men, Yudishtura, Rama, Arjuna, Solomon, most of the Old and New Testament characters; Achilles, Ulysses, Theseus, Prometheus, Hercules, Æneas, Plutarch's heroes; the Merlin of Celtic bards; the Cid, Arthur and his knights, Siegfried and Hagen in the Nibelungen; Roland and Oliver; Roustam in the Shah-Nemah; and so on to Milton's Satan, Cervantes' Don Quixote, Shakspere's Hamlet, Richard II., Lear, Marc Antony, &c., and the modern Faust. These, I say, are models, combined, adjusted to other standards than America's, but of priceless value to her and hers.

Among women, the goddesses of the Egyptian, Indian and Greek mythologies, certain Bible characters, especially the Holy Mother; Cleopatra, Penelope; the portraits of Brunhelde and Chriemhilde in the Nibelungen; Oriana, Una, &c.; the modern Consuelo, Walter Scott's Jeanie and Effie Deans, &c., &c. (Yet woman portray'd or outlin'd at her best, or as perfect human mother, does not hitherto, it seems to me, fully appear in literature.)

quite unawaken'd, notwithstanding the resonance and the many angry tempests out of which its syllables have come, from pen or tongue. It is a great word, whose history, I suppose, remains unwritten, because that history has yet to be enacted. It is, in some sort, younger brother of another great and often-used word, Nature, whose history also waits unwritten. As I perceive, the tendencies of our day, in the States, (and I entirely respect them,) are toward those vast and sweeping movements, influences, moral and physical, of humanity, now and always current over the planet, on the scale of the impulses of the elements. Then it is also good to reduce the whole matter to the consideration of a single self, a man, a woman, on permanent grounds. Even for the treatment of the universal, in politics, metaphysics, or anything, sooner or later we come down to one single, solitary soul.

There is, in sanest hours, a consciousness, a thought that rises, independent, lifted out from all else, calm, like the stars, shining eternal. This is the thought of identity—yours for you, whoever you are, as mine for me. Miracle of miracles, beyond statement, most spiritual and vaguest of earth's dreams, yet hardest basic fact, and only entrance to all facts. In such devout hours, in the midst of the significant wonders of heaven and earth, (significant only because of the Me in the centre,) creeds, conventions, fall away and become of no account before this simple idea. Under the luminousness of real vision, it alone takes possession, takes value. Like the shadowy dwarf in the fable, once liberated and look'd upon, it expands over the whole earth, and spreads to the roof of heaven.

The quality of BEING, in the object's self, according to its own central idea and purpose, and of growing therefrom and thereto—not criticism by other standards, and adjustments thereto—is the lesson of Nature. True, the full man wisely gathers, culls, absorbs; but if, engaged disproportionately in that, he slights or overlays the precious idiocrasy and special nativity and intention that he is, the man's self, the main thing, is a failure, however wide his general cultivation. Thus, in our times, refinement and delicatesse are not only attended to sufficiently, but threaten to eat us up, like a cancer. Already, the democratic genius watches, ill-pleased, these tendencies. Provision for a little healthy rudeness, savage virtue, justification of what one has in one's self, whatever it is, is demanded. Negative qualities, even deficiencies, would be a relief. Singleness and normal simplicity and separation, amid this more and more complex, more and more artificialized state of society—how pensively we yearn for them! how we would welcome their return!

In some such direction, then—at any rate enough to preserve the balance—we feel called upon to throw what weight we can, not for absolute reasons, but current ones. To prune, gather, trim, conform, and ever cram and stuff, and be genteel and proper, is the pressure of our days. While aware that much can be said even in behalf of all this, we perceive that we have not now to consider the question of what is demanded to serve a half-starved and barbarous nation, or set of nations, but what is most applicable, most pertinent, for numerous congeries of conventional, over-corpulent societies, already becoming stifled and rotten with flatulent, infidelistic literature, and polite conformity and art. In addition to establish'd sciences, we suggest a science as it were of healthy average personalism, on original-universal grounds, the object of which should be to raise up and supply through the States a copious race of superb American men and women, cheerful, religious, ahead of any yet known.

America has yet morally and artistically originated nothing. She seems singularly unaware that the models of persons, books, manners, &c., appropriate for former conditions and for European lands, are but exiles and exotics here. No current of her life, as shown on the surfaces of what is authoritatively called her society, accepts or runs into social or esthetic democracy; but all the currents set squarely against it. Never, in the Old World, was thoroughly upholster'd exterior appearance and show, mental and other, built entirely on the idea of caste, and on the sufficiency of mere outside acquisition—never were glibness, verbal intellect, more the test, the emulation—more loftily elevated as head and sample—than they are on the surface of our republican States this day. The writers of a time hint the mottoes of its gods. The word of the modern, say these voices, is the word Culture.

We find ourselves abruptly in close quarters with the enemy. This word Culture, or what it has come to represent, involves, by contrast, our whole theme, and has been, indeed, the spur, urging us to engagement. Certain questions arise. As now taught, accepted and carried out, are not the processes of culture rapidly creating a class of supercilious infidels, who believe in nothing? Shall a man lose himself in countless masses of adjustments, and be so shaped with reference to this, that, and the other, that the simply good and healthy and brave parts of him are reduced and clipp'd away, like the bordering of box in a garden? You can cultivate corn and roses and orchards—but who shall cultivate the mountain peaks, the ocean, and the tumbling gorgeousness of the clouds? Lastly—is the readily-given reply that culture only seeks to help, systematize, and put in attitude, the elements of fertility and power, a conclusive reply?

I do not so much object to the name, or word, but I should certainly insist, for the purposes of these States, on a radical change of category, in the distribution of precedence. I should demand a programme of culture, drawn out, not for a single class alone, or for the parlors or lecture-rooms, but with an eye to practical life, the west, the working-men, the facts of farms and jack-planes and engineers, and of the broad range of the women also of the middle and working strata, and with reference to the perfect equality of women, and of a grand and powerful motherhood. I should demand of this programme or theory a scope generous enough to include the widest human area. It must have for its spinal meaning the formation of a typical personality of character, eligible to the uses of the high average of men—and *not* restricted by conditions ineligible to the masses. The best culture will always be that of the manly and courageous instincts, and loving perceptions, and of self-respect—aiming to form, over this continent, an idiocrasy of universalism, which, true child of America, will bring joy to its mother, returning to her in her own spirit, recruiting myriads of offspring, able, natural, perceptive, tolerant, devout believers in her, America, and with some definite instinct why and for what she has arisen, most vast, most formidable of historic births, and is, now and here, with wonderful step, journeying through Time.

The problem, as it seems to me, presented to the New World, is, under permanent law and order, and after preserving cohesion, (ensemble-Individuality,) at all hazards, to vitalize man's free play of special Personalism, recognizing in it something that calls ever more to be consider'd, fed, and adopted as the substratum for the best that belongs to us, (government indeed is for it,) including the new esthetics of our future.

To formulate beyond this present vagueness—to help limn and put before us the species, or a specimen of the species, of the democratic ethnology of the future, is a work toward which the genius of our land, with peculiar encouragement, invites her well-wishers. Already certain limnings, more or less grotesque, more or less fading and watery, have appear'd. We too, (repressing doubts and qualms,) will try our hand.

Attempting, then, however crudely, a basic model or portrait of personality for general use for the manliness of the States, (and doubtless that is most useful which is most simple and comprehen-

sive for all, and toned low enough,) we should prepare the canvas
well beforehand. Parentage must consider itself in advance. (Will
the time hasten when fatherhood and motherhood shall become a
science—and the noblest science?) To our model, a clear-blooded,
strong-fibred physique, is indispensable; the questions of food,
drink, air, exercise, assimilation, digestion, can never be intermitted. Out of these we descry a well-begotten selfhood—in youth,
fresh, ardent, emotional, aspiring, full of adventure; at maturity,
brave, perceptive, under control, neither too talkative nor too
reticent, neither flippant nor sombre; of the bodily figure, the movements easy, the complexion showing the best blood, somewhat
flush'd, breast expanded, an erect attitude, a voice whose sound
outvies music, eyes of calm and steady gaze, yet capable also of
flashing—and a general presence that holds its own in the company
of the highest. (For it is native personality, and that alone, that
endows a man to stand before presidents or generals, or in any
distinguish'd collection, with *aplomb*—and *not* culture, or any knowledge or intellect whatever.)

With regard to the mental-educational part of our model, enlarge-
ment of intellect, stores of cephalic knowledge, &c., the concentration thitherward of all the customs of our age, especially in America,
is so overweening, and provides so fully for that part, that, important
and necessary as it is, it really needs nothing from us here—except,
indeed, a phrase of warning and restraint. Manners, costumes, too,
though important, we need not dwell upon here. Like beauty, grace
of motion, &c., they are results. Causes, original things, being
attended to, the right manners unerringly follow. Much is said,
among artists, of "the grand style," as if it were a thing by itself.
When a man, artist or whoever, has health, pride, acuteness, noble
aspirations, he has the motive-elements of the grandest style. The
rest is but manipulation, (yet that is no small matter.)

Leaving still unspecified several sterling parts of any model fit
for the future personality of America, I must not fail, again and
ever, to pronounce myself on one, probably the least attended to
in modern times—a hiatus, indeed, threatening its gloomiest con-
sequences after us. I mean the simple, unsophisticated Conscience,
the primary moral element. If I were asked to specify in what quarter
lie the grounds of darkest dread, respecting the America of our
hopes, I should have to point to this particular. I should demand
the invariable application to individuality, this day and any day, of
that old, ever-true plumb-rule of persons, eras, nations. Our triumphant modern civilizee, with his all-schooling and his wondrous

appliances, will still show himself but an amputation while this deficiency remains. Beyond, (assuming a more hopeful tone,) the vertebration of the manly and womanly personalism of our western world, can only be, and is, indeed, to be (I hope,) its all penetrating Religiousness.

The ripeness of Religion is doubtless to be looked for in this field of individuality, and is a result that no organization or church can ever achieve. As history is poorly retain'd by what the technists call history, and is not given out from their pages, except the learner has in himself the sense of the well-wrapt, never yet written, perhaps impossible to be written, history—so Religion, although casually arrested, and, after a fashion, preserv'd in the churches and creeds, does not depend at all upon them, but is a part of the identified soul, which, when greatest, knows not bibles in the old way, but in new ways—the identified soul, which can really confront Religion when it extricates itself entirely from the churches, and not before.

Personalism fuses this, and favors it. I should say, indeed, that only in the perfect uncontamination and solitariness of individuality may the spirituality of religion positively come forth at all. Only here, and on such terms, the meditation, the devout ecstasy, the soaring flight. Only here, communion with the mysteries, the eternal problems, whence? whither? Alone, and identity, and the mood—and the soul emerges, and all statements, churches, sermons, melt away like vapors. Alone, and silent thought and awe, and aspiration—and then the interior consciousness, like a hitherto unseen inscription, in magic ink, beams out its wondrous lines to the sense. Bibles may convey, and priests expound, but it is exclusively for the noiseless operation of one's isolated Self, to enter the pure ether of veneration, reach the divine levels, and commune with the unutterable.

To practically enter into politics is an important part of American personalism. To every young man, north and south, earnestly studying these things, I should here, as an offset to what I have said in former pages, now also say, that may-be to views of very largest scope, after all, perhaps the political, (perhaps the literary and sociological,) America goes best about its development its own way —sometimes, to temporary sight, appalling enough. It is the fashion among dillettants and fops (perhaps I myself am not guiltless,) to decry the whole formulation of the active politics of America, as beyond redemption, and to be carefully kept away from. See you that you do not fall into this error. America, it may be, is doing

very well upon the whole, notwithstanding these antics of the
parties and their leaders, these half-brain'd nominees, the many
ignorant ballots, and many elected failures and blatherers. It is the
dillettants, and all who shirk their duty, who are not doing well.
As for you, I advise you to enter more strongly yet into politics. I
advise every young man to do so. Always inform yourself; always
do the best you can; always vote. Disengage youself from parties.
They have been useful, and to some extent remain so; but the floating, uncommitted electors, farmers, clerks, mechanics, the masters
of parties—watching aloof, inclining victory this side or that side—
such are the ones most needed, present and future. For America,
if eligible at all to downfall and ruin, is eligible within herself, not
without; for I see clearly that the combined foreign world could
not beat her down. But these savage, wolfish parties alarm me.
Owning no law but their own will, more and more combative, less
and less tolerant of the idea of ensemble and of equal brotherhood,
the perfect equality of the States, the ever-overarching American
ideas, it behooves you to convey yourself implicitly to no party,
nor submit blindly to their dictators, but steadily hold yourself
judge and master over all of them.

So much, (hastily toss'd together, and leaving far more unsaid,)
for an ideal, or intimations of an ideal, toward American manhood. But the other sex, in our land, requires at least a basis of
suggestion.

I have seen a young American woman, one of a large family
of daughters, who, some years since, migrated from her meagre
country home to one of the northern cities, to gain her own support. She soon became an expert seamstress, but finding the employment too confining for health and comfort, she went boldly to
work for others, to house-keep, cook, clean, &c. After trying several
places, she fell upon one where she was suited. She has told me
that she finds nothing degrading in her position; it is not inconsistent with personal dignity, self-respect, and the respect of others.
She confers benefits and receives them. She has good health; her
presence itself is healthy and bracing; her character is unstain'd;
she has made herself understood, and preserves her independence,
and has been able to help her parents, and educate and get places
for her sisters; and her course of life is not without opportunities
for mental improvement, and of much quiet, uncosting happiness
and love.

I have seen another woman who, from taste and necessity con-
join'd, has gone into practical affairs, carries on a mechanical

business, partly works at it herself, dashes out more and more into real hardy life, is not abash'd by the coarseness of the contact, knows how to be firm and silent at the same time, holds her own with unvarying coolness and decorum, and will compare, any day, with superior carpenters, farmers, and even boatmen and drivers. For all that, she has not lost the charm of the womanly nature, but preserves and bears it fully, though through such rugged presentation.

Then there is the wife of a mechanic, mother of two children, a woman of merely passable English education, but of fine wit, with all her sex's grace and intuitions, who exhibits, indeed, such a noble female personality, that I am fain to record it here. Never abnegating her own proper independence, but always genially preserving it, and what belongs to it—cooking, washing, child-nursing, house-tending—she beams sunshine out of all these duties, and makes them illustrious. Physiologically sweet and sound, loving work, practical, she yet knows that there are intervals, however few, devoted to recreation, music, leisure, hospitality—and affords such intervals. Whatever she does, and wherever she is, that charm, that indescribable perfume of genuine womanhood attends her, goes with her, exhales from her, which belongs of right to all the sex, and is, or ought to be, the invariable atmosphere and common aureola of old as well as young.

My dear mother once described to me a resplendent person, down on Long Island, whom she knew in early days. She was known by the name of the Peacemaker. She was well toward eighty years old, of happy and sunny temperament, had always lived on a farm, and was very neighborly, sensible and discreet, an invariable and welcom'd favorite, especially with young married women. She had numerous children and grandchildren. She was uneducated, but possess'd a native dignity. She had come to be a tacitly agreed upon domestic regulator, judge, settler of difficulties, shepherdess, and reconciler in the land. She was a sight to draw near and look upon, with her large figure, her profuse snow-white hair, (uncoif'd by any head-dress or cap,) dark eyes, clear complexion, sweet breath, and peculiar personal magnetism.

The foregoing portraits, I admit, are frightfully out of line from these imported models of womanly personality—the stock feminine characters of the current novelists, or of the foreign court poems, (Ophelias, Enids, princesses, or ladies of one thing or another,) which fill the envying dreams of so many poor girls, and are accepted by our men, too, as supreme ideals of feminine excellence to be sought after. But I present mine just for a change.

Then there are mutterings, (we will not now stop to heed them
here, but they must be heeded,) of something more revolutionary.
The day is coming when the deep questions of woman's entrance
amid the arenas of practical life, politics, the suffrage, &c., will
not only be argued all around us, but may be put to decision, and
real experiment.

Of course, in these States, for both man and woman, we must
entirely recast the types of highest personality from what the oriental, feudal, ecclesiastical worlds bequeath us, and which yet possess the imaginative and esthetic fields of the United States, pictorial and melodramatic, not without use as studies, but making
sad work, and forming a strange anachronism upon the scenes
and exigencies around us. Of course, the old undying elements
remain. The task is, to successfully adjust them to new combinations, our own days. Nor is this so incredible. I can conceive a
community, to-day and here, in which, on a sufficient scale, the
perfect personalities, without noise meet; say in some pleasant
western settlement or town, where a couple of hundred best men and
women, of ordinary worldly status, have by luck been drawn together, with nothing extra of genius or wealth, but virtuous, chaste,
industrious, cheerful, resolute, friendly and devout. I can conceive
such a community organized in running order, powers judiciously
delegated—farming, building, trade, courts, mails, schools, elections, all attended to; and then the rest of life, the main thing,
freely branching and blossoming in each individual, and bearing
golden fruit. I can see there, in every young and old man, after his
kind, and in every woman after hers, a true personality, develop'd,
exercised proportionately in body, mind, and spirit. I can imagine
this case as one not necessarily rare or difficult, but in buoyant ac-
cordance with the municipal and general requirements of our times.
And I can realize in it the culmination of something better than any
stereotyped *eclat* of history or poems. Perhaps, unsung, undrama-
tized, unput in essays or biographies—perhaps even some such community already exists, in Ohio, Illinois, Missouri, or somewhere,
practically fulfilling itself, and thus outvying, in cheapest vulgar
life, all that has been hitherto shown in best ideal pictures.

In short, and to sum up, America, betaking herself to formative action, (as it is about time for more solid achievement, and
less windy promise,) must, for her purposes, cease to recognize a
theory of character grown of feudal aristocracies, or form'd by
merely literary standards, or from any ultramarine, full-dress for-

mulas of culture, polish, caste, &c., and must sternly promulgate
her own new standard, yet old enough, and accepting the old, the perennial elements, and combining them into groups, unities,
appropriate to the modern, the democratic, the west, and to the
practical occasions and needs of our own cities, and of the agricultural regions. Ever the most precious in the common. Ever the
fresh breeze of field, or hill, or lake, is more than any palpitation
of fans, though of ivory, and redolent with perfume; and the air
is more than the costliest perfumes.

And now, for fear of mistake, we may not intermit to beg our
absolution from all that genuinely is, or goes along with, even
Culture. Pardon us, venerable shade! if we have seem'd to speak
lightly of your office. The whole civilization of the earth, we know,
is yours, with all the glory and the light thereof. It is, indeed, in
your own spirit, and seeking to tally the loftiest teachings of it,
that we aim these poor utterances. For you, too, mighty minister!
know that there is something greater than you, namely, the fresh,
eternal qualities of Being. From them, and by them, as you, at
your best, we too evoke the last, the needed help, to vitalize our
country and our days. Thus we pronounce not so much against the
principle of culture; we only supervise it, and promulge along with
it, as deep, perhaps a deeper, principle. As we have shown the New
World including in itself the all-leveling aggregate of democracy,
we show it also including the all-varied, all-permitting, all-free
theorem of individuality, and erecting therefor a lofty and hitherto
unoccupied framework or platform, broad enough for all, eligible
to every farmer and mechanic—to the female equally with the
male—a towering selfhood, not physically perfect only—not satisfied with the mere mind's and learning's stores, but religious,
possessing the idea of the infinite, (rudder and compass sure amid
this troublous voyage, o'er darkest, wildest wave, through stormiest
wind, of man's or nation's progress)—realizing, above the rest, that
known humanity, in deepest sense, is fair adhesion to itself, for
purposes beyond—and that, finally, the personality of mortal life
is most important with reference to the immortal, the unknown, the
spiritual, the only permanently real, which as the ocean waits for
and receives the rivers, waits for us each and all.

Much is there, yet, demanding line and outline in our Vistas,
not only on these topics, but others quite unwritten. Indeed, we
could talk the matter, and expand it, through lifetime. But it is
necessary to return to our original premises In view of them, we

have again pointedly to confess that all the objective grandeurs of the world, for highest purposes, yield themselves up, and depend on mentality alone. Here, and here only, all balances, all rests. For the mind, which alone builds the permanent edifice, haughtily builds it to itself. By it, with what follows it, are convey'd to mortal sense the culminations of the materialistic, the known, and a prophecy of the unknown. To take expression, to incarnate, to endow a literature with grand and archetypal models—to fill with pride and love the utmost capacity, and to achieve spiritual meanings, and suggest the future—these, and these only, satisfy the soul. We must not say one word against real materials; but the wise know that they do not become real till touched by emotions, the mind. Did we call the latter imponderable? Ah, let us rather proclaim that the slightest song-tune, the countless ephemera of passions arous'd by orators and tale-tellers, are more dense, more weighty than the engines there in the great factories, or the granite blocks in their foundations.

Approaching thus the momentous spaces, and considering with reference to a new and greater personalism, the needs and possibilities of American imaginative literature, through the medium-light of what we have already broach'd, it will at once be appreciated that a vast gulf of difference separates the present accepted condition of these spaces, inclusive of what is floating in them, from any condition adjusted to, or fit for, the world, the America, there sought to be indicated, and the copious races of complete men and women, along these Vistas crudely outlined. It is, in some sort, no less a difference than lies between that long-continued nebular state and vagueness of the astronomical worlds, compared with the subsequent state, the definitely-form'd worlds themselves, duly compacted, clustering in systems, hung up there, chandeliers of the universe, beholding and mutually lit by each other's lights, serving for ground of all substantial foothold, all vulgar uses—yet serving still more as an undying chain and echelon of spiritual proofs and shows. A boundless field to fill! A new creation, with needed orbic works launch'd forth, to revolve in free and lawful circuits—to move, self-poised, through the ether, and shine like heaven's own suns! With such, and nothing less, we suggest that New World literature, fit to rise upon, cohere, and signalize in time, these States.

What, however, do we more definitely mean by New World literature? Are we not doing well enough here already? Are not the United States this day busily using, working, more printer's type, more presses, than any other country? uttering and absorbing more publications than any other? Do not our publishers fatten quicker and deeper? (helping themselves, under shelter of a delusive and sneaking law, or rather absence of law, to most of their forage, poetical, pictorial, historical, romantic, even comic, without money and without price—and fiercely resisting the timidest proposal to pay for it.) Many will come under this delusion—but my purpose is to dispel it. I say that a nation may hold and circulate rivers and oceans of very readable print, journals, magazines, novels, library-books, "poetry," &c.—such as the States to-day possess and circulate—of unquestionable aid and value—hundreds of new volumes annually composed and brought out here, respectable enough, indeed unsurpass'd in smartness and erudition—with further hundreds, or rather millions, (as by free forage or theft aforemention'd,) also thrown into the market—and yet, all the while, the said nation, land, strictly speaking, may possess no literature at all.

Repeating our inquiry, what, then, do we mean by real literature? especially the democratic literature of the future? Hard questions to meet. The clues are inferential, and turn us to the past. At best, we can only offer suggestions, comparisons, circuits.

It must still be reiterated, as, for the purpose of these memoranda, the deep lesson of history and time, that all else in the contributions of a nation or age, through its politics, materials, heroic personalities, military *eclat*, &c., remains crude, and defers, in any close and thorough-going estimate, until vitalized by national, original archetypes in literature. They only put the nation in form, finally tell anything—prove, complete anything—perpetuate anything. Without doubt, some of the richest and most powerful and populous communities of the antique world, and some of the grandest personalities and events, have, to after and present times, left themselves entirely unbequeath'd. Doubtless, greater than any that have come down to us, were among those lands, heroisms, persons, that have not come down to us at all, even by name, date, or location. Others have arrived safely, as from voyages over wide, century-stretching seas. The little ships, the miracles that have buoy'd them, and by incredible chances safely convey'd them, (or the best of them, their meaning and essence,) over long wastes, darkness, lethargy, ignorance, &c., have been a few inscriptions—a few immortal compositions, small in size, yet compassing what measureless values of reminiscence, contemporary portraitures, manners, idioms and beliefs, with deepest inference, hint and thought, to tie and touch forever the old, new body, and the old, new soul! These! and still these! bearing the freight so dear—dearer than pride—dearer than love. All the best experience of humanity, folded, saved, freighted to us here. Some of these tiny ships we call Old and New Testament, Homer, Eschylus, Plato, Juvenal, &c. Precious minims! I think, if we were forced to choose, rather than have you, and the likes of you, and what belongs to, and has grown of you, blotted out and gone, we could better afford, appalling as that would be, to lose all actual ships, this day fasten'd by wharf, or floating on wave, and see them, with all their cargoes, scuttled and sent to the bottom.

Gather'd by geniuses of city, race or age, and put by them in highest of art's forms, namely, the literary form, the peculiar combinations and the outshows of that city, age, or race, its particular modes of the universal attributes and passions, its faiths, heroes, lovers and gods, wars, traditions, struggles, crimes, emotions, joys, (or the subtle spirit of these,) having been pass'd on to us to illumine our own selfhood, and its experiences—what they supply, indispensable and highest, if taken away, nothing else in all the world's boundless storehouses could make up to us, or ever again return.

For us, along the great highways of time, those monuments stand —those forms of majesty and beauty. For us those beacons burn through all the nights. Unknown Egyptians, graving hieroglyphs; Hindus, with hymn and apothegm and endless epic; Hebrew prophet, with spirituality, as in flashes of lightning, conscience like red-hot iron, plaintive songs and screams of vengeance for tyrannies and enslavement; Christ, with bent head, brooding love and peace, like a dove; Greek, creating eternal shapes of physical and esthetic proportion; Roman, lord of satire, the sword, and the codex;— of the figures, some far off and veil'd, others nearer and visible; Dante, stalking with lean form, nothing but fibre, not a grain of superfluous flesh; Angelo, and the great painters, architects, musicians; rich Shakspere, luxuriant as the sun, artist and singer of feudalism in its sunset, with all the gorgeous colors, owner thereof, and using them at will; and so to such as German Kant and Hegel, where they, though near us, leaping over the ages, sit again, impassive, imperturbable, like the Egyptian gods. Of these, and the like of these, is it too much, indeed, to return to our favorite figure, and view them as orbs and systems of orbs, moving in free paths in the spaces of that other heaven, the kosmic intellect, the soul?

Ye powerful and resplendent ones! ye were, in your atmospheres, grown not for America, but rather for her foes, the feudal and the old—while our genius is democratic and modern. Yet could ye, indeed, but breathe your breath of life into our New World's nostrils—not to enslave us, as now, but, for our needs, to breed a spirit like your own—perhaps, (care we to say it?) to dominate, even destroy, what you yourselves have left! On your plane, and no less, but even higher and wider, must we mete and measure for to-day and here. I demand races of orbic bards, with unconditional uncompromising sway. Come forth, sweet democratic despots of the west!

By points like these we, in reflection, token what we mean by any land's or people's genuine literature. And thus compared and tested, judging amid the influence of loftiest products only, what do our current copious fields of print, covering in manifold forms, the United States, better, for an analogy, present, than, as in certain regions of the sea, those spreading, undulating masses of squid, through which the whale swimming, with head half out, feeds?

Not but that doubtless our current so-called literature, (like an endless supply of small coin,) performs a certain service, and may-be, too, the service needed for the time, (the preparation-service, as children learn to spell.) Everybody reads, and truly nearly everybody writes, either books, or for the magazines or journals. The matter has magnitude, too, after a sort. But is it really advancing? or, has it advanced for a long while? There is something impressive about the huge editions of the dailies and weeklies, the mountain-stacks of white paper piled in the press-vaults, and the proud, crashing, ten-cylinder presses, which I can stand and watch any time by the half hour. Then, (though the States in the field of imagination present not a single first-class work, nor a single great literatus,) the main objects, to amuse, to titillate, to pass away time, to circulate the news, and rumors of news, to rhyme and read rhyme, are yet attain'd, and on a scale of infinity. To-day, in books, in the rivalry of writers, especially novelists, success, (so-call'd,) is for him or her who strikes the mean flat average, the sensational appetite for stimulus, incident, persiflage, &c., and depicts, to the common calibre, sensual, exterior life. To such, or the luckiest of them, as we see, the audiences are limitless and profitable; but they cease presently. While this day, or any day, to workmen portraying interior or spiritual life, the audiences were limited, and often laggard—but they last forever.

Compared with the past, our modern science soars, and our journals serve—but ideal and even ordinary romantic literature, does not, I think, substantially advance. Behold the prolific brood of the contemporary novel, magazine-tale, theatre-play, &c. The same endless thread of tangled and superlative love-story, inherited, apparently from the Amadises and Palmerins of the 13th, 14th, and

15th centuries over there in Europe. The costumes and associations brought down to date, the seasoning hotter and more varied, the dragons and ogres left out—but the *thing*, I should say, has not advanced—is just as sensational, just as strain'd—remains about the same, nor more, nor less.

What is the reason our time, our lands, that we see no fresh local courage, sanity, of our own—the Mississippi, stalwart Western men, real mental and physical facts, Southerners, &c., in the body of our literature? especially the poetic part of it. But always, instead, a parcel of dandies and ennuyees, dapper little gentlemen from abroad, who flood us with their thin sentiment of parlors, parasols, piano-songs, tinkling rhymes, the five-hundredth importation—or whimpering and crying about something, chasing one aborted conceit after another, and forever occupied in dyspeptic amours with dyspeptic women. While, current and novel, the grandest events and revolutions, and stormiest passions of history, are crossing to-day with unparallel'd rapidity and magnificence over the stages of our own and all the continents, offering new materials, opening new vistas, with largest needs, inviting the daring launching forth of conceptions in literature, inspired by them, soaring in highest regions, serving art in its highest, (which is only the other name for serving God, and serving humanity,) where is the man of letters, where is the book, with any nobler aim than to follow in the old track, repeat what has been said before—and, as its utmost triumph, sell well, and be erudite or elegant?

Mark the roads, the processes, through which these States have arrived, standing easy, henceforth ever-equal, ever-compact, in their range today. European adventures? the most antique? Asiatic or African? old history—miracles—romances? Rather, our own unquestion'd facts. They hasten, incredible, blazing bright as fire. From the deeds and days of Columbus down to the present, and including the present—and especially the late Secession war—when I con them, I feel, every leaf, like stopping to see if I have not made a mistake, and fall'n on the splendid figments of some dream. But it is no dream. We stand, live, move, in the huge flow of our age's materialism—in its spirituality. We have had founded for us the most positive of lands. The founders have pass'd to other spheres—but what are these terrible duties they have left us?

Their politics the United States have, in my opinion, with all their faults, already substantially establish'd, for good, on their own native, sound, long-vista'd principles, never to be overturn'd, offering a sure basis for all the rest. With that, their future religious forms, sociology, literature, teachers, schools, costumes, &c., are of course to make a compact whole, uniform, on tallying principles. For how can we remain, divided, contradicting ourselves, this way?* I say we can only attain harmony and stability by consulting ensemble and the ethic purports, and faithfully building upon them. For the New World, indeed, after two grand stages of preparation-strata, I perceive that now a third stage, being ready for, (and without which the other two were useless,) with unmistakable signs appears. The First stage was the planning and putting on record the political foundation rights of immense masses of people—indeed all people—in the organization of republican National, State, and municipal governments, all constructed with reference to each, and each to all. This is the American programme, not for classes, but for universal man, and is embodied in the compacts of the Declaration of Independence, and, as it began and has now grown, with its amendments, the Federal Constitution—and in the State governments, with all their interiors, and with general suffrage; those having the sense not only of what is in themselves, but that their certain several things started, planted, hundreds of others in the same direction duly arise and follow. The Second stage relates to material prosperity, wealth, produce, labor-saving machines, iron, cotton, local, State and continental railways, intercommunication and trade with all lands, steamships, mining, general employment, organization of great cities, cheap appliances for comfort, numberless technical schools, books, newspapers, a currency for money circulation, &c. The Third stage, rising out of the previous ones, to make them and all illustrious, I, now, for one, promulge, announcing a native expression-spirit, getting into form, adult, and through mentality, for these States, self-contain'd, different from others, more expansive, more rich and free, to be evidenced by original authors and poets to come, by American personalities plenty of them, male and female, traversing the States, none excepted—and by native superber tableaux and growths of language, songs, operas, orations, lectures, architecture—and by a sublime and serious Religious Democracy sternly taking command, dis-

---

* Note, to-day, an instructive, curious spectacle and conflict. Science, (twin, in its fields, of Democracy in its)—Science, testing absolutely all thoughts, all works, has already burst well upon the world—a sun, mounting, most illuminating, most glorious—surely never again to set. But against it, deeply entrench'd, holding possession, yet remains, (not only through the churches and schools, but by imaginative literature, and unregenerate poetry,) the fossil theology of the mythic-materialistic, superstitious, untaught and credulous, fable-loving, primitive ages of humanity.

solving the old, sloughing off surfaces, and from its own interior
and vital principles, reconstructing, democratizing society.

For America, type of progress, and of essential faith in man,
above all his errors and wickedness—few suspect how deep, how
deep it really strikes. The world evidently supposes, and we have
evidently supposed so too, that the States are merely to achieve
the equal franchise, an elective government—to inaugurate the
respectability of labor, and become a nation of practical operatives,
law-abiding, orderly and well off. Yes, those are indeed parts of
the task of America; but they not only do not exhaust the pro-
gressive conception, but rather arise, teeming with it, as the mediums
of deeper, higher progress. Daughter of a physical revolution—
mother of the true revolutions, whch are of the interior life, and of
the arts. For so long as the spirit is not changed, any change of
appearance is of no avail.

The old men, I remember as a boy, were always talking of American independence. What is independence? Freedom from all laws
or bonds except those of one's own being, control'd by the universal
ones. To lands, to man, to woman, what is there at last to each,
but the inherent soul, nativity, idiocrasy, free, highest-poised, soaring
its own flight, following out itself?

At present, these States, in their theology and social standards,
(of greater importance than their political institutions,) are entirely
held possession of by foreign lands. We see the sons and daughters
of the New World, ignorant of its genius, not yet inaugurating the
native, the universal, and the near, still importing the distant, the
partial, and the dead. We see London, Paris, Italy—not original,
superb, as where they belong—but second-hand here, where they
do not belong. We see the shreds of Hebrews, Romans, Greeks;
but where, on her own soil, do we see, in any faithful, highest,
proud expression, America herself? I sometimes question whether
she has a corner in her own house.

Not but that in one sense, and a very grand one, good theology,
good art, or good literature, has certain features shared in common.
The combination fraternizes, ties the races—is, in many particulars,
under laws applicable indifferently to all, irrespective of climate or
date, and, from whatever source, appeals to emotions, pride, love,
spirituality, common to humankind. Nevertheless, they touch a
man closest, (perhaps only actually touch him,) even in these, in
their expression through autochthonic lights and shades, flavors,
fondnesses, aversions, specific incidents, illustrations, out of his own
nationality, geography, surroundings, antecedents, &c. The spirit

and the form are one, and depend far more on association, identity and place, than is supposed. Subtly interwoven with the materiality and personality of a land, a race—Teuton, Turk, Californian, or what not—there is always something—I can hardly tell what it is— history but describes the results of it—it is the same as the untellable look of some human faces. Nature, too, in her stolid forms, is full of it—but to most it is there a secret. This something is rooted in the invisible roots, the profoundest meanings of that place, race, or nationality; and to absorb and again effuse it, uttering words and products as from its midst, and carrying it into highest regions, is the work, or a main part of the work, of any country's true author, poet, historian, lecturer, and perhaps even priest and philosoph. Here, and here only, are the foundations for our really valuable and permanent verse, drama, &c.

But at present, (judged by any higher scale than that which finds the chief ends of existence to be to feverishly make money during one-half of it, and by some "amusement," or perhaps foreign travel flippantly kill time, the other half,) and consider'd with reference to purposes of patriotism, health, a noble personality, religion, and the democratic adjustments, all these swarms of poems, literary magazines, dramatic plays, resultant so far from American intellect, and the formation of our best ideas, are useless and a mockery. They strengthen and nourish no one, express nothing characteristic, give decision and purpose to no one, and suffice only the lowest level of vacant minds.

Of what is called the drama, or dramatic presentation in the United States, as now put forth at the theatres, I should say it deserves to be treated with the same gravity, and on a par with the questions of ornamental confectionery at public dinners, or the arrangement of curtains and hangings in a ball-room—nor more, nor less. Of the other, I will not insult the reader's intelligence, (once really entering into the atmosphere of these Vistas,) by supposing it necessary to show, in detail, why the copious dribble, either of our little or well-known rhymesters, does not fulfil, in any respect, the needs and august occasions of this land. America demands a poetry that is bold, modern, and all-surrounding and kosmical, as she is herself. It must in no respect ignore science or the modern, but inspire itself with science and the modern. It must bend its vision toward the future, more than the past. Like America, it must extricate itself from even the greatest models of the past, and, while courteous to them, must have entire faith in itself, and the products of its own democratic spirit only. Like her, it must place in the van, and hold up at all hazards, the banner of the divine pride of man in himself, (the radical foundation of the new religion.) Long enough have the People been listening to poems in which common humanity, deferential, bends low, humiliated, acknowledging superiors. But America listens to no such poems. Erect, inflated, and fully self-esteeming be the chant; and then America will listen with pleased ears.

Nor may the genuine gold, the gems, when brought to light at last, be probably usher'd forth from any of the quarters currently counted on. To-day, doubtless, the infant genius of American poetic expression, (eluding those highly-refined imported and gilt-edged themes, and sentimental and butterfly flights, pleasant to orthodox publishers—causing tender spasms in the coteries, and warranted not to chafe the sensitive cuticle of the most exquisitely artificial gossamer delicacy,) lies sleeping far away, happily unrecognized and uninjur'd by the coteries, the art-writers, the talkers and critics of the saloons, or the lecturers in the colleges—lies sleeping, aside, unrecking itself, in some western idiom, or native Michigan or Tennessee repartee, or stump-speech—or in Kentucky or Georgia, or the Carolinas—or in some slang or local song or allusion of the Manhattan, Boston, Philadelphia or Baltimore mechanic—or up in the Maine woods—or off in the hut of the California miner, or crossing the Rocky Mountains, or along the Pacific railroad—or on the breasts of the young farmers of the northwest, or Canada, or boatmen of the lakes. Rude and coarse nursing-beds, these; but only from such beginnings and stocks, indigenous here, may haply arrive, be grafted, and sprout, in time, flowers of genuine American aroma, and fruits truly and fully our own.

I say it were a standing disgrace to these States—I say it were a disgrace to any nation, distinguish'd above others by the variety and vastness of its territories, its materials, its inventive activity, and the splendid practicality of its people, not to rise and soar above others also in its original styles in literature and art, and its own supply of intellectual and esthetic masterpieces, archetypal, and consistent with itself. I know not a land except ours that has not, to some extent, however small, made its title clear. The Scotch have their born ballads, subtly expressing their past and present, and expressing character. The Irish have theirs. England, Italy, France, Spain, theirs. What has America? With exhaustless mines of the richest ore of epic, lyric, tale, tune, picture, &c., in the Four Years' War; with, indeed, I sometimes think, the richest masses of material ever afforded a nation, more variegated, and on a larger scale—the first sign of proportionate, native, imaginative Soul, and first-class works to match, is, (I cannot too often repeat,) so far wanting.

Long ere the second centennial arrives, there will be some forty to fifty great States, among them Canada and Cuba. When the present century closes, our population will be sixty or seventy millions. The Pacific will be ours, and the Atlantic mainly ours. There will be daily electric communication with every part of the globe. What an age! What a land! Where, elsewhere, one so great? The individuality of one nation must then, as always, lead the world. Can there be any doubt who the leader ought to be? Bear in mind, though, that nothing less than the mightiest original non-subordinated SOUL has ever really, gloriously led, or ever can lead. (This SOUL—its other name, in these Vistas, is LITERATURE.)

In fond fancy leaping those hundred years ahead, let us survey America's works, poems, philosophies, fulfilling prophecies, and giving form and decision to best ideals. Much that is now undream'd of, we might then perhaps see establish'd, luxuriantly cropping forth, richness, vigor of letters and of artistic expression, in whose products character will be a main requirement, and not merely erudition or elegance.

Intense and loving comradeship, the personal and passionate attachment of man to man—which, hard to define, underlies the lessons and ideals of the profound saviours of every land and age, and which seems to promise, when thoroughly develop'd, cultivated and recognized in manners and literature, the most substantial hope and safety of the future of these States, will then be fully express'd.*

A strong-fibred joyousness and faith, and the sense of health *al fresco*, may well enter into the preparation of future noble Amer-

---

*It is to the development, identification, and general prevalence of that fervid comradeship, (the adhesive love, at least rivaling the amative love hitherto possessing imaginative literature, if not going beyond it,) that I look for the counterbalance and offset of our materialistic and vulgar American democracy, and for the spiritualization thereof. Many will say it is a dream, and will not follow my inferences: but I confidently expect a time when there will be seen, running like a half-hid warp through all the myriad audible and visible worldly interests of America, threads of manly friendship, fond and loving, pure and sweet, strong and life-long, carried to degrees hitherto unknown—not only giving tone to individual character, and making it unprecedentedly emotional, muscular, heroic, and refined, but having the deepest relations to general politics. I say democracy infers such loving comradeship, as its most inevitable twin or counterpart, without which it will be incomplete, in vain, and incapable of perpetuating itself.

ican authorship. Part of the test of a great literatus shall be the absence in him of the idea of the covert, the lurid, the maleficent, the devil, the grim estimates inherited from the Puritans, hell, natural depravity, and the like. The great literatus will be known, among the rest, by his cheerful simplicity, his adherence to natural standards, his limitless faith in God, his reverence, and by the absence in him of doubt, ennui, burlesque, persiflage, or any strain'd and temporary fashion.

Nor must I fail, again and yet again, to clinch, reiterate more plainly still, (O that indeed such survey as we fancy, may show in time this part completed also!) the lofty aim, surely the proudest and the purest, in whose service the future literatus, of whatever field, may gladly labor. As we have intimated, offsetting the material civilization of our race, our nationality, its wealth, territories, factories, population, products, trade, and military and naval strength, and breathing breath of life into all these, and more, must be its moral civilization—the formulation, expression, and aidancy whereof, is the very highest height of literature. The climax of this loftiest range of civilization, rising above all the gorgeous shows and results of wealth, intellect, power, and art, as such—above even theology and religious fervor—is to be its development, from the eternal bases, and the fit expression, of absolute Conscience, moral soundness, Justice. Even in religious fervor there is a touch of animal heat. But moral conscientiousness, crystalline, without flaw, not Godlike only, entirely human, awes and enchants forever. Great is emotional love, even in the order of the rational universe. But, if we must make gradations, I am clear there is something greater. Power, love, veneration, products, genius, esthetics, tried by subtlest comparisons, analyses, and in serenest moods, somewhere fail, somehow become vain. Then noiseless, with flowing steps, the lord, the sun, the last ideal comes. By the names right, justice, truth, we suggest, but do not describe it. To the world of men it remains a dream, an idea as they call it. But no dream is it to the wise—but the proudest, almost only solid lasting thing of all. Its analogy in the material universe is what holds together this world, and every object upon it, and carries its dynamics on forever sure and safe. Its lack, and the persistent shirking of it, as in life, sociology, literature, politics business, and even sermonizing, these times, or any times, still leaves the abysm, the mortal flaw and smutch, mocking civilization to-day, with all its unquestion'd triumphs, and all the civilization so far known.*

_____

*I am reminded as I write that out of this very conscience, or idea of conscience, of intense moral right, and in its name and strain'd construction, the

Present literature, while magnificently fulfilling certain popular demands, with plenteous knowledge and verbal smartness, is profoundly sophisticated, insane, and its very joy is morbid. It needs tally and express Nature, and the spirit of Nature, and to know and obey the standards. I say the question of Nature, largely consider'd, involves the questions of the esthetic, the emotional, and the religious—and involves happiness. A fitly born and bred race, growing up in right conditions of out-door as much as indoor harmony, activity and development, would probably, from and in those conditions, find it enough merely *to live*—and would, in their relations to the sky, air, water, trees, &c., and to the countless common shows, and in the fact of life itself, discover and achieve happiness—with Being suffused night and day by wholesome extasy, surpassing all the pleasures that wealth, amusement, and even gratified intellect, erudition, or the sense of art, can give.

in the prophetic literature of these States (the reader of my speculations will miss their principal stress unless he allows well for the point that a new Literature, perhaps a new Metaphysics, certainly a new Poetry, are to be, in my opinion, the only sure and worthy supports and expressions of the American Democracy,) Nature, true Nature, and the true idea of Nature, long absent, must, above all, become fully restored, enlarged, and must furnish the pervading atmosphere to poems, and the test of all high literary and esthetic compositions. I do not mean the smooth walks, trimm'd hedges, poseys and nightingales of the English poets, but the whole orb, with its geologic history, the kosmos, carrying fire and snow, that rolls through the illimitable areas, light as a feather, though weighing billions of tons. Furthermore, as by what we now partially call Nature is intended, at most, only what is entertainable by the physical conscience, the sense of matter, and of good animal health—

---

worst fanaticisms, wars, persecutions, murders, &c., have yet, in all lands, in the past, been broach'd, and have come to their devilish fruition. Much is to be said—but I may say here, and in response, that side by side with the unflagging stimulation of the elements of religion and conscience must henceforth move with equal sway, science, absolute reason, and the general proportionate development of the whole man. These scientific facts, deductions, are divine too—precious counted parts of moral civilization, and, with physical health, indispensable to it, to prevent fanaticism. For abstract religion, I perceive, is easily led astray, ever credulous, and is capable of devouring, remorseless, like fire and flame. Conscience, too, isolated from all else, and from the emotional nature, may but attain the beauty and purity of glacial, snowy ice. We want, for these States, for the general character, a cheerful, religious fervor, endued with the ever-present modifications of the human emotions, friendship, benevolence, with a fair field for scientific inquiry, the right of individual judgment, and always the cooling influences of material Nature.

on these it must be distinctly accumulated, incorporated, that man, comprehending these, has, in towering superaddition, the moral and spiritual consciences, indicating his destination beyond the ostensible, the mortal.

To the heights of such estimate of Nature indeed ascending, we proceed to make observations for our Vistas, breathing rarest air. What is I believe called Idealism seems to me to suggest, (guarding against extravagance, and ever modified even by its opposite,) the course of inquiry and desert of favor for our New World metaphysics, their foundation of and in literature, giving hue to all.*

---

*The culmination and fruit of literary artistic expression, and its final fields of pleasure for the human soul, are in metaphysics, including the mysteries of the spiritual world, the soul itself, and the question of the immortal continuation of our identity. In all ages, the mind of man has brought up here—and always will. Here, at least, of whatever race or era, we stand on common ground. Applause, too, is unanimous, antique or modern. Those authors who work well in this field—though their reward, instead of a handsome percentage, or royalty, may be but simply the laurel-crown of the victors in the great Olympic games—will be dearest to humanity, and their works, however esthetically defective, will be treasur'd forever. The altitude of literature and poetry has always been religion—and always will be. The Indian Vedas, the Nackas of Zoroaster, the Talmud of the Jews, the Old Testament, the Gospel of Christ and his disciples, Plato's works, the Koran of Mohammed, the Edda of Snorro, and so on toward our own day, to Swedenborg, and to the invaluable contributions of Leibnitz, Kant and Hegel—these, with such poems only in which, (while singing well of persons and events, of the passions of man, and the shows of the material universe,) the religious tone, the consciousness of mystery, the recognition of the future, of the unknown, of Deity over and under all, and of the divine purpose, are never absent, but indirectly give tone to all— exhibit literature's real heights and elevations, towering up like the great mountains of the earth.

Standing on this ground—the last, the highest, only permanent ground—and sternly criticising, from it, all works, either of the literary, or any art, we have peremptorily to dismiss every pretensive production, however fine its esthetic or intellectual points, which violates or ignores, or even does not celebrate, the central divine idea of All, suffusing universe, of eternal trains of purpose, in the development, by however slow degrees, of the physical, moral, and spiritual kosmos. I say he has studied, meditated to no profit, whatever may be his mere erudition, who has not absorb'd this simple consciousness and faith. It is not entirely new—but it is for Democracy to elaborate it, and look to build upon and expand from it, with uncompromising reliance. Above the doors of teaching the inscription is to appear, Though little or nothing can be absolutely known, perceiv'd, except from a point of view which is evanescent, yet we know at least one permanency, that Time and Space, in the will of God, furnish successive chains, completions of material births and beginnings, solve all discrepancies, fears and doubts, and eventually fulfil happiness—and that the prophecy of those births, namely spiritual results, throws the true arch over all teaching, all science. The local considerations of sin, disease, deformity, ignorance, death, &c., and their measurement by the superficial mind, and ordinary legislation and theology, are to be met by science, boldly accepting, promulging

The elevating and etherealizing ideas of the unknown and of unreality must be brought forward with authority, as they are the legitimate heirs of the known, and of reality, and at least as great as their parents. Fearless of scoffing, and of the ostent, let us take our stand, our ground, and never desert it, to confront the growing excess and arrogance of realism. To the cry, now victorious—the cry of sense, science, flesh, incomes, farms, merchandise, logic, intellect, demonstrations, solid perpetuities, buildings of brick and iron, or even the facts of the shows of trees, earth, rocks, &c., fear not, my brethren, my sisters, to sound out with equally determin'd voice, that conviction brooding within the recesses of every envision'd soul—illusions! apparitions! figments all! True, we must not condemn the show, neither absolutely deny it, for the indispensability of its meanings; but how clearly we see that, migrate in soul to what we can already conceive of superior and spiritual points of view, and, palpable as it seems under present relations, it all and several might, nay certainly would, fall apart and vanish.

I hail with joy the oceanic, variegated, intense practical energy, the demand for facts, even the business materialism of the current age, our States. But wo to the age or land in which these things, movements, stopping at themselves, do not tend to ideas. As fuel to flame, and flame to the heavens, so must wealth, science, materialism—even this democracy of which we make so much—unerringly feed the highest mind, the soul. Infinitude the flight: fathomless the mystery. Man, so diminutive, dilates beyond the sensible universe, competes with, outcopes space and time, meditating even one great idea. Thus, and thus only, does a human being, his spirit, ascend above, and justify, objective Nature, which, probably nothing in itself, is incredibly and divinely serviceable, indispensable, real, here. And as the purport of objective Nature is doubtless folded, hidden, somewhere here—as somewhere here is what this globe and its manifold forms, and the light of day, and night's darkness, and life itself, with all its experiences, are for—it is here the great literature, especially verse, must get its inspiration and throbbing blood. Then may we attain to a poetry worthy the immortal soul of man, and which, while absorbing materials, and, in their own sense, the shows of Nature, will, above all, have, both directly and indirectly, a freeing, fluidizing, expanding, religious character, ex-

---

this faith, and planting the seeds of superber laws—of the explication of the physical universe through the spiritual—and clearing the way for a religion, sweet and unimpugnable alike to little child or great savan.

ulting with science, fructifying the moral elements, and stimulating aspirations, and meditations on the unknown.

The process, so far, is indirect and peculiar, and though it may be suggested, cannot be defined. Observing, rapport, and with intuition, the shows and forms presented by Nature, the sensuous luxuriance, the beautiful in living men and women, the actual play of passions, in history and life—and, above all, from those developments either in Nature or human personality in which power, (dearest of all to the sense of the artist,) transacts itself—out of these, and seizing what is in them, the poet, the esthetic worker in any field, by the divine magic of his genius, projects them, their analogies, by curious removes, indirections, in literature and art. (No useless attempt to repeat the material creation, by daguerreotyping the exact likeness by mortal mental means.) This is the image-making faculty, coping with material creation, and rivaling, almost triumphing over it. This alone, when all the other parts of a specimen of literature or art are ready and waiting, can breathe into it the breath of life, and endow it with identity.

"The true question to ask," says the librarian of Congress in a paper read before the Social Science Convention at New York, October, 1869, "The true question to ask respecting a book, is, *has it help'd any human soul?*" This is the hint, statement, not only of the great literatus, his book, but of every great artist. It may be that all works of art are to be first tried by their art qualities, their image-forming talent, and their dramatic, pictorial, plot-constructing, euphonious and other talents. Then, whenever claiming to be first-class works, they are to be strictly and sternly tried by their foundation in, and radiation, in the highest sense, and always indirectly, of the ethic principles, and eligibility to free, arouse, dilate.

As, within the purposes of the Kosmos, and vivifying all meteorology, and all the congeries of the mineral, vegetable and animal worlds—all the physical growth and development of man, and all the history of the race in politics, religions, wars, &c., there is a moral purpose, a visible or invisible intention, certainly underlying all—its results and proof needing to be patiently waited for—needing intuition, faith, idiosyncrasy, to its realization, which many, and especially the intellectual, do not have—so in the product, or congeries of the product, of the greatest literatus. This is the last, profoundest measure and test of a first-class literary or esthetic achievement, and when understood and put in force must fain, I say, lead to works, books, nobler than any hitherto known. Lo! Nature, (the only complete, actual poem,) existing calmly in the divine scheme, containing all, content, careless of the criticisms of a day, or these endless and wordy chatterers. And lo! to the consciousness of the soul, the permanent identity, the thought, the something, before which the magnitude even of democracy, art, literature, &c., dwindles, becomes partial, measurable—something that fully satisfies, (which those do not.) That something is the All, and the idea of All, with the accompanying idea of eternity, and of itself, the soul, buoyant, indestructible, sailing space forever, visiting every region, as a ship the sea. And again lo! the pulsations in all matter, all spirit, throbbing forever—the eternal beats, eternal systole and diastole of life in things—wherefrom I feel and know that death is not the ending, as was thought, but rather the real beginning —and that nothing ever is or can be lost, nor ever die, nor soul, nor matter.

In the future of these States must arise poets immenser far, and make great poems of death. The poems of life are great, but there must be the poems of the purports of life, not only in itself, but beyond itself. I have eulogized Homer, the sacred bards of Jewry, Eschylus, Juvenal, Shakspere, &c., and acknowledged their inestimable value. But, (with perhaps the exception, in some, not all respects, of the second-mention'd,) I say there must, for future and democratic purposes, appear poets, (dare I to say so?) of higher class even than any of those—poets not only possess'd of the religious fire and abandon of Isaiah, luxuriant in the epic talent of Homer, or for proud characters as in Shakspere, but consistent with the Hegelian formulas, and consistent with modern science. America needs, and the world needs, a class of bards who will, now and ever, so link and tally the rational physical being of man, with the ensembles of time and space, and with this vast and multiform show, Nature, surrounding him, ever tantalizing him, equally a part, and yet not a part of him, as to essentially harmonize, satisfy, and put at rest. Faith, very old, now scared away by science, must be restored, brought back by the same power that caused her departure— restored with new sway, deeper, wider, higher than ever. Surely, this universal ennui, this coward fear, this shuddering at death, these low, degrading views, are not always to rule the spirit pervading future society, as it has the past, and does the present. What the Roman Lucretius sought most nobly, yet all too blindly, negatively to do for his age and its successors, must be done positively by some great coming literatus, especially poet, who, while remaining fully poet, will absorb whatever science indicates, with spiritualism, and out of them, and out of his own genius, will compose the great poem of death. Then will man indeed confront Nature, and confront time and space, both with science, and *con amore*, and take his right place, prepared for life, master of fortune and misfortune. And then that which was long wanted will be supplied, and the ship that had it not before in all her voyages, will have an anchor.

There are still other standards, suggestions, for products of high literatuses. That which really balances and conserves the social and political world is not so much legislation, police, treaties, and dread of punishment, as the latent eternal intuitional sense, in humanity, of fairness, manliness, decorum, &c. Indeed, this perennial regulation, control, and oversight, by self-suppliance, is *sine qua non* to democracy; and a highest widest aim of democratic literature may well be to bring forth, cultivate, brace, and strengthen this sense, in individuals and society. A strong mastership of the general inferior self by the superior self, is to be aided, secured, indirectly, but surely, by the literatus, in his works, shaping, for individual or aggregate democracy, a great passionate body in and along with which goes a great masterful spirit.

And still, providing for contingencies, I fain confront the fact, the need of powerful native philosophs and orators and bards, these States, as rallying points to come, in times of danger, and to fend off ruin and defection. For history is long, long, long. Shift and turn the combinations of the statement as we may, the problem of the future of America is in certain respects as dark as it is vast. Pride, competition, segregation, vicious wilfulness, and license beyond example, brood already upon us. Unwieldy and immense, who shall hold in behemoth? who bridle leviathan? Flaunt it as we choose, athwart and over the roads of our progress loom huge uncertainty, and dreadful, threatening gloom. It is useless to deny it: Democracy grows rankly up the thickest, noxious, deadliest plants and fruits of all—brings worse and worse invaders—needs newer, larger, stronger, keener compensations and compellers.

Our lands, embracing so much, (embracing indeed the whole, rejecting none,) hold in their breast that flame also, capable of consuming themselves, consuming us all. Short as the span of our national life has been, already have death and downfall crowded close upon us—and will again crowd close, no doubt, even if warded off. Ages to come may never know, but I know, how narrowly during the late secession war—and more than once, and more than twice or thrice—our Nationality, (wherein bound up, as in a ship in a

storm, depended, and yet depend, all our best life, all hope, all
value,) just grazed, just by a hair escaped destruction. Alas! to
think of them! the agony and bloody sweat of certain of those hours!
those cruel, sharp, suspended crises!

Even to-day, amid these whirls, incredible flippancy, and blind
fury of parties, infidelity, entire lack of first-class captains and
leaders, added to the plentiful meanness and vulgarity of the ostensible masses—that problem, the labor question, beginning to
open like a yawning gulf, rapidly widening every year—what prospect have we? We sail a dangerous sea of seething currents, cross
and under-currents, vortices—all so dark, untried—and whither
shall we turn? It seems as if the Almighty had spread before this
nation charts of imperial destinies, dazzling as the sun, yet with
many a deep intestine difficulty, and human aggregate of cankerous
imperfection,—saying, lo! the roads, the only plans of development,
long and varied with all terrible balks and ebullitions. You said in
your soul, I will be empire of empires, overshadowing all else, past
and present, putting the history of old-world dynasties, conquests
behind me, as of no account—making a new history, a history of
democracy, making old history a dwarf—I alone inaugurating
largeness, culminating time. If these, O lands of America, are indeed
the prizes, the determinations of your soul, be it so. But behold the
cost, and already specimens of the cost. Thought you greatness was
to ripen for you like a pear? If you would have greatness, know that
you must conquer it through ages, centuries—must pay for it with
a proportionate price. For you too, as for all lands, the struggle,
the traitor, the wily person in office, scrofulous wealth, the surfeit
of prosperity, the demonism of greed, the hell of passion, the decay
of faith, the long postponement, the fossil-like lethargy, the ceaseless need of revolutions, prophets, thunderstorms, deaths, births,
new projections and invigorations of ideas and men.

Yet I have dream'd, merged in that hidden-tangled problem of
our fate, whose long unraveling stretches mysteriously through
time—dream'd out, portray'd, hinted already—a little or a larger
band—a band of brave and true, unprecedented yet—arm'd and
equipt at every point—the members separated, it may be, by different dates and States, or south, or north, or east, or west—Pacific,
Atlantic, Southern, Canadian—a year, a century here, and other
centuries there—but always one, compact in soul, conscience-con-
serving, God-inculcating, inspired achievers, not only in literature,
the greatest art, but achievers in all art—a new, undying order,
dynasty, from age to age transmitted—a band, a class, at least as

fit to cope with current years, our dangers, needs, as those who, for their times, so long, so well, in armor or in cowl, upheld and made illustrious, that far-back feudal, priestly world. To offset chivalry, indeed, those vanish'd countless knights, old altars, abbeys, priests, ages and strings of ages, a knightlier and more sacred cause to-day demands, and shall supply, in a New World, to larger, grander work, more than the counterpart and tally of them.

Arrived now, definitely, at an apex for these Vistas, I confess that the promulgation and belief in such a class or institution—a new and greater literatus order—its possibility, (nay certainty,) underlies these entire speculations—and that the rest, the other parts, as superstructures, are all founded upon it. It really seems to me the condition, not only of our future national and democratic development, but of our perpetuation. In the highly artificial and materialistic bases of modern civilization, with the corresponding arrangements and methods of living, the force-infusion of intellect alone, the depraving influences of riches just as much as poverty, the absence of all high ideals in character—with the long series of tendencies, shapings, which few are strong enough to resist, and which now seem, with steam-engine speed, to be everywhere turning out the generations of humanity like uniform iron castings—all of which, as compared with the feudal ages, we can yet do nothing better than accept, make the best of, and even welcome, upon the whole, for their oceanic practical grandeur, and their restless whole-sale kneading of the masses—I say of all this tremendous and dominant play of solely materialistic bearings upon current life in the United States, with the results as already seen, accumulating, and reaching far into the future, that they must either be confronted and met by at least an equally subtle and tremendous force-infusion for purposes of spiritualization, for the pure conscience, for genuine esthetics, and for absolute and primal manliness and womanliness— or else our modern civilization, with all its improvements, is in vain, and we are on the road to a destiny, a status, equivalent, in its real world, to that of the fabled damned.

Prospecting thus the coming unsped days, and that new order in them—marking the endless train of exercise, development, un-wind, in nation as in man, which life is for—we see, fore-indicated, amid these prospects and hopes, new law-forces of spoken and written language—not merely the pedagogue-forms, correct, regular, familiar with precedents, made for matters of outside propriety, fine words, thoughts definitely told out—but a language fann'd by the breath of Nature, which leaps overhead, cares mostly for

impetus and effects, and for what it plants and invigorates to grow—
tallies life and character, and seldomer tells a thing than suggests
or necessitates it. In fact, a new theory of literary composition for
imaginative works of the very first class, and especially for highest
poems, is the sole course open to these States. Books are to be
call'd for, and supplied, on the assumption that the process of
reading is not a half-sleep, but, in highest sense, an exercise, a
gymnast's struggle; that the reader is to do something for himself,
must be on the alert, must himself or herself construct indeed the
poem, argument, history, metaphysical essay—the text furnishing
the hints, the clue, the start or frame-work. Not the book needs so
much to be the complete thing, but the reader of the book does.
That were to make a nation of supple and athletic minds, well-
train'd, intuitive, used to depend on themselves, and not on a few
coteries of writers.

Investigating here, we see, not that it is a little thing we have, in
having the bequeath'd libraries, countless shelves of volumes,
records, &c.; yet how serious the danger, depending entirely on
them, of the bloodless vein, the nerveless arm, the false application,
at second or third hand. We see that the real interest of this people
of ours in the theology, history, poetry, politics, and personal
models of the past, (the British islands, for instance, and indeed
all the past,) is not necessarily to mould ourselves or our literature
upon them, but to attain fuller, more definite comparisons, warnings,
and the insight to ourselves, our own present, and our own far
grander, different, future history, religion, social customs, &c. We
see that almost everything that has been written, sung, or stated,
of old, with reference to humanity under the feudal and oriental
institutes, religions, and for other lands, needs to be re-written,
re-sung, re-stated, in terms consistent with the institution of these
States, and to come in range and obedient uniformity with them.

We see, as in the universes of the material kosmos, after meteorological, vegetable, and animal cycles, man at last arises, born
through them, to prove them, concentrate them, to turn upon them
with wonder and love—to command them, adorn them, and carry
them upward into superior realms—so, out of the series of the
preceding social and political universes, now arise these States. We
see that while many were supposing things established and completed, really the grandest things always remain; and discover that
the work of the New World is not ended, but only fairly begun.

We see our land, America, her literature, esthetics, &c., as, substantially, the getting in form, or effusement and statement, of
deepest basic elements and loftiest final meanings, of history and

man—and the portrayal, (under the eternal laws and conditions of beauty,) of our own physiognomy, the subjective tie and expression of the objective as from our own combination, continuation, and points of view—and the deposit and record of the national mentality, character, appeals, heroism, wars, and even liberties—where these, and all, culminate in native literary and artistic formulation, to be perpetuated; and not having which native, first-class formulation, she will flounder about, and her other, however imposing, eminent greatness, prove merely a passing gleam; but truly having which, she will understand herself, live nobly, nobly contribute, emanate, and, swinging, poised safely on herself, illumin'd and illuming, become a full-form'd world, and divine Mother not only of material but spiritual worlds, in ceaseless succession through time—the main thing being the average, the bodily, the concrete, the democratic, the popular, on which all the superstructures of the future are to permanently rest.

Preface, 1872,

to "As a Strong Bird on Pinions Free,'
(now "Thou Mother with thy Equal Brood," in permanent ed'n.)

THE impetus and ideas urging me, for some years past, to an utterance, or attempt at utterance, of New World songs, and an epic of Democracy, having already had their publish'd expression, as well as I can expect to give it, in "Leaves of Grass," the present and any future pieces from me are really but the surplusage forming after that volume, or the wake eddying behind it. I fulfill'd in that an imperious conviction, and the commands of my nature as total and irresistible as those which make the sea flow, or the globe revolve. But of this supplementary volume, I confess I am not so certain. Having from early manhood abandon'd the business pursuits and applications usual in my time and country, and obediently yielded myself up ever since to the impetus mention'd, and to the work of expressing those ideas, it may be that mere habit has got dominion of me, when there is no real need of saying any thing further But what is life but an experiment? and mortality but an exercise? with reference to results beyond. And so shall my poems be. If incomplete here, and superfluous there, *n'importe*—the earnest trial and persistent exploration shall at least be mine, and other success failing shall be success enough. I have been more anxious, anyhow, to suggest the songs of vital endeavor and manly evolution, and furnish something for races of outdoor athletes, than to make perfect rhymes, or reign in the parlors. I ventur'd from the beginning my own way, taking chances—and would keep on venturing.

I will therefore not conceal from any persons, known or unknown to me, who take an interest in the matter, that I have the ambition of devoting yet a few years to poetic composition. The mighty present age! To absorb and express in poetry, anything of it—of its world—America—cities and States—the years, the events of our Nineteenth century—the rapidity of movement—the violent contrasts, fluctuations of light and shade, of hope and fear—the entire revolution made by science in the poetic method—these great new underlying

525

facts and new ideas rushing and spreading everywhere;—truly a mighty age! As if in some colossal drama, acted again like those of old under the open sun, the Nations of our time, and all the characteristics of Civilization, seem hurrying, stalking across, flitting from wing to wing, gathering, closing up, toward some long-prepared, most tremendous denouement. Not to conclude the infinite scenas of the race's life and toil and happiness and sorrow, but haply that the boards be clear'd from oldest, worst incumbrances, accumulations, and Man resume the eternal play anew, and under happier, freer auspices. To me, the United States are important because in this colossal drama they are unquestionably designated for the leading parts, for many a century to come. In them history and humanity seem to seek to culminate. Our broad areas are even now the busy theatre of plots, passions, interests, and suspended problems, compared to which the intrigues of the past of Europe, the wars of dynasties, the scope of kings and kingdoms, and even the development of peoples, as hitherto, exhibit scales of measurement comparatively narrow and trivial. And on these areas of ours, as on a stage, sooner or later, something like an *eclaircissement* of all the past civilization of Europe and Asia is probably to be evolved.

The leading parts. Not to be acted, emulated here, by us again, that role till now foremost in history—not to become a conqueror nation, or to achieve the glory of mere military, or diplomatic, or commercial superiority—but to become the grand producing land of nobler men and women—of copious races, cheerful, healthy, tolerant, free—to become the most friendly nation, (the United States indeed)—the modern composite nation, form'd from all, with room for all, welcoming all immigrants—accepting the work of our own interior development, as the work fitly filling ages and ages to come;—the leading nation of peace, but neither ignorant nor incapable of being the leading nation of war;—not the man's nation only, but the woman's nation—a land of splendid mothers, daughters, sisters, wives.

Our America to-day I consider in many respects as but indeed a vast seething mass of *materials*, ampler, better, (worse also,) than previously known—eligible to be used to carry towards its crowning stage, and build for good, the great ideal nationality of the future, the nation of the body and the soul,*—no limit here

---

* The problems of the achievements of this crowning stage through future first-class National Singers, Orators, Artists, and others—of creating in litera-

to land, help, opportunities, mines, products, demands, supplies, &c.;—with (I think) our political organization, National, State, and Municipal, permanently establish'd, as far ahead as we can calculate—but, so far, no social, literary, religious, or esthetic organizations, consistent with our politics, or becoming to us— which organizations can only come, in time, through great democratic ideas, religion—through science, which now, like a new sunrise, ascending, begins to illuminate all—and through our own begotten poets and literatuses. (The moral of a late well-written book on civilization seems to be that the only real foundation-walls and bases—and also *sine qua non* afterward—of true and full civilization, is the eligibility and certainty of boundless products for feeding, clothing, sheltering everybody—perennial fountains of physical and domestic comfort, with intercommunication, and with civil and ecclesiastical freedom—and that then the esthetic and mental business will take care of itself. Well, the United States have establish'd this basis, and upon scales of extent, variety, vitality, and continuity, rivaling those of Nature; and have now to proceed to build an edifice upon it. I say this edifice is only to be fitly built by new literatures, especially the poetic. I say a modern image-making creation is indispensable to fuse and express the modern political and scientific creations—and then the trinity will be complete.)

When I commenced, years ago, elaborating the plan of my poems, and continued turning over that plan, and shifting it in my mind through many years, (from the age of twenty-eight to thirty-five,) experimenting much, and writing and abandoning much, one deep purpose underlay the others, and has underlain it and its execution ever since—and that has been the religious purpose. Amid many changes, and a formulation taking far different shape from what I at first supposed, this basic purpose has never been departed from in the composition of my verses. Not of course to exhibit itself in the old ways, as in writing hymns or psalms with an eye to the church-pew, or to express conventional pietism, or the sickly yearnings of devotees, but in new ways, and aiming at the widest sub-bases and inclusions of humanity, and tallying the fresh air of sea and land.

---

ture an *imaginative* New World, the correspondent and counterpart of the current Scientific and Political New Worlds,—and the perhaps distant, but still delightful prospect, (for our children, if not in our own day,) of delivering America, and indeed, all Christian lands everywhere, from the thin moribund and watery, but appallingly extensive nuisance of conventional poetry—by putting something really alive and substantial in its place—I have undertaken to grapple with, and argue, in the preceding "Democratic Vistas."

I will see, (said I to myself,) whether there is not, for my purposes as poet, a religion, and a sound religious germenancy in the average human race, at least in their modern development in the United States, and in the hardy common fibre and native yearnings and elements, deeper and larger, and affording more profitable returns, than all mere sects or churches—as boundless, joyous, and vital as Nature itself—a germenancy that has too long been unencouraged, unsung, almost unknown. With science, the old theology of the East, long in its dotage, begins evidently to die and disappear. But (to my mind) science—and may be such will prove its principal service—as evidently prepares the way for One indescribably grander —Time's young but perfect offspring—the new theology—heir of the West—lusty and loving, and wondrous beautiful. For America, and for to-day, just the same as any day, the supreme and final science is the science of God—what we call science being only its minister—as Democracy is, or shall be also. And a poet of America (I said) must fill himself with such thoughts, and chant his best out of them. And as those were the convictions and aims, for good or bad, of "Leaves of Grass," they are no less the intention of this volume. As there can be, in my opinion, no sane and complete personality, nor any grand and electric nationality, without the stock element of religion imbuing all the other elements, (like heat in chemistry, invisible itself, but the life of all visible life,) so there can be no poetry worthy the name without that element behind all. The time has certainly come to begin to discharge the idea of religion, in the United States, from mere ecclesiasticism, and from Sundays and churches and church-going, and assign it to that general position, chiefest, most indispensable, most exhilarating, to which the others are to be adjusted, inside of all human character, and education, and affairs. The people, especially the young men and women of America, must begin to learn that religion, (like poetry,) is something far, far different from what they supposed. It is, indeed too important to the power and perpetuity of the New World to be consign'd any longer to the churches, old or new, Catholic or Protestant—Saint this, or Saint that. It must be consign'd henceforth to democracy *en masse*, and to literature. It must enter into the poems of the nation. It must make the nation.

The Four Years' War is over—and in the peaceful, strong, exciting, fresh occasions of to-day, and of the future, that strange, sad war is hurrying even now to be forgotten. The camp, the drill, the lines of sentries, the prisons, the hospitals,—(ah! the hospitals!)— all have passed away—all seem now like a dream. A new race, a young and lusty generation, already sweeps in with oceanic currents, obliterating the war, and all its scars, its mounded graves, and all its reminiscences of hatred, conflict, death. So let it be obliterated. I say the life of the present and the future makes undeniable demands upon us each and all, south, north, east, west. To help put the United States (even if only in imagination) hand in hand, in one unbroken circle in a chant—to rouse them to the unprecedented gradeur of the part they are to play, and are even now playing—to the thought of their great future, and the attitude conform'd to it— especially their great esthetic, moral, scientific future, (of which their vulgar material and political present is but as the preparatory tuning of instruments by an orchestra,) these, as hitherto, are still, for me, among my hopes, ambitions.

"Leaves of Grass," already publish'd, is, in its intentions, the song of a great composite *democratic individual*, male or female. And following on and amplifying the same purpose, I suppose I have in mind to run through the chants of this volume, (if ever completed,) the thread-voice, more or less audible, of an aggregated, inseparable, unprecedented, vast, composite, electric *democratic nationality*.

Purposing, then, to still fill out, from time to time through years to come, the following volume, (unless prevented,) I conclude this preface to the first instalment of it, pencil'd in the open air, on my fifty-third birth-day, by wafting to you, dear reader, whoever you are, (from amid the fresh scent of the grass, the pleasant coolness of the forenoon breeze, the lights and shades of tree-boughs silently dappling and playing around me, and the notes of the cat-bird for undertone and accompaniment,) my true good-will and love.

W. W.

Washington, D. C., May 31, 1872.

Preface, 1876,

to the two-volume Centennial Edition

of L. of G. and "Two Rivulets."

AT the eleventh hour, under grave illness, I gatherup the pieces of prose and poetry left over since publishing, a while since, my first and main volume, "Leaves of Grass"—pieces, here, some new, some old—nearly all of them (sombre as many are, making this almost death's book) composed in by-gone atmospheres of perfect health—and preceded by the freshest collection, the little "Two Rivulets," now send them out, embodied in the present melange, partly as my contribution and outpouring to celebrate, in some sort, the feature of the time, the first centennial of our New World nationality—and then as chyle and nutriment to that moral, indissoluble union, equally representing all, and the mother of many coming centennials.

And e'en for flush and proof of our America—for reminder, just as much, or more, in moods of towering pride and joy, I keep my special chants of death and immortality* to stamp the coloring-

---

*PASSAGE TO INDIA.—As in some ancient legend-play, to close the plot and the hero's career, there is a farewell gathering on ship's deck and on shore, a loosing of hawsers and ties, a spreading of sails to the wind—a starting out on unknown seas, to fetch up no one knows whither—to return no more—and the curtain falls, and there is the end of it—so I have reserv'd that poem, with its cluster, to finish and explain much that, without them, would not be explain'd, and to take leave, and escape for good, from all that haspreceded them. (Then probably "Passage to India," and its cluster, are but freer vent and fuller expression to what, from the first, and so on throughout, more or less lurks in my writings, underneath every page, every line, everywhere.)

I am not sure but the last inclosing sublimation of race or poem is, what it thinks of death. After the rest has been comprehended and said, even the grandest—after those contributions to mightiest nationality, or to sweetest song, or to the best personalism, male or female, have been glean'd from the rich and varied themes of tangible life, and have been fully accepted and sung, and the pervading fact of visible existence, with the duty it devolves, is rounded and apparently completed, it still remains to be really completed by suffusing through the whole and several, that other pervading invisible fact, so large a finish of all, present and past. For terminus and temperer to all, they were originally written; and that shall be their office at the last.

---

part, (is it not the largest part?) of life here, combining the rest, and furnishing, for person or State, the only permanent and unitary meaning to all, even the meanest life, consistently with the dignity of the universe, in Time. As from the eligibility to this thought, and the cheerful conquest of this fact, flash forth the first distinctive proofs of the soul, so to me, (extending it only a little further,) the ultimate Democratic purports, the ethereal and spiritual ones, are to concentrate here, and as fixed stars, radiate hence. For, in my opinion, it is no less than this idea of immortality, above all other ideas, that is to enter into, and vivify, and give crowning religious stamp, to democracy in the New World.

It was originally my intention, after chanting in "Leaves of Grass" the songs of the body and existence, to then compose a further, equally needed volume, based on those convictions of perpetuity and conservation which, enveloping all precedents, make the unseen soul govern absolutely at last. I meant, while in a sort continuing the theme of my first chants, to shift the slides, and exhibit the problem and paradox of the same ardent and fully appointed personality entering the sphere of the resistless gravitation of spiritual law, and with cheerful face estimating death, not at all as the cessation, but as somehow what I feel it must be, the entrance upon by far the greatest part of existence, and something that life is at least as much for, as it is for itself. But the full construction of such a work is beyond my powers, and must remain for some bard in the future. The physical and the sensuous, in themselves or in their immediate continuations, retain holds upon me which I think are never entirely releas'd; and those holds I have not only not denied, but hardly wish'd to weaken.

Meanwhile, not entirely to give the go-by to my original plan, and far more to avoid a mark'd hiatus in it, than to entirely fulfil it, I end my books with thoughts, or radiations from thoughts, on death, immortality, and a free entrance into the spiritual world. In those thoughts, in a sort, I make the first steps or studies toward the mighty theme, from the point of view necessitated by my foregoing poems, and by modern science. In them I also seek to set the key-stone to my democracy's enduring arch. I recollate them now, for the press, in order to partially occupy and offset days of strange sickness, and the heaviest affliction and bereavement of my life; and I fondly please myself with the notion of leaving that cluster to you, O unknown reader of the future, as "something to remember me by," more especially than all else. Written in former days of perfect health, little did I think the pieces had the purport that now, under present circumstances, opens to me.

[As I write these lines, May 31, 1875, it is again early summer—again my birth-day—now my fifty-sixth. Amid the outside beauty and freshness, the sunlight and verdure of the delightful season, O how different the moral atmosphere amid which I now revise this Volume, from the jocund influence surrounding the growth and advent of "Leaves of Grass." I occupy myself, arranging these pages for publication, still envelopt in thoughts of the death two years since of my dear Mother, the most perfect and magnetic character, the rarest combination of practical, moral and spiritual, and the least selfish, of all and any I have ever known—and by me O so much the most deeply loved—and also under the physical affliction of a tedious attack of paralysis, obstinately lingering and keeping its hold upon me, and quite suspending all bodily activity and comfort.]

Under these influences, therefore, I still feel to keep "Passage to India" for last words even to this centennial dithyramb. Not as, in antiquity, at highest

For some reason—not explainable or definite to my own mind, yet secretly pleasing and satisfactory to it—I have not hesitated to embody in, and run through the volume, two altogether distinct veins, or strata—politics for one, and for the other, the pensive thought of immortality. Thus, too, the prose and poetic, the dual forms of the present book. The volume, therefore, after its minor episodes, probably divides into these two, at first sight far diverse, veins of topic and treatment. Three points, in especial, have become very dear to me, and all through I seek to make them again and again, in many forms and repetitions, as will be seen: 1. That the true growth-characteristics of the democracy of the New World are henceforth to radiate in superior literary, artistic and religious expressions, far more than in its republican forms, universal suffrage, and frequent elections, (though these are unspeakably important.) 2. That the vital political mission of the United States is, to practically solve and settle the problem of two sets of rights—the fusion, thorough compatibility and junction of individual State prerogatives, with the indispensable necessity of centrality and Oneness—the national identity power—the sovereign Union, relentless, permanently comprising all, and over all, and in that never yielding an inch: then 3d. Do we not, amid a general malaria of fogs and vapors, our day, unmistakably see two pillars of promise, with grandest, indestructible indications—one, that the morbid facts of American politics and society everywhere are but passing incidents and flanges of our unbounded impetus of growth? weeds, annuals, of the rank, rich soil—not central, enduring, perennial things? The other, that all the hitherto experience of the States, their first century, has been but preparation, adolescence—and that this Union is only now and henceforth, (*i.e.* since the secession war,) to enter on its full democratic career?

Of the whole, poems and prose, (not attending at all to chronological order, and with original dates and passing allusions in the heat and impression of the hour, left shuffled in, and undisturb'd,) the chants of "Leaves of Grass," my former volume, yet serve as the indispensable deep soil, or basis, out of which,

---

festival of Egypt, the noisome skeleton of death was sent on exhibition to the revelers, for zest and shadow to the occasion's joy and light—but as the marble statue of the normal Greeks at Elis, suggesting death in the form of a beautiful and perfect young man, with closed eyes, leaning on an inverted torch—emblem of rest and aspiration after action—of crown and point which all lives and poems should steadily have reference to, namely, the justified and noble termination of our identity, this grade of it, and outlet-preparation to another grade.

and out of which only, could come the roots and stems more definitely indicated by these later pages. (While that volume radiates physiology alone, the present one, though of the like origin in the main, more palpably doubtless shows the pathology which was pretty sure to come in time from the other.)

In that former and main volume, composed in the flush of my health and strength, from the age of 30 to 50 years, I dwelt on birth and life, clothing my ideas in pictures, days, transactions of my time, to give them positive place, identity—saturating them with that vehemence of pride and audacity of freedom necessary to loosen the mind of still-to-be-form'd America from the accumulated folds, the superstitions, and all the long, tenacious and stifling antidemocratic authorities of the Asiatic and European past—my enclosing purport being to express, above all artificial regulation and aid, the eternal bodily composite, cumulative, natural character of one's self.*

---

*Namely, a character, making most of common and normal elements, to the superstructure of which not only the precious accumulations of the learning and experiences of the Old World, and the settled social and municipal neccesities and current requirements, so long a-building, shall still faithfully contribute, but which at its foundations and carried up thence, and receiving its impetus from the democractic spirit, and accepting its gauge in all departments from the democratic formulas, shall again directly be vitalized by the perennial influences of Nature at first hand, and the old heroic stamina of Nature, the strong air of prairie and mountain, the dash of the briny sea, the primary antiseptics—of the passions, in all their fullest heat and potency, of courage, rankness, amativeness, and of immense pride. Not to lose at all, therefore, the benefits of artificial progress and civilization, but to re-occupy for Western tenancy the oldest though ever-fresh fields, and reap from them the savage and sane nourishment indispensable to a hardy nation, and the absence of which, threatening to become worse and worse, is the most serious lack and defect to-day of our New World literature.

Not but what the brawn of "Leaves of Grass" is, I hope, thoroughly spiritualized everywhere, for final estimate, but, from the very subjects, the direct effect is a sense of the life, as it should be, of flesh and blood, and physical urge, and animalism. While there are other themes, and plenty of abstract thoughts and poems in the volume—while I have put in it passing and rapid but actual glimpses of the great struggle between the nation and the slave-power, (1861–'65) as the fierce and bloody panorama of that contest unroll'd itself: while the whole book, indeed, revolves around that four years' war, which, as I was in the midst of it, becomes, in "Drum-Taps," pivotal to the rest entire—and here and there, before and afterward, not a few episodes and speculations—*that*—namely, to make a type-portrait for living, active, worldly, healthy personality, objective as well as subjective, joyful and potent, and modern and free, distinctively for the use of the United States, male and female, through the long future—has been, I say, my general object. (Probably, indeed, the whole of these varied songs, and all my writings, both volumes, only ring changes in some sort, on the ejaculation, How vast, how eligible, how joyful, how real, is a human being himself or herself.)

Estimating the American Union as so far, and for some time to come, in its yet formative condition, I bequeath poems and essays

Though from no definite plan at the time, I see now that I have unconsciously sought, by indirections at least as much as directions, to express the whirls and rapid growth and intensity of the United States, the prevailing tendency and events of the Nineteenth century, and largely the spirit of the whole current world, my time; for I feel that I have partaken of that spirit, as I have been deeply interested in all those events, the closing of long-stretch'd eras and ages, and, illustrated in the history of the United States, the opening of larger ones. (The death of President Lincoln, for instance, fitly, historically closes, in the civilization of feudalism, many old influences—drops on them, suddenly, a vast, gloomy, as it were, separating curtain.)

Since I have been ill, (1873–74–75,) mostly without serious pain, and with plenty of time and frequent inclination to judge my poems, (never composed with eye on the book-market, nor for fame, nor for any pecuniary profit,) I have felt temporary depression more than once, for fear that in "Leaves of Grass" the *moral* parts were not sufficiently pronounc'd. But in my clearest and calmest moods I have realized that as those "Leaves," all and several, surely prepare the way for, and necessitate morals, and are adjusted to them, just the same as Nature does and is, they are what, consistently with my plan, they must and probably should be. (In a certain sense, while the Moral is the purport and last intelligence of all Nature, there is absolutely nothing of the moral in the works, or laws, or shows of Nature. Those only lead inevitably to it—begin and necessitate it.)

Then I meant "Leaves of Grass," as publish'd, to be the Poem of average Identity, (of *yours*, whoever you are, now reading these lines.) A man is not greatest as victor in war, nor inventor or explorer, nor even in science, or in his intellectual or artistic capacity, or exemplar in some vast benevolence. To the highest democratic view, man is most acceptable in living well the practical life and lot which happens to him as ordinary farmer, sea-farer, mechanic, clerk, laborer, or driver—upon and from which position as a central basis or pedestal, while performing its labors, and his duties as citizen, son, husband, father, and employ'd person, he preserves his physique, ascends, developing, radiating himself in other regions—and especially where and when, (greatest of all, and nobler than the proudest mere genius or magnate in any field,) he fully realizes the conscience, the spiritual, the divine faculty, cultivated well, exemplified in all his deeds and words, through life, uncompromising to the end—a flight loftier than any of Homer's or Shakspere's—broader than all poems and bibles —namely, Nature's own, and in the midst of it, Yourself, your own Identity, body and soul. (All serves, helps—but in the centre of all, absorbing all, giving, for your purpose, the only meaning and vitality to all, master or mistress of all, under the law, stands Yourself.) To sing the Song of that law of average Identity, and of Yourself, consistently with the divine law of the universal, is a main intention of those "Leaves."

Something more may be added—for, while I am about it, I would make a full confession. I also sent out "Leaves of Grass" to arouse and set flowing in men's and women's hearts, young and old, endless streams of living, pulsating love and friendship, directly from them to myself, now and ever. To this terrible, irrepressible yearning, (surely more or less down underneath in most human souls)—this never–satisfied appetite for sympathy, and this boundless offering of sympathy—this universal democratic comradeship—this old, eternal, yet ever-new interchange of adhesiveness, so fitly emblematic of as nutriment and influences to help truly assimilate and harden, and especially to furnish something toward what the States most need of all, and which seems to me yet quite unsupplied in literature, namely, to show them, or begin to show them, themselves distinctively, and what they are for. For though perhaps the main points of all ages and nations are points of resemblance, and, even while granting evolution, are substantially the same, there are some vital things in which this Republic, as to its individualities, and as a compacted Nation, is to specially stand forth, and culminate modern humanity. And these are the very things it least morally and mentally knows—(though, curiously enough, it is at the same time faithfully acting upon them.)

I count with such absolute certainty on the great future of the United States—different from, though founded on, the past—that I have always invoked that future, and surrounded myself with it, before or while singing my songs. (As ever, all tends to followings—America, too, is a prophecy. What, even of the best and most successful, would be justified by itself alone? by the present, or the material ostent alone? Of men or States, few realize how much they live in the future. That, rising like pinnacles, gives its main significance to all You and I are doing to-day. Without it, there were little meaning in lands or poems—little purport in human lives. All ages, all Nations and States, have been such prophecies. But where any former ones with prophecy so broad, so clear, as our times, our lands—as those of the West?)

Without being a scientist, I have thoroughly adopted the conclusions of the great savans and experimentalists of our time, and of the last hundred years, and they have interiorly tinged the

---

America—I have given in that book, undisguisedly, declaredly, the openest expression. Besides, important as they are in my purpose as emotional expressions for humanity, the special meaning of the "Calamus" cluster of "Leaves of Grass," (and more or less running through the book, and cropping out in "Drum-Taps,") mainly resides in its political significance. In my opinion, it is by a fervent, accepted development of comradeship, the beautiful and sane affection of man for man, latent in all the young fellows, north and south, east and west—it is by this, I say, and by what goes directly and indirectly along with it, that the United States of the future, (I cannot too often repeat,) are to be most effectually welded together, intercalated, anneal'd into a living union.

Then, for enclosing clue of all, it is imperatively and ever to be borne in mind that "Leaves of Grass" entire is not to be construed as an intellectual or scholastic effort or poem mainly, but more as a radical utterance out of the Emotions and the Physique—an utterance adjusted to, perhaps born of, Democracy and the Modern—in its very nature regardless of the old conventions, and, under the great laws, following only its own impulses.

chyle of all my verse, for purposes beyond. Following the modern spirit, the real poems of the present, ever solidifying and expanding into the future, must vocalize the vastness and splendor and reality with which scientism has invested man and the universe, (all that is called creation,) and must henceforth launch humanity into new orbits, consonant with that vastness, splendor, and reality, (unknown to the old poems,) like new systems of orbs, balanced upon themselves, revolving in limitless space, more subtle than the stars. Poetry, so largely hitherto and even at present wedded to children's tales, and to mere amorousness, upholstery and superficial rhyme, will have to accept, and, while not denying the past, nor the themes of the past, will be revivified by this tremendous innovation, the kosmic spirit, which must henceforth, in my opinion, be the background and underlying impetus, more or less visible, of all first-class songs.

Only, (for me, at any rate, in all my prose and poetry,) joyfully accepting modern science, and loyally following it without the slightest hesitation, there remains ever recognized still a higher flight, a higher fact, the eternal soul of man, (of all else too,) the spiritual, the religious—which it is to be the greatest office of scientism, in my opinion, and of future poetry also, to free from fables, crudities and superstitions, and launch forth in renew'd faith and scope a hundred fold. To me, the worlds of religiousness, of the conception of the divine, and of the ideal, though mainly latent are just as absolute in humanity and the universe as the world of chemistry, or anything in the objective worlds. To me

> The prophet and the bard,
> Shall yet maintain themselves—in higher circles yet,
> Shall mediate to the modern, to democracy—interpret yet to them,
> God and eidólons.

To me, the crown of savantism is to be, that it surely opens the way for a more splendid theology, and for ampler and diviner songs. No year, nor even century, will settle this. There is a phase of the real, lurking behind the real, which it is all for. There is also in the intellect of man, in time, far in prospective recesses, a judgment, a last appellate court, which will settle it.

In certain parts in these flights, or attempting to depict or suggest them, I have not been afraid of the charge of obscurity, in either of my two volumes—because human thought, poetry or melody, must leave dim escapes and outlets—must possess a certain fluid, aerial character, akin to space itself, obscure to those of little or no imagination, but indispensable to the highest pur-

poses. Poetic style, when address'd to the soul, is less definite
form, outline, sculpture, and becomes vista, music, half-tints, and
even less than half-tints. True, it may be architecture; but again
it may be the forest wild-wood, or the best effect thereof, at twilight,
the waving oaks and cedars in the wind, and the impalpable odor.

Finally, as I have lived in fresh lands, inchoate, and in a revolutionary age, future-founding, I have felt to identify the points
of that age, these lands, in my recitatives, altogether in my own
way. Thus my form has strictly grown from my purports and
facts, and is the analogy of them. Within my time the United
States have emerged from nebulous vagueness and suspense, to full
orbic, (though varied,) decision—have done the deeds and achiev'd
the triumphs of half a score of centuries—and are henceforth to
enter upon their real history—the way being now, (*i. e.* since the
result of the Secession War,) clear'd of death-threatening impedi-
menta, and the free areas around and ahead of us assured and certain, which were not so before—(the past century being but preparations, trial voyages and experiments of the ship, before her starting
out upon deep water.)

In estimating my volumes, the world's current times and deeds,
and their spirit, must be first profoundly estimated. Out of the
hundred years just ending, (1776–1876,) with their genesis of inevitable wilful events, and new experiments and introductions,
and many unprecedented things of war and peace, (to be realized
better, perhaps only realized, at the remove of a century hence;)
out of that stretch of time, and especially out of the immediately
preceding twenty-five years, (1850–75,) with all their rapid changes,
innovations, and audacious movements—and bearing their own
inevitable wilful birth-marks—the experiments of my poems too
have found genesis.

W. W.

Poetry To-day In America—Shakspere— the Future

Strange as it may seem, the topmost proof of a race is its own born poetry. The presence of that, or the absence, each tells its story. As the flowering rose or lily, as the ripen'd fruit to a tree, the apple or the peach, no matter how fine the trunk, or copious or rich the branches and foliage, here waits *sine qua non* at last. The stamp of entire and finish'd greatness to any nation, to the American Republic among the rest, must be sternly withheld till it has put what it stands for in the blossom of original, first-class poems. No imitations will do.

And though no *esthetik* worthy the present condition or future certainties of the New World seems to have been outlined in men's minds, or has been generally called for, or thought needed, I am clear that until the United States have just such definite and native expressers in the highest artistic fields, their mere political, geographical, wealth-forming, and even intellectual eminence, however astonishing and predominant, will constitute but a more and more expanded and well-appointed body, and perhaps brain, with little or no soul. Sugar-coat the grim truth as we may, and ward off with outward plausible words, denials, explanations, to the mental inward perception of the land this blank is plain; a barren void exists. For the meanings and maturer purposes of these States are not the constructing of a new world of politics merely, and physical comforts for the million, but even more determinedly, in range with science and the modern, of a new world of democratic sociology and imaginative literature. If the latter were not establish'd for the States, to form their only permanent tie and hold, the first-named would be of little avail.

With the poems of a first-class land are twined, as weft with warp, its types of personal character, of individuality, peculiar, native, its own physiognomy, man's and woman's, its own shapes, forms, and manners, fully justified under the eternal laws of all forms, all manners, all times. The hour has come for democracy in America to inaugurate itself in the two directions specified—

autochthonic poems and personalities—born expressers of itself, its spirit alone, to radiate in subtle ways, not only in art, but the practical and familiar, in the transactions between employers and employ'd persons, in business and wages, and sternly in the army and navy, and revolutionizing them. I find nowhere a scope profound enough, and radical and objective enough, either for aggregates or individuals. The thought and identity of a poetry in America to fill, and worthily fill, the great void, and enhance these aims, electrifying all and several, involves the essence and integral facts, real and spiritual, of the whole land, the whole body. What the great sympathetic is to the congeries of bones, joints, heart, fluids, nervous system and vitality, constituting, launching forth in time and space a human being—aye, an immortal soul—such relation, and no less, holds true poetry to the single personality, or to the nation.

Here our thirty-eight States stand to-day, the children of past precedents, and, young as they are, heirs of a very old estate. One or two points we will consider, out of the myriads presenting themselves. The feudalism of the British Islands, illustrated by Shakspere—and by his legitimate followers, Walter Scott and Alfred Tennyson—with all its tyrannies, superstitions, evils, had most superb and heroic permeating veins, poems, manners; even its errors fascinating. It almost seems as if only that feudalism in Europe, like slavery in our own South, could outcrop types of tallest, noblest personal character yet—strength and devotion and love better than elsewhere—invincible courage, generosity, aspiration, the spines of all. Here is where Shakspere and the others I have named perform a service incalculably precious to our America. Politics, literature, and everything else, centers at last in perfect *personnel*, (as democracy is to find the same as the rest;) and here feudalism is unrival'd—here the rich and highest-rising lessons it bequeaths us—a mass of foreign nutriment, which we are to work over, and popularize and enlarge, and present again in our own growths.

Still there are pretty grave and anxious drawbacks, jeopardies, fears. Let us give some reflections on the subject, a little fluctuating, but starting from one central thought, and returning there again. Two or three curious results may plow up. As in the astronomical laws, the very power that would seem most deadly and destructive turns out to be latently conservative of longest, vastest future births and lives. We will for .nce briefly examine the just-named authors solely from a Western point of view. It may be, indeed, that we shall use the sun of English literature, and the brightest current stars of his system, mainly as pegs to hang some cogitations on, for home inspection.

As depicter and dramatist of the passions at their stormiest outstretch, though ranking high, Shakspere (spanning the arch wide enough) is equal'd by several, and excell'd by the best old Greeks, (as Æschylus.) But in portraying mediæval European lords and barons, the arrogant port, so dear to the inmost human heart, (pride! pride! dearest, perhaps, of all—touching us, too, of the States closest of all—closer than love,) he stands alone, and I do not wonder he so witches the world.

From first to last, also, Walter Scott and Tennyson, like Shakspere, exhale that principle of caste which we Americans have come on earth to destroy. Jefferson's verdict on the Waverley novels was that they turn'd and condens'd brilliant but entirely false lights and glamours over the lords, ladies, and aristocratic institutes of Europe, with all their measureless infamies, and then left the bulk of the suffering, down-trodden people contemptuously in the shade. Without stopping to answer this hornet-stinging criticism, or to repay any part of the debt of thanks I owe, in common with every American, to the noblest, healthiest, cheeriest romancer that ever lived, I pass on to Tennyson, his works.

Poetry here of a very high (perhaps the highest) order of verbal melody, exquisitely clean and pure, and almost always perfumed, like the tuberose, to an extreme of sweetness—sometimes not, however, but even then a camellia of the hot-house, never a common flower—the verse of inside elegance and high-life; and yet preserving amid all its super-delicatesse a smack of outdoors and outdoor folk. The old Norman lordhood quality here, too, cross'd with that Saxon fiber from which twain the best current stock of England springs—poetry that revels above all things in traditions of knights and chivalry, and deeds of derring-do. The odor of English social life in its highest range—a melancholy, affectionate, very manly, but dainty breed—pervading the pages like an invisible scent; the idleness, the traditions, the mannerisms, the stately *ennui;* the yearning of love, like a spinal marrow, inside of all; the costumes, brocade and satin; the old houses and furniture—solid oak, no mere veneering—the moldy secrets everywhere; the verdure, the ivy on the walls, the moat, the English landscape outside, the buzzing fly in the sun inside the window pane. Never one democratic page; nay, not a line, not a word; never free and *naïve* poetry, but involv'd, labor'd, quite sophisticated—even when the theme is ever so simple or rustic, (a shell, a bit of sedge, the commonest love-passage between a lad and lass,) the handling of the rhyme all showing the scholar and conventional gentleman; showing the laureate, too, the *attaché* of the throne, and most excellent, too; nothing better through the volumes than the dedication "to the Queen" at the beginning, and the other fine diction, "these to his memory" (Prince Albert's,) preceding "Idylls of the King."

Such for an off-hand summary of the mighty three that now, by the women, men, and young folk of the fifty millions given these States by their late census, have been and are more read than all others put together

We hear it said, both of Tennyson and another current leading literary illustrator of Great Britain, Carlyle—as of Victor Hugo in France—that not one of them is personally friendly or admirant toward America; indeed, quite the reverse. *N'importe.* That they (and more good minds than theirs) cannot span the vast revolutionary arch thrown by the United States over the centuries, fix'd in the present, launch'd to the endless future; that they cannot stomach the high-life-below-stairs coloring all our poetic and genteel social status so far—the measureless viciousness of the great radical Republic, with its ruffianly nominations and elections; its loud, ill-pitch'd voice, utterly regardless whether the verb agrees with the nominative; its fights, errors, eructations, repulsions, dishonesties, audacities; those fearful and varied and long-continued storm and stress stages (so offensive to the well-regulated college-bred mind) where with Nature, history, and time block out nationalities more powerful than the past, and to upturn it and press on to the future;— that they cannot understand and fathom all this, I say, is it to be wonder'd at? Fortunately, the gestation of our thirty-eight empires (and plenty more to come) proceeds on its course, on scales of area and velocity immense and absolute as the globe, and, like the globe itself, quite oblivious even of great poets and thinkers. But we can by no means afford to be oblivious of them.

The same of feudalism, its castles, courts, etiquettes, personalities. However they, or the spirits of them hovering in the air, might scowl and glower at such removes as current Kansas or Kentucky life and forms, the latter may by no means repudiate or leave out the former. Allowing all the evil that it did, we get, here and to-day, a balance of good out of its reminiscence almost beyond price.

Am I content, then, that the general interior chyle of our republic should be supplied and nourish'd by wholesale from foreign and antagonistic sources such as these? Let me answer that question briefly:

Years ago I thought Americans ought to strike out separate, and have expressions of their own in highest literature. I think so still, and more decidedly than ever. But those convictions are now strongly temper'd by some additional points, (perhaps the results of advancing age, or the reflections of invalidism.) I see that this world of the West, as part of all, fuses inseparably with the East, and with all, as time does—the ever new, yet old, old human race— "the same subject continued," as the novels of our grandfathers had it for chapter-heads. If we are not to hospitably receive and complete the inaugurations of the old civilizations, and change their small scale to the largest, broadest scale, what on earth are we for?

The currents of practical business in America, the rude, coarse, tussling facts of our lives, and all their daily experiences, need just the precipitation and tincture of this entirely different fancy world of lulling, contrasting, even feudalistic, anti-republican poetry and romance. On the enormous outgrowth of our unloos'd individualities, and the rank self-assertion of humanity here, may well fall these grace-persuading, *recherché* influences. We first require that individuals and communities shall be free; then surely comes a time when it is requisite that they shall not be too free. Although to such results in the future I look mainly for a great poetry native to us, these importations till then will have to be accepted, such as they are, and thankful they are no worse. The inmost spiritual currents of the present time curiously revenge and check their own compell'd tendency to democracy, and absorption in it, by mark'd leanings to the past—by reminiscences in poems, plots, operas, novels, to a far-off, contrary, deceased world, as if they dreaded the great vulgar gulf tides of to-day. Then what has been fifty centuries growing, working in, and accepted as crowns and apices for our kind, is not going to be pulled down and discarded in a hurry.

It is, perhaps, time we paid our respects directly to the honorable party, the real object of these preambles. But we must make *reconnaissance* a little further still. Not the least part of our lesson were to realize the curiosity and interest of friendly foreign experts,* and how our situation looks to them. "American poetry," says the

---

* A few years ago I saw the question, "Has America produced any great poem?" announced as prize-subject for the competition of some university in Northern Europe. I saw the item in a foreign paper and made a note of it; but being taken down with paralysis, and prostrated for a long season, the

London "Times,"* "is the poetry of apt pupils, but it is afflicted "from first to last with a fatal want of raciness. Bryant has been "long passed as a poet by Professor Longfellow; but in Long- "fellow, with all his scholarly grace and tender feeling, the defect "is more apparent than it was in Bryant. Mr. Lowell can overflow "with American humor when politics inspire his muse; but in the "realm of pure poetry he is no more American than a Newdigate "prize-man. Joaquin Miller's verse has fluency and movement and "harmony, but as for the thought, his songs of the sierras might "as well have been written in Holland."

Unless in a certain very slight contingency, the "Times" says: "American verse, from its earliest to its latest stages, seems an "exotic, with an exuberance of gorgeous blossom, but no principle "of reproduction. That is the very note and test of its inherent "want. Great poets are tortured and massacred by having their "flowers of fancy gathered and gummed down in the *hortus siccus* "of an anthology. American poets show better in an anthology "than in the collected volumes of their works. Like their audience "they have been unable to resist the attraction of the vast orbit of "English literature. They may talk of the primeval forest, but it "would generally be very hard from internal evidence to detect that "they were writing on the banks of the Hudson rather than on those "of the Thames. . . . . In fact, they have caught the English tone and "air and mood only too faithfully, and are accepted by the super- "ficially cultivated English intelligence as readily as if they were "English born. Americans themselves confess to a certain disap- "pointment that a literary curiosity and intelligence so diffused [as "in the United States] have not taken up English literature at the "point at which America has received it, and carried it forward "and developed it with an independent energy. But like reader like "poet. Both show the effects of having come into an estate they "have not earned. A nation of readers has required of its poets a "diction and symmetry of form equal to that of an old literature "like that of Great Britain, which is also theirs. No ruggedness, "however racy, would be tolerated by circles which, however super- "ficial their culture, read Byron and Tennyson."

---

matter slipp'd away, and I have never been able since to get hold of any essay presented for the prize, or report of the discussion, nor to learn for certain whether there was any essay or discussion, nor can I now remember the place. It may have been Upsala, or possibly Heidelberg. Perhaps some German or Scandinavian can give particulars. I think it was in 1872.

* In a long and prominent editorial, at the time, on the death of William Cullen Bryant.

The English critic, though a gentleman and a scholar, and friendly withall, is evidently not altogether satisfied, (perhaps he is jealous,) and winds up by saying: "For the English language to have been "enriched with a national poetry which was not English but Ameri-"can, would have been a treasure beyond price." With which, as whet and foil, we shall proceed to ventilate more definitely certain no doubt willful opinions.

Leaving unnoticed at present the great masterpieces of the antique, or anything from the middle ages, the prevailing flow of poetry for the last fifty or eighty years, and now at its height, has been and is (like the music) an expression of mere surface melody, within narrow limits, and yet, to give it its due, perfectly satisfying to the demands of the ear, of wondrous charm, of smooth and easy delivery, and the triumph of technical art. Above all things it is fractional and select. It shrinks with aversion from the sturdy, the universal, and the democratic.

The poetry of the future, (a phrase open to sharp criticism, and not satisfactory to me, but significant, and I will use it)—the poetry of the future aims at the free expression of emotion, (which means far, far more than appears at first,) and to arouse and initiate, more than to define or finish. Like all modern tendencies, it has direct or indirect reference continually to the reader, to you or me, to the central identity of everything, the mighty Ego. (Byron's was a vehement dash, with plenty of impatient democracy, but lurid and introverted amid all its magnetism; not at all the fitting, lasting song of a grand, secure, free, sunny race.) It is more akin, likewise, to outside life and landscape, (returning mainly to the antique feeling,) real sun and gale, and woods and shores—to the elements themselves—not sitting at ease in parlor or library listening to a good tale of them, told in good rhyme. Character, a feature far above style or polish—a feature not absent at any time, but now first brought to the fore—gives predominant stamp to advancing poetry. Its born sister, music, already responds to the same influences. "The music of the present, Wagner's, Gounod's, even the "later Verdi's, all tends toward this free expression of poetic emo-"tion, and demands a vocalism totally unlike that required for "Rossini's splendid roulades, or Bellini's suave melodies."

Is there not even now, indeed, an evolution, a departure from the masters? Venerable and unsurpassable after their kind as are the old works, and always unspeakably precious as studies, (for Americans more than any other people,) is it too much to say that by the shifted combinations of the modern mind the whole underlying theory of first-class verse has changed? "Formerly, during "the period term'd classic," says Sainte-Beuve, "when literature "was govern'd by recognized rules, he was consider'd the best "poet who had composed the most perfect work, the most beauti-"ful poem, the most intelligible, the most agreeable to read, the "most complete in every respect,—the Æneid, the Gerusalemme, a "fine tragedy. To-day, something else is wanted. For us the greatest "poet is he who in his works most stimulates the reader's imagina-"tion and reflection, who excites him the most himself to poetize. "The greatest poet is not he who has done the best; it is he who "suggests the most; he, not all of whose meaning is at first obvious, "and who leaves you much to desire, to explain, to study, much "to complete in your turn."

The fatal defects our American singers labor under are subordination of spirit, an absence of the concrete and of real patriotism, and in excess that modern æsthetic contagion a queer friend of mine calls the *beauty disease*. "The immoderate taste for beauty "and art," says Charles Baudelaire, "leads men into monstrous "excesses. In minds imbued with a frantic greed for the beautiful, "all the balances of truth and justice disappear. There is a lust, a "disease of the art faculties, which eats up the moral like a cancer."

Of course, by our plentiful verse-writers there is plenty of service perform'd, of a kind. Nor need we go far for a tally. We see, in every polite circle, a class of accomplish'd, good-natured persons, ("society," in fact, could not get on without them,) fully eligible for certain problems, times, and duties—to mix egg-nog, to mend the broken spectacles, to decide whether the stew'd eels shall precede the sherry or the sherry the stew'd eels, to eke our Mrs. A. B.'s parlor-tableaux with monk, Jew, lover, Puck, Prospero, Caliban, or what not, and to generally contribute and gracefully adapt their flexibilities and talents, in those ranges, to the world's service. But for real crises, great needs and pulls, moral or physical, they might as well have never been born.

Or the accepted notion of a poet would appear to be a sort of male odalisque, singing or piano-playing a kind of spiced ideas, second-hand reminiscences, or toying late hours at entertainments, in rooms stifling with fashionable scent. I think I haven't seen a new-publish'd, heathy, bracing, simple lyric in ten years. Not long ago, there were verses in each of three fresh monthlies, from leading authors, and in every one the whole central *motif* (perfectly serious) was the melancholiness of a marriageable young woman who didn't get a rich husband, but a poor one!

Besides its tonic and *al fresco* physiology, relieving such as this,
the poetry of the future will take on character in a more important
respect. Science, having extirpated the old stock-fables and superstitions, is clearing a field for verse, for all the arts, and even for
romance, a hundred-fold ampler and more wonderful, with the new
principles behind. Republicanism advances over the whole world.
Liberty, with Law by her side, will one day be paramount—will at
any rate be the central idea. Then only—for all the splendor and
beauty of what has been, or the polish of what is—then only will
the true poets appear, and the true poems. Not the satin and patch-
ouly of to-day, not the glorification of the butcheries and wars of
the past, nor any fight between Deity on one side and somebody
else on the other—not Milton, not even Shakspere's plays, grand
as they are. Entirely different and hitherto unknown classes of men,
being authoritatively called for in imaginative literature, will certainly appear. What is hitherto most lacking, perhaps most absolutely indicates the future. Democracy has been hurried on through
time by measureless tides and winds, resistless as the revolution of
the globe, and as far-reaching and rapid. But in the highest walks
of art it has not yet had a single representative worthy of it anywhere upon the earth.

Never had real bard a task more fit for sublime ardor and genius
than to sing worthily the songs these States have already indicated.
Their origin, Washington, '76, the picturesqueness of old times, the
war of 1812 and the sea-fights; the incredible rapidity of movement and breadth of area—to fuse and compact the South and
North, the East and West, to express the native forms, situations,
scenes, from Montauk to California and from the Saguenay to the
Rio Grande—the working out on such gigantic scales, and with
such a swift and mighty play of changing light and shade, of the
great problems of man and freedom,—how far ahead of the stereotyped plots, or gem-cutting, or tales of love, or wars of mere ambition! Our history is so full of spinal, modern germinal subjects—
one above all. What the ancient siege of Ilium, and the puissance
of Hector's and Agamemnon's warriors proved to Hellenic art and
literature, and all art and literature since, may prove the war of
attempted secession of 1861-'65 to the future æsthetics, drama,
romance, poems of the United States.

Nor could utility itself provide anything more practically serviceable to the hundred millions who, a couple of generations hence,
will inhabit within the limits just named, than the permeation of
a sane, sweet, autochthonous national poetry—must I say of a

kind that does not now exist? but which, I fully believe, will in time be supplied on scales as free as Nature's elements. (It is acknowledged that we of the States are the most materialistic and money-making people ever known. My own theory, while fully accepting this, is that we are the most emotional, spiritualistic, and poetry-loving people also.)

Infinite are the new and orbic traits waiting to be launch'd forth in the firmament that is, and is to be, America. Lately, I have wonder'd whether the last meaning of this cluster of thirty-eight States is not only practical fraternity among themselves—the only real *union*, (much nearer its accomplishment, too, than appears on the surface)—but for fraternity over the whole globe—that dazzling, pensive dream of ages! Indeed, the peculiar glory of our lands, I have come to see, or expect to see, not in their geographical or republican greatness, nor wealth or products, nor military or naval power, nor special, eminent names in any department, to shine with, or outshine, foreign special names in similar departments,—but more and more in a vaster, saner, more surrounding Comradeship, uniting closer and closer not only the American States, but all nations, and all humanity. That, O poets! is not that a theme worth chanting, striving for? Why not fix your verses henceforth to the gauge of the round globe? the whole race? Perhaps the most illustrious culmination of the modern may thus prove to be a signal growth of joyous, more exalted bards of adhesiveness, identically one in soul, but contributed by every nation, each after its distinctive kind. Let us, audacious, start it. Let the diplomats, as ever, still deeply plan, seeking advantages, proposing treaties between governments, and to bind them, on paper: what I seek is different, simpler. I would inaugurate from America, for this purpose, new formulas—international poems. I have thought that the invisible root out of which the poetry deepest in, and dearest to, humanity grows, is Friendship. I have thought that both in patriotism and song (even amid their grandest shows past) we have adhered too long to petty limits, and that the time has come to enfold the world.

Not only is the human and artificial world we have establish'd in the West a radical departure from anything hitherto known—not only men and politics, and all that goes with them—but Nature itself, in the main sense, its construction, is different. The same old font of type, of course, but set up to a text never composed or issued before. For Nature consists not only in itself, objectively, but at least just as much in its subjective reflection from the person, spirit, age, looking at it, in the midst of it, and absorbing it—faithfully sends back the characteristic beliefs of the time or individual—takes, and readily gives again, the physiognomy of any nation or literature—falls like a great elastic veil on a face, or like the molding plaster on a statue.

What is Nature? What were the elements, the invisible backgrounds and eidólons of it, to Homer's heroes, voyagers, gods? What all through the wanderings of Virgil's Æneas? Then to Shakspere's characters—Hamlet, Lear, the English-Norman kings, the Romans? What was Nature to Rousseau, to Voltaire, to the German Goethe in his little classical court gardens? In those presentments in Tennyson (see the "Idylls of the King"—what sumptuous, perfumed, arras-and-gold Nature, inimitably described, better than any, fit for princes and knights and peerless ladies—wrathful or peaceful, just the same—Vivien and Merlin in their strange dalliance, or the death-float of Elaine, or Geraint and the long journey of his disgraced Enid and himself through the wood, and the wife all day driving the horses,) as in all the great imported art-works, treatises, systems, from Lucretius down, there is a constantly lurking, often pervading something, that will have to be eliminated, as not only unsuited to modern democracy and science in America, but insulting to them, and disproved by them.*

Still, the rule and demesne of poetry will always be not the exterior, but interior; not the macrocosm, but microcosm; not Nature, but Man. I haven't said anything about the imperative need of a race of giant bards in the future, to hold up high to eyes of land and race the eternal antiseptic models, and to dauntlessly confront greed, injustice, and all forms of that wiliness and tyranny whose roots never die—(my opinion is, that after all the rest is advanced, *that* is what first-class poets are for; as, to their days and occasions, the Hebrew lyrists, Roman Juvenal, and doubtless the old singers of India, and the British Druids)—to counteract dangers, immensest ones, already looming in America—measureless corruption in politics—what we call religion, a mere mask of wax or lace;—for *ensemble*, that most cankerous, offensive of all earth's shows—a vast and varied community, prosperous and fat with wealth of money and products and business ventures—plenty

---

*Whatever may be said of the few principal poems—or their best passages—it is certain that the overwhelming mass of poetic works, as now absorb'd into human character, exerts a certain constipating, repressing, in-door, and artificial influence, impossible to elude—seldom or never that freeing, dilating, joyous one, with which uncramp'd Nature works on every individual without exception.

of mere intellectuality too—and then utterly without the sound, prevailing, moral and æsthetic health-action beyond all the money and mere intellect of the world.

Is it a dream of mine that, in times to come, west, south, east, north, will silently, surely arise a race of such poets, varied, yet one in soul—nor only poets, and of the best, but newer, larger prophets—larger than Judea's, and more passionate—to meet and penetrate those woes, as shafts of light the darkness?

As I write, the last fifth of the nineteenth century is enter'd upon, and will soon be waning. Now, and for a long time to come, what the United States most need, to give purport, definiteness, reason why, to their unprecedented material wealth, industrial products, education by rote merely, great populousness and intellectual activity, is the central, spinal reality, (or even the idea of it,) of such a democratic band of native-born-and-bred teachers, artists, *littérateurs*, tolerant and receptive of importations, but entirely adjusted to the West, to ourselves, to our own days, combinations, differences, superiorities. Indeed, I am fond of thinking that the whole series of concrete and political triumphs of the Republic are mainly as bases and preparations for half a dozen future poets, ideal personalities, referring not to a special class, but to the entire people, four or five millions of square miles.

Long, long are the processes of the development of a nationality. Only to the rapt vision does the seen become the prophecy of the unseen.* Democracy, so far attending only to the real, is not for the real only, but the grandest ideal—to justify the modern by that, and not only to equal, but to become by that superior to the past. On a comprehensive summing up of the processes and present and hitherto condition of the United States, with reference to their future, and the indispensable precedents to it, my point, below all

---

*Is there not such a thing as the philosophy of American history and politics? And if so, what is it? . . .Wise men say there are two sets of wills to nations and to persons—one set that acts and works from explainable motives—from teaching, intelligence, judgment, circumstance, caprice, emulation, greed, &c.— and then another set, perhaps deep, hidden, unsuspected, yet often more potent than the first, refusing to be argued with, rising as it were out of abysses, resistlessly urging on speakers, doers, communities, unwitting to themselves— the poet to his fieriest words—the race to pursue its loftiest ideal. Indeed, the paradox of a nation's life and career, with all its wondrous contradictions, can probably only be explain'd from these two wills, sometimes conflicting, each operating in its sphere, combining in races or in persons, and producing strangest results.

Let us hope there is (indeed, can there be any doubt there is?) this great

surfaces, and subsoiling them, is, that the bases and prerequisites
of a leading nationality are, first, at all hazards, freedom, worldly
wealth and products on the largest and most varied scale, common
education and intercommunication, and, in general, the passing
through of just the stages and crudities we have passed or are
passing through in the United States.

Then, perhaps, as weightiest factor of the whole business, and
of the main outgrowths of the future, it remains to be definitely
avow'd that the native-born middle-class population of quite all
the United States—the average of farmers and mechanics everywhere—the real, though latent and silent bulk of America, city or
country, presents a magnificent mass of material, never before
equaled on earth. It is this material, quite unexpress'd by literature
or art, that in every respect insures the future of the republic.
During the Secession War I was with the armies, and saw the rank
and file, North and South, and studied them for four years. I have
never had the least doubt about the country in its essential future since.

---

unconscious and abysmic second will also running through the average nationality and career of America. Let us hope that, amid all the dangers and defections
of the present, and through all the processes of the conscious will, it alone is the
permanent and sovereign force, destined to carry on the New World to fulfill its
destinies in the future—to resolutely pursue those destinies, age upon age; to
build, far, far beyond its past vision, present thought; to form and fashion, and
for the general type, men and women more noble, more athletic than the world
has yet seen; to gradually, firmly blend, from all the States, with all varieties, a
friendly, happy, free, religious nationality—a nationality not only the richest,
most inventive, most productive and materialistic the world has yet known, but
compacted indissolubly, and out of whose ample and solid bulk, and giving
purpose and finish to it, conscience, morals, and all the spiritual attributes, shall
surely rise, like spires above some group of edifices, firm-footed on the earth,
yet scaling space and heaven.

Great as they are, and greater far to be, the United States, too, are but a
series of steps in the eternal process of creative thought. And here is, to my
mind, their final justification, and certain perpetuity. There is in that sublime
process, in the laws of the universe—and, above all, in the moral law—something that would make unsatisfactory, and even vain and contemptible, all the
triumphs of war, the gains of peace, and the proudest worldly grandeur of all
the nations that have ever existed, or that (ours included) now exist, except
that we constantly see, through all their worldly career, however struggling and
blind and lame, attempts, by all ages, all peoples, according to their development, to reach, to press, to progress on, and ever farther on, to more and
more advanced ideals.

The glory of the republic of the United States, in my opinion, is to be that,
emerging in the light of the modern and the splendor of science, and solidly
based on the past, it is to cheerfully range itself, and its politics are henceforth
to come, under those universal laws, and embody them, and carry them out, to
serve them. And as only that individual becomes truly great who understands
well that, while complete in himself in a certain sense, he is but a part of the

Meantime, we can (perhaps) do no better than to saturate ourselves with, and continue to give imitations, yet awhile, of the
æsthetic models, supplies, of that past and of those lands we spring
from. Those wondrous stores, reminiscences, floods, currents! Let
them flow on, flow hither freely. And let the sources be enlarged,
to include not only the works of British origin, as now, but stately
and devout Spain, courteous France, profound Germany, the manly
Scandinavian lands, Italy's art race, and always the mystic Orient.
Remembering that at present, and doubtless long ahead, a certain
humility would well become us. The course through time of highest
civilization, does it not wait the first glimpse of our contribution
to its cosmic train of poems, bibles, first-class structures, perpetuities—Egypt and Palestine and India—Greece and Rome and
mediæval Europe—and so onward? The shadowy procession is not
a meagre one, and the standard not a low one. All that is mighty
in our kind seems to have already trod the road. Ah, never may
America forget her thanks and reverence for samples, treasures

---

divine, eternal scheme, and whose special life and laws are adjusted to move in
harmonious relations with the general laws of Nature, and especially with the
moral law, the deepest and highest of all, and the last vitality of man or state—so
the United States may only become the greatest and the most continuous, by
understanding well their harmonious relations with entire humanity and history,
and all their laws and progress, sublimed with the creative thought of Deity,
through all time, past, present, and future. Thus will they expand to the amplitude of their destiny, and become illustrations and culminating parts of the
cosmos, and of civilization.

No more considering the States as an incident, or series of incidents, however
vast, coming accidentally along the path of time, and shaped by casual emergencies as they happen to arise, and the mere result of modern improvements,
vulgar and lucky, ahead of other nations and times, I would finally plant, as
seeds, these thoughts or speculations in the growth of our republic—that it is
the deliberate culmination and result of all the past—that here, too, as in all
departments of the universe, regular laws (slow and sure in planting, slow and
sure in ripening) have controll'd and govern'd, and will yet control and govern;
and that those laws can no more be baffled or steer'd clear of, or vitiated, by
chance, or any fortune or opposition, than the laws of winter and summer, or
darkness and light.

The summing up of the tremendous moral and military perturbations of
1861–5, and their results—and indeed of the entire hundred years of the past
of our national experiment, from its inchoate movement down to the present
day (1780–1881)—is, that they all now launch the United States fairly forth,
consistently with the entirety of civilization and humanity, and in main sort
the representative of them, leading the van, leading the fleet of the modern and
democratic, on the seas and voyages of the future.

And the real history of the United States—starting from that great convulsive
struggle for unity, the secession war, triumphantly concluded, and *the South
victorious after all*—is only to be written at the remove of hundreds, perhaps a
thousand, years hence.

such as these—that other life-blood, inspiration, sunshine, hourly in use to-day, all days, forever, through her broad demesne!

All serves our New World progress, even the bafflers, head-winds, cross-tides. Through many perturbations and squalls, and much backing and filling, the ship, upon the whole, makes unmistakably for her destination. Shakspere has served, and serves, may-be, the best of any.

For conclusion, a passing thought, a contrast, of him who, in my opinion, continues and stands for the Shaksperean cultus at the present day among all English-writing peoples—of Tennyson, his poetry. I find it impossible, as I taste the sweetness of those lines, to escape the flavor, the conviction, the lush-ripening culmination, and last honey of decay (I dare not call it rottenness) of that feudalism which the mighty English dramatist painted in all the splendors of its noon and afternoon. And how they are chanted—both poets! Happy those kings and nobles to be so sung, so told! To run their course—to get their deeds and shapes in lasting pigments—the very pomp and dazzle of the sunset!

Meanwhile, democracy waits the coming of its bards in silence and in twilight—but 'tis the twilight of the dawn.

Specimen Days

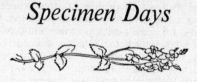

A HAPPY HOUR'S COMMAND

Down in the Woods, July 2d, 1882.—If I do it at all I must delay
no longer. Incongruous and full of skips and jumps as is that huddle
of diary-jottings, war-memoranda of 1862–'65, Nature-notes of
1877–'81, with Western and Canadian observations afterwards, all
bundled up and tied by a big string, the resolution and indeed
mandate comes to me this day, this hour,—(and what a day! what
an hour just passing! the luxury of riant grass and blowing breeze,
with all the shows of sun and sky and perfect temperature, never
before so filling me body and soul)—to go home, untie the bundle,
reel out diary-scraps and memoranda, just as they are, large or
small, one after another, into print-pages,* and let the melange's
lackings and wants of connection take care of themselves. It will
illustrate one phase of humanity anyhow; how few of life's days

---

* The pages from [560] to [573] are nearly verbatim an off-hand letter of mine in
January, 1882, to an insisting friend. Following, I give some gloomy experiences.
The war of attempted secession has, of course, been the distinguishing event of
my time. I commenced at the close of 1862, and continued steadily through
'63, '64, and '65, to visit the sick and wounded of the army, both on the field
and in the hospitals in and around Washington city. From the first I kept little
note-books for impromptu jottings in pencil to refresh my memory of names
and circumstances, and what was specially wanted, &c. In these I brief'd cases,
persons, sights, occurrences in camp, by the bedside, and not seldom by the
corpses of the dead. Some were scratch'd down from narratives I heard and
itemized while watching, or waiting, or tending somebody amid those scenes.
I have dozens of such little note-books left, forming a special history of those
years, for myself alone, full of associations never to be possibly said or sung.
I wish I could convey to the reader the associations that attach to these soil'd
and creas'd livraisons, each composed of a sheet or two of paper, folded small
to carry in the pocket, and fasten'd with a pin. I leave them just as I threw them
by after the war, blotch'd here and there with more than one blood-stain,
hurriedly written, sometimes at the clinique, not seldom amid the excitement of
uncertainty, or defeat, or of action, or getting ready for it, or a march. Most of
the pages from [578] to [636] are verbatim copies of those lurid and blood-
smutch'd little note-books.

Very different are most of the memoranda that follow. Some time after the
war ended I had a paralytic stroke, which prostrated me for several years. In
1876 I began to get over the worst of it. From this date, portions of several

553

and hours (and they not by relative value or proportion, but by chance) are ever noted. Probably another point too, how we give long preparations for some object, planning and delving and fashioning, and then, when the actual hour for doing arrives, find ourselves still quite unprepared, and tumble the thing together, letting hurry and crudeness tell the story better than fine work. At any rate I obey my happy hour's command, which seems curiously imperative. May-be, if I don't do anything else, I shall send out the most wayward, spontaneous, fragmentary book ever printed.

ANSWER TO AN INSISTING FRIEND

You ask for items, details of my early life—of genealogy and parentage, particularly of the women of my ancestry, and of its far back Netherlands stock on the maternal side—of the region where I was born and raised, and my father and mother before me, and theirs before them—with a word about Brooklyn and New York cities, the times I lived there as lad and young man. You say you want to get at these details mainly as the go-befores and embryons of "Leaves of Grass." Very good; you shall have at least some specimens of them all. I have often thought of the meaning of such things—that one can only encompass and complete matters of that kind by exploring behind, perhaps very far behind, themselves directly, and so into their genesis, antecedents, and cumulative stages. Then as luck would have it, I lately whiled away the tedium of a week's half-sickness and confinement, by collating these very items for another (yet unfulfill'd, probably abandon'd,) purpose; and if you will be satisfied with them, authentic in date-occurrence

---

seasons, especially summers, I spent at a secluded haunt down in Camden county, New Jersey—Timber creek, quite a little river (it enters from the great Delaware, twelve miles away)—with primitive solitudes, winding stream, recluse and woody banks, sweet-feeding springs, and all the charms that birds, grass, wild-flowers, rabbits and squirrels, old oaks, walnut trees, &c., can bring. Through these times, and on these spots, the diary from page 83 onward was mostly written.

The COLLECT afterward gathers up the odds and ends of whatever pieces I can now lay hands on, written at various times past, and swoops all together like fish in a net.

I suppose I publish and leave the whole gathering, first, from that eternal tendency to perpetuate and preserve which is behind all Nature, authors included; second, to symbolize two or three specimen interiors, personal and other, out of the myriads of my time, the middle range of the Nineteenth century in the New World; a strange, unloosen'd, wondrous time. But the book is probably without any definite purpose that can be told in a statement.

and fact simply, and told my own way, garrulous-like, here they are. I shall not hesitate to make extracts, for I catch at any thing to save labor; but those will be the best versions of what I want to convey.

GENEALOGY—VAN VELSOR AND WHITMAN

The later years of the last century found the Van Velsor family, my mother's side, living on their own farm at Cold Spring, Long Island, New York State, near the eastern edge of Queens county, about a mile from the harbor.* My father's side—probably the fifth generation from the first English arrivals in New England— were at the same time farmers on their own land—(and a fine domain it was, 500 acres, all good soil, gently sloping east and south, about one-tenth woods, plenty of grand old trees,) two or three miles off, at West Hills, Suffolk county. The Whitman name in the Eastern States, and so branching West and South, starts undoubtedly from one John Whitman, born 1602, in Old England, where he grew up, married, and his eldest son was born in 1629. He came over in the "True Love" in 1640 to America, and lived in Weymouth, Mass., which place became the mother-hive of the New-Englanders of the name: he died in 1692. His brother, Rev. Zechariah Whitman, also came over in the "True Love," either at that time or soon after, and lived at Milford, Conn. A son of this Zechariah, named Joseph, migrated to Huntington, Long Island, and permanently settled there. Savage's "Genealogical Dictionary" (vol. iv. p. 524) gets the Whitman family establish'd at Huntington, per this Joseph, before 1664. It is quite certain that from that beginning, and from Joseph, the West Hill Whitmans, and all others in Suffolk county, have since radiated, myself among the number. John and Zechariah both went to England and back again divers times; they had large families, and several of their children were born in the old country. We hear of the father of John and Zechariah, Abijah Whitman, who goes over into the 1500's, but we know little about him, except that he also was for some time in America.

These old pedigree-reminiscences come up to me vividly from a visit I made not long since (in my 63d year) to West Hills, and to the burial grounds of my ancestry, both sides. I extract from notes of that visit, written there and then:

---

* Long Island was settled first on the west end by the Dutch, from Holland, then on the east end by the English—the dividing line of the two nationalities being a little west of Huntington, where my father's folks lived, and where I was born.

THE OLD WHITMAN AND VAN VELSOR CEMETERIES

July 29, 1881.—After more than forty years' absence, (except a brief visit, to take my father there once more, two years before he died,) went down Long Island on a week's jaunt to the place where I was born, thirty miles from New York city. Rode around the old familiar spots, viewing and pondering and dwelling long upon them, everything coming back to me. Went to the old Whitman homestead on the upland and took a view eastward, inclining south, over the broad and beautiful farm lands of my grandfather (1780,) and my father. There was the new house (1810,) the big oak a hundred and fifty or two hundred years old; there the well, the sloping kitchen-garden, and a little way off even the well-kept remains of the dwelling of my great-grandfather (1750–'60) still standing, with its mighty timbers and low ceilings. Near by, a stately grove of tall, vigorous black-walnuts, beautiful, Apollo-like, the sons or grandsons, no doubt, of black-walnuts during or before 1776. On the other side of the road spread the famous apple orchard, over twenty acres, the trees planted by hands long mouldering in the grave (my uncle Jesse's,) but quite many of them evidently capable of throwing out their annual blossoms and fruit yet.

I now write these lines seated on an old grave (doubtless of a century since at least) on the burial hill of the Whitmans of many generations. Fifty and more graves are quite plainly traceable, and as many more decay'd out of all form—depress'd mounds, crumbled and broken stones, cover'd with moss—the gray and sterile hill, the clumps of chestnuts outside, the silence, just varied by the soughing wind. There is always the deepest eloquence of sermon or poem in any of these ancient graveyards of which Long Island has so many; so what must this one have been to me? My whole family history, with its succession of links, from the first settlement down to date, told here—three centuries concentrate on this sterile acre.

The next day, July 30, I devoted to the maternal locality, and if possible was still more penetrated and impress'd. I write this paragraph on the burial hill of the Van Velsors, near Cold Spring, the most significant depository of the dead that could be imagin'd, without the slightest help from art, but far ahead of it, soil sterile, a mostly bare plateau-flat of half an acre, the top of a hill, brush and well grown trees and dense woods bordering all around, very primitive, secluded, no visitors, no road (you cannot drive here, you have to bring the dead on foot, and follow on foot.) Two or three-score graves quite plain; as many more almost rubb'd out. My grandfather Cornelius and my grandmother Amy (Naomi) and numerous relatives nearer or remoter, on my mother's side, lie buried here. The scene as I stood or sat, the delicate and wild odor of the woods, a slightly drizzling rain, the emotional atmosphere of the place, and the inferr'd reminiscences, were fitting accompaniments.

THE MATERNAL HOMESTEAD

I went down from this ancient grave place eighty or ninety rods to the site of the Van Velsor homestead, where my mother was born (1795), and where every spot had been familiar to me as a child and youth (1825–'40.) Then stood there a long rambling, darkgray, shingle-sided house, with sheds, pens, a great barn, and much open road-space. Now of all those not a vestige left; all had been pull'd down, erased, and the plough and harrow pass'd over foundations, road-spaces and everything, for many summers; fenced in at present, and grain and clover growing like any other fine fields. Only a big hole from the cellar, with some little heaps of broken stone, green with grass and weeds, identified the place. Even the copious old brook and spring seem'd to have mostly dwindled away. The whole scene, with what it arous'd, memories of my young days there half a century ago, the vast kitchen and ample fireplace and the sitting-room adjoining, the plain furniture, the meals, the house full of merry people, my grandmother Amy's sweet old face in its Quaker cap, my grandfather "the Major," jovial, red, stout, with sonorous voice and characteristic physiognomy, with the actual sights themselves, made the most pronounc'd half-day's experience of my whole jaunt.

For there with all those wooded, hilly, healthy surroundings, my dearest mother, Louisa Van Velsor, grew up—(her mother, Amy Williams, of the Friends' or Quakers' denomination—the Williams family, seven sisters and one brother—the father and brother sailors, both of whom met their deaths at sea.) The Van Velsor people were noted for fine horses, which the men bred and train'd from blooded stock. My mother, as a young woman, was a daily and daring rider. As to the head of the family himself, the old race of the Netherlands, so deeply grafted on Manhattan island and in Kings and Queens counties, never yielded a more mark'd and full Americanized specimen than Major Cornelius Van Velsor.

TWO OLD FAMILY INTERIORS

Of the domestic and inside life of the middle of Long Island, at and just before that time, here are two samples:

"The Whitmans, at the beginning of the present century, lived in a long story-and-a-half farm-house, hugely timber'd, which is still standing. A great smoke-canopied kitchen, with vast hearth and chimney, form'd one end of the house. The existence of slavery in New York at that time, and the possession by the family of some twelve or fifteen slaves, house and field servants, gave things quite a patriarchal look. The young darkies could be seen, a swarm of them, toward sundown, in this kitchen, squatted in a circle on the floor, eating their supper of Indian pudding and milk. In the house, and in food and furniture, all was rude, but substantial. No carpets or stoves were known, and no coffee, and tea or sugar only for the women. Rousing wood fires gave both warmth and light on winter nights. Pork, poultry, beef, and all the ordinary vegetables and grains were plentiful. Cider was the men's common drink, and used at meals. The clothes were mainly homespun. Journeys were made by both men and women on horseback. Both sexes labor'd with their own hands—the men on the farm—the women in the house and around it. Books were scarce. The annual copy of the almanac was a treat, and was pored over through the long winter evenings. I must not forget to mention that both these families were near enough to the sea to behold it from the high places, and to hear in still hours the roar of the surf; the latter, after a storm, giving a peculiar sound at night. Then all hands, male and female, went down frequently on beach and bathing parties, and the men on practical expeditions for cutting salt hay, and for clamming and fishing."—*John Burroughs's* NOTES.

"The ancestors of Walt Whitman, on both the paternal and maternal sides, kept a good table, sustain'd the hospitalities, decorums, and an excellent social reputation in the county, and they were often of mark'd individuality. If space permitted, I should consider some of the men worthy special description; and still more of the women. His great-grandmother on the paternal side, for instance, was a large swarthy woman, who lived to a very old age. She smoked tobacco, rode on horseback like a man, managed the most vicious horse, and, becoming a widow in later life, went forth every day over her farm-lands, frequently in the saddle, directing the labor of her slaves, with language in which, on exciting occasions, oaths were not spared. The two immediate grand-mothers were, in the best sense, superior women. The maternal one (Amy Williams before marriage) was a Friend, or Quakeress, of sweet, sensible character, housewifely proclivities, and deeply intuitive and spiritual. The other, (Hannah Brush,) was an equally noble, perhaps stronger character, lived to be very old, had quite a family of sons, was a natural lady, was in early life a school-mistress, and had great solidity of mind. W. W. himself makes much of the women of his ancestry."—*The same.*

Out from these arrieres of persons and scenes, I was born May 31, 1819. And now to dwell awhile on the locality itself—as the successive growth-stages of my infancy, childhood, youth and man-hood were all pass'd on Long Island, which I sometimes feel as if I had incorporated. I roam'd, as boy and man, and have lived in nearly all parts, from Brooklyn to Montauk point.

PAUMANOK, AND MY LIFE ON IT AS CHILD AND YOUNG MAN

Worth fully and particularly investigating indeed this Paumanok, (to give the spot its aboriginal name,) stretching east through

Kings, Queens and Suffolk counties, 120 miles altogether—on the north Long Island sound, a beautiful, varied and picturesque series of inlets, "necks" and sea-like expansions, for a hundred miles to Orient point.* On the ocean side the great south bay dotted with countless hummocks, mostly small, some quite large, occasionally long bars of sand out two hundred rods to a mile-and-a-half from the shore. While now and then, as at Rockaway and far east along the Hamptons, the beach makes right on the island, the sea dashing up without intervention. Several light-houses on the shores east; a long history of wrecks tragedies, some even of late years. As a youngster, I was in the atmosphere and traditions of many of these wrecks—of one or two almost an observer. Off Hempstead beach for example, was the loss of the ship "Mexico" in 1840, (alluded to in "the Sleepers" in L. of G.) And at Hampton, some years later, the destruction of the brig "Elizabeth," a fearful affair, in one of the worst winter gales, where Margaret Fuller went down, with her husband and child.

Inside the outer bars or beach this south bay is everywhere comparatively shallow; of cold winters all thick ice on the surface. As a boy I often went forth with a chum or two, on those frozen fields, with hand-sled, axe and eel-spear, after messes of eels. We would cut holes in the ice, sometimes striking quite an eel-bonanza, and filling our baskets with great, fat, sweet, white-meated fellows. The scenes, the ice, drawing the hand-sled, cutting holes, spearing the eels, &c., were of course just such fun as is dearest to boyhood. The shores of this bay, winter and summer, and my doings there in early life, are woven all though L. of G. One sport I was very fond of was to go on a bay-party in summer to gather sea-gull's eggs. (The gulls lay two or three eggs, more than half the size of hen's eggs, right on the sand, and leave the sun's heat to hatch them.)

The eastern end of Long Island, the Peconic bay region, I knew quite well too—sail'd more than once around Shelter island, and down to Montauk—spent many an hour on Turtle hill by the old light-house, on the extreme point, looking out over the ceaseless roll of the Atlantic. I used to like to go down there and fraternize

---

*"Paumanok, (or Paumanake, or Paumanack, the Indian name of Long Island,) over a hundred miles long; shaped like a fish—plenty of sea shore, sandy, stormy, uninviting, the horizon boundless, the air too strong for invalids, the bays a wonderful resort for aquatic birds, the south-side meadows cover'd wth salt hay, the soil of the island generally tough, but good for the locust-tree, the apple orchard, and the blackberry, and with numberless springs of the sweetest water in the world. Years ago, among the bay-men—a strong, wild race, now extinct, or rather entirely changed—a native of Long Island was called a *Paumanacker*, or *Creole-Paumanacker*."—*John Burroughs.*

with the blue-fishers, or the annual squads of sea-bass takers. Sometimes, along Montauk peninsula, (it is some 15 miles long, and
good grazing,) met the strange, unkempt, half-barbarous herdsmen,
at that time living there entirely aloof from society or civilization,
in charge, on those rich pasturages, of vast droves of horses, kine
or sheep, own'd by farmers of the eastern towns. Sometimes, too,
the few remaining Indians, or half-breeds, at that period left on
Montauk peninsula, but now I believe altogether extinct.

More in the middle of the island were the spreading Hempstead
plains, then (1830–'40) quite prairie-like, open, uninhabited, rather
sterile, cover'd with kill-calf and huckleberry bushes, yet plenty of
fair pasture for the cattle, mostly milch-cows, who fed there by
hundreds, even thousands, and at evening, (the plains too were
own'd by the towns, and this was the use of them in common,)
might be seen taking their way home, branching off regularly in the
right places. I have often been out on the edges of these plains
toward sundown, and can yet recall in fancy the interminable cow
processions, and hear the music of the tin or copper bells clanking
far or near, and breathe the cool of the sweet and slightly aromatic
evening air, and note the sunset.

Through the same region of the island, but further east, extended
wide central tracts of pine and scrub-oak, (charcoal was largely
made here,) monotonous and sterile. But many a good day or half-
day did I have, wandering through those solitary cross-roads, inhaling the peculiar and wild aroma. Here, and all along the island and
its shores, I spent intervals many years, all seasons, sometimes riding, sometimes boating, but generally afoot, (I was always then a
good walker,) absorbing fields, shores, marine incidents, characters,
the bay-men, farmers, pilots—always had a plentiful acquaintance
with the latter, and with fishermen—went every summer on sailing
trips—always liked the bare sea-beach, south side, and have some
of my happiest hours on it to this day.

As I write, the whole experience comes back to me after the
lapse of forty and more years—the soothing rustle of the waves,
and the saline smell—boyhood's times, the clam-digging, barefoot,
and with trowsers roll'd up—hauling down the creek—the perfume
of the sedge-meadows—the hay-boat, and the chowder and fishing
excursions;—or, of later years, little voyages down and out New
York bay. in the pilot boats. Those same later years, also, while
living in Brooklyn, (1836–'50) I went regularly every week in the
mild seasons down to Coney island, at that time a long, bare unfre-
quented shore, which I had all to myself, and where I loved, after
bathing, to race up and down the hard sand, and declaim Homer or

Shakspere to the surf and sea-gulls by the hour. But I am getting ahead too rapidly, and must keep more in my traces.

MY FIRST READING—LAFAYETTE

From 1824 to '28 our family lived in Brooklyn in Front, Cranberry and Johnson streets. In the latter my father built a nice house for a home, and afterwards another in Tillary street. We occupied them, one after the other, but they were mortgaged, and we lost them. I yet remember Lafayette's visit.* Most of these years I went to the public schools. It must have been about 1829 or '30 that I went with my father and mother to hear Elias Hicks preach in a ball-room on Brooklyn heights. At about the same time employ'd as a boy in an office, lawyers', father and two sons, Clarke's, Fulton street, near Orange. I had a nice desk and window-nook to myself; Edward C. kindly help'd me at my handwriting and composition, and, (the signal event of my life up to that time,) subscribed for me to a big circulating library. For a time I now revel'd in romance-reading of all kinds; first, the "Arabian Nights," all the volumes, an amazing treat. Then, with sorties in very many other directions, took in Walter Scott's novels, one after another, and his poetry, (and continue to enjoy novels and poetry to this day.)

PRINTING OFFICE—OLD BROOKLYN

After about two years went to work in a weekly newspaper and printing office, to learn the trade. The paper was the "Long Island Patriot," owned by S. E. Clements, who was also postmaster. An old printer in the office, William Hartshorne, a revolutionary character, who had seen Washington, was a special friend of mine, and I had many a talk with him about long past times. The apprentices, including myself, boarded with his grand-daughter. I used occasionally to go out riding with the boss, who was very kind to us boys; Sundays he took us all to a great old rough, fortress-looking

---

* "On the visit of General Lafayette to this country, in 1824, he came over to Brooklyn in state, and rode through the city. The children of the schools turn'd out to join in the welcome. An edifice for a free public library for youths was just then commencing, and Lafayette consented to stop on his way and lay the corner-stone. Numerous children arriving on the ground, where a huge irregular excavation for the building was already dug, surrounded with heaps of rough stone, several gentlemen assisted in lifting the children to safe or convenient spots to see the ceremony. Among the rest, Lafayette, also helping the children, took up the five-year-old Walt Whitman, and pressing the child a moment to his breast, and giving him a kiss, handed him down to a safe spot in the excavation."—*John Burroughs.*

stone church, on Joralemon street, near where the Brooklyn city hall now is—(at that time broad fields and country roads everywhere around.*) Afterward I work'd on the "Long Island Star," Alden Spooner's paper. My father all these years pursuing his trade as carpenter and builder, with varying fortune. There was a growing family of children—eight of us—my brother Jesse the oldest, myself the second, my dear sisters Mary and Hannah Louisa, my brothers Andrew, George, Thomas Jefferson, and then my youngest brother, Edward, born 1835, and always badly crippled, as I am myself of late years.

GROWTH—HEALTH—WORK

I develop'd (1833–4–5) into a healthy, strong youth (grew too fast, though, was nearly as big as a man at 15 or 16.) Our family at this period moved back to the country, my dear mother very ill for a long time, but recover'd. All these years I was down Long Island more or less every summer, now east, now west, sometimes months at a stretch. At 16, 17, and so on, was fond of debating societies, and had an active membership with them, off and on, in Brooklyn and one or two country towns on the island. A most omnivorous novel-reader, these and later years, devour'd everything I could get. Fond of the theatre, also, in New York, went whenever I could—sometimes witnessing fine performances.

1836–7, work'd as compositor in printing offices in New York city. Then, when little more than eighteen, and for a while afterwards, went to teaching country schools down in Queens and Suffolk counties, Long Island, and "boarded round." (This latter I consider one of my best experiences and deepest lessons in human

---

*Of the Brooklyn of that time (1830–40) hardly anything remains, except the lines of the old streets. The population was then between ten and twelve thousand. For a mile Fulton street was lined with magnificent elm trees. The character of the place was thoroughly rural. As a sample of comparative values, it may be mention'd that twenty-five acres in what is now the most costly part of the city, bounded by Flatbush and Fulton avenues, were then bought by Mr. Parmentier, a French *emigré*, for $4000. Who remembers the old places as they were? Who remembers the old citizens of that time? Among the former were Smith & Wood's, Coe Downing's, and other public houses at the ferry, the old Ferry itself Love lane, the Heights as then, the Wallabout with the wooden bridge, and the road out beyond Fulton street to the old toll-gate. Among the latter were the majestic and genial General Jeremiah Johnson, with others, Gabriel Furman, Rev. E. M. Johnson, Alden Spooner, Mr. Pierrepont, Mr. Joralemon, Samuel Willoughbby, Jonathan Trotter, George Hall, Cyrus P. Smith, N. B. Morse, John Dikeman, Adrian Hegeman, William Udall, and old Mr. Duflon, with his military garden.

nature behind the scenes, and in the masses.) In '39, '40, I started and publish'd a weekly paper in my native town, Huntington. Then returning to New York city and Brooklyn, work'd on as printer and writer, mostly prose, but an occasional shy at "poetry."

MY PASSION FOR FERRIES

Living in Brooklyn or New York city from this time forward, my life, then, and still more the following years, was curiously identified with Fulton ferry, already becoming the greatest of its sort in the world for general importance, volume, variety, rapidity, and picturesqueness. Almost daily, later, ('50 to '60,) I cross'd on the boats, often up in the pilot-houses where I could get a full sweep, absorbing shows, accompaniments, surroundings. What oceanic currents, eddies, underneath—the great tides of humanity also, with ever-shifting movements. Indeed, I have always had a passion for ferries; to me they afford inimitable, streaming, never-failing, living poems. The river and bay scenery, all about New York island, any time of a fine day—the hurrying, splashing sea-tides—the changing panorama of steamers, all sizes, often a string of big ones outward bound to distant ports—the myriads of white-sail'd schooners, sloops, skiffs, and the marvellously beautiful yachts—the majestic sound boats as they rounded the Battery and came along towards 5, afternoon, eastward bound—the prospect off towards Staten island, or down the Narrows, or the other way up the Hudson—what refreshment of spirit such sights and experiences gave me years ago (and many a time since.) My old pilot friends, the Balsirs, Johnny Cole, Ira Smith, William White, and my young ferry friend, Tom Gere—how well I remember them all.

BROADWAY SIGHTS

Besides Fulton ferry, off and on for years, I knew and frequented Broadway—that noted avenue of New York's crowded and mixed humanity, and of so many notables. Here I saw, during those times, Andrew Jackson, Webster, Clay, Seward, Martin Van Buren, filibuster Walker, Kossuth, Fitz Greene Halleck, Bryant, the Prince of Wales, Charles Dickens, the first Japanese ambassadors, and lots of other celebrities of the time. Always something novel or inspiriting; yet mostly to me the hurrying and vast amplitude of those never-ending human currents. I remember seeing James Fenimore Cooper in a court-room in Chambers street, back of the city hall, where he was carrying on a law case—(I think it was a charge of

libel he had brought against some one.) I also remember seeing
Edgar A. Poe, and having a short interview with him, (it must
have been in 1845 or '6,) in his office, second story of a corner
building, (Duane or Pearl street.) He was editor and owner or
part owner of "the Broadway Journal." The visit was about a piece
of mine he had publish'd. Poe was very cordial, in a quiet way,
appear'd well in person, dress &c. I have a distinct and pleasing
remembrance of his looks, voice, manner and matter; very kindly
and human, but subdued, perhaps a little jaded. For another of
my reminiscences, here on the west side, just below Houston street,
I once saw (it must have been about 1832, of a sharp, bright January day) a bent, feeble but stout-built very old man, bearded,
swathed in rich furs, with a great ermine cap on his head, led and
assisted, almost carried, down the steps of his high front stoop (a
dozen friends and servants, emulous, carefully holding, guiding
him) and then lifted and tuck'd in a gorgeous sleigh, envelop'd in
other furs, for a ride. The sleigh was drawn by as fine a team of
horses as I ever saw. (You needn't think all the best animals are
brought up nowadays; never was such horseflesh as fifty years ago
on Long Island, or south, or in New York city; folks look'd for
spirit and mettle in a nag, not tame speed merely.) Well, I, a boy of
perhaps thirteen or fourteen, stopp'd and gazed long at the spectacle of that fur-swathed old man, surrounded by friends and servants, and the careful seating of him in the sleigh. I remember the
spirited, champing horses, the driver with his whip, and a fellow-
driver by his side, for extra prudence. The old man, the subject
of so much attention, I can almost see now. It was John Jacob
Astor.

The years 1846, '47, and there along, see me still in New York
city, working as writer and printer, having my usual good health
and a good time generally.

OMNIBUS JAUNTS AND DRIVERS

One phase of those days must by no means go unrecorded—
namely, the Broadway omnibuses, with their drivers. The vehicles
still (I write this paragraph in 1881) give a portion of the character
of Broadway—the Fifth avenue, Madison avenue, and Twenty-
third street lines yet running. But the flush days of the old Broadway stages, characteristic and copious, are over. The Yellow-birds,
the Red-birds, the original Broadway, the Fourth avenue, the
Knickerbocker, and a dozen others of twenty or thirty years ago,
are all gone. And the men specially identified with them, and giving

vitality and meaning to them—the drivers—a strange, natural, quick-eyed and wondrous race—(not only Rabelais and Cervantes would have gloated upon them, but Homer and Shakspere would)—how well I remember them, and must here give a word about them. How many hours, forenoons and afternoons—how many exhilarating night-times I have had—perhaps June or July, in cooler air—riding the whole length of Broadway, listening to some yarn, (and the most vivid yarns ever spun, and the rarest mimicry)—or perhaps I declaiming some stormy passage from Julius Cæsar or Richard, (you could roar as loudly as you chose in that heavy, dense, uninterrupted street-bass.) Yes, I knew all the drivers then, Broadway Jack, Dressmaker, Balky Bill, George Storms, Old Elephant, his brother Young Elephant (who came afterward,) Tippy, Pop Rice, Big Frank, Yellow Joe, Pete Callahan, Patsy Dee, and dozens more; for there were hundreds. They had immense qualities, largely animal—eating, drinking, women—great personal pride, in their way—perhaps a few slouches here and there, but I should have trusted the general run of them, in their simple good-will and honor, under all circumstances. Not only for comradeship, and sometimes affection—great studies I found them also. (I suppose the critics will laugh heartily, but the influence of those Broadway omnibus jaunts and drivers and declamations and escapades undoubtedly enter'd into the gestation of "Leaves of Grass.")

PLAYS AND OPERAS TOO

And certain actors and singers, had a good deal to do with the business. All through these years, off and on, I frequented the old Park, the Bowery, Broadway and Chatham-square theatres, and the Italian operas at Chambers-street, Astor-place or the Battery—many seasons was on the free list, writing for papers even as quite a youth. The old Park theatre—what names, reminiscences, the words bring back! Placide, Clarke, Mrs. Vernon, Fisher, Clara F., Mrs. Wood, Mrs. Seguin, Ellen Tree, Hackett, the younger Kean, Macready, Mrs. Richardson, Rice—singers, tragedians, comedians. What perfect acting! Henry Placide in "Napoleon's Old Guard" or "Grandfather Whitehead,"—or "the Provoked Husband" of Cibber, with Fanny Kemble as Lady Townley—or Sheridan Knowles in his own "Virginius"—or inimitable Power in "Born to Good Luck." These, and many more, the years of youth and onward. Fanny Kemble—name to conjure up great mimic scenes withall—perhaps the greatest. I remember well her rendering of Bianca in "Fazio," and Marianna in "the Wife." Nothing finer did ever stage exhibit—

the veterans of all nations said so, and my boyish heart and head felt it in every minute cell. The lady was just matured, strong, better than merely beautiful, born from the footlights, had had three years' practice in London and through the British towns, and then she came to give America that young maturity and roseate power in all their noon, or rather forenoon, flush. It was my good luck to see her nearly every night she play'd at the old Park—certainly in all her principal characters.

I heard, these years, well render'd, all the Italian and other operas in vogue, "Sonnambula," "the Puritans," "Der Freischutz," "Huguenots," "Fille d'Regiment," "Faust," "Etoile du Nord," "Poliuto," and others. Verdi's "Ernani," "Rigoletto," and "Trovatore," with Donnizetti's "Lucia" or "Favorita" or "Lucrezia," and Auber's "Massaniello," or Rossini's "William Tell" and "Gazza Ladra," were among my special enjoyments. I heard Alboni every time she sang in New York and vicinity—also Grisi, the tenor Mario, and the baritone Badiali, the finest in the world.

This musical passion follow'd my theatrical one. As boy or young man I had seen, (reading them carefully the day beforehand,) quite all Shakspere's acting dramas, play'd wonderfully well. Even yet I cannot conceive anything finer than old Booth in "Richard Third," or "Lear," (I don't know which was best,) or Iago, (or Pescara, or Sir Giles Overreach, to go outside of Shakspere)—or Tom Hamblin in "Macbeth"—or old Clarke, either as the ghost in "Hamlet," or as Prospero in "the Tempest," with Mrs. Austin as Ariel, and Peter Richings as Caliban. Then other dramas, and fine players in them, Forrest as Metamora or Damon or Brutus— John R. Scott as Tom Cringle or Rolla—or Charlotte Cushman's Lady Gay Spanker in "London Assurance." Then of some years later at Castle Garden, Battery, I yet recall the splendid seasons of the Havana musical troupe under Maretzek—the fine band, the cool sea-breezes, the unsurpass'd vocalism—Steffanone, Bosio, Truffi, Marini in "Marino Faliero," "Don Pasquale," or "Favorita." No better playing or singing ever in New York. It was here too I afterward heard Jenny Lind. (The Battery—its past associations— what tales those old trees and walks and sea-walls could tell!)

THROUGH EIGHT YEARS

In 1848, '49, I was occupied as editor of the "daily Eagle" newspaper, in Brooklyn. The latter year went off on a leisurely journey and working expedition (my brother Jeff with me) through all the middle States, and down the Ohio and Mississippi rivers. Lived awhile in New Orleans, and work'd there on the editorial staff of "daily Crescent" newspaper. After a time plodded back northward, up the Mississippi, and around to, and by way of the great lakes, Michigan, Huron, and Erie, to Niagara falls and lower Canada, finally returning through central New York and down the Hudson; traveling altogether probably 8000 miles this trip, to and fro. '51, '53, occupied in house-building in Brooklyn. (For a little of the first part of that time in printing a daily and weekly paper, "the Freeman.") '55, lost my dear father this year by death. Commenced putting "Leaves of Grass" to press for good, at the job printing office of my friends, the brothers Rome, in Brooklyn, after many MS. doings and undoings—(I had great trouble in leaving out the stock "poetical" touches, but succeeded at last.) I am now (1856–'7) passing through my 37th year.

SOURCES OF CHARACTER—RESUl TS—1860

To sum up the foregoing from the outset (and, of course, far, far more unrecorded,) I estimate three leading sources and formative stamps to my own character, now solidified for good or bad, and its subsequent literary and other outgrowth—the maternal nativity-stock brought hither from far-away Netherlands, for one, (doubtless the best)—the subterranean tenacity and central bony structure (obstinacy, wilfulness) which I get from my paternal English elements, for another—and the combination of my Long Island birth-spot, sea-shores, childhood's scenes, absorptions, with teeming Brooklyn and New York—with, I suppose, my experiences afterward in the secession outbreak, for the third.

For, in 1862, startled by news that my brother George, an officer in the 51st New York volunteers, had been seriously wounded (first Fredericksburg battle, December 13th,) I hurriedly went down to the field of war in Virginia. But I must go back a little.

OPENING OF THE SECESSION WAR

News of the attack on fort Sumter and *the flag* at Charleston harbor, S. C., was receiv'd in New York city late at night (13th April, 1861,) and was immediately sent out in extras of the newspapers. I had been to the opera in Fourteenth street that night, and after the performance was walking down Broadway toward twelve o'clock, on my way to Brooklyn, when I heard in the distance the loud cries of the newsboys, who came presently tearing and yelling up the street, rushing from side to side even more furiously than usual. I bought an extra and cross'd to the Metropolitan hotel (Niblo's) where the great lamps were still brightly blazing, and, with a crowd of others, who gather'd impromptu, read the news, which was evidently authentic. For the benefit of some who had no papers, one of us read the telegram aloud, while all listen'd silently and attentively. No remark was made by any of the crowd, which had increas'd to thirty or forty, but all stood a minute or two, I remember, before they dispers'd. I can almost see them there now, under the lamps at midnight again.

NATIONAL UPRISING AND VOLUNTEERING

I have said somewhere that the three Presidentiads preceding 1861 show'd how the weakness and wickedness of rulers are just as eligible here in America under republican, as in Europe under dynastic influences. But what can I say of that prompt and splendid wrestling with secession slavery, the arch-enemy personified, the instant he unmistakably show'd his face? The volcanic upheaval of the nation, after that firing on the flag at Charleston, proved for certain something which had been previously in great doubt, and at once substantially settled the question of disunion. In my judgment it will remain as the grandest and most encouraging spectacle yet vouchsafed in any age, old or new, to political progress and democracy. It was not for what came to the surface merely—though that was important—but what it indicated below, which was of eternal importance. Down in the abysms of New World humanity there had form'd and harden'd a primal hard-pan of national Union will, determin'd and in the majority, refusing to be tamper'd with or argued against, confronting all emergencies, and capable at any time of bursting all surface bonds, and breaking out like an earthquake. It is, indeed, the best lesson of the century, or of America, and it is a mighty privilege to have been part of it. (Two great spectacles, immortal proofs of democracy, unequall'd in all the history of the past, are furnish'd by the secession war—one at the beginning, the other at its close. Those are, the general, voluntary, arm'd upheaval, and the peaceful and harmonious disbanding of the armies in the summer of 1865.)

CONTEMPTUOUS FEELING

Even after the bombardment of Sumter, however, the gravity of the revolt, and the power and will of the slave States for a strong and continued military resistance to national authority, were not at all realized at the north, except by a few. Nine-tenths of the people of the free States look'd upon the rebellion, as started in South Carolina, from a feeling one-half of contempt, and the other half composed of anger and incredulity. it was not thought it would be join'd in by Virginia, North Carolina, or Georgia. A great and cautious national official predicted that it would blow over "in sixty days," and folks generally believ'd the prediction. I remember talking about it on a Fulton ferry–boat with the Brooklyn mayor, who said he only "hoped the Southern fire-eaters would commit some overt act of resistance, as they would then be at once so effectually squelch'd, we would never hear of secession again—but he was afraid they never would have the pluck to really do anything." I remember, too, that a couple of companies of the Thirteenth Brooklyn, who rendezvou'd at the city armory, and started thence as thirty days' men, were all provided with pieces of rope, conspicuously tied to their musket-barrels, with which to bring back each man a prisoner from the audacious South, to be led in a noose, on our men's early and triumphant return!

BATTLE OF BULL RUN, JULY, 1861

All this sort of feeling was destin'd to be arrested and revers'd by a terrible shock—the battle of first Bull Run—certainly, as we now know it, one of the most singular fights on record. (All battles, and their results, are far more matters of accident than is generally thought; but this was throughout a casualty, a chance. Each side supposed it had won, till the last moment. One had, in point of fact, just the same right to be routed as the other. By a fiction, or series of fictions, the national forces at the last moment exploded in a panic and fled from the field.) The defeated troops commenced pouring into Washington over the Long Bridge at daylight on Monday, 22d—day drizzling all through with rain. The Saturday and Sunday of the battle (20th, 21st,) had been parch'd and hot to an extreme—the dust, the grime and smoke, in layers, sweated in, follow'd by other layers again sweated in, absorb'd by those excited souls—their clothes all saturated with the clay-powder filling the air—stirr'd up everywhere on the dry roads and trodden fields by the regiments, swarming wagons, artillery, &c.—all the men with this coating of murk and sweat and rain, now recoiling back, pouring over the Long Bridge—a horrible march of twenty miles, returning to Washington baffled, humiliated, panic-struck. Where are the vaunts, and the proud boasts with which you went forth? Where are your banners, and your bands of music, and your ropes to bring back your prisoners? Well, there isn't a band playing—and there isn't a flag but clings ashamed and lank to its staff.

The sun rises, but shines not. The men appear, at first sparsely and shamed-faced enough, then thicker, in the streets of Washington—appear in Pennsylvania avenue, and on the steps and basement entrances. They come along in disorderly mobs, some in squads, stragglers, companies. Occasionally, a rare regiment, in perfect order, with its officers (some gaps, dead, the true braves,) marching in silence, with lowering faces, stern, weary to sinking, all black and dirty, but every man with his musket, and stepping alive; but these are the exceptions. Sidewalks of Pennsylvania avenue, Fourteenth street, &c., crowded, jamm'd with citizens, darkies, clerks, everybody, lookers-on; women in the windows, curious expressions from faces, as those swarms of dirt-cover'd return'd soldiers there (will they never end?) move by; but nothing said, no comments; (half our lookers-on secesh of the most venomous kind—they say nothing; but the devil snickers in their faces.) During the forenoon Washington gets all over motley with these defeated soldiers—queer-looking objects, strange eyes and faces, drench'd (the steady rain drizzles on all day) and fearfully worn, hungry, haggard, blister'd in the feet. Good people (but not over-many of them either,) hurry up something for their grub. They put wash-kettles on the fire, for soup, for coffee. They set tables on the side-walks—wagon-loads of bread are purchas'd, swiftly cut into stout chunks. Here are two aged ladies, beautiful, the first in the city for culture and charm, they stand with store of eating and drink at an improvis'd table of rough plank, and give food, and have the store replenish'd from their house every half-hour all that day; and there in the rain they stand, active, silent, white-hair'd, and give food, though the tears stream down their cheeks, almost without intermission, the whole time. Amid the deep excitement, crowds and motion, and desperate eagerness, it seems strange to see many, very many, of the soldiers sleeping—in the midst of all, sleeping sound. They drop down anywhere, on the steps of houses, up close by the basement or fences, on the sidewalk, aside on some vacant lot, and deeply sleep. A poor seventeen or eighteen year old boy lies there, on the stoop of a grand house; he sleeps so calmly, so profoundly. Some clutch their muskets firmly even in sleep. Some in squads; comrades, brothers, close together—and on them, as they lay, sulkily drips the rain.

As afternoon pass'd, and evening came, the streets, the barrooms, knots everywhere, listeners, questioners, terrible yarns, bugaboo, mask'd batteries, our regiment all cut up, &c.—stories and story-tellers, windy, bragging, vain centres of street-crowds. Resolution, manliness, seem to have abandon'd Washington. The principal hotel, Willard's, is full of shoulder-straps—thick, crush'd, creeping with shoulder-straps. (I see them, and must have a word with them. There you are, shoulder-straps!—but where are your companies? where are your men? Incompetents! never tell me of chances of battle, of getting stray'd, and the like. I think this is your work, this retreat, after all. Sneak, blow, put on airs there in Willard's sumptuous parlors and bar-rooms, or anywhere—no explanation shall save you. Bull Run is your work; had you been half or one-tenth worthy your men, this would never have happen'd.)

Meantime, in Washington, among the great persons and their entourage, a mixture of awful consternation, uncertainty, rage, shame, helplessness, and stupefying disappointment. The worst is not only imminent, but already here. In a few hours—perhaps before the next meal—the secesh generals, with their victorious hordes, will be upon us. The dream of humanity, the vaunted Union we thought so strong, so impregnable—lo! it seems already smash'd like a china plate. One bitter, bitter hour—perhaps proud America will never again know such an hour. She must pack and fly—no time to spare. Those white palaces—the dome-crown'd capitol there on the hill, so stately over the trees—shall they be left—or destroy'd first? For it is certain that the talk among certain of the magnates and officers and clerks and officials everywhere, for twenty-four hours in and around Washington after Bull Run, was loud and undisguised for yielding out and out, and substituting the southern rule, and Lincoln promptly abdicating and departing. If the secesh officers and forces had immediately follow'd, and by a bold Napoleonic movement had enter'd Washington the first day, (or even the second,) they could have had things their own way, and a powerful faction north to back them. One of our returning colonels express'd in public that night, amid a swarm of officers and gentlemen in a crowded room, the opinion that it was useless to fight, that the southerners had made their title clear, and that the best course for the national government to pursue was to desist from any further attempt at stopping them, and admit them again to the lead, on the best terms they were willing to grant. Not a voice was rais'd against this judgment, amid that large crowd of officers and gentlemen. (The fact is, the hour was one of the three or four of those crises we had then and afterward, during the fluctuations of four years, when human eyes appear'd at least just as likely to see the last breath of the Union as to see it continue.)

THE STUPOR PASSES—SOMETHING ELSE BEGINS

But the hour, the day, the night pass'd, and whatever returns, an hour, a day, a night like that can never again return. The President, recovering himself, begins that very night—sternly, rapidly sets about the task of reorganizing his forces, and placing them in positions for future and surer work. If there were nothing else of Abraham Lincoln for history to stamp him with, it is enough to send him with his wreath to the memory of all future time, that he endured that hour, that day, bitterer than gall—indeed a crucifixion day—that it did not conquer him—that he unflinchingly stemm'd it, and resolv'd to lift himself and the Union out of it.

Then the great New York papers at once appear'd, (commencing that evening, and following it up the next morning, and incessantly through many days afterwards,) with leaders that rang out over the land with the loudest, most reverberating ring of clearest bugles, full of encouragement, hope, inspiration, unfaltering defiance. Those magnificent editorials! they never flagg'd for a fortnight. The "Herald" commenced them—I remember the articles well. The "Tribune" was equally cogent and inspiriting—and the "Times," "Evening Post," and other principal papers, were not a whit behind. They came in good time, for they were needed. For in the humiliation of Bull Run, the popular feeling north, from its extreme of superciliousness, recoil'd to the depth of gloom and apprehension.

(Of all the days of the war, there are two especially I can never forget. Those were the day following the news, in New York and Brooklyn, of that first Bull Run defeat, and the day of Abraham Lincoln's death. I was home in Brooklyn on both occasions. The day of the murder we heard the news very early in the morning. Mother prepared breakfast—and other meals afterward—as usual; but not a mouthful was eaten all day by either of us. We each drank half a cup of coffee; that was all. Little was said. We got every newspaper morning and evening, and the frequent extras of that period, and pass'd them silently to each other.)

DOWN AT THE FRONT

FALMOUTH, VA., *opposite Fredericksburg, December 21, 1862.*— Begin my visits among the camp hospitals in the army of the Potomac. Spend a good part of the day in a large brick mansion on the banks of the Rappahannock, used as a hospital since the battle— seems to have receiv'd only the worst cases. Out doors, at the foot of a tree, within ten yards of the front of the house, I notice a heap of amputated feet, legs, arms, hands, &c., a full load for a one-horse cart. Several dead bodies lie near, each cover'd with its brown woolen blanket. In the door-yard, towards the river, are fresh graves, mostly of officers, their names on pieces of barrel-staves or broken boards, stuck in the dirt. (Most of these bodies were subsequently taken up and transported north to their friends.) The large mansion is quite crowded upstairs and down, everything impromptu, no system, all bad enough, but I have no doubt the best that can be done; all the wounds pretty bad, some frightful, the men in their old clothes, unclean and bloody. Some of the wounded are rebel soldiers and officers, prisoners. One, a Mississippian, a captain, hit badly in leg, I talk'd with some time; he ask'd me for papers, which I gave him. (I saw him three months afterward in Washington, with his leg amputated, doing well.) I went through the rooms, downstairs and up. Some of the men were dying. I had nothing to give at that visit, but wrote a few letters to folks home, mothers, &c. Also talk'd to three or four, who seem'd most susceptible to it, and needing it.

AFTER FIRST FREDERICKSBURG

December 23 to 31.—The results of the late battle are exhibited everywhere about here in thousands of cases, (hundreds die every day,) in the camp, brigade, and division hospitals. These are merely tents, and sometimes very poor ones, the wounded lying on the ground, lucky if their blankets are spread on layers of pine or hemlock twigs, or small leaves. No cots; seldom even a mattress. It is pretty cold. The ground is frozen hard, and there is occasional snow. I go around from one case to another. I do not see that I do much good to these wounded and dying; but I cannot leave them. Once in a while some youngster holds on to me convulsively, and I do what I can for him; at any rate, stop with him and sit near him for hours, if he wishes it.

Besides the hospitals, I also go occasionally on long tours through the camps, talking with the men, &c. Sometimes at night among the groups around the fires, in their shebang enclosures of bushes. These are curious shows, full of characters and groups. I soon get acquainted anywhere in camp, with officers or men, and am always well used. Sometimes I go down on picket with the regiments I know best. As to rations, the army here at present seems to be tolerably well supplied, and the men have enough, such as it is, mainly salt pork and hard tack. Most of the regiments lodge in the

flimsy little shelter-tents. A few have built themselves huts of logs
and mud, with fire-places.

January, '63.—Left camp at Falmouth, with some wounded, a
few days since, and came here by Aquia creek railroad, and so on
government steamer up the Potomac. Many wounded were with
us on the cars and boat. The cars were just common platform ones.
The railroad journey of ten or twelve miles was made mostly before
sunrise. The soldiers guarding the road came out from their tents
or shebangs of bushes with rumpled hair and half-awake look.
Those on duty were walking their posts, some on banks over us, others
down far below the level of the track. I saw large cavalry camps off
the road. At Aquia creek landing were numbers of wounded going
north. While I waited some three hours, I went around among
them. Several wanted word sent home to parents, brothers, wives,
&c., which I did for them, (by mail the next day from Washington.)
On the boat I had my hands full. One poor fellow died going up.

I am now remaining in and around Washington, daily visiting
the hospitals. Am much in Patent-office, Eighth street, H street,
Armory-square, and others. Am now able to do a little good, having
money, (as almoner of others home,) and getting experience. To-day,
Sunday afternoon and till nine in the evening, visited Campbell
hospital; attended specially to one case in ward 1, very sick with
pleurisy and typhoid fever, young man, farmer's son, D. F. Russell,
company E, 60th New York, downhearted and feeble; a long time
before he would take any interest; wrote a letter home to his mother,
in Malone, Franklin county, N. Y., at his request; gave him some
fruit and one or two other gifts; envelop'd and directed his letter,
&c. Then went thoroughly through ward 6, observ'd every case in
the ward, without, I think, missing one; gave perhaps from twenty
to thirty persons, each one some little gift, such as oranges, apples,
sweet crackers, figs, &c.

Thursday, Jan. 21.—Devoted the main part of the day to Armory-
square hospital; went pretty thoroughly through wards F, G, H,
and I; some fifty cases in each ward. In ward F supplied the men
throughout with writing paper and stamp'd envelope each; distributed in small portions, to proper subjects, a large jar of first-
rate preserv'd berries, which had been donated to me by a lady—
her own cooking. Found several cases I thought good subjects for
small sums of money, which I furnish'd. (The wounded men often
come up broke, and it helps their spirits to have even the small sum

I give them.) My paper and envelopes all gone, but distributed a good lot of amusing reading matter; also, as I thought judicious, tobacco, oranges, apples, &c. Interesting cases in ward I; Charles Miller, bed 19, company D, 53d Pennsylvania, is only sixteen years of age, very bright, courageous boy, left leg amputated below the knee; next bed to him, another young lad very sick; gave each appropriate gifts. In the bed above, also, amputation of the left leg; gave him a little jar of raspberries; bed 1, this ward, gave a small sum; also to a soldier on crutches, sitting on his bed near. . . . (I am more and more surprised at the very great proportion of youngsters from fifteen to twenty-one in the army. I afterwards found a still greater proportion among the southerners.)

Evening, same day, went to see D. F. R., before alluded to; found him remarkably changed for the better; up and dress'd—quite a triumph; he afterwards got well, and went back to his regiment. Distributed in the wards a quantity of note-paper, and forty or fifty stamp'd envelopes, of which I had recruited my stock, and the men were much in need.

FIFTY HOURS LEFT WOUNDED ON THE FIELD

Here is a case of a soldier I found among the crowded cots in the Patent-office. He likes to have some one to talk to, and we will listen to him. He got badly hit in his leg and side at Fredericksburg that eventful Saturday, 13th of December. He lay the succeeding two days and nights helpless on the field, between the city and those grim terraces of batteries; his company and regiment had been compell'd to leave him to his fate. To make matters worse, it happen'd he lay with his head slightly down hill, and could not help himself. At the end of some fifty hours he was brought off, with other wounded, under a flag of truce. I ask him how the rebels treated him as he lay during those two days and nights within reach of them—whether they came to him—whether they abused him? He answers that several of the rebels, soldiers and others, came to him at one time and another. A couple of them, who were together, spoke roughly and sarcastically, but nothing worse. One middle-aged man, however, who seem'd to be moving around the field, among the dead and wounded, for benevolent purposes, came to him in a way he will never forget; treated our soldier kindly, bound up his wounds, cheer'd him, gave him a couple of biscuits and a drink of whiskey and water; asked him if he could eat some beef. This good secesh, however, did not change our soldier's position, for it might have caused the blood to burst from the wounds, clotted and stagnated. Our soldier is from Pennsylvania; has had a pretty severe time; the wounds proved to be bad ones. But he retains a good heart, and is at present on the gain. (It is not uncommon for the men to remain on the field this way, one, two, or even four or five days.)

HOSPITAL SCENES AND PERSONS

Letter Writing.—When eligible, I encourage the men to write, and myself, when called upon, write all sorts of letters for them, (including love letters, very tender ones.) Almost as I reel off these memoranda, I write for a new patient to his wife. M. de F., of the 17th Connecticut, company H, has just come up (February 17th) from Windmill point, and is received in ward H, Armory-square. He is an intelligent looking man, has a foreign accent, black-eyed and hair'd, a Hebraic appearance. Wants a telegraphic message sent to his wife, New Canaan, Conn. I agree to send the message—but to make things sure I also sit down and write the wife a letter, and despatch it to the post-office immediately, as he fears she will come on, and he does not wish her to, as he will surely get well.

Saturday, January 30th.—Afternoon, visited Campbell hospital. Scene of cleaning up the ward, and giving the men all clean clothes—through the ward (6) the patients dressing or being dress'd—the naked upper half of the bodies—the good-humor and fun—the shirts, drawers, sheets of beds, &c., and the general fixing up for Sunday. Gave J. L. 50 cents.

Wednesday, February 4th.—Visited Armory-square hospital, went pretty thoroughly through wards E and D. Supplied paper and envelopes to all who wish'd—as usual, found plenty of men who needed those articles. Wrote letters. Saw and talk'd with two or three members of the Brooklyn 14th regt. A poor fellow in ward D, with a fearful wound in a fearful condition, was having some loose splinters of bone taken from the neighborhood of the wound. The operation was long, and one of great pain—yet, after it was well commenced, the soldier bore it in silence. He sat up, propp'd—was much wasted—had lain a long time quiet in one position (not for days only but weeks,) a bloodless, brown-skinn'd face, with eyes full of détermination—belong'd to a New York regiment. There was an unusual cluster of surgeons, medical cadets, nurses, &c., around his bed—I thought the whole thing was done with tenderness, and done well. In one case, the wife sat by the side of her husband, his sickness typhoid fever, pretty bad. In another, by the side of her son, a mother—she told me she had seven children, and this was the youngest. (A fine, kind, healthy, gentle mother, good-looking, not very old, with a cap on her head, and dress'd like home—what a charm it gave to the whole ward.) I liked the woman nurse in ward E—I noticed how she sat a long time by a poor fellow who had just had, that morning, in addition to his other sickness, bad hemorrhage—she gently assisted him, reliev'd him of the blood, holding a cloth to his mouth, as he coughed it up—he was so weak he could only just turn his head over on the pillow.

One young New York man, with a bright, handsome face, had been lying several months from a most disagreeable wound, receiv'd at Bull Run. A bullet had shot him right through the bladder, hitting him front, low in the belly, and coming out back. He had suffer'd much—the water came out of the wound, by slow but steady quantities, for many weeks—so that he lay almost constantly in a sort of puddle—and there were other disagreeable circumstances. He was of good heart, however. At present comparatively comfortable, had a bad throat, was delighted with a stick of horehound candy I gave him, with one or two other trifles.

PATENT-OFFICE HOSPITAL

February 23.—I must not let the great hospital at the Patent-office pass away without some mention. A few weeks ago the vast area of the second story of that noblest of Washington buildings was crowded close with rows of sick, badly wounded and dying soldiers. They were placed in three very large apartments. I went there many times. It was a strange, solemn, and, with all its features of suffering and death, a sort of fascinating sight. I go sometimes at night to soothe and relieve particular cases. Two of the immense apartments are fill'd with high and ponderous glass cases, crowded with models in miniature of every kind of utensil, machine or invention, it ever enter'd into the mind of man to conceive; and with curiosities and foreign presents. Between these cases are lateral openings, perhaps eight feet wide and quite deep, and in these were placed the sick, besides a great long double row of them up and down through the middle of the hall. Many of them were very bad cases, wounds and amputations. Then there was a gallery running above the hall in which there were beds also. It was, indeed, a curious scene, especially at night when lit up. The glass cases, the beds, the forms lying there, the gallery above, and the marble pavement under foot—the suffering, and the fortitude to bear it in various degrees—occasionally, from some, the groan that could not be repress'd—sometimes a poor fellow dying, with emaciated face and glassy eye,

the nurse by his side, the doctor also there, but no friend, no relative—such were the sights but lately in the Patent-office. (The
wounded have since been removed from there, and it is now vacant
again.)

THE WHITE HOUSE BY MOONLIGHT

February 24th.—A spell of fine soft weather. I wander about
a good deal, sometimes at night under the moon. To-night took
a long look at the President's house. The white portico—the palace-
like, tall, round columns, spotless as snow—the walls also—the
tender and soft moonlight, flooding the pale marble, and making
peculiar faint languishing shades, not shadows—everywhere a soft
transparent hazy, thin, blue moon-lace, hanging in the air—the
brilliant and extra-plentiful clusters of gas, on and around the façade,
columns, portico, &c.—everything so white, so marbly pure and
dazzling, yet soft—the White House of future poems, and of dreams
and dramas, there in the soft and copious moon—the gorgeous front,
in the trees, under the lustrous flooding moon, full of reality, full
of illusion—the forms of the trees, leafless, silent, in trunk and
myriad-angles of branches, under the stars and sky—the White House
of the land, and of beauty and night—sentries at the gates, and by
the portico, silent, pacing there in blue overcoats—stopping you
not at all, but eyeing you with sharp eyes, whichever way you move.

AN ARMY HOSPITAL WARD

Let me specialize a visit I made to the collection of barrack-
like one-story edifices, Campbell hospital, out on the flats, at the
end of the then horse railway route, on Seventh street. There is a
long building appropriated to each ward. Let us go into ward 6.
It contains to-day, I should judge, eighty or a hundred patients,
half sick, half wounded. The edifice is nothing but boards, well
whitewash'd inside, and the usual slender-framed iron bedsteads,
narrow and plain. You walk down the central passage, with a row
on either side, their feet towards you, and their heads to the wall.
There are fires in large stoves and the prevailing white of the walls
is reliev'd by some ornaments, stars, circles, &c., made of evergreens.
The view of the whole edifice and occupants can be taken at once,
for there is no partition. You may hear groans or other sounds of
unendurable suffering from two or three of the cots, but in the main
there is a quiet—almost a painful absence of demonstration; but the
pallid face, the dull'd eye, and the moisture on the lip, are demonstration enough. Most of these sick or hurt are evidently young

fellows from the country, farmers' sons, and such like. Look at the fine large frames, the bright and broad countenances and the many yet lingering proofs of strong constitution and physique. Look at the patient and mute manner of our American wounded as they lie in such a sad collection; representatives from all New England, and from New York, and New Jersey, and Pennsylvania—indeed from all the States and all the cities—largely from the west. Most of them are entirely without friends or acquaintances here—no familiar face, and hardly a word of judicious sympathy or cheer, through their sometimes long and tedious sickness, or the pangs of aggravated wounds.

A CONNECTICUT CASE

This young man in bed 25 is H. D. B., of the 27th Connecticut, company B. His folks live at Northford, near New Haven. Though not more than twenty-one, or thereabouts, he has knock'd much around the world, on sea and land, and has seen some fighting on both. When I first saw him he was very sick, with no appetite. He declined offers of money—said he did not need anything. As I was quite anxious to do something, he confess'd that he had a hankering for a good home-made rice pudding—thought he could relish it better than anything. At this time his stomach was very weak. (The doctor, whom I consulted, said nourishment would do him more good than anything; but things in the hospital, though better than usual, revolted him.) I soon procured B. his rice-pudding. A Washington lady, (Mrs. O'C.), hearing his wish, made the pudding herself, and I took it up to him the next day. He subsequently told me he lived upon it for three or four days. This B. is a good sample of the American eastern young man—the typical Yankee. I took a fancy to him, and gave him a nice pipe, for a keepsake. He receiv'd afterwards a box of things from home, and nothing would do but I must take dinner with him, which I did, and a very good one it was.

TWO BROOKLYN BOYS

Here in this same ward are two young men from Brooklyn, members of the 51st New York. I had known both the two as young lads at home, so they seem near to me. One of them, J. L., lies there with an amputated arm, the stump healing pretty well. (I saw him lying on the ground at Fredericksburg last December, all bloody, just after the arm was taken off. He was very phlegmatic about it, munching away at a cracker in the remaining hand—made no fuss.) He will recover, and thinks and talks yet of meeting the Johnny Rebs.

A SECESH BRAVE

The grand soldiers are not comprised in those of one side, any more than the other. Here is a sample of an unknown southerner, a lad of seventeen. At the War department, a few days ago, I witness'd a presentation of captured flags to the Secretary. Among others a soldier named Gant, of the 104th Ohio volunteers, presented a rebel battle-flag, which one of the officers stated to me was borne to the mouth of our cannon and planted there by a boy but seventeen years of age, who actually endeavor'd to stop the muzzle of the gun with fence-rails. He was kill'd in the effort, and the flag-staff was sever'd by a shot from one of our men.

THE WOUNDED FROM CHANCELLORSVILLE

May, '63.—As I write this, the wounded have begun to arrive from Hooker's command from bloody Chancellorsville. I was down among the first arrivals. The men in charge told me the bad cases were yet to come. If that is so I pity them, for these are bad enough. You ought to see the scene of the wounded arriving at the landing here at the foot of Sixth street, at night. Two boat loads came about half-past seven last night. A little after eight it rain'd a long and violent shower. The pale, helpless soldiers had been debark'd, and lay around on the wharf and neighborhood anywhere. The rain was, probably, grateful to them; at any rate they were exposed to it. The few torches light up the spectacle. All around—on the wharf, on the ground, out on side places—the men are lying on blankets, old quilts, &c., with bloody rags bound round heads, arms, and legs. The attendants are few, and at night few outsiders also—only a few hard-work'd transportation men and drivers. (The wounded are getting to be common, and people grow callous.) The men, whatever their condition, lie there, and patiently wait till their turn comes to be taken up. Near by, the ambulances are now arriving in clusters, and one after another is call'd to back up and take its load. Extreme cases are sent off on stretchers. The men generally make little or no ado, whatever their sufferings. A few groans that cannot be sup-press'd, and occasionally a scream of pain as they lift a man into the ambulance. To-day, as I write, hundreds more are expected, and to-morrow and the next day more, and so on for many days. Quite often they arrive at the rate of 1000 a day.

A NIGHT BATTLE, OVER A WEEK SINCE

May 12.—There was part of the late battle at Chancellorsville, (second Fredericksburg,) a little over a week ago, Saturday,

Saturday night and Sunday, under Gen. Joe Hooker, I would like
to give just a glimpse of—(a moment's look in a terrible storm at
sea—of which a few suggestions are enough, and full details impossible.) The fighting had been very hot during the day, and after
an intermission the latter part, was resumed at night, and kept up
with furious energy till 3 o'clock in the morning. That afternoon
(Saturday) an attack sudden and strong by Stonewall Jackson had
gain'd a great advantage to the southern army, and broken our lines,
entering us like a wedge, and leaving things in that position at dark.
But Hooker at 11 at night made a desperate push, drove the secesh
forces back, restored his original lines, and resumed his plans.
This night scrimmage was very exciting, and afforded countless
strange and fearful pictures. The fighting had been general both at
Chancellorsville and northeast at Fredericksburg. (We hear of
some poor fighting, episodes, skedaddling on our part. I think not
of it. I think of the fierce bravery, the general rule.) One corps, the
6th, Sedgewick's, fights four dashing and bloody battles in thirty-
six hours, retreating in great jeopardy, losing largely but maintaining
itself, fighting with the sternest desperation under all circumstances,
getting over the Rappahannock only by the skin of its teeth, yet
getting over. It lost many, many brave men, yet it took vengeance,
ample vengeance.

But it was the tug of Saturday evening, and through the night
and Sunday morning, I wanted to make a special note of. It was
largely in the woods, and quite a general engagement. The night
was very pleasant, at times the moon shining out full and clear, all
Nature so calm in itself, the early summer grass so rich, and foliage
of the trees—yet there the battle raging, and many good fellows lying
helpless, with new accessions to them, and every minute amid the
rattle of muskets and crash of cannon, (for there was an artillery
contest too,) the red life-blood oozing out from heads or trunks or
limbs upon that green and dew-cool grass. Patches of the woods
take fire, and several of the wounded, unable to move, are consumed
—quite large spaces are swept over, burning the dead also—some
of the men have their hair and beards singed—some, burns on their
faces and hands—others holes burnt in their clothing. The flashes
of fire from the cannon, the quick flaring flames and smoke, and the
immense roar—the musketry so general, the light nearly bright
enough for each side to see the other—the crashing, tramping of
men—the yelling—close quarters—we hear the secesh yells—our
men cheer loudly back, especially if Hooker is in sight—hand to
hand conflicts, each side stands up to it, brave, determin'd as demons,
they often charge upon us—a thousand deeds are done worth to

write newer greater poems on—and still the woods on fire—still
many are not only scorch'd—too many, unable to move, are burn'd
to death.

Then the camps of the wounded—O heavens, what scene is this?—
is this indeed *humanity*—these butchers' shambles? There are several
of them. There they lie, in the largest, in an open space in the woods,
from 200 to 300 poor fellows—the groans and screams—the odor
of blood, mixed with the fresh scent of the night, the grass, the
trees—that slaughter-house! O well is it their mothers, their sisters
cannot see them—cannot conceive, and never conceiv'd, these
things. One man is shot by a shell, both in the arm and leg—both
are amputated—there lie the rejected members. Some have their
legs blown off—some bullets through the breast—some indescribably
horrid wounds in the face or head, all mutilated, sickening, torn,
gouged out—some in the abdomen—some mere boys—many rebels,
badly hurt—they take their regular turns with the rest, just the same
as any—the surgeons use them just the same. Such is the camp of the
wounded—such a fragment, a reflection afar off of the bloody
scene—while over all the clear, large moon comes out at times
softly, quietly shining. Amid the woods, that scene of flitting souls—
amid the crack and crash and yelling sounds—the impalpable perfume of the woods—and yet the pungent, stifling smoke—the radiance of the moon, looking from heaven at intervals so placid—the
sky so heavenly—the clear-obscure up there, those buoyant upper
oceans—a few large placid stars beyond, coming silently and languidly out, and then disappearing—the melancholy, draperied night
above, around. And there, upon the roads, the fields, and in those
woods, that contest, never one more desperate in any age or land—
both parties now in force—masses—no fancy battle, no semi-play,
but fierce and savage demons fighting there—courage and scorn
of death the rule, exceptions almost none.

What history, I say, can ever give—for who can know—the
mad, determin'd tussle of the armies, in all their separate large
and little squads—as this—each steep'd from crown to toe in desperate, mortal purports? Who know the conflict, hand-to-hand—the
many conflicts in the dark, those shadowy-tangled, flashing-moon-
beam'd woods—the writhing groups and squads—the cries, the din,
the cracking guns and pistols—the distant cannon—the cheers and
calls and threats and awful music of the oaths—the indescribable
mix—the officers' orders, persuasions, encouragements—the devils
fully rous'd in human hearts—the strong shout, *Charge, men, charge*—
the flash of the naked sword, and rolling flame and smoke? And still
the broken, clear and clouded heaven—and still again the moonlight

pouring silvery soft its radiant patches over all. Who paint the scene, the sudden partial panic of the afternoon, at dusk? Who paint the irrepressible advance of the second division of the Third corps under Hooker himself, suddenly order'd up—those rapid-filing phantoms through the woods? Who show what moves there in the shadows, fluid and firm—to save, (and it did save,) the army's name, perhaps the nation? as there the veterans hold the field. (Brave Berry falls not yet—but death has mark'd him—soon he falls.)

UNNAMED REMAINS THE BRAVEST SOLDIER

Of scenes like these, I say, who writes—whoe'er can write the story? Of many a score—aye, thousands, north and south, of unwrit heroes, unknown heroisms, incredible, impromptu, first-class desperations—who tells? No history ever—no poem sings, no music sounds, those bravest men of all—those deeds. No formal general's report, nor book in the library, nor column in the paper, embalms the bravest, north or south, east or west. Unnamed, unknown, remain, and still remain, the bravest soldiers. Our manliest—our boys—our hardy darlings; no picture gives them. Likely, the typic one of them (standing, no doubt, for hundreds, thousands,) crawls aside to some bush-clump, or ferny tuft, on receiving his death-shot—there sheltering a little while, soaking roots, grass and soil, with red blood—the battle advances, retreats, flits from the scene, sweeps by—and there, haply with pain and suffering (yet less, far less, than is supposed,) the last lethargy winds like a serpent round him—the eyes glaze in death—none recks—perhaps the burial-squads, in truce, a week afterwards, search not the secluded spot—and there, at last, the Bravest Soldier crumbles in mother earth, unburied and unknown.

SOME SPECIMEN CASES

June 18th.—In one of the hospitals I find Thomas Haley, company M, 4th New York cavalry—a regular Irish boy, a fine specimen of youthful physical manliness—shot through the lungs—inevitably dying—came over to this country from Ireland to enlist—has not a single friend or acquaintance here—is sleeping soundly at this moment, (but it is the sleep of death)—has a bullet-hole straight through the lung. I saw Tom when first brought here, three days since, and didn't suppose he could live twelve hours—(yet he looks well enough in the face to a casual observer.) He lies there with his frame exposed above the waist, all naked, for coolness, a fine built man, the tan not yet bleach'd from his cheeks and neck. It is useless to talk to him, as with his sad hurt, and the stimulants they give him, and the utter strangeness of every object, face, furniture, &c., the poor fellow, even when awake, is like some frighten'd, shy animal. Much of the time he sleeps, or half sleeps. (Sometimes I thought he knew more than he show'd.) I often come and sit by him in perfect silence; he will breathe for ten minutes as softly and evenly as a young babe asleep. Poor youth, so handsome, athletic, with profuse beautiful shining hair. One time as I sat looking at him while he lay asleep, he suddenly, without the least start, awaken'd, open'd his eyes, gave me a long steady look, turning his face very slightly to gaze easier—one long, clear, silent look—a slight sigh—then turn'd back and went into his doze again. Little he knew, poor death-stricken boy, the heart of the stranger that hover'd near.

W. H. E., Co. F., 2d N. J.—His disease is pneumonia. He lay sick at the wretched hospital below Aquia creek, for seven or eight days before brought here. He was detail'd from his regiment to go there and help as nurse, but was soon taken down himself. Is an elderly, sallow-faced, rather gaunt, gray-hair'd man, a widower, with children. He express'd a great desire for good, strong green tea. An excellent lady, Mrs. W., of Washington, soon sent him a package; also a small sum of money. The doctor said give him the tea at pleasure; it lay on the table by his side, and he used it every day. He slept a great deal; could not talk much, as he grew deaf. Occupied bed 15, ward I, Armory. (The same lady above, Mrs. W., sent the men a large package of tobacco.)

J. G. lies in bed 52, ward I; is of company B, 7th Pennsylvania. I gave him a small sum of money, some tobacco, and envelopes. To a man adjoining also gave twenty-five cents; he flush'd in the face when I offer'd it—refused at first, but as I found he had not a cent, and was very fond of having the daily papers to read, I prest it on him. He was evidently very grateful, but said little.

J. T. L., of company F., 9th New Hampshire, lies in bed 37, ward I. Is very fond of tobacco. I furnish him some; also with a little money. Has gangrene of the feet; a pretty bad case; will surely have to lose three toes. Is a regular specimen of an old-fashion'd, rude, hearty, New England countryman, impressing me with his likeness to that celebrated singed cat, who was better than she look'd.

Bed 3, ward E, Armory, has a great hankering for pickles, something pungent. After consulting the doctor, I gave him a small bottle of horse-radish; also some apples; also a book. Some of the nurses are excellent. The woman-nurse in this ward I like very much. (Mrs. Wright—a year afterwards I found her in Mansion house hospital, Alexandria—she is a perfect nurse.)

In one bed a young man, Marcus Small, company K, 7th Maine—sick with dysentery and typhoid fever—pretty critical case—I talk with him often—he thinks he will die—looks like it indeed. I write a letter for him home to East Livermore, Maine—I let him talk to me a little, but not much, advise him to keep very quiet—do most of the talking myself—stay quite a while with him, as he holds on to my hand—talk to him in a cheering, but slow, low and measured manner—talk about his furlough, and going home as soon as he is able to travel.

Thomas Lindly, 1st Pennsylvania cavalry, shot very badly through the foot—poor young man, he suffers horribly, has to be constantly dosed with morphine, his face ashy and glazed, bright young eyes—I give him a large handsome apple, lay it in sight, tell him to have it roasted in the morning, as he generally feels easier then, and can eat a little breakfast. I write two letters for him.

Opposite, an old Quaker lady is sitting by the side of her son, Amer Moore, 2d U. S. artillery—shot in the head two weeks since, very low, quite rational—from hips down paralyzed—he will surely die. I speak a very few words to him every day and evening—he answers pleasantly—wants nothing—(he told me soon after he came about his home affairs, his mother had been an invalid, and he fear'd to let her know his condition.) He died soon after she came.

MY PREPARATIONS FOR VISITS

In my visits to the hospitals I found it was in the simple matter of personal presence, and emanating ordinary cheer and magnetism, that I succeeded and help'd more than by medical nursing, or delicacies, or gifts of money, or anything else. During the war I possess'd the perfection of physical health. My habit, when practicable, was to prepare for starting out on one of those daily or nightly tours of from a couple to four or five hours, by fortifying myself with previous rest, the bath, clean clothes, a good meal, and as cheerful an appearance as possible.

AMBULANCE PROCESSIONS

June 25, Sundown.—As I sit writing this paragraph I see a train of about thirty huge four-horse wagons, used as ambulances, fill'd with wounded, passing up Fourteenth street, on their way, probably, to Columbian, Carver, and mount Pleasant hospitals. This is the way the men come in now, seldom in small numbers, but almost always in these long, sad processions. Through the past

winter, while our army lay opposite Fredericksburg, the like
strings of ambulances were of frequent occurrence along Seventh
street, passing slowly up from the steamboat wharf, with loads
from Aquia creek.

BAD WOUNDS—THE YOUNG

The soldiers are nearly all young men, and far more American
than is generally supposed—I should say nine-tenths are native-
born. Among the arrivals from Chancellorsville I find a large
proportion of Ohio, Indiana, and Illinois men. As usual, there
are all sorts of wounds. Some of the men fearfully burnt from the
explosions of artillery caissons. One ward has a long row of officers,
some with ugly hurts. Yesterday was perhaps worse than usual.
Amputations are going on—the attendants are dressing wounds.
As you pass by, you must be on your guard where you look. I saw
the other day a gentleman, a visitor apparently from curiosity, in
one of the wards, stop and turn a moment to look at an awful wound
they were probing. He turn'd pale, and in a moment more he had
fainted away and fallen on the floor.

THE MOST INSPIRITING OF ALL WAR'S SHOWS

June 29.—Just before sundown this evening a very large cavalry
force went by—a fine sight. The men evidently had seen service.
First came a mounted band of sixteen bugles, drums and cymbals,
playing wild martial tunes—made my heart jump. Then the principal
officers, then company after company, with their officers at their
heads, making of course the main part of the cavalcade; then a long
train of men with led horses, lots of mounted negroes with special
horses—and a long string of baggage-wagons, each drawn by four
horses—and then a motley rear guard. It was a pronouncedly warlike and gay show; the sabres clank'd, the men look'd young and
healthy and strong; the electric tramping of so many horses on the
hard road, and the gallant bearing, fine seat, and bright faced appearance of a thousand and more handsome young American men, were
so good to see. An hour later another troop went by, smaller in
numbers, perhaps three hundred men. They too look'd like serviceable men, campaigners used to field and fight.

July 3.—This forenoon, for more than an hour, again long strings
of cavalry, several regiments, very fine men and horses, four or five
abreast. I saw them in Fourteenth street, coming in town from north.
Several hundred extra horses, some of the mares with colts, trotting

along. (Appear'd to be a number of prisoners too.) How inspiriting always the cavalry regiments. Our men are generally well mounted, feel good, are young, gay on the saddle, their blankets in a roll behind them, their sabres clanking at their sides. This noise and movement and the tramp of many horses' hoofs has a curious effect upon one. The bugles play—presently you hear them afar off, deaden'd, mix'd with other noises. Then just as they had all pass'd, a string of ambulances commenc'd from the other way, moving up Fourteenth street north, slowly wending along, bearing a large lot of wounded to the hospitals.

BATTLE OF GETTYSBURG

July 4th.—The weather to-day, upon the whole, is very fine, warm, but from a smart rain last night, fresh enough, and no dust, which is a great relief for this city. I saw the parade about noon, Pennsylvania avenue, from Fifteenth street down toward the capitol. There were three regiments of infantry, (I suppose the ones doing patrol duty here,) two or three societies of Odd Fellows, a lot of children in barouches, and a squad of policemen. (A useless imposition upon the soldiers—they have work enough on their backs without piling the like of this.) As I went down the Avenue, saw a big flaring placard on the bulletin board of a newspaper office, announcing "Glorious Victory for the Union Army!" Meade had fought Lee at Gettysburg, Pennsylvania, yesterday and day before, and repuls'd him most signally, taken 3,000 prisoners, &c. (I afterwards saw Meade's despatch, very modest, and a sort of order of the day from the President himself, quite religious, giving thanks to the Supreme, and calling on the people to do the same.) I walk'd on to Armory hospital—took along with me several bottles of blackberry and cherry syrup, good and strong, but innocent. Went through several of the wards, announc'd to the soldiers the news from Meade, and gave them all a good drink of the syrups with ice water, quite refreshing—prepar'd it all myself, and serv'd it around. Meanwhile the Washington bells are ringing their sundown peals for Fourth of July, and the usual fusilades of boys' pistols, crackers, and guns.

A CAVALRY CAMP

I am writing this, nearly sundown, watching a cavalry company (acting Signal service,) just come in through a shower, making their night's camp ready on some broad, vacant ground, a sort of hill, in full view opposite my window. There are the men in their yellow-striped jackets. All are dismounted; the freed horses stand with drooping heads and wet sides; they are to be led off presently in groups, to water. The little wall-tents and shelter tents spring up quickly. I see the fires already blazing, and pots and kettles over them. Some among the men are driving in tent-poles, wielding their axes with strong, slow blows. I see great huddles of horses, bundles of hay, groups of men (some with unbuckled sabres yet on their sides,) a few officers, piles of wood, the flames of the fires, saddles, harness, &c. The smoke streams upward, additional men arrive and dismount —some drive in stakes, and tie their horses to them; some go with buckets for water, some are chopping wood, and so on.

July 6th.—A steady rain, dark and thick and warm. A train of six-mule wagons has just pass'd bearing pontoons, great square-end flat-boats, and the heavy planking for overlaying them. We hear that the Potomac above here is flooded, and are wondering whether Lee will be able to get back across again, or whether Meade will indeed break him to pieces. The cavalry camp on the hill is a ceaseless field of observation for me. This forenoon there stand the horses, tether'd together, dripping, steaming, chewing their hay. The men emerge from their tents, dripping also. The fires are half quench'd.

July 10th.—Still the camp opposite—perhaps fifty or sixty tents. Some of the men are cleaning their sabres (pleasant to-day,) some brushing boots, some laying off, reading, writing—some cooking, some sleeping. On long temporary cross-sticks back of the tents are cavalry accoutrements—blankets and overcoats are hung out to air—there are the squads of horses tether'd, feeding, continually stamping and whisking their tails to keep off flies. I sit long in my third story window and look at the scene—a hundred little things going on—peculiar objects connected with the camp that could not be described, any one of them justly, without much minute drawing and coloring in words.

A NEW YORK SOLDIER

This afternoon, July 22d, I have spent a long time with Oscar F. Wilber, company G, 154th New York, low with chronic diarrhœa, and a bad wound also. He asked me to read him a chapter in the New Testament. I complied, and ask'd him what I should read. He said, "Make your own choice." I open'd at the close of one of the first books of the evangelists, and read the chapters describing the latter hours of Christ, and the scenes at the crucifixion. The poor, wasted young man ask'd me to read the following chapter also, how Christ rose again. I read very slowly, for Oscar was feeble. It pleased him very much, yet the tears were in his eyes. He ask'd me if I enjoy'd religion. I said, "Perhaps not, my dear, in the way you mean, and yet, may-be, it is the same thing." He said, "It is my chief reliance." He talk'd of death, and said he did not fear it. I said, "Why, Oscar, don't you think you will get well?" He said, "I may, but it is not probable." He spoke calmly of his condition. The wound was very bad, it discharg'd much. Then the diarrhœa had prostrated him, and I felt that he was even then the same as dying. He behaved very manly and affectionate. The kiss I gave him as I was about leaving he return'd fourfold. He gave me his mother's address, Mrs. Sally D. Wilber, Alleghany post-office, Cattaraugus county, N. Y. I had several such interviews with him. He died a few days after the one just described.

HOME-MADE MUSIC

August 8th.—To-night, as I was trying to keep cool, sitting by a wounded soldier in Armory-square, I was attracted by some pleasant singing in an adjoining ward. As my soldier was asleep, I left him, and entering the ward where the music was, I walk'd half-way down and took a seat by the cot of a young Brooklyn friend, S. R., badly wounded in the hand at Chancellorsville, and who has suffer'd much, but at that moment in the evening was wide awake and comparatively easy. He had turn'd over on his left side to get a better view of the singers, but the mosquito-curtains of the adjoining cots obstructed the sight. I stept round and loop'd them all up, so that he had a clear show, and then sat down again by him, and look'd and listen'd. The principal singer was a young lady-nurse of one of the wards, accompanying on a melodeon, and join'd by the lady-nurses of other wards. They sat there, making a charming group, with their handsome, healthy faces, and standing up a little behind them were some ten or fifteen of the convalescent soldiers, young men, nurses, &c., with books in their hands, singing. Of course it was not such a performance as the great soloists at the New York opera house take a hand in, yet I am not sure but I receiv'd as much pleasure under the circumstances, sitting there, as I have had from the best Italian compositions, express'd by world-famous performers. The men lying up and down the hospital, in their cots, (some badly wounded—some never to rise thence,) the cots themselves, with their drapery of white curtains, and the shadows down the lower and upper parts of the ward; then the silence of the men, and the attitudes they took—the whole was a sight to look around upon again and again. And there sweetly rose those voices up to the high, whitewash'd wooden roof, and pleasantly the roof sent it all back again. They sang very well, mostly quaint old songs and declamatory hymns, to fitting tunes. Here, for instance:

> My days are swiftly gliding by, and I a pilgrim stranger,
> Would not detain them as they fly, those hours of toil and danger;
> For O we stand on Jordan's strand, our friends are passing over,
> And just before, the shining shore we may almost discover.
>
> We'll gird our loins my brethren dear, our distant home discerning,
> Our absent Lord has left us word, let every lamp be burning,
> For O we stand on Jordan's strand, our friends are passing over,
> And just before, the shining shore we may almost discover.

ABRAHAM LINCOLN

August 12th.—I see the President almost every day, as I happen to live where he passes to or from his lodgings out of town. He never sleeps at the White House during the hot season, but has quarters at a healthy location some three miles north of the city, the Soldiers' home, a United States military establishment. I saw him this morning about 8½ coming in to business, riding on Vermont avenue, near L street. He always has a company of twenty-five or thirty cavalry, with sabres drawn and held upright over their shoulders. They say this guard was against his personal wish, but he let his counselors have their way. The party makes no great show in uniform or horses. Mr. Lincoln on the saddle generally rides a good-sized, easy-going gray horse, is dress'd in plain black, somewhat rusty and dusty, wears a black stiff hat, and looks about as ordinary in attire, &c., as the commonest man. A lieutenant, with yellow straps, rides at his left, and following behind, two by two, come the cavalry men, in their yellow-striped jackets. They are generally going at a slow trot, as that is the pace set them by the one they wait upon. The sabres and accoutrements clank, and the entirely unornamental *cortége* as it trots towards Lafayette square arouses no sensation, only some curious stranger stops and gazes. I see very plainly ABRAHAM LINCOLN's dark brown face, with the deep-cut lines, the eyes, always to me with a deep latent sadness in the expression. We have got so that we exchange bows, and very cordial ones. Sometimes the President goes and comes in an open barouche. The cavalry always accompany him, with drawn sabres. Often I notice as he goes out evenings—and sometimes in the morning, when he returns early—he turns off and halts at the large and handsome residence of the Secretary of War, on K street, and holds conference there. If in his barouche, I can see from my window he does not alight, but sits in his vehicle, and Mr. Stanton comes out to attend him. Sometimes one of his sons, a boy of ten or twelve, accompanies him, riding at his right on a pony. Earlier in the summer I occasionally saw the President and his wife, toward the latter part of the afternoon, out in a barouche, on a pleasure ride through the city. Mrs. Lincoln was dress'd in complete black, with a long crape veil. The equipage is of the plainest kind, only two horses, and they nothing extra. They pass'd me once very close, and I saw the President in the face fully, as they were moving slowly, and his look, though abstracted, happen'd to be directed steadily in my eye. He bow'd and smiled, but far beneath his smile I noticed well the expression I have alluded to. None of the artists or pictures has caught the deep, though subtle and indirect expression of this man's face. There is something else there. One of the great portrait painters of two or three centuries ago is needed.

HEATED TERM

There has lately been much suffering here from heat; we have had it upon us now eleven days. I go around with an umbrella and a fan. I saw two cases of sun-stroke yesterday, one in Pennsylvania avenue, and another in Seventh street. The City railroad company loses some horses every day. Yet Washington is having a livelier August, and is probably putting in a more energetic and satisfactory summer, than ever before during its existence. There is probably more human electricity, more population to make it, more business, more light-heartedness, than ever before. The armies that swiftly circumambiated from Fredericksburg—march'd, struggled, fought, had out their mighty clinch and hurl at Gettysburg—wheel'd, circumambiated again, return'd to their ways, touching us not, either at their going or coming. And Washington feels that she has pass'd the worst; perhaps feels that she is henceforth mistress. So here she sits with her surrounding hills spotted with guns, and is conscious of a character and identity different from what it was five or six short weeks ago, and very considerably pleasanter and prouder.

SOLDIERS AND TALKS

Soldiers, soldiers, soldiers, you meet everywhere about the city, often superb-looking men, though invalids dress'd in worn uniforms, and carrying canes or crutches. I often have talks with them, occasionally quite long and interesting. One, for instance, will have been all through the peninsula under McClellan—narrates to me the fights, the marches, the strange, quick changes of that eventful campaign, and gives glimpses of many things untold in any official reports or books or journals. These, indeed, are the things that are genuine and precious. The man was there, has been out two years, has been through a dozen fights, the superflous flesh of talking is long work'd off him, and he gives me little but the hard meat and sinew. I find it refreshing, these hardy, bright, intuitive, American young men, (experienc'd soldiers with all their youth.) The vocal play and significance moves one more than books. Then there hangs something majestic about a man who has borne his part in battles, especially if he is very quiet regarding it when you desire him to unbosom. I am continually lost at the absence of blowing and blowers among these old-young American militaries. I have found some man or other who has been in every battle since the war began, and have talk'd with them about each one in every part of the United States, and many of the engagements on the rivers and harbors too. I find men here from every State in the Union, without exception. (There are more Southerners, especially border State men, in the Union army than is generally supposed.*) I now doubt whether one can get a fair idea of what this war practically is, or what genuine America is, and her character, without some such experience as this I am having.

DEATH OF A WISCONSIN OFFICER

Another characteristic scene of that dark and bloody 1863, from notes of my visit to Armory-square hospital, one hot but pleasant summer day. In ward H we approach the cot of a young lieutenant of one of the Wisconsin regiments. Tread the bare board floor lightly here, for the pain and panting of death are in this cot. I saw the lieutenant when he was first brought here from Chancellorsville, and have been with him occasionally from day to day and night to night. He had been getting along pretty well till night before last, when a sudden hemorrhage that could not be stopt came upon him, and to-day it still continues at intervals. Notice that water-pail by the side of the bed, with a quantity of blood and bloody pieces of muslin, nearly full; that tells the story. The poor young man is struggling

---

* MR. GARFIELD (*In the House of Representatives, April 15, '79.*) "Do gentle-men know that (leaving out all the border States) there were fifty regiments and seven companies of white men in our army fighting for the Union from the States that went into rebellion? Do they know that from the single State of Kentucky more Union soldiers fought under our flag than Napoleon took into the battle of Waterloo? more than Wellington took with all the allied armies against Napoleon? Do they remember that 186,000 color'd men fought under our flag against the rebellion and for the Union, and that of that number 90,000 were from the States which went into rebellion?"

painfully for breath, his great dark eyes with a glaze already upon them, and the choking faint but audible in his throat. An attendant sits by him, and will not leave him till the last; yet little or nothing can be done. He will die here in an hour or two, without the presence of kith or kin. Meantime the ordinary chat and business of the ward a little way off goes on indifferently. Some of the inmates are laughing and joking, others are playing checkers or cards, others are reading, &c.

I have noticed through most of the hospitals that as long as there is any chance for a man, no matter how bad he may be, the surgeon and nurses work hard, sometimes with curious tenacity, for his life, doing everything, and keeping somebody by him to exucute the doctor's orders, and minister to him every minute night and day. See that screen there. As you advance through the dusk of early candle-light, a nurse will step forth on tip-toe, and silently but imperiously forbid you to make any noise, or perhaps to come near at all. Some soldier's life is flickering there, suspended between recovery and death. Perhaps at this moment the exhausted frame has just fallen into a light sleep that a step might shake. You must retire. The neighboring patients must move in their stocking feet. I have been several times struck with such mark'd efforts—everything bent to save a life from the very grip of the destroyer. But when that grip is once firmly fix'd, leaving no hope or chance at all, the surgeon abandons the patient. If it is a case where stimulus is any relief, the nurse gives milk-punch or brandy, or whatever is wanted, *ad libitum*. There is no fuss made. Not a bit of sentimentalism or whining have I seen about a single death-bed in hospital or on the field, but generally impassive indifference. All is over, as far as any efforts can avail; it is useless to expend emotions or labors. While there is a prospect they strive hard—at least most surgeons do; but death certain and evident, they yield the field.

HOSPITALS ENSEMBLE

Aug., Sep., and Oct., '63.—I am in the habit of going to all, and to Fairfax seminary, Alexandria, and over Long bridge to the great Convalescent camp. The journals publish a regular directory of them—a long list. As a specimen of almost any one of the larger of these hospitals, fancy to yourself a space of three to twenty acres of ground, on which are group'd ten or twelve very large wooden barracks, with, perhaps, a dozen or twenty, and sometimes more than that number, small buildings, capable altogether of accommodating from five hundred to a thousand or fifteen hundred persons.

Sometimes these wooden barracks or wards, each of them perhaps
from a hundred to a hundred and fifty feet long, are rang'd in a
straight row, evenly fronting the street; others are plann'd so to
form an immense V; and others again are ranged around a hollow
square. They make altogether a huge cluster, with the additional
tents, extra wards for contagious diseases, guard-houses, sutler's
stores, chaplains's house; in the middle will probably be an edifice
devoted to the offices of the surgeon in charge and the ward surgeons,
principal attachés, clerks &c. The wards are either letter'd alpha-
betically, ward G, ward K, or else numerically, 1, 2, 3, &c. Each has
its ward surgeon and corps of nurses. Of course, there is, in the
aggregate, quite a muster of employés, and over all the surgeon in
charge. Here in Washington, when these army hospitals are all
fill'd, (as they have been already several times,) they contain a
population more numerous in itself than the whole of the Washington of ten or fifteen years ago. Within sight of the capitol, as I write,
are some thirty or forty such collections, at times holding from fifty
to seventy thousand men. Looking from any eminence and studying
the topography in my rambles, I use them as landmarks. Through
the rich August verdure of the trees, see that white group of buildings off yonder in the outskirts; then another cluster half a mile to
the left of the first; then another a mile to the right, and another a
mile beyond, and still another between us and the first. Indeed, we
can hardly look in any direction but these clusters are dotting the
landscape and environs. That little town, as you might suppose it,
off there on the brow of a hill, is indeed a town, but of wounds,
sickness and death. It is Finley hospital, northeast of the city, on
Kendall green, as it used to be call'd. That other is Campbell hospital. Both are large establishments. I have known these two alone to
have from two thousand to twenty-five hundred inmates. Then there
is Carver hospital, larger still, a wall'd and military city regularly
laid out, and guarded by squads of sentries. Again, off east, Lincoln
hospital, a still larger one; and half a mile further Emory hospital.
Still sweeping the eye around down the river toward Alexandria,
we see, to the right, the locality where the Convalescent camp stands,
with its five, eight, or sometimes ten thousand inmates. Even all
these are but a portion. The Harewood, Mount Pleasant, Armory-
square, Judiciary hospitals, are some of the rest, and all large collections.

A SILENT NIGHT RAMBLE

October 20th.—To-night, after leaving the hospital at 10 o'clock,
(I had been on self-imposed duty some five hours, pretty closely

confined,) I wander'd a long time around Washington. The night was sweet, very clear, sufficiently cool, a voluptuous half-moon, slightly golden, the space near it of a transparent blue-gray tinge. I walk'd up Pennsylvania avenue, and then to Seventh street, and a long while around the Patent-office. Somehow it look'd rebukefully strong, majestic, there in the delicate moonlight. The sky, the planets, the constellations all so bright, so calm, so expressively silent, so soothing, after those hospital scenes. I wander'd to and fro till the moist moon set, long after midnight.

SPiRITUAL CHARACTERS AMONG THE SOLDIERS

Every now and then, in hospital or camp, there are beings I meet—specimens of unworldliness, disinterestedness, and animal purity and heroism—perhaps some unconscious Indianian, or from Ohio or Tennessee—on whose birth the calmness of heaven seems to have descended, and whose gradual growing up, whatever the circumstances of work-life or change, or hardship, or small or no education that attended it, the power of a strange spiritual sweetness, fibre and inward health, have also attended. Something veil'd and abstracted is often a part of the manners of these beings. I have met them, I say, not seldom in the army, in camp, and in the hospitals. The Western regiments contain many of them. They are often young men, obeying the events and occasions about them, marching, soldiering, fighting, foraging, cooking, working on farms or at some trade before the war—unaware of their own nature, (as to that, who is aware of his own nature?) their companions only understanding that they are different from the rest, more silent, "something odd about them," and apt to go off and meditate and muse in solitude.

CATTLE DROVES ABOUT WASHINGTON

Among other sights are immense droves of cattle with their drivers, passing through the streets of the city. Some of the men have a way of leading the cattle by a peculiar call, a wild, pensive hoot, quite musical, prolong'd, indescribable, sounding something between the cooing of a pigeon and the hoot of an owl. I like to stand and look at the sight of one of these immense droves—a little way off—(as the dust is great.) There are always men on horseback, cracking their whips and shouting—the cattle low—some obstinate ox or steer attempts to escape—then a lively scene—the mounted men, always excellent riders and on good horses, dash after the recusant, and wheel and turn—a dozen mounted drovers, their great slouch'd,

broad-brim'd hats, very picturesque—another dozen on foot—
everybody cover'd with dust—long goads in their hands—an immense drove of perhaps 1000 cattle—the shouting, hooting, movement, &c.

HOSPITAL PERPLEXITY

To add to other troubles, amid the confusion of this great army
of sick, it is almost impossible for a stranger to find any friend
or relative, unless he has the patient's specific address to start upon.
Besides the directory printed in the newspapers here, there are one
or two general directories of the hospitals kept at provost's headquarters, but they are nothing like complete; they are never up to
date, and, as things are, with the daily streams of coming and going
and changing, cannot be. I have known cases, for instance such as a
farmer coming here from northern New York to find a wounded
brother, faithfully hunting round for a week, and then compell'd
to leave and go home without getting any trace of him. When he got
home he found a letter from the brother giving the right address.

DOWN AT THE FRONT

CULPEPER, VA., *Feb. '64.*—Here I am pretty well down toward
the extreme front. Three or four days ago General S., who is now
in chief command, (I believe Meade is absent, sick,) moved a strong
force southward from camp as if intending business. They went to
the Rapidan; there has since been some manœuvring and a little
fighting, but nothing of consequence. The telegraphic accounts
given Monday morning last, make entirely too much of it, I should
say. What General S. intended we here know not, but we trust in
that competent commander. We were somewhat excited, (but not
so very much either,) on Sunday, during the day and night, as orders
were sent out to pack up and harness, and be ready to evacuate, to
fall back towards Washington. But I was very sleepy and went to
bed. Some tremendous shouts arousing me during the night, I went
forth and found it was from the men above mention'd, who were
returning. I talk'd with some of the men; as usual I found them full
of gayety, endurance, and many fine little outshows, the signs of
the most excellent good manliness of the world. It was a curious
sight to see those shadowy columns moving through the night. I
stood unobserv'd in the darkness and watch'd them long. The mud
was very deep. The men had their usual burdens, overcoats, knapsacks, guns and blankets. Along and along they filed by me, with
often a laugh, a song, a cheerful word, but never once a murmur.

It may have been odd, but I never before so realized the majesty and reality of the American people *en masse*. It fell upon me like a great awe. The strong ranks moved neither fast nor slow. They had march'd seven or eight miles already through the slipping unctuous mud. The brave First corps stopt here. The equally brave Third corps moved on to Brandy station. The famous Brooklyn 14th are here, guarding the town. You see their red legs actively moving everywhere. Then they have a theatre of their own here. They give musical performances, nearly everything done capitally. Of course the audience is a jam. It is good sport to attend one of these entertainments of the 14th. I like to look around at the soldiers, and the general collection in front of the curtain, more than the scene on the stage.

PAYING THE BOUNTIES

One of the things to note here now is the arrival of the paymaster with his strong box, and the payment of bounties to veterans re-enlisting. Major H. is here to-day, with a small mountain of green-backs, rejoicing the hearts of the 2d division of the First corps. In the midst of a rickety shanty, behind a little table, sit the major and clerk Eldridge, with the rolls before them, and much moneys. A re-enlisted man gets in cash about $200 down, (and heavy instal-ments following, as the pay-days arrive, one after another.) The show of the men crowding around is quite exhilarating; I like to stand and look. They feel elated, their pockets full, and the en-suing furlough, the visit home. It is a scene of sparkling eyes and flush'd cheeks. The soldier has many gloomy and harsh experiences, and this makes up for some of them. Major H. is order'd to pay first all the re-enlisted men of the First corps their bounties and back pay, and then the rest. You hear the peculiar sound of the rustling of the new and crisp greenbacks by the hour, through the nimble fingers of the major and my friend clerk E.

RUMORS, CHANGES, &C.

About the excitement of Sunday, and the orders to be ready to start, I have heard since that the said orders came from some cau-tious minor commander, and that the high principalities knew not and thought not of any such move; which is likely. The rumor and fear here intimated a long circuit by Lee, and flank attack on our right. But I cast my eyes at the mud, which was then at its deepest and palmiest condition, and retired composely to rest. Still it is about time for Culpeper to have a change. Authorities have chased each other here like clouds in a stormy sky. Before the first Bull Run this was the rendezvous and camp of instruction of the secession troops. I am stopping at the house of a lady who has witness'd all the eventful changes of the war, along this route of contending armies. She is a widow, with a family of young children, and lives here with her sister in a large handsome house. A number of army officers board with them.

VIRGINIA

Dilapidated, fenceless, and trodden with war as Virginia is, wherever I move across her surface, I find myself rous'd to surprise and admiration. What capacity for products, improvements, human life, nourishment and expansion. Everywhere that I have been in the Old Dominion, (the subtle mockery of that title now!) such thoughts have fill'd me. The soil is yet far above the average of any of the northern States. And how full of breadth the scenery, everywhere distant mountains, everywhere convenient rivers. Even yet prodigal in forest woods, and surely eligible for all the fruits, orchards, and flowers. The skies and atmosphere most luscious, as I feel certain, from more than a year's residence in the State, and movements hither and yon. I should say very healthy, as a general thing. Then a rich and elastic quality, by night and by day. The sun rejoices in his strength, dazzling and burning, and yet, to me, never unpleasantly weakening. It is not the panting tropical heat, but invigorates. The north tempers it. The nights are often unsurpassable. Last evening (Feb. 8,) I saw the first of the new moon, the outlined old moon clear along with it; the sky and air so clear, such transparent hues of color, it seem'd to me I had never really seen the new moon before. It was the thinnest cut crescent possible. It hung delicate just above the sulky shadow of the Blue mountains. Ah, if it might prove an omen and good prophecy for this unhappy State.

SUMMER OF 1864

I am back again in Washington, on my regular daily and nightly rounds. Of course there are many specialties. Dotting a ward here and there are always cases of poor fellows, long-suffering under obstinate wounds, or weak and dishearten'd from typhoid fever, or the like; mark'd cases, needing special and sympathetic nourishment. These I sit down and either talk to, or silently cheer them up. They always like it hugely, (and so do I.) Each case has its pecularities, and needs some new adaptation. I have learnt to thus conform—learnt a good deal of hospital wisdom. Some of the poor young chaps, away from home for the first time in their lives, hunger and thirst for affection; this is sometimes the only thing that will reach their condition. The men like to have a pencil, and something to write in. I have given them cheap pocket-diaries, and almanacs for 1864, interleav'd with blank paper. For reading I generally have some old pictorial magazines or story papers—they are always acceptable. Also the morning or evening papers of the day. The best books I do not give, but lend to read through the wards, and then take them to others, and so on; they are very punctual about returning the books. In these wards, or on the field, as I thus continue to go round, I have come to adapt myself to each emergency, after its kind or call, however trivial, however solemn, every one justified and made real under its circumstances—not only visits and cheering talk and little gifts—not only washing and dressing wounds, (I have some cases where the patient is unwilling any one should do this but me)—but passages from the Bible, expounding them, prayer at the bedside, explanations of doctrine, &c. (I think I see my friends smiling at this confession, but I was never more in earnest in my life.) In camp and everywhere, I was in the habit of reading or giving recitations to the men. They were very fond of it, and liked declamatory poetical pieces. We would gather in a large group by ourselves, after supper, and spend the time in such readings, or in talking, and occasionally by an amusing game called the game of twenty questions.

A NEW ARMY ORGANIZATION FIT FOR AMERICA

It is plain to me out of the events of the war, north and south, and out of all considerations, that the current military theory, practice, rules and organization, (adopted from Europe from the feudal institutes, with, of course, the "modern improvements," largely from the French,) though tacitly follow'd, and believ'd in by the officers generally, are not at all consonant with the United States, nor our people, nor our days. What it will be I know not—but I know that as entire an abnegation of the present military system, and the naval too, and a building up from radically different root-bases and centres appropriate to us, must eventually result, as that our political system has resulted and become establish'd, different from feudal Europe, and built up on itself from original, perennial, democratic premises. We have undoubtedly in the United States, the greatest military power—an exhaustless, intelligent, brave and reliable rank and file—in the world, any land, perhaps all lands.

The problem is to organize this in the manner fully appropriate to it, to the principles of the republic, and to get the best service out of it. In the present struggle, as already seen and review'd, probably three-fourths of the losses, men, lives, &c., have been sheer superfluity, extravagance, waste.

DEATH OF A HERO

I wonder if I could ever convey to another—to you, for instance, reader dear—the tender and terrible realities of such cases, (many, many happen'd,) as the one I am now going to mention. Stewart C. Glover, company E, 5th Wisconsin—was wounded May 5, in one of those fierce tussles of the Wilderness—died May 21—aged about 20. He was a small and beardless young man—a splendid soldier—in fact almost an ideal American, of his age. He had serv'd nearly three years, and would have been entitled to his discharge in a few days. He was in Hancock's corps. The fighting had about ceas'd for the day, and the general commanding the brigade rode by and call'd for volunteers to bring in the wounded. Glover responded among the first—went out gayly—but while in the act of bearing in a wounded sergeant to our lines, was shot in the knee by a rebel sharpshooter; consequence, amputation and death. He had resided with his father, John Glover, an aged and feeble man, in Batavia, Genesee county, N. Y., but was at school in Wisconsin, after the war broke out, and there enlisted—soon took to soldier-life, liked it, was very manly, was belov'd by officers and comrades. He kept a little diary, like so many of the soldiers. On the day of his death he wrote the following in it, *to-day the doctor says I must die—all is over with me—ah, so young to die.* On another blank leaf he pencill'd to his brother, *dear brother Thomas, I have been brave but wicked—pray for me.*

HOSPITAL SCENES.—INCIDENTS

It is Sunday afternoon, middle of summer, hot and oppressive, and very silent through the ward. I am taking care of a critical case, now lying in a half lethargy. Near where I sit is a suffering rebel, from the 8th Louisiana; his name is Irving. He has been here a long time, badly wounded, and lately had his leg amputated; it is not doing very well. Right opposite me is a sick soldier-boy, laid down with his clothes on, sleeping, looking much wasted, his pallid face on his arm. I see by the yellow trimming on his jacket that he is a cavalry boy. I step softly over and find by his card that he is named

William Cone, of the 1st Maine cavalry, and his folks live in Skowhegan.

Ice Cream Treat.—One hot day toward the middle of June, I gave the inmates of Carver hospital a general ice cream treat, purchasing a large quantity, and, under convoy of the doctor or head nurse, going around personally through the wards to see to its distribution.

An Incident.—In one of the fights before Atlanta, a rebel soldier, of large size, evidently a young man, was mortally wounded top of the head, so that the brains partially exuded. He lived three days, lying on his back on the spot where he first dropt. He dug with his heel in the ground during that time a hole big enough to put in a couple of ordinary knapsacks. He just lay there in the open air, and with little intermission kept his heel going night and day. Some of our soldiers then moved him to a house, but he died in a few minutes.

Another.—After the battles at Columbia, Tennessee, where we repuls'd about a score of vehement rebel charges, they left a great many wounded on the ground, mostly within our range. Whenever any of these wounded attempted to move away by any means, generally by crawling off, our men without exception brought them down by a bullet. They let none crawl away, no matter what his condition.

A YANKEE SOLDIER

As I turn'd off the Avenue one cool October evening into Thirteenth street, a soldier with knapsack and overcoat stood at the corner inquiring his way. I found he wanted to go part of the road in my direction, so we walk'd on together. We soon fell into conversation. He was small and not very young, and a tough little fellow, as I judged in the evening light, catching glimpses by the lamps we pass'd. His answers were short, but clear. His name was Charles Carroll; he belong'd to one of the Massachusetts regiments and was born in or near Lynn. His parents were living, but were very old. There were four sons, and all had enlisted. Two had died of starvation and misery in the prison at Andersonville, and one had been kill'd in the west. He only was left. He was now going home, and by the way he talk'd I inferr'd that his time was nearly out. He made great calculations on being with his parents to comfort them the rest of their days.

UNION PRISONERS SOUTH

Michael Stansbury, 48 years of age, a sea-faring man, a southerner by birth and raising, formerly captain of U. S. light ship

Long Shoal, station'd at Long Shoal point, Pamlico sound—though a southerner, a firm Union man—was captur'd Feb. 17, 1863, and has been nearly two years in the Confederate prisons; was at one time order'd releas'd by Governor Vance, but a rebel officer re-arrested him; then sent on to Richmond for exchange—but instead of being exchanged was sent down (as a southern citizen, not a soldier,) to Salisbury, N. C., where he remain'd until lately, when he escap'd among the exchang'd by assuming the name of a dead soldier, and coming up via Wilmington with the rest. Was about sixteen months in Salisbury. Subsequent to October, '64, there were about 11,000 Union prisoners in the stockade; about 100 of them southern unionists, 200 U. S. deserters. During the past winter 1500 of the prisoners, to save their lives, join'd the confederacy, on con- dition of being assign'd merely to guard duty. Out of the 11,000 not more than 2500 came out; 500 of these were pitiable, helpless wretches—the rest were in a condition to travel. There were often 60 dead bodies to be buried in the morning; the daily average would be about 40. The regular food was a meal of corn, the cob and husk ground together, and sometimes once a week a ration of sorghum molasses. A diminutive ration of meat might possibly come once a month, not oftener. In the stockade, containing the 11,000 men, there was a partial show of tents, not enough for 2000. A large proportion of the men lived in holes in the ground, in the utmost wretchedness. Some froze to death, others had their hands and feet frozen. The rebel guards would occasionally, and on the least pretence, fire into the prison from mere demonism and wan- tonness. All the horrors that can be named, starvation, lassitude, filth, vermin, despair, swift loss of self-respect, idiocy, insanity, and frequent murder, were there. Stansbury has a wife and child living in Newbern—has written to them from here—is in the U. S. light- house employ still—(had been home to Newbern to see his family, and on his return to the ship was captured in his boat.) Has seen men brought there to Salisbury as hearty as you ever see in your life—in a few weeks completely dead gone, much of it from thinking on their condition—hope all gone. Has himself a hard, sad, strangely deaden'd kind of look, as of one chill'd for years in the cold and dark, where his good manly nature had no room to exercise itself.

DESERTERS

Oct. 24.—Saw a large squad of our own deserters, (over 300) surrounded with a cordon of arm'd guards, marching along Penn- sylvania avenue. The most motley collection I ever saw, all sorts of rig, all sorts of hats and caps, many fine-looking young fellows, some of them shame-faced, some sickly, most of them dirty, shirts very dirty and long worn, &c. They tramp'd along without order, a huge huddling mass, not in ranks. I saw some of the spectators laughing, but I felt like anything else but laughing. These deserters are far more numerous than would be thought. Almost every day I see squads of them, sometimes two or three at a time, with a small guard; sometimes ten or twelve, under a larger one. (I hear that desertions from the army now in the field have often averaged 10,000 a month. One of the commonest sights in Washington is a squad of deserters.)

A GLIMPSE OF WAR'S HELL-SCENES

In one of the late movements of our troops in the valley, (near Upperville, I think,) a strong force of Moseby's mounted guerillas attack'd a train of wounded, and the guard of cavalry convoying them. The ambulances contain'd about 60 wounded, quite a number of them officers of rank. The rebels were in strength, and the capture of the train and its partial guard after a short snap was effectually accomplish'd. No sooner had our men surrender'd, the rebels instantly commenced robbing the train and murdering their prisoners, even the wounded. Here is the scene or a sample of it, ten minutes after. Among the wounded officers in the ambulances were one, a lieutenant of regulars, and another of higher rank. These two were dragg'd out on the ground on their backs, and were now surrounded by the guerillas, a demoniac crowd, each member of which was stabbing them in different parts of their bodies. One of the officers had his feet pinn'd firmly to the ground by bayonets stuck through them and thrust into the ground. These two officers, as afterwards found on examination, had receiv'd about twenty such thrusts, some of them through the mouth, face, &c. The wounded had all been dragg'd (to give a better chance also for plunder,) out of their wagons; some had been effectually dispatch'd, and their bodies were lying there lifeless and bloody. Others, not yet dead, but horribly mutilated, were moaning or groaning. Of our men who surrender'd, most had been thus maim'd or slaughter'd.

At this instant a force of our cavalry, who had been following the train at some interval, charged suddenly upon the secesh captors, who proceeded at once to make the best escape they could. Most of them got away, but we gobbled two officers and seventeen men, in the very acts just described. The sight was one which admitted of little discussion, as may be imagined. The seventeen cap-

tur'd men and two officers were put under guard for the night, but
it was decided there and then that they should die. The next morning
the two officers were taken in the town, separate places, put in the
centre of the street, and shot. The seventeen men were taken to an
open ground, a little one side. They were placed in a hollow square,
half-encompass'd by two of our cavalry regiments, one of which
regiments had three days before found the bloody corpses of three
of their men hamstrung and hung up by the heels to limbs of trees
by Moseby's guerillas, and the other had not long before had twelve
men, after surrendering, shot and then hung by the neck to limbs
of trees, and jeering inscriptions pinn'd to the breast of one of the
corpses, who had been a sergeant. Those three, and those twelve,
had been found, I say, by these environing regiments. Now, with
revolvers, they form'd the grim cordon of the seventeen prisoners.
The latter were placed in the midst of the hollow square, unfasten'd,
and the ironical remark made to them that they were now to be
given "a chance for themselves." A few ran for it. But what use?
From every side the deadly pills came. In a few minutes the seventeen
corpses strew'd the hollow square. I was curious to know whether
some of the Union soldiers, some few, (some one or two at least
of the youngsters,) did not abstain from shooting on the helpless
men. Not one. There was no exultation, very little said, almost
nothing, yet every man there contributed his shot.

Multiply the above by scores, aye hundreds—verify it in all the
forms that different circumstances, individuals, places, could afford—
light it with every lurid passion, the wolf's, the lion's lapping thirst
for blood—the passionate, boiling volcanoes of human revenge for
comrades, brothers slain—with the light of burning farms, and heaps
of smutting, smouldering black embers—and in the human heart
everywhere black, worse embers—and you have an inkling of this
war.

GIFTS—MONEY—DISCRIMINATION

As a very large proportion of the wounded came up from the
front without a cent of money in their pockets, I soon discover'd
that it was about the best thing I could do to raise their spirits, and
show them that somebody cared for them, and practically felt a
fatherly or brotherly interest in them, to give them small sums in
such cases, using tact and discretion about it. I am regularly supplied
with funds for this purpose by good women and men in Boston,
Salem, Providence, Brooklyn, and New York. I provide myself with
a quantity of bright new ten-cent and five-cent bills, and, when I
think it incumbent, I give 25 or 30 cents, or perhaps 50 cents, and

occasionally a still larger sum to some particular case. As I have started this subject, I take opportunity to ventilate the financial question. My supplies, altogether voluntary, mostly confidential, often seeming quite Providential, were numerous and varied. For instance, there were two distant and wealthy ladies, sisters, who sent regularly, for two years, quite heavy sums, enjoining that their names should be kept secret. The same delicacy was indeed a frequent condition. From several I had *carte blanche.* Many were entire strangers. From these sources, during from two to three years, in the manner described, in the hospitals, I bestowed, as almoner for others, many, many thousands of dollars. I learn'd one thing conclusively—that beneath all the ostensible greed and heartlessness of our times there is no end to the generous benevolence of men and women in the United States, when once sure of their object. Another thing became clear to me—while *cash* is not amiss to bring up the rear, tact and magnetic sympathy and unction are, and ever will be, sovereign still.

ITEMS FROM MY NOTE BOOKS

Some of the half-eras'd, and not over-legible when made, memoranda of things wanted by one patient or another, will convey quite a fair idea. D. S. G., bed 52, wants a good book; has a sore, weak throat; would like some horehound candy; is from New Jersey, 28th regiment. C. H. L., 145th Pennsylvania, lies in bed 6, with jaundice and erysipelas; also wounded; stomach easily nauseated; bring him some oranges, also a little tart jelly; hearty, full-blooded young fellow—(he got better in a few days, and is now home on a furlough.) J. H. G., bed 24, wants an undershirt, drawers, and socks; has not had a change for quite a while; is evidently a neat, clean boy from New England—(I supplied him; also with a comb, toothbrush, and some soap and towels; I noticed afterward he was the cleanest of the whole ward.) Mrs. G., lady-nurse, ward F, wants a bottle of brandy—has two patients imperatively requiring stimulus —low with wounds and exhaustion. (I supplied her with a bottle of first-rate brandy from the Christian commission rooms.)

A CASE FROM SECOND BULL RUN

Well, poor John Mahay is dead. He died yesterday. His was a painful and long-lingering case, (see p. [583] *ante.*) I have been with him at times for the past fifteen months. He belonged to company

A, 101st New York, and was shot through the lower region of the
abdomen at second Bull Run, August, '62. One scene at his bedside
will suffice for the agonies of nearly two years. The bladder had
been perforated by a bullet going entirely through him. Not long
since I sat a good part of the morning by his bedside, ward E,
Armory square. The water ran out of his eyes from the intense
pain, and the muscles of his face were distorted, but he utter'd
nothing except a low groan now and then. Hot moist cloths were
applied, and reliev'd him somewhat. Poor Mahay, a mere boy in
age, but old in misfortune. He never knew the love of parents, was
placed in infancy in one of the New York charitable institutions,
and subsequently bound out to a tyrannical master in Sullivan
county, (the scars of whose cowhide and club remain'd yet on his
back.) His wound here was a most disagreeable one, for he was a
gentle, cleanly, and affectionate boy. He found friends in his hospital life, and, indeed, was a universal favorite. He had quite a
funeral ceremony.

ARMY SURGEONS—AID DEFICIENCIES

I must bear my most emphatic testimony to the zeal, manliness,
and professional spirit and capacity, generally prevailing among
the surgeons, many of them young men, in the hospitals and the
army. I will not say much about the exceptions, for they are few;
(but I have met some of those few, and very incompetent and airish
they were). I never ceas'd to find the best men, and the hardest and
most disinterested workers, among the surgeons in the hospitals.
They are full of genius, too. I have seen many hundreds of them
and this is my testimony. There are, however, serious deficiencies,
wastes, sad want of system, in the commissions, contributions, and
in all the voluntary, and a great part of the governmental nursing,
edibles, medicines, stores, &c. (I do not say surgical atttendance,
because the surgeons cannot do more than human endurance permits.) Whatever puffing accounts there may be in the papers of the
North, this is the actual fact. No thorough previous preparation,
no system, no foresight, no genius. Always plenty of stores, no
doubt, but never where they are needed, and never the proper application. Of all harrowing experiences, none is greater than that of
the days following a heavy battle. Scores, hundreds of the noblest
men on earth, uncomplaining, lie helpless, mangled, faint, alone,
and so bleed to death, or die from exhaustion, either actually untouch'd at all, or merely the laying of them down and leaving them,
when there ought to be means provided to save them.

THE BLUE EVERYWHERE

This city, its suburbs, the capitol, the front of the White House, the places of amusement, the Avenue, and all the main streets, swarm with soldiers this winter, more than ever before. Some are out from the hospitals, some from the neighboring camps, &c. One source or another, they pour plenteously, and make, I should say, the mark'd feature in the human movement and costume-appearance of our national city. Their blue pants and overcoats are everywhere. The clump of crutches is heard up the stairs of the paymasters' offices, and there are characteristic groups around the doors of the same, often waiting long and wearily in the cold. Toward the latter part of the afternoon, you see the furlough'd men, sometimes singly, sometimes in small squads, making their way to the Baltimore depot. At all times, except early in the morning, the patrol detachments are moving around, especially during the earlier hours of evening, examining passes, and arresting all soldiers without them. They do not question the one-legged, or men badly disabled or maim'd, but all others are stopt. They also go around evenings through the auditoriums of the theatres, and make officers and all show their passes, or other authority, for being there.

A MODEL HOSPITAL

Sunday, January 29th, 1865.—Have been in Armory-square this afternoon. The wards are very comfortable, new floors and plaster walls, and models of neatness. I am not sure but this is a model hospital after all, in important respects. I found several sad cases of old lingering wounds. One Delaware soldier, William H. Millis, from Bridgeville, whom I had been with after the battles of the Wilderness, last May, where he receiv'd a very bad wound in the chest, with another in the left arm, and whose case was serious (pneumonia had set in) all last June and July, I now find well enough to do light duty. For three weeks at the time mention'd he just hovered between life and death.

BOYS IN THE ARMY

As I walk'd home about sunset, I saw in Fourteenth street a very young soldier, thinly clad, standing near the house I was about to enter. I stopt a moment in front of the door and call'd him to me. I knew that an old Tennessee regiment, and also an Indiana regiment, were temporarily stopping in new barracks, near Fourteenth street. This boy I found belonged to the Tennessee regiment. But I could hardly believe he carried a musket. He was but 15 years old, yet had been twelve months a soldier, and had borne his part in several battles, even historic ones. I ask'd him if he did not suffer from the cold, and if he had no overcoat. No, he did not suffer from cold, and had no overcoat, but could draw one whenever he wish'd. His father was dead, and his mother living in some part of East Tennessee; all the men were from that part of the country. The next forenoon I saw the Tennessee and Indiana regiments marching down the Avenue. My boy was with the former, stepping along with the rest. There were many other boys no older. I stood and watch'd them as they tramp'd along with slow, strong, heavy, regular steps. There did not appear to be a man over 30 years of age, and a large proportion were from 15 to perhaps 22 or 23. They had all the look of veterans, worn, stain'd, impassive, and a certain unbent, lounging gait, carrying in addition to their regular arms and knapsacks, frequently a frying-pan, broom, &c. They were all of pleasant physiognomy; no refinement, nor blanch'd with intellect, but as my eye pick'd them, moving along, rank by rank, there did not seem to be a single repulsive, brutal or markedly stupid face among them.

BURIAL OF A LADY NURSE

Here is an incident just occurr'd in one of the hospitals. A lady named Miss or Mrs. Billings, who has long been a practical friend of soldiers, and nurse in the army, and had become attached to it in a way that no one can realize but him or her who has had experience, was taken sick, early this winter, linger'd some time, and finally died in the hospital. It was her request that she should be buried among the soldiers, and after the military method. This request was fully carried out. Her coffin was carried to the grave by soldiers, with the usual escort, buried, and a salute fired over the grave. This was at Annapolis a few days since.

FEMALE NURSES FOR SOLDIERS

There are many women in one position or another, among the hospitals, mostly as nurses here in Washington, and among the military stations; quite a number of them young ladies acting as volunteers. They are a help in certain ways, and deserve to be mention'd with respect. Then it remains to be distinctly said that few or no young ladies, under the irresistible conventions of society, answer the practical requirements of nurses for soldiers. Middle-aged or healthy and good condition'd elderly women, mothers of children, are always best. Many of the wounded must be handled. A hundred things which cannot be gainsay'd, must occur and must be done. The presence of a good middle-aged or elderly woman, the magnetic touch of hands, the expressive features of the mother, the silent soothing of her presence, her words, her knowledge and privileges arrived at only through having had children, are precious and final qualifications. It is a natural faculty that is required; it is not merely having a genteel young woman at a table in a ward. One of the finest nurses I met was a red-faced illiterate old Irish woman; I have seen her take the poor wasted naked boys so tenderly up in her arms. There are plenty of excellent clean old black women that would make tip-top nurses.

SOUTHERN ESCAPEES

Feb. 23, '65.—I saw a large procession of young men from the rebel army, (deserters they are call'd, but the usual meaning of the word does not apply to them,) passing the Avenue to-day. There were nearly 200, come up yesterday by boat from James river. I stood and watch'd them as they shuffled along, in a slow, tired, worn sort of way; a large proportion of light-hair'd, blonde, light gray-eyed young men among them. Their costumes had a dirt-stain'd uniformity; most had been originally gray; some had articles of our uniform, pants on one, vest or coat on another; I think they were mostly Georgia and North Carolina boys. They excited little or no attention. As I stood quite close to them, several good looking enough youths, (but O what a tale of misery their appearance told,) nodded or just spoke to me, without doubt divining pity and father-liness out of my face, for my heart was full enough of it. Several of the couples trudg'd along with their arms about each other, some probably brothers, as if they were afraid they might somehow get separated. They nearly all look'd what one might call simple, yet intelligent, too. Some had pieces of old carpet, some blankets, and others old bags around their shoulders. Some of them here and there had fine faces, still it was a procession of misery. The two hundred had with them about half a dozen arm'd guards. Along this week I saw some such procession, more or less in numbers, every day, as they were brought up by the boat. The government does what it can for them, and sends them north and west.

Feb. 27.—Some three or four hundred more escapees from the confederate army came up on the boat. As the day has been very pleasant indeed, (after a long spell of bad weather,) I have been wandering around a good deal, without any other object than to be out-doors and enjoy it; have met these escaped men in all directions. Their apparel is the same ragged, long-worn motley as before described. I talk'd with a number of the men. Some are quite bright and stylish, for all their poor clothes—walking with an air, wearing their old head-coverings on one side, quite saucily. I find the old, unquestionable proofs, as all along the past four years, of the un-scrupulous tyranny exercised by the secession government in con-scripting the common people by absolute force everywhere, and paying no attention whatever to the men's time being up—keeping them in military service just the same. One gigantic young fellow, a Georgian, at least six feet three inches high, broad-sized in pro-portion, attired in the dirtiest, drab, well-smear'd rags, tied with strings, his trousers at the knees all strips and streamers, was com-placently standing eating some bread and meat. He appear'd con-tented enough. Then a few minutes after I saw him slowly walking along. It was plain he did not take anything to heart.

Feb. 28.—As I pass'd the military headquarters of the city, not far from the President's house, I stopt to interview some of the crowd of escapees who were lounging there. In appearance they were the same as previously mention'd. Two of them, one about 17, and the other perhaps 25 or '6, I talked with some time. They were from North Carolina, born and rais'd there, and had folks there. The elder had been in the rebel service four years. He was first conscripted for two years. He was then kept arbitrarily in the ranks. This is the case with a large proportion of the secession army. There was nothing downcast in these young men's manners; the younger had been soldiering about a year; he was conscripted; there were six brothers (all the boys of the family) in the army, part of them as conscripts, part as volunteers; three had been kill'd; one had es-caped about four months ago, and now this one had got away; he was a pleasant and well-talking lad, with the peculiar North Carolina idiom (not at all disagreeable to my ears.) He and the elder one were of the same company, and escaped together—and wish'd to remain together. They thought of getting transportation away to Missouri, and working there; but were not sure it was judicious. I advised farm work for the present. The younger had made six dollars on the boat, with some tobacco he brought; he had three and a half left. The elder had nothing; I gave him a trifle. Soon after, met John Wormley, 9th Alabama, a West Tennessee rais'd boy, parents both dead—had the look of one for a long time on short allowance— said very little—chew'd tobacco at a fearful rate, spitting in propor-tion—large clear dark-brown eyes, very fine—didn't know what to make of me—told me at last he wanted much to get some clean underclothes, and a pair of decent pants. Didn't care about coat or hat fixings. Wanted a chance to wash himself well, and put on the underclothes. I had the very great pleasure of helping him to accomplish all those wholesome designs.

March 1st.—Plenty more butternut or clay-color'd escapees every day. About 160 came in to-day, a large portion South Carolinians. They generally take the oath of allegiance, and are sent north, west, or extreme south-west if they wish. Several of them told me that the desertions in their army, of men going home, leave or no leave, are far more numerous than their desertions to our side. I saw a very forlorn looking squad of about a hundred, late this afternoon, on their way to the Baltimore depot.

THE CAPITOL BY GAS-LIGHT

To-night I have been wandering awhile in the capitol, which is all lit up. The illuminated rotunda looks fine. I like to stand aside and look a long, long while, up at the dome; it comforts me somehow. The House and Senate were both in session till very late. I look'd in upon them, but only a few moments; they were hard at work on tax and appropriation bills. I wander'd through the long and rich corridors and apartments under the Senate; an old habit of mine, former winters, and now more satisfaction than ever. Not many persons down there, occasionally a flitting figure in the distance.

THE INAUGURATION

March 4.—The President very quietly rode down to the capitol in his own carriage, by himself, on a sharp trot, about noon, either because he wish'd to be on hand to sign bills, or to get rid of marching in line with the absurd procession, the muslin temple of liberty, and pasteboard monitor. I saw him on his return, at three o'clock, after the performance was over. He was in his plain two-horse barouche, and look'd very much worn and tired; the lines, indeed, of vast responsibilities, intricate questions, and demands of life and death, cut deeper than ever upon his dark brown face; yet all the old goodness, tenderness, sadness, and canny shrewdness, underneath the furrows. (I never see that man without feeling that he is one to become personally attach'd to, for his combination of purest, heartiest tenderness, and native western form of manliness.) By his side sat his little boy, of ten years. There were no soldiers, only a lot of civilians on horseback, with huge yellow scarfs over their shoulders, riding around the carriage. (At the inauguration four years ago, he rode down and back again surrounded by a dense mass of arm'd cavalrymen eight deep, with drawn sabres; and there were sharp-shooters station'd at every corner on the route.) I ought to make mention of the closing levee of Saturday night last. Never before was such a compact jam in front of the White House—all the grounds fill'd, and away out to the spacious sidewalks. I was there, as I took a notion to go—was in the rush inside with the crowd—surged along the passage-ways, the blue and other rooms, and through the great east room. Crowds of country people, some very funny. Fine music from the Marine band, off in a side place. I saw Mr. Lincoln, drest all in black, with white kid gloves and a claw-hammer coat, receiving, as in duty bound, shaking hands, looking very disconsolate, and as if he would give anything to be somewhere else.

ATTITUDE OF FOREIGN GOVERNMENTS DURING THE WAR

Looking over my scraps, I find I wrote the following during 1864. The happening to our America, abroad as well as at home, these years, is indeed most strange. The democratic republic has paid her to-day the terrible and resplendent compliment of the united wish of all the nations of the world that her union should be broken, her future cut off, and that she should be compell'd to descend to the level of kindgoms and empires ordinarily great. There is certainly not one government in Europe but is now watching the war in this country, with the ardent prayer that the United States may be effectually split, crippled, and dismember'd by it. There is not one but would help toward that dismemberment, if it dared. I say such is the ardent wish to-day of England and of France, as governments, and of all the nations of Europe, as governments. I think indeed it is to-day the real, heartfelt wish of all the nations of the world, with the single exception of Mexico—Mexico, the only one to whom we have ever really done wrong, and now the only one who prays for us and for our triumph, with genuine prayer. Is it not indeed strange? America, made up of all, cheerfully from the beginning opening her arms to all, the result and justifier of all, of Britain, Germany, France and Spain—all here--the accepter, the friend, hope, last resource and general house of all—she who has harm'd none, but been bounteous to so many, to millions, the mother of strangers and exiles, all nations—should now I say be paid this dread compliment of general governmental fear and hatred. Are we indignant? alarm'd? Do we feel jeopardized? No; help'd, braced, concentrated, rather. We are all too prone to wander from ourselves, to affect Europe, and watch her frowns and smiles. We need this hot lesson of general hatred, and henceforth must never forget it. Never again will we trust the moral sense nor abstract friendliness of a single *government* of the old world.

THE WEATHER.—DOES IT SYMPATHIZE WITH THESE TIMES?

Whether the rains, the heat and cold, and what underlies them all, are affected with what affects man in masses, and follow his play of passionate action, strain'd stronger than usual, and on a larger scale than usual—whether this, or no, it is certain that there is now, and has been for twenty months or more, on this American continent north, many a remarkable, many an unprecedented expression of the subtile world of air above us and around us. There, since this war, and the wide and deep national agitation, strange analogies, different combinations, a different sunlight, or absence of it; different products even out of the ground. After every great battle, a great storm. Even civic events the same. On Saturday last, a forenoon like whirling demons, dark, with slanting rain, full of rage; and then the afternoon, so calm, so bathed with flooding splendor from heaven's most excellent sun, with atmosphere of sweetness; so clear, it show'd the stars, long, long before they were due. As the President came out on the capitol portico, a curious little white cloud, the only one in that part of the sky, appear'd like a hovering bird, right over him.

Indeed, the heavens, the elements, all the meteorological influences, have run riot for weeks past. Such caprices, abruptest alternation of frowns and beauty, I never knew. It is a common remark that (as last summer was different in its spells of intense heat from any preceding it,) the winter just completed has been without parallel. It has remain'd so down to the hour I am writing. Much of the daytime of the past month was sulky, with leaden heaviness, fog, interstices of bitter cold, and some insane storms. But there have been samples of another description. Nor earth nor sky ever knew spectacles of superber beauty than some of the nights lately here. The western star, Venus, in the earlier hours of evening, has never been so large, so clear; it seems as if it told something, as if it held rapport indulgent with humanity, with us Americans. Five or six nights since, it hung close by the moon, then a little past its first quarter. The star was wonderful, the moon like a young mother. The sky, dark blue, the transparent night, the planets, the moderate west wind, the elastic temperature, the miracle of that great star, and the young and swelling moon swimming in the west, suffused

the soul. Then I heard, slow and clear, the deliberate notes of a
bugle come up out of the silence, sounding so good through the
night's mystery, no hurry, but firm and faithful, floating along,
rising, falling leisurely, with here and there a long-drawn note; the
bugle, well play'd, sounding tattoo, in one of the army hospitals
near here, where the wounded (some of them personally so dear
to me,) are lying in their cots, and many a sick boy come down to
the war from Illinois, Michigan, Wisconsin, Iowa, and the rest.

INAUGURATION BALL

March 6.—I have been up to look at the dance and supper-rooms,
for the inauguration ball at the Patent office; and I could not help
thinking, what a different scene they presented to my view a while
since, fill'd with a crowded mass of the worst wounded of the war,
brought in from second Bull Run, Antietam, and Fredericksburg.
To-night, beautiful women, perfumes, the violins' sweetness, the
polka and the waltz; then the amputation, the blue face, the groan,
the glassy eye of the dying, the clotted rag, the odor of wounds and
blood, and many a mother's son amid strangers, passing away untended there, (for the crowd of the badly hurt was great, and much
for nurse to do, and much for surgeon.)

SCENE AT THE CAPITOL

I must mention a strange scene at the capitol, the hall of Representatives, the morning of Saturday last, (March 4th.) The day
just dawn'd, but in half-darkness, everything dim, leaden, and
soaking. In that dim light, the members nervous from long drawn
duty, exhausted, some asleep, and many half asleep. The gas-light,
mix'd with the dingy day-break, produced an unearthly effect. The
poor little sleepy, stumbling pages, the smell of the hall, the members with heads leaning on their desks, the sounds of the voices
speaking, with unusual intonations—the general moral atmosphere
also of the close of this important session—the strong hope that
the war is approaching its close—the tantalizing dread lest the hope
may be a false one—the grandeur of the hall itself, with its effect
of vast shadows up toward the panels and spaces over the galleries—
all made a mark'd combination.

In the midst of this, with the suddenness of a thunderbolt, burst
one of the most angry and crashing storms of rain and hail ever
heard. It beat like a deluge on the heavy glass roof of the hall, and
the wind literally howl'd and roar'd. For a moment, (and no wonder,)

the nervous and sleeping Representatives were thrown into confusion. The slumberers awaked with fear, some started for the doors, some look'd up with blanch'd cheeks and lips to the roof, and the little pages began to cry; it was a scene. But it was over almost as soon as the drowsied men were actually awake. They recover'd themselves; the storm raged on, beating, dashing, and with loud noises at times. But the House went ahead with its business then, I think, as calmly and with as much deliberation as at any time in its career. Perhaps the shock did it good. (One is not without impression, after all, amid these members of Congress, of both the Houses, that if the flat routine of their duties should ever be broken in upon by some great emergency involving real danger, and calling for first-class personal qualities, those qualities would be found generally forthcoming, and from men not now credited with them.)

A YANKEE ANTIQUE

March 27, 1865.—Sergeant Calvin F. Harlowe, company C, 29th Massachusetts, 3d brigade, 1st division, Ninth corps—a mark'd sample of heroism and death, (some may say bravado, but I say *heroism*, of grandest, oldest order)—in the late attack by the rebel troops, and temporary capture by them, of fort Steadman, at night. The fort was surprised at dead of night. Suddenly awaken'd from their sleep, and rushing from their tents, Harlowe, with others, found himself in the hands of the secesh—they demanded his surrender—he answer'd, *Never while I live.* (Of course it was useless. The others surrender'd; the odds were too great.) Again he was ask'd to yield, this time by a rebel captain. Though surrounded, and quite calm, he again refused, call'd sternly to his comrades to fight on, and himself attempted to do so. The rebel captain then shot him—but at the same instant he shot the captain. Both fell together mortally wounded. Harlowe died almost instantly. The rebels were driven out in a very short time. The body was buried next day, but soon taken up and sent home, (Plymouth county, Mass.) Harlowe was only 22 years of age—was a tall, slim, dark-hair'd, blue-eyed young man—had come out originally with the 29th; and that is the way he met his death, after four years' campaign. He was in the Seven Days fight before Richmond, in second Bull Run, Antietam, first Fredericksburg, Vicksburg, Jackson, Wilderness, and the campaigns following—was as good a soldier as ever wore the blue, and every old officer in the regiment will bear that testimony. Though so young, and in a common rank, he had a spirit as resolute and brave as any hero in the books, ancient or modern—It was too great to say the words "I surrender"—and so he died. (When I think of such things, knowing them well, all the vast and complicated events of the war, on which history dwells and makes its volumes, fall aside, and for the moment at any rate I see nothing but young Calvin Harlowe's figure in the night, disdaining to surrender.)

WOUNDS AND DISEASES

The war is over, but the hospitals are fuller than ever, from former and current cases. A large majority of the wounds are in the arms and legs. But there is every kind of wound, in every part of the body. I should say of the sick, from my observation, that the prevailing maladies are typhoid fever and the camp fevers generally, diarrhœa, catarrhal affections and bronchitis, rheumatism and pneumonia. These forms of sickness lead; all the rest follow. There are twice as many sick as there are wounded. The deaths range from seven to ten per cent. of those under treatment.*

DEATH OF PRESIDENT LINCOLN

April 16, '65.—I find in my notes of the time, this passage on the death of Abraham Lincoln: He leaves for America's history and biography, so far, not only its most dramatic reminiscence—he leaves, in my opinion, the greatest, best, most characteristic, artistic, moral personality. Not but that he had faults, and show'd them in the Presidency; but honesty, goodness, shrewdness, conscience, and (a new virtue, unknown to other lands, and hardly yet really known here, but the foundation and tie of all, as the future will grandly develop,) UNIONISM, in its truest and amplest sense, form'd the hard-pan of his character. These he seal'd with his life. The tragic splendor of his death, purging, illuminating all, throws round his form, his head, an aureole that will remain and will grow brighter through time, while history lives, and love of country lasts. By many has this Union been help'd; but if one name, one man, must be pick'd out, he, most of all, is the conservator of it, to the future. He was assassinated—but the Union is not assassinated—*ça ira!* One falls, and another falls. The soldier drops, sinks like a wave—but the ranks of the ocean eternally press on. Death does its work, obliterates a hundred, a thousand—President, general, captain, private—but the Nation is immortal.

---

* In the U. S. Surgeon-General's office since, there is a formal record and treatment of 253,142 cases of wounds by government surgeons. What must have been the number unofficial, indirect—to say nothing of the Southern armies?

SHERMAN'S ARMY'S JUBILATION—ITS SUDDEN STOPPAGE

When Sherman's armies, (long after they left Atlanta,) were marching through South and North Carolina—after leaving Savannah, the news of Lee's capitulation having been receiv'd—the men never mov'd a mile without from some part of the line sending up continued, inspiriting shouts. At intervals all day long sounded out the wild music of those peculiar army cries. They would be commenc'd by one regiment or brigade, immediately taken up by others, and at length whole corps and armies would join in these wild triumphant choruses. It was one of the characteristic expressions of the western troops, and became a habit, serving as a relief and outlet to the men—a vent for their feelings of victory, returning peace, &c. Morning, noon, and afternoon, spontaneous, for occasion or without occasion, these huge, strange cries, differing from any other, echoing through the open air for many a mile, expressing youth, joy, wildness, irrepressible strength, and the ideas of advance and conquest, sounded along the swamps and uplands of the South, floating to the skies. ('There never were men that kept in better spirits in danger of defeat—what then could they do in victory?' —said one of the 15th corps to me, afterwards.) This exuberance continued till the armies arrived at Raleigh. There the news of the President's murder was receiv'd. Then no more shouts or yells, for a week. All the marching was comparatively muffled. It was very significant—hardly a loud word or laugh in many of the regiments. A hush and silence pervaded all.

NO GOOD PORTRAIT OF LINCOLN

Probably the reader has seen physiognomies (often old farmers, sea-captains, and such) that, behind their homeliness, or even ugliness, held superior points so subtle, yet so palpable, making the real life of their faces almost as impossible to depict as a wild perfume or fruit-taste, or a passionate tone of the living voice—and such was Lincoln's face, the peculiar color, the lines of it, the eyes, mouth, expression. Of technical beauty it had nothing—but to the eye of a great artist it furnished a rare study, a feast and fascination. The current portraits are all failures—most of them caricatures.

RELEAS'D UNION PRISONERS FROM SOUTH

The releas'd prisoners of war are now coming up from the southern prisons. I have seen a number of them. The sight is worse than any sight of battle-fields, or any collection of wounded, even the bloodiest. There was, (as a sample,) one large boat load, of several hundreds, brought about the 25th, to Annapolis; and out of the whole number only three individuals were able to walk from the boat. The rest were carried ashore and laid down in one place or another. Can those be *men*—those little livid brown, ash-streak'd, monkey-looking dwarfs?—are they really not mummied, dwindled corpses? They lay there, most of them, quite still, but with a horrible look in their eyes and skinny lips (often with not enough flesh on the lips to cover their teeth.) Probably no more appalling sight was ever seen on this earth. (There are deeds, crimes, that may be forgiven; but this is not among them. It steeps its perpetrators in blackest, escapeless, endless damnation. Over 50,000 have been compell'd to die the death of starvation—reader, did you ever try to realize what *starvation* actually is?—in those prisons—and in a land of plenty.) An indescribable meanness, tyranny, aggravating course of insults, almost incredible—was evidently the rule of treatment through all the southern military prisons. The dead there are not to be pitied as much as some of the living that come from there—if they can be call'd living—many of them are mentally imbecile, and will never recuperate.*

---

* *From a review of* "ANDERSONVILLE, A STORY OF SOUTHERN MILITARY PRISONS," *published serially in the* "*Toledo Blade*," *in 1879, and afterwards in book form.*

"There is a deep fascination in the subject of Andersonville—for that Golgotha, in which lie the whitening bones of 13,000 gallant young men, represents the dearest and costliest sacrifice of the war for the preservation of our national unity. It is a type, too, of its class. Its more than hundred hecatombs of dead represent several times that number of their brethren, for whom the prison gates of Belle Isle, Danville, Salisbury, Florence, Columbia, and Cahaba open'd only in eternity. There are few families in the North who have not at least one dear relative or friend among these 60,000 whose sad fortune it was to end their service for the Union by lying down and dying for it in a southern prison pen. The manner of their death, the horrors that cluster'd thickly around every moment of their existence, the loyal, unfaltering steadfastness with which they endured all that fate had brought them, has never been adequately told. It was not with them as with their comrades in the field, whose every act was perform'd in the presence of those whose duty it was to observe such matters and report them to the world. Hidden from the view of their friends in the north by the impenetrable veil which the military operations of the rebels drew around the so-called confederacy, the people knew next to nothing of their career or their sufferings. Thousands died there less heeded even than the hundreds who perish'd on the battle-field. Grant did not lose as many men kill'd outright, in the terrible campaign from the Wilderness to the James river—43 days of desperate fighting—as died in July and August in Andersonville. Nearly twice as many died in that prison as fell from the day that Grant cross'd the Rapidan, till he settled down in the trenches before Petersburg. More than four times as many Union dead lie under the solemn soughing pines about that forlorn little

DEATH OF A PENNSYLVANIA SOLDIER

Frank H. Irwin, company E, 93d Pennsylvania—died May 1, '65—My letter to his mother.—Dear madam: No doubt you and Frank's friends have heard the sad fact of his death in hospital here, through his uncle, or the lady from Baltimore, who took his things. (I have not seen them, only heard of them visiting Frank.) I will write you a few lines—as a casual friend that sat by his death-bed. Your son, corporal Frank H. Irwin, was wounded near fort Fisher, Virginia, March 25th, 1865—the wound was in the left knee, pretty bad. He was sent up to Washington, was receiv'd in ward C, Armory-square hospital, March 28th—the wound became worse, and on the 4th of April the leg was amputated a little above the knee—the operation was perform'd by Dr. Bliss, one of the best surgeons in the army—he did the whole operation himself—there was a good deal of bad matter gather'd—the bullet was found in the knee. For a couple of weeks afterwards he was doing pretty well.

---

village in southern Georgia, than mark the course of Sherman from Chattanooga to Atlanta. The nation stands aghast at the expenditure of life which attended the two bloody campaigns of 1864, which virtually crush'd the confederacy, but no one remembers that more Union soldiers died in the rear of the rebel lines than were kill'd in the front of them. The great military events which stamp'd out the rebellion drew attention away from the sad drama which starvation and disease play'd in those gloomy pens in the far recesses of sombre southern forests."

From a letter of "Johnny Bouquet," in N. Y. Tribune, March 27, '81
"I visited at Salisbury, N. C., the prison pen or the site of it, from which nearly 12,000 victims of southern politicians were buried, being confined in a pen without shelter, exposed to all the elements could do, to all the disease herding animals together could create, and to all the starvation and cruelty an incompetent and intense caitiff government could accomplish. From the conversation and almost from the recollection of the northern people this place has dropp'd, but not so in the gossip of the Salisbury people, nearly all of whom say that the half was never told; that such was the nature of habitual outrage here that when Federal prisoners escaped the townspeople harbor'd them in their barns, afraid the vengeance of God would fall on them, to deliver even their enemies back to such cruelty. Said one old man at the Boyden House, who join'd in the conversation one evening: 'There were often men buried out of that prison pen still alive. I have the testimony of a surgeon that he has seen them pull'd out of the dead cart with their eyes open and taking notice, but too weak to lift a finger. There was not the least excuse for such treatment, as the confederate government had seized every sawmill in the region, and could just as well have put up shelter for these prisoners as not, wood being plentiful here. It will be hard to make any honest man in Salisbury say that there was the slightest necessity for those prisoners having to live in old tents, caves and holes half-full of water. Representations were made to the Davis government against the officers in charge of it, but no attention was paid to them. Promotion was the punishment for cruelty there. The inmates were skeletons. Hell could have no terrors for any man who died there, except the inhuman keepers.' "

I visited and sat by him frequently, as he was fond of having me. The last ten or twelve days of April I saw that his case was critical. He previously had some fever, with cold spells. The last week in April he was much of the time flighty—but always mild and gentle. He died first of May. The actual cause of death was pyæmia, (the absorption of the matter in the system instead of its discharge.) Frank, as far as I saw, had everything requisite in surgical treatment, nursing, &c. He had watches much of the time. He was so good and well-behaved and affectionate, I myself liked him very much. I was in the habit of coming in afternoons and sitting by him, and soothing him, and he liked to have me—liked to put his arm out and lay his hand on my knee—would keep it so a long while. Toward the last he was more restless and flighty at night—often fancied himself with his regiment—by his talk sometimes seem'd as if his feelings were hurt by being blamed by his officers for something he was entirely innocent of—said, "I never in my life was thought capable of such a thing, and never was." At other times he would fancy himself talking as it seem'd to children or such like, his relatives I suppose, and giving them good advice; would talk to them a long while. All the time he was out of his head not one single bad word or idea escaped him. It was remark'd that many a man's conversation in his senses was not half as good as Frank's delirium. He seem'd quite willing to die—he had become very weak and had suffer'd a good deal, and was perfectly resign'd, poor boy. I do not know his past life, but I feel as if it must have been good. At any rate what I saw of him here, under the most trying circumstances, with a painful wound, and among strangers, I can say that he behaved so brave, so composed, and so sweet and affectionate, it could not be surpass'd. And now like many other noble and good men, after serving his country as a soldier, he has yielded up his young life at the very outset in her service. Such things are gloomy—yet there is a text. "God doeth all things well"—the meaning of which, after due time, appears to the soul.

I thought perhaps a few words, though from a stranger, about your son, from one who was with him at the last, might be worth while—for I loved the young man, though I but saw him immediately to lose him. I am merely a friend visiting the hospitals occasionally to cheer the wounded and sick.   **W. W.**

THE ARMIES RETURNING

May 7.—Sunday.—To-day as I was walking a mile or two south of Alexandria, I fell in with several large squads of the returning

Western army, (*Sherman's men* as they call'd themselves,) about
a thousand in all, the largest portion of them half sick, some con-
valescents, on their way to a hospital camp. These fragmentary
excerpts, with the unmistakable Western physiognomy and idioms,
crawling along slowly—after a great campaign, blown this way, as
it were, out of their latitude—I mark'd with curiosity, and talk'd
with off and on for over an hour. Here and there was one very sick;
but all were able to walk, except some of the last, who had given
out, and were seated on the ground, faint and despondent. These
I tried to cheer, told them the camp they were to reach was only a
little way further over the hill, and so got them up and started,
accompanying some of the worst a little way, and helping them, or
putting them under the support of stronger comrades.

May 21.—Saw General Sheridan and his cavalry to-day; a strong,
attractive sight; the men were mostly young, (a few middle-aged,)
superb-looking fellows, brown, spare, keen, with well-worn clothing,
many with pieces of water-proof cloth around their shoulders,
hanging down. They dash'd along pretty fast, in wide close ranks,
all spatter'd with mud; no holiday soldiers; brigade after brigade.
I could have watch'd for a week. Sheridan stood on a balcony, under
a big tree, coolly smoking a cigar. His looks and manner impress'd
me favorably.

May 22.—Have been taking a walk along Pennsylvania avenue
and Seventh street north. The city is full of soldiers, running around
loose. Officers everywhere, of all grades. All have the weather-beaten
look of practical service. It is a sight I never tire of. All the armies
are now here (or portions of them,) for to-morrow's review. You
see them swarming like bees everywhere.

THE GRAND REVIEW

For two days now the broad spaces of Pennsylvania avenue along
to Treasury hill, and so by detour around to the President's house,
and so up to Georgetown, and across the aqueduct bridge, have been
alive with a magnificent sight, the returning armies. In their wide
ranks stretching clear across the Avenue, I watch them march or
ride along, at a brisk pace, through two whole days—infantry,
cavalry, artillery—some 200,000 men. Some days afterwards one or
two other corps; and then, still afterwards, a good part of Sherman's
immense army, brought up from Charleston, Savannah, &c.

WESTERN SOLDIERS

May 26-7.—The streets, the public buildings and grounds of
Washington, still swarm with soldiers from Illinois, Indiana, Ohio

Missouri, Iowa, and all the Western States. I am continually meeting and talking with them. They often speak to me first, and always show great sociability, and glad to have a good interchange of chat. These Western soldiers are more slow in their movements, and in their intellectual quality also; have no extreme alertness. They are larger in size, have a more serious physiognomy, are continually looking at you as they pass in the street. They are largely animal, and handsomely so. During the war I have been at times with the Fourteenth, Fifteenth, Seventeenth, and Twentieth Corps. I always feel drawn toward the men, and like their personal contact when we are crowded close together, as frequently these days in the street-cars. They all think the world of General Sherman; call him "old Bill," or sometimes "uncle Billy."

A SOLDIER ON LINCOLN

May 28.—As I sat by the bedside of a sick Michigan soldier in hospital to-day, a convalescent from the adjoining bed rose and came to me, and presently we began talking. He was a middle-aged man, belonged to the 2d Virginia regiment, but lived in Racine, Ohio, and had a family there. He spoke of President Lincoln, and said: "The war is over, and many are lost. And now we have lost the best, the fairest, the truest man in America. Take him altogether, he was the best man this country ever produced. It was quite a while I thought very different; but some time before the murder, that's the way I have seen it." There was deep earnestness in the soldier. (I found upon further talk he had known Mr. Lincoln personally, and quite closely, years before.) He was a veteran; was now in the fifth year of his service; was a cavalry man, and had been in a good deal of hard fighting.

TWO BROTHERS ONE SOUTH, ONE NORTH

May 28-9.—I staid to-night a long time by the bedside of a new patient, a young Baltimorean, aged about 19 years, W. S. P., (2d Maryland, southern,) very feeble, right leg amputated, can't sleep hardly at all—has taken a great deal of morphine, which, as usual, is costing more than it comes to. Evidently very intelligent and well bred—very affectionate—held on to my hand, and put it by his face, not willing to let me leave. As I was lingering, soothing him in his pain, he says to me suddenly, "I hardly think you know who I am—I don't wish to impose upon you—I am a rebel soldier." I said I did not know that, but it made no difference. Visiting him daily for about two weeks after that, while he lived, (death had mark'd him, and he was quite alone,) I loved him much, always kiss'd him, and he did me. In an adjoining ward I found his brothei, an officer of rank, a Union soldier, a brave and religious man, (Col. Clifton K. Prentiss, sixth Maryland infantry, Sixth corps, wounded in one of the engagements at Petersburg, April 2—linger'd, suffer'd much, died in Brooklyn, Aug. 20, '65.) It was in the same battle both were hit. One was a strong Unionist, the other Secesh; both fought on their respective sides, both badly wounded, and both brought together here after a separation of four years. Each died for his cause.

SOME SAD CASES YET

May 31.—James H. Williams, aged 21, 3d Virginia cavalry.— About as mark'd a case of a strong man, brought low by a complication of diseases, (laryngitis, fever, debility and diarrhœa,) as I have ever seen—has superb physique, remains swarthy yet, and flushed and red with fever—is altogether flighty—flesh of his great breast and arms tremulous, and pulse pounding away with treble quickness—lies a good deal of the time in a partial sleep, but with low muttering and groans—a sleep in which there is no rest. Powerful as he is, and so young, he will not be able to stand many more days of the strain and sapping heat of yesterday and to-day. His throat is in a bad way, tongue and lips parch'd. When I ask him how he feels, he is able just to articulate, "I feel pretty bad yet, old man," and looks at me with his great bright eyes. Father, John Williams, Millensport, Ohio.

June 9–10.—I have been sitting late to-night by the bedside of a wounded captain, a special friend of mine, lying with a painful fracture of left leg in one of the hospitals, in a large ward partially vacant. The lights were put out, all but a little candle, far from where I sat. The full moon shone in through the windows, making long, slanting silvery patches on the floor. All was still, my friend too was silent, but could not sleep; so I sat there by him, slowly wafting the fan, and occupied with the musings that arose out of the scene, the long shadowy ward, the beautiful ghostly moonlight on the floor, the white beds, here and there an occupant with huddled form, the bed-clothes thrown off. The hospitals have a number of cases of sun-stroke and exhaustion by heat, from the late reviews. There are many such from the Sixth corps, from the hot parade of day before yesterday. (Some of these shows cost the lives of scores of men.)

Sunday, Sep. 10.—Visited Douglas and Stanton hospitals. They are quite full. Many of the cases are bad ones, lingering wounds, and old sickness. There is a more than usual look of despair on the countenances of many of the men; hope has left them. I went through the wards, talking as usual. There are several here from the confederate army whom I had seen in other hospitals, and they recognized me. Two were in a dying condition.

CALHOUN'S REAL MONUMENT

In one of the hospital tents for special cases, as I sat to-day tending a new amputation, I heard a couple of neighboring soldiers talking to each other from their cots. One down with fever, but improving, had come up belated from Charleston not long before. The other was what we now call an "old veteran," (*i. e.*, he was a Connecticut youth, probably of less than the age of twenty-five years, the four last of which he had spent in active service in the war in all parts of the country.) The two were chatting of one thing and another. The fever soldier spoke of John C. Calhoun's monument, which he had seen, and was describing it. The veteran said: "I have seen Calhoun's monument. That you saw is not the real monument. But I have seen it. It is the desolated, ruined south; nearly the whole generation of young men between seventeen and thirty destroyed or maim'd; all the old families used up—the rich impoverish'd, the plantations cover'd with weeds, the slaves unloos'd and become the masters, and the name of southerner blacken'd with every shame—all that is Calhoun's real monument."

HOSPITALS CLOSING

October 3.—There are two army hospitals now remaining. I went to the largest of these (Douglas) and spent the afternoon and evening. There are many sad cases, old wounds, incurable sickness, and some of the wounded from the March and April battles before Richmond. Few realize how sharp and bloody those closing battles were. Our men exposed themselves more than usual; press'd ahead without urging. Then the southerners fought with extra desperation. Both sides knew that with the successful chasing of the rebel cabal from Richmond, and the occupation of that city by the national troops, the game was up. The dead and wounded were unusually many. Of the wounded the last lingering driblets have been brought to hospital here. I find many rebel wounded here, and have been extra busy to-day 'tending to the worst cases of them with the rest.

Oct., Nov. and Dec., '65—Sundays.—Every Sunday of these months visited Harewood hospital out in the woods, pleasant and recluse, some two and a half or three miles north of the capitol. The situation is healthy, with broken ground, grassy slopes and patches of oak woods, the trees large and fine. It was one of the most extensive of the hospitals, now reduced to four or five partially occupied wards, the numerous others being vacant. In November, this became the last military hospital kept up by the government, all the others being closed. Cases of the worst and most incurable wounds, obstinate illness, and of poor fellows who have no homes to go to, are found here.

Dec. 10—Sunday.—Again spending a good part of the day at Harewood. I write this about an hour before sundown. I have walk'd out for a few minutes to the edge of the woods to soothe myself with the hour and scene. It is a glorious, warm, golden-sunny, still afternoon. The only noise is from a crowd of cawing crows, on some trees three hundred yards distant. Clusters of gnats swimming and dancing in the air in all directions. The oak leaves are thick under the bare trees, and give a strong and delicious perfume. Inside the wards everything is gloomy. Death is there. As I enter'd, I was confronted by it the first thing; a corpse of a poor soldier, just dead, of typhoid fever. The attendants had just straighten'd the limbs, put coppers on the eyes, and were laying it out.

The roads.—A great recreation, the past three years, has been in taking long walks out from Washington, five, seven, perhaps ten miles and back; generally with my friend Peter Doyle, who is as fond of it as I am. Fine moonlight nights, over the perfect military roads, hard and smooth—or Sundays—we had these delightful walks, never to be forgotten. The roads connecting Washington and the numerous forts around the city, made one useful result, at any rate, out of the war.

TYPICAL SOLDIERS

Even the typical soldiers I have been personally intimate with,—it seems to me if I were to make a list of them it would be like a city directory. Some few only have I mention'd in the foregoing pages—most are dead—a few yet living. There is Reuben Farwell, of Michigan, (little 'Mitch;') Benton H. Wilson, color-bearer, 185th New York; Wm. Stansberry; Manvill Winterstein, Ohio; Bethuel Smith; Capt. Simms, of 51st New York, (kill'd at Petersburg mine explosion,) Capt. Sam. Pooley and Lieut. Fred. McReady, same reg't. Also, same reg't., my brother, George W. Whitman—in active service all through, four years, re-enlisting twice—was promoted, step by step, (several times immediately after battles,) lieutenant, captain, major and lieut. colonel—was in the actions at Roanoke, Newbern, 2d Bull Run, Chantilly, South Mountain, Antietam, Fredericksburg, Vicksburg, Jackson, the bloody conflicts of the Wilderness, and at Spottsylvania, Cold Harbor, and afterwards around Petersburg; at one of these latter was taken prisoner, and pass'd four or five months in secesh military prisons, narrowly escaping with life, from a severe fever, from starvation and half-nakedness in the winter. (What a history that 51st New York had! Went out early—march'd, fought everywhere—was in storms at sea, nearly wreck'd—storm'd forts—tramp'd hither and yon in Virginia, night and day, summer of '62—afterwards Kentucky and Mississippi—re-enlisted—was in all the engagements and campaigns, as above.) I strengthen and comfort myself much with the certainty that the capacity for just such regiments, (hundreds, thousands of them) is inexhaustible in the United States, and that there isn't a county nor a township in the republic—nor a street in any city—but could turn out, and on occasion, would turn out lots of just such typical soldiers, whenever wanted.

"CONVULSIVENESS"

As I have look'd over the proof-sheets of the preceding pages, I have once or twice fear'd that my diary would prove, at best, but a batch of convulsively written reminiscences. Well, be it so. They are but parts of the actual distraction, heat, smoke and excitement of those times. The war itself, with the temper of society preceding it, can indeed be best described by that very word *convulsiveness*.

THREE YEARS SUMM'D UP

During those three years in hospital, camp or field, I made over six hundred visits or tours, and went, as I estimate, counting all, among from eighty thousand to a hundred thousand of the wounded and sick, as sustainer of spirit and body in some degree, in time of need. These visits varied from an hour or two, to all day or night; for with dear or critical cases I generally watch'd all night. Sometimes I took up my quarters in the hospital, and slept or watch'd there several nights in succession. Those three years I consider the greatest privilege and satisfaction, (with all their feverish excitements and physical deprivations and lamentable sights,) and, of course, the most profound lesson of my life. I can say that in my ministerings I comprehended all, whoever came in my way, northern or southern, and slighted none. It arous'd and brought out and decided un-dream'd-of depths of emotion. It has given me my most fervent views of the true *ensemble* and extent of the States. While I was with wounded and sick in thousands of cases from the New England States, and from New York, New Jersey, and Pennsylvania, and from Michigan, Wisconsin, Ohio, Indiana, Illinois, and all the Western States, I was with more or less from all the States, North and South, without exception. I was with many from the border States, especially from Maryland and Virginia, and found, during those lurid years 1862–63, far more Union southerners, especially Tennesseans, than is supposed. I was with many rebel officers and men among our wounded, and gave them always what I had, and tried to cheer them the same as any. I was among the army teamsters considerably, and, indeed, always found myself drawn to them. Among the black soldiers, wounded or sick, and in the contraband camps, I also took my way whenever in their neighborhood, and did what I could for them.

THE MILLION DEAD, TOO, SUMM'D UP

The dead in this war—there they lie, strewing the fields and woods and valleys and battle-fields of the south—Virginia, the Peninsula—Malvern hill and Fair Oaks—the banks of the Chick-ahominy—the terraces of Fredericksburg—Antietam bridge—the grisly ravines of Manassas—the bloody promenade of the Wilder-ness—the vaarieties of the *strayed* dead, (the estimate of the War department is 25,000 national soldiers kill'd in battle and never buried at all, 5,000 drown'd—15,000 inhumed by strangers, or on the march in haste, in hitherto unfound localities—2,000 graves cover'd by sand and mud by Mississippi freshets, 3,000 carried away by caving-in of banks, &c.,)—Gettysburg, the West, Southwest—Vicksburg—Chattanooga—the trenches of Petersburg—the num-berless battles, camps, hospitals everywhere—the crop reap'd by the mighty reapers, typhoid, dysentery, inflammations—and blackest and loathesomest of all, the dead and living burial-pits, the prison-pens of Andersonville, Salisbury, Belle-Isle, &c., (not Dante's pictured hell and all its woes, its degradations, filthy torments, excell'd those prisons)—the dead, the dead, the dead—*our* dead—or South or North, ours all, (all, all, all, finally dear to me)—or East or West—Atlantic coast or Mississippi valley—somewhere they crawl'd to die, alone, in bushes, low gullies, or on the sides of hills—(there, in secluded spots, their skeletons, bleach'd bones, tufts of hair, buttons, fragments of clothing, are occasionally found yet)—our young

men once so handsome and so joyous, taken from us—the son from
the mother, the husband from the wife, the dear friend from the
dear friend—the clusters of camp graves, in Georgia, the Carolinas,
and in Tennessee—the single graves left in the woods or by the roadside, (hundreds, thousands, obliterated)—the corpses floated down
the rivers, and caught and lodged, (dozens, scores, floated down the
upper Potomac, after the cavalry engagements, the pursuit of Lee,
following Gettysburg)—some lie at the bottom of the sea—the
general million, and the special cemeteries in almost all the States—
the infinite dead—(the land entire saturated, perfumed with their
impalpable ashes' exhalation in Nature's chemistry distill'd, and
shall be so forever, in every future grain of wheat and ear of corn,
and every flower that grows, and every breath we draw)—not only
Northern dead leavening Southern soil—thousands, aye tens of
thousands, of Southerners, crumble to-day in Northern earth.

And everywhere among these countless graves—everywhere in
the many soldier Cemeteries of the Nation, (there are now, I believe, over seventy of them)—as at the time in the vast trenches,
the depositories of slain, Northern and Southern, after the great
battles—not only where the scathing trail passed those years, but
radiating since in all the peaceful quarters of the land—we see,
and ages yet may see, on monuments and gravestones, singly or in
masses, to thousands or tens of thousands, the significant word
Unknown.

(In some of the cemeteries nearly *all* the dead are unknown.
At Salisbury, N. C., for instance, the known are only 85, while
the unknown are 12,027, and 11,700 of these are buried in trenches.
A national monument has been put up here, by order of Congress,
to mark the spot—but what visible, material monument can ever
fittingly commemorate that spot?)

THE REAL WAR WILL NEVER GET IN THE BOOKS

And so good-bye to the war. I know not how it may have been,
or may be, to others—to me the main interest I found, (and still, on
recollection, find,) in the rank and file of the armies, both sides, and
in those specimens amid the hospitals, and even the dead on the
field. To me the points illustrating the latent personal character and
eligibilities of these States, in the two or three millions of American
young and middle-aged men, North and South, embodied in those
armies—and especially the one-third or one-fourth of their number,
stricken by wounds or disease at some time in the course of the
contest—were of more significance even than the political interests

involved. (As so much of a race depends on how it faces death, and how it stands personal anguish and sickness. As, in the glints of emotions under emergencies, and the indirect traits and asides in Plutarch, we get far profounder clues to the antique world than all its more formal history.)

Future years will never know the seething hell and the black infernal background of countless minor scenes and interiors, (not the official surface-courteousness of the Generals, not the few great battles) of the Secession war; and it is best they should not—the real war will never get in the books. In the mushy influences of current times, too, the fervid atmosphere and typical events of those years are in danger of being totally forgotten. I have at night watch'd by the side of a sick man in the hospital, one who could not live many hours. I have seen his eyes flash and burn as he raised himself and recurr'd to the cruelties on his surrender'd brother, and mutilations of the corpse afterward. (See, in the preceding pages, the incident at Upperville—the seventeen kill'd as in the description, were left there on the ground. After they dropt dead, no one touch'd them—all were made sure of, however. The carcasses were left for the citzens to bury or not, as they chose.)

Such was the war. It was not a quadrille in a ball-room. Its interior history will not only never be written—its practicality, minutiæ of deeds and passions, will never be even suggested. The actual soldier of 1862-'65, North and South, with all his ways, his incredible dauntlessness, habits, practices, tastes, language, his fierce friendship, his appetite, rankness, his superb strength and animality, lawless gait, and a hundred unnamed lights and shades of camp, I say, will never be written—perhaps must not and should not be.

The preceding notes may furnish a few stray glimpses into that life, and into those lurid interiors, never to be fully convey'd to the future. The hospital part of the drama from '61 to '65, deserves indeed to be recorded. Of that many-threaded drama, with its sudden and strange surprises, its confounding of prophecies, its moments of despair, the dread of foreign interference, the interminable campaigns, the bloody battles, the mighty and cumbrous and green armies, the drafts and bounties—the immense money expenditure, like a heavy-pouring constant rain—with, over the whole land, the last three years of the struggle, an unending, universal mourning-wail of women, parents, orphans—the marrow of the tragedy concentrated in those Army Hospitals—(it seem'd sometimes as if the whole interest of the land, North and South, was one vast central hospital, and all the rest of the affair but flanges)—those forming

the untold and unwritten history of the war—infinitely greater—
(like life's) than the few scraps and distortions that are ever told or
written. Think how much, and of importance, will be—how much,
civic and military, has already been—buried in the grave, in eternal
darkness.

AN INTERREGNUM PARAGRAPH

Several years now elapse before I resume my diary. I continued
at Washington working in the Attorney-General's department
through '66 and '67, and some time afterward. In February '73 I
was stricken down by paralysis, gave up my desk, and migrated to
Camden, New Jersey, where I lived during '74 and '75, quite unwell—
but after that began to grow better; commenc'd going for weeks at a
time, even for months, down in the country, to a charmingly recluse
and rural spot along Timber creek, twelve or thirteen miles from
where it enters the Delaware river. Domicil'd at the farm-house of
my friends, the Staffords, near by, I lived half the time along this
creek and its adjacent fields and lanes. And it is to my life here that I,
perhaps, owe partial recovery (a sort of second wind, or semi-
renewal of the lease of life) from the prostration of 1874–'75. If the
notes of that outdoor life could only prove as glowing to you, reader
dear, as the experience itself was to me. Doubtless in the course of
the following, the fact of invalidism will cròp out, (I call myself
a half-Paralytic these days, and reverently bless the Lord it is no
worse,) between some of the lines—but I get my share of fun and
healthy hours, and shall try to indicate them. (The trick is, I find,
to tone your wants and tastes low down enough, and make much of
negatives, and of mere daylight and the skies.)

NEW THEMES ENTERED UPON

1876, *'77.*—I find the woods in mid-May and early June my
best places for composition.* Seated on logs or stumps there, or

---

*Without apology for the abrupt change of field and atmosphere—after
what I have put in he preceding fifty or sixty pages—temporary episodes,
thank heaven!—I restore my book to the bracing and buoyant equilibrium of
concrete outdoor Nature, the only permanent reliance for sanity of book or
human life.

Who knows, (I have it in my fancy, my ambition,) but the pages now ensuing
may carry ray of sun, or smell of grass or corn, or call of bird, or gleam of stars
by night, or snow-flakes falling fresh and mystic, to denizen of heated city
house, or tired workman or workwoman?—or may-be in sick-room or prison—
to serve as cooling breeze, or Nature's aroma, to some fever'd mouth or latent
pulse.

resting on rails, nearly all the following memoranda have been jotted down. Wherever I go, indeed, winter or summer, city or country, alone at home or traveling, I must take notes—(the ruling passion strong in age and disablement, and even the approach of—but I must not say it yet.) Then underneath the following excerpta—crossing the *t*'s and dotting the *i*'s of certain moderate movements of late years—I am fain to fancy the foundations of quite a lesson learn'd. After you have exhausted what there is in business, politics, conviviality, love, and so on—have found that none of these finally satisfy, or permanently wear—what remains? Nature remains; to bring out from their torpid recesses, the affinities of a man or woman with the open air, the trees, fields, the changes of seasons—the sun by day and the stars of heaven by night. We will begin from these convictions. Literature flies so high and is so hotly spiced, that our notes may seem hardly more than breaths of common air, or draughts of water to drink. But that is part of our lesson.

Dear, soothing, healthy, restoration-hours—after three confining years of paralysis—after the long strain of the war, and its wounds and death.

ENTERING A LONG FARM-LANE

As every man has his hobby-liking, mine is for a real farm-lane fenced by old chestnut rails gray-green with dabs of moss and lichen, copious weeds and briers growing in spots athwart the heaps of stray-pick'd stones at the fence bases—irregular paths worn between, and horse and cow tracks—all characteristic accompaniments marking and scenting the neighborhood in their seasons—apple-tree blossoms in forward April—pigs, poultry, a field of August buckwheat, and in another the long flapping tassels of maize—and so to the pond, the expansion of the creek, the secluded-beautiful, with young and old trees, and such recesses and vistas.

TO THE SPRING AND BROOK

So, still sauntering on, to the spring under the willows—musical—as soft clinking glasses—pouring a sizeable stream, thick as my neck, pure and clear, out from its vent where the bank arches over like a great brown shaggy eyebrow or mouth-roof—gurgling, gurgling ceaselessly—meaning, saying something, of course (if one could only translate it)—always gurgling there, the whole year through—never giving out—oceans of mint, blackberries in summer

—choice of light and shade—just the place for my July sun-baths and water-baths too—but mainly the inimitable soft sound-gurgles of it, as I sit there hot afternoons. How they and all grow into me, day after day—everything in keeping—the wild, just-palpable perfume, and the dapple of leaf-shadows, and all the natural-medicinal, elemental-moral influences of the spot.

Babble on, O brook, with that utterance of thine! I too will express what I have gather'd in my days and progress, native, subterranean, past—and now thee. Spin and wind thy way—I with thee, a little while, at any rate. As I haunt thee so often, season by season thou knowest, reckest not me, (yet why be so certain? who can tell?)—but I will learn from thee, and dwell on thee—receive, copy, print from thee.

AN EARLY SUMMER REVEILLE

Away then to loosen, to unstring the divine bow, so tense, so long. Away, from curtain, carpet, sofa, book—from "society"— from city house, street, and modern improvements and luxuries— away to the primitive winding, aforementioned wooded creek, with its untrimm'd bushes and turfy banks—away from ligatures, tight boots, buttons, and the whole cast-iron civilizee life—from entourage of artificial store, machine, studio, office, parlor—from tailordom and fashion's clothes—from any clothes, perhaps, for the nonce, the summer heats advancing, there in those watery, shaded solitudes. Away, thou soul, (let me pick thee out singly, reader dear, and talk in perfect freedom, negligently, confidentially,) for one day and night at least, returning to the naked source-life of us all—to the breast of the great silent savage all-acceptive Mother Alas! how many of us are so sodden—how many have wander'd so far away, that return is almost impossible.

But to my jottings, taking them as they come, from the heap, without particular selection. There is little consecutiveness in dates. They run any time within nearly five or six years. Each was carelessly pencilled in the open air, at the time and place. The printers will learn this to some vexation perhaps, as much of their copy is from those hastily-written first notes.

BIRDS MIGRATING AT MIDNIGHT

Did you ever chance to hear the midnight flight of birds passing through the air and darkness overhead, in countless armies, changing their early or late summer habitat? It is something not to be forgotten. A friend called me up just after 12 last night to mark the peculiar noise of unusually immense flocks migrating north (rather late this year.) In the silence, shadow and delicious odor of the hour, (the natural perfume belonging to the night alone,) I thought it rare music. You could *hear* the characteristic motion—once or twice "the rush of mighty wings," but oftener a velvety rustle, long drawn out—sometimes quite near—with continual calls and chirps, and some song-notes. It all lasted from 12 till after 3. Once in a while the species was plainly distinguishable; I could make out the bobolink, tanager, Wilson's thrush, white-crown'd sparrow, and occasionally from high in the air came the notes of the plover.

BUMBLE-BEES

May-month—month of swarming, singing, mating birds—the bumble-bee month—month of the flowering lilac—(and then my own birth-month.) As I jot this paragraph, I am out just after sunrise, and down towards the creek. The lights, perfumes, melodies—the blue birds, grass birds and robins, in every direction—the noisy, vocal, natural concert. For undertones, a neighboring wood-pecker tapping his tree, and the distant clarion of chanticleer. Then the fresh earth smells—the colors, the delicate drabs and thin blues of the perspective. The bright green of the grass has receiv'd an added tinge from the last two days' mildness and moisture. How the sun silently mounts in the broad, clear sky, on his day's journey! How the warm beams bathe all, and come streaming kissingly and almost hot on my face.

A while since the croaking of the pond frogs and the first white of the dog-wood blossoms. Now the golden dandelions in endless profusion, spotting the ground everywhere. The white cherry and pear-blows—the wild violets, with their blue eyes looking up and saluting my feet, as I saunter the wood-edge—the rosy blush of budding apple-trees—the light-clear emerald hue of the wheat-fields—the darker green of the rye—a warm elasticity pervading the air—the cedar-bushes profusely deck'd with their little brown apples—the summer fully awakening—the convocation of black birds, garrulous flocks of them, gathering on some tree, and making the hour and place noisy as I sit near.

Later.—Nature marches in procession, in sections, like the corps of an army. All have done much for me, and still do. But for the last two days it has been the great wild bee, the humble-bee, or "bumble," as the children call him. As I walk, or hobble, from the farm-house down to the creek, I traverse the before-mention'd lane, fenced by old rails, with many splits, splinters, breaks, holes, &c., the choice habitat of those crooning, hairy insects. Up and down and by and between these rails, they swarm and dart and fly in countless myriads. As I wend slowly along, I am often accompanied with a moving cloud of them. They play a leading part in my morning, midday or sunset rambles, and often dominate the landscape in a way I never before thought of—fill the long lane, not by scores or hundreds only, but by thousands. Large and vivacious and swift, with wonderful momentum and a loud swelling perpetual hum, varied now and then by something almost like a shriek, they dart to and fro, in rapid flashes, chasing each other, and (little things as they are,) conveying to me a new and pronounc'd sense of strength, beauty, vitality and movement. Are they in their mating season? or what is the meaning of this plenitude, swiftness, eagerness, display? As I walk'd, I thought I was follow'd by a particular swarm, but upon observation I saw that it was a rapid succession of changing swarms, one after another.

As I write, I am seated under a big wild-cherry tree—the warm day temper'd by partial clouds and a fresh breeze, neither too heavy nor light—and here I sit long and long, envelop'd in the deep musical drone of these bees, flitting, balancing, darting to and fro about me by hundreds—big fellows with light yellow jackets, great glistening swelling bodies, stumpy heads and gauzy wings—humming their perpetual rich mellow boom. (Is there not a hint in it for a musical composition, of which it should be the back-ground? some bumble-bee symphony?) How it all nourishes, lulls me, in the way most needed; the open air, the rye-fields, the apple orchards. The last two days have been faultless in sun, breeze, temperature and everything; never two more perfect days, and I have enjoy'd them wonderfully. My health is somewhat better, and my spirit at peace. (Yet the anniversary of the saddest loss and sorrow of my life is close at hand.)

Another jotting, another perfect day: forenoon, from 7 to 9, two hours envelop'd in sound of bumble-bees and bird-music. Down in the apple-trees and in a neighboring cedar were three or four russet-back'd thrushes, each singing his best, and roulading in ways I never heard surpass'd. Two hours I abandon myself to hearing them, and indolently absorbing the scene. Almost every bird I notice has a special time in the year—sometimes limited to a few days—when it sings its best; and now is the period of these russet-backs. Meanwhile, up and down the lane, the darting, droning, musical bumble-bees. A great swarm again for my entourage as I return home, moving along with me as before.

As I write this, two or three weeks later, I am sitting near the brook under a tulip tree, 70 feet high, thick with the fresh verdure of its young maturity—a beautiful object—every branch, every leaf perfect. From top to bottom, seeking the sweet juice in the blossoms, it swarms with myriads of these wild bees, whose loud and steady humming makes an undertone to the whole, and to my mood and the hour. All of which I will bring to a close by extracting the following verses from Henry A. Beer's little volume:

> "As I lay yonder in tall grass
> A drunken bumble-bee went past
> Delirious with honey toddy.
> The golden sash about his body
> Scarce kept it in his swollen belly
> Distent with honeysuckle jelly.
> Rose liquor and the sweet-pea wine
> Had fill'd his soul with song divine;
> Deep had he drunk the warm night through,
> His hairy thighs were wet with dew.
> Full many an antic he had play'd
> While the world went round through sleep and shade.
> Oft had he lit with thirsty lip
> Some flower-cup's nectar'd sweets to sip,
> When on smooth petals he would slip,
> Or over tangled stamens trip,
> And headlong in the pollen roll'd,
> Crawl out quite dusted o'er with gold;
> Or else his heavy feet would stumble
> Against some bud, and down he'd tumble
> Amongst the grass; there lie and grumble
> In low, soft bass—poor maudlin bumble!"

CEDAR-APPLES

As I journey'd to-day in a light wagon ten or twelve miles through the country, nothing pleas'd me more, in their homely beauty and novelty (I had either never seen the little things to such advantage, or had never noticed them before) than that peculiar fruit, with its profuse clear-yellow dangles of inch-long silk or yarn, in boundless profusion spotting the dark-green cedar bushes—contrasting well with their bronze tufts—the flossy shreds covering the knobs all over, like a shock of wild hair on elfin pates. On my ramble afterward down by the creek I pluck'd one from its bush, and shall keep it. These cedar-apples last only a little while however, and soon crumble and fade.

SUMMER SIGHTS AND INDOLENCIES

June 10th.—As I write, 5½ P. M., here by the creek, nothing can exceed the quiet splendor and freshness around me. We had a heavy shower, with brief thunder and lightning, in the middle of the day; and since, overhead, one of those not uncommon yet indescribable skies (in quality, not details or forms) of limpid blue, with rolling silver-fringed clouds, and a pure-dazzling sun. For underlay, trees in fulness of tender foliage—liquid, reedy, long-drawn notes of birds—based by the fretful mewing of a querulous cat-bird, and the pleasant chippering-shriek of two kingfishers. I have been watching the latter the last half hour, on their regular evening frolic over and in the stream; evidently a spree of the liveliest kind. They pursue each other, whirling and wheeling around, with many a jocund downward dip, splashing the spray in jets of diamonds—and then off they swoop, with slanting wings and graceful flight, sometimes so near me I can plainly see their dark-gray feather-bodies and milk-white necks.

SUNDOWN PERFUME—QUAIL-NOTES—THE HERMIT-THRUSH

June 19th, 4 to 6½ P. M.—Sitting alone by the creek—solitude here, but the scene bright and vivid enough—the sun shining, and quite a fresh wind blowing (some heavy showers last night,) the grass and trees looking their best—the clear-obscure of different greens, shadows, half-shadows, and the dappling glimpses of the water, through recesses—the wild flageolet-note of a quail near by— the just-heard fretting of some hylas down there in the pond— crows cawing in the distance—a drove of young hogs rooting in soft ground near the oak under which I sit—some come sniffing near me, and then scamper away, with grunts. And still the clear notes of the quail—the quiver of leaf-shadows over the paper as I write—the sky aloft, with white clouds, and the sun well declining to the west—the swift darting of many sand-swallows coming and going, their holes in a neighboring marl-bank—the odor of the cedar and oak, so palpable, as evening approaches—perfume, color, the bronze-and-gold of nearly ripen'd wheat—clover-fields, with honey-scent—the well-up maize, with long and rustling leaves—the great patches of thriving potatoes, dusky green, fleck'd all over with white blossoms—the old, warty, venerable oak above me—and ever, mix'd with the dual notes of the quail, the soughing of the wind through some near-by pines.

As I rise for return, I linger long to a delicious song-epilogue (is it the hermit-thrush?) from some bushy recess off there in the swamp, repeated leisurely and pensively over and over again. This, to the circle-gambols of the swallows flying by dozens in concentric rings in the last rays of sunset, like flashes of some airy wheel.

A JULY AFTERNOON BY THE POND

The fervent heat, but so much more endurable in this pure air—the white and pink pond-blossoms, with great heart-shaped leaves; the glassy waters of the creek, the banks, with dense bushery, and the picturesque beeches and shade and turf; the tremulous, reedy call of some bird from recesses, breaking the warm, indolent, half-voluptuous silence; an occasional wasp, hornet, honey-bee or bumble (they hover near my hands or face, yet annoy me not, nor I them, as they appear to examine, find nothing, and away they go)—the vast space of the sky overhead so clear, and the buzzard up there sailing his slow whirl in majestic spirals and discs; just over the surface of the pond, two large slate-color'd dragon-flies, with wings of lace, circling and darting and occasionally balancing themselves quite still, their wings quivering all the time, (are they not showing off for my amusement?)—the pond itself, with the sword-shaped calamus; the water snakes—occasionally a flitting blackbird, with red dabs on his shoulders, as he darts slantingly by—the sounds that bring out the solitude, warmth, light and shade—the quawk of some pond duck—(the crickets and grasshoppers are mute in the noon heat, but I hear the song of the first cicadas;)—then at some distance the rattle and whirr of a reaping machine as the horses draw it on a rapid walk through a rye field on the opposite side of the creek—(what was the yellow or light-brown bird, large as a young hen, with short neck and long-stretch'd legs I just saw, in flapping and awkward flight over there through the trees?)—the prevailing delicate, yet palpable, spicy, grassy, clovery perfume to my nostrils; and over all, encircling all, to my sight and soul, the free space of the sky, transparent and blue—and hovering there in the west, a mass of white-gray fleecy clouds the sailors call "shoals of mackerel"—the sky, with silver swirls like locks of toss'd hair, spreading, expanding—a vast voiceless, formless simulacrum—yet may-be the most real reality and formulator of everything—who knows?

LOCUSTS AND KATYDIDS

Aug. 22.—Reedy monotones of locust, or sounds of katydid—I hear the latter at night, and the other both day and night. I thought the morning and evening warble of birds delightful; but I find I can listen to these strange insects with just as much pleasure. A single locust is now heard near noon from a tree two hundred feet off, as I write—a long whirring, continued, quite loud noise graded in distinct whirls, or swinging circles, increasing in strength and rapidity up to a certain point, and then a fluttering, quietly tapering fall.

Each strain is continued from one to two minutes. The locust-song is very appropriate to the scene—gushes, has meaning, is masculine, is like some fine old wine, not sweet, but far better than sweet.

But the katydid—how shall I describe its piquant utterances? One sings from a willow-tree just outside my open bedroom window, twenty yards distant; every clear night for a fortnight past has sooth'd me to sleep. I rode through a piece of woods for a hundred rods the other evening, and heard the katydids by myriads—very curious for once; but I like better my single neighbor on the tree.

Let me say more about the song of the locust, even to repetition; a long, chromatic, tremulous crescendo, like a brass disk whirling round and round, emitting wave after wave of notes, beginning with a certain moderate beat or measure, rapidly increasing in speed and emphasis, reaching a point of great energy and significance, and then quickly and gracefully dropping down and out. Not the melody of the singing-bird—far from it; the common musician might think without melody, but surely having to the finer ear a harmony of its own; monotonous—but what a swing there is in that brassy drone, round and round, cymball ne—or like the whirling of brass quoits.

THE LESSON OF A TREE

Sept 1.—I should not take either the biggest or the most picturesque tree to illustrate it. Here is one of my favorites now before me, a fine yellow poplar, quite straight, perhaps 90 feet high, and four thick at the butt. How strong, vital, enduring! how dumbly eloquent! What suggestions of imperturbability and *being*, as against the human trait of mere *seeming*. Then the qualities, almost emotional, palpably artistic, heroic, of a tree; so innocent and harmless, yet so savage. It *is*, yet says nothing. How it rebukes by its tough and equable serenity all weathers, this gusty-temper'd little whiffet, man, that runs indoors at a mite of rain or snow. Science (or rather half-way science) scoffs at reminiscence of dryad and hamadryad, and of trees speaking. But, if they don't, they do as well as most speaking, writing, poetry, sermons—or rather they do a great deal better. I should say indeed that those old dryad-reminiscences are quite as true as any, and profounder than most reminiscences we get. ("Cut this out," as the quack mediciners say, and keep by you.) Go and sit in a grove or woods, with one or more of those voiceless companions, and read the foregoing, and think.

One lesson from affiliating a tree—perhaps the greatest moral lesson anyhow from earth, rocks, animals, is that same lesson of inherency, of *what is*, without the least regard to what the looker on (the critic) supposes or says, or whether he likes or dislikes. What worse—what more general malady pervades each and all of us, our literature, education, attitude toward each other, (even toward ourselves,) than a morbid trouble about *seems*, (generally temporarily seems too,) and no trouble at all, or hardly any, about the sane, slow-growing, perennial, real parts of character, books, friendship, marriage—humanity's invisible foundations and hold-together? (As the all-basis, the nerve, the great-sympathetic, the plenum within humanity, giving stamp to everything, is necessarily invisible.)

Aug. 4, 6 P. M.—Lights and shades and rare effects on tree-foliage and grass—transparent greens, grays, &c., all in sunset pomp and dazzle. The clear beams are now thrown in many new places, on the quilted, seam'd, bronze-drab, lower tree-trunks, shadow'd except at this hour—now flooding their young and old columnar rugged-ness with strong light, unfolding to my sense new amazing features of silent, shaggy charm, the solid bark, the expression of harmless impassiveness, with many a bulge and gnarl unreck'd before. In the revealings of such light, such exceptional hour, such mood, one does not wonder at the old story fables, (indeed, why fables?) of people falling into love-sickness with trees, seiz'd extatic with the mystic realism of the resistless silent strength in them—*strength*, which after all is perhaps the last, completest, highest beauty.

Trees I am familiar with here

Oaks, (many kinds—one sturdy old fellow, vital, green, bushy, five feet thick at the butt, I sit under every day.)
Cedars, plenty.
Tulip·trees, (*Liriodendron*, is of the magnolia family—I have seen it in Michigan and south-ern Illinois, 140 feet high and 8 feet thick at the butt*; does not transplant well; best rais'd from seeds—the lumbermen call it yellow poplar.)
Sycamores.
Gum-trees, both sweet and sour.
Beeches.

---

* There is a tulip poplar within sight of Woodstown, which is twenty feet around, three feet from the ground, four feet across about eighteen feet up the trunk, which is broken off about three or four feet higher up. On the south side an arm has shot out from which rise two stems, each to about ninety-one or ninety-two feet from the ground. Twenty-five (or more) years since the cavity in the butt was large enough for, and nine men at one time, ate dinner therein. It is supposed twelve to fifteen men could now, at one time, stand within its trunk. The severe winds of 1877 and 1878 did not seem to damage it, and the two stems send out yearly many blossoms, scenting the air immedi-ately about it with their sweet perfume. It is entirely unprotected by other trees, on a hill.—*Woodstown, N. J.*, "*Register*," *April 15, '79.*

Black-walnuts.	Dogwood.
Sassafras.	Pine.
Willows.	the Elm.
Catalpas.	Chestnut.
Persimmons.	Linden.
Mountain-ash.	Aspen.
Hickories.	Spruce.
Maples, many kinds.	Hornbeam.
Locusts.	Laurel.
Birches.	Holly.

AUTUMN SIDE-BITS

Sept. 20.—Under an old black oak, glossy and green, exhaling aroma—amid a grove the Albic druids might have chosen—envelop'd in the warmth and light of the noonday sun, and swarms of flitting insects—with the harsh cawing of many crows a hundred rods away—here I sit in solitude, absorbing, enjoying all. The corn, stack'd in its cone-shaped stacks, russet-color'd and sere—a large field spotted thick with scarlet-gold pumpkins—an adjoining one of cabbages, showing well in their green and pearl, mottled by much light and shade—melon patches, with their bulging ovals, and great silver-streak'd, ruffled, broad-edged leaves—and many an autumn sight and sound beside—the distant scream of a flock of guinea-hens—and pour'd over all the September breeze, with pensive cadence through the tree tops.

Another Day.—The ground in all directions strew'd with *debris* from a storm. Timber creek, as I slowly pace its banks, has ebb'd low, and shows reaction from the turbulent swell of the late equinoctial. As I look around, I take account of stock—weeds and shrubs, knolls, paths, occasional stumps, some with smooth'd tops, (several I use as seats of rest, from place to place, and from one I am now jotting these lines,)—frequent wildflowers, little white, star-shaped things, or the cardinal red of the lobelia, or the cherry-ball seeds of the perennial rose, or the many-threaded vines winding up and around trunks of trees.

Oct. 1, 2, and 3.—Down every day in the solitude of the creek. A serene autumn sun and westerly breeze today (3d) as I sit here, the water surface prettily moving in wind-ripples before me. On a stout old beech at the edge, decayed and slanting, almost fallen to the stream, yet with life and leaves in its mossy limbs, a gray squirrel, exploring, runs up and down, flirts his tail, leaps to the ground, sits on his haunches upright as he sees me, (a Darwinian hint?) and then races up the tree again.

Oct. 4—Cloudy and coolish; signs of incipient winter. Yet pleasant here, the leaves thick-falling, the ground brown with them already; rich coloring, yellows of all hues, pale and dark-green, shades from lightest to richest red—all set in and toned down by the prevailing brown of the earth and gray of the sky. So, winter is coming; and I yet in my sickness. I sit here amid all these fair sights and vital influences, and abandon myself to that thought, with its wandering trains of speculation.

THE SKY—DAYS AND NIGHTS—HAPPINESS

Oct. 20.—A clear, crispy day—dry and breezy air, full of oxygen. Out of the sane, silent, beauteous miracles that envelope and fuse me—trees, water, grass, sunlight, and early frost—the one I am looking at most to-day is the sky. It has that delicate, transparent blue, peculiar to autumn, and the only clouds are little or larger white ones, giving their still and spiritual motion to the great concave. All through the earlier day (say from 7 to 11) it keeps a pure, yet vivid blue. But as noon approaches the color gets lighter, quite gray for two or three hours—then still paler for a spell, till sundown—which last I watch dazzling through the interstices of a knoll of big trees—darts of fire and a gorgeous show of light-yellow, liver-color and red, with a vast silver glaze askant on the water—the transparent shadows, shafts, sparkle, and vivid colors beyond all the paintings ever made.

I don't know what or how, but it seems to me mostly owing to these skies, (every now and then I think, while I have of course seen them every day of my life, I never really saw the skies before,) I have had this autumn some wondrously contented hours—may I not say perfectly happy ones? As I've read, Byron just before his death told a friend that he had known but three happy hours during his whole existence. Then there is the old German legend of the king's bell, to the same point. While I was out there by the wood, that beautiful sunset through the trees, I thought of Byron's and the bell story, and the notion started in me that I was having a happy hour. (Though perhaps my best moments I never jot down; when they come I cannot afford to break the charm by inditing memoranda. I just abandon myself to the mood, and let it float on, carrying me in its placid extasy.)

What is happiness, anyhow? Is this one of its hours, or the like of it?—so impalpable—a mere breath, an evanescent tinge? I am not sure—so let me give myself the benefit of the doubt. Hast

Thou, pellucid, in Thy azure depths, medicine for case like mine?
(Ah, the physical shatter and troubled spirit of me the last three
years.) And dost Thou subtly mystically now drip it through the
air invisibly upon me?

Night of Oct. 28.—The heavens unusually transparent—the stars
out by myriads—the great path of the Milky Way, with its branch,
only seen of very clear nights—Jupiter, setting in the west, looks
like a huge hap-hazard splash, and has a little star for companion.

> Clothed in his white garments,
> Into the round and clear arena slowly entered the brahmin,
> Holding a little child by the hand,
> Like the moon with the planet Jupiter in a cloudless night-sky.
> *Old Hindu Poem*

Early in November.—At its farther end the lane already described
opens into a broad grassy upland field of over twenty acres, slightly
sloping to the south. Here I am accustom'd to walk for sky views
and effects, either morning or sundown. To-day from this field my
soul is calm'd and expanded beyond description, the whole forenoon by the clear blue arching over all, cloudless, nothing particular, only sky and daylight. Their soothing accompaniments,
autumn leaves, the cool dry air, the faint aroma—crows cawing in
the distance—two great buzzards wheeling gracefully and slowly
far up there—the occasional murmur of the wind, sometimes quite
gently, then threatening through the trees—a gang of farm-laborers
loading corn-stalks in a field in sight, and the patient horses waiting.

COLORS—A CONTRAST

Such a play of colors and lights, different seasons, different hours
of the day—the lines of the far horizon where the faint-tinged edge
of the landscape loses itself in the sky. As I slowly hobble up the
lane toward day-close, an incomparable sunset shooting in molten
sapphire and gold, shaft after shaft, through the ranks of the long-
leaved corn, between me and the west.

Another day.—The rich dark green of the tulip-trees and the oaks,
the gray of the swamp-willows, the dull hues of the sycamores and
black-walnuts, the emerald of the cedars (after rain,) and the light
yellow of the beeches.

NOVEMBER 8, '76

The forenoon leaden and cloudy, not cold or wet, but indicating
both. As I hobble down here and sit by the silent pond, how different

from the excitement amid which, in the cities, millions of people are now waiting news of yesterday's Presidential election, or receiving and discussing the result—in this secluded place uncared-for, unknown.

CROWS AND CROWS

Nov. 14.—As I sit here by the creek, resting after my walk, a warm languor bathes me from the sun. No sound but a cawing of crows, and no motion but their black flying figures from overhead, reflected in the mirror of the pond below. Indeed a principal feature of the scene to-day is these crows, their incessant cawing, far or near, and their countless flocks and processions moving from place to place, and at times almost darkening the air with their myriads. As I sit a moment writing this by the bank, I see the black, clear-cut reflection of them far below, flying through the watery looking-glass, by ones, twos, or long strings. All last night I heard the noises from their great roost in a neighboring wood.

A WINTER DAY ON THE SEA-BEACH

One bright December mid-day lately I spent down on the New Jersey sea-shore, reaching it by a little more than an hour's railroad trip over the old Camden and Atlantic. I had started betimes, fortified by nice strong coffee and a good breakfast (cook'd by the hands I love, my dear sister Lou's—how much better it makes the victuals taste, and then assimilate, strengthen you, perhaps make the whole day comfortable afterwards.) Five or six miles at the last, our track enter'd a broad region of salt grass meadows, intersected by lagoons, and cut up everywhere by watery runs. The sedgy perfume, delightful to my nostrils, reminded me of "the mash" and south bay of my native island. I could have journey'd contentedly till night through these flat and odorous sea-prairies. From half-past 11 till 2 I was nearly all the time along the beach, or in sight of the ocean, listening to its hoarse murmur, and inhaling the bracing and welcome breezes. First, a rapid five-mile drive over the hard sand—our carriage wheels hardly made dents in it. Then after dinner (as there were nearly two hours to spare) I walk'd off in another direction, (hardly met or saw a person,) and taking possession of what appear'd to have been the reception-room of an old bath-house range, had a broad expanse of view all to myself—quaint, refreshing, unimpeded—a dry area of sedge and Indian grass immediately before and around me—space, simple, unornamented space. Distant vessels, and the far-off, just visible trailing smoke of an inward bound

steamer; more plainly, ships, brigs, schooners, in sight, most of
them with every sail set to the firm and steady wind.

The attractions, fascinations there are in sea and shore! How
one dwells on their simplicity, even vacuity! What is it in us, arous'd
by those indirections and directions? That spread of waves and
gray-white beach, salt, monotonous, senseless—such an entire absence of art, books, talk, elegance—so indescribably comforting,
even this winter day—grim, yet so delicate-looking, so spiritual—
striking emotional, impalpable depths, subtler than all the poems,
paintings, music, I have ever read, seen, heard. (Yet let me be fair,
perhaps it is because I have read those poems and heard that
music.)

SEA-SHORE FANCIES

Even as a boy, I had the fancy, the wish, to write a piece, perhaps
a poem, about the sea-shore—that suggesting, dividing line, contact, junction, the solid marrying the liquid—that curious, lurking
something, (as doubtless every objective form finally becomes to
the subjective spirit,) which means far more than its mere first sight,
grand as that is—blending the real and ideal, and each made portion
of the other. Hours, days, in my Long Island youth and early
manhood, I haunted the shores of Rockaway or Coney island, or
away east to the Hamptons or Montauk. Once, at the latter place,
(by the old lighthouse, nothing but sea-tossings in sight in every
direction as far as the eye could reach,) I remember well, I felt that
I must one day write a book expressing this liquid, mystic theme.
Afterward, I recollect, how it came to me that instead of any special
lyrical or epical or literary attempt, the sea-shore should be an
invisible *influence*, a pervading gauge and tally for me, in my composition. (Let me give a hint here to young writers. I am not sure
but I have unwittingly follow'd out the same rule with other powers
besides sea and shores—avoiding them, in the way of any dead set
at poetizing them, as too big for formal handling—quite satisfied
if I could indirectly show that we have met and fused, even if only
once, but enough—that we have really aborb'd each other and
understand each other.)

There is a dream, a picture, that for years at intervals, (sometimes quite long ones, but surely again, in time,) has come noiselessly up before me, and I really believe, fiction as it is, has enter'd
largely into my practical life—certainly into my writings, and shaped
and color'd them. It is nothing more or less than a stretch of interminable white-brown sand, hard and smooth and broad, with

the ocean perpetually, grandly, rolling in upon it, with slow-measured sweep, with rustle and hiss and foam, and many a thump as of low bass drums. This scene, this picture, I say, has risen before me at times for years. Sometimes I wake at night and can hear and see it plainly.

IN MEMORY OF THOMAS PAINE

Spoken at Lincoln Hall, Philadelphia, Sunday, Jan. 28, '77, for 140th anniversary of T. P.'s birth-day.

Some thirty-five years ago, in New York city, at Tammany hall, of which place I was then a frequenter, I happen'd to become quite well acquainted with Thomas Paine's perhaps most intimate chum, and certainly his later years' very frequent companion, a remarkably fine old man, Col. Fellows, who may yet be remember'd by some stray relics of that period and spot. If you will allow me, I will first give a description of the Colonel himself. He was tall, of military bearing, aged about 78 I should think, hair white as snow, clean-shaved on the face, dress'd very neatly, a tail-coat of blue cloth with metal buttons, buff vest, pantaloons of drab color, and his neck, breast and wrists showing the whitest of linen. Under all circumstances, fine manners; a good but not profuse talker, his wits still fully about him, balanced and live and undimm'd as ever. He kept pretty fair health, though so old. For employment—for he was poor—he had a post as constable of some of the upper courts. I used to think him very picturesque on the fringe of a crowd holding a tall staff, with his erect form, and his superb, bare, thick-hair'd, closely-cropt white head. The judges and young lawyers, with whom he was ever a favorite, and the subject of respect, used to call him Aristides. It was the general opinion among them that if manly rectitude and the instincts of absolute justice remain'd vital anywhere about New York City Hall, or Tammany, they were to be found in Col. Fellows. He liked young men, and enjoy'd to leisurely talk with them over a social glass of toddy, after his day's work, (he on these occasions never drank but one glass,) and it was at reiterated meetings of this kind in old Tammany's back parlor of those days, that he told me much about Thomas Paine. At one of our interviews he gave me a minute account of Paine's sickness and death. In short, from those talks, I was and am satisfied that my old friend, with his mark'd advantages, had mentally, morally and emotionally gauged the author of "Common Sense," and besides giving me a good portrait of his appearance and manners, had taken the true measure of his interior character.

Paine's practical demeanor, and much of his theoretical belief, was a mixture of the French and English schools of a century ago, and the best of both. Like most old-fashion'd people, he drank a glass or two every day, but was no tippler, nor intemperate, let alone being a drunkard. He lived simply and economically, but quite well—was always cheery and courteous, perhaps occasionally a little blunt, having very positive opinions upon politics, religion, and so forth. That he labor'd well and wisely for the States in the trying period of their parturition, and in the seeds of their character, there seems to me no question. I dare not say how much of what our Union is owning and enjoying to-day—its independence—its ardent belief in, and substantial practice of, radical human rights—and the severance of its government from all ecclesiastical and superstitious dominion—I dare not say how much of all this is owing to Thomas Paine, but I am inclined to think a good portion of it decidedly is.

But I was not going either into an analysis or eulogium of the man. I wanted to carry you back a generation or two, and give you by indirection a moment's glance—and also to ventilate a very earnest and I believe authentic opinion, nay conviction, of that time, the fruit of the interviews I have mention'd, and of questioning and cross-questioning, clench'd by my best information since, that Thomas Paine had a noble personality, as exhibited in presence, face, voice, dress, manner, and what may be call'd his atmosphere and magnetism, especially the later years of his life. I am sure of it. Of the foul and foolish fictions yet told about the circumstances of his decease, the absolute fact is that as he lived a good life, after its kind, he died calmly and philosophically, as became him. He served the embryo Union with most precious service—a service that every man, woman and child in our thirty-eight States is to some extent receiving the benefit of to-day—and I for one here cheerfully, reverently throw my pebble on the cairn of his memory. As we all know, the season demands—or rather, will it ever be out of season? —that America learn to better dwell on her choicest possession, the legacy of her good and faithful men—that she well preserve their fame, if unquestion'd—or, if need be, that she fail not to dissipate what clouds have intruded on that fame, and burnish it newer, truer and brighter, continually.

A TWO HOURS' ICE-SAIL

Feb. 3, '77.—From 4 to 6 P. M. crossing the Delaware, (back again at my Camden home,) unable to make our landing, through the ice; our boat stanch and strong and skilfully piloted, but old and sulky, and poorly minding her helm. (*Power*, so important in poetry and war, is also first point of all in a winter steamboat, with long stretches of ice-packs to tackle.) For over two hours we bump'd and beat about, the invisible ebb, sluggish but irresistible, often carrying us long distances against our will. In the first tinge of dusk, as I look'd around, I thought there could not be presented a more chilling, arctic, grim-extended, depressing scene. Everything was yet plainly visible; for miles north and south, ice, ice, ice, mostly broken, but some big cakes, and no clear water in sight. The shores, piers, surfaces, roofs, shipping, mantled with snow. A faint winter vapor hung a fitting accompaniment around and over the endless whitish spread, and gave it just a tinge of steel and brown.

Feb. 6.—As I cross home in the 6 P. M. boat again, the transparent shadows are filled everywhere with leisurely falling, slightly slanting, curiously sparse but very large, flakes of snow. On the shores, near and far, the glow of just-lit gas-clusters at intervals. The ice, sometimes in hummocks, sometimes floating fields, through which our boat goes crunching. The light permeated by that peculiar evening haze, right after sunset, which sometimes renders quite distant objects so distinctly.

SPRING OVERTURES—RECREATIONS

Feb. 10.—The first chirping, almost singing, of a bird to-day. Then I noticed a couple of honey-bees spirting and humming about the open window in the sun.

Feb. 11.—In the soft rose and pale gold of the declining light, this beautiful evening, I heard the first hum and preparation of awakening spring—very faint—whether in the earth or roots, or starting of insects, I know not—but it was audible, as I lean'd on a rail (I am down in my country quarters awhile,) and look'd long at the western horizon. Turning to the east, Sirius, as the shadows deeppen'd, came forth in dazzling splendor. And great Orion; and a little to the north-east the big Dipper, standing on end.

Feb. 20.—A solitary and pleasant sundown hour at the pond, exercising arms, chest, my whole body, by a tough oak sapling thick as my wrist, twelve feet high—pulling and pushing, inspiring the good air. After I wrestle with the tree awhile, I can feel its young sap and virtue welling up out of the ground and tingling through me from crown to toe, like health's wine. Then for addition and variety I launch forth in my vocalism; shout declamatory pieces, sentiments, sorrow, anger, &c., from the stock poets or plays—or inflate my lungs and sing the wild tunes and refrains I heard of the blacks down south, or patriotic songs I learn'd in the army. I make the echoes ring, I tell you! As the twilight fell, in a pause of these ebullitions, an owl somewhere the other side of the creek sounded *too-oo-oo-oo-oo*, soft and pensive (and I fancied a little sarcastic) repeated four or five times. Either to applaud the negro songs—or perhaps an ironical comment on the sorrow, anger, or style of the stock poets.

ONE OF THE HUMAN KINKS

How is it that in all the serenity and lonesomeness of solitude, away off here amid the hush of the forest, alone, or as I have found in prairie wilds, or mountain stillness, one is never entirely without the instinct of looking around, (I never am, and others tell me the same of themselves, confidentially,) for somebody to appear, or start up out of the earth, or from behind some tree or rock? Is it a lingering, inherited remains of man's primitive wariness, from the wild animals? or from his savage ancestry far back? It is not at all nervousness or fear. Seems as if something unknown were possibly lurking in those bushes, or solitary places. Nay, it is quite certain there is—some vital unseen presence.

AN AFTERNOON SCENE

Feb. 22.—Last night and to-day rainy and thick, till mid-afternoon, when the wind chopp'd round, the clouds swiftly drew off like curtains, the clear appear'd, and with it the fairest, grandest, most wondrous rainbow I ever saw, all complete, very vivid at its earth-ends, spreading vast effusions of illuminated haze, violet, yellow, drab-green, in all directions overhead, through which the sun beam'd—an indescribable utterance of color and light, so gorgeous yet so soft, such as I had never witness'd before. Then its continuance: a full hour pass'd before the last of those earth-ends disappear'd. The sky behind was all spread in translucent blue, with many little white clouds and edges. To these a sunset, filling, dominating the esthetic and soul senses, sumptuously, tenderly, full. I end this note by the pond, just light enough to see, through the evening shadows, the western reflections in its water-mirror surface, with inverted figures of trees. I hear now and then the *flup* of a pike leaping out, and rippling the water.

THE GATES OPENING

April 6.—Palpable spring indeed, or the indications of it. I am sitting in bright sunshine, at the edge of the creek, the surface just rippled by the wind. All is solitude, morning freshness, negligence. For companions my two kingfishers sailing, winding, darting, dipping, sometimes capriciously separate, then flying together. I hear their guttural twittering again and again; for awhile nothing but that peculiar sound. As noon approaches other birds warm up. The reedy notes of the robin, and a musical passage of two parts, one a clear delicious gurgle, with several other birds I cannot place. To which is join'd, (yes, I just hear it,) one low purr at intervals from some impatient hylas at the pond-edge. The sibilant murmur of a pretty stiff breeze now and then through the trees. Then a poor little dead leaf, long frost-bound, whirls from somewhere up aloft in one wild escaped freedom-spree in space and sunlight, and then dashes down to the waters, which hold it closely and soon drown it out of sight. The bushes and trees are yet bare, but the beeches have their wrinkled yellow leaves of last season's foliage largely left, frequent cedars and pines yet green, and the grass not without proofs of coming fulness. And over all a wonderfully fine dome of clear blue, the play of light coming and going, and great fleeces of white clouds swimming so silently.

THE COMMON EARTH, THE SOIL

The soil, too—let others pen-and-ink the sea, the air, (as I sometimes try)—but now I feel to choose the common soil for theme—naught else. The brown soil here, (just between winter-close and opening spring and vegetation)—the rain-shower at night, and the fresh smell next morning—the red worms wriggling out of the ground—the dead leaves, the incipient grass, and the latent life underneath—the effort to start something—already in shelter'd spots some little flowers—the distant emerald show of winter wheat and the rye fields—the yet naked trees, with clear interstices, giving prospects hidden in summer—the tough fallow and the plow-team, and the stout boy whistling to his horses for encouragement—and there the dark fat earth in long slanting stripes upturn'd.

BIRDS AND BIRDS AND BIRDS

A little later—bright weather.—An unusual melodiousness, these days, (last of April and first of May) from the blackbirds; indeed all sorts of birds, darting, whistling, hopping or perch'd on trees. Never before have I seen, heard, or been in the midst of, and got so flooded and saturated with them and their performances, as this

current month. Such oceans, such successions of them. Let me make
a list of those I find here:

Black birds (plenty,)	Meadow-larks (plenty,)
Ring doves,	Cat-birds (plenty,)
Owls,	Cuckoos,
Woodpeckers,	Pond snipes (plenty,)
King-birds,	Cheewinks,
Crows (plenty,)	Quawks,
Wrens,	Ground robins,
Kingfishers,	Ravens,
Quails,	Gray snipes,
Turkey-buzzards,	Eagles,
Hen-hawks,	High-holes,
Yellow birds,	Herons,
Thrushes,	Tits,
Reed birds,	Woodpigeons.

Early came the

Blue birds,	Meadow-lark,
Killdeer,	White-bellied swallow,
Plover,	Sandpiper,
Robin,	Wilson's thrush,
Woodcock,	Flicker.

FULL-STARR'D NIGHTS

May 21.—Back in Camden. Again commencing one of those unusually transparent, full-starr'd, blue-black nights, as if to show
that however lush and pompous the day may be, there is something
left in the not-day that can outvie it. The rarest, finest sample of
long-drawn-out clear-obscure, from sundown to 9 o'clock. I went
down to the Delaware, and cross'd and cross'd. Venus like blazing
silver well up in the west. The large pale thin crescent of the new
moon, half an hour high, sinking languidly under a bar-sinister of
cloud, and then emerging. Arcturus right overhead. A faint fragrant
sea-odor wafted up from the south. The gloaming, the temper'd
coolness, with every feature of the scene, indescribably soothing
and tonic—one of those hours that give hints to the soul, impossible
to put in a statement. (Ah, where would be any food for spirituality
without night and the stars?) The vacant spaciousness of the air,
and the veil'd blue of the heavens, seem'd miracles enough.

As the night advanc'd it changed its spirit and garments to ampler
stateliness. I was almost conscious of a definite presence, Nature
silently near. The great constellation of the Water-Serpent stretch'd
its coils over more than half the heavens. The Swan with outspread
wings was flying down the Milky Way. The northern Crown, the

Eagle, Lyra, all up there in their places. From the whole dome shot down points of light, rapport with me, through the clear blue-black. All the usual sense of motion, all animal life, seem'd discarded, seem'd a fiction; a curious power, like the placid rest of Egyptian gods, took possession, none the less potent for being impalpable. Earlier I had seen many bats, balancing in the luminous twilight, darting their black forms hither and yon over the river; but now they altogether disappear'd. The evening star and the moon had gone. Alertness and peace lay calmly couching together through the fluid universal shadows.

Aug. 26.—Bright has the day been, and my spirits an equal *forzando*. Then comes the night, different, inexpressibly pensive, with its own tender and temper'd splendor. Venus lingers in the west with a voluptuous dazzle unshown hitherto this summer. Mars rises early, and the red sulky moon, two days past her full; Jupiter at night's meridian, and the long curling-slanted Scorpion stretching full view in the south, Aretus-neck'd. Mars walks the heavens lord-paramount now; all through this month I go out after supper and watch for him; sometimes getting up at midnight to take another look at his unparallel'd lustre. (I see lately an astronomer has made out through the new Washington telescope that Mars has certainly one moon, perhaps two.) Pale and distant, but near in the heavens. Saturn precedes him.

MULLEINS AND MULLEINS

Large, placid mulleins, as summer advances, velvety in texture, of a light greenish-drab color, growing everywhere in the fields— at first earth's big rosettes in their broad-leav'd low cluster-plants, eight, ten, twenty leaves to a plant—plentiful on the fallow twenty-acre lot, at the end of the lane, and especially by the ridge-sides of the fences—then close to the ground, but soon springing up—leaves as broad as my hand, and the lower ones twice as long—so fresh and dewy in the morning—stalks now four or five, even seven or eight feet high. The farmers, I find, think the mullein a mean unworthy weed, but I have grown to a fondness for it. Every object has its lesson, enclosing the suggestion of everything else—and lately I sometimes think all is concentrated for me in these hardy, yellow-flower'd weeds. As I come down the lane early in the morning, I pause before their soft wool-like fleece and stem and broad leaves, glittering with countless diamonds. Annually for three summers now, they and I have silently return'd together; at such long intervals I stand or sit among them, musing—and woven with the rest, of so many hours and moods of partial rehabilitation—of my sane or sick spirit, here as near at peace as it can be.

DISTANT SOUNDS

The axe of the wood-cutter, the measured thud of a single thresh-ing-flail, the crowing of chanticleer in the barn-yard, (with invariable responses from other barn-yards,) and the lowing of cattle—but most of all, or far or near, the wind—through the high tree-tops, or through low bushes, laving one's face and hands so gently, this balmy-bright noon, the coolest for a long time, (Sept. 2)—I will not call it *sighing*, for to me it is always a firm, sane, cheery expression, though a monotone, giving many varieties, or swift or slow, or dense or delicate. The wind in the patch of pine woods off there—how sibilant. Or at sea, I can imagine it this moment, tossing the waves, with spirts of foam flying far, and the free whistle, and the scent of the salt—and that vast paradox somehow with all its action and restless-ness conveying a sense of eternal rest.

Other adjuncts.—But the sun and moon here and these times. As never more wonderful by day, the gorgeous orb imperial, so vast, so ardently, lovingly hot—so never a more glorious moon of nights, especially the last three or four. The great planets too—Mars never before so flaming bright, so flashing-large, with slight yellow tinge, (the astronomers say—is it true?—nearer to us than any time the past century)—and well up, lord Jupiter, (a little while since close by the moon)—and in the west, after the sun sinks, voluptuous Venus, now languid and shorn of her beams, as if from some divine excess.

A SUN-BATH—NAKEDNESS

Sunday, Aug. 27.—Another day quite free from mark'd pros-tration and pain. It seems indeed as if peace and nutriment from heaven subtly filter into me as I slowly hobble down these country lanes and across fields, in the good air—as I sit here in solitude with Nature—open, voiceless, mystic, far removed, yet palpable, eloquent Nature. I merge myself in the scene, in the perfect day. Hovering over the clear brook-water, I am sooth'd by its soft gurgle in one place, and the hoarser murmurs of its three-foot fall in another. Come, ye disconsolate, in whom any latent eligibility is left—come get the sure virtues of creek-shore, and wood and field. Two months (July and August, '77,) have I absorb'd them, and they begin to make a new man of me. Every day, seclusion—every day at least two or three hours of freedom, bathing, no talk, no bonds, no dress, no books, no *manners*.

Shall I tell you, reader, to what I attribute my already much-restored health? That I have been almost two years, off and on, without drugs and medicines, and daily in the open air. Last summer I found a particularly secluded little dell off one side by my creek, originally a large dug-out marl-pit, now abandon'd, fill'd with bushes, trees, grass, a group of willows, a straggling bank, and a spring of delicious water running right through the middle of it, with two or three little cascades. Here I retreated every hot day, and follow it up this summer. Here I realize the meaning of that old fellow who said he was seldom less alone than when alone. Never before did I get so close to Nature; never before did she come so close to me. By old habit, I pencill'd down from to time to time, almost automatically, moods, sights, hours, tints and outlines, on the spot. Let me specially record the satisfaction of this current forenoon, so serene and primitive, so conventionally exceptional, natural.

An hour or so after breakfast I wended my way down to the recesses of the aforesaid dell, which I and certain thrushes, cat-birds, &c., had all to ourselves. A light south-west wind was blowing through the tree-tops. It was just the place and time for my Adamic air-bath and flesh-brushing from head to foot. So hanging clothes on a rail near by, keeping old broadbrim straw on head and easy shoes on feet, havn't I had a good time the last two hours! First with the stiff-elastic bristles rasping arms, breast, sides, till they turn'd scarlet—then partially bathing in the clear waters of the running brook—taking everything very leisurely, with many rests and pauses—stepping about barefooted every few minutes now and then in some neighboring black ooze, for unctuous mud-bath to my feet—a brief second and third rinsing in the crystal running waters—rubbing with the fragrant towel—slow negligent promenades on the turf up and down in the sun, varied with occasional rests, and further frictions of the bristle-brush—sometimes carrying my portable chair with me from place to place, as my range is quite extensive here, nearly a hundred rods, feeling quite secure from intrusion, (and that indeed I am not at all nervous about, if it accidentally happens.)

As I walk'd slowly over the grass, the sun shone out enough to show the shadow moving with me. Somehow I seem'd to get identity with each and every thing around me, in its condition. Nature was naked, and I was also. It was too lazy, soothing, and joyous-equable to speculate about. Yet I might have thought somehow in this vein: Perhaps the inner never lost rapport we hold with earth, light, air, trees, &c., is not to be realized through eyes and mind only, but through the whole corporeal body, which I will not have blinded or bandaged any more than the eyes. Sweet, sane, still Nakedness in Nature!—ah if poor, sick, prurient humanity in cities might really know you once more! Is not nakedness then indecent? No, not inherently. It is your thought, your sophistication, your fear, your respectability, that is indecent. There come moods when these clothes of ours are not only too irksome to wear, but are themselves indecent. Perhaps indeed he or she to whom the free exhilarating extasy of nakedness in Nature has never been eligible (and how many thousands there are!) has not really known what purity is—nor what faith or art or health really is. (Probably the whole curriculum of first-class philosophy, beauty, heroism, form, illustrated by the old Hellenic race—the highest height and deepest depth known to civilization in those departments—came from their natural and religious idea of Nakedness.)

Many such hours, from time to time, the last two summers—I attribute my partial rehabilitation largely to them. Some good people may think it a feeble or half-crack'd way of spending one's time and thinking. May-be it is.

THE OAKS AND I

Sept. 5, '77.—I write this, 11 A. M., shelter'd under a dense oak by the bank, where I have taken refuge from a sudden rain. I came down here, (we had sulky drizzles all the morning, but an hour ago a lull,) for the before-mention'd daily and simple exercise I am fond of—to pull on that young hickory sapling out there—to sway and yield to its tough-limber upright stem—haply to get into my old sinews some of its elastic fibre and clear sap. I stand on the turf and take these health-pulls moderately and at intervals for nearly an hour, inhaling great draughts of fresh air. Wandering by the creek, I have three or four naturally favorable spots where I rest—besides a chair I lug with me and use for more deliberate occasions. At other spots convenient I have selected, besides the hickory just named, strong and limber boughs of beech or holly, in easy-reaching distance, for my natural gymnasia, for arms, chest, trunk-muscles. I can soon feel the sap and sinew rising through me, like mercury to heat. I hold on boughs or slender trees caressingly there in the sun and shade, wrestle with their innocent stalwartness—and *know* the virtue thereof passes from them into me. (Or may-be we interchange—may-be the trees are more aware of it all than I ever thought.)

But now pleasantly imprison'd here under the big oak—the rain dripping, and the sky cover'd with leaden clouds—nothing but the pond on one side, and the other a spread of grass, spotted with the milky blossoms of the wild carrot—the sound of an axe wielded at some distant wood-pile—yet in this dull scene, (as most folks would call it,) why am I so (almost) happy here and alone? Why would any intrusion, even from people I like, spoil the charm? But am I alone? Doubtless there comes a time—perhaps it has come to me—when one feels through his whole being, and pronouncedly the emotional part, that identity between himself subjectively and Nature objectively which Schelling and Fichte are so fond of pressing. How it is I know not, but I often realize a presence here—in clear moods I am certain of it, and neither chemistry nor reasoning nor esthetics will give the least explanation. All the past two summers it has been strengthening and nourishing my sick body and soul, as never before. Thanks, invisible physician, for thy silent delicious medicine, thy day and night, thy waters and thy airs, the banks, the grass, the trees, and e'en the weeds!

A QUINTETTE

While I have been kept by the rain under the shelter of my great oak, (perfectly dry and comfortable, to the rattle of the drops all around,) I have pencill'd off the mood of the hour in a little quintette, which I will give you:

> At vacancy with Nature,
> Acceptive and at ease,
> Distilling the present hour,
> Whatever, wherever it is,
> And over the past, oblivion.

Can you get hold of it, reader dear? and how do you like it anyhow?

THE FIRST FROST—MEMS

Where I was stopping I saw the first palpable frost, on my sunrise walk, October 6; all over the yet-green spread a light blue-gray veil, giving a new show to the entire landscape. I had but little time to notice it, for the sun rose cloudless and mellow-warm, and as I returned along the lane it had turn'd to glittering patches of wet. As I walk I notice the bursting pods of wild-cotton, (Indian hemp they call it here,) with flossy-silky contents, and dark red-brown seeds—a startled rabbit—I pull a handful of the balsamic life-everlasting and stuff it down in my trowsers-pocket for scent.

THREE YOUNG MEN'S DEATHS

December 20.—Somehow I got thinking to-day of young men's deaths—not at all sadly or sentimentally, but gravely, realistically, perhaps a little artistically. Let me give the following three cases from budgets of personal memoranda, which I have been turning over, alone in my room, and resuming and dwelling on, this rainy afternoon. Who is there to whom the theme does not come home? Then I don't know how it may be to others, but to me not only is there nothing gloomy or depressing in such cases—on the contrary, as reminiscences, I find them soothing, bracing, tonic.

ERASTUS HASKELL.—[I just transcribe verbatim from a letter written by myself in one of the army hospitals, 16 years ago, during the secession war.] *Washington, July 28, 1863.*—Dear M.,—I am writing this in the hospital, sitting by the side of a soldier, I do not expect to last many hours. His fate has been a hard one—he seems to be only about 19 or 20—Erastus Haskell, company K, 141st N. Y.—has been out about a year, and sick or half-sick more than half that time—has been down on the peninsula—was detail'd to go in the band as fifer-boy. While sick, the surgeon told him to keep up with the rest—(probably work'd and march'd too long.) He is a shy, and seems to me a very sensible boy—has fine manners—never complains—was sick down on the peninsula in an old storehouse—typhoid fever. The first week this July was brought up here—journey very bad, no accommodations, no nourishment, nothing but hard jolting, and exposure enough to make a well man sick; (these fearful journeys do the job for many)—arrived here July 11th—a silent dark-skinn'd Spanish-looking youth, with large very dark blue eyes, peculiar looking. Doctor F. here made light of his sickness—said he would recover soon, &c.; but I thought very different, and told F. so repeatedly; (I came near quarreling with him about it from the first)—but he laugh'd and would not listen to me. About four days ago, I told Doctor he would in my opinion lose the boy without doubt—but F. again laugh'd at me. The next day he changed his opinion—I brought the head surgeon of the post—he said the boy would probably die, but they would make a hard fight for him.

The last two days he has been lying panting for breath—a pitiful sight. I have been with him some every day or night since he arrived. He suffers a great deal with the heat—says little or nothing—is flighty the last three days, at times—knows me always, however—calls me "Walter"—(sometimes calls the name over and over and over again, musingly, abstractedly, to himself.) His father lives at Breesport, Chemung county, N. Y., is a mechanic with large family—is a steady, religous man; his mother too is living. I have written to them, and shall write again to-day—Erastus has not receiv'd a word from home for months.

As I sit here writing to you, M., I wish you could see the whole scene. This young man lies within reach of me, flat on his back, his hands clasp'd across his breast, his thick black hair cut close; he is dozing, breathing hard, every breath a spasm—it looks so cruel. He is a noble youngster,—I consider him past all hope. Often there is no one with him for a long while. I am here as much as possible.

WILLIAM ALCOTT, fireman. *Camden, Nov., 1874.*—Last Monday afternoon his widow, mother, relatives, mates of the fire department, and his other friends, (I was one, only lately it is true, but our love grew fast and close, the days and nights of those eight weeks by the chair of rapid decline, and the bed of death,) gather'd to the funeral of this young man, who had grown up, and was well-known here. With nothing special, perhaps, to record, I would give a word or two to his memory. He seem'd to me not an inappropriate specimen in character and elements, of that bulk of the average good American race that ebbs and flows perennially beneath this scum of eructations on the surface. Always very quiet in manner, neat in person and dress, good temper'd—punctual and industrious at his work, till he could work no longer—he just lived his steady, square, unobtrusive life, in its own humble sphere, doubtless unconscious of itself. (Though I think there were currents of emotion and intellect undevelop'd beneath, far deeper than his acquaintances ever suspected—or than he himself ever did.) He was no talker. His troubles, when he had any, he kept to himself. As there was nothing querulous about him in life, he made no complaints during his last sickness. He was one of those persons that while his associates never thought of attributing any particular talent or grace to him, yet all insensibly, really, liked Billy Alcott.

I, too, loved him. At last, after being with him quite a good deal—after hours and days of panting for breath, much of the time unconscious, (for though the consumption that had been lurking in his system, once thoroughly started, made rapid progress, there was still great vitality in him, and indeed for four or five days he lay dying, before the close,) late on Wednesday night, Nov. 4th, where we surrounded his bed in silence, there came a lull—a longer drawn breath, a pause, a faint sigh—another—a weaker breath, another sigh—a pause again and just a tremble—and the face of the poor wasted young man (he was just 26,) fell gently over, in death, on my hand, on the pillow.

CHARLES CASWELL.—[I extract the following, verbatim, from a letter to me dated September 29, from my friend John Burroughs, at Esopus-on-Hudson, New York State.] S. was away when your picture came, attending his sick brother, Charles—who has since died—an event that has sadden'd me much. Charlie was younger than S., and a most attractive young fellow. He work'd at my father's, and had done so for two years. He was about the best specimen of a young country farm-hand I ever knew. You would have loved him. He was like one of your poems. With his great strength, his blond hair, his cheerfulness and contentment, his universal good will, and his silent manly ways, he was a youth hard to match. He was murder'd by an old doctor. He had typhoid fever, and the old fool bled him twice. He lived to wear out the fever, but had not strength to rally. He was out of his head nearly all the time. In the morning, as he died in the afternoon, S. was standing over him, when Charlie put up his arms around S.'s neck, and pull'd his face down and kiss'd him. S. said he knew then the end was near. (S. stuck to him day and night to the last.) When I was home in August, Charlie was cradling on the hill, and it was a picture to see him walk through the grain. All work seem'd play to him. He had no vices, any more than Nature has, and was belov'd by all who knew him.

I have written thus to you about him, for such young men belong to you; he was of your kind. I wish you could have known him. He had the sweetness of a child, and the strength and courage and readiness of a young Viking. His mother and father are poor; they have a rough, hard farm. His mother works in the field with her husband when the work presses. She has had twelve children.

FEBRUARY DAYS

February 7, 1878.—Glistening sun to-day, with slight haze, warm enough, and yet tart, as I sit here in the open air, down in my country retreat, under an old cedar. For two hours I have been idly wandering around the woods and pond, lugging my chair, picking out choice spots to sit awhile—then up and slowly on again. All is peace here. Of course, none of the summer noises or vitality; to-day hardly even the winter ones. I amuse myself by exercising my voice in recitations, and in ringing the changes on all the vocal and alphabetical sounds. Not even an echo; only the cawing of a solitary crow, flying at some distance. The pond is one bright, flat spread, without a ripple—a vast Claude Lorraine glass, in which I study the sky, the light, the leafless trees, and an occasional crow, with flapping wings, flying overhead. The brown fields have a few white patches of snow left.

Feb. 9.—After an hour's ramble, now retreating, resting, sitting close by the pond, in a warm nook, writing this, shelter'd from the breeze, just before noon. The *emotional* aspects and influences of Nature! I, too, like the rest, feel these modern tendencies (from all the prevailing intellections, literature and poems,) to turn everything to pathos, ennui, morbidity, dissatisfaction, death. Yet how clear it is to me that those are not the born results, influences of Nature at all, but of one's own distorted, sick or silly soul. Here, amid this wild, free scene, how healthy, how joyous, how clean and vigorous and sweet!

Mid-afternoon.—One of my nooks is south of the barn, and here I am sitting now, on a log, still basking in the sun, shielded from the wind. Near me are the cattle, feeding on corn-stalks. Occasionally a cow or the young bull (how handsome and bold he is!) scratches and munches the far end of the log on which I sit. The fresh milky odor is quite perceptible, also the perfume of hay from the barn. The perpetual rustle of dry corn-stalks, the low sough of the wind round the barn gables, the grunting of pigs, the distant whistle of a locomotive, and occasional crowing of chanticleers, are the sounds.

Feb. 19.—Cold and sharp last night—clear and not much wind—the full moon shining, and a fine spread of constellations and little and big stars—Sirius very bright, rising early, preceded by many-orb'd Orion, glittering, vast, sworded, and chasing with his dog. The earth hard frozen, and a stiff glare of ice over the pond. Attracted by the calm splendor of the night, I attempted a short walk, but was driven back by the cold. Too severe for me also at 9 o'clock, when I came out this morning, so I turn'd back again. But now, near noon, I have walk'd down the lane, basking all the way in the sun (this farm has a pleasant southerly exposure,) and here I am, seated under the lee of a bank, close by the water. There are blue-birds already flying about, and I hear much chirping and twittering and two or three real songs, sustain'd quite awhile, in the mid-day brilliance and warmth. (There! that is a true carol, coming out boldly and repeatedly, as if the singer meant it.) Then as the noon strengthens, the reedy trill of the robin—to my ear the most cheering of bird-notes. At intervals, like bars and breaks (out of the low murmur that in any scene, however quiet, is never entirely absent to a delicate ear,) the occasional crunch and cracking of the ice-glare congeal'd over the creek, as it gives way to the sunbeams—sometimes with low sigh—sometimes with indignant, obstinate tug and snort.

(Robert Burns says in one of his letters: "There is scarcely any earthly object gives me more—I do not know if I should call it pleasure—but something which exalts me—something which enrap tures me—than to walk in the shelter'd side of a wood in a cloudy winter day, and hear the stormy wind howling among the trees, and raving over the plain. It is my best season of devotion." Some of his most characteristic poems were composed in such scenes and seasons.)

A MEADOW LARK

March 16.—Fine, clear, dazzling morning, the sun an hour high, the air just tart enough. What a stamp in advance my whole day receives from the song of that meadow lark perch'd on a fence-stake twenty rods distant! Two or three liquid-simple notes, repeated at intervals, full of careless happiness and hope. With its peculiar shimmering-slow progress and rapid-noiseless action of the wings, it flies on a ways, lights on another stake, and so on to another, shimmering and singing many minutes.

SUNDOWN LIGHTS

May 6, 5 P. M.—This is the hour for strange effects in light and shade—enough to make a colorist go delirious—long spokes of molten silver sent horizontally through the trees (now in their brightest tenderest green,) each leaf and branch of endless foliage a lit-up miracle, then lying all prone on the youthful-ripe, interminable grass, and giving the blades not only aggregate but individual splendor, in ways unknown to any other hour. I have particular spots where I get these effects in their perfection. One broad splash lies on the water, with many a rippling twinkle, offset by the rapidly deepening black-green murky-transparent shadows behind, and at intervals all along the banks. These, with great shafts of horizontal fire thrown among the trees and along the grass as the sun lowers, give effects more and more peculiar, more and more superb, unearthly, rich and dazzling.

THOUGHTS UNDER AN OAK—A DREAM

June 2.—This is the fourth day of a dark northeast storm, wind and rain. Day before yesterday was my birthday. I have now enter'd on my 60th year. Every day of the storm, protected by overshoes and a waterproof blanket, I regularly come down to the pond, and ensconce myself under the lee of the great oak; I am here now writing these lines. The dark smoke-color'd clouds roll in furious silence athwart the sky; the soft green leaves dangle all round me; the wind steadily keeps up its hoarse, soothing music over my head—Nature's mighty whisper. Seated here in solitude I have been musing over my life—connecting events, dates, as links of a chain, neither sadly nor cheerily, but somehow, to-day here under the oak, in the rain, in an unusually matter-of-fact spirit.

But my great oak—sturdy, vital, green—five feet thick at the butt. I sit a great deal near or under him. Then the tulip tree near by— the Apollo of the woods—tall and graceful, yet robust and sinewy, inimitable in hang of foliage and throwing-out of limb; as if the beauteous, vital, leafy creature could walk, if it only would. (I had a sort of dream-trance the other day, in which I saw my favorite trees step out and promenade up, down and around, very curiously— with a whisper from one, leaning down as he pass'd me, *We do all this on the present occasion, exceptionally, just for you.*)

CLOVER AND HAY PERFUME

July 3d, 4th, 5th.—Clear, hot, favorable weather—has been a good summer—the growth of clover and grass now generally mow'd. The familiar delicious perfume fills the barns and lanes. As you go along you see the fields of grayish white slightly tinged with yellow, the loosely stack'd grain, the slow-moving wagons passing, and farmers in the fields with stout boys pitching and loading the sheaves. The corn is about beginning to tassel. All over the middle and southern states the spear-shaped battalia, multitudinous, curving, flaunting —long, glossy, dark-green plumes for the great horseman, earth. I hear the cheery notes of my old acquaintance Tommy quail; but too late for the whip-poor-will, (though I heard one solitary lingerer night before last.) I watch the broad majestic flight of a turkey-buzzard, sometimes high up, sometimes low enough to see the lines of his form, even his spread quills, in relief against the sky. Once or twice lately I have seen an eagle here at early candle-light flying low.

AN UNKNOWN

June 15.—To-day I noticed a new large bird, size of a nearly grown hen—a haughty, white-bodied dark-wing'd hawk—I suppose a hawk from his bill and general look—only he had a clear, loud, quite musical, sort of bell-like call, which he repeated again and again, at intervals, from a lofty dead tree-top, overhanging the water. Sat there a long time, and I on the opposite bank watching him. Then he darted down, skimming pretty close to the stream—

rose slowly, a magnificent sight, and sail'd with steady wide-spread wings, no flapping at all, up and down the pond two or three times, near me, in circles in clear sight, as if for my delectation. Once he came quite close over my head; I saw plainly his hook'd bill and hard restless eyes.

BIRD-WHISTLING

How much music (wild, simple, savage, doubtless, but so tart-sweet,) there is in mere whistling. It is four-fifths of the utterance of birds. There are all sorts and styles. For the last half-hour, now, while I have been sitting here, some feather'd fellow away off in the bushes has been repeating over and over again what I may call a kind of throbbing whistle. And now a bird about the robin size has just appear'd, all mulberry red, flitting among the bushes—head, wings, body, deep red, not very bright—no song, as I have heard. *4 o'clock:* There is a real concert going on around me—a dozen different birds pitching in with a will. There have been occasional rains, and the growths all show its vivifying influences. As I finish this, seated on a log close by the pond-edge, much chirping and trilling in the distance, and a feather'd recluse in the woods near by is singing deliciously—not many notes, but full of music of almost human sympathy—continuing for a long, long while.

HORSE-MINT

Aug. 22.—Not a human being, and hardly the evidence of one, in sight. After my brief semi-daily bath, I sit here for a bit, the brook musically brawling, to the chromatic tones of a fretful cat-bird somewhere off in the bushes. On my walk hither two hours since, through fields and the old lane, I stopt to view, now the sky, now the mile-off woods on the hill, and now the apple orchards. What a contrast from New York's or Philadelphia's streets! Every-where great patches of dingy-blossom'd horse-mint wafting a spicy odor through the air, (especially evenings.) Everywhere the flowering boneset, and the rose-bloom of the wild bean.

THREE OF US

July 14.—My two kingfishers still haunt the pond. In the bright sun and breeze and perfect temperature of to-day, noon, I am sitting here by one of the gurgling brooks, dipping a French water-pen in the limpid crystal, and using it to write these lines, again watching the feather'd twain, as they fly and sport athwart the water, so close, almost touching into its surface. Indeed there seem to be three of us. For nearly an hour I indolently look and join them while they dart and turn and take their airy gambols, sometimes far up the creek disappearing for a few moments, and then surely returning again, and performing most of their flight within sight of me, as if they knew I appreciated and absorb'd their vitality, spirituality, faithfulness, and the rapid, vanishing, delicate lines of moving yet quiet electricity they draw for me across the spread of the grass, the trees, and the blue sky. While the brook babbles, babbles, and the shadows of the boughs dapple in the sunshine around me, and the cool west by-nor'-west wind faintly soughs in the thick bushes and tree tops.

Among the objects of beauty and interest now beginning to appear quite plentifully in this secluded spot, I notice the humming-bird. the dragon-fly with its wings of slate-color'd gauze, and many varieties of beautiful and plain butterflies, idly flapping among the plants and wild posies. The mullein has shot up out of its nest of broad leaves, to a tall stalk towering sometimes five or six feet high, now studded with knobs of golden blossoms. The milk-weed, (I see a great gorgeous creature of gamboge and black lighting on one as I write,) is in flower, with its delicate red fringe; and there are profuse clusters of a feathery blossom waving in the wind on taper stems. I see lots of these and much else in every direction, as I saunter or sit. For the last half hour a bird has persistently kept up a simple, sweet, melodious song, from the bushes. (I have a positive conviction that some of these birds sing, and others fly and flirt about here, for my especial benefit.)

DEATH OF WILLIAM CULLEN BRYANT

New York City.—Came on from West Philadelphia, June 13, in the 2 P. M. train to Jersey city, and so across and to my friends, Mr. and Mrs. J. H. J., and their large house, large family (and large hearts,) amid which I feel at home, at peace—away up on Fifth avenue, near Eighty-sixth street, quiet, breezy, overlooking the dense woody fringe of the park—plenty of space and sky, birds chirping, and air comparatively fresh and odorless. Two hours before starting, saw the announcement of William Cullen Bryant's funeral, and felt a strong desire to attend. I had known Mr. Bryant over thirty years ago, and he had been markedly kind to me. Off and on, along that time for years as they pass'd, we met and chatted together. I thought him very sociable in his way, and a man to become attach'd to. We were both walkers, and when I work'd in Brooklyn he several times came over, middle of afternoons, and we took rambles miles long, till dark, out towards Bedford or Flatbush, in company. On these occasions he gave me clear accounts of scenes in Europe—the cities, looks, architecture, art, especially Italy—where he had travel'd a good deal.

June 14.—The Funeral.—And so the good, stainless, noble old citizen and poet lies in the closed coffin there—and this is his funeral. A solemn, impressive, simple scene, to spirit and senses. The remarkable gathering of gray heads, celebrities—the finely render'd anthem, and other music—the church, dim even now at approaching noon, in its light from the mellow-stain'd windows—the pronounc'd eulogy on the bard who loved Nature so fondly, and sung so well her shows and seasons—ending with these appropriate well-known lines:

> I gazed upon the glorious sky,
>   And the green mountains round,
> And thought that when I came to lie
>   At rest within the ground,
> 'Twere pleasant that in flowery June,
> When brooks send up a joyous tune,
>   And groves a cheerful sound,
> The sexton's hand, my grave to make,
> The rich green mountain turf should break.

JAUNT UP THE HUDSON

June 20th.—On the "Mary Powell," enjoy'd everything beyond precedent. The delicious tender summer day, just warm enough—the constantly changing but ever beautiful panorama on both sides of the river—(went up near a hundred miles)—the high straight walls of the stony Palisades—beautiful Yonkers, and beautiful Irvington—the never-ending hills, mostly in rounded lines, swathed with verdure, —the distant turns, like great shoulders in blue veils—the frequent gray and brown of the tall-rising rocks—the river itself, now narrowing, now expanding—the white sails of the many sloops, yachts, &c., some near, some in the distance—the rapid succession of handsome villages and cities, (our boat is a swift traveler, and makes few stops)—the Race—picturesque West Point, and indeed all along—the costly and often turreted mansions forever showing in some cheery light color, through the woods—make up the scene.

HAPPINESS AND RASPBERRIES

June 21.—Here I am, on the west bank of the Hudson, 80 miles north of New York, near Esopus, at the handsome, roomy, honeysuckle-and-rose-embower'd cottage of John Burroughs. The place, the perfect June days and nights, (leaning toward crisp and cool,) the hospitality of J. and Mrs. B., the air, the fruit, (especially my favorite dish, currants and raspberries, mixed, sugar'd, fresh and ripe from the bushes—I pick 'em myself)—the room I occupy at night, the perfect bed, the window giving an ample view of the Hudson and the opposite shores, so wonderful toward sunset, and the rolling music of the RR. trains, far over there—the peaceful rest—the early Venus-heralded dawn—the noiseless splash of sunrise, the light and warmth indescribably glorious, in which, (soon as the sun is well up,) I have a capital rubbing and rasping with the flesh-brush—with an extra scour on the back by Al. J., who is here with us—all inspiriting my invalid frame with new life, for the day. Then, after some whiffs of morning air, the delicious coffee of Mrs. B., with the cream, strawberries, and many substantials, for breakfast.

A SPECIMEN TRAMP FAMILY

June 22.—This afternoon we went out (J. B., Al. and I) on quite a drive around the country. The scenery, the perpetual stone fences, (some venerable old fellows, dark-spotted with lichens)—the many fine locust-trees—the runs of brawling water, often over descents of rock—these, and lots else. It is lucky the roads are first-rate here, (as they are,) for it is up or down hill everywhere, and sometimes steep enough. B. has a tip-top horse, strong, young, and both gentle and fast. There is a great deal of waste land and hills on the river edge of Ulster county, with a wonderful luxuriance of wild flowers and bushes—and it seems to me I never saw more vitality of trees—eloquent hemlocks, plenty of locusts and fine maples, and the balm of Gilead, giving out aroma. In the fields and along the road-sides unusual crops of the tall-stemm'd wild daisy, white as milk and yellow as gold.

We pass'd quite a number of tramps, singly or in couples—one squad, a family in a rickety one-horse wagon, with some baskets evidently their work and trade—the man seated on a low board, in front, driving—the gauntish woman by his side, with a baby well bundled in her arms, its little red feet and lower legs sticking out right towards us as we pass'd—and in the wagon behind, we saw two (or three) crouching little children. It was a queer, taking, rather sad picture. If I had been alone and on foot, I should have stopp'd and held confab. But on our return nearly two hours afterward, we found them a ways further along the same road, in a lonesome open spot, haul'd aside, unhitch'd, and evidently going to camp for the night. The freed horse was not far off, quietly cropping the grass. The man was busy at the wagon, the boy had gather'd some dry wood, and was making a fire—and as we went a little further we met the woman afoot. I could not see her face, in its great sun-bonnet, but somehow her figure and gait told misery, terror, destitution. She had the rag-bundled, half-starv'd infant still in her arms, and in her hands held two or three baskets, which she had evidently taken to the next house for sale. A little barefoot five-year old girl-child, with fine eyes, trotted behind her, clutching her gown. We stopp'd, asking about the baskets, which we bought. As we paid the money, she kept her face hidden in the recesses of her bonnet. Then as we started, and stopp'd again, Al., (whose sympathies were evidently arous'd,) went back to the camping group to get another basket. He caught a look of her face, and talk'd with her a little. Eyes, voice and manner were those of a corpse, animated by electricity. She was quite young—the man she was traveling with, middle-aged. Poor woman—what story was it, out of her fortunes, to account for that inexpressibly scared way, those glassy eyes, and that hollow voice?

MANHATTAN FROM THE BAY

June 25.—Returned to New York last night. Out to-day on the waters for a sail in the wide bay, southeast of Staten island—a rough, tossing ride, and a free sight—the long stretch of Sandy Hook, the highlands of Navesink, and the many vessels outward and inward bound. We came up through the midst of all, in the full sun. I especially enjoy'd the last hour or two. A moderate sea-breeze had set in; yet over the city, and the waters adjacent, was a thin haze, concealing nothing, only adding to the beauty. From my point of view, as I write amid the soft breeze, with a sea-temperature, surely nothing on earth of its kind can go beyond this show. To the left the North river with its far vista—nearer, three or four war-ships, anchor'd peacefully—the Jersey side, the banks of Weehawken, the Palisades, and the gradually receding blue, lost in the distance—to the right the East river—the mast-hemm'd shores—the grand obelisk-like towers of the bridge, one on either side, in haze, yet plainly defin'd, giant brothers twain, throwing free graceful interlinking loops high across the tumbled tumultuous current below—(the tide is just changing to its ebb)—the broad water-spread everywhere crowded—no, not crowded, but thick as stars in the sky—with all sorts and sizes of sail and steam vessels, plying ferry-boats, arriving and departing coasters, great ocean Dons, iron-black, modern, magnificent in size and power, fill'd with their incalculable value of human life and precious merchandise—with here and there, above all, those daring, careening things of grace and wonder, those white and shaded swift-darting fish-birds, (I wonder if shore or sea elsewhere can outvie them,) ever with their slanting spars, and fierce, pure, hawk-like beauty and motion—first-class New York sloop or schooner yachts, sailing, this fine day, the free sea in a good wind. And rising out of the midst, tall-topt, ship-hemm'd modern, American, yet strangely oriental, V-shaped Manhattan, with its compact mass, its spires, its cloud-touching edifices group'd at the centre—the green of the trees, and all the white, brown and gray of the architecture well blended, as I see it, under a miracle of limpid sky, delicious light of heaven above, and June haze on the surface below.

HUMAN AND HEROIC NEW YORK

The general subjective view of New York and Brooklyn—(will not the time hasten when the two shall be municipally united in one, and named Manhattan?)—what I may call the human interior and exterior of these great seething oceanic populations, as I get it in this visit, is to me best of all. After an absence of many years, (I went away at the outbreak of the secession war, and have never been back to stay since,) again I resume with curiosity the crowds, the streets I knew so well, Broadway, the ferries, the west side of the city, democratic Bowery—human appearances and manners as seen in all these, and along the wharves, and in the perpetual travel of the horse-cars, or in the crowded excursion steamers, or in Wall and Nassau streets by day—in the places of amusement at night—bubbling and whirling and moving like its own environment of waters—endless humanity in all phases—Brooklyn also—taken in for the last three weeks. No need to specify minutely—enough to say that (making all allowances for the shadows and side-streaks of a million-headed-city) the brief total of the impressions, the human qualities, of these vast cities, is to me comforting, even heroic, beyond statement. Alertness, generally fine physique, clear eyes that look straight at you, a singular combination of reticence and self-possession, with good nature and friendliness—a prevailing range of according manners, taste and intellect, surely beyond any else-where upon earth—and a palpable outcropping of that personal comradeship I look forward to as the subtlest, strongest future hold of this many-item'd Union—are not only constantly visible here in these mighty channels of men, but they form the rule and average.

To-day, I should say—defiant of cynics and pessimists, and with a full knowledge of all their exceptions—an appreciative and perceptive study of the current humanity of New York gives the directest proof yet of successful Democracy, and of the solution of that parodox, the eligibility of the free and fully developed individual with the paramount aggregate. In old age, lame and sick, pondering for years on many a doubt and danger for this republic of ours—fully aware of all that can be said on the other side—I find in this visit to New York, and the daily contact and rapport with its myriad people, on the scale of the oceans and tides, the best, most effective medicine my soul has yet partaken—the grandest physical habitat and surroundings of land and water the globe affords—namely, Manhattan island and Brooklyn, which the future shall join in one city—city of superb democracy, amid superb surroundings.

HOURS FOR THE SOUL

July 22d, 1878.—Living down in the country again. A wonderful conjunction of all that goes to make those sometime miracle-hours after sunset—so near and yet so far. Perfect, or nearly perfect days, I notice, are not so very uncommon; but the combinations that make perfect nights are few, even in a life time. We have one of those perfections to-night. Sunset left things pretty clear; the larger stars were visible soon as the shades allow'd. A while after 8, three or four great black clouds suddenly rose, seemingly from different points, and sweeping with broad swirls of wind but no thunder, underspread the orbs from view everywhere, and indicated a violent heat-storm. But without storm, clouds, blackness and all, sped and vanish'd as suddenly as they had risen; and from a little after 9 till 11 the atmosphere and the whole show above were in that state of exceptional clearness and glory just alluded to. In the northwest turned the Great Dipper with its pointers round the Cynosure. A little south of east the constellation of the Scorpion was fully up, with red Antares glowing in its neck; while dominating, majestic Jupiter swam, an hour and a half risen, in the east—(no moon till after 11.) A large part of the sky seem'd just laid in great splashes of phosphorus. You could look deeper in, farther through, than usual; the orbs thick as heads of wheat in a field. Not that there was any special brilliancy either—nothing near as sharp as I have seen of keen winter nights, but a curious general luminousness throughout to sight, sense, and soul. The latter had much to do with it. (I am convinced there are hours of Nature, especially of the atmosphere, mornings and evenings, address'd to the soul.

Night transcends, for that purpose, what the proudest day can do.) Now, indeed, if never before, the heavens declared the glory of God. It was to the full the sky of the Bible, of Arabia, of the prophets, and of the oldest poems. There, in abstraction and stillness, (I had gone off by myself to absorb the scene, to have the spell unbroken,) the copiousness, the removedness, vitality, loose-clear-crowdedness, of that stellar concave spreading overhead, softly absorb'd into me, rising so free, interminably high, stretching east, west, north, south—and I, though but a point in the centre below, embodying all.

As if for the first time, indeed, creation noiselessly sank into and through me its placid and untellable lesson, beyond—O, so infinitely beyond!—anything from art, books, sermons, or from science, old or new. The spirit's hour—religion's hour—the visible suggestion of God in space and time—now once definitely indicated, if never again. The untold pointed at—the heavens all paved with it. The Milky Way, as if some superhuman symphony, some ode of universal vagueness, disdaining syllable and sound—a flashing glance of Deity, address'd to the soul. All silently—the indescribable night and stars—far off and silently.

THE DAWN.—*July 23.*—This morning, between one and two hours before sunrise, a spectacle wrought on the same background, yet of quite different beauty and meaning. The moon well up in the heavens, and past her half, is shining brightly—the air and sky of that cynical-clear, Minerva-like quality, virgin cool—not the weight of sentiment or mystery, or passion's ecstasy indefinable—not the religious sense, the varied All, distill'd and sublimated into one, of the night just described. Every star now clear-cut, showing for just what it is, there in the colorless ether. The character of the heralded morning, ineffably sweet and fresh and limpid, but for the esthetic sense alone, and for purity without sentiment. I have itemized the night—but dare I attempt the cloudless dawn? (What subtle tie is this between one's soul and the break of day? Alike, and yet no two nights or morning shows ever exactly alike.) Preceded by an immense star, almost unearthly in its effusion of white plendor, with two or three long unequal spoke-rays of diamond radiance, shedding down through the fresh morning air below—an hour of this, and then the sunrise.

THE EAST.—What a subject for a poem! Indeed, where else a more pregnant, more splendid one? Where one more idealistic-real, more subtle, more sensuous-delicate? The East, answering all lands, all ages, peoples; touching all senses, here, immediate, now—and yet so indescribably far off—such retrospect! The East

—long-stretching—so losing itself—the orient, the gardens of Asia, the womb of history and song—forth-issuing all those strange, dim cavalcades—

> Florid with blood, pensive, rapt with musings, hot with passion,
> Sultry with perfume, with ample and flowing garments,
> With sunburnt visage, intense soul and glittering eyes.

Always the East—old, how incalculably old! And yet here the same—ours yet, fresh as a rose, to every morning, every life, to-day—and always will be.

Sept. 17.—Another presentation—same theme—just before sunrise again, (a favorite hour with me.) The clear gray sky, a faint glow in the dull liver-color of the east, the cool fresh odor and the moisture—the cattle and horses off there grazing in the fields—the star Venus again, two hours high. For sounds, the chirping of crickets in the grass, the clarion of chanticleer, and the distant cawing of an early crow. Quietly over the dense fringe of cedars and pines rises that dazzling, red, transparent disk of flame, and the low sheets of white vapor roll and roll into dissolution.

THE MOON.—*May 18.*—I went to bed early last night, but found myself waked shortly after 12, and, turning awhile sleepless and mentally feverish, I rose, dress'd myself, sallied forth and walk'd down the lane. The full moon, some three or four hours up—a sprinkle of light and less-light clouds just lazily moving—Jupiter an hour high in the east, and here and there throughout the heavens a random star appearing and disappearing. So, beautifully veil'd and varied—the air, with that early-summer perfume, not at all damp or raw—at times Luna languidly emerging in richest brightness for minutes, and then partially envelop'd again. Far off a whippoor-will plied his notes incessantly. It was that silent time between 1 and 3.

The rare nocturnal scene, how soon it sooth'd and pacified me! Is there not something about the moon, some relation or reminder, which no poem or literature has yet caught! (In very old and primitive ballads I have come across lines or asides that suggest it.) After a while the clouds mostly clear'd, and as the moon swam on, she carried, shimmering and shifting, delicate color-effects of pellucid green and tawny vapor. Let me conclude this part with an extract, (some writer in the 'Tribune," May 16, 1878:)

No one ever gets tired of the moon. Goddess that she is by dower of her eternal beauty, she is a true woman by her tact—knows the charm of being seldom seen, of coming by surprise and staying but a little while; never wears the same dress two nights running, nor all the night the same way; commends herself to the matter-of-fact people by her usefulness, and makes her uselessness adored by poets, artists, and all lovers in all lands; lends herself to every symbolism and to every emblem; is Diana's bow and Venus's mirror and Mary's throne; is a sickle, a scarf, an eyebrow, his face or her face, as look'd at by her or by him; is the madman's hell, the poet's heaven, the baby's toy, the philosopher's study; and while her admirers follow her footsteps, and hang on her lovely looks, she knows how to keep her woman's secret—her other side—unguess'd and unguessable.

Furthermore.—February 19, 1880.—Just before 10 P.M. cold and entirely clear again, the show overhead, bearing southwest, of wonderful and crowded magnificence. The moon in her third quarter—the clusters of the Hyades and Pleiades, with the planet Mars between—in full crossing sprawl in the sky the great Egyptian X, (Sirius, Procyon, and the main stars in the constellations of the Ship, the Dove, and of Orion;) just north of east Bootes, and in his knee Arcturus, an hour high, mounting the heaven, ambitiously large and sparkling, as if he meant to challenge with Sirius the stellar supremacy.

With the sentiment of the stars and moon such nights I get all the free margins and indefiniteness of music or poetry, fused in geometry's utmost exactness.

STRAW-COLOR'D AND OTHER PSYCHES

Aug. 4.—A pretty sight! Where I sit in the shade—a warm day, the sun shining from cloudless skies, the forenoon well advanc'd— I look over a ten-acre field of luxuriant clover-hay, (the second crop)—the livid-ripe red blossoms and dabs of August brown thickly spotting the prevailing dark-green. Over all flutter myriads of light-yellow butterflies, mostly skimming along the surface, dipping and oscillating, giving a curious animation to the scene. The beautiful, spiritual insects! straw-color'd Psyches! Occasionally one of them leaves his mates, and mounts, perhaps spirally, perhaps in a straight line in the air, fluttering up, up, till literally out of sight. In the lane as I came along just now I noticed one spot, ten feet square or so, where more than a hundred had collected, holding a revel, a gyration-dance, or butterfly good-time, winding and circling, down and across, but always keeping within the limits. The little creatures have come out all of a sudden the last few days, and are now very plentiful. As I sit outdoors, or walk, I hardly look around without somewhere seeing two (always two) fluttering through the air in amorous dalliance. Then their inimitable color, their fragility, peculiar motion—and that strange, frequent way of one leaving the crowd and mounting up, up in the free ether, and apparently never returning. As I look over the field, these yellow-wings everywhere mildly sparkling, many snowy blossoms of the wild carrot gracefully bending on their tall and taper stems—while for sounds, the distant guttural screech of a flock of guinea-hens comes shrilly yet somehow musically to my ears. And now a faint growl of heat-thunder in the north—and ever the low rising and falling wind-purr from the tops of the maples and willows.

Aug. 20.—Butterflies and butterflies, (taking the place of the bumble-bees of three months since, who have quite disappear'd,) continue to flit to and fro, all sorts, white, yellow, brown, purple—now and then some gorgeous fellow flashing lazily by on wings like artists' palettes dabb'd with every color. Over the breast of the pond I notice many white ones, crossing, pursuing their idle capricious flight. Near where I sit grows a tall-stemm'd weed topt with a profusion of rich scarlet blossoms, on which the snowy insects alight and dally, sometimes four or five of them at a time. By-and-by a humming-bird visits the same, and I watch him coming and going, daintily balancing and shimmering about. These white butterflies give new beautiful contrasts to the pure greens of the August foliage, (we have had some copious rains lately,) and over the glistening bronze of the pond-surface. You can tame even such insects; I have one big and handsome moth down here, knows and comes to me, likes me to hold him up on my extended hand.

Another Day, later.—A grand twelve-acre field of ripe cabbages with their prevailing hue of malachite green, and floating-flying over and among them in all directions myriads of these same white butterflies. As I came up the lane to-day I saw a living globe of the same, two to three feet in diameter, many scores cluster'd together and rolling along in the air, adhering to their ball-shape, six or eight feet above the ground.

A NIGHT REMEMBRANCE

Aug. 25, 9–10 a. m.—I sit by the edge of the pond, everything quiet, the broad polish'd surface spread before me—the blue of the heavens and the white clouds reflected from it—and flitting across, now and then, the reflection of some flying bird. Last night I was down here with a friend till after midnight; everything a miracle of splendor—the glory of the stars, and the completely rounded moon —the passing clouds, silver and luminous-tawny—now and then masses of vapory illuminated scud—and silently by my side my dear friend. The shades of the trees, and patches of moonlight on the grass—the softly blowing breeze, and just-palpable odor of the neighboring ripening corn—the indolent and spiritual night, inexpressibly rich, tender, suggestive—something altogether to filter through one's soul, and nourish and feed and soothe the memory long afterwards.

WILD FLOWERS

This has been and is yet a great season for wild flowers; oceans of them line the roads through the woods, border the edges of the water-runlets, grow all along the old fences, and are scatter'd in profusion over the fields. An eight-petal'd blossom of gold-yellow, clear and bright, with a brown tuft in the middle, nearly as large as a silver half-dollar, is very common; yesterday on a long drive I noticed it thickly lining the borders of the brooks everywhere. Then there is a beautiful weed cover'd with blue flowers, (the blue of the old Chinese teacups treasur'd by our grand-aunts,) I am continually stopping to admire—a little larger than a dime, and very plentiful. White, however, is the prevailing color. The wild carrot I have spoken of; also the fragrant life-everlasting. But there are all hues and beauties, especially on the frequent tracts of half-open scrub-oak and dwarf-cedar hereabout—wild asters of all colors. Notwithstanding the frost-touch the hardy little chaps maintain themselves in all their bloom. The tree-leaves, too, some of them are beginning to turn yellow or drab or dull green. The deep wine-color of the sumachs and gum-trees is already visible, and the straw-color of the dog-wood and beech. Let me give the names of some of these perennial blossoms and friendly weeds I have made acquaintance with hereabout one season or another in my walks:

wild azalea,	dandelions,
wild honeysuckle,	yarrow,
wild roses,	coreopsis,
golden rod,	wild pea,
larkspur,	woodbine,
early crocus,	elderberry,
sweet flag, (great patches of it,)	poke-weed,
creeper, trumpet-flower,	sun-flower,
scented marjoram,	chamomile,
snakeroot,	violets,
Solomon's seal,	clematis,
sweet balm,	bloodroot,
mint, (great plenty,)	swamp magnolia,
wild geranium,	milk-weed,
wild heliotrope,	wild daisy, (plenty,)
burdock,	wild chrysanthemum.

A CIVILITY TOO LONG NEGLECTED

The foregoing reminds me of something. As the individualities I would mainly portray have certainly been slighted by folks who make pictures, volumes, poems, out of them—as a faint testimonial of my own gratitude for many hours of peace and comfort in half-sickness, (and not by any means sure but they will somehow get wind of the compliment,) I hereby dedicate the last half of these Specimen Days to the

bees,
black-birds,
dragon-flies,
pond-turtles,
mulleins, tansy, peppermint,
moths (great and little, some splendid fellows,)
glow-worms, (swarming millions of them indescribably strange and beautiful at night over the pond and creek,)
water-snakes,
crows,
millers,
mosquitoes,
butterflies,
wasps and hornets,
cat birds (and all other birds,)
cedars,
tulip-trees (and all other trees,)
and to the spots and memories of those days, and of the creek.

DELAWARE RIVER—DAYS AND NIGHTS

April 5, 1879.—With the return of spring to the skies, airs, waters of the Delaware, return the sea-gulls. I never tire of watching their broad and easy flight, in spirals, or as they oscillate with slow un-flapping wings, or look down with curved beak, or dipping to the water after food. The crows, plenty enough all through the winter, have vanish'd with the ice. Not one of them now to be seen. The steamboats have again come forth—bustling up, handsome, freshly painted, for summer work—the Columbia, the Edwin Forrest, (the Republic not yet out,) the Reybold, the Nelly White, the Twilight, the Ariel, the Warner, the Perry, the Taggart, the Jersey Blue—even the hulky old Trenton—not forgetting those saucy little bull-pups of the current, the steamtugs.

But let me bunch and catalogue the affair—the river itself, all the way from the sea—cape Island on one side and Henlopen light on the other—up the broad bay north, and so to Philadelphia, and on further to Trenton;—the sights I am most familiar with, (as I live a good part of the time in Camden, I view matters from that outlook)—the great arrogant, black, full-freighted ocean steamers, inward or outward bound—the ample width here between the two cities, intersected by Windmill island—an occasional man-of-war, sometimes a foreigner, at anchor, with her guns and port-holes; and the boats, and the brown-faced sailors, and the regular oar-strokes, and the gay crowds of "visiting day"—the frequent large and handsome three-masted schooners, (a favorite style of marine build, hereabout of late years,) some of them new and very jaunty, with their white-gray sails and yellow pine spars—the sloops dashing along in a fair wind—(I see one now, coming up, under broad canvas, her gaff-topsail shining in the sun, high and picturesque—what a thing of beauty amid the sky and waters!)—the crowded wharf-ships along the city—the flags of different nationalities, the sturdy English cross on its ground of blood, the French tricolor, the banner of the great North German empire, and the Italian and the Spanish colors—sometimes, of an afternoon, the whole scene enliven'd by a fleet of yachts, in a half calm, lazily returning from a race down at Gloucester;—the neat, rakish, revenue steamer "Hamilton" in mid-stream, with her perpendicular stripes flaunting aft—and, turning the eyes north, the long ribands of fleecy-white steam, or dingy-black smoke, stretching far, fan-shaped, slanting diagonally across from the Kensington or Richmond shores, in the west-by-south-west wind.

SCENES ON FERRY AND RIVER—LAST WINTER'S NIGHTS

Then the Camden ferry. What exhilaration, change, people, business, by day. What soothing, silent, wondrous hours, at night, crossing on the boat, most all to myself—pacing the deck, alone, forward or aft. What communion with the waters, the air, the exquisite *chiaroscuro*—the sky and stars, that speak no word, nothing to the intellect, yet so eloquent, so communicative to the soul. And the ferry men—little they know how much they have been to me, day and night—how many spells of listlessness, ennui, debility, they and their hardy ways have dispell'd. And the pilots—captains Hand, Walton, and Giberson by day, and captain Olive at night; Eugene Crosby, with his strong young arm so often supporting, circling, convoying me over the gaps of the bridge, through impediments, safely aboard. Indeed all my ferry friends—captain Frazee the superintendent, Lindell, Hiskey, Fred Rauch, Price, Watson, and a dozen more. And the ferry itself, with its queer scenes—sometimes children suddenly born in the waiting-houses (an actual fact—and more than once)—sometimes a masquerade party, going over at night, with a band of music, dancing and whirling like mad on the broad deck, in their fantastic dresses; sometimes the astronome , Mr. Whitall, (who posts me up in points about the stars by a living lesson there and then, and answering every question)—sometimes a prolific family group, eight, nine, ten, even twelve! (Yesterday, as I cross'd, a mother, father, and eight children, wating in the ferry-house, bound westward somewhere.)

I have mention'd the crows. I always watch them from the boats. They play quite a part in the winter scenes on the river, by day

Their black splatches are seen in relief against the snow and ice everywhere at that season—sometimes flying and flapping—sometimes on little or larger cakes, sailing up or down the stream. One day the river was mostly clear—only a single long ridge of broken ice making a narrow stripe by itself, running along down the current for over a mile, quite rapidly. On this white stripe the crows were congregated, hundreds of them—a funny procession—("half mourning" was the comment of some one.)

Then the reception room, for passengers waiting—life illustrated thoroughly. Take a March picture I jotted there two or three weeks since. Afternoon, about 3¼ o'clock, it begins to snow. There has been a matinee performance at the theater—from 4¼ to 5 comes a stream of homeward bound ladies. I never knew the spacious room to present a gayer, more lively scene—handsome, well-drest Jersey women and girls, scores of them, streaming in for nearly an hour— the bright eyes and glowing faces, coming in from the air—a sprinkling of snow on bonnets or dresses as they enter—the five or ten minutes' waiting—the chatting and laughing—(women can have capital times among themselves, with plenty of wit, lunches, jovial abandon)—Lizzie, the pleasant-manner'd waiting-room woman— for sound, the bell-taps and steam-signals of the departing boats with their rhythmic break and undertone—the domestic pictures, mothers with bevies of daughters, (a charming sight)—children, countrymen—the railroad men in their blue clothes and caps—all the various characters of city and country represented or suggested. Then outside some belated passenger frantically running, jumping after the boat. Towards six o'clock the human stream gradually thickening—now a pressure of vehicles, drays, piled railroad crates— now a drove of cattle, making quite an excitement, the drovers with heavy sticks, belaboring the steaming sides of the frighten'd brutes. Inside the reception room, business bargains, flirting, love-making, *eclaircissements*, proposals—pleasant, sober-faced Phil coming in with his burden of afternoon papers—or Jo, or Charley (who jump'd in the dock last week, and saved a stout lady from drowning,) to replenish the stove, after clearing it with long crow-bar poker.

Besides all this "comedy human," the river affords nutriment of a higher order. Here are some of my memoranda of the past winter, just as pencill'd down on the spot.

A January Night.—Fine trips across the wide Delaware to-night. Tide pretty high, and a strong ebb. River, a little after 8, full of ice, mostly broken, but some large cakes making our strong-timber'd steamboat hum and quiver as she strikes them. In the clear moonlight they spread, strange, unearthly, silvery, faintly glistening, as far as I can see. Bumping, trembling, sometimes hissing like a thousand snakes, the tide-procession, as we wend with or through it, affording a grand undertone, in keeping with the scene. Overhead, the splendor indescribable; yet something haughty, almost supercilious, in the night. Never did I realize more latent sentiment, almost *passion*, in those silent interminable stars up there. One can understand, such a night, why, from the days of the Pharaohs or Job, the dome of heaven, sprinkled with planets, has supplied the subtlest, deepest criticism on human pride, glory, ambition.

Another Winter Night.—I don't know anything more *filling* than to be on the wide firm deck of a powerful boat, a clear, cool, extra-moonlight night, crushing proudly and resistlessly through this thick, marbly, glistening ice. The whole river is now spread with it—some immense cakes. There is such weirdness about the scene—partly the quality of the light, with its tinge of blue, the lunar twilight—only the large stars holding their own in the radiance of the moon. Temperature sharp, comfortable for motion, dry, full of oxygen. But the sense of power—the steady, scornful, imperious urge of our strong new engine, as she ploughs her way through the big and little cakes.

Another.—For two hours I cross'd and recross'd, merely for pleasure—for a still excitement. Both sky and river went through several changes. The first for awhile held two vast fan-shaped echelons of light clouds, through which the moon waded, now radiating, carrying with her an aureole of tawny transparent brown, and now flooding the whole vast with clear vapory light-green, through which, as through an illuminated veil, she moved with measur'd womanly motion. Then, another trip, the heavens would be absolutely clear, and Luna in all her effulgence. The Big Dipper in the north, with the double star in the handle much plainer than common. Then the sheeny track of light in the water, dancing and rippling. Such transformations; such pictures and poems, inimitable.

Another.—I am studying the stars, under advantages, as I cross to-night. (It is late in February, and again extra clear.) High toward the west, the Pleiades, tremulous with delicate sparkle, in the soft heavens. Aldebaran, leading the V-shaped Hyades—and overhead Capella and her kids. Most majestic of all, in full display in the high South, Orion, vast-spread, roomy, chief histrion of the stage, with his shiny yellow rosette on his shoulder, and his three Kings—and a little to the east, Sirius, calmly arrogant, most wondrous single star. Going late ashore, (I couldn't give up the beauty and soothingness of the night,) as I staid around, or slowly wander'd,

I heard the echoing calls of the railroad men in the West Jersey depot yard, shifting and switching trains, engines, &c.; amid the general silence otherways, and something in the acoustic quality of the air, musical, emotional effects, never thought of before. I linger'd long and long, listening to them.

Night of March 18, '79.—One of the calm, pleasantly cool, exquisitely clear and cloudless, early spring nights—the atmosphere again that rare vitreous blue-black, welcom'd by astronomers. Just at 8, evening, the scene overhead of certainly solemnest beauty, never surpass'd. Venus nearly down in the west, of a size and lustre as if trying to outshow herself, before departing. Teeming, maternal orb—I take you again to myself. I am reminded of that spring preceding Abraham Lincoln's murder, when I, restlessly haunting the Potomac banks, around Washington city, watch'd you, off there, aloof, moody as myself:

As we walk'd up and down in the dark blue so mystic,
As we walk'd in silence the transparent shadowy night,
As I saw you had something to tell, as you bent to me night after night,
As you droop from the sky low down, as if to my side, (while the other stars
    all look'd on,)
As we wander'd together the solemn night.

With departing Venus, large to the last, and shining even to the edge of the horizon, the vast dome presents, at this moment, such a spectacle! Mercury was visible just after sunset—a rare sight. Arcturus is now risen, just north of east. In calm glory all the stars of Orion hold the place of honor, in meridian, to the south—with the Dog-star a little to the left. And now, just rising, Spica, late, low and slightly veil'd. Castor, Regulus and the rest, all shining unusually clear, (no Mars or Jupiter or moon till morning.) On the edges of the river, many lamps twinkling—with two or three huge chimneys, a couple of miles up, belching forth molten, steady flames, volcano-like, illuminating all around—and sometimes an electric or calcium, its Dante-Inferno gleams, in far shafts, terrible, ghastly-powerful. Of later May nights, crossing, I like to watch the fishermen's little buoy-lights—so pretty, so dreamy—like corpse candles—undulating delicate and lonesome on the surface of the shadowy waters, floating with the current.

THE FIRS1 SPRING DAY ON CHESTNUT STREET

Winter relaxing its hold, has already allow'd us a foretaste of spring. As I write, yesterday afternoon's softness and brightness (after the morning fog, which gave it a better setting, by contrast,) show'd Chestnut street—say between Broad and Fourth—to more advantage in its various asides, and all its stores, and gay-dress'd crowds generally, than for three months past. I took a walk there between one and two. Doubtless, there were plenty of hard-up folks along the pavements, but nine-tenths of the myriad-moving human panorama to all appearance seem'd flush, well-fed, and fully-provided. At all events it was good to be on Chestnut street yesterday. The peddlers on the sidewalk—("sleeve-buttons, three for five cents") —the handsome little fellow with canary-bird whistles—the cane men, toy men, toothpick men—the old woman squatted in a heap on the cold stone flags, with her basket of matches, pins and tape— the young negro mother, sitting, begging, with her two little coffee-color'd twins on her lap—the beauty of the cramm'd conservatory of rare flowers, flaunting reds, yellows, snowy lilies, incredible orchids, at the Baldwin mansion near Twelfth street—the show of fine poultry, beef, fish, at the restaurants—the china stores, with glass and statuettes—the luscious tropical fruits—the street cars plodding along, with their tintinnabulating bells—the fat, cab-looking, rapidly driven one-horse vehicles of the post-office, squeez'd full of coming or going letter-carriers, so healthy and handsome and manly-looking, in their gray uniforms—the costly books, pictures, curiosities, in the windows—the gigantic policemen at most of the corners—will all be readily remember'd and recognized as features of this principal avenue of Philadelphia. Chestnut street, I have discover'd, is not without individuality, and its own points, even when compared with the great promenade-streets of other cities. I have never been in Europe, but acquired years' familiar experience with New York's, (perhaps the world's,) great thoroughfare, Broadway, and possess to some extent a personal and saunterer's knowledge of St. Charles street in New Orleans, Tremont street, in Boston, and the broad trottoirs of Pennsylvania avenue in Washington. Of course it is a pity that Chestnut were not two or three times wider; but the street, any fine day, shows vividness, motion, variety, not easily to be surpass'd. (Sparkling eyes, human faces, magnetism, well-dress'd women, ambulating to and fro—with lots of fine things in the windows—are they not about the same, the civilized world over?)

> How fast the flitting figures come!
> The mild, the fierce, the stony face,
> Some bright with thoughtless smiles—and some
> Where secret tears have left their trace.

A few days ago one of the six-story clothing stores along here

had the space inside its plate-glass show-window partition'd into
a little corral, and litter'd deeply with rich clover and hay, (I could
smell the odor outside,) on which reposed two magnificent fat
sheep, full-sized but young—the handsomest creatures of the kind
I ever saw. I stopp'd long and long, with the crowd, to view them—
one lying down chewing the cud, and one standing up, looking out,
with dense-fringed patient eyes. Their wool, of a clear tawny color,
with streaks of glistening black—altogether a queer sight amidst
that crowded promenade of dandies, dollars and drygoods.

UP THE HUDSON TO ULSTER COUNTY

April 23.—Off to New York on a little tour and*visit. Leaving
the hospitable, home-like quarters of my valued friends, Mr. and
Mrs. J. H. Johnston—took the 4 P. M. boat, bound up the Hudson,
100 miles or so. Sunset and evening fine. Especially enjoy'd the
hour after we passed Cozzens's landing—the night lit by the crescent
moon and Venus, now swimming in tender glory, and now hid by
the high rocks and hills of the western shore, which we hugg'd
close. (Where I spend the next ten days is in Ulster county and its
neighborhood, with frequent morning and evening drives, observations of the river, and short rambles.)

April 24—Noon.—A little more and the sun would be oppressive.
The bees are out gathering their bread from willows and other trees.
I watch them returning, darting through the air or lighting on the
hives, their thighs covered with the yellow forage. A solitary robin
sings near. I sit in my shirt sleeves and gaze from an open bay-win-
dow on the indolent scene—the thin haze, the Fishkill hills in the
distance—off on the river, a sloop with slanting mainsail, and two
or three little shad-boats. Over on the railroad opposite, long freight
trains, sometimes weighted by cylinder-tanks of petroleum, thirty,
forty, fifty cars in a string, panting and rumbling along in full view,
but the sound soften'd by distance.

DAYS AT J. B.'S—TURF-FIRES—SPRING SONGS

April 26.—At sunrise, the pure clear sound of the meadow lark.
An hour later, some notes, few and simple, yet delicious and perfect,
from the bush-sparrow—towards noon, the reedy trill of the robin.
To-day is the fairest, sweetest yet—penetrating warmth—a lovely
veil in the air, partly heat-vapor and partly from the turf-fires
everywhere in patches on the farms. A group of soft maples near
by silently bursts out in crimson tips, buzzing all day with busy

bees. The white sails of sloops and schooners glide up or down the river; and long trains of cars, with ponderous roll, or faint bell notes, almost constantly on the opposite shore. The earliest wild flowers in the woods and fields, spicy arbutus, blue liverwort, frail anemone, and the pretty white blossoms of the bloodroot. I launch out in slow rambles, discovering them. As I go along the roads I like to see the farmers' fires in patches, burning the dry brush, turf, debris. How the smoke crawls along, flat to the ground, slanting, slowly rising, reaching away, and at last dissipating. I like its acrid smell—whiffs just reaching me—welcomer than French perfume.

The birds are plenty; of any sort, or of two or three sorts, curiously, not a sign, till suddenly some warm, gushing, sunny April (or even March) day—lo! there they are, from twig to twig, or fence to fence, flirting, singing, some mating, preparing to build. But most of them *en passant*—a fortnight, a month in these parts, and then away. As in all phases, Nature keeps up her vital, copious, eternal procession. Still, plenty of the birds hang around all or most of the season—now their love-time, and era of nest-building. I find flying over the river, crows, gulls and hawks. I hear the afternoon shriek of the latter, darting about, preparing to nest. The oriole will soon be heard here, and the twanging *meoeow* of the cat-bird; also the king-bird, cuckoo and the warblers. All along, there are three peculiarly characteristic spring songs—the meadow-lark's, so sweet, so alert and remonstrating (as if he said, "don't you see?" or, "can't you understand?")—the cheery, mellow, human tones of the robin—(I have been trying for years to get a brief term, or phrase, that would identify and describe that robin-call)—and the amorous whistle of the high-hole. Insects are out plentifully at midday.

April 29.—As we drove lingering along the road we heard, just after sundown, the song of the wood-thrush. We stopp'd without a word, and listen'd long, The delicious notes—a sweet, artless, voluntary, simple anthem, as from the flute-stops of some organ, wafted through the twilight—echoing well to us from the perpendicular high rock, where, in some thick young trees' recesses at the base, sat the bird—fill'd our senses, our souls.

MEETING A HERMIT

I found in one of my rambles up the hills a real hermit, living in a lonesome spot, hard to get at, rocky, the view fine, with a little patch of land two rods square. A man of youngish middle age, city born and raised, had been to school, had travel'd in Europe and California. I first met him once or twice on the road, and pass'd the time of day, with some small talk; then, the third time, he ask'd me to go along a bit and rest in his hut (an almost unprecedented compliment, as I heard from others afterwards.) He was of Quaker stock, I think, talk'd with ease and moderate freedom, but did not unbosom his life, or story, or tragedy, or whatever it was.

AN ULSTER COUNTY WATERFALL

I jot this mem. in a wild scene of woods and hills, where we have come to visit a waterfall. I never saw finer or more copious hemlocks, many of them large, some old and hoary. Such a sentiment to them, secretive, shaggy—what I call weather-beaten and let-alone—a rich underlay of ferns, yew sprouts and mosses, beginning to be spotted with the early summer wild-flowers. Enveloping all, the monotone and liquid gurgle from the hoarse impetuous copious fall—the greenish-tawny, darkly transparent waters, plunging with velocity down the rocks, with patches of milk-white foam—a stream of hurrying amber, thirty feet wide, risen far back in the hills and woods, now rushing with volume—every hundred rods a fall, and sometimes three or four in that distance. A primitive forest, druidical, solitary and savage—not ten visitors a year—broken rocks everywhere— shade overhead, thick underfoot with leaves—a just palpable wild and delicate aroma.

WALTER DUMONT AND HIS MEDAL

As I saunter'd along the high road yesterday, I stopp'd to watch a man near by, ploughing a rough stony field with a yoke of oxen. Usually there is much geeing and hawing, excitement, and continual noise and expletives, about a job of this kind. But I noticed how different, how easy and wordless, yet firm and sufficient, the work of this young ploughman. His name was Walter Dumont, a farmer, and son of a farmer, working for their living. Three years ago, when the steamer "Sunnyside" was wreck'd of a bitter icy night on the west bank here, Walter went out in his boat—was the first man on hand with assistance—made a way through the ice to shore, connected a line, perform'd work of first-class readiness, daring, danger, and saved numerous lives. Some weeks after, one evening when he was up at Esopus, among the usual loafing crowd at the country store and post-office, there arrived the gift of an unexpected official gold medal for the quiet hero. The impromptu presentation was made to him on the spot, but he blush'd, hesitated as he took it, and had nothing to say.

HUDSON RIVER SIGHTS

It was a happy thought to build the Hudson river railroad right along the shore. The grade is already made by nature; you are sure of ventilation one side—and you are in nobody's way. I see, hear, the locomotives and cars, rumbling, roaring, flaming, smoking, constantly, away off there, night and day—less than a mile distant, and in full view by day. I like both sight and sound. Express trains thunder and lighten along; of freight trains, most of them very long, there cannot be less than a hundred a day. At night far down you see the headlight approaching, coming steadily on like a meteor. The river at night has its special character-beauties. The shad-fishermen go forth in their boats and pay out their nets—one sitting forward, rowing, and one standing up aft dropping it properly—marking the line with little floats bearing candles, conveying, as they glide over the water, an indescribable sentiment and doubled brightness. I like to watch the tows at night too, with their twinkling lamps, and hear the husky panting of the steamers; or catch the sloops' and schooners' shadowy forms, like phantoms, white, silent, indefinite, out there. Then the Hudson of a clear moonlight night.

But there is one sight the very grandest. Sometimes in the fiercest driving storm of wind, rain, hail or snow, a great eagle will appear over the river, now soaring with steady and now overhended wings—always confronting the gale, or perhaps cleaving into, or at times literally *sitting* upon it. It is like reading some first-class natural tragedy or epic, or hearing martial trumpets. The splendid bird enjoys the hubbub—is adjusted and equal to it—finishes it so artistically. His pinions just oscillating—the position of his head and neck—his resistless, occasionally varied flight—now a swirl, now an upward movement—the black clouds driving—the angry wash below—the hiss of rain, the wind's piping (perhaps the ice colliding, grunting)—he tacking or jibing—now, as it were, for a change, abandoning himself to the gale, moving with it with such velocity—and now, resuming control, he comes up against it, lord of the situation and the storm—lord, amid it, of power and savage joy.

Sometimes (as at present writing,) middle of sunny afternoon, the old "Vanderbilt" steamer stalking ahead—I plainly hear her rhythmic, slushing paddles—drawing by long hawsers an immense and varied following string, ("an old sow and pigs," the river folks call it.) First comes a big barge, with a house built on it, and spars towering over the roof; then canal boats, a lengthen'd, clustering train, fasten'd and link'd together—the one in the middle, with high staff, flaunting a broad and gaudy flag—others with the almost invariable lines of new-wash'd clothes, drying; two sloops and a schooner aside the tow—little wind, and that adverse—with three long, dark, empty barges bringing up the rear. People are on the boats: men lounging, women in sun-bonnets, children, stovepipes with streaming smoke.

TWO CITY AREAS, CERTAIN HOURS

NEW YORK, *May 24, '79.*—Perhaps no quarters of this city (I have return'd again for awhile,) make more brilliant, animated, crowded, spectacular human presentations these fine May afternoons than the two I am now going to describe from personal observation. First: that area comprising Fourteenth street (especially the short range between Broadway and Fifth avenue) with Union square, its adjacencies, and so retrostretching down Broadway for half a mile. All the walks here are wide, and the spaces ample and free—now flooded with liquid gold from the last two hours of powerful sunshine. The whole area at 5 o'clock, the days of my observations, must have contain'd from thirty to forty thousand finely-dress'd people, all in motion, plenty of them good-looking, many beautiful women, often youths and children, the latter in groups with their nurses—the trottoirs everywhere close-spread, thick-tangled, (yet no collision, no trouble,) with masses of bright color, action, and tasty toilets; (surely the women dress better than ever before, and the men do too.) As if New York would show these afternoons what it can do in its humanity, its choicest physique and physiognomy, and its countless prodigality of locomotion, dry goods, glitter, magnetism, and happiness.

Second: also from 5 to 7 P. M. the stretch of Fifth avenue, all the way from the Central Park exits at Fifty-ninth street, down to Fourteenth, especially along the high grade by Fortieth street, and down the hill. A Mississippi of horses and rich vehicles, not by dozens and scores, but hundreds and thousands—the broad avenue filled and cramm'd with them—a moving, sparkling, hurrying crush, for more than two miles. (I wonder they don't get block'd, but I believe they never do.) Altogether it is to me the marvel sight of New York. I like to get in one of the Fifth avenue stages and ride up, stemming the swift-moving procession. I doubt if London or Paris or any city in the world can show such a carriage carnival as I have seen here five or six times these beautiful May afternoons.

CENTRAL PARK WALKS AND TALKS

May 16 to 22.—I visit Central Park now almost every day, sitting, or slowly rambling, or riding around. The whole place presents its very best appearance this current month—the full flush of the trees, the plentiful white and pink of the flowering shrubs, the emerald green of the grass spreading everywhere, yellow dotted still with dandelions—the specialty of the plentiful gray rocks, peculiar to these grounds, cropping out, miles and miles—and over all the beauty and purity, three days out of four, of our summer skies. As I sit, placidly, early afternoon, off against Ninetieth street, the police-man, C. C., a well-form'd sandy-complexion'd young fellow, comes over and stands near me. We grow quite friendly and chatty forth-with. He is a New Yorker born and raised, and in answer to my questions tells me about the life of a New York Park policeman, (while he talks keeping his eyes and ears vigilantly open, occasionally pausing and moving where he can get full views of the vistas of the road, up and down, and the spaces around.) The pay is $2.40 a day (seven days to a week)—the men come on and work eight hours straight ahead, which is all that is required of them out of the twenty-four. The position has more risks than one might suppose—for instance if a team or horse runs away (which happens daily) each man is expected not only to be prompt, but to waive safety and stop wildest nag or nags)—*do it*, and don't be thinking of your bones or face)—give the alarm-whistle too, so that other guards may repeat, and the vehicles up and down the tracks be warn'd. Injuries to the men are continually happening. There is much alert-ness and quiet strength. (Few appreciate, I have often thought, the Ulyssean capacity, derring do, quick readiness in emergencies, prac-ticality, unwitting devotion and heroism, among our American young men and working-people—the firemen, the railroad em-ployés, the steamer and ferry men, the police, the conductors and drivers—the whole splendid average of native stock, city and coun-try.) It is good work, though; and upon the whole, the Park force members like it. They see life, and the excitement keeps them up. There is not so much difficulty as might be supposed from tramps, roughs, or in keeping people "off the grass." The worst trouble of the regular Park employé is from malarial fever, chills, and the like.

A FINE AFTERNOON, 4 TO 6

Ten thousand vehicles careering through the Park this perfect afternoon. Such a show! and I have seen all—watch'd it narrowly, and at my leisure. Private barouches, cabs and coupés, some fine horseflesh—lapdogs, footmen, fashions, foreigners, cockades on hats, crests on panels—the full oceanic tide of New York's wealth and "gentility." It was an impressive, rich, interminable circus on a grand scale, full of action and color in the beauty of the day, under the clear sun and moderate breeze. Family groups, couples, single drivers—of course dresses generally elegant—much "style," (yet perhaps little or nothing, even in that direction, that fully justified itself.) Through the windows of two or three of the richest carriages I saw faces almost corpse-like, so ashy and listless. Indeed the whole affair exhibited less of sterling America, either in spirit or countenance, than I had counted on from such a select mass-spectacle. I suppose, as a proof of limitless wealth, leisure, and the aforesaid "gentility," it was tremendous. Yet what I saw those hours (I took two other occasions, two other afternoons to watch the same scene,) confirms a thought that haunts me every additional glimpse I get of our top-loftical general or rather exceptional phases of wealth and fashion in this country—namely, that they are ill at ease, much too conscious, cased in too many cerements, and far from happy—that there is nothing in them which we who are poor and plain need at all envy, and that insted of the perennial smell of the grass and woods and shores, their typical redolence is of soaps and essences, very rare may be, but suggesting the barber shop—something that turns stale and musty in a few hours anyhow.

Perhaps the show on the horseback road was prettiest. Many groups (threes a favorite number,) some couples, some singly—many ladies—frequently horses or parties dashing along on a full run—fine riding the rule—a few really first-class animals. As the afternoon waned, the wheel'd carriages grew less, but the saddle-riders seemed to increase. They linger'd long—and I saw some charming forms and faces.

DEPARTING OF THE BIG STEAMERS

May 15.—A three hours' bay-trip from 12 to 3 this afternoon, accompanying "the City of Brussels" down as far as the Narrows, in behoof of some Europe-bound friends, to give them a good send off. Our spirited little tug, the "Seth Low," kept close to the great black "Brussels," sometimes one side, sometimes the other, always up to her, or even pressing ahead, (like the blooded pony accompanying the royal elephant.) The whole affair, from the first, was an animated, quick-passing, characteristic New York scene; the large, good-looking, well-dress'd crowd on the wharf-end—men and women come to see their friends depart, and bid them God-speed—the ship's sides swarming with passengers—groups of bronze-faced sailors, with uniform'd officers at their posts—the quiet directions, as she quickly unfastens and moves out, prompt to a minute

—the emotional faces, adieus and fluttering handkerchiefs, and many smiles and some tears on the wharf—the answering faces, smiles, tears and fluttering handkerchiefs, from the ship—(what can be subtler and finer than this play of faces on such occasions in these responding crowds?—what go more to one's heart?)—the proud, steady, noiseless cleaving of the grand oceaner down the bay—we speeding by her side a few miles, and then turning, wheeling, amid a babel of wild hurrahs, shouted partings, ear-splitting steam whistles, kissing of hands and waving of handkerchiefs.

This departing of the big steamers, noons or afternoons—there is no better medicine when one is listless or vapory. I am fond of going down Wednesdays and Saturdays—their more special days— to watch them and the crowds on the wharves, the arriving passengers, the general bustle and activity, the eager looks from the faces, the clear-toned voices, (a travel'd foreigner, a musician, told me the other day she thinks an American crowd has the finest voices in the world,) the whole look of the great, shapely black ships themselves, and their groups and lined sides—in the setting of our bay with the blue sky overhead. Two days after the above I saw the "Britannic," the "Donau," the "Helvetia" and the "Schiedam" steam out, all off for Europe—a magnificent sight.

TWO HOURS ON THE MINNESOTA

From 7 to 9, aboard the United States school-ship Minnesota, lying up the North river. Captain Luce sent his gig for us about sundown, to the foot of Twenty-third street, and receiv'd us aboard with officer-like hospitality and sailor heartiness. There are several hundred youths on the Minnsota to be train'd for efficiently manning the government navy. I like the idea much; and, so far as I have seen to-night, I like the way it is carried out on this huge vessel. Below, on the gun-deck, were gather'd nearly a hundred of the boys, to give us some of their singing exercises, with a melodeon accompaniment, play'd by one of their number. They sang with a will. The best part, however, was the sight of the young fellows themselves. I went over among them before the singing began, and talk'd a few minutes informally. They are from all the States; I asked for the Southerners, but could only find one, a lad from Baltimore. In age, apparently, they range from about fourteen years to nineteen or twenty. They are all of American birth, and have to pass a rigid medical examination; well-grown youths, good flesh, bright eyes, looking straight at you, healthy, intelligent, not a slouch among them, nor a menial—in every one the promise of a man. I have been to many public aggregations of young and old, and of schools and colleges, in my day, but I confess I have never been so near satisfied, so comforted, (both from the fact of the school itself, and the splendid proof of our country, our composite race, and the sample-promises of its good average capacities, its future,) as in the collection from all parts of the United States on this navy training ship. ("Are there going to be *any men* there?" was the dry and pregnant reply of Emerson to one who had been crowding him with the rich material statistics and possibilities of some western or Pacific region.)

May 26.—Aboard the Minnesota again. Lieut. Murphy kindly came for me in his boat. Enjoy'd specially those brief trips to and fro—the sailors, tann'd, strong, so bright and able-looking, pulling their oars in long side-swing, man-of-war style, as they row'd me across. I saw the boys in companies drilling with small arms; had a talk with Chaplain Rawson. At 11 o'clock all of us gathered to breakfast around a long table in the great ward room—I among the rest—a genial, plentiful, hospitable affair every way—plenty to eat, and of the best; became acquainted with several new officers. This second visit, with its observations, talks, (two or three at random with the boys,) confirm'd my first impressions.

MATURE SUMMER DAYS AND NIGHTS

Aug. 4.—Forenoon—as I sit under the willow shade, (have retreated down in the country again,) a little bird is leisurely dousing and flirting himself amid the brook almost within reach of me. He evidently fears me not—takes me for some concomitant of the neighboring earthy banks, free bushery and wild weeds. *6 p. m.*—The last three days have been perfect ones for the season, (four nights ago copious rains, with vehement thunder and lightning.) I write this sitting by the creek watching my two kingfishers at their sundown sport. The strong, beautiful, joyous creatures! Their wings glisten in the slanted sunbeams as they circle and circle around, occasionally dipping and dashing the water, and making long stretches up and down the creek. Wherever I go over fields, through lanes, in by-places, blooms the white-flowering wild-carrot, its delicate pat of snow-flakes crowning its slender stem, gracefully oscillating in the breeze.

EXPOSITION BUILDING—NEW CITY HALL—RIVER TRIP

PHILADELPHIA, *Aug. 26.*—Last night and to-night of unsurpass'd clearness, after two days' rain; moon splendor and star splendor.

Being out toward the great Exposition building, West Philadelphia, I saw it lit up, and thought I would go in. There was a ball, democratic but nice; plenty of young couples waltzing and quadrilling—music by a good string-band. To the sight and hearing of these—to moderate strolls up and down the roomy spaces—to getting off aside, resting in an arm-chair and looking up a long while at the grand high roof with its graceful and multitudinous work of iron rods, angles, gray colors, plays of light and shade, receding into dim outlines—to absorbing (in the intervals of the string band,) some capital voluntaries and rolling caprices from the big organ at the other end of the building—to sighting a shadow'd figure or group or couple of lovers every now and then passing some near or farther aisle—I abandon'd myself for over an hour.

Returning home, riding down Market street in an open summer car, something detain'd us between Fifteenth and Broad, and I got out to view better the new, three-fifths-built marble edifice, the City Hall, of magnificent proportions—a majestic and lovely show there in the moonlight—flooded all over, façades, myriad silver-white lines and carv'd heads and mouldings, with the soft dazzle—silent, weird, beautiful—well, I know that never when finish'd will that magnificent pile impress one as it impress'd me those fifteen minutes.

To-night, since, I have been long on the river. I watch the C-shaped Northern Crown, (with the star Alshacca that blazed out so suddenly, alarmingly, one night a few years ago.) The moon in her third quarter, and up nearly all night. And there, as I look eastward, my long-absent Pleiades, welcome again to sight. For an hour I enjoy the soothing and vital scene to the low splash of waves—new stars steadily, noiselessly rising in the east.

As I cross the Delaware, one of the deck-hands, F. R., tells me how a woman jump'd overboard and was drown'd a couple of hours since. It happen'd in mid-channel—she leap'd from the forward part of the boat, which went over her. He saw her rise on the other side in the swift running water, throw her arms and closed hands high up, (white hands and bare forearms in the moonlight like a flash,) and then she sank. (I found out afterwards that this young fellow had promptly jump'd in, swam after the poor creature, and made, though unsuccessfully, the bravest efforts to rescue her; but he didn't mention that part at all in telling me the story.)

SWALLOWS ON THE RIVER

Sept. 3.—Cloudy and wet, and wind due east; air without palpable fog, but very heavy with moisture—welcome for a change.

Forenoon, crossing the Delaware, I noticed unusual numbers of
swallows in flight, circling, darting, graceful beyond description,
close to the water. Thick, around the bows of the ferry-boat as she
lay tied in her slip, they flew; and as we went out I watch'd beyond
the pier-heads, and across the broad stream, their swift-winding
loop-ribands of motion, down close to it, cutting and intersecting.
Though I had seen swallows all my life, seem'd as though I never
before realized their peculiar beauty and character in the landscape.
(Some time ago, for an hour, in a huge old country barn, watching
these birds flying, recall'd the 22d book of the Odyssey, where
Ulysses slays the suitors, bringing things to *eclaircissement*, and
Minerva, swallow-bodied, darts up through the spaces of the hall,
sits high on a beam, looks complacently on the show of slaughter,
and feels in her element, exulting, joyous.)

BEGIN A LONG JAUNT WEST

The following three or four months (Sept. to Dec. '79) I made
quite a western journey, fetching up at Denver, Colorado, and penetrating the Rocky Mountain region enough to get a good notion
of it all. Left West Philadelphia after 9 o'clock one night, middle of
September, in a comfortable sleeper. Oblivious of the two or three
hundred miles across Pennsylvania; at Pittsburgh in the morning to
breakfast. Pretty good view of the city and Birmingham—fog and
damp, smoke, coke-furnaces, flames, discolor'd wooden houses, and
vast collections of coal-barges. Presently a bit of fine region, West
Virginia, the Panhandle, and crossing the river, the Ohio. By day
through the latter State—then Indiana—and so rock'd to slumber
for a second night, flying like lightning through Illinois.

IN THE SLEEPER

What a fierce weird pleasure to lie in my berth at night in the
luxurious palace-car, drawn by the mighty Baldwin—embodying,
and filling me, too, full of the swiftest motion, and most resistless
strength! It is late, perhaps midnight or after—distances join'd like
magic—as we speed through Harrisburg, Columbus, Indianapolis.
The element of danger adds zest to it all. On we go, rumbling and
flashing, with our loud whinnies thrown out from time to time, or
trumpet-blasts, into the darkness. Passing the homes of men, the
farms, barns, cattle—the silent villages. And the car itself, the
sleeper, with curtains drawn and lights turn'd down—in the berths
the slumberers, many of them women and children—as on, on, on,

691 to one of our

we fly like lightning through the night—how strangely sound and sweet they sleep! (They say the French Voltaire in his time designated the grand opera and a ship of war the most signal illustrations of the growth of humanity's and art's advance beyond primitive barbarism. Perhaps if the witty philosopher were here these days, and went in the same car with perfect bedding and feed from New York to San Francisco, he would shift his type and sample to one of our American sleepers.)

MISSOURI STATE

We should have made the run of 960 miles from Philadelphia to St. Louis in thirty-six hours, but we had a collision and bad locomotive smash about two-thirds of the way, which set us back. So merely stopping over night that time in St. Louis, I sped on westward. As I cross'd Missouri State the whole distance by the St. Louis and Kansas City Northern Railroad, a fine early autumn day, I thought my eyes had never looked on scenes of greater pastoral beauty. For over two hundred miles successive rolling prairies, agriculturally perfect view'd by Pennsylvania and New Jersey eyes, and dotted here and there with fine timber. Yet fine as the land is, it isn't the finest portion; (there is a bed of impervious clay and hard-pan beneath this section that holds water too firmly, "drowns the land in wet weather, and bakes it in dry," as a cynical farmer told me.) South are some richer tracts, though perhaps the beauty-spots of the State are the northwestern counties. Altogether, I am clear, (now, and from what I have seen and learn'd since,) the Missouri, in climate, soil, relative situation, wheat, grass, mines, railroads, and every important materialistic respect, stands in the front rank of the Union. Of Missouri averaged politically, and socially I have heard all sorts of talk, some pretty severe—but I should have no fear myself of getting along safely and comfortably anywhere among the Missourians. They raise a good deal of tobacco. You see at this time quantities of the light greenish-gray leaves pulled and hanging out to dry on temporary frameworks or rows of sticks. Looks much like the mullein familiar to eastern eyes.

LAWRENCE AND TOPEKA, KANSAS

We thought of stopping in Kansas City, but when we got there we found a train ready and a crowd of hospitable Kansians to take us on to Lawrence, to which I proceeded. I shall not soon forget my good days in L., in company with Judge Usher and his sons, (especially John and Linton,) true westerners of the noblest type. Nor the similar days in Topeka. Nor the brotherly kindness of my RR. friends there, and the city and State officials. Lawrence and Topeka are large, bustling, half-rural, handsome cities. I took two or three long drives about the latter, drawn by a spirited team over smooth roads.

THE PRAIRIES

And an Undeliver'd Speech

At a large popular meeting at Topeka—the Kansas State Silver Wedding, fifteen or twenty thousand people—I had been erroneously bill'd to deliver a poem. As I seem'd to be made much of, and wanted to be good-natured, I hastily pencill'd out the following little speech. Unfortunately, (or fortunately,) I had such a good time and rest, and talk and dinner, with the U. boys, that I let the hours slip away and didn't drive over to the meeting and speak my piece. But here it is just the same:

"My friends, your bills announce me as giving a poem; but I have no poem— have composed none for this occasion. And I can honestly say I am now glad of it. Under these skies resplendent in September beauty—amid the peculiar landscape you are used to, but which is new to me—these interminable and stately prairies—in the freedom and vigor and sane enthusiasm of this perfect western air and autumn sunshine—it seems to me a poem would be almost an impertinence. But if you care to have a word from me, I should speak it about these very prairies; they impress me most, of all the objective shows I see or have seen on this, my first real visit to the West. As I have roll'd rapidly hither for more than a thousand miles, through fair Ohio, through bread-raising Indiana and Illinois—through ample Missouri, that contains and raises everything; as I have partially explor'd your charming city during the last two days, and, standing on Oread hill, by the university, have launch'd my view across broad expanses of living green, in every direction—I have again been most impress'd, I say, and shall remain for the rest of my life most impress'd, with that feature of the topography of your western central world—that vast Something, stretching out on its own unbounded scale, unconfined, which there is in these prairies, combining the real and ideal, and beautiful as dreams.

"I wonder indeed if the people of this continental inland West know how much of first-class *art* they have in these prairies—how original and all your own—how much of the influences of a character for your future humanity, broad, patriotic, heroic and new? how entirely they tally on land the grandeur and superb monotony of the skies of heaven, and the ocean with its waters? how freeing, soothing, nourishing they are to the soul?

"Then is it not subtly they who have given us our leading modern Americans, Lincoln and Grant?—vast-spread, average men—their foregrounds of character altogether practical and real, yet (to those who have eyes to see) with finest backgrounds of the ideal, towering high as any. And do we not see, in them, foreshadowings of the future races that shall fill these prairies?

"Not but what the Yankee and Atlantic States, and every other part—Texas, and the States flanking the south-east and the Gulf of Mexico—the Pacific shore empire—the Territories and Lakes, and the Canada line (the day is not yet, but it will come, including Canada entire)—are equally and integrally and indissolubly this Nation, the *sine qua non* of the human, political and commercial New World. But this favor'd central area of (in round numbers) two thousand miles square seems fated to be the home both of what I would call America's distinctive ideas and distinctive realities.''

ON TO DENVER—A FRONTIER INCIDENT

The jaunt of five or six hundred miles from Topeka to Denver took me through a variety of country, but all unmistakably prolific, western, American, and on the largest scale. For a long distance we follow the line of the Kansas river, (I like better the old name, Kaw,) a stretch of very rich, dark soil, famed for its wheat, and call'd the Golden Belt—then plains and plains, hour after hour—Ellsworth county, the centre of the State—where I must stop a moment to tell a characteristic story of early days—scene the very spot where I am passing—time 1868. In a scrimmage at some public gathering in the town, A. had shot B. quite badly, but had not kill'd him. The sober men of Ellsworth conferr'd with one another and decided that A. deserv'd punishment. As they wished to set a good example and establish their reputation the reverse of a Lynching town, they open an informal court and bring both men before them for deliberate trial. Soon as this trial begins the wounded man is led forward to give his testimony. Seeing his enemy in durance and unarm'd, B. walks suddenly up in a fury and shoots A. through the head—shoots him dead. The court is instantly adjourn'd, and its unanimous members, without a word of debate, walk the murderer B. out, wounded as he is, and hang him.

In due time we reach Denver, which city I fall in love with from the first, and have that feeling confirm'd, the longer I stay there. One of my pleasantest days was a jaunt, via Platte cañon, to Leadville.

AN HOUR ON KENOSHA SUMMIT

Jottings from the Rocky Mountains, mostly pencill'd during a day's trip over the South Park RR., returning from Leadville, and especially the hour we were detain'd, (much to my satisfaction,) at Kenosha summit. As afternoon advances, novelties, far-reaching splendors, accumulate under the bright sun in this pure air. But I had better commence with the day.

The confronting of Platte cañon just at dawn, after a ten miles' ride in early darkness on the rail from Denver—the seasonable stoppage at the entrance of the cañon, and good breakfast of eggs, trout, and nice griddle-cakes—then as we travel on, and get

well in the gorge, all the wonders, beauty, savage power of the
scene—the wild stream of water, from sources of snows, brawling
continually in sight one side—the dazzling sun, and the morning
lights on the rocks—such turns and grades in the track, squirming
around corners, or up and down hills—far glimpses of a hundred
peaks, titanic necklaces, stretching north and south—the huge
rightly-named Dome-rock—and as we dash along, others similar,
simple, monolithic, elephantine.

AN EGOTISTICAL "FIND"

"I have found the law of my own poems," was the unspoken
but more-and-more decided feeling that came to me as I pass'd,
hour after hour, amid all this grim yet joyous elemental abandon
—this plenitude of material, entire absence of art, untrammel'd
play of primitive Nature—the chasm, the gorge, the crystal mountain
stream, repeated scores, hundreds of miles—the broad handling
and absolute uncrampedness—the fantastic forms, bathed in transparent browns, faint reds and grays, towering sometimes a thousand,
sometimes two or three thousand feet high—at their tops now and
then huge masses pois'd , and mixing with the clouds, with only their
outlines, hazed in misty lilac, visible. ("In Nature's grandest shows,"
says an old Dutch writer, an ecclesiastic, "amid the ocean's depth,
if so might be, or countless worlds rolling above at night, a man thinks
of them, weighs all, not for themselves or the abstract, but with
reference to his own personality, and how they may affect him or color
his destinies.")

NEW SENSES—NEW JOYS

We follow the stream of amber and bronze brawling along its
bed, with its frequent cascades and snow-white foam. Through
the cañon we fly—mountains not only each side, but seemingly,
till we get near, right in front of us—every rood a new view flashing,
and each flash defying description—on the almost perpendicular
sides, clinging pines, cedars, spruces, crimson sumach bushes, spots
of wild grass—but dominating all, those towering rocks, rocks,
rocks, bathed in delicate vari-colors, with the clear sky of autumn
overhead. New senses, new joys, seem develop'd. Talk as you like,
a typical Rocky Mountain cañon, or a limitless sea-like stretch of
the great Kansas or Colorado plains, under favoring circumstances,
tallies, perhaps expresses, certainly awakes, those grandest and
sublest element-emotions in the human soul, that all the marble

temples and sculptures from Phidias to Thorwaldsen—all paintings, poems, reminiscences, or even music, probably never can.

STEAM-POWER, TELEGRAPHS, &C.

I get out on a ten minutes' stoppage at Deer creek, to enjoy the unequal'd combination of hill, stone and wood. As we speed again, the yellow granite in the sunshine, with natural spires, minarets, castellated perches far aloft—then long stretches of straight-upright palisades, rhinoceros color—then gamboge and tinted chromos. Ever the best of my pleasures the cool-fresh Colorado atmosphere, yet sufficiently warm. Signs of man's restless advent and pioneerage, hard as Nature's face is—deserted dug-outs by dozens in the side-hills—the scantling hut, the telegraph-pole, the smoke of some impromptu chimney or outdoor fire—at intervals little settlements of log-houses, or parties of surveyors or telegraph builders, with their comfortable tents. Once, a canvas office where you could send a message by electricity anywhere around the world! Yes, pronounc'd signs of the man of latest dates, dauntlessly grappling with these grisliest shows of the old kosmos. At several places steam saw-mills, with their piles of logs and boards, and the pipes puffing. Occasionally Platte cañon expanding into a grassy flat of a few acres. At one such place, toward the end, where we stop, and I get out to stretch my legs, as I look skyward, or rather mountain-topward, a huge hawk or eagle (a rare sight here) is idly soaring, balancing along the ether, now sinking low and coming quite near, and then up again in stately-languid circles—then higher, higher, slanting to the north, and gradually out of sight.

AMERICA'S BACK-BONE

I jot these lines literally at Kenosha summit, where we return, afternoon, and take a long rest, 10,000 feet above sea-level. At this immense height the South Park stretches fifty miles before me. Mountainous chains and peaks in every variety of perspective, every hue of vista, fringe the view, in nearer, or middle, or far-dim distance, or fade on the horizon. We have now reach'd, penetrated the Rockies, (Hayden calls it the Front Range,) for a hundred miles or so; and though these chains spread away in every direction, specially north and south, thousands and thousands farther, I have seen specimens of the utmost of them, and know henceforth at least what they are, and what they look like. Not themselves alone, for they typify stretches and areas of half the globe—are, in fact, the vertebræ or back-bone of our hemisphere. As the anatomists say a man is only a spine, topp'd, footed, breasted and radiated, so the whole Western world is, in a sense, but an expansion of these mountains. In South America they are the Andes, in Central America and Mexico the Cordilleras, and in our States they go under different names—in California the Coast and Cascade ranges—thence more eastwardly the Sierra Nevadas—but mainly and more centrally here the Rocky Mountains proper, with many an elevation such as Lincoln's, Grey's, Harvard's, Yale's, Long's and Pikes' peaks, all over 14,000 feet high. (East, the highest peaks of the Alleghanies, the Adirondacks, the Cattskills, and the White Mountains, range from 2000 to 5500 feet—only Mount Washington, in the latter, 6300 feet.)

THE PARKS

In the midst of all here, lie such beautiful contrasts as the sunken basins of the North, Middle, and South Parks, (the latter I am now on one side of, and overlooking,) each the size of a large, level, almost quadrangular, grassy, western county, wall'd in by walls of hills, and each park the source of a river. The ones I specify are the largest in Colorado, but the whole of that State, and of Wyoming, Utah, Nevada and western California, through their sierras and ravines, are copiously mark'd by similar spreads and openings, many of the small ones of paradisiac loveliness and perfection, with their offsets of mountains, streams, atmosphere and hues beyond compare.

ART FEATURES

Talk, I say again, of going to Europe, of visiting the ruins of feudal castles, or Coliseum remains, or kings' palaces—when you can come *here*. The alternations one gets, too; after the Illinois and Kansas prairies of a thousand miles—smooth and easy areas of the corn and wheat of ten million democratic farms in the future—here start up in every conceivable presentation of shape, these non-utilitarian piles, coping the skies, emanating a beauty, terror, power, more than Dante or Angelo ever knew. Yes, I think the chyle of not only poetry and painting, but oratory, and even the metaphysics and music fit for the New World, before being finally assimilated, need first and feeding visits here.

Mountain streams.—The spiritual contrast and etheriality of the whole region consist largely to me in its never-absent peculiar streams—the snows of inaccessible upper areas melting and running down through the gorges continually. Nothing like the water of pastoral plains, or creeks with wooded banks and turf, or anything of the kind elsewhere. The snapes tnat eiement takes in the shows of the globe cannot be fully understood by an artist until he has studieu these unique rivulets.

Aerial effects.—But perhaps as I gaze around me the rarest sight of all is in atmospheric hues. The prairies—as I cross'd them in my journey hither—and these mountains and parks, seem to me to afford new lights and shades. Everywhere the aerial gradations and sky-effects inimitable; nowhere else such perspectives, such transparent lilacs and grays. I can conceive of some superior landscape painter, some fine colorist, after sketching awhile out here, discarding all his previous work, delightful to stock exhibition amateurs, as muddy, raw and artificial. Near one's eye ranges an infinite variety; high up, the bare whitey-brown, above timber line; in certain spots afar patches of snow any time of year; (no trees, no flowers, no birds, at those chilling altitudes.) As I write I see the Snowy Range through the blue mist, beautiful and far off. I plainly see the patches of snow.

DENVER IMPRESSIONS

Through the long-lingering half-light of the most superb of evenings we return'd to Denver, where I staid several days leisurely exploring, receiving impressions, with which I may as well taper off this memorandum, itemizing what I saw there. The best was the men, three-fourths of them large, able, calm, alert, American. And cash! why they create it here. Out in the smelting works, (the biggest and most improv'd ones, for the precious metals, in the world,) I saw long rows of vats, pans, cover'd by bubbling-boiling water, and fill'd with pure silver, four or five inches thick, many thousand dollars' worth in a pan. The foreman who was showing me shovel'd it carelessly up with a little wooden shovel, as one might toss beans. Then large silver bricks, worth $2000 a brick, dozens of piles, twenty in a pile. In one place in the mountains, at a mining camp, I had a few days before seen rough bullion on the ground in the open air, like the confectioner's pyramids at some swell dinner in New York. (Such a sweet morsel to roll over with a poor author's pen and ink—and appropriate to slip in here— that the silver product of Colorado and Utah, with the gold product of California, New Mexico, Nevada and Dakota, foots up an addition to the world's coin of considerably over a hundred millions every year.)

A city, this Denver, well-laid out—Laramie street, and 15th and 16th and Champa streets, with others, particularly fine—some with tall storehouses of stone or iron, and windows of plate-glass—all the streets with little canals of mountain water running along the sides—plenty of people, "business," modernness—yet not without a certain racy wild smack, all its own. A place of fast horses, (many mares with their colts,) and I saw lots of big greyhounds for antelope hunting. Now and then groups of miners, some just come in, some starting out, very picturesque.

One of the papers here interview'd me, and reported me as saying off-hand: "I have lived in or visited all the great cities on the Atlantic third of the republic—Boston, Brooklyn with its hills, New Orleans, Baltimore, stately Washington, broad Philadelphia, teeming Cincinnati and Chicago, and for thirty years in that wonder, wash'd by hurried and glittering tides, my own New York, not only the New World's but the world's city—but, newcomer to Denver as I am, and threading its streets, breathing its air, warm'd by its sunshine, and having what there is of its human as well as aerial ozone flash'd upon me now for only three or four days, I am very much like a man feels sometimes toward certain people he meets with, and warms to, and hardly knows why. I, too, can hardly tell why, but as I enter'd the city in the slight haze of a late September afternoon, and have breath'd its air, and slept well o' nights, and have roam'd or rode leisurely, and watch'd the comers and goers at the hotels, and absorb'd the climatic magnetism of this curiously attractive region, there has steadily grown upon me a feeling of affection for the spot, which, sudden as it is, has become so definite and strong that I must put it on record."

So much for my feeling toward the Queen city of the plains and peaks, where she sits in her delicious rare atmosphere, over 5000 feet above sea-level, irrigated by mountain streams, one way looking east over the prairies for a thousand miles, and having the other, westward, in constant view by day, draped in their violet haze, mountain tops innumerable. Yes, I fell in love with Denver, and even felt a wish to spend my declining and dying days there.

I TURNED SOUTH—AND THEN EAST AGAIN

Leave Denver at 8 A. M. by the Rio Grande RR. going south. Mountains constantly in sight in the apparently near distance, veil'd slightly, but still clear and very grand—their cones, colors, sides, distinct against the sky—hundreds, it seem'd thousands, interminable necklaces of them, their tops and slopes hazed more or less slightly in that blue-gray, under the autumn sun, for over a hundred miles—the most spiritual show of objective Nature I ever beheld, or ever thought possible. Occasionally the light strengthens, making a contrast of yellow-tinged silver on one side, with dark and shaded gray on the other. I took a long look at Pike's peak, and was a little disappointed. (I suppose I had expected something stunning.) Our view over plains to the left stretches amply, with corrals here and there, the frequent cactus and wild sage, and herds of cattle feeding. Thus about 120 miles to Pueblo. At that town we board the comfortable and well-equipt Atchison, Topeka and Santa Fe RR., now striking east.

UNFULFILL'D WANTS—THE ARKANSAS RIVER

I had wanted to go to the Yellowstone river region—wanted specially to see the National Park, and the geysers and the "hoo-doo" or goblin land of that country; indeed, hesitated a little at Pueblo, the turning point—wanted to thread the Veta pass—wanted to go over the Santa Fe trail away southwestward to New Mexico—but turn'd and set my face eastward—leaving behind me whetting glimpse-tastes of southeastern Colorado, Pueblo, Bald mountain, the Spanish peaks, Sangre de Christos, Mile-Shoe-curve (which my veteran friend on the locomotive told me was "the boss railroad curve of the universe,") fort Garland on the plains, Veta, and the three great peaks of the Sierra Blancas.

The Arkansas river plays quite a part in the whole of this region—I see it, or its high-cut rocky northern shore, for miles, and cross and recross it frequently, as it winds and squirms like a snake. The plains vary here even more than usual—sometimes a long sterile stretch of scores of miles—then green, fertile and grassy, an equal length. Some very large herds of sheep. (One wants new words in writing about these plains, and all the inland American West—the terms, *far*, *large*, *vast*, &c., are insufficient.)

A SILENT LITTLE FOLLOWER—THE COREOPSIS

Here I must say a word about a little follower, present even now before my eyes. I have been accompanied on my whole journey from Barnegat to Pike's Peak by a pleasant floricultural friend, or rather millions of friends—nothing more or less than a hardy little yellow five-petal'd September and October wild-flower, growing I think everywhere in the middle and northern United States. I had seen it on the Hudson and over Long Island, and along the banks of the Delaware and through New Jersey, (as years ago up the Connecticut, and one fall by Lake Champlain.) This trip it follow'd me regularly, with its slender stem and eyes of gold, from Cape May to the Kaw valley, and so through tne cañons and to these plains. In Missouri I saw immense fields all bright with it. Toward western Illinois I woke up one morning in the sleeper and the first thing when I drew the curtain of my berth and look'd out was its pretty countenance and bending neck.

Sept. 25th.—Early morning—still going east after we leave Sterling, Kansas, where I stopp'd a day and night. The sun up about half an hour; nothing can be fresher or more beautiful than this time, this region. I see quite a field of my yellow flower in full bloom. At intervals dots of nice two-story houses, as we ride swiftly by. Over the immense area, flat as a floor, visible for twenty miles in every direction in the clear air, a prevalence of autumn-drab and reddish-tawny herbage—sparse stacks of hay and enclosures, breaking the landscape—as we rumble by, flocks of prairie-hens starting up. Between Sterling and Florence a fine country. (Remembrances to E. L., my old-young soldier friend of war times, and his wife and boy at S.)

THE PRAIRIES AND GREAT PLAINS IN POETRY

(*After traveling Illinois, Missouri, Kansas and Colorado*)

Grand as the thought that doubtless the child is already born who will see a hundred millions of people, the most prosperous and advanc'd of the world, inhabiting these Prairies, the great Plains, and the valley of the Mississippi, I could not help thinking it would be grander still to see all those inimitable American areas fused in the alembic of a perfect poem, or other esthetic work, entirely western, fresh and limitless—altogether our own, without a trace or taste of Europe's soil, reminiscence, technical letter or spirit. My days and nights, as I travel here—what an exhilaration!—not the air alone, and the sense of vastness, but every local sight and feature. Everywhere something characteristic—the cactuses, pinks, buffalo grass, wild sage—the receding perspective, and the far circle-line of the horizon all times of day, especially forenoon—the clear, pure, cool, rarefied nutriment for the lungs, previously quite unknown—the black patches and streaks left by surface-conflagrations—the deep-plough'd furrow of the "fire-guard"—the slanting snow-racks built all along to shield the railroad from winter drifts—the prairie-dogs and the herds of antelope—the curious "dry rivers"—occasionally a "dug-out" or corral—Fort Riley and Fort Wallace—those towns of the northern plains, (like ships on the sea,) Eagle-Tail, Coyoté, Cheyenne, Agate, Monotoyn, Kit Carson—with ever the ant-hill and the buffalo-wallow—ever the herds of cattle and the cow-boys ("cow-punchers") to me a strangely interesting class, bright-eyed as hawks, with their swarthy complexions and their broad-brimm'd hats—apparently always on horseback, with loose arms slightly raised and swinging as they ride.

THE SPANISH PEAKS—EVENING ON THE PLAINS

Between Pueblo and Bent's fort, southward, in a clear afternoon sun-spell I catch exceptionally good glimpses of the Spanish peaks. We are in southeastern Colorado—pass immense herds of cattle as our first-class locomotive rushes us along—two or three times crossing the Arkansas, which we follow many miles, and of which river I get fine views, sometimes for quite a distance, its stony, upright, not very high, palisade banks, and then its muddy flats. We pass Fort Lyon—lots of adobie houses—limitless pasturage, appropriately fleck'd with those herds of cattle—in due time the declining sun in the west—a sky of limpid pearl over all—and so evening on the great plains. A calm, pensive, boundless landscape—the perpendicular rocks of the north Arkansas, hued in twilight—a thin line of violet on the southwestern horizon—the palpable coolness and slight aroma—a belated cow-boy with some unruly member of his herd—an emigrant wagon toiling yet a little further, the horses slow and tired—two men, apparently father and son, jogging along on foot—and around all the indescribable *chiaroscuro* and sentiment, (profounder than anything at sea,) athwart these endless wilds

AMERICA'S CHARACTERISTIC LANDSCAPE

Speaking generally as to the capacity and sure future destiny of that plain and prairie area (larger than any European kingdom) it is the inexhaustible land of wheat, maize, wool, flax, coal, iron, beef and pork, butter and cheese, apples and grapes—land of ten million virgin farms—to the eye at present wild and unproductive—yet experts say that upon it when irrigated may easily be grown enough wheat to feed the world. Then as to scenery (giving my own thought and feeling,) while I know the standard claim is that Yosemite, Niagara falls, the upper Yellowstone and the like, afford the greatest natural shows, I am not so sure but the Prairies and Plains, while less stunning at first sight, last longer, fill the esthetic sense fuller, precede all the rest, and make North America's characteristic landscape.

Indeed through the whole of this journey, with all its shows and varieties, what most impress'd me, and will longest remain with me, are these same prairies. Day after day, and night after night, to my eyes, to all my senses—the esthetic one most of all—they silently and broadly unfolded. Even their simplest statistics are sublime.

EARTH'S MOST IMPORTANT STREAM

The valley of the Mississippi river and its tributaries, (this stream and its adjuncts involve a big part of the question,) comprehends more than twelve hundred thousand square miles, the greater part prairies. It is by far the most important stream on the globe, and would seem to have been marked out by design, slow-flowing from north to south, through a dozen climates, all fitted for man's healthy occupancy, its outlet unfrozen all the year, and its line forming a safe, cheap continental avenue for commerce and passage from the north temperate to the torrid zone. Not even the mighty Amazon (though larger in volume) on its line of east and west—not the Nile in Africa, nor the Danube in Europe, nor the three great rivers of China, compare with it. Only the Mediterranean sea has play'd some such part in history, and all through the past, as the Mississippi is destined to play in the future. By its demesnes, water'd and welded by its branches, the Missouri, the Ohio, the Arkansas, the Red, the Yazoo, the St. Francis and others, it already compacts twenty-five millions of people, not merely the most peaceful and money-making, but the most restless and warlike on earth. Its valley, or reach, is rapidly concentrating the political power of the American Union. One almost thinks it *is* the Union—or soon will be. Take it out, with its radiations, and what would be left? From the car windows through Indiana, Illinois, Missouri, or stopping some days along the Topeka and Santa Fe road, in southern Kansas, and indeed wherever I went, hundreds and thousands of miles through this region, my eyes feasted on primitive and rich meadows, some of them partially inhabited, but far, immensely far more untouch'd, unbroken—and much of it more lovely and fertile in its unplough'd innocence than the fair and valuable fields of New York's, Pennsylvania's, Maryland's or Virginia's richest farms.

PRAIRIE ANALOGIES—THE TREE QUESTION

The word Prairie is French, and means literally meadow. The cosmical analogies of our North American plains are the Steppes of Asia, the Pampas and Llanos of South America, and perhaps the Saharas of Africa. Some think the plains have been originally lake-beds; others attribute the absence of forests to the fires that almost annually sweep over them—(the cause, in vulgar estimation, of Indian summer.) The tree question will soon become a grave one. Although the Atlantic slope, the Rocky mountain region, and the southern portion of the Mississippi valley, are well wooded, there are here stretches of hundreds and thousands of miles where either not a tree grows, or often useless destruction has prevail'd; and the matter of the cultivation and spread of forests may well be press'd upon thinkers who look to the coming generations of the prairie States.

MISSISSIPPI VALLEY LITERATURE

Lying by one rainy day in Missouri to rest after quite a long exploration—first trying a big volume I found there of "Milton, Young, Gray, Beattie and Collins," but giving it up for a bad job—enjoying however for awhile, as often before, the reading of Walter Scott's poems, "Lay of the Last Minstrel," "Marmion," and so on—I stopp'd and laid down the book, and ponder'd the thought of a poetry that should in due time express and supply the teeming region I was in the midst of, and have briefly touch'd upon. One's mind needs but a moment's deliberation anywhere in the United States to see clearly enough that all the prevalent book and library poets, either as imported from Great Britain, or follow'd and *doppel-gang'd* here, are foreign to our States, copiously as they are read by us all. But to fully understand not only how absolutely in opposition to our times and lands, and how little and cramp'd, and what anachronisms and absurdities many of their pages are, for American purposes, one must dwell or travel awhile in Missouri, Kansas and Colorado, and get rapport with their people and country.

Will the day ever come—no matter how long deferr'd—when those models and lay-figures from the British islands—and even the precious traditions of the classics—will be reminiscences, studies only? The pure breath, primitiveness, boundless prodigality and amplitude, strange mixture of delicacy and power, of continence, of real and ideal, and of all original and first-class elements, of these prairies, the Rocky mountains, and of the Mississippi and Missouri rivers—will they ever appear in, and in some sort form a standard for our poetry and art? (I sometimes think that even the ambition of my friend Joaquin Miller to put them in, and illustrate them, places him ahead of the whole crowd.)

Not long ago I was down New York bay, on a steamer, watching the sunset over the dark green heights of Navesink, and viewing all that inimitable spread of shore, shipping and sea, around Sandy hook. But an intervening week or two, and my eyes catch the shadowy outlines of the Spanish peaks. In the more than two thousand miles between, though of infinite and paradoxical variety, a curious and absolute fusion is doubtless steadily annealing, compacting, identifying all. But subtler and wider and more solid, (to produce such compaction,) than the laws of the States, or the common ground of Congress or the Supreme Court, or the grim welding of our national wars, or the steel ties of railroads, or all the kneading and fusing processes of our material and business history, past or present, would in my opinion be a great throbbing, vital, imaginative work, or series of works, or literature, in constructing which the Plains, the Prairies, and the Mississippi river, with the demesnes of its varied and ample valley, should be the concrete background, and America's humanity, passions, struggles, hopes, there and now—an *eclaircissement* as it is and is to be, on the stage of the New World, of all Time's hitherto drama of war, romance and evolution— should furnish the lambent fire, the ideal.

AN INTERVIEWER'S-ITEM

Oct. 17, '79.—To-day one of the newspapers of St. Louis prints the following informal remarks of mine on American, especially Western literature: "We called on Mr. Whitman yesterday and after a somewhat desultory conversation abruptly asked him: 'Do you think we are to have a distinctively American literature?' 'It seems to me,' said he, 'that our work at present is to lay the foundations of a great nation in products, in agriculture, in commerce, in networks of intercommunication, and in all that relates to the comforts of vast masses of men and families, with freedom of speech, ecclesiasticism, &c. These we have founded and are carrying out on a grander scale than ever hitherto, and Ohio, Illinois, Indiana, Missouri, Kansas and Colorado, seem to me to be the seat and field of these very facts and ideas. Materialistic prosperity in all its varied forms, with those other points that I mentioned, intercommunication and freedom, are first to be attended to. When those have their results and get settled, then a literature worthy of us will begin to be defined. Our American superiority and vitality are in the bulk of our people, not in a gentry like the old world. The greatness of our army during the secession war, was in the rank and file, and so with the nation.

Other lands have their vitality in a few, a class, but we have it in the bulk of the people. Our leading men are not of much account and never have been, but the average of the people is immense, beyond all history. Sometimes I think in all departments, literature and art included, that will be the way our superiority will exhibit itself. We will not have great individuals or great leaders, but a great average bulk, unprecedentedly great.' "

THE WOMEN OF THE WEST

Kansas City.—I am not so well satisfied with what I see of the women of the prairie cities. I am writing this where I sit leisurely in a store in Main street, Kansas city, a streaming crowd on the sidewalks flowing by. The ladies (and the same in Denver) are all fashionably drest, and have the look of "gentility" in face, manner and action, but they do *not* have, either in physique or the mentality appropriate to them, any high native originality of spirit or body, (as the men certainly have, appropriate to them.) They are "intellectual" and fashionable, but dyspeptic-looking and generally doll-like; their ambition evidently is to copy their eastern sisters. Something far different and in advance must appear, to tally and complete the superb masculinity of the West, and maintain and continue it.

THE SILENT GENERAL

Sept. 28, '79.—So General Grant, after circumambiating the world, has arrived home again—landed in San Francisco yesterday, from the ship City of Tokio from Japan. What a man he is! what a history! what an illustration—his life—of the capacities of that American individuality common to us all. Cynical critics are wondering "what the people can see in Grant" to make such a hubbub about. They aver (and it is no doubt true) that he has hardly the average of our day's literary and scholastic culture, and absolutely no pronounc'd genius or conventional eminence of any sort. Correct: but he proves how an average western farmer, mechanic, boatman, carried by tides of circumstances, perhaps caprices, into a position of incredible military or civic responsibilities, (history has presented none more trying, no born monarch's, no mark more shining for attack or envy,) may steer his way fitly and steadily through them all, carrying the country and himself with credit year after year— command over a million armed men—fight more than fifty pitch'd battles—rule for eight years a land larger than all the kingdoms of Europe combined—and then, retiring, quietly (with a cigar in his mouth) make the promenade of the whole world, through its courts and coteries, and kings and czars and mikados, and splendidest glitters and etiquettes, as phlegmatically as he ever walk'd the portico of a Missouri hotel after dinner. I say all this is what people like—and I am sure I like it. Seems to me it transcends Plutarch. How those old Greeks, indeed, would have seized on him! A mere plain man—no art, no poetry—only practical sense, ability to do, or try his best to do, what devolv'd upon him. A common trader, money-maker, tanner, farmer of Illinois—general for the republic, in its terrific struggle with itself, in the war of attempted secession—President following, (a task of peace, more difficult than the war itself)—nothing heroic, as the authorities put it—and yet the greatest hero. The gods, the destinies, seem to have concentrated upon him.

PRESIDENT HAYES'S SPEECHES

Sept. 30.—I see President Hayes has come out West, passing quite informally from point to point, with his wife and a small cortege of big officers, receiving ovations, and making daily and sometimes double-daily addresses to the people. To these addresses—all impromptu, and some would call them ephemeral—I feel to devote a momorandum. They are shrewd, good-natur'd, face-to-face speeches, on easy topics not to deep; but they give me some revised ideas of oratory—of a new, opportune theory and practice of that art, quite changed from the classic rules, and adapted to our days, our occasions, to American democracy, and to the swarming populations of the West. I hear them criticised as wanting in dignity, but to me they are just what they should be, considering all the circumstances, who they come from, and who they are address'd to. Underneath, his objects are to compact and fraternize the States, encourage their materialistic and industrial development, soothe and expand their self-poise, and tie all and each with resistless double ties not only of intertrade barter, but human comradeship.

From Kansas city I went on to St. Louis, where I remain'd nearly three months, with my brother T. J. W., and my dear nieces.

ST. LOUIS MEMORANDA

Oct., Nov., and Dec., '79.—The points of St. Louis are its position, its absolute wealth, (the long accumulations of time and trade, solid riches, probaby a higher average thereof than any city,) the unrivall'd amplitude of its well-laid out environage of broad plateaus, for future expansion—and the great State of which it is the head. It fuses northern and southern qualities, perhaps native and foreign ones, to perfection, rendezvous the whole stretch of the Mississippi and Missouri rivers, and its American electricity goes well with its German phlegm. Fourth, Fifth and Third streets are store-streets, showy, modern, metropolitan, with hurrying crowds, vehicles, horse-cars, hubbub, plenty of people, rich goods, plate-glass windows, iron fronts often five or six stories high. You can purchase anything in St. Louis (in most of the big western cities for the matter of that) just as readily and cheaply as in the Atlantic marts. Often in going about the town you see reminders of old, even decay'd civilization. The water of the west, in some places, is not good, but they make it up here by plenty of very fair wine, and inexhaustible quantities of the best beer in the world. There are immense establishments for slaughtering beef and pork—and I saw flocks of sheep, 5000 in a flock. (In Kansas city I had visited a packing establishment that kills and packs an average of 2500 hogs a day the whole year round, for export. Another in Atchison, Kansas, same extent; others nearly equal elsewhere. And just as big ones here.)

NIGHTS ON THE MISSISSIPPI

Oct. 29th, 30th, and 31st.—Wonderfully fine, with the full harvest moon, dazzling and silvery. I have haunted the river every night lately, where I could get a look at the bridge by moonlight. It is indeed a structure of perfection and beauty unsurpassable, and I never tire of it. The river at present is very low; I noticed to-day it had much more of a blue-clear look than usual. I hear the slight ripples, the air is fresh and cool, and the view, up or down, wonderfully clear, in the moonlight. I am out pretty late: it is so fascinating, dreamy. The cool night-air, all the influences, the silence, with those far-off eternal stars, do me good. I have been quite ill of late. And so, well-near the centre of our national demesne, these night views of the Mississippi.

UPON OUR OWN LAND

"Always, after supper, take a walk half a mile long," says an old proverb, dryly adding, "and if convenient let it be upon your own land." I wonder does any other nation but ours afford opportunity for such a jaunt as this? Indeed has any previous period afforded it? No one, I discover, begins to know the real geographic, democratic, indissoluble American Union in the present, or suspect it in the future, until he explores these Central States, and dwells awhile observantly on their prairies, or amid their busy towns, and the mighty father of waters. A ride of two or three thousand miles, "on one's own land," with hardly a disconnection, could certainly be had in no other place than the United States, and at no period before this. If you want to see what the railroad is, and how civilization and progress date from it—how it is the conqueror of crude nature, which it turns to man's use, both on small scales and on the largest—come hither to inland America.

I return'd home, east, Jan. 5, 1880, having travers'd, to and fro and across, 10,000 miles and more. I soon resumed my seclusions down in the woods, or by the creek, or gaddings about cities, and an occasional disquisition, as will be seen following.

EDGAR POE'S SIGNIFICANCE

Jan. 1, '80.—In diagnosing this disease called humanity—to assume for the nonce what seems a chief mood of the personality and writings of my subject—I have thought that poets, somewhere or other on the list, present the most mark'd indications. Comprehending artists in a mass, musicians, painters, actors, and so on, and considering each and all of them as radiations or flanges of that furious whirling wheel, poetry, the centre and axis of the whole, where else indeed may we so well investigate the causes, growths, tally-marks of the time—the age's matter and malady?

By common consent there is nothing better for man or woman than a perfect and noble life, morally without flaw, happily balanced in activity, physically sound and pure, giving its due proportion, and no more, to the sympathetic, the human emotional element—a life, in all these, unhasting, unresting, untiring to the end. And yet there is another shape of personality dearer far to the artist-sense, (which likes the play of strongest lights and shades,) where the perfect character, the good, the heroic, although never attain'd, is never lost sight of, but through failures, sorrows, temporary downfalls, is return'd to again and again, and while often violated, is passionately adhered to as long as mind, muscles, voice, obey the power we call volition. This sort of personality we see more or less in Burns, Byron, Schiller, and George Sand. But we do not see it in Edgar Poe. (All this is the result of reading at intervals the last three days a new volume of his poems—I took it on my rambles down by the pond, and by degrees read it all through there.)

While to the character first outlined the service Poe renders is certainly that entire contrast and contradiction which is next best to fully exemplifying it.

Almost without the first sign of moral principle, or of the concrete or its heroisms, or the simpler affections of the heart, Poe's verses illustrate an intense faculty for technical and abstract beauty, with the rhyming art to excess, an incorrigible propensity toward nocturnal themes, a demoniac undertone behind every page—and, by final judgment, probably belong among the electric lights of imaginative literature, brilliant and dazzling, but with no heat. There is an indescribable magnetism about the poet's life and reminiscences, as well as the poems. To one who could work out their subtle retracing and retrospect, the latter would make a close tally no doubt between the author's birth and antecedents, his childhood and youth, his physique, his so-call'd education, his studies and associates, the literary and social Baltimore, Richmond, Philadelphia and New York, of those times—not only the places and circumstances in themselves, but often, very often, in a strange spurning of, and reaction from them all.

The following from a report in the Washington "Star" of November 16, 1875, may afford those who care for it something further of my point of view toward this interesting figure and influence of our era. There occurr'd about that date in Baltimore a public reburial of Poe's remains, and dedication of a monument over the grave:

"Being in Washington on a visit at the time, 'the old gray' went over to Baltimore, and though ill from paralysis, consented to hobble up and silently take a seat on the platform, but refused to make any speech, saying, 'I have felt a strong impulse to come over and be here to-day myself in memory of Poe, which I have obey'd, but not the slightest impulse to make a speech, which, my dear friends, must also be obeyed.' In an informal circle, however, in conversation after the ceremonies, Whitman said: 'For a long while, and until lately, I had a distaste for Poe's writings. I wanted, and still want for poetry, the clear sun shining, and fresh air blowing—the strength and power of health, not of delirium, even amid the stormiest passions—with always the background of the eternal moralities. Non-complying with these requirements, Poe's genius has yet conquer'd a special recognition for itself, and I too have come to fully admit it, and appreciate it and him.

" 'In a dream I once had, I saw a vessel on the sea, at midnight, in a storm. It was no great full-rigg'd ship, nor majestic steamer, steering firmly through the gale, but seem'd one of those superb little schooner yachts I had often seen lying anchor'd, rocking so jauntily, in the waters around New York, or up Long Island sound—now flying uncontroll'd with torn sails and broken spars through the wild sleet and winds and waves of the night. On the deck was a slender, slight, beautiful figure, a dim man, apparently enjoying all the terror, the murk, and the dislocation of which he was the centre and the victim. That figure of my lurid dream might stand for Edgar Poe, his spirit, his fortunes, and his poems—themselves all lurid dreams.' "

Much more may be said, but I most desired to exploit the idea put at the beginning. By its popular poets the calibres of an age, the weak spots of its embankments, its sub-currents, (often more significant than the biggest surface ones,) are unerringly indicated. The lush and the weird that have taken such extraordinary possession of nineteenth century verse-lovers—what mean they? The inevitable tendency of poetic culture to morbidity, abnormal beauty —the sickliness of all technical thought or refinement in itself— the abnegation of the perennial and democratic concretes at first hand, the body, the earth and sea, sex and the like—and the substitution of something for them at second or third hand—what bearings have they on current pathological study?

BEETHOVEN'S SEPTETTE

Feb. 11, '80.—At a good concert to-night in the foyer of the opera house, Philadelphia—the band a small but first-rate one. Never did music more sink into and soothe and fill me—never so prove its soul-rousing power, its impossibility of statement. Especially in the rendering of one of Beethoven's master septettes by the well-chosen and perfectly-combined instruments (violins, viola, clarionet, horn, 'cello and contrabass,) was I carried away, seeing, absorbing many wonders. Dainty abandon, sometimes as if Nature laughing on a hillside in the sunshine; serious and firm monotonies, as of winds; a horn sounding through the tangle of the forest, and the dying echoes; soothing floating of waves, but presently rising in surges, angrily lashing, muttering, heavy; piercing peals of laughter, for interstices; now and then weird, as Nature herself is in certain moods—but mainly spontaneous, easy, careless— often the sentiment of the postures of naked children playing or sleeping. It did me good even to watch the violinists drawing their bows so masterly—every motion a study. I allow'd myself, as I sometimes do, to wander out of myself. The conceit came to me of a copious grove of singing birds, and in their midst a simple harmonic duo, two human souls, steadily asserting their own pensiveness, joyousness.

A HINT OF WILD NATURE

Feb. 13.—As I was crossing the Delaware to-day, saw a large flock of wild geese, right overhead, not very high up, ranged in V-shape, in relief against the noon clouds of light smoke-color. Had a capital though momentary view of them, and then of their course on and on southeast, till gradually fading—(my eyesight yet first rate for the open air and its distances, but I use glasses for reading.) Queer thoughts melted into me the two or three minutes, or less, seeing these creatures cleaving the sky—the spacious, airy realm—even the prevailing smoke-gray color everywhere, (no sun shining)—the waters below—the rapid flight of the birds, appearing just for a minute—flashing to me such a hint of the whole spread of Nature, with her eternal unsophisticated freshness, her never-visited recesses of sea, sky, shore—and then disappearing in the distance.

LOAFING IN THE WOODS

March 8.—I write this down in the country again, but in a new spot, seated on a log in the woods, warm, sunny, midday. Have been loafing here deep among the trees, shafts of tall pines, oak, hickory, with a thick undergrowth of laurels and grapevines—the ground cover'd everywhere by debris, dead leaves, breakage, moss—everything solitary, ancient, grim. Paths (such as they are) leading hither and yon—(how made I know not, for nobody seems to come here, nor man nor cattle-kind.) Temperature to-day about 60, the wind through the pine-tops; I sit and listen to its hoarse sighing above (and to the *stillness*) long and long, varied by aimless rambles in the old roads and paths, and by exercise-pulls at the young saplings, to keep my joints from getting stiff. Blue-birds, robins, meadow-larks begin to appear.

Next day, 9th.—A snowstorm in the morning, and continuing most of the day. But I took a walk over two hours, the same woods and paths, amid the falling flakes. No wind, yet the musical low murmur through the pines, quite pronounced, curious, like water-falls, now still'd, now pouring again. All the senses, sight, sound, smell, delicately gratified. Every snowflake lay where it fell on the evergreens, holly-trees, laurels, &c., the multitudinous leaves and branches piled, bulging-white, defined by edge-lines of emerald—the tall straight columns of the plentiful bronze-topt pines—a slight resinous odor blending with that of the snow. (For there is a scent to everything, even the snow, if you can only detect it—no two places, hardly any two hours, anywhere, exactly alike. How different the odor of noon from midnight, or winter from summer, or a windy spell from a still one.)

A CONTRALTO VOICE

May 9, Sunday.—Visit this evening to my friends the J.'s—good supper, to which I did justice—lively chat with Mrs. J. and

I. and J. As I sat out front on the walk afterward, in the evening
air, the church-choir and organ on the corner opposite gave Luther's
hymn, *Ein feste burg*, very finely. The air was borne by a rich contralto. For nearly half an hour there in the dark, (there was a good
string of English stanzas,) came the music, firm and unhurried, with
long pauses. The full silver star-beams of Lyra rose silently over the
church's dim roof-ridge. Vari-color'd lights from the stain'd glass
windows broke through the tree-shadows. And under all—under the
Northern Crown up there, and in the fresh breeze below, and the
chiaroscuro of the night, that liquid-full contralto.

SEEING NIAGARA TO ADVANTAGE

June 4, '80.—For really seizing a great picture or book, or piece
of music, or architecture, or grand scenery—or perhaps for the
first time even the common sunshine, or landscape, or may be even
the mystery of identity, most curious mystery of all—there comes
some lucky five minutes of a man's life, set amid a fortuitous con-
currence of circumstances, and bringing in a brief flash the culmination of years of reading and travel and thought. The present
case about two o'clock this afternoon, gave me Niagara, its superb
severity of action and color and majestic grouping, in one short,
indescribable show. We were very slowly crossing the Suspension
bridge—not a full stop anywhere, but next to it—the day clear,
sunny, still—and I out on the platform. The falls were in plain view
about a mile off, but very distinct, and no roar—hardly a murmur.
The river tumbling green and white, far below me; the dark high
banks, the plentiful umbrage, many bronze cedars, in shadow; and
tempering and arching all the immense materiality, a clear sky overhead, with a few white clouds, limpid, spiritual, silent. Brief, and
as quiet as brief, that picture—a remembrance always afterwards.
Such are the things, indeed, I lay away with my life's rare and blessed
bits of hours, reminiscent, past—the wild sea-storm I once saw one
winter day, off Fire island—the elder Booth in Richard, that famous
night forty years ago in the old Bowery—or Alboni in the children's
scene in Norma—or night-views, I remember, on the field, after
battles in Virginia—or the peculiar sentiment of moonlight and stars
over the great Plains, western Kansas—or scooting up New York
bay, with a stiff breeze and a good yacht, off Navesink. With
these, I say, I henceforth place that view, that afternoon, that combination complete, that five minutes' perfect absorption of Niagara
—not the great majestic gem alone by itself, but set complete in all
its varied, full indispensable surroundings.

JAUNTING TO CANADA

To go back a little, I left Philadelphia, 9th and Green streets, at 8 o'clock P.M., June 3, on a first-class sleeper, by the Lehigh Valley (North Pennsylvania) route, through Bethlehem, Wilkesbarre, Waverly, and so (by Erie) on through Corning to Hornellsville, where we arrived at 8, morning, and had a bounteous breakfast. I must say I never put in such a good night on any railroad track—smooth, firm, the minimum of jolting, and all the swiftness compatible with safety. So without change to Buffalo, and thence to Clifton, where we arrived early afternoon; then on to London, Ontario, Canada, in four more—less than twenty-two hours altogether. I am domiciled at the hospitable house of my friends Dr. and Mrs. Bucke, in the ample and charming garden and lawns of the asylum.

SUNDAY WITH THE INSANE

June 6.—Went over to the religious services (Episcopal) main Insane asylum, held in a lofty, good-sized hall, third story. Plain boards, whitewash, plenty of cheap chairs, no ornament or color, yet all scrupulously clean and sweet. Some three hundred persons present, mostly patients. Everything, the prayers, a short sermon, the firm, orotund voice of the minister, and most of all, beyond any portraying or suggesting, *that audience,* deeply impress'd me. I was furnish'd with an arm-chair near the pulpit, and sat facing the motley, yet perfectly well-behaved and orderly congregation. The quaint dresses and bonnets of some of the women, several very old and gray, here and there like the heads in old pictures. O the looks that came from those faces! There were two or three I shall probably never forget. Nothing at all markedly repulsive or hideous—strange enough I did not see one such. Our common humanity, mine and yours, everywhere:

"The same old blood—the same red, running blood;"

yet behind most, an inferr'd arriere of such storms, such wrecks, such mysteries, fires, love, wrong, greed for wealth, religious problems, crosses—mirror'd from those crazed faces (yet now temporarily so calm, like still waters,) all the woes and sad happenings of life and death—now from every one the devotional element radiating —was it not, indeed, *the peace of God that passeth all understanding,* strange as it may sound? I can only say that I took long and searching eye-sweeps as I sat there, at it seem'd so, rousing unprecedented thoughts, problems unanswerable. A very fair choir, and melodeon accompaniment. They sang "Lead, kindly light," after the sermon. Many join'd in the beautiful hymn, to which the minister read the introductory text, *"In the daytime also He led them with a cloud, and all the night with a light of fire."* Then the words:

> Lead, kindly light, amid the encircling gloom,
>> Lead thou me on.
> The night is dark, and I am far from home;
>> Lead thou me on.
> Keep thou my feet; I do not ask to see
> The distant scene; one step enough for me.
>
> I was not ever thus, nor pray'd that thou
>> Should'st lead me on;
> I lov'd to choose and see my path; but now
>> Lead thou me on.
> I loved the garish day, and spite of fears
> Pride ruled my will; remember not past years.

A couple of days after, I went to the "Refractory building," under special charge of Dr. Beemer, and through the wards pretty thoroughly, both the men's and women's. I have since made many other visits of the kind through the asylum, and around among the detach'd cottages. As far as I could see, this is among the most advanced, perfected, and kindly and rationally carried on, of all its kind in America. It is a town in itself, with many buildings and a thousand inhabitants.

I learn that Canada, and especially this ample and populous province, Ontario, has the very best and plentiest benevolent institutions in all departments.

REMINISCENCE OF ELIAS HICKS

June 8.—To-day a letter from Mrs. E. S. L., Detroit, accompanied in a little post-office roll by a rare old engraved head of Elias Hicks, (from a portrait in oil by Henry Inman, painted for J. V. S., must have been 60 years or more ago, in New York)— among the rest the following excerpt about E. H. in the letter:

"I have listen'd to his preaching so often when a child, and sat with my mother at social gatherings where he was the centre, and every one so pleas'd and stirr'd by his conversation. I hear that you contemplate writing or speaking about him, and I wonder'd whether you had a picture of him. As I am the owner of two, I send you one."

GRAND NATIVE GROWTH

In a few days I go to lake Huron, and may have something to say of that region and people. From what I already see, I should say the young native population of Canada was growing up, forming a hardy, democratic, intelligent, radically sound, and just as American, good-natured and *individualistic* race, as the average range of best specimens among us. As among us, too, I please myself by considering that this element, though it may not be the majority, promises to be the leaven which must eventually leaven the whole lump.

A ZOLLVEREIN BETWEEN THE U. S. AND CANADA

Some of the more liberal of the presses here are discussing the question of a zollverein between the United States and Canada. It is proposed to form a union for commercial purposes—to altogether abolish the frontier tariff line, with its double sets of custom house officials now existing between the two countries, and to agree upon one tariff for both, the proceeds of this tariff to be divided between the two governments on the basis of population. It is said that a large proportion of the merchants of Canada are in favor of this step, as they believe it would materially add to the business of the country, by removing the restrictions that now exist on trade between Canada and the States. Those persons who are opposed to the measure believe that it would increase the material welfare of the country, but it would loosen the bonds between Canada and England; and this sentiment overrides the desire for commercial prosperity. Whether the sentiment can continue to bear the strain put upon it is a question. It is thought by many that commercial considerations must in the end prevail. It seems also to be generally agreed that such a zollverein, or common customs union, would bring practically more benefits to the Canadian provinces than to the United States. (It seems to me a certainty of time, sooner or later, that Canada shall form two or three grand States, equal and independent, with the rest of the American Union. The St. Lawrence and lakes are not for a frontier line, but a grand interior or mid-channel.)

THE ST. LAWRENCE LINE

August 20.—Premising that my three or four months in Canada were intended, among the rest, as an exploration of the line of the St. Lawrence, from lake Superior to the sea, (the engineers here insist upon considering it as one stream, over 2000 miles long, including lakes and Niagara and all)—that I have only partially carried out my programme; but for the seven or eight hundred miles so far fulfill'd, I find that the *Canada question* is absolutely control'd by this vast water line, with its first-class features and points of trade, humanity, and many more—here I am writing this nearly a thousand miles north of my Philadelphia starting-point (by way of Montreal and Quebec) in the midst of regions that go to a further extreme of grimness, wildness of beauty, and a sort of still and pagan *scaredness*, while yet Christian, inhabitable, and partially fertile, than perhaps any other on earth. The weather remains perfect; some might call it a little cool, but I wear my old gray overcoat and find it just right. The days are full of sunbeams and oxygen. Most of the forenoons and afternoons I am on the forward deck of the steamer.

THE SAVAGE SAGUENAY

Up these black waters, over a hundred miles—always strong, deep, (hundreds of feet, sometimes thousands,) ever with high, rocky hills for banks, green and gray—at times a little like some parts of the Hudson, but much more pronounc'd and defiant. The hills rise higher—keep their ranks more unbroken. The river is straighter and of more resolute flow, and its hue, though dark as ink, exquisitely polish'd and sheeny under the August sun. Different, indeed, this Saguenay from all other rivers—different effects—a bolder, more vehement play of lights and shades. Of a rare charm of singleness and simplicity. (Like the organ-chant at midnight from the old Spanish convent, in "Favorita"—one strain only, simple and monotonous and unornamented—but indescribably penetrating and grand and masterful.) Great place for echoes: while our steamer was tied at the wharf at Tadousac (taj-oo-sac) waiting, the escape-pipe letting off steam, I was sure I heard a band at the hotel up in the rocks—could even make out some of the tunes. Only when our pipe stopp'd, I knew what caused it. Then at cape Eternity and Trinity rock, the pilot with his whistle producing similar marvellous results, echoes indescribably weird, as we lay off in the still bay under their shadows.

CAPES ETERNITY AND TRINITY

But the great, haughty, silent capes themselves; I doubt if any crack points, or hills, or historic places of note, or anything of the kind elsewhere in the world, outvies these objects—(I write while I am before them face to face.) They are very simple, they do not startle—at least they did not me—but they linger in one's memory forever. They are placed very near each other, side by side, each a mountain rising flush out of the Saguenay. A good thrower could

throw a stone on each in passing—at least it seems so. Then they
are as distinct in form as a perfect physical man or a perfect physical
woman. Cape Eternity is bare, rising, as just said, sheer out of the
water, rugged and grim (yet with an indescribable beauty) nearly
two thousand feet high. Trinity rock, even a little higher, also rising
flush, top-rounded like a great head with close-cut verdure of hair.
I consider myself well repaid for coming my thousand miles to get
the sight and memory of the unrivall'd duo. They have stirr'd me
more profoundly than anything of the kind I have yet seen. If
Europe or Asia had them, we should certainly hear of them in all
sorts of sent-back poems, rhapsodies, &c., a dozen times a year
through our papers and magazines.

CHICOUTIMI AND HA-HA BAY

No indeed—life and travel and memory have offer'd and will
preserve to me no deeper-cut incidents, panorama, or sights to cheer
my soul, than these at Chicoutimi and Ha-ha bay, and my days
and nights up and down this fascinating savage river—the rounded
mountains, some bare and gray, some dull red, some draped close
all over with matted green verdure or vines—the ample, calm,
eternal rocks everywhere—the long streaks of motley foam, a milk-
white curd on the glistening breast of the stream—the little two-
masted schooner, dingy yellow, with patch'd sails, set wing-and-
wing, nearing us, coming saucily up the water with a couple of
swarthy, black-hair'd men aboard—the strong shades falling on the
light gray or yellow outlines of the hills all through the forenoon, as
we steam within gunshot of them—while ever the pure and delicate
sky spreads over all. And the splendid sunsets, and the sights of
evening—the same old stars, (relatively a little different, I see, so
far north) Arcturus and Lyra, and the Eagle, and great Jupiter like
a silver globe, and the constellation of the Scorpion. Then northern
lights nearly every night.

THE INHABITANTS—GOOD LIVING

Grim and rocky and black-water'd as the demesne hereabout is,
however, you must not think genial humanity, and comfort, and
good-living are not to be met. Before I began this memorandum I
made a first-rate breakfast of sea-trout, finishing off with wild raspberries. I find smiles and courtesy everywhere—physiognomies in
general curiously like those in the United States—(I was astonish'd
to find the same resemblance all through the province of Quebec.)

In general the inhabitants of this rugged country (Charlevoix, Chicoutimi and Tadousac counties, and lake St. John region) a simple, hardy population, lumbering, trapping furs, boating, fishing, berry-picking and a little farming. I was watching a group of young boatmen eating their early dinner—nothing but an immense loaf of bread, had apparently been the size of a bushel measure, from which they cut chunks with a jack-knife. Must be a tremendous winter country this, when the solid frost and ice fully set in.

CEDAR-PLUMS LIKE—NAMES

(Back again in Camden and down in Jersey)

One time I thought of naming this collection "Cedar-Plums Like" (which I still fancy wouldn't have been a bad name, nor inappropriate.) A melange of loafing, looking, hobbling, sitting, traveling— a little thinking thrown in for salt, but very little—not only summer but all seasons—not only days but nights—some literary meditations—books, authors examined, Carlyle, Poe, Emerson tried, (always under my cedar-tree, in the open air, and never in the library)— mostly the scenes everybody sees, but some of my own caprices, meditations, egotism—truly an open air and mainly summer formation—singly, or in cluster—wild and free and somewhat acrid— indeed more like cedar-plums than you might guess at first glance.

But do you know what they are? (To city man, or some sweet parlor lady, I now talk.) As you go along roads, or barrens, or across country, anywhere through these States, middle, eastern, western, or southern, you will see, certain seasons of the year, the thick woolly tufts of the cedar mottled with bunches of china-blue berries, about as big as fox-grapes. But first a special word for the tree itself: everybody knows that the cedar is a healthy, cheap, democratic wood, streak'd red and white—an evergreen—that it is not a *cultivated* tree—that it keeps away moths—that it grows inland or seaboard, all climates, hot or cold, any soil—in fact rather prefers sand and bleak side spots—content if the plough, the fertilizer and the trimming-axe, will but keep away and let it alone. After a long rain, when everything looks bright, often have I stopt in my wood-saunters, south or north, or far west, to take in its dusky green, wash'd clean and sweet, and speck'd copiously with its fruit of clear, hardy blue. The wood of the cedar is of use—but what profit on earth are those sprigs of acrid plums? A question impossible to answer satisfactorily. True, some of the herb doctors give them for stomachic affections, but the remedy is as bad as the disease. Then in my rambles down in Camden county I once found an old crazy woman gathering the clusters with zeal and joy. She show'd, as I was told afterward, a sort of infatuation for them, and every year placed and kept profuse bunches high and low about her room. They had a strange charm on her uneasy head, and effected docility and peace. (She was harmless, and lived near by with her well-off married daughter.) Whether there is any connection between those bunches, and being out of one's wits, I cannot say, but I myself entertain a weakness for them. Indeed, I love the cedar, anyhow—its naked ruggedness, its just palpable odor, (so different from the perfumer's best,) its silence, its equable acceptance of winter's cold and summer's heat, of rain or drouth—its shelter to me from those, at times—its associations—(well, I never could explain *why* I love anybody, or anything.) The service I now especially owe to the cedar is, while I cast around for a name for my proposed collection, hesitating, puzzled—after rejecting a long, long string, I lift my eyes, and lo! the very term I want. At any rate, I go no further—I tire in the search. I take what some invisible kind spirit has put before me. Besides, who shall say there is not affinity enough between (at least the bundle of sticks that produced) many of these pieces, or granulations, and those blue berries? their uselessness growing wild—a certain aroma of Nature I would so like to have in my pages—the thin soil whence they come—their content in being let alone—their stolid and deaf repugnance to answering questions, (this latter the nearest, dearest trait affinity of all.)

Then reader dear, in conclusion, as to the point of the name for the present collection, let us be satisfied to *have* a name—something to identify and bind it together, to concrete all its vegetable, mineral, personal memoranda, abrupt raids of criticism, crude gossip of philosophy, varied sands and clumps—without bothering ourselves because certain pages do not present themselves to you or me as coming under their own name with entire fitness or amiability. (It is a profound, vexatious, never-explicable matter—this of names. I have been exercised deeply about it my whole life.*)

---

*In the pocket of my receptacle-book I find a list of suggested and rejected names for this volume, or parts of it—such as the following:

> *As the wild bee hums in May,*
> *& August mulleins grow,*
> *& Winter snow-flakes fall,*
> *& stars in the sky roll round.*

> *Away from Books—away from Art,*
> *Now for the Day and Night—the lesson done,*
> *Now for the Sun and Stars.*

After all of which the name "Cedar-Plums Like" got its nose put out of joint; but I cannot afford to throw away what I pencill'd down the lane there, under the shelter of my old friend, one warm October noon. Besides, it wouldn't be civil to the cedar tree.

DEATH OF THOMAS CARLYLE

Feb. 10, '81.—And so the flame of the lamp, after long wasting and flickering, has gone out entirely.

As a representative author, a literary figure, no man else will bequeath to the future more significant hints of our stormy era, its fierce paradoxes, its din, and its struggling parturition periods, than Carlyle. He belongs to our own branch of the stock too; neither Latin nor Greek, but altogether Gothic. Rugged, mountainous, volcanic, he was himself more a French revolution than any of his volumes. In some repects, so far in the Nineteenth century, the best equipt, keenest mind, even from the college point of view, of all Britain; only he had an ailing body. Dyspepsia is to be traced in every page, and now and then fills the page. One may include among the lessons of his life—even though that life stretch'd to amazing length—how behind the tally of genius and morals stands the stomach, and gives a sort of casting vote.

Two conflicting agonistic elements seem to have contended in the man, sometimes pulling him different ways like wild horses. He was a cautious, conservative Scotchman, fully aware what a fœtid gas-bag much of modern radicalism is; but then his great heart demanded reform, demanded change—often terribly at odds with his scornful brain. No author ever put so much wailing and despair into his books, sometimes palpable, oftener latent. He reminds me of that passage in Young's poems where as death presses

---

Notes of a half-Paralytic,
Week in and Week out,
Embers of Ending Days,
Ducks and Drakes,
Flood Tide and Ebb,
Gossip at Early Candle-light,
Echoes and Escapades,
Such as I.....Evening Dews,
Notes after Writing a Book,
Far and Near at 63,
Drifts and Cumulus,
Maize-Tassels.....Kindlings,
Fore and Aft.....Vestibules,
Scintilla at 60 and after,
Sands on the Shores of 64,

As Voices in the Dusk, from Speakers
  far or hid,
Autochthons.....Embryons,
Wings-and-Wing,
Notes and Recallés,
Only Mulleins and Bumble-Bees,
Pond-Babble.....Tête-à-Têtes,
Echoes of a Life in the l9th Century
  in the New World,
Flanges of Fifty Years,
Abandons.....Hurry Notes,
A Life-Mosaic.....Native Moments,
Types and Semi-Tones,
Oddments.....Sand-Drifts,
Again and Again.

closer and closer for his prey, the soul rushes hither and thither, appealing, shrieking, berating, to escape the general doom.

Of short-comings, even positive blur–spots, from an American point of view, he had serious share.

Not for his merely literary merit, (though that was great)—not as "maker of books," but as launching into the self-complacent atmosphere of our days a rasping, questioning, dislocating agitation and shock, is Carlyle's final value. It is time the English-speaking peoples had some true idea about the verteber of genius, namely power. As if they must always have it cut and bias'd to the fashion, like a lady's cloak! What a needed service he performs! How he shakes our comfortable reading circles with a touch of the old Hebraic anger and prophecy—and indeed it is just the same. Not Isaiah himself more scornful, more threatening: "The crown of pride, the drunkards of Ephraim, shall be trodden under feet: And the glorious beauty which is on the head of the fat valley shall be a fading flower." (The word prophecy is much misused; it seems narrow'd to prediction merely. That is not the main sense of the Hebrew word translated "prophet;" it means one whose mind bubbles up and pours forth as a fountain, from inner, divine spontaneities revealing God. Prediction is a very minor part of prophecy. The great matter is to reveal and outpour the God-like suggestions pressing for birth in the soul. This is briefly the doctrine of the Friends or Quakers.)

Then the simplicity and amid ostensible frailty the towering strength of this man—a hardy oak knot, you could never wear out—an old farmer dress'd in brown clothes, and not handsome—his very foibles fascinating. Who cares that he wrote about Dr. Francia, and "Shooting Niagara"—and "the Nigger Question,"—and didn't at all admire our United States? (I doubt if he ever thought or said half as bad words about us as we deserve.) How he splashes like leviathan in the seas of modern literature and politics! Doubtless, respecting the latter, one needs first to realize, from actual observation, the squalor, vice and doggedness ingrain'd in the bulk-population of the British Islands, with the red tape, the fatuity, the flunkeyism everywhere, to understand the last meaning in his pages. Accordingly, though he was no chartist or radical, I consider Carlyle's by far the most indignant comment or protest anent the fruits of feudalism to-day in Great Britain—the increasing poverty and degradation of the homeless, landless twenty millions, while a few thousands, or rather a few hundreds, possess the entire soil, the money, and the fat berths. Trade and shipping, and clubs and culture, and prestige, and guns, and a fine select class of gentry and aristocracy, with every modern improvement, cannot begin to salve or defend such stupendous hoggishness.

The way to test how much he has left his country were to consider, or try to consider, for a moment, the array of British thought, the resultant *ensemble* of the last fifty years, as existing to-day, *but with Carlyle left out.* It would be like an army with no artillery. The show were still a gay and rich one—Byron, Scott, Tennyson, and many more—horsemen and rapid infantry, and banners flying— but the last heavy roar so dear to the ear of the train'd soldier, and that settles fate and victory, would be lacking.

For the last three years we in America have had transmitted glimpses of a thin-bodied, lonesome, wifeless, childless, very old man, lying on a sofa, kept out of bed by indomitable will, but, of late, never well enough to take the open air. I have noted this news from time to time in brief descriptions in the papers. A week ago I read such an item just before I started out for my customary evening stroll between eight and nine. In the fine cold night, unusually clear, (Feb. 5, '81,) as I walked some open grounds adjacent, the condition of Carlyle, and his approaching—perhaps even then actual—death, filled me with thoughts eluding statement, and curiously blending with the scene. The planet Venus, an hour high in the west, with all her volume and lustre recover'd, (she has been shorn and languid for nearly a year,) including an additional sentiment I never noticed before—not merely voluptuous, Paphian, steeping, fascinating—now with calm commanding seriousness and hauteur—the Milo Venus now. Upward to the zenith, Jupiter, Saturn, and the moon past her quarter, trailing in procession, with the Pleiades following, and the constellation Taurus, and red Aldebaran. Not a cloud in heaven. Orion strode through the southeast, with his glittering belt—and a trifle below hung the sun of the night, Sirius. Every star dilated, more vitreous, nearer than usual. Not as in some clear nights when the larger stars entirely outshine the rest. Every little star or cluster just as distinctly visible, and just as nigh. Berenice's hair showing every gem, and new ones. To the northeast and north, the Sickle, the Goat and kids, Cassiopea, Castor and Pollux, and the two Dippers. While through the whole of this silent indescribable show, inclosing and bathing my whole receptivity, ran the thought of Carlyle dying. (To soothe and spiritualize, and, as far as may be, solve the mysteries of death and genius, consider them under the stars at midnight.)

And now that he has gone hence, can it be that Thomas Carlyle, soon to chemically dissolve in ashes and by winds, remains an identity still? In ways perhaps eluding all the statements, lore and speculations of ten thousand years—eluding all possible statements to mortal sense—does he yet exist, a definite, vital being, a spirit, an individual—perhaps now wafted in space among those stellar systems, which, suggestive and limitless as they are, merely edge more limitless, far more suggestive systems? I have no doubt of it. In silence, of a fine night, such questions are answer'd to the soul, the best answers that can be given. With me, too, when depress'd by some specially sad event, or tearing problem, I wait till I go out under the stars for the last voiceless satisfaction.

Later Thoughts and Jottings

CARLYLE FROM AMERICAN POINTS OF VIEW

There is surely at present an inexplicable *rapport* (all the more piquant from its contradictoriness) between that deceas'd author and our United States of America—no matter whether it lasts or not.* As we Westerners assume definite shape, and result in formations and fruitage unknown before, it is curious with what a new sense our eyes turn to representative outgrowths of crises and personages in the Old World. Beyond question, since Carlyle's death, and the publication of Froude's memoirs, not only the interest in his books, but every personal bit regarding the famous Scotchman— his dyspepsia, his buffetings, his parentage, his paragon of a wife, his career in Edinburgh, in the lonesome nest on Craigenputtock moor, and then so many years in London—is probably wider and livelier to-day in this country than in his own land. Whether I succeed or no, I, too, reaching across the Atlantic and taking the man's dark fortune-telling of humanity and politics, would offset it all, (such is the fancy that comes to me,) by a far more profound horoscope-casting of those themes—G. G. Hegel's.†

---

*It will be difficult for the future—judging by his books, personal dis-sympathies, &c.,—to account for the deep hold this author has taken on the present age, and the way he has color'd its method and thought. I am certainly at a loss to account for it all as affecting myself. But there could be no view, or even partial picture, of the middle and latter part of our Nineteenth century, that did not markedly include Thomas Carlyle. In his case (as so many others, literary productions, works of art, personal identities, events,) there has been an impalpable something more effective than the palpable. Then I find no better text, (it is always important to have a definite, special, even oppositional, living man to start from,) for sending out certain speculations and comparisons for home use. Let us see what they amount to—those reactionary doctrines, fears, scornful analyses of democracy—even from the most erudite and sincere mind of Europe.

†Not the least mentionable part of the case, (a streak, it may be, of that humor with which history and fate love to contrast their gravity,) is that although neither of my great authorities during their lives consider'd the Unite*d*

First, about a chance, a never–fulfill'd vacuity of this pale cast
of thought—this British Hamlet from Cheyne row, more puzzling
than the Danish one, with his contrivances for settling the broken
and spavin'd joints of the world's government, especially in its democratic dislocation. Carlyle's grim fate was cast to live and dwell in,
and largely embody, the parturition agony and qualms of the old
order, amid crowded accumulations of ghastly morbidity, giving
birth to the new. But conceive of him (or his parents before him)
coming to America, recuperated by the cheering realities and activity of our people and country—growing up and delving face-to-
face resolutely among us here, especially at the West—inhaling and
exhaling our limitless air and eligibilities—devoting his mind to the
theories and developments of this Republic amid its practical facts
as exemplified in Kansas, Missouri, Illinois, Tennessee, or Louisiana.
I say *facts*, and face-to-face confrontings—so different from books,
and all those quiddities and mere reports in the libraries, upon which
the man (it was wittily said of him at the age of thirty, that there
was no one in Scotland who had glean'd so much and seen so little,)
almost wholly fed, and which even his sturdy and vital mind but
reflected at best.

Something of the sort narrowly escaped happening. In 1835, after
more than a dozen years of trial and non-success, the author of
"Sartor Resartus" removing to London, very poor, a confirmed
hypochondriac, "Sartor" universally scoffed at, no literary prospects
ahead, deliberately settled on one last casting-throw of the literary
dice—resolv'd to compose and launch forth a book on the subject
of *the French Revolution*—and if that won no higher guerdon or
prize than hitherto, to sternly abandon the trade of author forever,
and emigrate for good to America. But the venture turn'd out a
lucky one, and there was no emigration.

Carlyle's work in the sphere of literature as he commenced and
carried it out, is the same in one or two leading respects that Immanuel Kant's was in speculative philosophy. But the Scotchman had
none of the stomachic phlegm and never–perturb'd placidity of the
Konigsberg sage, and did not, like the latter, understand his own
limits, and stop when he got to the end of them. He clears away
jungle and poison–vines and underbrush—at any rate hacks val-
iantly at them, smiting hip and thigh. Kant did the like in his sphere,

---

States worthy of serious mention, all the principal works of both might not
inappropriately be this day collected and bound up under the conspicuous
title: "*Speculations for the use of North America, and Democracy there, with
the relations of the same to Metaphysics, including Lessons and Warnings
(encouragements too, and of the vastest) from the Old World to the New.*"

and it was all he profess'd to do; his labors have left the ground fully prepared ever since—and greater service was probably never perform'd by mortal man. But the pang and hiatus of Carlye seems to me to consist in the evidence everywhere that amid a whirl of fog and fury and cross-purposes, he firmly believ'd he had a clue to the medication of the world's ills, and that his bounden mission was to exploit it.*

There were two anchors, or sheet-anchors, for steadying, as a last resort, the Carlylean ship. One will be specified presently. The other, perhaps the main, was only to be found in some mark'd form of personal force, an extreme degree of competent urge and will, a man or men "born to command." Probably there ran through every vein and current of the Scotchman's blood something that warm'd up to this kind of trait and character above aught else in the world, and which makes him in my opinion the chief celebrater and promulger of it in literature—more than Plutarch, more than Shakspere. The great masses of humanity stand for nothing—at least nothing but nebulous raw material; only the big planets and shining suns for him. To ideas almost invariably languid or cold, a number-one forceful personality was sure to rouse his eulogistic passion and savage joy. In such case, even the standard of duty hereinafter rais'd, was to be instantly lower'd and vail'd. All that is comprehended under the terms republicanism and democracy were distasteful to him from the first, and as he grew older they became hateful and contemptible. For an undoubtedly candid and penetrating faculty such as his, the bearings he persistently ignored were marvellous. For instance, the promise, nay certainty of the democratic principle, to each and every State of the current world, not so much of helping it to perfect legislators and excutives, but as the only effectual method for surely, however slowly, training people on a large scale toward voluntarily ruling and managing themselves (the ultimate aim of political and all other development)—to gradually reduce the fact of *governing* to its minimum, and to subject all its staffs and their doings to the telescopes and microscopes of committees and parties—and greatest of all, to afford (not stagnation and obedient content, which went well enough with the feudalism and ecclesiasticism of the antique and

---

*I hope I shall not myself fall into the error I charge upon him, of prescribing a specific for indispensable evils. My utmost pretension is probably but to offset that old claim of the exclusively curative power of first-class individual men, as leaders and rulers, by the claims, and general movement and result, of ideas. Something of the latter kind seems to me the distinctive theory of America, of democracy, and of the modern—or rather, I should say, it *is* democracy, and *is* the modern.

medieval world, but) a vast and sane and recurrent ebb and tide
action for those floods of the great deep that have henceforth
palpably burst forever their old bounds—seem never to have enter'd
Carlyle's thought. It was splendid how he refus'd any compromise
to the last. He was curiously antique. In that harsh, picturesque,
most potent voice and figure, one seems to be carried back from the
present of the British islands more than two thousand years, to the
range between Jerusalem and Tarsus. His fullest best biographer
justly says of him:

"He was a teacher and prophet, in the Jewish sense of the word. The
prophecies of Isaiah and Jeremiah have become a part of the permanent
spiritual inheritance of mankind, because events proved that they had inter-
preted correctly the signs of their own times, and their prophecies were fulfill'd.
Carlyle, like them, believ'd that he had a special message to deliver to the
present age. Whether he was correct in that belief, and whether his message
was a true message, remains to be seen. He has told us that our most cherish'd
ideas of political liberty, with their kindred corollaries, are mere illusions, and
that the progress which has seem'd to go along with them is a progress towards
anarchy and social dissolution. If he was wrong, he has misused his powers.
The principles of his teachings are false. He has offer'd himself as a guide upon
a road of which he had no knowledge; and his own desire for himself would be
the speediest oblivion both of his person and his works. If, on the other hand,
he has been right; if, like his great predecessors, he has read truly the tendencies
of this modern age of ours, and his teaching is authenticated by facts, then
Carlyle, too, will take his place among the inspired seers."

To which I add an amendment that under no circumstances, and
no matter how completely time and events disprove his lurid
vaticinations, should the English-speaking world forget this man,
nor fail to hold in honor his unsurpass'd conscience, his unique
method, and his honest fame. Never were convictions more earnest
and genuine. Never was there less of a flunkey or temporizer. Never
had political progressivism a foe it could more heartily respect.

The second main point of Carlyle's utterance was the idea of
duty being done. (It is simply a new codicil—if it be particularly
new, which is by no means certain—on the time-honor'd bequest
of dynasticism, the mould-eaten rules of legitimacy and kings.) He
seems to have been impatient sometimes to madness when reminded by persons who thought at least as deeply as himself, that
this formula, though precious, is rather a vague one, and that
there are many other considerations to a philosophical estimate of
each and every department either in general history or individual
affairs.

Altogether, I don't know anything more amazing than these
persistent strides and throbbings so far through our Nineteenth
century of perhaps its biggest, sharpest, and most erudite brain, in

defiance and discontent with everything; contemptuously ignoring, (either from constitutional inaptitude, ignorance itself, or more likely because he demanded a definite cure-all here and now,) the only solace and solvent to be had.

There is, apart from mere intellect, in the make-up of every superior human identity, (in its moral completeness, considered as *ensemble,* not for that moral alone, but for the whole being, including physique,) a wondrous something that realizes without argument, frequently without what is called education, (though I think it the goal and apex of all education deserving the name)—an intuition of the absolute balance, in time and space, of the whole of this multifarious, mad chaos of fraud, frivolity, hoggishness—this revel of fools, and incredible make-believe and general unsettledness, we call *the world;* a soul-sight of that divine clue and unseen thread which holds the whole congeries of things, all history and time, and all events, however trivial, however momentous, like a leash'd dog in the hand of the hunter. Such soul-sight and root-centre for the mind—mere optimism explains only the surface or fringe of it— Carlyle was mostly, perhaps entirely without. He seems instead to have been haunted in the play of his mental action by a spectre, never entirely laid from first to last, (Greek scholars, I believe, find the same mocking and fantastic apparition attending Aristophanes, his comedies,)—the spectre of world-destruction.

How largest triumph or failure in human life, in war or peace, may depend on some little hidden centrality, hardly more than a drop of blood, a pulse-beat, or a breath of air! It is certain that all these weighty matters, democracy in America, Carlyleism, and the temperament for deepest political or literary exploration, turn on a simple point in speculative philosophy.

The most profound theme that can occupy the mind of man— the problem on whose solution science, art, the bases and pursuits of nations, and everything else, including intelligent human happiness, (here to-day, 1882, New York, Texas, California, the same as all times, all lands,) subtly and finally resting, depends for competent outset and argument, is doubtless involved in the query: What is the fusing explanation and tie—what the relation between the (radical, democratic) Me, the human identity of understanding, emotions, spirit, &c., on the one side, of and with the (conservative) Not Me, the whole of the material objective universe and laws, with what is behind them in time and space, on the other side? Immanuel Kant, though he explain'd, or partially explain'd, as may be said, the laws of the human understanding, left this question an open one. Schelling's answer, or suggestion of answer, is (and very valuable and important, as far as it goes,) that the same general and particular intelligence, passion, even the standards of right and wrong, which exist in a conscious and formulated state in man, exist in an unconscious state, or in perceptible analogies, throughout the entire universe of external Nature, in all its objects large or small, and all its movements and processes—thus making the impalpable human mind, and concrete Nature, notwithstanding their duality and separation, convertible, and in centrality and essence one. But G. F. Hegel's fuller statement of the matter probably remains the last best word that has been said upon it, up to date. Substantially adopting the scheme just epitomized, he so carries it out and fortifies it and merges everything in it, with certain serious gaps now for the first time fill'd, that it becomes a coherent metaphysical system, and substantial answer (as far as there can be any answer) to the foregoing question—a system which, while I distinctly admit that the brain of the future may add to, revise, and even entirely reconstruct, at any rate beams forth to-day, in its entirety, illuminating the thought of the universe, and satisfying the mystery thereof to the human mind, with a more consoling scientific assurance than any yet.

According to Hegel the whole earth, (an old nucleus-thought, as in the Vedas, and no doubt before, but never hitherto brought so absolutely to the front, fully surcharged with modern scientism and facts, and made the sole entrance to each and all,) with its infinite variety, the past, the surroundings of to-day or what may happen in the future, the contrarieties of material with spiritual, and of natural with artificial, are all, to the eye of the *ensemblist*, but necessary sides and unfoldings, different steps or links, in the endless process of Creative thought, which, amid numberless apparent failures and contradictions, is held together by central and never-broken unity—not contradictions or failures at all, but radiations of one consistent and eternal purpose; the whole mass of everything steadily, unerringly tending and flowing toward the permanent *utile* and *morale*, as rivers to oceans. As life is the whole law and incessant effort of the visible universe, and death only the other or invisible side of the same, so the *utile*, so truth, so health, are the continuous-immutable laws of the moral universe, and vice and disease, with all their perturbations, are but transient, even if ever so prevalent expressions.

To politics throughout, Hegel applies the like catholic standard and faith. Not any one party, or any one form of government, is absolutely and exclusively true. Truth consists in the just relations of objects to each other. A majority or democracy may rule as outrageously and do as great harm as an oligarchy or despotism—though far less likely to do so. But the great evil is either a violation of the relations just referr'd to, or of the moral law. The specious, the unjust, the cruel, and what is called the unnatural, though not only permitted but in a certain sense, (like shade to light,) inevitable in the divine scheme, are by the whole constitution of that scheme, partial, inconsistent, temporary, and though having ever so great an ostensible majority, are certainly destin'd to failure, after causing great suffering.

Theology, Hegel translates into science.* All apparent contra-dictions in the statement of the Deific nature by different ages, nations, churches, points of view, are but fractional and imperfect expressions of one essential unity, from which they all proceed—crude endeavors or distorted parts, to be regarded both as distinct and united. In short (to put it in our own form, or summing up,) that thinker or analyzer or overlooker who by an inscrutable combina-tion of train'd wisdom and natural intuition most fully accepts in perfect faith the moral unity and sanity of the creative scheme, in history, science, and all life and time, present and future, is both the truest cosmical devotee or religioso, and the profoundest phil-osopher. While he who, by the spell of himself and his circumstance, sees darkness and despair in the sum of the workings of God's providence, and who, in that, denies or prevaricates, is, no matter how much piety plays on his lips, the most radical sinner and infidel.

I am the more assured in recounting Hegel a little freely here,† not only for offsetting the Carlylean letter and spirit—cutting it out all and several from the very roots, and below the roots—but to counterpoise, since the late death and deserv'd apotheosis of Darwin, the tenets of the evolutionists. Unspeakably precious as those are to biology, and henceforth indispensable to a right aim and estimate in study, they neither comprise or explain everything—and the last word or whisper still remains to be breathed, after the utmost of those claims, floating high and forever above them all,

* I am much indebted to J. Gostick's abstract.

† I have deliberately repeated it all, not only in offset to Carlyle's ever-lurking pessimism and world-decadence, but as presenting the most thoroughly *American points of view* I know. In my opinion the above formulas of Hegel are an essential and crowning justification of New World democracy in the creative realms of time and space. There is that about them which only the vastness, the multiplicity and the vitality of America would seem able to com-prehend, to give scope and illustration to, or to be fit for, or even originate. It is strange to me that they were born in Germany, or in the old world at all. While a Carlyle, I should say, is quite the legitimate European product to be expected.

and above technical metaphysics. While the contributions which German Kant and Fichte and Schelling and Hegel have bequeath'd to humanity—and which English Darwin has also in his field—are indispensable to the erudition of America's future, I should say that in all of them, and the best of them, when compared with the lightning flashes and flights of the old prophets and *exaltés*, the spiritual poets and poetry of all lands, (as in the Hebrew Bible,) there seems to be, nay certainly is, something lacking—something cold, a failure to satisfy the deepest emotions of the soul—a want of living glow, fondness, warmth, which the old *exaltés* and poets supply, and which the keenest modern philosophers so far do not.

Upon the whole, and for our purposes, this man's name certainly belongs on the list with the just-specified, first-class moral physicians of our current era—and with Emerson and two or three others— though his prescription is drastic, and perhaps destructive, while theirs is assimilating, normal and tonic. Feudal at the core, and mental offspring and radiation of feudalism as are his books, they afford ever-valuable lessons and affinities to democratic America. Nations or individuals, we surely learn deepest from unlikeness, from a sincere opponent, from the light thrown even scornfully on dangerous spots and liabilities. (Michel Angelo invoked heaven's special protection against his friends and affectionate flatterers; palpable foes he could manage for himself.) In many particulars Carlyle was indeed, as Froude terms him, one of those far-off Hebraic utterers, a new Micah or Habbakuk. His words at times bubble forth with abysmic inspiration. Always precious, such men; as precious now as any time. His rude, rasping, taunting, contra- dictory tones—what ones are more wanted amid the supple, pol- ish'd, money-worshipping, Jesus-and-Judas-equalizing, suffrage- sovereignty echoes of current America? He has lit up our Nineteenth century with the light of a powerful, penetrating, and perfectly honest intellect of the first-class, turn'd on British and European politics, social life, literature, and representative personages—thor- oughly dissatisfied with all, and mercilessly exposing the illness of all. But while he announces the malady, and scolds and raves about it, he himself, born and bred in the same atmosphere, is a mark'd illustration of it.

A COUPLE OF OLD FRIENDS—A COLERIDGE BIT

Latter April.—Have run down in my country haunt for a couple of days, and am spending them by the pond. I had already dis-

cover'd my kingfisher here (but only one—the mate not here yet.)
This fine bright morning, down by the creek, he has come out for
a spree, circling, flirting, chirping at a round rate. While I am
writing these lines he is disporting himself in scoots and rings over
the wider parts of the pond, into whose surface he dashes, once or
twice making a loud *souse*—the spray flying in the sun—beautiful!
I see his white and dark-gray plumage and peculiar shape plainly,
as he has deign'd to come very near me. The noble, graceful bird!
Now he is sitting on the limb of an old tree, high up, bending over
the water—seems to be looking at me while I memorandize. I almost
fancy he knows me. *Three days later.*—My second kingfisher is here
with his (or her) mate. I saw the two together flying and whirling
around. I had heard, in the distance, what I thought was the clear
rasping staccato of the birds several times already—but I couldn't
be sure the notes came from both until I saw them together. To-day
at noon they appear'd, but apparently either on business, or for a
little limited exercise only. No wild frolic now, full of free fun and
motion, up and down for an hour. Doubtless, now they have cares,
duties, incubation responsibilities. The frolics are deferr'd till sum-
mer-close.

I don't know as I can finish to-day's memorandum better than
with Coleridge's lines, curiously appropriate in more ways than
one:

> "All Nature seems at work—slugs leave their lair,
> The bees are stirring—birds are on the wing,
> And winter, slumbering in the open air,
> Wears on his smiling face a dream of spring;
> And I, the while, the sole unbusy thing,
> Nor honey make, nor pair, nor build, nor sing."

A WEEK'S VISIT TO BOSTON

May 1, '81.—Seems as if all the ways and means of American
travel to-day had been settled, not only with reference to speed and
directness, but for the comfort of women, children, invalids, and
old fellows like me. I went on by a through train that runs daily
from Washington to the Yankee metropolis without change. You
get in a sleeping-car soon after dark in Philadelphia, and after
ruminating an hour or two, have your bed made up if you like,
draw the curtains, and go to sleep in it—fly on through Jersey to
New York—hear in your half-slumbers a dull jolting and bumping
sound or two—are unconsciously toted from Jersey city by a midnight steamer around the Battery and under the big bridge to the
track of the New Haven road—resume your flight eastward, and

early the next morning you wake up in Boston. All of which was my experience. I wanted to go to the Revere house. A tall unknown gentleman, (a fellow-passenger on his way to Newport he told me, I had just chatted a few moments before with him,) assisted me out through the depot crowd, procured a hack, put me in it with my traveling bag, saying smilingly and quietly, "Now I want you to let this be *my* ride," paid the driver, and before I could remonstrate bow'd himself off.

The occasion of my jaunt, I suppose I had better say here, was for a public reading of "the death of Abraham Lincoln" essay, on the sixteenth anniversary of that tragedy; which reading duly came off, night of April 15. Then I linger'd a week in Boston—felt pretty well (the mood propitious, my paralysis lull'd)—went around everywhere, and saw all that was to be seen, especially human beings. Boston's immense material growth—commerce, finance, commission stores, the plethora of goods, the crowded streets and sidewalks—made of course the first surprising show. In my trip out West, last year, I thought the wand of future prosperity, future empire, must soon surely be wielded by St. Louis, Chicago, beautiful Denver, perhaps San Francisco; but I see the said wand stretch'd out just as decidedly in Boston, with just as much certainty of staying; evidences of copious capital—indeed no centre of the New World ahead of it, (half the big railroads in the West are built with Yankees' money, and they take the dividends.) Old Boston with its zigzag streets and multitudinous angles, (crush up a sheet of letter-paper in your hand, throw it down, stamp it flat, and that is a map of old Boston)—new Boston with its miles upon miles of large and costly houses—Beacon street, Commonwealth avenue, and a hundred others. But the best new departures and expansions of Boston, and of all the cities of New England, are in another direction.

THE BOSTON OF TO-DAY

In the letters we get from Dr. Schliemann (interesting but fishy) about his excavations there in the far-off Homeric area, I notice cities, ruins, &c., as he digs them out of their graves, are certain to be in layers—that is to say, upon the foundation of an old concern, very far down indeed, is always another city or set of ruins, and upon that another superadded—and sometimes upon that still another— each representing either a long or rapid stage of growth and development, different from its predecessor, but unerringly growing out of and resting on it. In the moral, emotional, heroic, and human growths, (the main of a race in my opinion,) something of this kind has certainly taken place in Boston. The New England metropolis of to-day may be described as sunny, (there is something else that makes warmth, mastering even winds and meteorologies, though those are not to be sneez'd at,) joyous, receptive, full of ardor, sparkle, a certain element of yearning, magnificently tolerant, yet not to be fool'd; fond of good eating and drinking—costly in costume as its purse can buy; and all through its best average of houses, streets, people, that subtle something (generally thought to be climate, but it is not—it is something indefinable in *the race*, the turn of its development) which effuses behind the whirl of animation, study, business, a happy and joyous public spirit, as distinguish'd from a sluggish and saturnine one. Makes me think of the glints we get (as in Symonds's books) of the jolly old Greek cities. Indeed there is a good deal of the Hellenic in B., and the people are getting handsomer too—padded out, with freer motions, and with color in their faces. I never saw (although this is not Greek) so many *fine-looking gray hair'd women.* At my lecture I caught myself pausing more than once to look at them, plentiful everywhere through the audience—healthy and wifely and motherly, and wonderfully charming and beautiful—I think such as no time or land but ours could show.

MY TRIBUTE TO FOUR POETS

April 16.—A short but pleasant visit to Longfellow. I am not one of the calling kind, but as the author of "Evangeline" kindly took the trouble to come and see me three years ago in Camden, where I was ill, I felt not only the impulse of my own pleasure on that occasion, but a duty. He was the only particular eminence I called on in Boston, and I shall not soon forget his lit-up face and glowing warmth and courtesy, in the modes of what is called the old school.

And now just here I feel the impulse to interpolate something about the mighty four who stamp this first American century with its birth-marks of poetic literature. In a late magazine one of my reviewers, who ought to know better, speaks of my "attitude of contempt and scorn and intolerance" toward the leading poets— of my "deriding" them, and preaching their "uselessness." If anybody cares to know what I think—and have long thought and avow'd—about them, I am entirely willing to propound. I can't imagine any better luck befalling these States for a poetical beginning and initiation than has come from Emerson, Longfellow, Bryant and Whittier. Emerson, to me, stands unmistakably at the head, but for the others I am at a loss where to give any precedence. Each illustrious, each rounded, each distinctive. Emerson for his sweet, vital-tasting melody, rhym'd philosophy, and poems as amber-clear as the honey of the wild bee he loves to sing. Longfellow for rich color, graceful forms and incidents—all that makes life beautiful and love refined—competing with the singers of Europe on their own ground, and, with one exception, better and finer work than that of any of them. Bryant pulsing the first interior verse-throbs of a mighty world—bard of the river and the wood, ever conveying a taste of open air, with scents as from hayfields, grapes, birch-borders—always lurkingly fond of threnodies—beginning and ending his long career with chants of death, with here and there through all, poems, or passages of poems, touching the highest universal truths, enthusiasms, duties—morals as grim and eternal, if not as stormy and fateful, as anythig in Eschylus. While in Whittier, with his special themes—(his outcropping love of heroism and war, for all his Quakerdom, his verses at times like the measur'd step of Cromwell's old veterans)—in Whittier lives the zeal, the moral energy, that founded New England—the splendid rectitude and ardor of Luther, Milton, George Fox—I must not, dare not, say the wilfulness and narrowness—though doubtless the world needs now, and always will need, almost above all, just such narrowness and wilfulness.

MILLET'S PICTURES—LAST ITEMS

April 18.—Went out three or four miles to the house of Quincy Shaw, to see a collection of J. F. Millet's pictures. Two rapt hours. Never before have I been so penetrated by this kind of expression. I stood long and long before "the Sower." I believe what the picture-men designate "the first Sower," as the artist executed a second copy, and a third, and, some think, improved in each. But I doubt it. There is something in this that could hardly be caught again—a sublime murkiness and original pent fury. Besides this masterpiece, there were many others. (I shall never forget the simple evening scene, "Watering the Cow,") all inimitable, all perfect as pictures, works of mere art; and then it seem'd to me, with that last impalpable ethic purpose from the artist (most likely unconscious to himself) which I am always looking for. To me all of them told the full story of what went before and necessitated the great French revolution—the long precedent crushing of the masses of a heroic people into the earth, in abject poverty, hunger—every right denied, humanity attempted to be put back for generations—yet Nature's

force, titanic here, the stronger and hardier for that repression—
waiting terribly to break forth, revengeful—the pressure on the
dykes, and the bursting at last—the storming of the Bastile—the
execution of the king and queen—the tempest of massacres and
blood. Yet who can wonder?

> Could we wish humanity different?
> Could we wish the people made of wood or stone?
> Or that there be no justice in destiny or time?

The true France, base of all the rest, is certainly in these pictures.
I comprehend "Field-People Reposing," "the Diggers," and "the
Angelus" in this opinion. Some folks always think of the French as
a small race, five or five and a half feet high, and ever frivolous and
smirking. Nothing of the sort. The bulk of the personnel of France,
before the revolution, was large-sized, serious, industrious as now,
and simple. The revolution and Napoleon's wars dwarf'd the standard of human size, but it will come up again. If for nothing else, I
should dwell on my brief Boston visit for opening to me the new
world of Millet's pictures. Will America ever have such an artist
out of her own gestation, body, soul?

Sunday, April 17.—An hour and a half, late this afternoon, in
silence and half light, in the great nave of Memorial hall, Cambridge, the walls thickly cover'd with mural tablets, bearing the
names of students and graduates of the university who fell in the
secession war.

April 23.—It was well I got away in fair order, for if I had staid
another week I should have been killed with kindness, and with
eating and drinking.

BIRDS—AND A CAUTION

May 14.—Home again; down temporarily in the Jersey woods.
Between 8 and 9 A.M. a full concert of birds, from different quarters,
in keeping with the fresh scent, the peace, the naturalness all around
me. I am lately noticing the russet-back, size of the robin or a trifle
less, light breast and shoulders, with irregular dark stripes—tail
long—sits hunch'd up by the hour these days, top of a tall bush, or
some tree, singing blithely. I often get near and listen, as he seems
tame; I like to watch the working of his bill and throat, the quaint
sidle of his body, and flex of his long tail. I hear the woodpecker,
and night and early morning the shuttle of the whip-poor-will—
noons, the gurgle of thrush delicious, and *meo-o-ow* of the cat-bird.
Many I cannot name; but I do not very particularly seek informa-

tion. (You must not know too much, or be too precise or scientific about birds and trees and flowers and water-craft; a certain free margin, and even vagueness—perhaps ignorance, credulity—helps your enjoyment of these things, and of the sentiment of feather'd, wooded, river, or marine Nature generally. I repeat it—don't want to know too exactly, or the reasons why. My own notes have been written off-hand in the latitude of middle New Jersey. Though they describe what I saw—what appear'd to me—I dare say the expert ornithologist, botanist or entomologist will detect more than one slip in them.)

SAMPLES OF MY COMMON-PLACE BOOK

I ought not to offer a record of these days, interests, recuperations, without including a certain old, well-thumb'd common-place book,* filled with favorite excerpts, I carried in my pocket for three summers, and absorb'd over and over again, when the mood invited. I find so much in having a poem or fine suggestion sink into me (a little

---

* *Samples of my common-place book down at the creek:*

I have—says old Pindar—many swift arrows in my quiver which speak to the wise, though they need an interpreter to the thoughtless.

Such a man as it takes ages to make, and ages to understand.
H. D. Thoreau.

If you hate a man, don't kill him, but let him live.—*Buddhistic.*

Famous swords are made of refuse scraps, thought worthless.

Poetry is the only verity—the expression of a sound mind speaking after the ideal—and not after the apparent.—*Emerson.*

The form of oath among the Shoshone Indians is, "The earth hears me. The sun hears me. Shall I lie?"

The true test of civilization is not the census, nor the size of cities, nor the crops—no, but the kind of a man the country turns out.—*Emerson.*

> The whole wide ether is the eagle's sway:
> The whole earth is a brave man's fatherland.—*Euripides.*

> Spices crush'd, their pungence yield,
>   Trodden scents their sweets respire;
> Would you have its strength reveal'd?
>   Cast the incense in the fire.

Matthew Arnold speaks of "the huge Mississippi of falsehood called History."

> The wind blows north, the wind blows south,
>   The wind blows east and west;
> No matter how the free wind blows,
>   Some ship will find it best.

then goes a great ways) prepar'd by these vacant sane and natural influences.

Preach not to others what they should eat, but eat as becomes you, and be silent.—*Epictetus.*

Victor Hugo makes a donkey meditate and apostrophize thus:

> My brother, man, if you would know the truth,
> We both are by the same dull walls shut in;
> The gate is massive and the dungeon strong.
> But you look through the key-hole out beyond,
> And call this knowledge; yet have not at hand
> The key wherein to turn the fatal lock.

"William Cullen Bryant surprised me once," relates a writer in a New York paper, "by saying that prose was the natural language of composition, and he wonder'd how anybody came to write poetry."

> Farewell! I did not know thy worth;
> But thou art gone, and now 'tis prized:
> So angels walk'd unknown on earth,
> But when they flew were recognized.—*Hood.*

John Burroughs, writing of Thoreau, says: "He improves with age—in fact requires age to take off a little of his asperity, and fully ripen him. The world likes a good hater and refuser almost as well as it likes a good lover and accepter —only it likes him farther off."

Louise Michel at the burial of Blanqui, (1881)

Blanqui drill'd his body to subjection to his grand conscience and his noble passions, and commencing as a young man, broke with all that is sybaritish in modern civilization. Without the power to sacrifice self, great ideas will never bear fruit.

> Out of the leaping furnace flame
> A mass of molten silver came;
> Then, beaten into pieces three,
> Went forth to meet its destiny.
> The first a crucifix was made,
> Within a soldier's knapsack laid;
> The second was a locket fair,
> Where a mother kept her dead child's hair;
> The third—a bangle, bright and warm,
> Around a faithless woman's arm.
>
> A mighty pain to love it is,
> And 'tis a pain that pain to miss;
> But of all pain the greatest pain,
> It is to love, but love in vain.

Maurice F. Egan on De Guérin

> A pagan heart, a Christian soul had he,
> He follow'd Christ, yet for dead Pan he sigh'd,
> Till earth and heaven met within his breast:
> As if Theocritus in Sicily
> Had come upon the Figure crucified,
> And lost his gods in deep, Christ-given rest.

MY NATIVE SAND AND SALT ONCE MORE

July 25, '81.—Far Rockaway, L. I.—A good day here, on a
jaunt, amid the sand and salt, a steady breeze setting in from the
sea, the sun shining, the sedge-odor, the noise of the surf, a mixture
of hissing and booming, the milk-white crests curling over. I had a
leisurely bath and naked ramble as of old, on the warm-gray shore-
sands, my companions off in a boat in deeper water—(I shouting
to them Jupiter's menaces against the gods, from Pope's Homer.)

July 28—to Long Branch.—8½ A.M., on the steamer "Plymouth Rock," foot of 23d street, New York, for Long Branch.
Another fine day, fine sights, the shores, the shipping and bay—
everything comforting to the body and spirit of me. (I find the
human and objective atmosphere of New York city and Brooklyn more affiliative to me than any other.) *An hour later*—Still
on the steamer, now sniffing the salt very plainly—the long pulsating *swash* as our boat steams seaward—the hills of Navesink
and many passing vessels—the air the best part of all. At Long
Branch the bulk of the day, stopt at a good hotel, took all very

---

> And if I pray, the only prayer
>   That moves my lips for me,
> Is, leave the mind that now I bear,
>   And give me Liberty.—*Emily Brontë.*

> I travel on not knowing,
>   I would not if I might;
> I would rather walk with God in the dark,
>   Than go alone in the light;
> I would rather walk with Him by faith
>   Than pick my way by sight.

Prof. Huxley in a late lecture

I myself agree with the sentiment of Thomas Hobbes, of Malmesbury, that
"the scope of all speculation is the performance of some action or thing to be
done." I have not any very great respect for, or interest in, mere "knowing,"
as such.

Prince Metternich

Napoleon was of all men in the world the one who most profoundly despised
the race. He had a marvellous insight into the weaker sides of human nature,
(and all our passions are either foibles themselves, or the cause of foibles.) He
was a very small man of imposing character. He was ignorant, as a sub-lieuten-
ant generally is: a remarkable instinct supplied the lack of knowledge. From
his mean opinion of men, he never had any anxiety lest he should go wrong.
He ventur'd everything, and gain'd thereby an immense step toward success.
Throwing himself upon a prodigious arena, he amaz'd the world, and made
himself master of it, while others cannot even get so far as being masters of
their own hearth. Then he went on and on, until he broke his neck.

leisurely, had an excellent dinner, and then drove for over two hours about the place, especially Ocean avenue, the finest drive one can imagine, seven or eight miles right along the beach. In all directions costly villas, palaces, millionaires—(but few among them I opine like my friend George W. Childs, whose personal integrity, generosity, unaffected simplicity, go beyond all worldly wealth.)

HOT WEATHER NEW YORK

August.—In the big city awhile. Even the height of the dog-days, there is a good deal of fun about New York, if you only avoid fluster, and take all the buoyant wholesomeness that offers. More comfort, too, than most folks think. A middle-aged man, with plenty of money in his pocket, tells me that he has been off for a month to all the swell places, has disburs'd a small fortune, has been hot and out of kilter everywhere, and has return'd home and lived in New York city the last two weeks quite contented and happy. People forget when it is hot here, it is generally hotter still in other places. New York is so situated, with the great ozonic brine on both sides, it comprises the most favorable health-chances in the world. (If only the suffocating crowding of some of its tenement houses could be broken up.) I find I never sufficiently realized how beautiful are the upper two-thirds of Manhattan island. I am stopping at Mott Haven, and have been familiar now for ten days with the region above One-hundredth street, and along the Harlem river and Washington heights. Am dwelling a few days with my friends, Mr. and Mrs. J. H. J., and a merry housefull of young ladies. Am putting the last touches on the printer's copy of my new volume of "Leaves of Grass"—the completed book at last. Work at it two or three hours, and then go down and loaf along the Harlem river; have just had a good spell of this recreation. The sun sufficiently veil'd, a soft south breeze, the river full of small or large shells (light taper boats) darting up and down, some singly, now and then long ones with six or eight young fellows practicing—very inspiriting sights. Two fine yachts lie anchor'd off the shore. I linger long, enjoying the sundown, the glow, the streak'd sky, the heights, distances, shadows.

Aug. 10.—As I haltingly ramble an hour or two this forenoon by the more secluded parts of the shore, or sit under an old cedar half way up the hill, the city near in view, many young parties gather to bathe or swim, squads of boys, generally twos or threes, some larger ones, along the sand-bottom, or off an old pier close by. A peculiar and pretty carnival—at its height a hundred lads or young men, very democratic, but all decent behaving. The laughter, voices, calls, responses—the springing and diving of the bathers from the great string-piece of the decay'd pier, where climb or stand long ranks of them, naked, rose-color'd, with movements, postures ahead of any sculpture. To all this, the sun, so bright, the dark-green shadow of the hills the other side, the amber-rolling waves, changing as the tide comes in to a transparent tea-color—the frequent splash of the playful boys, sousing—the glittering drops sparkling, and the good western breeze blowing.

"CUSTER'S LAST RALLY"

Went to-day to see this just-finish'd painting by John Mulvany, who has been out in far Dakota, on the spot, at the forts, and among the frontiersmen, soldiers and Indians, for the last two years, on purpose to sketch it in from reality, or the best that could be got of it. Sat for over an hour before the picture, completely absorb'd in the first view. A vast canvas, I should say twenty or twenty-two feet by twelve, all crowded, and yet not crowded, conveying such a vivid play of color, it takes a little time to get used to it. There are no tricks; there is no throwing of shades in masses; it is all at first painfully real, overwhelming, needs good nerves to look at it. Forty or fifty figures, perhaps more, in full finish and detail in the midground, with three times that number, or more, through the rest— swarms upon swarms of savage Sioux, in their war-bonnets, frantic, mostly on ponies, driving through the background, through the smoke, like a hurricane of demons. A dozen of the figures are wonderful. Altogether a western, autochthonic phase of America, the frontiers, culminating, typical, deadly, heroic to the uttermost—nothing in the books like it, nothing in Homer, nothing in Shakspere; more grim and sublime than either, all native, all our own, and all a fact. A great lot of muscular, tan-faced men, brought to bay under terrible circumstances—death ahold of them, yet every man undaunted, not one losing his head, wringing out every cent of the pay before they sell their lives. Custer (his hair cut short) stands in the middle, with dilated eye and extended arm, aiming a huge cavalry pistol. Captain Cook is there, partially wounded, blood on the white handkerchief around his head, aiming his carbine coolly, half kneeling—(his body was afterwards found close by Custer's.) The slaughter'd or half-slaughter'd horses, for breastworks, make a peculiar feature. Two dead Indians, herculean, lie in the foreground, clutching their Winchester rifles, very characteristic. The many soldiers, their faces and attitudes, the carbines, the broad-brimm'd western hats, the powder-smoke in puffs, the dying horses with their rolling eyes almost human in their agony, the clouds of war bonneted Sioux in the background, the figures of Custer and Cook— with indeed the whole scene, dreadful, yet with an attraction and beauty that will remain in my memory. With all its color and fierce action, a certain Greek continence pervades it. A sunny sky and clear light envelop all. There is an almost entire absence of the stock traits of European war pictures. The physiognomy of the work is realistic and Western. I only saw it for an hour or so; but it needs to be seen many times—needs to be studied over and over again. I could look on such a work at brief intervals all my life without tiring; it is very tonic to me; then it has an ethic purpose below all, as all great art must have. The artist said the sending of the picture abroad, probably to London, had been talk'd of. I advised him if it went abroad to take it to Paris. I think they might appreciate it there—nay, they certainly would. Then I would like to show Messieur Crapeau that some things can be done in America as well as others.

SOME OLD ACQUAINTANCES—MEMORIES

Aug. 16.—"Chalk a big mark for to-day," was one of the sayings of an old sportsman-friend of mine, when he had had unusually good luck—come home thoroughly tired, but with satisfactory results of fish or birds. Well, to-day might warrant such a mark for me. Everything propitious from the start. An hour's fresh stimulation, coming down ten miles of Manhattan island by railroad and 8 o'clock stage. Then an excellent breakfast at Pfaff's restaurant, 24th street. Our host himself, an old friend of mine, quickly appear'd on the scene to welcome me and bring up the news, and, first opening a big fat bottle of the best wine in the cellar, talk about ante-bellum times, '59 and '60, and the jovial suppers at his then Broadway place, near Bleecker street. Ah the friends and names and frequenters, those times, that place. Most are dead—Ada Clare, Wilkins, Daisy Sheppard, O'Brien, Henry Clapp, Stanley, Mullin, Wood, Brougham, Arnold—all gone And there Pfaff and I, sitting opposite each other at the little table, gave a remembrance to them in a style they would have themselves fully confirm'd, namely, big, brimming, fill'd-up champagne-glasses, drain'd in abstracted silence, very leisurely, to the last drop. (Pfaff is a generous German *restaurateur*, silent, stout, jolly, and I should say the best selecter of champagne in America.)

A DISCOVERY OF OLD AGE

Perhaps the best is always cumulative. One's eating and drinking one wants fresh, and for the nonce, right off, and have done
with it—but I would not give a straw for that person or poem,
or friend, or city, or work of art, that was not more grateful the
second time than the first—and more still the third. Nay, I do
not believe any grandest eligibility ever comes forth at first. In
my own experience, (persons, poems, places, characters,) I discover the best hardly ever at first, (no absolute rule about it, however,) sometimes suddenly bursting forth, or stealthily opening to me,
perhaps after years of unwitting familiarity, unappreciation,
usage.

A VISIT, AT THE LAST— TO R. W. EMERSON

Concord, Mass.—Out here on a visit—elastic, mellow, Indian-
summery weather. Came to-day from Boston, (a pleasant ride of
40 minutes by steam, through Somerville, Belmont, Waltham, Stony
Brook, and other lively towns,) convoy'd by my friend F. B. Sanborn,
and to his ample house, and the kindness and hospitality of Mrs. S.
and their fine family. Am writing this under the shade of some old
hickories and elms, just after 4 P.M., on the porch, within a stone's
throw of the Concord river. Off against me, across stream, on a
meadow and side-hill, haymakers are gathering and wagoning-in
probably their second or third crop. The spread of emerald-green
and brown, the knolls, the score or two of little haycocks dotting
the meadow, the loaded-up wagons, the patient horses, the slow-
strong action of the men and pitchforks—all in the just-waning
afternoon, with patches of yellow sun-sheen, mottled by long
shadows—a cricket shrilly chirping, herald of the dusk—a boat with
two figures noiselessly gliding along the little river, passing under the
stone bridge-arch—the slight settling haze of aerial moisture, the
sky and the peacefulness expanding in all directions and overhead—
fill and soothe me.

Same evening.—Never had I a better piece of luck befall me:
a long and blessed evening with Emerson, in a way I couldn't
have wish'd better or different. For nearly two hours he has been
placidly sitting where I could see his face in the best light, near me.
Mrs. S.'s back-parlor well fill'd with people, neighbors, many fresh
and charming faces, women, mostly young, but some old. My friend
A. B. Alcott and his daughter Louisa were there early. A good deal
of talk, the subject Henry Thoreau—some new glints of his life and
fortunes, with letters to and from him—one of the best by Margaret

Fuller, others by Horace Greeley, Channing, &c.—one from Thoreau himself, most quaint and interesting. (No doubt I seem'd very stupid to the room-full of company, taking hardly any part in the conversation; but I had "my own pail to milk in," as the Swiss proverb puts it.) My seat and the relative arrangement were such that, without being rude, or anything of the kind, I could just look squarely at E., which I did a good part of the two hours. On entering, he had spoken very briefly and politely to several of the company, then settled himself in his chair, a trifle push'd back, and, though a listener and apparently an alert one, remain'd silent through the whole talk and discussion. A lady friend quietly took a seat next him, to give special attention. A good color in his face, eyes clear, with the well-known expression of sweetness, and the old clear-peering aspect quite the same.

Next Day.—Several hours at E.'s house, and dinner there. An old familiar house, (he has been in it thirty-five years,) with surroundings, furnishment, roominess and plain elegance and fullness, signifying democratic ease, sufficient opulence, and an admirable old-fashioned simplicity—modern luxury, with its mere sumptuousness and affectation, either touch'd lightly upon or ignored altogether. Dinner the same. Of course the best of the occasion (Sunday, September 18, '81) was the sight of E. himself. As just said, a healthy color in the cheeks, and good light in the eyes, cheery expression, and just the amount of talking that best suited, namely, a word or short phrase only where needed, and almost always with a smile. Besides Emerson himself, Mrs. E., with their daughter Ellen, the son Edward and his wife, with my friend F. S. and Mrs. S., and others, relatives and intimates. Mrs. Emerson, resuming the subject of the evening before, (I sat next to her,) gave me further and fuller information about Thoreau, who, years ago, during Mr. E.'s absence in Europe, had lived for some time in the family, by invitation.

OTHER CONCORD NOTATIONS

Though the evening at Mr. and Mrs. Sanborn's, and the memorable family dinner at Mr. and Mrs. Emerson's, have most pleasantly and permanently fill'd my memory, I must not slight other notations of Concord. I went to the old Manse, walk'd through the ancient garden, enter'd the rooms, noted the quaintness, the unkempt grass and bushes, the little panes in the windows, the low ceilings, the spicy smell, the creepers embowering the light. Went to the Concord battle ground, which is close by, scann'd French's statue, "the Minute Man" read Emerson's poetic inscription on the

base, linger'd a long while on the bridge, and stopp'd by the grave
of the unnamed British soldiers buried there the day after the fight
in April '75. Then riding on, (thanks to my friend Miss M. and her
spirited white ponies, she driving them) a half hour at Hawthorne's
and Thoreau's graves. I got out and went up of course on foot, and
stood a long while and ponder'd. They lie close together in a pleasant
wooded spot well up the cemetery hill, "Sleepy Hollow." The flat
surface of the first was densely cover'd by myrtle, with a border of
arbor-vitæ, and the other had a brown headstone, moderately
elaborate, with inscriptions. By Henry's side lies his brother John,
of whom much was expected, but he died young. Then to Walden
pond, that beautifully embower'd sheet of water, and spent over an
hour there. On the spot in the woods where Thoreau had his solitary
house is now quite a cairn of stones, to mark the place; I too carried
one and deposited on the heap. As we drove back, saw the "School
of Philosophy," but it was shut up, and I would not have it open'd
for me. Near by stopp'd at the house of W. T. Harris, the Hegelian,
who came out, and we had a pleasant chat while I sat in the wagon.
I shall not soon forget those Concord drives, and especially that
charming Sunday forenoon one with my friend Miss M., and the
white ponies.

BOSTON COMMON—MORE OF EMERSON

Oct. 10–13.—I spend a good deal of time on the Common, these
delicious days and nights—every mid-day from 11:30 to about 1—
and almost every sunset another hour. I know all the big trees,
especially the old elms along Tremont and Beacon streets, and have
come to a sociable-silent understanding with most of them, in the
sunlit air, (yet crispy-cool enough,) as I saunter along the wide un-
paved walks. Up and down this breadth by Beacon street, between
these same old elms, I walk'd for two hours, of a bright sharp
February mid-day twenty-one years ago, with Emerson, then in
his prime, keen, physically and morally magnetic, arm'd at every
point, and when he chose, wielding the emotional just as well as the
intellectual. During those two hours he was the talker and I the
listener. It was an argument-statement, reconnoitring, review, attack,
and pressing home, (like an army corps in order, artillery, cavalry,
infantry,) of all that could be said against that part (and a main part)
in the construction of my poems, "Children of Adam." More precious than gold to me that dissertation—it afforded me, ever after,
this strange and paradoxical lesson; each point of E.'s statement
was unanswerable, no judge's charge ever more complete or con-

vincing, I could never hear the points better put—and then I felt down in my soul the clear and unmistakable conviction to disobey all, and pursue my own way. "What have you to say then to such things?" said E., pausing in conclusion. "Only that while I can't answer them at all, I feel more settled than ever to adhere to my own theory, and exemplify it," was my candid response. Whereupon we went and had a good dinner at the American House. And thenceforward I never waver'd or was touch'd with qualms, (as I confess I had been two or three times before).

AN OSSIANIC NIGHT—DEAREST FRIENDS

Nov., '81.—Again back in Camden. As I cross the Delaware in long trips to-night, between 9 and 11, the scene overhead is a peculiar one—swift sheets of flitting vapor-gauze, follow'd by dense clouds throwing an inky pall on everything. Then a spell of that transparent steel-gray black sky I have noticed under similar circumstances, on which the moon would beam for a few moments with calm lustre, throwing down a broad dazzle of highway on the waters; then the mists careering again. All silently, yet driven as if by the furies they sweep along, sometimes quite thin, sometimes thicker— a real Ossianic night—amid the whirl, absent or dead friends, the old, the past, somehow tenderly suggested—while the Gael-strains chant themselves from the mists—["Be thy soul blest, O Carril! in the midst of thy eddying winds. O that thou woulds't come to my hall when I am alone by night! And thou dost come, my friend. I hear often thy light hand on my harp, when it hangs on the distant wall, and the feeble sound touches my ear. Why dost thou not speak to me in my grief, and tell me when I shall behold my friends? But thou passest away in thy murmuring blast; the wind whistles through the gray hairs of Ossian."]

But most of all, those changes of moon and sheets of hurrying vapor and black clouds, with the sense of rapid action in weird silence, recall the far-back Erse belief that such above were the preparations for receiving the wraiths of just-slain warriors— ["We sat that night in Selma, round the strength of the shell. The wind was abroad in the oaks. The spirit of the mountain roar'd. The blast came rustling through the hall, and gently touch'd my harp. The sound was mournful and low, like the song of the tomb. Fingal heard it the first. The crowded sighs of his bosom rose. Some of my heroes are low, said the gray-hair'd king of Morven. I hear the sound of death on the harp. Ossian, touch the trembling string. Bid the sorrow rise, that their spirits may fly with joy to

Morven's woody hills. I touch'd the harp before the king; the sound was mournful and low. Bend forward from your clouds, I said, ghosts of my fathers! bend. Lay by the red terror of your course. Receive the falling chief; whether he comes from a distant land, or rises from the rolling sea. Let his robe of mist be near; his spear that is form'd of a cloud. Place a half-extinguish'd meteor by his side, in the form of a hero's sword. And oh! let his countenance be lovely, that his friends may delight in his presence. Bend from your clouds, I said, ghosts of my fathers, bend. Such was my song in Selma, to the lightly trembling harp."]

How or why I know not, just at the moment, but I too muse and think of my best friends in their distant homes—of William O'Connor, of Maurice Bucke, of John Burroughs, and of Mrs. Gilchrist—friends of my soul—stanchest friends of my other soul, my poems.

ONLY A NEW FERRY BOAT

Jan. 12, '82.—Such a show as the Delaware presented an hour before sundown yesterday evening, all along between Philadelphia and Camden, is worth weaving into an item. It was full tide, a fair breeze from the southwest, the water of a pale tawny color, and just enough motion to make things frolicsome and lively. Add to these an approaching sunset of unusual splendor, a broad tumble of clouds, with much golden haze and profusion of beaming shaft and dazzle. In the midst of all, in the clear drab of the afternoon light, there steam'd up the river the large, new boat, "the Wenonah," as pretty an object as you could wish to see, lightly and swiftly skimming along, all trim and white, cover'd with flags, transparent red and blue, streaming out in the breeze. Only a new ferry-boat, and yet in its fitness comparable with the prettiest products of Nature's cunning, and rivaling it. High up in the transparent ether gracefully balanced and circled four or five great sea hawks, while here below, amid the pomp and picturesqueness of sky and river, swam this creation of artificial beauty and motion and power, in its way no less perfect.

DEATH OF LONGFELLOW

Camden, April 3, '82.—I have just return'd from an old forest haunt, where I love to go occasionally away from parlors, pavements, and the newspapers and magazines—and where, of a clear forenoon, deep in the shade of pines and cedars and a tangle of old laurel-trees and vines, the news of Longfellow's death first reach'd me. For want of anything better, let me lightly twine a sprig of the sweet ground-ivy trailing so plentifully through the dead leaves at my feet, with reflections of that half hour alone, there in the silence, and lay it as my contribution on the dead bard's grave.

Longfellow in his voluminous works seems to me not only to be eminent in the style and forms of poetical expression that mark the present age, (an idiosyncrasy, almost a sickness, of verbal melody,) but to bring what is always dearest as poetry to the general human heart and taste, and probably must be so in the nature of things. He is certainly the sort of bard and counteractant most needed for our materialistic, self-assertive, money-worshipping, Anglo-Saxon races, and especially for the present age in America— an age tyrannically regulated with reference to the manufacturer, the merchant, the financier, the politician and the day workman— for whom and among whom he comes as the poet of melody, courtesy, deference—poet of the mellow twilight of the past in Italy, Germany, Spain, and in Northern Europe—poet of all sympathetic gentleness—and universal poet of women and young people. I should have to think long if I were ask'd to name the man who has done more, and in more valuable directions, for America.

I doubt if there ever was before such a fine intuitive judge and selecter of poems. His translations of many German and Scandinavian pieces are said to be better than the vernaculars. He does not urge or lash. His influence is like good drink or air. He is not tepid either, but always vital, with flavor, motion, grace. He strikes a splendid average, and does not sing exceptional passions, or humanity's jagged escapades. He is not revolutionary, brings nothing offensive or new, does not deal hard blows. On the contrary, his songs soothe and heal, or if they excite, it is a healthy and agreeable excitement. His very anger is gentle, is at second hand, (as in the "Quadroon Girl" and the "Witnesses.")

There is no undue element of pensiveness in Longfellow's strains. Even in the early translation, the Manrique, the movement is as of strong and steady wind or tide, holding up and buoying. Death is not avoided through his many themes, but there is something almost winning in his original verses and renderings on that dread subject—as, closing "the Happiest Land" dispute,

> And then the landlord's daughter
> Up to heaven rais'd her hand,
> And said, "Ye may no more contend,
> There lies the happiest land."

To the ungracious complaint-charge of his want of racy nativity
and special originality, I shall only say that America and the world
may well be reverently thankful—can never be thankful enough—
for any such singing-bird vouchsafed out of the centuries, without
asking that the notes be different from those of other songsters;
adding what I have heard Longfellow himself say, that ere the New
World can be worthily original, and announce herself and her own
heroes, she must be well saturated with the originality of others, and
respectfully consider the heroes that lived before Agamemnon.

STARTING NEWSPAPERS

Reminiscences—(From the "Camden Courier.")—As I sat taking
my evening sail across the Delaware in the staunch ferryboat
"Beverly," a night or two ago, I was join'd by two young reporter
friends. "I have a message for you," said one of them; "the C. folks
told me to say they would like a piece sign'd by your name, to go in
their first number. Can you do it for them?" "I guess so," said I;
"what might it be about?" "Well, anything on newspapers, or perhaps what you've done yourself, starting them." And off the boys
went, for we had reach'd the Philadelphia side. The hour was fine
and mild, the bright half-moon shining; Venus, with excess of
splendor, just setting in the west, and the great Scorpion rearing
its length more than half up in the southeast. As I cross'd leisurely for
an hour in the pleasant night-scene, my young friend's words brought
up quite a string of reminiscences.

I commenced when I was but a boy of eleven or twelve writing
sentimental bits for the old "Long Island Patriot," in Brooklyn;
this was about 1832. Soon after, I had a piece or two in George P.
Morris's then celebrated and fashionable "Mirror," of New York
city. I remember with what half-suppress'd excitement I used to
watch for the big, fat, red-faced, slow-moving, very old English
carrier who distributed the "Mirror" in Brooklyn; and when I got
one, opening and cutting the leaves with trembling fingers. How it
made my heart double-beat to see *my piece* on the pretty white
paper, in nice type.

My first real venture was the "Long Islander," in my own beautiful
town of Huntington, in 1839. I was about twenty years old. I had
been teaching country school for two or three years in various
parts of Suffolk and Queens counties, but liked printing; had been
at it while a lad, learn'd the trade of compositor, and was encouraged
to start a paper in the region where I was born. I went to New York,
bought a press and types, hired some little help, but did most of

the work myself, including the press-work. Everything seem'd turning out well; (only my own restlessness prevented me gradually establishing a permanent property there.) I bought a good horse, and every week went all round the country serving my papers, devoting one day and night to it. I never had happier jaunts—going over to south side, to Babylon, down the south road, across to Smithtown and Comac, and back home. The experiences of those jaunts, the dear old-fashion'd farmers and their wives, the stops by the hayfields, the hospitality, nice dinners, occasional evenings, the girls, the rides through the brush, come up in my memory to this day.

I next went to the "Aurora" daily in New York city—a sort of free lance. Also wrote regularly for the "Tattler," an evening paper. With these and a little outside work I was occupied off and on, until I went to edit the "Brooklyn Eagle," where for two years I had one of the pleasantest sits of my life—a good owner, good pay, and easy work and hours. The troubles in the Democratic party broke forth about those times (1848–'49) and I split off with the radicals; which led to rows with the boss and "the party," and I lost my place.

Being now out of a job, I was offer'd impromptu, (it happen'd between the acts one night in the lobby of the old Broadway theatre near Pearl street, New York city,) a good chance to go down to New Orleans on the staff of the "Crescent," a daily to be started there with plenty of capital behind it. One of the owners, who was north buying material, met me walking in the lobby, and though that was our first acquaintance, after fifteen minutes' talk (and a drink) we made a formal bargain, and he paid me two hundred dollars down to bind the contract and bear my expenses to New Orleans. I started two days afterwards; had a good leisurely time, as the paper wasn't to be out in three weeks. I enjoy'd my journey and Louisiana life much. Returning to Brooklyn a year or two afterward I started the "Freeman," first as a weekly, then daily. Pretty soon the secession war broke out, and I, too, got drawn in the current southward, and spent the following three years there, (as memorandized preceding.)

Besides starting them as aforementioned, I have had to do, one time or another, during my life, with a long list of papers, at divers places, sometimes under queer circumstances. During the war, the hospitals at Washington, among other means of amusement, printed a little sheet among themselves, surrounded by wounds and death, the "Armory Square Gazette," to which I contributed. The same long afterward, casually, to a paper—I think it was call'd the "Jimplecute"—out in Colorado where I stopp'd at the time. When I was in Quebec province, in Canada, in 1880, I went into the queerest little old French printing office near Tadousac. It was far more primitive and ancient than my Camden friend William Kurtz's place up on Federal street. I remember, as a youngster, several characteristic old printers of a kind hard to be seen these days.

THE GREAT UNREST OF WHICH WE ARE PART

My thoughts went floating on vast and mystic currents as I sat to-day in solitude and half-shade by the creek—returning mainly to two principal centres. One of my cherish'd themes for a never-achiev'd poem has been the two impetuses of man and the universe—in the latter, creation's incessant unrest,* exfoliation, (Darwin's evolution, I suppose.) Indeed, what is Nature but change, in all its visible, and still more its invisible processes? Or what is humanity 'n its faith, love, heroism, poetry, even morals, but *emotion*?

BY EMERSON'S GRAVE

May 6, 82.—We stand by Emerson's new-made grave without sadness—indeed a solemn joy and faith, almost hauteur—our soul-benison no mere

"Warrior, rest, thy task is done,"

for one beyond the warriors of the world lies surely symboll'd here. A just man, poised on himself, all-loving, all-inclosing, and sane and clear as the sun. Nor does it seem so much Emerson himself we are here to honor—it is conscience, simplicity, culture, humanity's attributes at their best, yet applicable if need be to average affairs, and eligible to all. So used are we to suppose a heroic death can only come from out of battle or storm, or mighty personal contest, or amid dramatic incidents or danger, (have we not been taught so for ages by all the plays and poems?) that few even of those who most sympathizingly mourn Emerson's late departure will fully appreciate

---

*"Fifty thousand years ago the constellation of the Great Bear or Dipper was a starry cross; a hundred thousand years hence the imaginary Dipper will be upside down, and the stars which form the bowl and handle will have changed places. The misty nebulæ are moving, and besides are whirling around in great spirals, some one way, some another. Every molecule of matter in the whole universe is swinging to and fro; every particle of ether which fills space is in jelly-like vibration. Light is one kind of motion, heat another, electricity another, magnetism another, sound another. Every human sense is the result of motion; every perception, every thought is but motion of the molecules of the brain translated by that incomprehensible thing we call mind. The processes of growth, of existence, of decay, whether in words, or in the minutest organisms, are but motion."

the ripen'd grandeur of that event, with its play of calm and fitness, like evening light on the sea.

How I shall henceforth dwell on the blessed hours when, not long since, I saw that benignant face, the clear eyes, the silently smiling mouth, the form yet upright in its great age—to the very last, with so much spring and cheeriness, and such an absence of decrepitude, that even the term *venerable* hardly seem'd fitting.

Perhaps the life now rounded and completed in its mortal development, and which nothing can change or harm more, has its most illustrious halo, not in its splendid intellectual or esthetic products, but as forming in its entirety one of the few, (alas! how few!) perfect and flawless excuses for being, of the entire literary class.

We can say, as Abraham Lincoln at Gettysburg, It is not we who come to consecrate the dead—we reverently come to receive, if so it may be, some consecration to ourselves and daily work from him.

AT PRESENT WRITING—PERSONAL

A letter to a German friend—extract

May 31, '82.—"From to-day I enter upon my 64th year. The paralysis that first affected me nearly ten years ago, has since remain'd, with varying course—seems to have settled quietly down, and will probably continue. I easily tire, am very clumsy, cannot walk far; but my spirits are first-rate. I go around in public almost every day—now and then take long trips, by railroad or boat, hundreds of miles—live largely in the open air—am sunburnt and stout, (weight 190)—keep up my activity and interest in life, people, progress, and the questions of the day. About two-thirds of the time I am quite comfortable. What mentality I ever had remains entirely unaffected; though physically I am a half-paralytic, and likely to be so, long as I live. But the principal object of my life seems to have been accomplish'd—I have the most devoted and ardent of friends, and affectionate relatives—and of enemies I really make no account."

AFTER TRYING A CERTAIN BOOK

I tried to read a beautifully printed and scholarly volume on "the Theory of Poetry," received by mail this morning from England—but gave it up at last for a bad job. Here are some capricious pencillings that follow'd, as I find them in my notes:

In youth and maturity Poems are charged with sunshine and

varied pomp of day; but as the soul more and more takes precedence, (the sensuous still included,) the Dusk becomes the poet's atmosphere. I too have sought, and ever seek, the brilliant sun, and make my songs according. But as I grow old, the half-lights of evening are far more to me.

The play of Imagination, with the sensuous objects of Nature for symbols, and Faith—with Love and Pride as the unseen impetus and moving-power of all, make up the curious chess-game of a poem.

Common teachers or critics are always asking "What does it mean?" Symphony of fine musician, or sunset, or sea-waves rolling up the beach—what do they mean? Undoubtedly in the most subtle-elusive sense they mean something—as love does, and religion does, and the best poem;—but who shall fathom and define those meanings? (I do not intend this as a warrant for wildness and frantic escapades—but to justify the soul's frequent joy in what cannot be defined to the intellectual part, or to calculation.)

At its best, poetic lore is like what may be heard of conversation in the dusk, from speakers far or hid, of which we get only a few broken murmurs. What is not gather'd is far more—perhaps the main thing.

Grandest poetic passages are only to be taken at free removes, as we sometimes look for stars at night, not by gazing directly toward them, but off one side.

(*To a poetic student and friend.*)—I only seek to put you in rapport. Your own brain, heart, evolution, must not only understand the matter, but largely supply it.

FINAL CONFESSIONS—LITERARY TESTS

So draw near their end these garrulous notes. There have doubtless occurr'd some repetitions, technical errors in the consecutiveness of dates, in the minutiæ of botanical, astronomical, &c., exactness, and perhaps elsewhere;—for in gathering up, writing, peremptorily dispatching copy, this hot weather, (last of July and through August, '82,) and delaying not the printers, I have had to hurry along, no time to spare. But in the deepest veracity of all—in reflections of objects, scenes, Nature's out-pourings, to my senses and receptivity, as they seem'd to me—in the work of giving those who care for it, some authentic glints, specimen-days of my life—and in the *bona fide* spirit and relations, from author to reader, on all the subjects design'd, and as far as they go, I feel to make unmitigated claims.

The synopsis of my early life, Long Island, New York city, and so forth, and the diary-jottings in the Secession war, tell their own story. My plan in starting what constitutes most of the middle of the book, was originally for hints and data of a Nature-poem that should carry one's experiences a few hours, commencing at noon-flush, and so through the after-part of the day—I suppose led to such idea by my own life-afternoon now arrived. But I soon found I could move at more ease, by giving the narrative at first hand. (Then there is a humiliating lesson one learns, in serene hours, of a fine day or night. Nature seems to look on all fixed-up poetry and art as something almost impertinent.)

Thus I went on, years following, various seasons and areas, spinning forth my thought beneath the night and stars, (or as I was confined to my room by half-sickness,) or at midday looking out upon the sea, or far north steaming over the Saguenay's black breast, jotting all down in the loosest sort of chronological order, and here printing from my impromptu notes, hardly even the seasons group'd together, or anything corrected—so afraid of dropping what smack of outdoors or sun or starlight might cling to the lines, I dared not try to meddle with or smooth them. Every now and then (not often, but for a foil,) I carried a book in my pocket—or perhaps tore out from some broken or cheap edition a bunch of loose leaves; most always had something of the sort ready, but only took it out when the mood demanded. In that way, utterly out of reach of literary conventions, I re-read many authors.

I cannot divest my appetite of literature, yet I find myself eventually trying it all by Nature—*first premises* many call it, but really the crowning results of all, laws, tallies and proofs. (Has it never occurr'd to any one how the last deciding tests applicable to a book are entirely outside of technical and grammatical ones, and that any truly first-class production has little or nothing to do with the rules and calibres of ordinary critics? or the bloodless chalk of Allibone's Dictionary? I have fancied the ocean and the daylight, the mountain and the forest, putting their spirit in a judgment on our books. I have fancied some disembodied human soul giving its verdict.)

NATURE AND DEMOCRACY— -MORALITY

Democracy most of all affiliates with the open air, is sunny and hardy and sane only with Nature—just as much as Art is. Something is required to temper both—to check them, restrain them from excess, morbidity. I have wanted, before departure, to bear special testimony to a very old lesson and requisite. American Democracy, in its myriad personalities, in factories, work-shops, stores, offices— through the dense streets and houses of cities, and all their manifold sophisticated life—must either be fibred, vitalized, by regular contact with out-door light and air and growths, farm-scenes, animals, fields, trees, birds, sun-warmth and free skies, or it will certainly dwindle and pale. We cannot have grand races of mechanics, work people, and commonalty, (the only specific purpose of America,) on any less terms. I conceive of no flourishing and heroic elements of Democracy in the United States, or of Democracy maintaining itself at all, without the Nature-element forming a main part—to be its health-element and beauty-element—to really underlie the whole politics, sanity, religion and art of the New World.

Finally, the morality: "Virtue," said Marcus Aurelius, "what is it, only a living and enthusiastic sympathy with Nature?" Perhaps indeed the efforts of the true poets, founders, religions, literatures, all ages, have been, and ever will be, our time and times to come, essentially the same—to bring people back from their persistent strayings and sickly abstractions, to the costless average, divine, original concrete.

Index of Poem Titles